The Cambridge History of Latin America is a large-scale, collaborative, multi-volume history of Latin America during the five centuries from the first contacts between Europeans and the native peoples of the Americas in the late fifteenth and early sixteenth centuries to the present.

Latin America: Politics and Society Since 1930 consists of chapters from Part 2 of Volume VI of *The Cambridge History.* Together they provide a comprehensive account of Latin American politics and political and social movements in Latin America since 1930. Each chapter is accompanied by a bibliographical essay.

LATIN AMERICA
POLITICS AND SOCIETY SINCE 1930

The following titles drawn from
The Cambridge History of Latin America edited by Leslie Bethell
are available in hardcover and paperback:

Colonial Spanish America

Colonial Brazil

The Independence of Latin America

Spanish America after Independence, *c.* 1820–*c.* 1870

Brazil: Empire and First Republic, 1822–1930

Latin America: Economy and Society, 1870–1930

Mexico Since Independence

Central America Since Independence

Cuba: A Short History

Chile Since Independence

Argentina Since Independence

Ideas and Ideologies in Twentieth Century Latin America

A Cultural History of Latin America

Latin America: Economy and Society Since 1930

Latin America: Politics and Society Since 1930

LATIN AMERICA
POLITICS AND SOCIETY
SINCE 1930

edited by

LESLIE BETHELL
St. Antony's College, Oxford

CAMBRIDGE
UNIVERSITY PRESS

PUBLISHED BY THE PRESS SYNDICATE OF THE UNIVERSITY OF CAMBRIDGE
The Pitt Building, Trumpington Street, Cambridge CB2 1RP, United Kingdom

CAMBRIDGE UNIVERSITY PRESS
The Edinburgh Building, Cambridge CB2 2RU, United Kingdom
40 West 20th Street, New York, NY 10011-4211, USA
10 Stamford Road, Oakleigh, Melbourne 3166, Australia

© Cambridge University Press 1998

First published 1998

Printed in the United States of America

Typeset in Garamond

Library of Congress Cataloging-in-Publication Data

Latin America : politics and society since 1930 / edited by Leslie Bethell.
p.   cm.
Consists of chapters from pt. 2 of v. 6 of The Cambridge history of Latin America.
Includes bibliographical references (p.   ) and index.
Contents: Democracy in Latin America since 1930 / Jonathan Hartlyn
and Arturo Valenzuela – A note on citizenship in Latin America /
Laurence Whitehead – The left in Latin America since *c.* 1920 / Alan
Angell – The military in Latin American politics since 1930 / Alain
Rouquie and Stephen Suffern – Urban labour movements in Latin
America since 1930 / Ian Roxborough – Rural mobilizations in Latin
America since *c.* 1920 / Guillermo de la Peña.
ISBN 0-521-59390-5 (hard). – ISBN 0-521-59582-7 (pbk.)
1. Latin America – Politics and government – 20th century.
I. Bethell, Leslie.   II. Cambridge history of Latin America.
F1414.L2793   1997
980.03′3 – dc21   97-11735
                                                                      CIP

*A catalog record for this book is available from
the British Library*

ISBN 0 521 59390 5 hardback
ISBN 0 521 59582 7 paperback

CONTENTS

PREFACE

The Cambridge History of Latin America is a large-scale, collaborative, multi-volume history of Latin America during the five centuries from the first contacts between Europeans and the native peoples of the Americas in the late fifteenth and early sixteenth centuries to the present.

Latin America: Politics and Society Since 1930 brings together six chapters from *The Cambridge History of Latin America* Volume VI, Part 2. The authors survey the advance of (as well as the setbacks suffered by) democracy in Latin America; the successes and failures of the Latin American Left, both democratic and non-democratic; the military in Latin American politics – military interventions and coups, military regimes, and problems of transition to civilian rule; the urban working class and urban labour movements, with emphasis on their role in politics; and rural mobilizations and rural violence, especially in Mexico, Central America, and the Andes. Each chapter is accompanied by a bibliographical essay.

The aim is to provide in a single 'student edition' a comprehensive survey of Latin American politics and Latin American political and social movements since 1930.

LATIN AMERICA
POLITICS AND SOCIETY SINCE 1930

Part One

POLITICS

1

DEMOCRACY IN LATIN AMERICA
SINCE 1930*

INTRODUCTION

Latin America has often been viewed as a continent where in the nineteenth and twentieth centuries the formal architecture of democracy has been a thinly veiled facade for civilian and military tyrants who have imposed their will on conservative and backward peoples. Such a view of the origins and development of democracy is partial and misleading. The struggle to consolidate representative regimes, accept the legitimacy of opposition, expand citizenship, and affirm the rule of law has been a continuous and uneven process – on both sides of the Atlantic – for two centuries. The central, but often elusive, guiding principle has been the concept of popular sovereignty, the notion that legitimate government is generated by a free citizenry and is accountable to it for its policies and actions. In Latin America, as in Europe and North America, the quest for these liberal ideals has been a permanent aspiration, if often challenged by political disorder, civil war, human rights abuses, dictatorship and, in the twentieth century, alternative visions for organizing the political community, including fascism and Marxism.

By the early decades of the twentieth century, most of the major countries of Latin America had managed to establish at least 'oligarchical democracies', that is to say, regimes, in which presidents and national assemblies derived from open, if not fully fair, political competition for the support of limited electorates, according to prescribed constitutional rules and which were largely comparable to the restricted representative

*We gratefully acknowledge comments by Manuel Alcántara, Michael Coppedge, Bolivar Lamounier, Fabrice Lehoucq, Cynthia McClintock, Carina Perelli, and members of the University of North Carolina comparative politics discussion group, especially Evelyne Huber, Gary Marks and Lars Schoultz. Eduardo Feldman helped compile the bibliographical essay. We owe a special debt of gratitude to Leslie Bethell for his patience and indispensable editorial advice.

regimes in Europe of the same period. Argentina (from 1916) and Uruguay (from 1918) were democracies with universal male suffrage. However, in Latin America, as in Europe, the advent of world depression in the 1930s unleashed forces that undermined the progress of representative government. At the end of the Second World War there was a brief period of democratization. But democracies were swept away in the late 1940s and early 1950s. Another, more profound turn to democratic rule occurred in the late 1950s. But during the 1960s and 1970s numerous countries returned to military rule, often for long periods. Only in the late 1970s and 1980s was there a significant retreat from direct military control of government throughout the region. Most Latin American countries entered the 1990s under democratic government. During the half century from the 1930s to the 1980s there was no uniform pattern. While the majority of the small nations of Central America and regional giants such as Argentina, Brazil and Mexico fell far short of the ideal of democratic construction, other countries such as Chile, Costa Rica, Uruguay, Colombia and Venezuela experienced long periods of democratic government.

We define 'democracy' or 'political democracy' as incorporating three critical dimensions. The first, to use Robert Dahl's term, is contestation.[1] In a democracy the government is constituted by leaders who successfully compete for the vote of the citizenry in regularly scheduled elections. The essence of contestation is the acceptance of the legitimacy of political opposition; the right to challenge incumbents and replace them in the principal positions of political auuthority. Contestation requires state protection for the freedom of expression and association and the existence of regular, free and fair elections capable of translating the will of the citizenry into leadership options. Particularly significant for political contestation is the development of consolidated party systems, in which the interaction among parties follows a predictable pattern and their electoral strengths remain within stable parameters. Parties promote distinct programs or ideologies, sponsor individuals for elected office, and serve as critical links between civil society and the state.

The second dimension is constitutionalism, or respect for the constitu-

---

[1] We are indebted to Robert Dahl's influential work for the first and third points in this characterization of democracy. See Robert Dahl, *Polyarchy: Participation and Opposition* (New Haven, Conn., 1971). The definition of democracy that emphasizes the importance of competition for political leadership as a critical element stems from Joseph A. Schumpeter's pioneering work *Capitalism, Socialism and Democracy* (New York, 1942).

tional order, embodied in constitutional documents and/or practices, often in contravention with the strict application of the principle of majority rule. It is in this sense that contemporary democracies must be understood as 'constitutional democracies'. A constitutional democracy, while guaranteeing the right of opposition to challenge incumbents by appealing for the support of a majority of the citizenry, defines and restricts the powers of governmental authorities. It also places limits on the hegemony of electoral majorities or their representatives, with a view to protecting the rights and preferences of individuals and minorities, the options of future majorities, and the very institutions of democracy itself. These institutions and rules vary and include such provisions as restrictions on presidential reelection and the partial insulation of judicial, electoral and security organs from elected leadership. They also include the use of qualified legislative majorities and complex ratification mechanisms when fundamental changes in the nation's constitution and basic laws are at stake. Finally, they make provisions for power sharing and minority representation, an essential element for the protection of opposition and encouragement of the concept of a 'loyal opposition'. In practice, constitutional democracies diverge on the degree to which contingent majorities or their representatives are constrained by constitutional and legal restrictions.

The third dimension is inclusiveness or participation. By definition democracies are based on the concept of popular sovereignty. As democracies evolve, the constitutional provisions for citizenship broaden to include larger proportions of the adult population, through the elimination of restrictions on suffrage based on property, literacy, gender, race or ethnicity. Changes in formal rules, including residency and registration requirements and the effective involvement of the population in politics through the expansion of parties and movements lead, over time, to full inclusiveness.

A constitutional democracy may be viewed as consolidated when contestation and respect for the constitutional order are widely accepted by both elites and mass publics and citizenship and effective electoral participation have been extended to all adults with minimum qualifications. This is a procedural definition of democracy. It is often supplemented by a conception of citizenship that incorporates formal equality (universal suffrage) and legal protection from abusive state power, but also includes notions of sufficient levels of material satisfaction and levels of education that participation can be deemed meaningful rather than largely manipulated.

The theoretical literature in the social sciences provides few adequate guide-posts for understanding the early development and consolidation of democracy in Latin America. The dominant perspectives have tended to view the success or failure of democracy as being directly related to broader cultural and economic forces. Cultural explanations drew on the legacy of Roman Catholicism and the Iberian colonial experiences to argue that liberal democracy would find infertile soil in conservative societies characterized by hierarchical social relations and deference to absolute authority. In such societies, even as they entered the modern world and achieved significant levels of industrialization, strong-man rule and corporatist political structures were more likely to flourish than representative institutions based on individualistic notions such as 'one person, one vote'.

From an economic perspective, the modernization school of the 1950s and 1960s held that economic development and industrialization would encourage social differentiation and higher levels of education, contributing to political pluralism and the gradual but inevitable success of democratic practices. By contrast, the dependency school of the 1960s and 1970s, implied that liberal democracy would be thwarted by a pattern of economic exchange which placed economic and political power in the hands of a small oligarchy, while discouraging the development of bourgeois and middle-class groups and strong states necessary for the growth of democratic institutions and practices. Industrialization and economic development, rather than encouraging the development of pro-democracy middle sectors, contributed to authoritarian responses by those very sectors who, in alliance with elites, the military and international capital, sought to thwart the rising power of working class and popular groups who threatened their privileges.

Broad cultural and economic factors, such as effective national integration, a vigorous civil society with a dense network of groups and associations, steady socio-economic development and reductions in inequalities may facilitate the development of democratic institutions and practices. Our review of the pattern of democratic development in Latin America suggests, however, that cultural and socio-economic factors are at best contributory conditions, not necessary ones. Taken alone they cannot account for the significant variations in the experience with democratic development in the hemisphere and are particularly incapable of accounting for notable deviant cases. Thus, they fail to explain why Chile, one of the most traditional and 'dependent' societies in the region was able to structure relatively competitive and predictable patterns of political contestation before the advent of similar patterns in many European coun-

For some Latin American republics these two processes were clear and distinct: stable practices permitting political contestation were established in the nineteenth or early twentieth centuries, prior to the advent of pressures for mass participation. This permitted a more gradual and ordered, if not controlled, process of enlargement of the political community in the aftermath of the 1929 Depression, helping to guarantee a greater degree of political continuity. For others, the challenge of contestation and inclusiveness came simultaneously, increasing the level of uncertainty and the risks for established actors in acceding to 'popular sovereignty' as the defining element of political power.

Although central to the consolidation of democracy, it would be misleading to imply that the ongoing challenges of forging democracy revolve exclusively around contestation and inclusiveness. Societies may face severe economic and social challenges or international shocks that can tax the survival of any political regime. The inability of democratic institutions to address fundamental problems resulting from civil conflict or severe economic crisis can undermine the legitimacy of representative institutions leading the way for authoritarian outcomes. Governance – how regime leaders analyse problems and the policy choices they make, especially in the economic field – can have profound effects on legitimacy, effectiveness and performance and thus on democracy. The challenges to democracy can also derive from the very functioning of political institutions. Governmental deadlock and paralysis stemming from minority governments and executive legislative conflict, or from the politics of outbidding by contending foes unwilling to compromise or stand up to anti-democratic forces can have independent effects, initiating or aggravating economic and social problems, thus contributing to 'unsolvable' problems (in Juan Linz's terms) that often accelerate regime breakdown. Weak or corrupt parties can aggravate a political crisis by providing no real authority or decisional capacity. Covert or overt support for conspiratorial alliances between political leaders and military elements, in contravention of the dictates of the electorate, severely undermines the democratic rules of the game, particularly in times of crisis.

In most countries democracy has always had to confront a 'violence option', exercised by forces resisting change (usually conservative landed interests or business groups allied with the military), from forces advocating a disruption of the status quo (insurrectionary socialism) and occasionally from an often ideologically muddled populism. The first group, though sometimes acting in the name of democracy, has usually justified the use of violence in terms of preventing anarchy, the rise of Communism or economic collapse. Very few coups in Latin America since 1930 have occurred without the active conspiracy of key political actors, including parties, seeking to advance their fortunes and defend their privileges through violence on failing to secure adequate electoral support. No Latin American country, with the exception of Costa Rica where the armed forces were abolished in 1949, has successfully institutionalized a model of democratic control of the military or enshrined adequate constitutional measures to prevent civilian manipulation of the armed forces. The second and third groups have often presented competing images of democracy to the procedural, political definition discussed above, focussed more on social and economic conditions and rights and stressing the 'majoritarian' imperatives of democracy over and above the constitutional limitations on the majority. On the right, order and economic growth compete with democracy; in populism and on the left, popular aspirations for inclusion and social justice clash with it. The willingness of the right to distort democratic procedures and violate its rules has often led to its denigration, feeding the doubts of populists and of the left about the possibilities for reform if they abide by the democratic 'rules of the game'.

Thus, even in democratic periods many countries in the region may be more accurately characterized as semi-democratic, rather than fully democratic, because of constraints on constitutionalism, contestation or inclusiveness, including occasional outright electoral fraud and manipulation. And some Latin American countries – for example Argentina, Brazil and Peru – can be characterized for part of the period since 1930 as possessing hybrid democratic-authoritarian regimes, noteworthy for the persistent interference in politics of the military and powerful economic interests, and by frequent direct, if brief, military intervention. In these three countries there was also the proscription for long periods of a particular leader or movement (Perón and the Peronists in Argentina, the Communist Party in Brazil and Haya de la Torre and APRA [Alianza Popular Revolucionaria Americana] in Peru).

It follows also that the process of democratic construction is reversible. Not only Argentina, Brazil and Peru, but in the early 1970s countries with long traditions of constitutional rule and respect for the electoral process such as Chile and Uruguay experienced profound regime breakdowns. For sure, these processes can be affected by international shocks or the demonstration effect of a series of regime breakdowns that encourage and even legitimize the actions of anti-democratic forces. This explains, in part, the cyclical nature of some of the patterns of regime change in the region. But, their precise impact necessarily differed in accordance with the internal dynamics within each country.

The chapter will next focus on broad themes of constitutional development in Latin America and especially what we have called the dilemma of presidentialism. This will be followed by discussions of political parties and party systems and of citizenship and electoral participation. The second part of the chapter consists of an account of the democratic experience of Latin America in the period from 1930 to 1990. Here we will focus specifically on the five countries which, although none was immune from civil war or military coup, together account for around half of the continent's years of democracy in this period: Chile, Uruguay, Costa Rica, Venezuela and Colombia, as well as the three countries that come next in terms of their experience of democracy: Argentina, Brazil and Peru. These eight countries are quite diverse and have distinctly different political histories and democratic experiences. All the larger and economically more developed countries of the region, except for Mexico, are included. Taken together they represented in 1985 approximately 65 per cent of the population of Latin America, 70 per cent of its GDP and 75 per cent of its value added in manufacturing.

The omission of Mexico is justified by the particular nature of Mexico's political system and political history in the period since the revolution of 1910. Mexico has had the longest experience of constitutional stability of any Latin American country in the period under review. The progressive constitution of 1917 had an important impact on the rest of Latin America and on the development of socio-political thought in the region. Here is a civilian regime (after 1940), essentially inclusionary, with a long established record of elections and some important constitutional restrictions on power, notably a strict prohibition on presidential re-election. For many decades its hegemonic party of the revolution has been capable of winning elections without recourse to fraud (though it still often acceded to it) as it successfully forged a multi-class, integrative coalition. Other parties have been countenanced, or even carefully buttressed, in order to give the appearance of opposition and to enhance democratic legitimacy, as appeals to revolutionary myths have become increasingly difficult to sustain over time. However, implicit in the notion of democracy is the possibility of the alternation of power. It is widely agreed that what Mexico has developed is a successful one-party authoritarian regime which has only begun to liberalize itself in the last decade of the century. Mexico's experience with democratic politics in the period from 1930 to 1990 was limited.[2]

PRESIDENTIAL CONSTITUTIONALISM

Spanish America's break with Spain during the first quarter of the nineteenth century was marked by the ascendancy of forces committed to the principles of republicanism and the revolutionary notion that political authority stems from the will of the citizenry rather than the divine right of kings. Liberal principles found a tenuous hold in Latin America before they took root in much of Europe. And the most compelling model for Latin American reformers was the constitution of the United States of America, a compact which had provided the former British colonies with a novel and yet stable government for a generation. Over a fairly narrow timespan, from 1811 (Chile, Colombia, Venezuela) through 1830 (Uruguay), seventeen countries issued republican constitutions inspired, to a greater or lesser degree, by the document drafted in Philadelphia in 1787.[3] Only Brazil when it separated from Portugal in 1822 retained a monarchical system. And even Brazil, after the Empire was abolished in 1889, adopted a republican constitution (1891) with striking parallels to the U.S. constitution.

To be sure there were other important influences on Latin America's founding fathers. French constitutional principles and legal doctrines, expressed in documents such as the liberal Spanish constitution of 1812, found their way into many of the region's fundamental laws. Distinctively French and Spanish influences are apparent in such institutions and practices as Councils of State, administrative courts, interior ministries, local and provincial administrative structures, and ministerial counter-signatures to authenticate presidential decrees. In its transition from traditional to rational legal authority, in Max Weber's terms, Latin America also drew on Roman Law, stemming from the heritage of Spanish colonial institutions and the legal innovations of the Napoleonic

---

[2] We recognize that had we included a more comprehensive overview of the region, including Haiti, Cuba, the Dominican Republic, and the countries of Central America, the trajectory of democracy would be less optimistic. In these countries highly stratified social structures, sharp disparities in power, weakness of political process and institutions and intervention by the United States, mitigated against the establishment of constitutional democracy.

[3] Cuba and Panama promulgated their first constitutions shortly after their independence, in 1901 and 1904 respectively.

codes. Following the precepts of the French Enlightenment, Latin American leaders believed that the law could ensure order and progress, a belief which would gain even wider currency as the intellectual and political elite embraced positivism in the last decades of the nineteenth century. This faith in legal constructs contributed to a penchant for rewriting constitutions, when the law seemed unable to mould political reality, and reformers or usurpers sought to find a better fit between legal precepts and political reality.

Despite the strong continental influence, the U.S. constitutional framework was decisive in charting the basic institutions of republican government in the new states. Concerned with the danger of tyranny, as their North American counterparts had been, the Latin Americans embraced presidential government, a system based on the doctrine of separation of powers, of checks and balances aimed both at curbing the power of executives and dampening the passions of elected assemblies. Under this governmental formula presidents and congresses could both claim popular legitimacy. Nevertheless, executives served fixed terms of office and were not dependent on legislative majorities for their survival. While the rest of the world that adopted democratic forms evolved towards parliamentarism, the Western Hemisphere (with the exception of Canada and the British Caribbean) became the continent of presidentialism.[4]

In emulating the United States document most Latin American constitution drafters opted for bicameral legislatures in which the lower house would reflect more the principle of 'one man one vote', and the upper house would represent designated geographical areas without regard to population size. Curiously, this bicameral formula, closely tied to the concept of federalism in North America, was implemented largely in unitary regimes throughout the region. Venezuela (1811), Argentina (1853), Brazil (1891) and Mexico (1824) adopted federal constitutions, but the aim was to balance regional interests with central authority, rather than create a 'compact' between states claiming a measure of sovereignty. Unicameral legislatures were favoured in Ecuador and in the Central American countries of Costa Rica, Guatemala, Honduras and El Salvador.

In the post-1930 period, even in the eight countries with the greatest exposure to democracy to which we are paying special attention, the adoption of a new constitution sometimes reflected an authoritarian

---

[4] Only Liberia (1847) and the Philippines (1935) would adopt the U.S. model prior to the Second World War and the proliferation of new states with the break-up of the European empires.

leader's effort to legitimize and/or extend his rule. Examples include Perón in Argentina (1949), Vargas in Brazil (1934, 1937), Pinochet in Chile (1980), Terra in Uruguay (1934), and Gómez (1931), López Contreras (1936) and Pérez Jiménez (1953) in Venezuela. Pinochet's success in imposing a new constitution through a plebiscite in 1980 gave him legitimacy in the eyes of key military and civilian constituencies, without which he would have had greater difficulty perpetuating his rule. On the other hand, some attempts to impose new constitutions backfired, helping to channel opposition to authoritarian regimes, as in Colombia in 1953 and Uruguay in 1980.

It would be erroneous, however, to imply that all constitutional changes, particularly in this recent period, have been minor, short-lived, ignored, or implemented to further the immediate goals of authoritarian rulers, although this has been true in some cases (and more so for the twelve other Latin American countries not extensively considered here). New or revised constitutions have marked important turning points in modifying governmental institutions and functions, generating new political rights, expanding inclusiveness, and promoting social and economic rights. In this sense, they have reflected larger social, economic and political changes, but once promulgated have also promoted changing norms and practices in the political community. New constitutions have often been generated at democratic 'turning points', as part of a broader process of democratic transition. In Peru in 1978 and Brazil in 1986, elections to Constituent Assemblies permitted authoritarian regimes to gauge and seek to limit (unsuccessfully) the strength of opposition forces. New constitutions, or major revisions of previous ones, have resulted from transitions in five of the eight countries under review since 1930: in Brazil (the 1946 and 1988 Constitutions), in Costa Rica (the 1949 Constitution), in Peru (the 1979 Constitution), in Uruguay (the 1942 Constitution), and in Venezuela (the 1947 and 1961 constitutions). In Colombia, all key aspects of the coalition National Front agreement facilitating a transition became part of the Constitution by a 1957 plebiscite (except for presidential alternation which resulted from a 1959 constitutional reform), and the incorporation of guerrilla groups into the country's political process and pressures for democratizing reforms were key impulses leading to a Constituent Assembly and a new Constitution in 1991. Table 1.1 lists the constitutions of the eight countries under review in this chapter since 1930.

Constitutions in Latin America, reflecting the influence of the North American Bill of Rights and the French Declaration of the Rights of Man,

Table 1.1. *Constitutions in Latin America*

Country	First constitution	Total no. of constitutions	Constitutions since 1930
Argentina	1819	4	1949; 1957; (1972); (1982)*
Brazil	1824	8	1934; 1937; 1946; 1967, 1969; 1988
Chile	1811	11	1980
Colombia	1811	12	(1936) (1957) (1968); 1991
Costa Rica	1825	9	1949
Peru	1823	13	1933; 1979
Uruguay	1830	5	1934; (1942); 1952; 1966
Venezuela	1811	24	1931; 1936; 1947; 1953; 1961

*Reinstatement of 1957 Constitution.
Sources: William W. Pierson and Federico G. Gil, *Governments of Latin America* (New York, 1957); Larry Diamond, Juan Linz and Seymour Martin Lipset (eds), *Democracy in Developing Countries,* Vol. IV, *Latin America* (Boulder, Colo., 1989).
Dates in parentheses are those of major amendments to the existing constitutional text.

called for the protection of individual rights, liberties and property for individuals defined as 'citizens'. The best exemplar of a 'liberal' constitution was the Argentine document of 1853. The 1917 Mexican Constitution, drafted at Querétaro in the course of the revolution incorporated into fundamental law a broad range of social and labour rights (for example, Articles 27 and 123) designed to subordinate individual rights to collective needs. The Mexican Constitution also dramatically curtailed the rights and privileges of the Catholic Church. Throughout the 1930s and 1940s, most countries in Latin America followed the Mexican example, incorporating social, educational and labor charters into their constitutions, stressing the 'social function of property' over individual property rights. Guarantees of these and other rights have tended to increase over time in both number and specificity, adding to the length and complexity of modern day Latin American constitutions; this is particularly true of three recent examples, the constitutions of Peru (1980), Brazil (1988) and Colombia (1991). Thus, constitutions came to reflect the same corporatist and social philosophy that inspired the continent's legal codes, as well as the hope that the constitutional expression of rights would be a step toward their realization, a hope which has all too often fallen far short of the mark.

One of the central issues determined by a constitution is a country's form of government. Presidential authority is the distinctive element in the formal structures of Latin American constitutional democracy. Although presidentialism became ingrained in the constitutional practice of the hemisphere, political instability and institutional conflict led to significant regime modifications which changed the character, if not the essence, of executive authority over time. These conflicts often revolved around two closely inter-related issues, the appropriate powers and authority of the president as a plebiscitarian figure, and the nature of executive-legislative relations, conflicts which reflected the broader struggles for power and influence in Latin American society, both within and outside of constitutional parameters. In this regard, Latin American constitutional history paralleled that of much of Europe.

Latin America's quest for the proper relationship between executive and legislative power has been stormy and contradictory. Most of the countries in the region have been governed, at one point or another, by strong-man rule. During periods of constitutional government, every country experienced significant conflicts between presidents intent on making a mark on history, and legislative bodies concerned with checking the executive branch and asserting congressional prerogatives. It is a serious error to minimize the degree to which institutional rivalries contributed to the perennial difficulties of Latin American presidential regimes. By contrast with a parliamentary regime, in presidential regimes both the executive and the legislature claim popular legitimacy, blaming the other for its problems. Increased executive prerogatives encouraged greater governmental deadlock as executives sought to impose their vision of the society's future on reluctant legislatures and powerful political interests. Often this conflict reflected the uneasy relations between political oppositions and governmental parties, with their monopoly over spoils and political power.

We should stress that in discussing Latin American constitutionalism we are dealing with constitutional rules applicable to legitimate governments, not with the practices or legal claims of unconstitutional regimes. This distinction is important because the frequent reference to strong executives in Latin America often ignores the difference between constitutional leaders and political usurpers. It is the premise of this chapter that constitutional executives in Latin America have been far less powerful than generally assumed.

The tendency towards increased executive authority in the aftermath of the 1929 Depression was a global process, affecting democratic as well as authoritarian governments. The power of presidents, prime ministers and dictators expanded as central governments became managers of vast bureaucratic organizations aimed at providing welfare and promoting economic development. The critique of the 'liberal' state, from both left and right, led to increased demand for states with 'developmentalist' ideologies. In Latin America, as well as Europe, democratic values emphasizing political rights, competition, and participation became less important than state capacity. The link between presidentialism, centralization of power and a technocratic impulse to insulate decision-making within the executive branch, encouraged after the Second World War by international assistance programmes, tended to relegate elected assemblies to a decidedly secondary role.

By mid-century Latin American presidents had gained considerable rule-making powers. The constitutions in force in countries like Argentina, Brazil, Colombia, Costa Rica, Chile, Peru, Uruguay and Venezuela provided the executive with broad 'initiative' in the formation of laws. In many cases executives gained exclusive prerogatives in formulating budget and wage legislation, while legislatures were sharply restricted in their authority to amend such legislation. Executives also gained broad latitude in issuing decrees, or decree laws with the force of law, on matters as diverse as national defence and public order, public finances and the creation of new agencies and governmental positions. This latitude came either through direct constitutional provisions, through congressionally delegated authority, or simply through executive fiat.

The growing strength of executive authority in constitutional governments, however, did not translate into a significant expansion of real power, or a notable increase in governmental efficacy. Although in some cases, constitutional presidents were able to exert quasi-dictatorial power, for the most part, the occupants of the office in Latin America have experienced a frustrating sense of weakness and inability to act. Success of executives varied depending on a multiplicity of factors including the strength of political parties, the viability of state institutions, the constraints on presidential prerogatives from autonomous and decentralized agencies, and the challenges to presidential authority from powerful societal groups and military establishments. The viability of presidentialism in Latin America was most seriously affected, however, by the inability of chief executives to command majority support from the population and majorities in the legislature. Either because of multiparty configurations, or because presidential parties or coalitions often crumbled in mid-term, presidents uniformly found it difficult to enact governmental programmes, leading to serious executive-legislature stalemate and paralysis, which encouraged instability and military intervention. A review of seventy-one presidents elected in relatively fair constitutionally prescribed contests in South America from 1930 to 1990 reveals that only twenty-seven (38 per cent) were elected by a majority of the citizenry. Nor in the overwhelming majority of cases did the president's own party hold a majority of seats in the legislature. Minority presidents and significant executive-legislative conflicts were important factors in democratic breakdowns (whether by presidential *auto-golpe* – coup d'etat by those already in office – or by military coup) in Argentina (1943), Brazil (1964), Chile (1973), Colombia (1949), Peru (1968 and 1992), and Uruguay (1933 and 1973).

The perennial conflict between constitutional powers contributed to a significant constitutional counter-trend designed to curb presidential prerogatives and establish a more balanced executive-legislative relationship. These include limitations on presidential terms, the development of congressional mechanisms to ensure executive accountability, the introduction of collegiate executives, and the elaboration of pacts aimed at reducing executive prerogatives and political conflict through co-participation or governance.

Whereas the United States did not restrict presidential re-election until 1951, following a period in which Franklin D. Roosevelt had been re-elected three times, most of the countries of Latin America adopted restrictions on presidential tenure much earlier. Uruguay prohibited immediate presidential reelection under the 1830 Constitution, a norm that was suspended in 1934 but re-adopted in 1942. Under the 1833 Constitution, Chile restricted the president to two terms and in 1871 barred immediate reelection; the 1925 and 1980 constitutions specified one term without immediate re-election. Argentina's 1853 Constitution also prohibited immediate re-election. Perón succeeded in changing this norm in 1949 to permit his own re-election in 1952. However, the Peronist Constitution was nullified following his overthrow in 1955; the 1957 Constitution reinstated the 1853 text with some modifications. In Costa Rica in 1859, in reaction to the ten-year control of the presidency by a single individual, a new constitution reduced presidential terms to three years and imposed limits on presidential re-election, through these were not always followed; subsequent constitutions continued limits on immediate presidential re-election, though presidential terms were extended to four years; in 1969, presidential re-election was flatly prohibited (except for those who had been elected to the presidency prior to 1969). In Brazil, immediate presidential reelection was prohibited by the First Republic's constitution of 1891. A 1910 constitutional reform in Colombia, on the heels of a period of dictatorship, decreed direct presidential elections for a four-year term with no immediate re-election, while also assuring minority representation in the legislature; the constitution promulgated in 1991 flatly prohibited re-election. In Venezuela, where only with the 1947 Constitution could voters elect the president directly, the constitution of 1961 specified five-year presidential terms, with former presidents being eligible for re-election only after the lapse of a ten-year period. In reaction to the *oncenio* of Augusto Leguía (1919–30), the 1933 Peruvian Constitution prohibited immediate presidential re-election, further stipulating that any official who even proposed a change would be forced to resign immediately and be permanently barred from any public office; this provision was changed to a straight prohibition of re-election by the 1979 Constitution. The only countries in Latin America which continued in 1990 to permit immediate re-election were countries with traditions of 'dictatorial re-election', namely Haiti, Nicaragua and the Dominican Republic.[5]

The noted constitutional scholar Karl Loewenstein, in an article published in 1949, distinguished three different types of presidential regimes in place in Latin America: pure presidentialism, attenuated presidentialism, and approximate parliamentarism.[6] Pure presidentialism, where presidents could name their cabinets at will without their being subject to congressional control, characterized Argentina, Brazil and Colombia, although Brazil would briefly adopt a parliamentary system after the resignation of Jânio Quadros in 1961.[7] In countries with attenuated presidentialism, the constitution required the president to share power with his ministers who, as members of a Cabinet Council, helped formulate policy and provided written consent for its execution (examples included Cuba, 1940; Bolivia, 1945; El Salvador, 1945 and Venezuela, 1947). Ministers, however, were neither collectively nor individually responsible to the legislature, even though they might be required to appear before parliament to defend policies.

---

[5] In 1993, reflecting continuing frustrations with executive-legislative conflicts, and the desire for 'strong leadership' in the context of severe socio-economic as well as political crisis, President Fujimori in Peru was able to have a new constitution approved by referendum permitting his immediate re-election, even as President Menem in Argentina was seeking to alter the constitution in order to provide for his reelection in 1995.

[6] Karl Lowenstein, 'The Presidency Outside the United States', *Journal of Politics*, 11, 1 (1949).

[7] The 1991 Colombian Constitution permitted not only the interpellation, but also the censure of ministers.

In what Lowenstein called approximate parliamentarism, the president, while retaining the right to name ministers without congressional approval, shared executive responsibility with a cabinet which was individually or collectively subject to congressional censure. Chile was a case in point. As early as the 1840s, ministers were summoned to the Chilean congress to answer interpellations and were censured for not following the wishes of congressional majorities. Although the 1925 Constitution was designed to re-establish a strong executive after thirty years of legislative supremacy, the congress retained the right to censure ministers and cabinets, forcing presidents to continue to bargain with party and congressional leaders in forming his cabinets. As a result, Chile had considerable cabinet instability. Presidents Juan Antonio Ríos (1942–6), Carlos Ibáñez (1952–8) and Salvador Allende (1970–3), each had five major cabinet changes during their time in office. Ríos' cabinets lasted an average of only six and a half months, Ibañez' seven months and Allende's less than six months. In the confrontational Allende years, the president was forced to replace or reassign numerous ministers because of congressional censure or threats of censure. The 1853 Argentine constitution permitted the legislature to force cabinet officers to appear before it for questioning. In Costa Rica, the 1871 Constitution provided for participation of ministers in congressional debates, without the right to vote. The 1933 Peruvian Constitution (and later the 1979 document), authorized the legislature to summon ministers to congressional debates, subject them to interpellations, and force their resignation through censures. The Uruguayan Constitutions of 1934, 1967 and 1983 also permitted ministerial censures, although the legislature was required to approve it with a two-thirds majority. In most constitutions, ministers were also required to countersign presidential acts, either individually or collectively, in order for these to become valid.

The Peruvian and Uruguayan constitutions went even further by introducing parliamentary practices stipulating that the president could dissolve the chamber of deputies in case of political stalemate. In the Uruguayan case (Constitutions of 1934, 1967 and 1983), the president could dissolve the congress and call new elections if the legislature failed to muster enough votes to approve a motion of censure. If the new parliament, elected after dissolution, proceeded to adopt the same motion of censure, the president would be forced to resign. Although chief executives have threatened to make use of the power of dissolution, none has followed through on the threat. This was due mostly to the continuous dominance of the Colorado party in both the executive and legislative branches in the period up until 1952 and the unwillingness of members of congress to risk losing their seats.

In Peru, under both the 1933 and 1979 constitutions, the president could dissolve the congress if it expressed a vote of no confidence in three successive cabinets during one term. For only one year in the period from 1933 to 1962 were parliamentary checks on presidential authority used effectively in Peru when APRA, which had succeeded in obtaining a legislative majority, broke with President José Luís Bustamante (1945–8). The ensuing stalemate, however, contributed directly to General Odría's coup d'etat. During the administration of Manuel Prado (1956–62), APRA also gained a majority, but chose not to challenge the president for fear of creating the same impasse. This more compliant behaviour did little good as Prado was overthrown by the military anyway for allowing APRA to compete and emerge as the country's strongest party. President Alberto Fujimori dissolved the Peruvian congress in 1992 on the pretext that the congress was blocking his programme and censuring his ministers. His action, however, was clearly unconstitutional as the legislature did not censure three cabinets in succession. While the Chilean Constitution of 1980 also gave the president the power to dissolve the legislature, this provision was eliminated in the amendments approved in 1989, after General Augusto Pinochet was defeated in the plebiscite of 1988.[8]

The most original effort to move away from pure presidentialism in Latin America was the Uruguayan experiment with a plural executive, a constitutional formula which retained the basic concept of separation of powers, while reducing the primacy of the executive. The first experiment in collegial governance, which lasted from 1919 to 1933, divided executive responsibility between a president, charged with the nation's foreign relations and internal order, and a nine member bi-annually elected council, charged with administering domestic policy. Two-thirds of the seats of the National Council of Administration were assigned to the party with the most votes; one third to the principal opposition force. The plural executive contributed to breaking the long tradition of civil conflicts in Uruguayan history, encouraging the growth of democratic practices and the legitimacy of opposition forces. Executive leadership was cumbersome, however, and led to inevitable tensions between the president and the Council, tensions which would not survive the deep economic crisis of

---

[8] Similar parliamentary provisions were included in the Cuban constitutional reforms of 1940. See William S. Stokes, 'The Cuban Parliamentary System in Action, 1940–1947', *Journal of Politics*, 11, 2 (1949). They were also included in the Venezuelan constitution of 1947.

the 1929 Depression. On 31 March 1933, President Gabriel Terra's 'coup d'etat' dissolved the Council, closed the congress, and scheduled elections for a new constituent assembly. The 1934 Constitution, approved in a national plebiscite, reintroduced the presidential system.

In 1951, Uruguayans once again modified the constitution, returning to the formula of a popularly elected nine-member plural executive, this time without the figure of the president. The principal rationale for the reform remained the same. Uruguayans feared the consequences of political competition which gave all of the spoils to one party, preferring a mechanism designed to share political power with the minority party. A collegial executive also made it easier for Uruguay's powerful party factions to attain some representation in the executive. The concept of power-sharing, following the two-thirds/one-third formula, was extended to departments, para-statal bodies, public corporations and state commissions.[9] Uruguay's second experiment with a collegial executive would last until 1966, when the presidential system was reintroduced with the concurrence of 52 per cent of the voters, at a time when Uruguay was drifting into a serious economic and political crisis.

Uruguay is a notable example of constitutional engineering aimed at curbing executive authority and encouraging direct participation of the opposition in governing the country. It comes closer to a 'consociational' 'solution' to the problem of executive primacy and destructive competition than to a parliamentary 'solution'. The latter appears more appropriate in multi-party contexts where the executive may not enjoy a majority in the legislature and must deal with shifting parliamentary coalitions in attempting to govern. A consociational approach seems more appropriate in two party contexts, where one party is likely to win both the executive and the congress, shutting out all opposition.

Venezuela, through the Pact of Punto Fijo (1958) and other inter-party agreements, also sought to minimize inter-party conflict by providing for direct representation of opposition parties in important government posts. And, in Chile, in both the first and second post-Pinochet presidential elections, Christian Democrats and Socialists sought to reduce inter-party conflict and insure their victory by presenting a single presidential candidate and negotiating jointly their congressional lists. It was Colombia, however, that resorted to the most far-reaching form of consociational

---

[9] Russell H. Fitzgibbon, 'Adoption of a Collegiate Executive in Uruguay', *Journal of Politics*, 14, 4 (1952).

arrangements in attempting to curb the effects of the monopoly of executive power by one party in a two-party system. The constitutional changes approved in the 1957 plebiscite and a 1959 constitutional reform led to the alternation of the presidency between the two major parties from 1958 to 1974 and ensured complete parity in the distribution of executive, legislative and even judicial posts. Coming after the destructive violence in the aftermath of the 1948 *bogotazo* and the military interregnum of Gustavo Rojas Pinilla (1953–7), the National Front permitted the re-establishment of civilian authority. Particularly in Colombia, but also in the other countries that resorted to a 'consociational' formula to restrict executive authority and minimize party confrontation, the price of greater political stability was a restriction on competition, the exclusion of third parties and the dampening of democratic participation.

PARTIES AND PARTY SYSTEMS

Political parties play a critical role in constitutional democracies with regard to both contestation and inclusiveness. They serve as organizers of electoral challenges to authority. They are also the links between political elites and the citizenry, mobilizing participation, articulating demands and aggregating political interests. The process of party formation, the particular role which individual parties play at different conjunctures and the overall strength and viability of parties and party systems are important factors in understanding the success or failure of democracy.

Independent Latin America's early political parties or proto-parties had crystallized by the second half of the nineteenth century into national networks loosely grouped into Conservatives and Liberals representing rival landowning and commercial elites with their respective followings. Conservatives tended to defend centralization of power and the privileges of the Catholic Church and oppose free trade; Liberals sought a more secular, decentralized and market-oriented order. Regional, family and personalistic struggles for power, however, overshadowed the apparent ideological differences. Only in Chile, Uruguay and Colombia, did these 'parties of notables' approximate to modern parties by the end of the century, as intra-elite competition expanded from the legislative arena through networks of regional and local elites, and eventually became mass based party organizations.

Although the Conservative-Liberal cleavage affected most countries to a greater or lesser extent, subsequent waves of party formation were much more deeply affected by national experiences, including the path and extent of industrialization and urbanization and the resulting class conflict, the degree of competitiveness of the political system at the time of the expansion of mass suffrage, and the response of traditional parties and leaders to the challenges of creating political movements that went beyond coteries of notables to incorporate the middle class, and subsequently the working class, into the political system.

Chile was unique in developing a multi-party system that incorporated both Communist and Socialist parties.[10] As Samuel Valenzuela notes, in Chile, it was the existence of competitive politics and log-rolling alliances during the 'Parliamentary Republic', a time of expansion of mass suffrage and working-class activism, which permitted the incorporation of parties of the left into the established political process. While labour was being repressed at the plant level, political competition at the electoral level provided strong incentives for Communist and Socialist proto-parties to organize and compete in local and congressional elections, rather than opt for the more daunting 'revolutionary' route to power. This electoral 'option' was made possible by splits among the traditional parties, particularly the willingness of the middle-class Radicals to build alliances with the left at the local level in exchange for electoral support at the national level, aimed at overtaking the political hegemony of the Conservatives and Liberals.[11] By 1938, the strength of the Chilean institutional system would permit the country to elect by the narrowest of margins Latin America's only Popular Front government. The uneasy alliance of the left would later find its expression in the failed candidacies of Salvador Allende under the Frente de Acción Popular and, in 1970, his successful election to the presidency under the banner of the Unidad Popular.

In Uruguay and Colombia the traditional parties were able to maintain their dominant position. The absence of both a strong labour challenge equivalent to that of Chile's mining sector, and an electorally established party of the centre such as the Chilean Radicals intent on breaking the monopoly of the traditional conservatives, made it easier for the Uruguayan and Colombian parties to co-opt new movements, and join in a common strategy to curb the growth of parties of the left and independent

---

[10] For extensive discussion of the Latin American Communist and Socialist parties and their role in democratic politics as well as armed revolutionary struggle, see the essay by Alan Angell in this volume.

[11] Samuel Valenzuela, 'Labor Movement Formation and Politics: The Chilean and French cases in comparative perspective, 1850–1950' (Ph.D. Dissertation, Columbia University, 1979).

populist parties, even as they engaged in periodic and violent inter-party struggles. In each case, one of the traditional parties became a predominant party (the Colorados in Uruguay early in the century and the Liberals in Colombia in the 1930s) as it instituted a series of reforms, successfully coopting important elements of the popular sectors. In both cases, the factionalization of the two traditional parties permitted populist expressions to emerge within the party system.

In Uruguay, strong inter-party rivalries persisted and contributed to the breakdowns of 1933 and 1973. Uruguay sought to mitigate these rivalries by encouraging the politics of conciliation and compromise through the adoption of formal mechanisms for party agreement such as the collegial executive, described above, and various formulas for power sharing between the majority and minority party. This resort to consociational solutions, however, alienated minority sectors of the population which sought expression in alternative parties such as the Christian Democrats and, more significantly, the Communist party. In alliance with dissident Colorados, they helped build the Frente Amplio to the point where in the 1970s, and once again in the 1990s, the left has constituted a strong 'third force' in Uruguayan party politics. Uruguay's peculiar 'double simultaneous' voting system also undermined the legitimacy of political institutions by reinforcing party fragmentation and permitting the election of minority candidates.

In Colombia, the Liberal Party under Alfonso López (1934–8) enacted a series of constitutional and other reforms that responded to the growing crisis in the country while serving narrow partisan purposes. These reforms limited the influence of the Church, expanded the electorate in urban areas where the party was strong, and increased the party's support base within labour. Conservatives did not actively protest the enactment of universal male suffrage by the Liberal dominated Congress because they hoped the measure would potentially help them more than the Liberals mobilize voters in the still predominantly rural country with assistance from the local clergy. However, the eruption of new social forces and new ideologies over the 1930s and 1940s in the context of continuing fears of single-party hegemony in a strongly presidentialist system accelerated polarization and violence in the country eventually leading to the undeclared civil war known as *la violencia,* regime breakdown (1949) and eventually military rule (1953–7).

The established order was challenged in several countries not only by parties of the left, but also by populist parties and movements. These provided a broad nationalist, anti-imperialist message that appealed to both middle-sector and working-class constituencies. They were often personalistic, built around charismatic leaders who sought to inspire their followers through emotional and dramatic appeals. At the same time, their message was directed largely to urban 'masses' rather than to specific classes, and the policies they advocated were reformist, nationalist, statist, and biased to the urban sector, rather than revolutionary. Populist parties often advocated import-substitution industrialization, workplace reforms and extension of state services in health and social security; at the same time, when in power they sought to control through state channels the popular mobilization they helped to generate. To conservative forces, these parties and movements were often seen as 'demagogic', while for the Communists and other leftist parties, they were viewed as 'charlatans duping the masses'. Although attacked as 'safety valves' by leftists, these parties were often not perceived in that fashion by economically dominant groups.[12] Their message appeared to fuse both progressive and reactionary elements. Because their style was personalistic and emotional, and because they combined both elements of mobilization and control while often maintaining only an ambiguous commitment to liberal democracy (often in mirror-image fashion to right wing groups in their own country), these parties and movements have been very difficult to label in conventional right-left ideological terms. Populist parties that maintained themselves over time – such as the Acción Democrática (AD) in Venezuela, the Partido de Liberación Nacional (PLN) in Costa Rica, APRA in Peru, and the Peronists in Argentina – usually moderated their radical rhetoric, reached out to a greater variety of social groups, sought to institutionalize (although, sometimes only minimally) their party structures and reduced (even if partially) the charismatic and emotional nature of their appeals.

Populism varied tremendously across the continent in terms of its importance, ability to gain power and commitment to democratic values. In Venezuela and Costa Rica, the populist parties that emerged at the end of the Second World War – AD led by Rómulo Betancourt and the PLN led by José 'Pepe' Figueres – became electorally predominant and key institutional actors in their respective democracies. Elsewhere, populist parties either established themselves as only ambiguously democratic actors in hostile environments (Argentina and Peru), or never fully institutionalized

---

[12] See Paul Drake, 'Conclusion: a requiem for populism?' in Michael Conniff (ed.), *Latin American Populism in Comparative Perspective* (Albuquerque, N.Mex., 1982).

themselves (Brazil). What could arguably be called the continent's first populist party, APRA in Peru (founded in 1924), was unable to attain power directly until 1985, as it faced a significant veto from the armed forces, not unlike the Peronists in Argentina. In the face of unremitting violence from the armed forces and other opponents, APRA was equivocal in its defence of political democracy, even as its founder and leader until his death, Víctor Raúl Haya de la Torre, made continual political compromises with erstwhile enemies in a vain effort to gain power that also generated numerous splits within his own movement. Unlike Acción Democrática and the Partido de Liberación Nacional, the Alianza Popular Revolucionaria Americana was never clearly a majority party in its formative years.

In Argentina and Brazil, populist parties were in effect built from 'above', as two authoritarian leaders, Perón and Vargas, opted to create political movements from their positions in power. At the same time, the reforms they instituted generated enormous popular support, eventually enabling each of them to win a democratic election (in the case of Perón, more than once). Vargas' movement, however, never effectively consolidated itself as a political party in the way that Peronism eventually did, although one of the parties he created, the Partido Trabalhista Brasileiro (PTB), grew steadily from 1945 to 1964. Brazil's party system was becoming increasingly fragmented and radicalized during this period of democratic experimentation. The large mass appeal of Peronism in Argentina, even more than APRA in Peru, created difficult dilemmas for elites anxious to legitimate the political process through elections while vetoing Peronist access to power.

In several countries, populist movements or parties were essentially personalist vehicles that did not survive the death or decline of their founder. This was particularly true of those created around former strongmen, such as Rojas' Alianza Nacional Popular (ANAPO) in Colombia, the Unión Nacional Odriísta (UNO) in Peru, and Ibáñez' Agrario Laborismo in Chile. Others revolved around significant political personalities or individuals suddenly thrust into positions of leadership, such as Jóvito Villalba or Wolfgang Larrazábal in Venezuela. As suggested by these examples from Venezuela, where following a long period of personalistic authoritarianism and the dictatorship of Pérez Jiménez, AD and Comité de Organización Política Electoral Independiente (COPEI), a Christian Democratic party, established themselves after 1958 as dominant and powerful intermediaries between a weak civil society and the state, more ephemeral movements appeared in countries which eventually moved to established party systems.

In addition to leftist and populist parties, from the late 1940s, a number of parties inspired by Catholic social doctrine began to emerge in Latin America. Christian Democratic parties became especially influential in Chile, in Venezuela, and eventually in Costa Rica. Smaller Christian Democratic parties were formed in Peru, Colombia and other countries, but never gained much importance.

The Chilean Partido Demócrata Cristiano (PDC) traces its origins to the 1930s when the youth wing of the Conservative party, heavily influenced by the progressive social doctrines of the Catholic church, split away to form the National Falange. The party's fortunes gradually improved as the Catholic church broke its alliance with the right, embracing a more progressive line that paralleled the reformist bent of the Falangist leadership. With church support, the Falange joined with several minor groups to form the PDC in 1957. In 1964, with the support of the right which feared the election of Marxist Salvador Allende, party leader Eduardo Frei was elected president on a platform proclaiming a 'third way' between Marxism and capitalism, a form of 'communitarian' socialism of cooperatives and worker self-managed enterprises. Although the party grew significantly during Frei's presidency, and succeeded in obtaining the largest vote of any single party in contemporary history in the 1965 congressional election, the Christian Democrats were not able to overcome the tripartite division of Chilean politics. Its candidate in the 1970 election, Radomiro Tomic, lost to Allende, coming in third with 27.8 per cent of the total vote. In the aftermath of the military regime, however, the party re-emerged as Chile's largest, with approximately 35 per cent of the electorate, shedding many of its 'communitarian' principles and embracing free-market economics with a more 'human face'.

The roots of the Christian Democratic COPEI in Venezuela lie in divisions in the Venezuelan student movement in the 1920s and 1930s, and were inspired by anti-Communism and Catholic social doctrine. When it was founded in 1946, it hoped to capture certain anti-party sentiment, and thus it named itself the 'Committee of Independent Electoral Political Organization'. The party was soon identified as the defender of the Church against the increasingly militant and radical AD. However, following the 1948 coup, COPEI distanced itself and eventually opposed the Pérez Jiménez dictatorship; by 1953 most of its party leaders were either imprisoned or in exile. COPEI's collaboration with AD in the 1958–63 period may have helped provide assurances to conservative Catholic elements and to parts of the military; at the same time, it provided the party with significant access to public resources and inroads into the labour and other popular sector movements. Increasingly, by emphasizing economic nationalism and social justice and moving away from a militant anti-Communism, its ideological positions overlapped with those of AD, as it also moved toward becoming a 'catch-all' party. The party captured the presidency in 1968 and in 1978.

In Costa Rica, a cluster of opposition parties eventually merged into the Partido Unidad Social Cristiana (PUSC) in 1984 around a Social Christian ideology to combat the more successful PLN. The convenience of an alternative ideology to that of social-democracy, and of an international organization and outside support and legitimacy in the form of the Christian Democracy Union as an alternative to the Socialist International, played a role. As with Venezuela's COPEI, the positions and policies of the PUSC were centrist and popular in content. The party captured the presidency with Rafael Calderón Fournier in 1990.

Thus, there is considerable variation in Latin American party systems. With the exception of the highly articulated single party in authoritarian Mexico, strong and cohesive parties are found in countries with the longest trajectory of elections and democratic alternation in power (Chile, Uruguay, Colombia, Costa Rica and Venezuela). Weak and diffuse parties are prevalent in countries where frequent military coups and authoritarian interludes have interrupted party continuity and undermined efforts to develop organizational coherence and leadership development (Peru, Brazil and Argentina).

There is no clear association between party strength and the degree of ideological or programmatic organization. Chile and Venezuela have been characterized by strong parties, but whereas the Chilean parties have had highly differentiated ideological orientations, remaining close to Otto Kirchheimer's ideal type of the early European 'mass integration party', Venezuela's parties share similar programmatic orientations and come closer to the 'catch all' model of more recent European parties seeking primarily to maximize their electoral fortunes.[13] Costa Rica resembles Venezuela in this regard. Although the major parties in Colombia and Uruguay are far less differentiated ideologically than the Chilean parties,

---

[13] Otto Kirchheimer, 'The Transformation of the Western European Party Systems', in Joseph LaPalombara and Myron Weiner (eds), *Political Parties and Political Development* (Princeton, N.J., 1966).

the strong levels of inherited party identification, going back farther than many European parties, prevented them from becoming fully 'catch-all' electoral machines.

Patron–client patterns of authority have long characterized parties in Latin America, particularly in Brazil and Colombia where rural *coroneis* and *gamonales* held sway at the local level as the crucial link between party leaders and voters. But, even in Chile, with its membership based ideological parties, the electoral fortunes of parties depended on a complex network of lower level 'brokers' who turned out voters based on a combination of particularistic and programmatic appeals. At the turn of the century urban politics in many Latin American countries were characterized by corrupt city machines and 'rotten boroughs' not too dissimilar to their counterparts in Europe and North America. Patterns of electoral corruption based on clientelistic politics lasted well into mid-century in most countries, as party and civil service reforms were slow to emerge.

Finally, party systems in Latin America have varied considerably with regard to the number of parties which garner the vast bulk of the votes cast. Several countries, including Colombia, Costa Rica, Uruguay and Venezuela, tend towards single-party dominant or two-party systems, reflecting the legacy of the generations-old struggle to control the presidency, a winner-take-all prize with vast patronage powers, the salience of class cleavages in society at the time of the expansion of mass suffrage and the ability of traditional parties to incorporate new groups. Argentina and Peru have had more fragmented multi-party systems, in a playing field that was less than democratic, with Argentina moving towards a two-party system by the end of the period and Peru experiencing severe party disintegration. Chile is unusual for its multi-party system which owes its formation to the major generative 'cleavages': centre–periphery, church–state, employer–worker. Brazil has also tended to multi-partyism, with parties closely built on clientelistic networks and the fundamental axis of power found at the state and even local level.

Where parties consolidated themselves as electoral organizations with congressional representation before the development of a strong state or of well-organized societal interests, as in Chile, Colombia and Uruguay, they tended to become powerful intermediaries between civil society and the state, further strengthening democratic rules of the game. In countries such as Argentina, Peru and, to a lesser extent Brazil, where the expansion of the suffrage or competitive electoral politics was delayed or thwarted by authoritarian interludes, interest groups established stronger corporatist patterns of direct access to the state, a pattern which would undermine the strength of parties and democratic practices and encourage populist appeals. Argentina and Peru were also characterized by a 'stalemated' party system because of constraints placed upon the participation of Apristas and Peronists by non-democratic forces, with Peru's party system more inchoate and volatile than that of Argentina. Of the eight countries, Peru and especially Brazil have had the weakest parties and party systems. Until, the emergence of the Partido dos Trabalhadores (PT) in the 1980s, Brazil had no single party with the institutional coherence of APRA in Peru. Indeed, one scholar has argued that Brazil may have the most underdeveloped parties and party system of any country with an equivalent level of economic development in the world.[14]

Looking back from a vantage point in the 1990s, the importance of the stability of party systems and of the number of parties to the consolidation of democracy in Latin America appears evident. A stable party system may be said to exist where a country's major parties are institutionalized, adopt a coherent position vis-à-vis the state and society, and effectively incorporate all relevant groups in society, including economically dominant groups, employing a mix of ideological, programmatic and clientelistic appeals, and where the interactions between or among those parties occur with an expected regularity and with electoral strengths within more or less understood parameters. The experience of the eight countries under review suggests that in presidential systems democracy is much more likely to be successful where such a stable party system revolves around two or two and a half parties; Chile is a partial exception.[15] Obversely, those countries with shifting party loyalties, inchoate party systems and greater electoral volatility appear less likely to be on the road toward democratic consolidation as we conclude this time period.

There appears to be three requirements for a strong party system. The first is that a country's political parties have a degree of institutionalization and coherence at a level at least similar to those of the state and of organizations in civil society. For most of the period since 1930, parties in

---

[14] Scott Mainwaring, 'Brazilian Party Underdevelopment', *Political Science Quarterly*, 107, 4 (1992): 677–707 and 'Brazil: weak parties, feckless democracy', in Scott Mainwaring and Timothy R. Scully (eds), *Building Democratic Institutions: Parties and Party Systems in Latin America* (Stanford, Cal., 1993).

[15] In a two-party system, each of the parties would be expected to be able to win a presidential election, even if one of these parties usually gains presidential office. In a two-and-a-half-party system, there would be a third party which receives some consistent percentage of the vote and maintains a minority presence in the legislature but is not considered a significant contender to win the presidency.

Brazil have been overshadowed by the state; in contrast, in Argentina, they appear to have been by dominated by corporative actors in society. In Peru, parties appear to have been overshadowed at first by social actors, then by the state, and then again by social movements and organizations. Colombia and Uruguay appear to have traditional parties with an initially strong but diminishing influence over sectors in civil society. Venezuela and especially Chile are the clearest examples of countries with strong parties in the terms employed here. Secondly, for a strong party system, these parties have to include broad sectors of the population, preferably relying on a mix of appeals. Parties that rely purely on ideological or programmatic appeals may encourage an excessive sectarianism and polarization in society; those that rely almost exclusively on clientelism or specific material benefits may ultimately breed excessive corruption and cynicism about the political process, encouraging some social groups increasingly to employ means outside of electoral channels to express their political demands. During the Allende (1970–3) years, the Chilean political parties approximated the former. In the years prior to 1973 the two traditional Uruguayan parties approached the latter, as did the traditional Colombian parties in the late 1970s and 1980s. Thirdly, it is important that economically dominant groups consider themselves represented in the political party system, either through a viable conservative party or through adequate presence or influence in one or two other parties, whether of a 'catch-all' or primarily middle-sector orientation. In Argentina, the absence of such a conservative party or such a presence in other parties has commonly been noted as one factor facilitating military coups.

It is in situations where a society's multiple interests are represented by a large number of parties, particularly where these parties are strongly ideological, that a parliamentary system would appear to be of particular assistance in potentially mitigating explosive political conflict. In presidential systems, cohesiveness and centripetal competition are much more likely to occur in a two-party system. However, these two parties are more likely to be of the 'catch-all' nature, may rely more strongly on clientelist and brokerage claims and may become factionalized and incoherent. In this context, seeming stability at the electoral level may well disguise the fact that parties are not adequately representing societal interests and conflict is likely to express itself through other, often violent, means, as appears to have been the case in Colombia and Uruguay. Societies with potentially explosive conflicts may well be better off having these expressed in the political arena through a multiplicity of parties than through what may be perceived as an extremely constrained two-party system; and in this case, a parliamentary system would be preferable to presidentialism.

ELECTIONS AND THE SUFFRAGE

If democratic constitutions, and a greater willingness by all major actors to adhere to the rules specified within them, and parties and party systems, are crucial to the evolution of political democracy in Latin America, so is the existence of regular, free, fair and open competitive elections. Such elections are a necessary condition for democracy, through not a sufficient one. Elections are insufficient by themselves to insure democracy because of their sporadic nature and the need for citizens to be able freely to express specific policy preferences through other means. The construction of citizenship and of democratic participation also depends upon the creation and enrichment of a dense network of associations and organizations and of opportunities for voluntary involvement in community and national affairs whose exploration is beyond the scope of this chapter.

Genuinely competitive elections in Latin America have often been problematic. Primarily as a direct consequence of military coups or the illegal extension of presidential terms of office, elections have not always been *regular* occurrences. Even when held, elections have not always been fully *free* either in permitting all opposition parties to participate or in the sense of assuring opposition forces freedom to campaign and to mobilize, access to the mass media and no discrimination with regard to the use of state resources. They have also not always been *fair* in terms of permitting all voters equal access to the polls or in terms of accurately reporting actual vote counts. Here, the development of respected, autonomous electoral oversight agencies and of mechanisms such as a single, secret ballot, have been critical. Certainly, elections have not always been *open,* as we shall see, in the sense of being held in conditions of universal suffrage.

In nineteenth-century Latin America, voting was often a public, oral act, with registration rolls controlled by local government officials. Only gradually and in an uneven process as suffrage expanded did voting also become secret and mechanisms to reduce fraud become more effective. The extent to which legal text and political reality approximated each other have varied by country and period. In legal terms, the secret ballot was introduced in Colombia in 1853, though patron–client relations, coercion and other forms of fraud severely limited the effectiveness of suffrage.

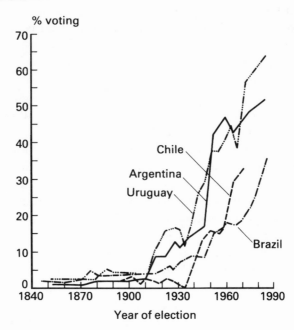

Figure I.I. *Southern Cone and Brazil population voting in presidential elections, 1846–1984*

Source: Enrique C. Ochoa, 'The Rapid Expansion of Voter Participation in Latin America: Presidential Elections, 1845–1986', *Statistical Abstract of Latin America* 25 (Los Angeles, 1987): 869–91.

Parties were responsible for providing their own ballots on election day until 1988. Argentina introduced the secret ballot in 1912, a reality that was respected until openly fraudulent elections were carried out in the 1930s. However, by the 1960s fraud of a large-scale nature was not feasible.

Uruguay was not the first country in Latin America to introduce the secret ballot (in 1918), but it was probably the first in which the fit between legal text and political reality became effectively closer. In Chile, the vote has been secret since at least 1925, though a single ballot (which minimizes the opportunity for fraud, especially among illiterates) was not introduced until 1958. In Costa Rica, the vote has been secret since 1925 and a more effective system of configuing voter rolls was established in 1927, but it was only with the establishment of the Supreme Electoral Tribunal under the 1949 Constitution that the spectre of electoral fraud diminished effectively. Peru and Brazil legally enacted the secret ballot in 1931 and 1932, respectively, but like Colombia in that period, there was considerable variance between law and practice. In Venezuela, the vote was made secret and universal in 1946.

The expansion of suffrage is a crucial element in the development of any democracy. All of the countries surveyed in this chapter expanded their citizenship rights through constitutional and other legal changes and experienced significant increases in popular participation from the 1930s to the 1990s. Visual evidence of this expansion is provided in Figures 1.1 and 1.2, based on electoral turnout as a percentage of a country's population in presidential elections. This is an admittedly imperfect indicator as turnout is dependent upon numerous factors including geography, population dispersion, legal restrictions on voting, the prevalence of fraud and the age profile of a country's population. However, the data do help to

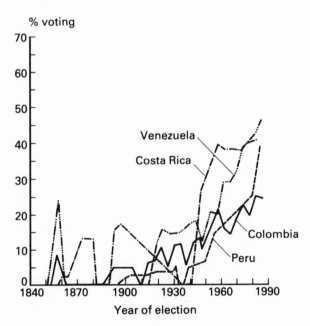

Figure 1.2. *Andean Region and Costa Rica population voting in presidential elections, 1845–1986*

Source: Enrique C. Ochoa, 'The Rapid Expansion of Voter Participation in Latin America: Presidential Elections, 1845–1986', *Statistical Abstract of Latin America* 25 (Los Angeles, 1987): 869–91.

Table 1.2. *Expansion of the suffrage in Latin America*

Country	Both property and literacy requirements removed	Women enfranchised	Voting obligatory	Illiteracy rates (15+)		
				c.1950	c.1960	c. 1985
Argentina	1912	1947	1912	14	9	4
Brazil	1985	1932	1932[†]	51	40	22
Chile	1970	1949	1958	20	16	6
Colombia	1936	1954	No	38	27	12
Costa Rica	1949	1949	1936*	21	16	6
			1959			
Peru	1979	1955	1963	–	39	15
Uruguay	1918	1932	1967	–	10	6
Venezuela	1947	1945	1958	49	37	13

Notes: [†] The Electoral Code of 1932 established severe penalties against those eligible to vote who failed to register, though it did not use the expression 'obligatory voting'.
* A law was passed in 1936, but was subsequently suspended. In 1959, obligatory voting was placed in the constitutional text.
Sources: Enrique C. Ochoa, 'The Rapid Expansion of Voter Participation in Latin America: Presidential Elections, 1845–1986', *Statistical Abstract of Latin America,* 25 (Los Angeles, Cal., 1987); on adult illiteracy (1950 and 1960), *Statistical Abstract of Latin America* 22 (Los Angeles, Cal., 1984); on adult illiteracy (1985), *Statistical Abstract of Latin America* 27 (Los Angeles, Cal., 1989); Harold Davis (ed.), *Government and Politics in Latin America* (New York, 1968); Bolivar Lamounier, personal communication; Fabrice Lehoucq, personal communication.

highlight dramatic changes within a country and contrast the evolution of participation across countries.

As is to be expected electoral turnout is greatest in those countries with higher levels of socio-economic development, stronger political parties and party systems, and well-institutionalized electoral agencies reflecting the greater extension of the rule of law: all of these are clearly factors related to citizenship. One additional feature with a direct impact on electoral turnout is the provision of mandatory voting requirements. These political factors sometimes outweigh the socio-economic ones in explaining levels of electoral participation.

As Figures 1.1 and 1.2 also illustrate, most countries experienced dramatic spurts in participation in different historical moments. These almost always reflected changes in electoral laws that facilitated the incorporation of previously excluded electorates. Table 1.2 provides information on the elimination of property and literacy requirements for voting and on the extension of the right to vote to women at the national level.

By the end of the period, Uruguay had the highest levels of electoral participation of the eight countries. This reflects at least in part the relative age of its population as well as mandatory voting requirements, although the strength and nature of its party system has undoubtedly also played a role. Women were granted the right to vote relatively early in Uruguay, in 1932, and there has been a dramatic steady climb in electoral participation since the 1934 election. There was a particularly sharp increase between the 1966 and 1971 elections, the first one in which voting was obligatory, but this probably also reflects the entry of a new party, growing mobilization and polarization of the party system. Chile, in sharp contrast to Uruguay, is probably the country whose electoral participation rates over this period are lowest given expectations based on such factors as level of socio-economic development and strength of the country's party system. The significant growth in participation between the elections of 1946 and 1964, reflect most directly the enfranchisement of women in 1949 and other electoral law changes (themselves a consequence of more complex social and political pressures). Agreements across parties to structure joint lists tended to discourage pressures to expand participation to illiterates and rural voters, slowing the movement toward universal suffrage until 1970. Even following the dramatic 1970 electoral reforms, Chile's electoral turnout rate remained below 35 per cent.

Colombia, Venezuela and Costa Rica moved toward universal male suffrage at approximately the same time, in 1936, 1947 and 1949, respectively. However, Costa Rica and Venezuela shared certain similarities in the timing and steady increase in their electorate, with Colombia presenting a significantly different pattern. By the end of the period, Costa Rica and Venezuela both had electoral participation rates above 40 per cent. Costa Rica witnessed spurts in participation between the contested 1948 elections that led to a brief civil war and enactment of a new constitution and the subsequent elections of 1953. The new constitution instituted universal suffrage and set the voting age at twenty years. This was followed by an equally dramatic expansion of the electorate between the 1958 and the 1962 elections as voting became mandatory. The electorate has continued to grow steadily since then, and in 1974 the voting age was lowered to eighteen years of age. Venezuela had no history of competitive presidential elections in the twentieth century until the election of 1947 under universal suffrage. Another sharp spurt in electoral participation came with the subsequent elections of 1958, when voting became obligatory, and growth in electoral participation has been fairly steady since then

reflecting legal requirements and successful incorporation of the population by the political parties.

In this context of generally, and often sharply, increasing voter participation rates, Colombia stands out as somewhat anomalous. Although it also
has an upward trend, it is both more moderate and more uneven than for
any of the other seven countries examined here. This is probably largely a
consequence of the demobilizing strategies of the two traditional parties in
the absence of mandatory voting requirements; indeed, Colombia is the
only country of the eight that has never mandated compulsory voting for
eligible voters. Low points in the 1920s, 1930s and 1940s reflect elections
in which one or the other party refused to present its own candidate. The
surge in 1958 was a consequence of the enfranchisement of women, simpli-
fied registration requirements, and enthusiasm for the return to civilian
rule under the coalition National Front governments.

Argentina's pattern of electoral participation most resembles that of
neighbouring Uruguay, as Figure 1.1 suggests, although its record of
democracy places it with Brazil and Peru. It has one of the earliest shifts to
universal male suffrage in Latin America, a relatively older population and
relatively higher per capita income. The first increase in participation in
Argentina appeared in 1916 with the change in electoral laws and the
entry of the Radical party into electoral life. However, the country's
democratic experience was arrested in the 1930s. A second spurt in participation took place in 1951, reflecting the enfranchisement of women
(1947), Peronist mobilization and perhaps some fraud. Downward fluctuations occurred subsequently, particularly when the Peronists were excluded until the democratization of the 1980s.

From the 1930s to the 1980s both Brazil and Peru had steadily climb-
ing participation rates from very low historical levels, especially once
women and illiterates were granted the right to vote and voting became
mandatory. Women were enfranchised (and the voting age lowered to
eighteen years) in Brazil in 1932, and in Peru in 1955. Voting has been
mandatory in Brazil since 1931, and in Peru since 1963. With the highest
levels of illiteracy of the eight countries (22 per cent and 15 per cent,
respectively in 1985, see Table 1.2), Brazil and Peru were the last to
remove property and literacy requirements to vote (in 1979 in Peru and in
1985 in Brazil). Under Peru's 1979 Constitution, which lowered the
voting age from 21 to 18, voting was made compulsory for illiterates.
Voting was also made compulsory for illiterates in Brazil in 1985, but the
1988 Constitution, which lowered the voting age to sixteen, made voting

optional for illiterates and for those under eighteen and over seventy years of age. Brazil's dramatic expansion in voter participation is unusual in that it took place for the most part during a period of military rule (1964–85), when direct congressional (but not presidential) elections were held every four years. It reflects the incorporation of many previously excluded rural electorates, as well as increased interest generated in the second half of the period by the possibilities of democratization.

Thus, by the end of this period, all eight countries under review had universal suffrage. By itself, however, this fact tells us little about their over-all democratic experience. In some countries, such as Uruguay, universal suffrage came relatively early and was largely respected. But in Argentina, the first of these eight countries to enact universal male suffrage, for most of the 1930s fraudulent elections grossly distorted the constitutional process, and from the late 1950s until the 1970s the country was ruled by outright military regimes or by hybrid regimes under which the dominant Peronist party was largely barred from presenting its candidates for office. Universal male suffrage came earlier in Colombia than in Costa Rica or Venezuela, but for much of the period Colombia was not only under a state of siege, its democracy was hamstrung by a weak state and judiciary and a restrictive coalition between its two dominant political parties. In contrast, universal suffrage came relatively late in Chile. In spite of this, until the 1973 military coup the country experienced a degree of political pluralism and competition, a richness of party diversity and respect for the rule of law which set it apart from nearly all others.

DEMOCRATIC EXPERIENCES

Considering in broad terms the relative success of their democratic experience in terms of the three elements central to any definition of democracy (as discussed in the Introduction) – contestation, constitutional order, and inclusiveness – in the period since 1930, the eight countries we are examining fall into three broad groupings. The first comprises the two countries with the richest history of democratic contestation and constitutional order on the continent: Uruguay and Chile. Uruguay's move toward direct, secret, universal male suffrage came early. Chile's came late, but its record of democratic contestation and respect for the rule of law was impressive. Both had among the strongest democratic party systems on the continent, even though, illustrating the diversity of political arrangements congruent with democracy, the nature of their parties and party systems are considerably different. However, even Chile and Uruguay seriously blemished their democratic records as they both succumbed to particularly brutal military rule in 1973. Uruguay returned to democratic rule in 1984, Chile not until 1990.

A second group of countries consists of Venezuela and Costa Rica, and more ambiguously of Colombia. Each of these countries had a less successful historical experience with constitutional order and with contestation than either Chile or Uruguay. However, they experienced a major crisis of democracy in the 1940s and/or 1950s which helped resolve in a lasting fashion the issue of toleration of a democratic opposition, threw up new parties (particularly in Venezuela and Costa Rica), and brought effective progress in the incorporation of new sectors of the population into the country's political life. Colombia is a marginal member of this group because of the severe restrictions on contestation imposed in the post-1958 National Front period, its relatively low effective inclusiveness, and then by its levels of state disaggregation. Like Uruguay, however, Colombia has a strong party system built on parties with deep roots in the nineteenth century. In contrast to the other five countries none of these three succumbed to military rule at any time during the 1960s, 1970s or 1980s.

The third set of countries comprises Argentina, Brazil and Peru. For much of the period since 1930, when they were not governed by outright authoritarian regimes, they had hybrid democratic-authoritarian regimes in which the fear or the reality of potential military intervention was a constant factor that entered into the calculations of major political actors. Argentina is the most anomalous member of this group. Based on its history of contestation and inclusiveness prior to 1930, Argentina might have been expected to have a strong democratic record after 1930. The tragic reversal of Argentina's democracy (at least until the 1980s) raises considerable doubts about simple evolutionary arguments regarding the link between modernization and democracy unmediated by political factors. Brazil experimented with statist and corporatist politics during the Estado Novo (1937–45). Both Brazil and Peru came under military rule in the 1960s. They had (and have) the weakest and most fragmented party systems of the eight countries. They were the last to expand the suffrage to all adults, including illiterates.

Not a single one of these eight countries with the most democratic experiences in the region was able to maintain even a hybrid or semi-democratic regime for the entire period from 1930 to 1990 (see Table 1.3).

Table 1.3. *Regime classification, 1930–90. Years democratic (D),*
semi-democratic (SD) or hybrid (H)

Country	Years
Argentina	1932–43 (SD); 1946–51 (D); 1958–66 (H); 1973–6 (D); 1983– (D)
Brazil	1945–64 (H); 1985–9 (SD); 1990– (D)
Chile	1932–58 (SD); 1958–73 (D); 1990– (SD)
Colombia	1930–49 (SD); 1958– (SD)
Costa Rica	1930–48 (SD); 1949– (D)
Peru	1939–48 (H); 1956–68 (H); 1980– (D)
Uruguay	1930–3 (D); 1942–73 (D); 1984– (D)
Venezuela	1945–8 (D); 1958–68 (SD); 1968– (D)

Notes: Democratic: constitutional rule, high contestation, high inclusion (universal male suffrage or high literacy offsetting restrictions).

Semi-democratic: constitutional restrictions on contestation (e.g., the National Front in Colombia) or on suffrage (see Table 1.2), or *de facto* restrictions on contestation (e.g., the 1958 Pact of Punto Fijo in Venezuela or fraud and clientelist manipulation of electorates, such as in Argentina or Colombia in the 1930s), but generally competitive, open elections determining key governmental posts.

Hybrid: Extensive military interference and frequent direct military intervention.

Sources: Larry Diamond, Juan Linz and Seymour Martin Lipset (eds), *Democracy in Developing Countries,* Vol. IV: *Latin America* (Boulder, Col. 1989); Dietrich Rueschemeyer, Evelyne Huber Stephens and John D. Stephens, *Capitalist Development and Democracy* (Chicago, 1992).

In the period from the late 1920s to the mid-1950s, Latin American democracies were affected by three significant international events: the Depression of the 1930s, the victory of the Allies and therefore of 'democracy' over fascism in the Second World War, and the advent of the Cold War. In the 1930s, coups reflected fears by elites of potential mass mobilization and protest in the face of economic crisis. Some of these coups, particularly later in the decade, reflected as well fears of Marxism and fascist disdain for democratic procedures. At the same time, Marxist and populist ideologies often viewed democracy as a corrupt enterprise only benefitting a narrow oligarchy. In the push toward more active mass participation in their countries' economic, social and political life, some viewed constitutional democracy as an obstacle. In turn, elites and their military allies came to fear the majoritarian impulse for change.

Six of the eight countries under review experienced military coups in the throes of the Depression. In all countries, the 1930s brought gradual economic recovery and the beginning of significant economic and social change with profound political implications. As in Europe, they were tumultuous years, marked by widespread political unrest as para-military groups of the right and left clashed in the streets and students and workers mastered the techniques of mass demonstrations. Social and economic progress, be it under the guise of fascism or of Marxism, was seen as a more important value than the preservation or development of liberal democratic institutions. After 1933, five of the countries under review were governed by dictatorships (Argentina, Brazil, Peru, Uruguay and Venezuela). Chile, which had experienced authoritarian rule and military activism at the onset of the Great Depression, bucked the trend by returning to constitutional rule in 1932. Colombia and Costa Rica managed to avoid constitutional breakdown, even though both countries experienced significant political change. Indeed, Colombia in 1930 managed a key test of contestation for the first time – the peaceful transfer of power from one political party (the Conservatives) to another (the Liberals), although this led to a new single party hegemony and the regime was unable to survive a second such transfer of power in 1946.

It is important not to exaggerate the political discontinuity of the period. The military coups that took place in both Chile and Uruguay, rather than leading to sharp breaks with those countries' political evolution, represented serious but passing setbacks. In neither case did authoritarian rule involve the wholesale dismantling of political parties or the replacement of civilian leaders by autonomous military organizations. Military men remained essentially obedient to political authority and once the authoritarian interlude ended, politics was restored to the parties and leaders of the past. In Venezuela, rule by *caudillos* was part of a long political history in what was the least democratic of these eight countries. The dictator Juan Vicente Gómez had been in power since 1908. After his death in 1935, two more generals held office for a decade before authoritarianism was successfully challenged by democratic forces. In the case of Peru, which had already experienced the dictatorship of Augusto B. Leguía before the Depression, military rule in the 1930s did mark the breakdown of 'oligarchical democracy', and the eruption of the populist APRA on the political scene would have new and far reaching political consequences.

Only in Argentina and Brazil did the military coups of 1930 lead to qualitative breaks with the past. In the case of Argentina, it meant the onset of a period of political reversal, in which conservative groups reassumed direct political control and employed fraudulent political means to maintain control for over a decade, once again barring opposition elements from participation and thwarting new societal groups, more particularly the working class, until Perón's dramatic rise to power in the mid-1940s. Argentina, which had been the most developed country in Latin America in the early decades of the century, would be the last major country to incorporate the working class. In Brazil, the demise of the old republic inaugurated a period of political experimentation under Getúlio Vargas which culminated in 1937 with the establishment of a modern authoritarian corporatist state, the Estado Novo (1937–45). The Estado Novo served, among other things, to link the working class through its unions to the state.[16]

By the mid-1940s, authoritarian regimes had run their course. Constitutional regimes returned to power in Peru in 1939, in Uruguay in 1942, in Venezuela and Brazil 1945. Throughout the continent, the end of the Second World War – widely viewed as a victory of democracy over fascism – strengthened democratic forces, as well as forces on the left.[17] And, with the election of February 1946 in Argentina, a short-lived democratic 'moment' was experienced by all eight countries under review simultaneously.

However, although Perón was elected president in open and fair elections in 1946, his rule declined steadily into authoritarian practices. Elsewhere, the onset of the Cold War led to a 'chilling' of democratic rights. In particular, the proscription of Communist parties – the party was declared illegal in Brazil in 1947; in Chile, Colombia, Costa Rica and Peru in 1948; and in Venezuela in 1950 – limited democratic contestation and participation.[18] Then in the late 1940s and early 1950s came a new cycle of authoritarianism. Coups or attempted coups and civil wars overthrew or undermined democratic regimes in five of the eight countries – Peru (1948), Venezuela (1948), Costa Rica (1948–9), Colombia (1948–53) and Brazil (1954–5). In Argentina Perón, who had been democratically elected in 1946, had turned authoritarian by the time he was overthrown by the military in 1955. New elite fears of populist majoritarianism and exclusion

---

[16] On labour and politics, democratic and authoritarian, in Argentina and Brazil and five of the other countries which are discussed in this chapter (Chile, Uruguay, Colombia, Venezuela and Peru), see Ruth Berins Collier and David Collier, *Shaping the Political Arena: Critical Junctures, the Labor Movement, and Regime Dynamics in Latin America* (Princeton, N.J., 1991.)

[17] On the advance and retreat of democracy in the mid-1940s, see Leslie Bethell and Ian Roxborough (eds), *Latin America between the Second World War and the Cold War, 1944–48* (Cambridge, 1992).

[18] Although most communist parties were subsequently legalized, in Brazil and the Southern Cone they suffered new proscriptions during the periods of military rule in the 1960s and 1970s.

from power in a democratic presidential system (either actual as in Argentina or Venezuela or potential as in Costa Rica or Peru) and institutional and constitutional conflicts, interacted with the advent of the Cold War and the sometimes ambiguous relationship toward democracy of the parties of the left and populist movement themselves. Military groups became important actors in a complex, but often predictable, political process in which party elites often sought to maximize their interests with a resort to force when they failed, or feared they might fail, at the ballot box.

Even so, in Costa Rica the aftermath of the 1948–9 Civil War planted the seeds for a stronger party system, toleration for the opposition, free and fair elections, and the elimination of the military as a factor in politics. Costa Rica was henceforth Latin America's model democracy. Brazil's limited post-war democracy survived the crisis following the suicide of Getúlio Vargas in 1954 – the ex-dictator Vargas had been democratically elected in 1950 – at least until the crisis of the early 1960s. Perón had been removed from office in 1955 in a self-proclaimed Revolución Libertadora, and Frondizi was elected president in 1958, though this did not bring stable democracy to Argentina. The retreat from power of Rojas Pinilla in 1957 and Odría and Pérez Jiménez in 1958 brought a transition from military rule and a restoration of constitutional government in Colombia, Peru and Venezuela respectively. In 1959, for the first time since 1948, all eight countries were again political democracies, even if several had significant restrictions. It was in that year that journalist Tad Szulc published a book entitled *The Twilight of the Tyrants.*

Ironically, 1959 was the year of the Cuban Revolution that so profoundly altered perceptions throughout Latin America and posed new threats and challenges to Latin American democracy. It brought to power the first socialist government in the western hemisphere. It raised questions about the ability of 'formal' 'bourgeois' democracy as against revolution to bring about social and economic change. It helped spur profound changes in both the military – toward focussing more on internal security and counter-insurgency – and the Church – helping to foster the currents of liberation theology. It radicalized not only intellectuals and students but also workers and peasants throughout Latin America.

Guerrilla movements emerged or were strengthened in Colombia, Peru and Venezuela, and an urban guerrilla appeared in Uruguay. Radical insurrectionary movements appeared to combat the military governments in Brazil and in Argentina. And in Chile, several radical splinter parties developed armed movements. Only Costa Rica appeared immune to this phenomenon. Although many of these guerrilla movements were inspired by Marxist ideologies and spawned by communist or socialist movements, some split off from populist movements as these sought to increase their electoral base and gain acceptance among economically dominant and culturally conservative groups. In Venezuela, the MIR broke away from AD and eventually turned to armed rebellion in coalition with other leftist groups in the early 1960s; in Argentina, the Montoneros wrapped themselves in the Peronist legacy; in Colombia, the M-19 emerged in the early 1970s in part from ANAPO and tried to use it as a mass base; in Peru, at several points radicalized groups broke from APRA to turn to insurgency.

At the same time, the Cuban Revolution encouraged anti-Communist democratic reformist movements, anxious to bring about peaceful changes in order to prevent revolutionary violence. The United States, through its Alliance for Progress, sought both to encourage reformist constitutional governments and to bolster the military as the most effective answer to appeals of the revolutionary left. Arthur Schlesinger Jr. has recalled a common view of the time: 'the future of Latin America . . . lay between the Castro road and the Betancourt road'.[19] Leaders such as the Liberals Lleras Camargo and Lleras Restrepo in Colombia, Betancourt in Venezuela, Belaúnde in Peru, and Frei in Chile were widely lauded. As this list suggests, many of these leaders came from reformist wings of traditional parties, from populist parties, or from the increasingly influential Christian Democratic parties.

Ultimately, however, the 1960s and the 1970s brought neither leftist revolution – by and large neither the rural nor the urban masses proved revolutionary – nor democratic progress to Latin America. The support of business elites for democracy remained contingent on calculations regarding the kind of regime that could best defend their interests. Many elements of the middle class, fearing a threat from below to their interests came to favor the restriction of democratic rights. An increasingly self-confident professional military, trained and equipped by the United States, showed greater concern about internal as opposed to external security threats. Over a half-dozen military coups took place in the region in the first five years of the Alliance for Progress, including in Argentina, Brazil and Peru, even as leftist insurrectionary movements failed in Venezuela, Peru and Colombia (as well as in other countries).

[19] 18 October 1989 letter to Tony Smith, cited in Tony Smith, 'The Alliance for Progress: the 1960s', in Abraham F. Lowenthal (ed.), *Exporting Democracy: The United States and Latin America* (Baltimore, Md., 1991), p. 87, n. 12.

Although unheralded at the time, the 1964 Brazilian coup was to be the first of a series of coups in Latin America carried out by the military as an institution, aiming to change fundamentally not only economic and social policy, but the political system as well. In seizing power, the Brazilian military showed contempt for stalemated democratic politics and populist appeals, while implementing repressive policies to stave off the revolutionary left. The Brazilian coup marked a qualitative change in military rule on the continent, inaugurating a government which viewed itself not simply as a referee, but as a revolutionary force seeking to forge a new political and economic order at sharp variance from the Cuban model.

Similar regimes seeking to transform politics and society were imposed on Argentina twice (with the coups of 1966 and 1976) and on Chile and Uruguay in 1973, the breakdown of democracy in Chile marking the end of a unique attempt to implement socialism through the ballot box. The 'bureaucratic-authoritarian' military regimes in Brazil, Argentina, Chile and Uruguay (to use Guillermo O'Donnell's term) were justified politically by the need to respond to the 'threat' of communism or demagogic populism in the context of leftist mobilization from below, while imposing economic stabilization and efficiency to ensure investor confidence and renewed and more vigorous growth.[20] These regimes sought to demobilize and if possible depoliticize their population. Because the perceived threat from below of previously organized groups was greater in the 1970s than in the 1960s, the extent of repression in Chile, Uruguay and Argentina (after 1976) was greater than that of the regime in Brazil. Intrinsic to the nature of these regimes, particularly those that appeared in the 1970s, was their analysis of the perceived faults of democracy, and especially the way in which politicians appealed in demagogic, corrupt and clientelist fashion to protect industrialists and organized labour.

The Peruvian coup of 1968 was also executed by a military high command with a mission, but unlike its counterparts in the Southern Cone which sought to implement conservative fiscal and economic policies and to restrict political participation, the Peruvian military attempted broad scale social reforms and popular mobilization.

The military 'reformers' of the 1960s and 1970s, however, left their countries with a decidedly mixed legacy. Brazilian society experienced fundamental transformations under military rule, but only in Chile was

---

[20] See David Collier (ed.), *The New Authoritarianism in Latin America* (Princeton, N.J., 1979), chapter by O'Donnell.

bureaucratic authoritarianism successful in fundamentally transforming the blueprint of the interventionist state and laying the groundwork for a successful strategy of export-led development. All of the military regimes failed in implementing their agendas for political reform, including fundamental transformations of the party system and the development of highly restricted democracies under military tutelage. The Peruvian military also failed in implementing reforms capable of revitalizing the economy and pre-empting the rise of insurrectionary opposition. And, the democratic governments that followed the military regimes of Argentina, Chile and Uruguay, in particular, had the difficult dilemma of seeking to balance the right to know the truth about human rights violations and punish those responsible, with the risk of threatening democratic stability by encouraging a new military coup.

At the end of the 1970s only three of the eight countries under review – Costa Rica, Colombia and Venezuela – maintained democratic systems, and Colombian democracy was seriously challenged by the growing threat of the narcotics trade and rural guerrilla movements. However, during the following decade, the military withdrew from power in Peru (1980), Argentina (1983), Uruguay (1984), Brazil (1985) and Chile (1990). At the beginning of the 1990s, all eight countries were again experiencing democratic rule.

The strength of the parties and party systems in both Chile and Uruguay were the central basis for continued optimism regarding the future of democracy in these countries following their transition out of military dictatorship. Argentina appeared to be moving gradually toward a more stable polity with the establishment of a two-party system and dramatic but still incomplete, economic restructuring. Peru, however, was in the midst of a devastating economic crisis and a cruel insurrectionary challenge which aggravated the weakness and stalemate of democratic institutions. There was a question mark also over Brazil, where weak political parties and political leadership had not been able to structure the necessary governing coalitions able to place the country's economy in order and begin to deal with daunting social problems.

Let us now review the democratic experience of each of the eight countries from the late 1950s to the early 1990s.[21]

---

[21] Political histories can be found in other volumes of the *Cambridge History of Latin America:* chapter on Costa Rica in *CHLA* Vol. VII (1990); chapters on Argentina, Chile, Colombia, Peru, Uruguay and Venezuela in *CHLA* Volume VIII (1991); and chapters on Brazil in *CHLA* Vol. IX (forthcoming).

Chile

Chile functioned relatively well as a democracy with the broadest spectrum of parties in Latin America from the early 1930s to the early 1970s. It was only as the Christian Democratic party became a more rigid and ideological centre, and the parties of the right and the left became equally more polarized and ideologized in the post-Cuban Revolution era, that Chile's multi-party system became unmanageable. For much of the time prior to the Allende years, the 'glue' of brokerage and of clientelist politics at the local level across the entire party spectrum helped to offset the more ideologized and polarized debates and conflicts at the national level. This suggests that in countries with deep societal divisions, there are substantial benefits to multi-party systems, as they can more effectively express and channel political demands, so long as a balance between ideological and brokerage politics may be sustained and the polarizing risks of presidentialism can be managed.

In the 1960s the political centre of gravity in Chile's highly polarized party system shifted decidedly to the left. The Radicals were displaced in the political centre by the surging Christian Democrats which took a decidedly reformist position, arguing that they represented a third way between socialism and capitalism. Fearing that the left would win, if the centre and right ran candidates on separate slates in the 1964 presidential race, Chile's right-wing parties reluctantly supported Eduardo Frei, the Christian Democratic candidate, who won with an absolute majority of votes, defeating Salvador Allende, the candidate of the left. Frei moved forcefully to implement his 'revolution in liberty', with significant support from the United States government. The Christian Democrats were confident that their reformist policies would help them break the traditional 'three thirds' division of Chilean politics, eroding the strength of both right and left. The right felt betrayed by the party they had voted for, in particular bitterly opposing the agrarian reform efforts and its rural unionization programme, which they saw as breaking the old covenant of Chilean politics which permitted the right to retain a strong presence on the land and control rural labour. The left was also threatened by the Christian Democrats aggressive state-sponsored efforts to expand the union movement and mobilize shanty-town dwellers.

Although the Christian Democrats were successful in implementing many of their programmes, they did not succeed in becoming a majority party capable of perpetuating itself in power. To the surprise even of the left, in the 1970 race, Allende, won 36 per cent of the vote, a smaller percentage than he had received in 1964, but enough to give him a plurality in the three-way race. Rather than recount the tragic story of escalating polarization that eventually led to the 1973 coup, it may be useful to emphasize the fact that if Chile had had a parliamentary regime rather than a presidential one, Allende might well have lost a vote of no-confidence in parliament, rather than committing suicide in the wake of a bloody coup that marked the interruption of Chilean democracy for seventeen years.

Chile's parties appeared to have learned a painful lesson from the events of the 1970s. In the 1990 presidential elections that marked the democratic transition, Patricio Aylwin, a Christian Democrat, presided over a broad centre left coalition, including the Socialist Party. He inherited a constitution which provided him with strong executive powers but which, at the same time, contained many anti-democratic elements, particularly those which barred the president from appointing or removing military commanders and gave the armed forces virtual autonomy. Without a majority in the Senate, due to the institution of appointed senators specified in the Constitution of 1980, he had to proceed with great caution in adopting a programme of reforms, dealing with the former military dictator Augusto Pinochet who retained his post as army commander, and addressing the issue of human rights violations. Under its new democracy Chile retained a multi-party system, although one that appeared less polarized than in the past. The continued presence of the communist party, although reduced in size, and the persistence of authoritarianism of right-wing forces on the right with little commitment to democracy, meant that ideological distance was still a factor in Chilean politics. In the 1993 presidential race, the centre-left coalition that defeated Pinochet succeeded in once again capturing the presidency with the election of Eduardo Frei Ruiz-Tagle, the former president's son.

Uruguay

Uruguay, during this period, demonstrates both the strengths and weaknesses of its particular combination of presidentialism and two-party politics. The interaction between its constrained party system and electoral rules clearly played a role in the 1973 democratic breakdown, as did the emerging strength of the leftist third party, the Frente Amplio. Yet, the return to democracy in the 1980s was facilitated by the continuing strength and relative moderation of the country's two historic parties.

Although the Blanco party captured the executive for the first time in modern history in 1958, as Uruguayans demonstrated their concern for the country's decline, Uruguay's perennial second party was not able to capitalize on its term in office to gain a permanent advantage. In the 1966 election, the Colorados regained the upper-hand in an election which also marked a return to the presidential system, after experimentation with a plural executive since 1951, in the hope that strong leadership could help overcome the country's economic decline and political crisis.

While other countries in the region spawned rural guerrilla movements encouraged by the Cuban example, Uruguay's highly sophisticated urban society saw the emergence of Latin America's most celebrated urban guerrillas, the Tupamaros. Attracting idealistic students and professional people with dwindling prospects for personal advancement in Uruguay's limping welfare state economy, the Tupamaros enjoyed surprising support among the population at large. The leftward trend in Uruguayan society was demonstrated by the important gains of the Frente Amplio, a broad coalition of far and moderate left groups in the 1971 presidential race. At the same time, the country's peculiar electoral system permitted the most right-wing candidate, with clear minority support, to win the presidency. The government of Juan María Bordaberry (1972–6) continued its predecessor's practice of involving the armed forces more deeply in counterinsurgency activities, finally declaring a state of internal war in 1972 which would lead to the defeat the Tupamaros. However, congressional opposition to the growing interventionism of the state and Bordaberry's exercise of unilateral executive authority, finally encouraged the president to dissolve the congress in 1973 with the support of right-wing elements in both parties and the military. His action, however, eventually lead to the imposition of a repressive authoritarian regime and direct military involvement in the ruling of the country.

The transition process in the 1980s was replete with difficulties, particularly as a leading National Party leader, Wilson Ferreira, was arrested by the military in June 1984. The final agreement was a *reforma pactada* in which both sides made concessions, culminating in the Naval Club Agreements. The opposition had to accept Ferreira's continued imprisonment, while promising the armed forces no legal retribution. The armed forces in turn permitted a return to the previous institutional order with open elections scheduled for November 1984. One of the most significant aspects of the civil-military dialogue was the direct participation of the Frente Amplio, a necessary development given the National party's refusal to participate. Thus, military officers were forced to deal with leaders of the left in seeking a compromise that was acceptable to a majority of Uruguayans. The Frente Amplio obtained 20 per cent of the vote in the presidential contest, a comparable figure to the 1971 race, underscoring the fact that Uruguay's party system had been fully restored, although it was becoming less of a two-party system than in the past.

The return to civilian rule presented new president Julio María Sanguinetti (1985–90), a Colorado journalist and party leader, with enormous challenges. A wave of strikes and labour demands made it difficult to address the nation's economic problems. Co-operation from the opposition National party, though, made it possible to institute economic measures and reforms. Civil-military relations remained his most vexing problem. Honoring a pledge to put an end to the liability of the military for human rights abuses, the government, with support of the Nationals, approved an amnesty law which would exonerate military officers from prosecution as earlier laws had done for the Tupamaros. The government's action elicited a bitter response from thousands of Uruguayans and the Frente Amplio who forced a plebiscite on the issue. The results in the end favoured the government 57 per cent to 43 per cent, putting to rest the difficult issue of justice and retribution. The 1989 presidential race was won by Luis Alberto Lacalle, a National leader, after strong intra-party conflicts had reduced the Colorado's chances of retaining the presidency. The Frente Amplio demonstrated its continued strength by winning the key mayoral post in Montevideo. Thus, Uruguay entered the 1990s a democracy once again, with a two-and-a-half party system.

The transitions from military rule in the late 1950s in Colombia and Venezuela had some important similarities. In both cases, political pacts were signed among the opposition parties providing each other with mutual assurances that they would not seek to govern hegemonically. In this way, the central issue of contestation was resolved, though the solution was eventually to lead to different kinds of challenges to the respective regimes. In both cases a predominant party (the Liberals in Colombia, AD in Venezuela) purposefully underplayed its potential power in order to facilitate the transition. Assurances were also given to economic actors and to the Church that their interests would be respected. In that sense, both

were conservative transitions that helped insure that economically dominant groups would not feel threatened and perhaps turn to the military,
yet in that way also limiting possibilities that major social or economic
reforms would be enacted. At the same time, significant differences in the
nature of these pacts and in the political economies of these two countries
help explain why Colombia was a country torn by political turmoil and
violence in the 1980s while Venezuela had a more successful – though far
from trouble-free – democracy.

Colombia

In Colombia, rigid guarantees under the National Front agreement –
constitutionally enshrined by a 1957 plebiscite – insured that neither
Liberals nor Conservatives would be excluded from power, while also
blocking access to potential new parties. Party leaders agreed to complete parity in the three branches of government. Congress, departmental assemblies and municipal councils would all automatically be
half-Liberal and half-Conservative, as would be the judiciary; cabinet
posts, governors and mayors would also be divided equally between the
two parties. Furthermore, most legislation would require a two-thirds
majority for approval. Finally, because Conservatives could not agree on a
candidate for the 1958 elections and because the presidency was such a
major post, they agreed to alternation in the presidency from 1958 to
1974 (thus assuring the Conservatives the last presidency).

The agreement was enacted by elite negotiation and was intended to
demobilize sectarian party followers and end the rural violence. Immobilism induced by the restrictive National Front rules and fear of popular
protests led most of the National Front governments to rule under state of
siege regulations. Neither significant redistributive reforms nor dramatic
strengthening of popular sector organizations took place (though these did
not deteriorate as in many other Latin American countries). Thus, the
nature of the country's democracy remained qualified throughout this
period.

The National Front period had the characteristics of a one-party and a
multi-party, as well as of a two-party system. Because presidents were
required to be of one designated party in each of the elections from 1958
through 1970, bi-partisan agreement was necessary. This official National
Front candidate thus headed a bi-partisan government that appeared to be
of a single party. Within each party, however, factions emerged opposed to

the National Front. Because most legislation required a two-thirds majority for passage until 1968, the existence of these various factions necessitated extensive negotiation on the part of the president with what appeared to be a squabbling multi-party system. Throughout this period, however, and even into the late 1970s and 1980s, by which time nearly all of the formal National Front requirements of coalition rule were lifted, the two traditional parties retained remarkably consistent percentages of the over-all vote in elections.

However, as a result of a profound socio-economic transformation in this period (the result of urbanization, industrialization, population growth, and increased literacy) as well as the National Front agreement itself, the sectarian identification of the country's population with the two political parties declined significantly. The centrality of the parties to the country's political life declined, even as they retained a near monopoly in the electoral arena. Non-electoral forms of opposition emerged or were strengthened – labour confederations independent of the two parties, civic protest movements and guerrilla movements. However, coalition rule remained attractive, for different reasons, to regional party leaders (access to patronage), major economic groups (access to policy-making) and international actors (insulation of decision-making).

Successive administrations were embroiled in questions of constitutional change, political reform and response to guerrilla violence. Complicating these efforts was the reality of drug trafficking, which weakened the state, emboldened guerrilla groups and elements of the security forces alike, led to the assassination of popular sector leaders, leftist party activists, journalists and high government officials and spurred sentiments of cynicism and despair. This period of stalemate, violence and despair, however, was punctuated by a most remarkable event, the enactment in 1991 of a new Constitution in which all elements of coalition rule which had remained since 1974 were dismantled. It was prepared by a Constituent Assembly in which representatives of a recently reincorporated guerrilla group (the M-19 Democratic Alliance) had a major presence. For the first time, a Colombian Constitution was the product of significant public discussion, negotiation and compromise.

Venezuela

Venezuela's political pact among major parties in 1958 was neither as rigid or exclusive as Colombia's, nor did it form part of the country's

Constitution. However, the parties (excluding the Communist party) agreed to a common programme which sought to provide assurances to economic and Church elites. Thus, though AD handily won the 1958 elections, Betancourt (1958–63) governed in conjunction with opposition parties, collaborating particularly with Rafael Caldera of COPEI. As revolutionary guerrillas emerged, some from the disgruntled youth wing of the AD, Betancourt successfully portrayed himself as a coalition builder of the centre and the right against this radicalized left. However, also unlike Colombia, rather than seeking to demobilize the country's population, the major Venezuelan parties maintained a vigorous institutional life; they actively sought to organize the country's growing electorate especially in urban areas where they were weak and to sustain a strong presence in labour and professional associations.

The 1968 and 1973 elections marked major turning points. Unlike Colombia, which found itself stalemated by coalition rule well into the 1980s, in 1969 COPEI formed a single-party government. Eventually, Caldera was able to assure co-operation with AD in Congress on selected issues. Under Caldera, guerrillas were successfully reincorporated into the democratic process, and leftist parties were legalized. Targeted government expenditures facilitated by oil revenues, effective assurances regarding the physical integrity of former guerrilla leaders and widespread legitimacy for democratic institutions in the country all facilitated the process. Finally, Caldera's administration set the stage for the effective dominance by AD and COPEI of the country's electoral landscape. From the 1973 elections, which were won by AD's Carlos Andrés Pérez, the two parties consistently received more than 80 per cent of the vote. They became 'catch-all' parties with overlapping social bases, ideological views and policy positions.

However, during Carlos Andrés Pérez's second term (1989–93), the fragility of even a seemingly consolidated democracy such as that of Venezuela became apparent. A contingent of junior military officers led two failed uprisings, one of which nearly succeeded in assassinating the president. To the horror of party leaders, however, the attempted coups found a strong echo in public opinion. The country was reeling from a difficult process of economic restructuring following the boom and bust years of the oil bonanza and then the debt crisis. Underlying the economic and social discontent was a sense that the two political parties were led by corrupt cliques who had grown distant from their mass following, generating more of a government by parties (*partidocracia*) than by people (*democracia*). That is to say party leaders, due to their control over the party organization and the placement of names on lists for elected offices, held too much power over potential candidates. These candidates, then, sought to curry favour as much with the party leadership as with their potential electorate. Internal governance within the parties was far from a democratic process itself. Finally, there was discontent with the seeming corruption, cronyism and self-serving mutual support that the two major parties provided for each other. When corruption charges reached the president himself Pérez was impeached, providing the country with a constitutional safety valve to the most serious crisis of confidence in the nation's fundamental institutions since the establishment of democracy in 1958. The extent and the permance of the damage to the country's two major parties, AD and COPEI, remained unclear. Rafael Caldera (president in 1968–73), broke with COPEI to run successfully an independent campaign for the presidency in 1993, the most serious threat to the two-party system in Venezuela since its consolidation in 1968.

Costa Rica

In Costa Rica, with Venezuela one of the two most successful democracies in Latin America since the 1950s, a two-party system emerged only gradually. Following the 1948 civil war the PLN (founded in 1951), played a dominant role in Costa Rican politics. However, after the overwhelming victory of Figueres, in the 1953 presidential elections, divisions within the PLN facilitated a victory by an opposition candidate in 1958. The PLN went on to win five of the subsequent seven presidential elections, with the opposition winning only in 1966 and in 1978. For the 1978 elections, a number of the opposition parties banded together in an informal coalition known as the Unity Opposition. By 1984, they had formally joined together into a single party, the Partido Unidad Social Cristiana-PUSC. The 'winner-take-all' logic of presidentialism and the predominant position of the PLN helped drive them together. The strong two-party system logic is evident in the fact that in the four presidential elections from 1974 to 1986, the two top candidates received an average percentage vote of 89 per cent.

Throughout the 1980s Costa Rica confronted the difficult challenge of restructuring its economy and shrinking down the relatively generous state services it had been able to extend to its population. During most of this decade it was led by the PLN which finally lost to the increasingly more unified opposition in the 1990 elections. Buffeted as it was both by international economic challenges as well as Cold War policies of the United States toward Nicaragua (which, however, did generate increased aid flows to the country), Costa Rica was unquestionably helped by the fact that it had eliminated its armed forces (in 1949) and that democratic processes had attained high levels of legitimacy within the population as a whole.

Argentina

The overthrow of Perón in Argentina in 1955 lead to another dismal chapter in the volatile politics of twentieth-century Argentina. Over the next thirty-five years no president would end his constitutional term in office to make way for an elected successor. The Radical party, the dominant party for two decades before the 1930s, was not only frag-mented but formally organized into opposing political parties. The Justicialista (Peronist) Party, was legally proscribed (with its leader in exile) and also fractionalized. From exile, Perón cast a large shadow over all other parties and groups, as he retained the surprising loyalty of a majority of Argentines. Because Perón remained anathema to the mili-tary establishment, Argentine politics, in Guillermo O'Donnell's words, would continue to be an 'insoluble game'. Without the support of the electorate, every government, constitutional or unconstitutional, lacked popular legitimacy and found it very difficult to impose any sense of authority. Nor could a government elected in a contest which barred the Peronists seek such legitimacy by establishing a bridge to the Peronists, lest it incur the wrath of the military. This is what happened to the Radical President Arturo Frondizi, elected in 1958, who was deposed in 1962, after permitting Peronist participation in provincial elections. Although less open to the Peronists, Arturo Illia suffered the same fate four years later.

The 1966 coup, which resulted in the designation of General Juan Carlos Onganía as president with broad dictatorial powers, marked the beginning of Argentina's first version of a bureaucratic authoritarian re-gime. Its marked failure finally led a subsequent military ruler to seek accommodation with opposition political leaders, including Perón. These overtures finally led to the eventual return of the seventy-eight-year-old leader to the presidency in September 1973 amid great fanfare and hope.

But the ailing *caudillo* was not able to cope with runaway inflation and the serious polarization of Argentine society, including within his own party. With his death only ten months later, the economic and political crisis in the country spun further out of control under the hapless rule of Perón's wife, Isabel Martínez, who assumed the presidency in her capacity as Vice-president, until her overthrow in 1976 ushering in Argentina's second bureaucratic-authoritarian military regime.

The 1982 invasion of the Malvinas/Falkland islands in a vain effort by the military to distract attention from growing domestic problems, and the military's subsequent ignominious defeat facilitated a rapid transition to democracy on the opposition's terms. In October 1983, Raúl Alfonsín, the leader of the Radical party, won the presidency, inflicting the first electoral loss ever on the Peronists. Alfonsín, with courage and determination, confronted the military over past human rights abuses, permitting the justice system to try and convict top military leaders, including ex-president General Jorge Videla, for their crimes. Several military revolts were contained as the citizenry made it clear that it would not stand for military adventurism. In working with the opposition Peronists, Alfonsín also showed a strong determination to put aside the politics of destructive competition and begin constructive political competition. Radical party successes in the 1985 congressional and state elections suggested that Argentina had begun to move away from the dominant single party configuration which had characterized its politics for so long, particularly after the rise of Perón.

Alfonsín's downfall proved to be the intractable Argentine economy. A successful stabilization programme unravelled as his government proved unwilling to stick by unpopular measures during election time. More fundamentally, Alfonsín did not fully understand the serious structural difficulties of the Argentine economy, with a bloated and inefficient public sector and a weak and dependent private sector used to surviving with state subsidies and favourable regulations. Ironically, it would be up to Alfonsín's successor, Peronist Carlos Menem, elected in 1989, to control hyperinflation and to embark on the difficult task of dismantling most of the legacy left by the populist years of Juan Perón. Menem's personalistic style did not bode well for the institutionalization of politics, but at the beginning of the 1990s Argentina appeared to have a viable democracy based on an emerging two-party system with both the Radical and Justicialista (Peronist) parties having strong roots in Argentine society.

Peru

In Peru, the party system has been notoriously weak and prone to fragmentation during this period. In no election did the two top parties ever receive 80 per cent or more of the vote. Since 1980, in no successive presidential elections have the same two parties been first or second in the polls. However, as we have seen, Peru possessed one coherent party, APRA, throughout this period, and other parties have been significant for more limited periods of time. For most of its history, APRA (founded in 1924) has been either illegal or in serious conflict with the military; indeed the party was officially illegal for twenty-one of its first twenty-five years. Furthermore, APRA's own democratic credentials have been questionable, though after the disastrous failure of the 1948 revolt and the repression of the Odría years, the party by the late 1950s was far more committed to seeking power through elections. APRA, moreover, retained a high degree of popularity with the electorate. Thus, like Argentina, democracy in Peru confronted a serious predicament: free elections were likely to lead to the victory of a party that was unacceptable to the military.

APRA's desperate search for acceptability and for power led it over the years to agree to serve as junior partners in electoral coalitions with other forces. This included one with Manuel Prado, a moderate businessman, in the 1956 elections. Prado's personalist party largely did not survive his presidency to any significant extent – unlike General Odría's Unión Nacional Odriísta (UNO). And the Communists and other leftist parties, though they did make some inroads into the labour movement, did not have much electoral impact. The 1956 election marked the appearance of Fernando Belaúnde's Acción Popular-AP party, with a reformist platform similar to that of the much smaller Christian Democratic party. These parties appealed to new urban working-class and middle-sector groups and elements of the peasantry freed from traditional forms of domination. APRA, because of its legal constraints and alliance with Prado, failed to incorporate these new elements of the electorate and thus was unable to become a majority party. In the 1962 elections, Haya de la Torre, though he finished first, was unable to garner the one-third of the vote necessary to be declared winner outright. As the Peruvian Congress debated the outcome, the military intervened and supervised new elections in 1963. In these, Belaúnde emerged victorious with 39 per cent of the vote (to Haya's 34 per cent and Odría's 24 per cent). For most of Belaúnde's presidency,

APRA formed an alliance in the opposition with UNO, in spite of the brutal repression APRA had confronted at Odría's hands in the 1950s. By the time APRA realized the seriousness of the immobilism and drift it helped create, it was too late to stop the military coup of 1968. Ironically, military perceptions that APRA had now become too conservative to govern Peru, linked to fears that APRA would be likely to win the 1969 elections, played a role in the coup.

In the 1960s, APRA increasingly lost adherents to a more radical faction, parts of which ultimately formed a guerrilla movement. And, in 1967, progressive factions of both the AP and the Christian Democrats broke away frustrated by Belaúnde's inability to carry out reforms. But it was the multiple social and economic changes induced by the military after 1968, combined with subsequent economic decline and the military's resort to more repressive tactics, which fed a dramatic growth in leftist parties and movements and to further ties between the labour movement and the left. The emergence of the electoral left, in the form of a broad coalition of forces within the United Left (IU – *Izquierda Unida*), was first apparent in elections for the 1978 Constituent Assembly; with 36.3 per cent the IU received the plurality of the vote. However, the left did not fare as well in the subsequent three presidential elections: the IU received 17 per cent of the vote in 1980, 25 per cent in 1985, and (divided by two) 10.9 per cent in 1990.

These three elections illustrate dramatically the weakness and volatility of the party system in the face of the country's most severe economic crisis, compounded by the challenges of confronting the Shining Path (*Sendero Luminoso*) guerrillas and the additional violence and corruption associated with drug trafficking. AP, victorious in the 1980 presidential elections with 45.4 per cent of the vote, received only 7.3 per cent of the vote in 1985. And APRA, which won the 1985 elections with 53.4 per cent of the vote, fell to only 19.1 per cent in the 1990 elections. Prior to the division and collapse of the electoral left, the 1990 elections appeared to presage the complete polarization of the country's political system. In the end, further reflecting party weakness, the two top vote getters in the first round of the elections, Alberto Fujimori and Mario Vargas Llosa, were essentially figures from outside of the political parties with little or no prior political experience. And, in spite of his late entry into the race, the politically unknown Fujimori won the second round election and assumed the presidency. Although the new president won 62.5 per cent of the vote in the second round, his own supporters obtained only 16.9 per cent of the seats in the Chamber of Deputies. The fragmentation of the traditional parties combined with Fujimori's hostility towards parties and politicians led to an increased personalization of the regime and overt hostility between the executive and the legislature controlled by the opposition. On 5 April 1992, Fujimori, with backing from the military, closed down the Congress. Although his action was popular with a citizenry reeling with Peru's economic crisis and the violence of the Shining Path, it did not augur well for the consolidation of democratic institutions.

Brazil

The military officers, who in 1964 brought to an abrupt end Brazil's first (and until the 1980s only) experiment in multi-party democratic politics, justified their seizure of power as a last resort, aimed at bringing an end to what they saw as a corrupt politics, racked by polarization and instability, contributing to economic decline. Although at first they proclaimed their intention to remain in office temporarily, as long as it took to remove the offending politicians, by their second year in office, and in the face of opposition parties' successes in state elections, they made clear their intention to stay longer in order to implement their 'revolutionary' programme.

Throughout its long history (1964–85), the Brazilian military regime was a curious combination of dictatorship and restricted democratic rule. Although political leaders were banned, the press censored and the trade unions repressed, the military government permitted the continued operation of an elected congress, albeit with limited authority. The activities of parties were curbed, but the regime sought to develop a new party system, grouping previous parties and factions into two party organizations, Aliança Renovadora Nacional-ARENA and Movimento Democrático Brasileiro-MDB, one pro-government, the other a loyal opposition. The implicit assumption was that a moderate two-party system, following the U.S. model, could be instituted and designed to stabilize the political process. Presidents were appointed for fixed terms in office by the military, but ratified by an electoral college of elected officials. While the armed forces as an institution had considerable say in the choice of the executive and influenced policy, they did not as an institution govern directly, delegating authority to predominantly urban political leaders and their coteries of technocrats and advisers, although for close to five years after the imposition of the exclusionary Fifth Institutional Act in 1968, military leaders governed with little consultation, cracking down on opponents and destroying an incipient guerrilla movement.

With the selection of General Ernesto Geisel (1974–9) the military government began a lengthy process of decompression, amid mounting economic difficulties provoked in part by the sharp increases in petroleum prices. In an attempt to quell growing discontent and burgeoning demands, Geisel sought to liberalize gradually, retaining governmental control through an elaborate effort at political engineering, ranging from the manipulation of electoral and party rules to restrictions on political expression and campaigning. By 1982, elections were open to other parties, including the Partido dos Trabalhadores (PT) under Luis Inácio da Silva (Lula). Although their ability to compete fairly was circumscribed, the growth of new, mostly weak parties meant that the simple two party system envisioned by the military had changed into a shifting and volatile multi-party system reminiscent of the situation before 1964.

Although the military government refused to permit direct presidential elections, an electoral college selected opposition leader Tancredo Neves president in 1985, effectively ending military rule. Neves' death, however, before assuming his office was a serious blow to Brazilian democracy. His vice-president, José Sarney, who assumed power, was a weaker man with far less democratic legitimacy. He presided over a long-drawn out and unwieldy constitutional reform crisis, at a time of mounting economic difficulties exacerbated by Brazil's colossal external debt. In 1989, Brazilians, including illiterates enfranchised for the first time in 1985 and newly enfranchised sixteen and seventeen year-olds, finally went to the polls to elect a president in direct elections. The polarization of the campaign was evident in the strong showings of veteran leftist leader Leonel Brizola and especially of Lula. In a run-off, however, Lula was defeated by Fernando Collor de Mello, a governor from a small state who surged in the polls thanks to his television campaign and anti-corruption platform.

Collor would prove to be a disastrous president. With weak political support of his own he was not able to reach out to opposition leaders in the congress to form a viable governing coalition to address the country's serious inflationary pressures and lacklustre economic performance. And, before he had completed half of his term in office, Collor was further weakened by serious accusations of corruption which eventually led to his impeachment and forced him from office, undermining efforts to consolidate a democratic constitutional order. Brazil under Collor illustrates the problems that weak multi-partyism in combination with presidentialism represents for countries seeking to institutionalize and consolidate democracy.

CONCLUSION

In this chapter, we have reviewed the experience of the eight Latin American countries with the most democratic experience in the twentieth century in the context of two historical cycles: from the late 1920s to the late 1950s (with a sub-cycle in the mid to late 1940s) and from the late 1950s to the late 1980s. Each began with a predominance of civilian regimes many of which succumbed to military rule only to return subsequently to rule by civilians. If the 1930s were a decade in which numerous weak oligarchic democracies were swept away, the 1980s were a decade in which equally weak mass democracies, their future still uncertain, were reinstated.

It is our premise that regardless of the immediate future of democracy in many countries of Latin America, its evolution has been either too readily dismissed or handled with excessively facile generalizations. The enduring nature of democracy as an ideal and as a set of institutions and practices, however imperfect, has often been misrepresented. Latin American countries have had decades of experimentation with elections, political parties of varying ideological persuasions, national and provincial assemblies and elected national, regional and local governments. Although constitutions have often been violated, most countries in the region are highly legalistic and take seriously constitutional precepts, even when they do not adhere to them. Despite many challenges both ideological and political, the legitimacy of democracy as the most appropriate institutional arrangement for governing a country and resolving conflicts peacefully is a central part of the heritage of Latin American political culture since independence. Even though the record of democracy in Latin America is decidedly mixed, a historical review indicates that it has retained a permanence on the continent – as an aspiration, as an option, and as a set of institutions and practices.

By contrast with much of Europe, the development and consolidation of democracy in Latin America in the twentieth century has not been complicated by fundamental disagreements over territory or the essence of nationhood. Moreover, with the partial exception of countries like Peru, Bolivia and Guatemala, with multiple languages and large indigenous populations that have failed to become fully integrated into national life, the multiple ethnic, linguistic, religious and historic divisions which complicated the consolidation of national authority in Europe have been largely absent. Regional, political and personal rivalries did fuel nineteenth-century civil strife, but these conflicts revolved primarily around competing claims for power and the establishment of national authority, not around competing definitions of the national community itself. The countries of Latin America are largely nations of immigrants in which citizenship is defined through birth or individual choice, not prior ethnic identity or religious faith. Even the divisive Church/state issue revolved around the degree of Church control over secular life, not around competing faiths, each seeking to impose their own truth value on others. In these ways the challenge of creating a political community for much of Latin America was far less daunting than for Germany, Holland, Belgium, Spain, Ireland or Czechoslovakia.

The American continent is the continent of republican government and presidential democracy. The countries of Latin America (Brazil excepted) share with the United States the experience of being the oldest continuous republics of the contemporary world. The establishment of political authority in the nineteenth century, and often into the twentieth, was, however, thwarted by complex regional, economic, political and personal rivalries. The twin threats to constitutional order feared most by the founding fathers of the United States, executive tyranny and the fear of a tyranny of the majority, would severely challenge constitutional order in the southern hemisphere.

By the 1920s, a century after independence, constitutional governments predominated in the regions, although many were quite restricted both in terms of contestation and inclusiveness. But, ten coups in the period 1930–3 meant that for most of the 1930s fifteen dictatorships cast their shadow over five surviving democracies. In the period following the Second World War, a war which was fought to preserve and defend democracy there was a brief resurgence of democracy in Latin America, as the number of constitutional governments increased to eleven. These regimes proved vulnerable, however, to the direct involvement of the military in political affairs, often in tacit or overt support of particular civilian contenders. By the late 1940s and early 1950s democratic regimes were once again outnumbered by ten outright dictatorships, in some cases as a direct reflection of the Cold War and growing concern over the increased power of the left. Military governments, however, generally viewed their role as referees of the political process rather than permanent rulers, making way for elected civilian regimes. Thus, by 1959 only four countries in the region were governed by military regimes, the most auspicious moment for democracy since the late 1920s.

The pendulum swung sharply back in the 1960s in the aftermath of the Cuban Revolution and this time the nature of dictatorship changed in qualitative terms. Between 1962 and 1964 eight military takeovers took place. Military coups in Brazil, Argentina, Peru, Chile and Uruguay inaugurated bureaucratic authoritarian or other military regimes which sought to rebuild the institutional order, either in direct response to threats from the left or in an attempt to preempt that threat. During the 1970s, depending upon the year, there were from twelve to sixteen authoritarian governments in Latin America, most intent on modernizing and transforming their societies by excluding not only the old politicians but the citizenry as well. Then, in the 1980s, in the throes of the worst economic crisis since the 1929 Depression, the most dramatic political reversal took place on the continent since the 1930s. By 1990, and for the first time in its history, all of the countries of the region with the exception of Cuba were led by elected presidents according to constitutionally prescribed provisions, however circumscribed the democratic nature of many of these regimes. Crises in the early 1990s in Haiti, Venezuela, Peru and Guatemala signalled the continued fragility of democracy on the continent in the last decade of the century.

In this context, we have explored the democratic experience of eight countries in the region (all the major countries except Mexico, and including Costa Rica). Our review suggests that no simple set of economic, cultural or historical determinants appears to explain satisfactorily the evolution of democracy in Latin America. Its construction is a complex process, subject to many challenges and reversals. Rather than being condemned to authoritarianism by inherited cultural patterns or requiring the prior development of democratic citizens, our review suggests that democracy and democratic practices engender, over time, patterns of behaviour and values which help configure democratic societies. The timing and sequence of attempts to resolve the challenges of contestation and inclusiveness are important factors in considering alternative patterns of democratic development. Nor is it possible to ignore the effects on democracy of socio-economic change and external shocks such as the 1929 Depression, the Second World War, the Cold War and Cuban Revolution. Democratic failures in Latin America in the period after 1930 reflect the continuous struggle to enlarge political access for sectors excluded from participation.

Although the underlying social forces and conflicts generated by profound change affected the prospects of democratic consolidation, our review suggests that the prospects for democracy were also significantly affected by political variables. These have a greater degree of autonomy from underlying social, economic and international forces than much of the literature has assumed. Democratic consolidation was affected by the lack of fairness of fundamental rules, such as those defining the electoral process, and the systematic exclusion of oppositions from the spoils of government. Aggravating the problem of democratic governability was the gridlock resulting from the separation of powers in which minority or lame-duck presidents and hostile parliamentary majorities frequently clashed, each claiming to be the legitimate representative of the people. Political leadership was also decisive at major turning points, as suggested by the examples of Figueres in Costa Rica and Betancourt in Venezuela.

A central feature differentiating the eight countries was the strength and principal characteristics of their party systems. Consolidated democracies possess institutionalized parties and stable party systems, in which the interaction among parties follows predictable patterns. With the partial exception of Chile's multi-party system, presidential democracies with two or two and a half party systems have functioned best. And, those countries with the most inchoate party systems and volatile party formations had the weakest experience with democracy.

As Latin America moves towards the twenty-first century, new burdens are being placed on old and nascent democracies. International economic globalization and domestic transformations are causing state shrinking and restructuring, a movement toward open markets, a growing informalization of the economy and a weakening of historic social actors such as trade unions and social movements. Economic and social dislocation has increased electoral volatility, often contributing to the personalization of power. These wrenching changes appeared to be affecting the social underpinnings of democracy in some countries, limiting the possibilities for improving the quality of life and the strength and variety of organizations in society that enhance citizenship and enrich democracy. And yet, for the first time since the Russian Revolution, democracy as a form of government has strong international ideological support and is embraced by a broad range of domestic actors. New multilateral efforts for the support of democracy on the continent, and a shift in U.S. policy away from a Cold War imperative to one that defines democracy as a cardinal objective of foreign policy, provides critical international support for domestic actors intent on preserving democratic practices. Thus, fragile democracies may well survive socio-economic challenges and political and institutional dead-locks that in earlier periods might have led to military intervention.

Our review of democracy on the continent through the prism of these eight countries also suggests that evaluations of trends in the region which focus on short time-frames are misleading if the phenomenon to be explained is democratic consolidation. These studies may yield useful insights regarding different transitional patterns, but we have sought to emphasize not the heady but temporary triumphalism of democratic transitions, but the steady, difficult, uneven but real history of the forging of constitutional democracy and democratic institutions in the region. Even though democratic institutions are still fragile and often besieged in much of Latin America, they have been, and will continue to be, a permanent option.

A NOTE ON CITIZENSHIP IN
LATIN AMERICA

The chapter on the development of state organization in Latin America, published in *The Cambridge History of Latin America* Volume VI, Part 2 and (in an abridged form) in *Latin America: Economy and Society Since 1930,* focussed on the phase of national integration that followed the collapse of liberal internationalism in the 1930s. It therefore downplayed the questions of individual rights that are often thought to constitute the core of liberal republicanism. However justified this simplification may be for most Latin American countries during most of the period from the 1930s, it proves to be a considerable handicap when attempting to explain the evolution of state organization during the 1980s. From a broader perspective we need a complementary study of the intermittent, fragmentary and unequal appearance – and disappearance – of citizenship rights in the interstices between state organization and the realm of private life. But so far we lack a history of the faltering emergence of an increasingly well-defined 'public sphere' in Latin American society, even though this almost certainly constitutes a critical factor differentiating the 'populism' of the 1940s and 1950s from the fragile 'democratizations' of the 1980s.

Put simply, there are two possible relationships between the state and the people. Viewing them as *subjects,* the state's main concern is with securing their compliance (and perhaps therefore providing for their security); as *citizens,* they acquire rights which the state is supposed to uphold. At the beginning of the period under study most of the population of Latin America were little more than subjects; at the end they were rather less than full citizens.

The most essential point to stress about the stereotyped 'oligarchic' state before 1930 was the extremely restricted circle of participants in public life. In some countries these may have formed a very close knit elite who acted together effectively to pursue their interests (hard to distinguish from the 'national' interest) and who ensured that the state apparatus was used purposively in accordance with their objectives. In other countries there may have been deep regional, economic or ideological divisions within the elite, with the result that public policies seemed confused and contradictory, and the state apparatus was kept ineffective. There were also cases where external economic or strategic interests constrained state organization; and of course cases where the fear of rejection or rebellion from below posed 'oligarchical' circles with special problems. But whether the form of political organization was 'liberal-constitutional' or 'dictatorial' or 'decentralized anti-statist' the objective conditions were usually lacking for massive state intrusion into social life. There was generally insufficient territorial control, inadequate administrative capacity, and too few public resources to permit anything but a relatively unstructured relationship between state and civil society. It would be tempting to label this relationship 'liberal' (which was indeed how many contemporary observers described it) except that in the processes of state building and market promoting these states often proved highly authoritarian towards specific social groups and quite effectively interventionist on certain economic issues. It so happened, of course, that the prevailing international economic system, and the associated ideological currents, were fully supportive of this state of affairs, but in any case there was little choice. In its extreme form the oligarchic state was structurally incapable of providing social benefits (or even formal political representation) to the great majority of the population; it was also incapable of imposing oppressive rational control (often even a minimum of law and order) throughout its domain; and its entrepreneurial capabilities were extremely limited.

Prior to 1930 a reasonably full and predictable range of civic rights were enjoyed in much of Latin America (excepting post-revolutionary Mexico) by a relatively well-defined and of course restricted sector of the population. Propertied, educated European-looking males usually belonged to this category; almost all others did not. Much has been written about the 'rise of the middle sectors' notably in the 1920s, and this can frequently be re-expressed in terms of limited pressure from rather precisely demarcated groups (bank clerks, teachers, railway workers, printers) to accede to the privileged status of citizen hitherto confined to their betters. Sometimes these groups might be viewed as the advance guard for a much broader swathe of claimants (as indeed they proved to be in Mexico, and were thought to within the Radical Party of Argentina). On the other hand, it was often more realistic to see them as potential allies of the status quo, who could usually be co-opted in small parcels and at fairly low cost. Periodically, of course, it would be necessary to mount clear displays of authority that removed all doubt in the minds of those who were to be excluded from citizenship that the door had been barred against them. For example, a number of the political changes of the early thirties period can be interpreted in this way, including the 1930 coups in Argentina and Bolivia, the 1932 massacre in El Salvador, and the consolidation of dictatorships in the Dominican Republic and Nicaragua. Equally it must be recognized that within the restricted elite enjoying civic rights there was also a considerable degree of hierarchy and conflict. Certainly some of the most privileged and traditional sectors were inclined to assign themselves not just rights but over-weening privileges, not just equality before the law but a proprietory ownership of the judicial and administrative system. Nevertheless, both in theory and to a significant extent in practice, there was a workable set of republican institutions and customs in place to cater for a restricted (some would say 'oligarchical') system of citizenship.

If this schematic account of 1930 is accepted, an analysis of the subsequent development of Latin American citizenship would have to characterize a subsequent phase of expanded *social* rights (often accompanied by restrictions on individual *civic* rights – sometimes described in terms of 'populism' or 'corporatism'); the incorporation of broader social strata into aspects of public life (usually in tranches, with the rural poor left far behind the urban working class, and indeed not typically included until after the Cuban revolution); with phases of disorderly mobilization and governmental overload followed by further episodes of closure, in which even the most basic citizen rights (*habeas corpus,* for example) might be summarily withdrawn; leading in the 1980s to a renewed affirmation of constitutional principles (this time expressed in more authentically universalist terms) and a dimunition of collective social rights and identities combined with a – possibly just rhetorical – reassertion of an individualistic ethic of citizenship. (Clearly, this compressed summary is too abstract to capture the texture of political development in individual countries.)

A few summary points must suffice to link this discussion to the chapter on the development of state organization. First, it emerges that throughout the region and the period under review normative conceptions of a participatory constitutional republicanism retained strong appeal. Initially only an oligarchy had enjoyed the benefits of this system, and even at the end of our period efforts to extend the coverage of citizenship rights were still most uneven and imperfect. Nevertheless, the aspiration remained powerfully intact, and exerted a strong constraint on those administrations and elites which attempt to disregard it. Second, there would seem to be a rather close affinity between 'inward orientated' development, national integration, and the populist mode of collective mobilization and incorporation. Arguably then, the switch back from nationalism to re-integration in international markets at the end of the period seems directly associated with the affirmation of a more individualistic and privatized image of citizenship. Third, whereas the normal assumption about liberal regimes is that they either uphold a fairly standard and universal model of citizenship rights throughout the society, or they collapse and citizenship collapses with them, in Latin America the more typical pattern has been for declaratory rights to bear rather little relationship to social realities, both under liberal and under illiberal regimes. In either case most subjects experience insecurity and unpredictability in their rights; citizenship is a promise which must be repeatedly renegotiated; there are no reliable guarantors, or stable rules of inclusion/exclusion. Finally, the institutions and modalities of state organization that expanded most during the inward-looking phase of development were subsequently most exposed to curtailment. In contrast other state institutions – the courts, the Congress, the municipalities – which had seemed to flourish under the oligarchic constitutionalism, which lasted until the 1920s, and that had tended to atrophy thereafter, may enjoy the prospect of a renaissance under new conditions of liberal internationalism.

The historical evidence required to flesh out this interpretation is barely available, although in principle it could be assembled. All that can be attempted here is an illustrative discussion of examples of state organization to promote citizenship. We begin with a brief sketch of Argentine social policy (with particular emphasis on the post-Peronist period). Argentine experience is of more general significance because so much emphasis was placed on the extension of *social* rights, to the relative neglect of those other aspects of citizenship that many analysts (following T. H. Marshall) have regarded as integral and indeed prior to welfare provision. Marshall, of course, considered that there were three elements to full citizenship – first came civil rights (equality before the law); second came political rights (electoral sovereignty); and then third came the provision of sufficient means to enable all people to engage in full social participation. In Argentina the third element was emphasized to the neglect of the first, and in conditions under which the second was put in jeopardy. Only after 1983 were political rights more securely upheld, and the dilapidated state of the Argentine judiciary is such that equality before the law remains very much a laggard, even in the early 1990s. The second example is a more comparative analysis of the strengthening of electoral procedures in contemporary Latin America. One illustrates the decline of a celebrated model of populist incorporation; the second highlights the role of the state as guarantor of the integrity of the suffrage.

Argentine social policy merits attention because the first Perón governments made exceptionally ambitious and comprehensive efforts to extend a certain range of citizenship rights to a very large proportion of the formerly non-incorporated population of the republic.[1] The long-term consequences of these ambitious and forceful social policies testify to their impact. Peronism became an apparently ineradicable mass political movement, and for the ensuing forty years Argentine politics were obsessed with the question whether or not the rights associated with the Peronist period should be extended, withdrawn, or in some way redesigned.

The contrast between the universalist principles normally associated with the construction of a 'welfare state' and the more particularist and paternalist emphasis of Argentine social welfare provision, even during the 'golden age' of early Peronism, has attracted the attention of researchers. Argentine social policies since the restoration of democracy in 1983 underscore the progressive degeneration of the welfare system and the virtual abandonment of attempts to provide a minimum social network for all Argentine citizens[2] – a process further accentuated by the democratically elected Peronist administration after 1989. Thus, the strengthening of Argentine political rights appears to have been offset by an atrophy of the social dimension of citizenship and a continuing disinterest in the rule of law, such that full citizenship remains elusive even in this once most prosperous and 'modern' of Latin American republics.

More generally, the social dimension of citizenship has been in retreat in most of Latin America, at least since the debt crisis of 1982. At the same time narrowly political rights have been generalized and entrenched as never before. By the end of our period competitive elections based on universal suffrage had become the principal method for renewing or replacing governmental authorities both at national level and also locally. (Even

[1] For example, female suffrage was granted and Eva Perón became a symbol of hope, not just for the poor in general but for poor women in particular. The complex issue of gender cannot be omitted from discussions of citizenship. For further discussion of women's movements and women's rights, including the vote, see Asunción Lavrin, 'Women in Twentieth Century Latin American Society', *The Cambridge History of Latin America* Vol. VI, Part 2 (1994).

[2] Georges Midré, 'Bread or Solidarity? Argentine Social Policies, 1983–1990', *Journal of Latin American Studies,* 24, 2 (1992), pp. 343–73.

in Mexico the electorate began to acquire a relatively independent voice, at least in some contests, and in Nicaragua in 1990 a clean election held under strong international scrutiny closed the revolutionary phase of political mobilization.) It requires a considerable degree of state organization to arrange the electoral process such that all eligible voters are properly registered in a timely manner, and that the votes are recorded and counted by impartial officers who observe standardized procedure throughout the entire territory. If the public administration can be organized to achieve this regularly and with 'transparency', then a basis can be established for the performance of other state functions that could eventually give rise to a fuller recognition of citizenship rights. One very notable feature of the initiatives that have recently been taken in the electoral arena, is that in a surprising variety of cases it has proved possible to uphold the 'rule of law' for everyone, without privilege or exception. Electoral contests are struggles for power and resources that could easily give rise to partiality and extra-legal conflict. Historically, indeed, the typical Latin American election has been of this kind. Yet by the early 1990s it was frequently proving possible for the state to organize extremely large and complex electoral processes without major taint of manipulation or illegality. Part of the reason for this was the establishment of specialized voter registration offices and electoral courts that were effectively insulated from the vices of incompetence, irresponsibility and delay associated with much of the rest of the public administration and the judicial system.[3] Such demonstration that all Latin American states are capable of establishing the complex structures required to guarantee the integrity of the suffrage must enhance the prospects for eventual reform or reinforcement of state capacity relating to other areas of citizenship.

These brief historical sketches serve merely to illustrate some of the themes that would require attention in any serious analysis of the relationship between state organization and the implantation of citizenship rights in contemporary Latin America. They also underline the fact that even in the early 1990s full citizenship remained an elusive and weakly adminis-

---

[3] A celebrated example was the Tribunal Supremo de Elecciones y Registro Civil, established in Costa Rica in 1949, which by 1986 employed 574 staff, and which issued every Costa Rican citizen over eighteen years of age with an identity card valid for ten years, including a photograph, that must be shown on demand. See Rafael Villegas Antillón, *El Tribunal Supremo de Elecciones y El Registro Civil de Costa Rica* (San José, 1987). The Costa Rican model has been widely imitated, and CAPEL performs the specialized function of promoting Latin America-wide exchange of expertise and experience in this area, including the provision of international observers for many regional elections. See, for example, their other Cuadernos, such as Julio Brea Franco, *Administración y Elecciones: La Experiencia Dominicana de 1986* (San José, 1987).

tered aspiration for most of the population under study. The 'collective social rights' that were promoted during the phase of inward-looking populist government seem bound to fade under the impact of international competition and fiscal austerity. A more individualistic and market-driven approach to citizenship may prove as unbalanced and artificial as the form that preceded it, but that is speculation for the future. What can already be noted is that the underlying rationale of this approach is to reduce the separation between public bureaucracy and civil society, by rendering the state more accountable and responsive to 'customer demand' and by reducing its discretionality. In some quarters the project may even be to cause the state (as a distinct coercive entity) to 'wither away' under market and social control. But the new rationale may be too neat. For example, given the gulf between 'citizen demands' and government resources, fragile democracies may seek to increase rather than diminish some forms of discretionality. And even if this approach remains in fashion Latin America will require an enhancement of state organization and state capacities across a considerable range of activities, before the subject population can acquire any decent and secure level of citizenship.

2

THE LEFT IN LATIN AMERICA
SINCE *c.* 1920*

The simplest way of writing the history of the Left in Latin America would be to restrict analysis to Communist and Socialist parties. These parties shared common ideological assumptions drawn from Marxism, and common political practices influenced by Leninism. If there was broad agreement about ends, however, the parties of the orthodox Marxist Left profoundly disagreed about means. This led to conflict and division. Between, and indeed within, the parties of the Left there was fierce, and often unresolved, debate over how power was to be attained, the extent to which liberal democratic rights should be respected, and the way that economy, society and the political system should be organized. In other words, there neither was, nor is, one united Left. Relations between the many groups, parties and movements that have claimed to be the true Left have frequently been hostile, even violently so. Competition between them has sometimes been more intense than with the parties of the Right. If the story of the Left is in part a story of heroic and patient struggle against terrible odds, it is also in part a story of sectarianism and personal rivalries, and of petty mindedness. It is nevertheless a story central to the political development of most Latin American countries in the twentieth century.

Defining the Left solely in terms of parties of Marxist inspiration and structure is, as will be argued, incomplete. None the less, the starting point for any historical discussion of the Left in Latin America has to be the Communist parties of the various republics. The Communist party has special claims to historical importance because of the universality of its

* I would like to thank Victor Hugo Acuña, Carol Graham, María D'Alva Kinzo, Robert Leiken, Juan Maiguascha, Nicola Miller, José Alvaro Moises, Marco Palacios, Diego Urbaneja, Laurence Whitehead and Samuel Valenzuela, for their comments and help, and, particularly, Malcolm Deas for his criticisms and James Dunkerley for his encouragement.

claims, its existence in almost every Latin American country, and its international links with the Soviet Union. In no small measure the importance of communism in Latin America derives from the impact of the Bolshevik Revolution. Communist parties in Latin America were seen as the direct representatives of an international movement of world revolution giving them an importance beyond their specific electoral appeal or political power. The issues regarded as central by the communist movement were widely accepted as central by other groups on the Left even when they profoundly rejected the specific interpretation offered by the communists. The political power and influence of the communist movement was inflated by the attention of the Right which crystallized its opposition to reform in its attacks on the ideas of the communists, and demonstrated its hostility to those ideas by repression of the Left.

Yet from the early days of communism in Latin America the movement suffered from internal problems as well as difficulties created by repressive governments. The Communist parties began their history of expulsions of dissidents, and experienced early defections, because of the Stalin – Trotsky disputes, and Trotskyism, though never a serious organizational challenge to the parties, remained an ideological alternative with some appeal. More seriously, there was tension between international communism closely guided by Moscow and insisting on complete loyalty, and a more indigenous or Latin American communism identified in the 1920s with the ideas of the Peruvian socialist, José Carlos Mariátegui (1895–1930). Unorthodox and revolutionary Latin American Marxism received its most potent political expression in the Cuban revolution, and later in the Nicaraguan revolution.

There were, in addition to the Communist parties, a number of Socialist parties in Latin America which at least in the case of Argentina and Chile received more electoral support than their major rivals on the Left. If these Socialist parties paid tribute to Marxism as a method of interpreting reality, their political practice was largely electoral and parliamentary, and they sought to distinguish themselves from the communists by appealing to a broader social constituency, and by stressing their national rather than international roots. In general, however, communism pre-dated the Socialist parties, and the schisms that occurred in Europe between social democracy and revolutionary Marxism-Leninism were not repeated in Latin America, with the exception of Argentina, and the possible exception of Chile where the Partido Democrático also resembled European social democracy before the rise of communism.

The political space occupied in Europe by social democracy would be occupied in Latin America by nationalist populist parties. The nature of these parties reveals the problem in searching for an adequate definition of the Left. They drew heavily upon Marxist ideas and Leninist practice, though their relations with the orthodox parties of the Left varied from close co-operation to bitter rivalry. Moreover, populist parties were never constrained by ideological orthodoxy. The Peruvian Alianza Popular Revolucionaria Americana (APRA), founded in 1924 by Víctor Raúl Haya de la Torre whose ideological and political debates with Mariátegui constitute one of the high points of Marxist discussion in Latin America, subsequently ranged widely across the political spectrum. It could be argued that the crucial and continuous political problem for the orthodox Left was the nature of its relationships with such parties of greater ideological flexibility and greater political appeal. Although to describe these parties as populist begs many questions, it does point to features which differentiate them from the orthodox parties of the Left. They had a stronger vocation for power, enjoyed broader social appeal, and had more flexible and politically astute leaders. Examples of such parties would include, besides APRA, Acción Democrática (AD) in Venezuela, the Partido Peronista in Argentina, the Colorados in Uruguay, the Partido Trabalhista Brasileiro (PTB) of Vargas in Brazil, and the Liberal party of Colombia. These parties were capable of arousing the fierce devotion and life-long loyalty of rank and file members held to be typical of firm believers in communism. At the same time, their policies and tactics did not suffer from what Gabriel Palma has called the real weakness of the Latin American Left, 'the mechanical determination of internal by external structures'.[1]

Marxist ideas were also a strong influence on governments that were far from being on the orthodox Left. For example, the government of President Lázaro Cárdenas in Mexico from 1934 to 1940 enacted a reform programme inspired by socialist ideas, with its nationalization of the oil companies, its experiment in workers control in the railways, its plans for a socialist educational system, and its support for the Republican cause in the Spanish Civil War. Yet the Mexican Communist Party, though it enjoyed more influence under Cárdenas than at any time before or since in its history, was used by Cárdenas in order to bolster what under subsequent Presidents became a markedly anti-communist regime. Later in the

---

[1] Gabriel Palma, 'Dependency: a formal theory of underdevelopment or a methodology for the analysis of concrete situations of underdevelopment?' *World Development*, 6, 7/8 (1978), p. 900.

century, the Peruvian military government of President Juan Velasco Alvarado from 1968 to 1975 began as a government strongly influenced by the prevailing ideas of the Marxist Left.

The Left faced the central problem that what it regarded as its 'natural' social base, above all workers and peasants, was much more likely to support populist parties, or even political movements of the Right. There were times of relative success in devising a strategy that would attract to the Left the social movements of the urban and rural poor – for example, the Popular Front movements of the 1930s, the impressive mobilization that followed the end of the Second World War, and the period that followed the success of the Cuban Revolution. But there were longer periods when the Left suffered political isolation and marginalization, and not only because of persecution. It could be argued that the real influence of Marxism in Latin America has been felt not so much through the parties of the Left, but at the level of ideology and as a stimulus to political mobilization and action, not least in the trade union movement and among students and intellectuals, including, from the 1960s, radical Catholics.

If the starting point for the history of Marxism in Latin America has to be the communist movement founded after the Bolshevik Revolution, then a second phase in that history begins with the Cuban revolution of 1959. Indeed the Cuban revolution was central to the politics of the Left of many Third World countries outside Latin America, as it seemed to offer the possibility of a successful national liberation struggle against what had been regarded as overwhelming odds. It also galvanized the politics of the Left in Europe and the United States, and led to a renewed interest in the problems of under-development. The excitement was not permanent however, and enthusiasm declined as Cuba failed to live up to the unrealistic hopes invested in it by the international Left. The long-term effect of Cuba was to fragment the Left between those who still believed in achieving socialism through peaceful means, and those who formed revolutionary movements that sought to seize power through political violence.

The Cuban model of achieving power looked less and less relevant to the Left of the major countries of Latin America as the first wave of guerrilla movements were defeated in the 1960s. The hopes of the Left revived as the victory of Salvador Allende and the Unidad Popular in Chile in 1970 seemed to offer the possibility of a peaceful road to socialism. But the abrupt ending of that experiment by the coup of 1973 marked a reversal of the fortunes of the Left in Latin America, only partially mitigated by the success of the Sandinista revolution in Nicaragua. The collapse of the Latin American military regimes in the 1980s brought political and ideological benefits to the Right rather than to the Left, not least because that collapse coincided with the ending of international communism as a viable political force. Nevertheless, the future of the Left in Latin America in 1990 looked less bleak than in many other parts of the world as there was a renewal of interest in democratic socialism associated with the struggle for citizenship rights by a variety of social movements whose ideological inspiration was varied and eclectic, but underpinned by a strong demand for equality and participation.

THE LEFT AND THE COMINTERN

The Russian Revolution occurred at a time appropriate for the development of communist movements in Latin America. The end of the First World War had brought about an economic recession. Unemployment increased, real wages declined and in several countries there were waves of strikes, often repressed with considerable violence. Organized labour in the more developed countries of the continent had since the late nineteenth century come under the influence of a wide variety of anarchists, syndicalists and libertarian socialists, often European immigrants coming to Latin America to seek work and to escape political persecution. Radical ideologies were not therefore new to the miners, port workers, transport workers and textile workers who constituted the bulk of organized labour. What was new about communism was the prestige it derived from the Russian Revolution, the discipline of its militants, and the sense of being part of an international revolutionary movement, of being participants in a single grand strategy of world revolution. In Latin America Marxism became equated with Soviet communism, and specifically with a Leninist model of political organization – a model that proved attractive even to political movements like APRA that did not belong to the Communist International.

Communism in Latin America was under the ideological and tactical tutelage of the Communist International (Comintern) from the time of its formation in 1919 until its demise in 1943. Of course, factors such as distance, lack of information, the preoccupation of the Comintern with other parts of the world, and the obscurity of some of the smaller countries in Latin America could amount in practice to a fair degree of independence: this was so, for example, for the Communist party in Costa Rica. Moreover, there were often differences between the public pronouncements of a party and what it did in practice. But the intention was that Latin American communism would loyally play its allotted role in the world revolution.

Armed with doctrinal certainties, Communist parties in Latin America could see a local reversal as insignificant in the forward march of international communism, or even as a positive contribution to the international revolution. Local parties were to act as disciplined units of the international movement, and thus there could be no real conflict between the local movement and the Communist International. Although rapid changes of international policy under Stalin produced tensions and doubts among local parties, such questioning was swept aside as the advance of fascism, and above all the outbreak of the Spanish Civil War cast the communist movement in the role of defender of the cause of democracy as well as socialism.

The impact of the Russian Revolution, and the undoubted heroism of many of the early communists helps to explain why so many intellectuals became identified with communism even when they may not actually have become party members. Moreover, commitment to the ideology of Marxism involved Latin American intellectuals in the contemporary debates about revolution and art in Europe, especially in France. They were undoubtedly influenced by the avant garde movements that sought to combine revolutionary forms in the arts with leftist political struggle. The French novelist Henri Barbusse and his *Clarté* movement had many imitators in Latin America. Leading Latin American intellectuals spent years in Europe, either in exile or voluntarily. José Carlos Mariátegui, and Haya de la Torre were both profoundly influenced by their European experiences.

Many intellectuals participated actively in the life of their national Communist parties. In some parties the bulk of the leadership and a substantial part of the membership came from the ranks of the radical middle classes, which is not surprising given the insignificant size of the urban working class in many countries. Pablo Neruda in Chile and César Vallejo in Peru were outstanding poets who were loyal members of their national Communist parties; in Mexico at one time three painters, Diego Rivera, David Siquieros and Xavier Guerrero were members of the central committee of the party; the novelist Jorge Amado, the painter Cándido Portinari, and the architect Oscar Niemeyer were members of the Brazilian Communist Party. Many intellectuals, as well as party members were

invited to the Soviet Union, and on their return reinforced the idea of the
Soviet Union as not far short of a workers paradise. The long-standing
commitment of such intellectuals to their respective Communist parties
created a culture of Marxism which pervaded intellectual life, and later,
the universities. But not all, not even a majority, of intellectuals were
Marxists. Many found radical populist movements such as Aprismo more
attractive, others related closely to the Mexican Revolution, and there
many who were apolitical or conservative.

One reason perhaps why intellectuals were attracted to join the Communist party was because it was a mirror image of that other all embracing creed, the Catholic Church.[2] In the words of Carlos Fuentes, 'We are
the sons of rigid ecclesiastical societies. This is the burden of Latin
America – to go from one church to another, from Catholicism to Marxism, with all its dogma and ritual.'[3] Communism like Catholicism was a
universal and total faith. Moscow replaced Rome as the centre of dogma
and inspiration. Communism like Catholicism needed its guiding elite
to lead the masses. Communism like Catholicism was anti-liberal and
mistrustful of the market as the guiding economic principle. Communists like Catholics suffered at the hands of persecutors. Such analogies
can be pushed too far, but there is some truth in them, and of course not
only for Latin America: clericalism tends to create anti-clericalism, and
in the twentieth century, Marxism was a powerful expression of anti-
clericalism. European intellectuals who joined the Communist party at
its most Stalinist phase did so knowing that it demanded total devotion
and commitment. Party members knew that dissent could mean expulsion, and political impotence: it was better to conceal doubts, and to
submerge them in overall loyalty to the party. Not all party members
could do so, and there was a steady stream of expulsions and defections.
The early schismatics were often called and often claimed to be Trotskyists, though they (and their accusers) were vague about the issues at stake
in the wider international movement.

From their inception Communist parties in Latin America suffered from
systematic and sustained repression. The Brazilian Communist Party enjoyed only one period of legality from the time of its foundation in 1922 to

[2] However, it is equally plausible to see communism as an extension of positivist beliefs into the
twentieth century. The notion of progress, of laws governing social development, of the need for an
enlightened elite were concepts that transferred easily from nineteenth-century positivism into
twentieth-century communism. In both positivism and communism an enlightened elite was cast to
play a crucial role as the group best able to interpret the laws of historical progress.

[3] Quoted in Nicola Miller, *Soviet Relations with Latin America* (Cambridge, 1989), p. 24.

the end of the Second World War, and thereafter was legal only between 1945 to 1947 and after 1985. The ferocity of repression was often out of all proportion to the real threat posed. Numerous actions in Central America, where governments could often rely on support from the United States in the repression of real, or even of imaginary, communist movements, demonstrated the brutality of the response to demands that fell far short of revolutionary threats to the existing order. Yet repression directed against communist movements may have had the effect of increasing the loyalty of those who had made their initial commitment to the cause. Certainly the life of Miguel Marmol, with its story of exile, imprisonment, torture and clandestinity seems to bear out that for this Salvadorean communist the more he was repressed, the more his commitment to the party increased.[4] If repression reduced the possibilities of the party becoming a mass party, it may well have increased the strength of the party as a disciplined elite.

The limits to the influence of the Left were not only, perhaps not even primarily set by repression. The major belief system in Latin America was Catholicism, and the fierce hostility of the Church to Marxism (and even to liberalism) was bound to limit the appeal of radical movements especially among the popular sectors outside the union movement, and among women. Even in the labour movement there were in practice considerable obstacles to the creation of a communist base. In the first place, organized labour was only a small proportion of a working population which was largely rural or artisanal, and ethic divisions inside the work force could further weaken its unity. Second, there were many competitors for the political allegiance of labour, and some, such as APRA in Peru or the Colombian Liberal Party in the 1930s, were more attractive than the Marxist parties. The Colombian Liberal Party successfully absorbed the promising socialist movement in the 1920s and 1930s, claiming socialism as part of the Liberal tradition. The structure of the coffee economy in Colombia favoured the development of a petty bourgeois individualism more at home in the traditional parties than in Marxist movements. Catholic unions were by no means an inconsiderable force. Third, the state in many Latin American countries made considerable effort to incorporate potentially powerful unions and to suffocate radical movements. The legal institutional framework for industrial relations that developed in the twenties and thirties, contributed initially to the control of the economic

---

[4] See Roque Dalton, *Miguel Marmol* (New York, 1987).

demands of the working class and then to the subordination of the labour movement to the state. In Mexico, despite the reformism of the Cárdenas presidency, there was little possibility that the state apparatus would allow the organized labour movement to escape from its embrace. And where the state was unable to co-opt labour – either because labour was strong enough to resist, or because the state was too weak to co-opt effectively – repression remained a formidable obstacle to the growth of the unions.

Marxist movements faced not only the threat of a state repression and incorporation, but also the challenge of radical populist movements, which, while they may have drawn on socialism, also expressed nationalist sentiments, appealed across the social spectrum, did not necessarily arouse the hostility of the Church and military (though most did in their early days), and did not demand the total doctrinal commitment of the communist movements. Above all these movements – Aprismo in Peru, Acción Democrática in Venezuela – explicitly appealed to the middle class and that large and important sector of artisans whose political actions were often militant, but by no means were the expression of Marxist ideas or faith.

These popular, multi-class movements did not repudiate liberal values so fiercely as the communists. They used ambiguity as a populist device to incorporate as much support as possible. They spoke of the people rather than of class, a posture which could be anti-capitalist without embracing its polar opposite, communism. Such populist parties had a vocation for immediate power while the communists stressed the need to wait for objective conditions to mature. Populist parties had to appeal to a broad electorate rather than a vanguard, and this meant appealing to the electorally vital middle class. This vocation for power, and the broader appeal of these movements made them a more immediate threat than the Communist parties. The repression suffered by the APRA party, for example, was at times equal in intensity, if not greater than that suffered by the Communist party. Communism was a long-term threat in Peru: Aprismo was an immediate and more dangerous one.

The appeal of these populist movements tended to diminish the possibilities for the development of Socialist parties outside the communist movement, except in the developed countries of the Southern Cone. In Chile and Argentina such parties regularly received more votes than the Communist parties; as early as 1916 and 1922 the Argentine Socialist Party received 9 per cent of the vote in the presidential elections. Nevertheless, Socialist parties were generally in the ideological shadow of the communists, and rarely commanded the union support given to the communists. The Argentine Socialist Party was weakened by two divisions: one in 1918 led to the formation of the Argentine Communist Party, and another in 1927 led to the formation of the Partido Socialista Independiente which supported the Conservative governments of the 1930s. Although the Socialist party won substantial representation in Congress (forty-three deputies in 1931) its pursuit of parliamentary tactics did not prosper in the 'infamous decade' of electoral fraud. The Socialist party had little support among the growing industrial unions. It commanded some following among the workers of the traditional agro-exporting sectors, but even here its attitude to the unions tended to be distant and patronizing, and the unions had little influence on party policy. It was more a party of the Buenos Aires consumers than of the urban workers, and it was hardly surprising that it lost its influence in the labour movement to the communists, and later to Perón.[5]

Socialist parties had limited appeal to the working class let alone to the peasantry. They were seen as too European, too intellectual and too middle class. They lacked the political experience and tactical flexibility of less doctrinaire parties such as the Radicals in Argentina and Chile, APRA and Acción Democrática, and the Uruguayan Colorado Party with its extensive programmes of welfare legislation. The Socialist parties were too committed to parliamentary tactics in countries, such as Argentina or Brazil, where such tactics were not always the most appropriate way of winning adherents to socialism. They lacked the international appeal of the Communist parties, and with the exception of Chile did not build up union support to the extent of the Communist parties.

The unusual emergence of a strong Socialist party in Chile in the 1930s is explained by the combination of several factors: a firmly entrenched constitutional system which allowed parties to operate freely in the parliamentary and electoral arenas; a social structure in which an unusually large middle class provided an electoral base for the Socialist party; a union movement attracted by socialist support for legal registration when the advantages of that registration were being contested by a Communist party then committed to an ultra-left stance; and by popular admiration

[5] Charles Hale has written of the Argentine socialist party, 'It approached workers as consumers not as producers: it adhered to free trade: it made no distinction between foreign and native capital; it hesitated on the abolition of private property. Since the party never asserted effective control over workers, who were mostly non-voting foreigners, both socialism and the labour movement floundered in the years after 1920'. 'Political and Social Ideas in Latin America, 1870–1930', in *Cambridge History of Latin America*, Vol. IV (1986), p. 429.

for the daring leadership of Marmaduke Grove who seized power in 1932 to establish a twelve-day Socialist Republic.

The leaders of the Comintern never seriously expected that a Marxist-Leninist revolution could succeed in Latin America before it did in Europe. Latin America was therefore reduced to a secondary and supportive role to the struggles of the European and Asian working classes.[6] The Comintern analysis of Latin America started from the perspective of the capitalist countries and not of those of Latin America itself. Thus it was stated that the revolution in the backward countries had to be democratic-bourgeois. But in view of the weakness and dependent character of the bourgeoisie in Latin America, the revolution had to be carried out by the proletariat, organized in a separate party, independent of the bourgeoisie and petty bourgeoisie, but, in a manner not specified, finding allies in the agricultural proletariat, separating this group from petty bourgeois influences. If this were not daunting enough for the tiny Latin American proletariat, its task was also to constitute workers councils (soviets) to create a system of dual power.

Parties that deviated from these guidelines were criticized and suffered sanctions. In the late 1920s promising developments in Colombia and Ecuador of parties based on trade unions, making an attempt to build up support in the population at large rather than just in the workplace, were brought to an end by fiat from the Comintern. The Comintern placed impossible tasks upon the shoulders of a handful of militants. Although the Comintern created agencies in Latin America such as the Buro Latinoamericano based in Buenos Aires, this was totally insufficient to deal with the problems facing the parties of Latin America. The Comintern had more pressing problems elsewhere than in Latin America, and inadequate resources. Rumours of Moscow gold to finance revolutions were largely just that, rumours. Incentives, to adopt the slogan of the Cuban Revolution, were moral rather than material, with the free trip to the Soviet Union a coveted prize. Many issues debated by the Comintern such as the character of the revolution, the nature of the party, the tasks of revolutionary movements in backward societies remained unresolved in Latin America. This lack of resolution was scarcely surprising as the overall strategy of the Comintern varied from policies of extreme leftism to rightist opportunism. In the early Mexican Communist Party there were endless, even

[6] This section relies heavily on Rodolfo Cerdas, *La Hoz y el Machete: La Internacional Comunista, América Latina, y la Revolución en Centroamérica* (San José, 1986); Eng. trans., 1993.

violent, debates over whether the party should be a mass or elite party, a worker party or a worker peasant alliance – and the issues were never resolved.

There were criticisms of the Comintern from inside, notably from M. N. Roy who pointed out the profound differences between the so-called colonial societies themselves, and who argued forcefully that the Comintern had to come to terms with the phenomenon of nationalist struggle, in which sectors of the petty bourgeoisie were playing an important role. But the major failing of the Comintern was the inability to come to terms with the peasant problem. Theoretically and organizationally the Communist parties were parties for, if not always of, the working class. Their conception of a Leninist revolutionary party not only excluded but was downright suspicious of the peasantry at a time when the overwhelming sector of the working population was rural. By isolating the party from the peasantry in the interests of class purity, the parties were denied influence in the major part of the population.

The most original Marxist attempt to incorporate the peasantry into an overall revolutionary coalition came from Mariátegui, who envisioned for Peru a united front labour movement, and a legal Socialist party that would embrace a wide coalition of peasants, Indians, agricultural workers, artisans and intellectuals as well as more orthodox working-class occupations. This broad front would be directed by a secret cell within the party linked to the Comintern. He stressed the need to organize broad sectors of the population, and was opposed to the utopian scheme of the Comintern to establish autonomous republics for the Quechua and Aymara 'nationalities' as they were defined by the Comintern.[7] His emphasis upon the social base of Marxism parallels the ideas of Gramsci rather than Lenin. Like Gramsci, he insisted that socialism had to be based upon the moral transformation of the people. But such unorthodox approaches were not welcome and Mariátegui, arguably the most original socialist theoretician of Latin America was roundly condemned by the Comintern, not least for being a 'populist'.

Mariátegui's debate was not only with Comintern orthodoxy but also with Aprismo, the movement founded by Haya de la Torre and which spread far beyond Peru to offer an original synthesis of nationalism, Marx-

---

[7] See Harry Vanden, 'Mariátegui, Marxismo, Comunismo and Other Bibliographical Notes', *Latin American Research Review*, 14, 3 (1979): 61–86.

ism and *indigenismo*. Haya attempted to adapt Marxism to local Latin American conditions, as Lenin did for Russia; indeed his political vision drew heavily upon Lenin's model of a revolutionary party vanguard – arguably more than did the Marxism of Mariátegui. Leninism was attractive to parties like APRA as a theory of how to seize power in conditions of economic backwardness, as an explanation of the power of imperialism and the consequent weakness of national class structures, and as a justification of the vanguard role to be played, not by a social class, but by an elite and disciplined political party. But in Haya's case, the appeal of his party was not directed so much to the urban workers or peasants as to the middle class. Haya argued that, 'in Indoamerica we have not had time to create a powerful and autonomous bourgeoisie, strong enough to displace the latifundista classes'. He added that the middle classes are the 'first to be affected by imperialist expansion, and from them excellent leaders and strong citizens movements have been formed'. It was necessary therefore to unite 'the three classes oppressed by imperialism: our young industrial proletariat, our vast and ignorant peasantry, and our impoverished middle classes'. He was proposing not only the alliance of the proletariat with the middle classes but also the amalgam within a single political party of manual and intellectual workers.[8]

Mariátegui had been a member of APRA, which he left in 1928 to form the Socialist Party. The differences between Mariátegui and Haya were profound, and their debate had a resonance well beyond Peru and the time in which it took place. Haya's attitude to the peasantry was close to the orthodox Marxist judgement which combined elements of disdain for their lack of revolutionary potential with paternalistic prescriptions for their involvement with the revolutionary movement. Mariátegui, by contrast, admired the peasantry for their capacity to survive in the harshest conditions and saw in their organizations the seeds of a future Peruvian socialism. Haya emphasized the role of the central state in the creation of the nation: Mariátegui preferred to start by developing civil society – only then could power be attained. Haya's view of power was altogether more military and elitist, and he legitimized insurrection to seize state power as a central policy of APRA. His vision of the party was disciplined, authoritarian and vertical, and with himself as the Peruvian Lenin. Mariátegui's version of the party was altogether broader, more participatory and

---

[8] Haya de la Torre, *Treinta Años de Aprismo* (Mexico, D.F., 1956), pp. 29, 54.

pluralist – a view that was rejected by the Comintern and indeed by many
of own fellow members of the Peruvian Socialist Party. Mariátegui died
only two years after founding the Socialist Party, with many of his disagreements with the Comintern unresolved. The ideological influence of Mariátegui was very great, but APRA was much more important politically
than the party that Mariátegui founded. Haya's ideas, the force of his
personality, and the support he aroused amongst the impoverished middle
classes of Peru made his movement a formidable political force, and in
exile his ideas and personality had a strong influence in a number of Latin
American countries.

In the radical politics of Cuba in the first decades after independence,
the ideas of José Martí (1835–95) were of great influence. Martí is more
difficult to associate with the Marxist camp than Mariátegui for his ideas
appealed to the liberal bourgeoisie as well as the radical Left. Indeed his
appeal lay in the way in which he wove a number of ideological strands
into a political message that was intensely nationalistic yet was also international. He was the ideological inspiration for the Cuban liberation
struggle, but put that struggle into a Latin American and even an international context as a struggle of the oppressed for liberty and equality. He
drew upon the ideas of Karl Krause, a minor and eccentric German
philosopher of the early nineteenth century who was influential in Spain,
as well as socialism and anarchism. His belief in progress was strongly
positivist, and his passionate moral belief in the cause he championed
made his ideas attractive to Cuban radicals of many persuasions. Like
Mariátegui he provided an authentic national radicalism in contrast with
the orthodoxy of the Comintern ideologists.

Whatever the shortcomings of the Comintern's strategy in Latin America, it should be stressed that the issues debated by the Comintern remained central to the debate over socialism in Latin America at least until
the 1980s. Debate revolved around the character of the revolution; the role
of different social classes; the extent to which the leading class, the proletariat, could make alliances with other classes; whether involvement in
electoral politics could result in socialism or merely served to strengthen
the capitalist order; the class position of the military; and above all,
perhaps, the character of the Communist party itself. These questions
seized the imagination of revolutionaries and reformers well beyond the
membership of the Communist party. As Manuel Caballero has argued, it
is something of a paradox that an institution, the Comintern, that was

intended above all to exert practical influence in the making of the revolution exercised its real significance at the level of ideological debate.[9]

Two of the most dramatic episodes in the history of the Left during the period of the Comintern were the insurrections in El Salvador and Nicaragua. Communism in Central America had not faced rivalry in the union movement from anarchism or syndicalism, in part because of the weak development of urban occupations, in part because of the ferocity of dictatorial regimes, and in part because of the relative absence of European migration from the anarchist centres of Italy and Spain. The first Communist parties emerged just before the 1929 depression and were thus in a position to take advantage of popular grievances that developed with the onset of the crisis. But this also led ruling groups to associate worker and peasant disturbances with the communists and to take correspondingly severe measures against what were still Communist parties in their infancy.[10]

The Salvadorean Communist Party was constituted formally in 1930, at a meeting, according to the memoirs of Miguel Marmol, held on a secluded beach in order to evade the police. The international nature of the party was clear from its inception, and an important role was played by a Mexican Comintern agent, Jorge Fernández Anaya. Comintern influences were channelled through the Salvadorean section of the International Red Aid, one of the front organizations created by the Comintern to mobilize widespread support.

Hardly had the party begun to organize when it was faced with the dilemma of how to turn massive peasant protest into a revolution, which according to the lines laid down by the Comintern had to be democratic and bourgeois. Peasant grievances had grown dramatically in El Salvador, for not only had the peasantry increasingly been dispossessed from their communal lands, but the miserable salaries they earned in the coffee harvest fell sharply with the onset of the international economic crisis in 1929. Anger over the abolition of the communal lands, and resentment at their treatment on the coffee estates provided a powerful communal grievance which, mixed with the collectivist rhetoric of the Communist party, led to one of the major rural protests in Latin America. But the possibility of repeating the Soviet Revolution in El Salvador was remote. The urban

---

[9] This is the theme of Manuel Caballero, *Latin America and the Comintern, 1919–1943* (Cambridge, 1986).

[10] On Central America, see James Dunkerley, *Power in the Isthmus: a Political History of Modern Central America* (London, 1988), esp. chs. 6 and 8 for Nicaragua and El Salvador.

and rural movements possessed quite distinct characteristics, and in the urban areas the Communist party was simply too weak to mount a successful insurrection, and, as it bitterly commented afterwards, the expected support from sectors of the supposedly disillusioned military was simply a self-deception on the part of the Communist leadership. Moreover, an insurrection directed against the bourgeoisie was an unlikely start to launch a bourgeois democratic revolution. Protest in the rural areas was massive, but was not controlled by the Communist party. Above all the party simply ignored the military aspects of a successful insurrection. The verdict of Marmol is worth quoting, 'When I recall the events of 1932 in El Salvador, I realise that we still grasped revolutionary concepts as simple fetishes and images, as abstract entities independent of reality, and not as real guides to practical action. In 1932 we made a communist insurrection in order to struggle for a bourgeois democratic programme. We established soviets in some parts of the country, but in their content they were but municipal bodies of bourgeois origin. Well, we paid dearly for not comprehending the practical application of our concepts.'[11]

What in the end was remarkable about the 1932 insurrection in El Salvador was the scope of the counter-repression in which an estimated 30,000 peasants were killed. The repression effectively ended Communist party activities in the country for the next twelve years, and left that party with a marked reluctance to undertake rural guerrilla activities in the future. The Communist party only abandoned the peaceful road in 1980, much later than the other revolutionary forces.

In Sandino's uprising in Nicaragua, Comintern aid was channelled through another front organization, the Anti-Imperialist League.[12] But Sandino and his movement were ideologically eclectic, and refused to conform to the principles laid down by the Comintern for the correct way to advance the revolution. Nor did Sandino accept the dictates of the Apristas either, though he drew some support and inspiration from a movement that was at that time more international than Peruvian. Sandino also drew upon anarchism, for his movement was anti-clerical and anti-authoritarian, and, influenced by contemporary developments in Mexico, he hoped to create a broad progressive multi-class alliance. But he also

---

[11] Dalton, *Miguel Marmol*, p. 246.

[12] The Anti-Imperialist League was one of a number of front organizations created by the Comintern to mobilize support, essentially from intellectuals who were not Communist party members. The Anti-Imperialist League was created in 1928 with its main offices in the United States and Mexico. It held several international congresses of writers, artists and intellectuals. Haya de la Torre was but one leading Latin American active in the League in its early days.

was attracted by more eccentric ideas, especially the spiritualism of the Magnetic Spiritual School of the Universal Commune, and indeed Sandino was the School's official representative in Nicaragua.[13] Relations with the Comintern agent, the Salvadorean Farabundo Martí broke down as Sandino asserted the nationalist and multi-class nature of the revolution he wanted to lead. It is doubtful if the Comintern contributed much to the revolutionary process inside Nicaragua, but it did attract international attention to the figure of Sandino and his struggle, and generated sympathy for the cause. Later the Comintern would denounce Sandino for his efforts to reach an understanding with the Mexican government at a time when the Mexican Communist Party was in open opposition. But by then Sandino had already attracted attention as one of the leaders of the colonial rebellion against imperialist domination. Yet the Comintern failed to read the lessons of the Sandino experience, namely the powerful mobilizing character of nationalism, and the need to fuse both political and military strategies.

The only Communist party in Central America that survived the repression of the 1930s was in Costa Rica. This party gained little influence over the peasantry, but was influential among sectors of the provincial petty bourgeoisie, among urban workers and artisans, and plantation workers. It was able to operate in a relatively open political system, ignored by the Comintern which saw better opportunities for revolution elsewhere. Its policies were moderate, and in the union field economistic. The party thrived in a country whose political structure encouraged the formation of multi-class alliances to push for radical reforms, and where an anti-American protectionist nationalism was very strong. What identity it had as a Communist party came from its sympathy with the Soviet Union, especially when the Comintern was urging the formation of popular fronts. The Costa Rican Communist Party may not have conformed to the prescriptions of the Comintern, but the party was able to operate consistently and openly in contrast to its dormant existence for decades after the depression in the rest of Central America.[14] However, at the same time as one group of radicals drew the lesson from the effects of the depression that there was need for a Communist party, another group drew their inspiration from the ideas of Aprismo. This group latter evolved into the PLN (Partido de Liberación Nacional) whose reformist and nationalist policies,

[13] Donald Hodges, *Intellectual Foundations of the Nicaraguan Revolution* (Austin, Tex., 1986), p. 6.
[14] Rodolfo Cerdas, *La Hoz y el Machete*, pp. 328, 350.

and triumph in the civil war of 1948, established it as the dominant political party in Costa Rica in the second half of the twentieth century.

In Cuba, the development of a strong Communist party took place in a national political context in which many groups were arguing for radical reforms. By the 1920s the expectations of the first generation of independent Cubans had not been fulfilled. There were powerful and unsatisfied sentiments of anti-imperialism and nationalism. Demands for social reform were linked to denunciations of the corruption of the political class. Students, intellectuals and former soldiers of the Liberation Army organized and issued radical manifestos. The first national labour organization was founded in 1925 (the Confederación Nacional Obrera de Cuba) along with the Cuban Communist Party.[15] But Cuba's Communist party, though powerful, faced formidable challenges from other parties such as the Authentic Cuban Revolutionary Party (PRC-Auténtico) whose legitimacy came from its involvement in the 1933 Revolution, and which also established a powerful presence in the labour movement.

Outside Central America, the major attempt by the Left at seizing power took place in Brazil in 1935, though the explanation for the timing and the motives of the participants remains confused, perhaps reflecting the internal feuds then taking place within the Comintern leadership in Moscow. The Brazilian Communist Party was unusual in the extent to which it had evolved from anarchism, rather than socialism, and in the extent to which it had intimate relations with military officers, following the rebellions of the *tenentes* in the 1920s. The 1935 insurrection was more of a *pronunciamento* than an attempt at revolution. Luis Carlos Prestes, a leader of the *tenentes* revolt of 1924, had impressed the Comintern as a strong leader who might pull off a revolution, but at the same time be more amenable to Comintern control than an independent Communist party. One of the consequences of Prestes' 'Long March' (1924–7) was the rejection of a peasant-based revolutionary strategy. The episode had convinced Prestes of the lack of consciousness among the peasantry, and of the power and ferocity of the landlord class. If, therefore, control over the state was best achieved by military power, then it seemed to make sense to the Comintern to use elements of the military to try to conquer the state. But there is also evidence that the coup attempt in 1935 served the interests of the government more than that of the would be revolutionar-

---

[15] Louis A. Pérez Jr., 'Cuba, c. 1930–1959', in *Cambridge History of Latin America*, Vol. VII (1990), p. 421.

ies, allowing Vargas to rule virtually as a dictator, justified by the 'red menace'.

In 1935 the Comintern abandoned the extremism of the 'Third Period', during which the enemy had been defined as revisionist socialism, replacing this with a policy of building Popular Fronts to halt the spread of fascism. Indeed so anxious did Moscow become during the Second World War to offer olive branches to possible allies (including dictators) that the Comintern itself was dissolved in 1943.

The Popular Front policy, and political radicalism in Latin America, was given a sharp impetus with the outbreak of the Spanish Civil War. The effect of the Spanish Civil War in a number of countries was to add a new dimension and a new intensity to domestic political conflict as both Left and Right identified with opposite sides in that war. What it also did was to contribute to internal divisions on the left as Stalinists and Trotsky-ists offered rival interpretations of the international conflict, and contrasting strategies to respond to it.

The Spanish Civil War provided a real opportunity for communist inspired movements to mobilize the support of artists and intellectuals. In the country that did most to help the Republican cause, Mexico, the most prominent organization mobilizing support for Spain was the League of Revolutionary Writers and Artists, led by a Mexican communist, and secretly funded by the government of Lázaro Cárdenas. The influx of prominent Republican exiles to Mexico after the war stimulated the radical Left in that country. Nevertheless, Spain is best seen as another example of the official party of the Mexican revolution using the Left as a useful ally.[16]

Among the many Latin American intellectuals whose political commitment was profoundly influenced by the war, and by the assassination of the Spanish poet Federico García Lorca, was Pablo Neruda. Witnessing the struggles in Spain inside the Republican camp between different groups, Neruda wrote that, 'the communists were the only organised force that created an army capable of confronting the Italians, the Germans, the Moors and the Falange. And they were, at the same time, the moral force that maintained the resistance and the anti-fascist struggle. Simply: one

---

[16] T.G. Powell, 'Mexico', in Mark Falcoff and Frederick B. Pike (eds), *The Spanish Civil War, 1936–1939; American Hemispheric Perspectives* (Lincoln, Neb., 1982). Such was the continuing mythology that on a visit to Spain in 1977, the Mexican President López Portillo said that 'the civil war myth continues to play a major role in sustaining the PRI's self-image as a popularly approved, legitimate political regime' (p. 54).

had to make a choice. This is what I did in those days, and I have never regretted a decision taken in the midst of the despair and hope of that tragic epoch.'[17] Many Latin Americans fought in Spain, and returned to Latin America impressed by the discipline and dedication of the communist battalions. In the Dominican Republic, the local Communist party was formed by a group of Spanish communist exiles who migrated there at the end of the civil war. Of an estimated 900 refugees from Spain to that country, well over 100 were communists, who became active in creating a number of front organizations.[18] Two Republican exiles, Alberto Bayo and Abraham Guillén, played important roles in the developments of guerrilla movements in Nicaragua and in the Southern Cone in the 1960s. Literary figures from Spain who settled in Latin America helped to strengthen the continuity between the intellectual avant garde and political radicalism. Influence was not all one way, however. The Argentine communist, Víctor Codovilla, operated in Spain as the Comintern agent 'Medina', and was important in the Spanish Communist Party.

The country in which the Popular Front strategy had most effect was in Chile, where the Communist party achieved outstanding growth relative to other parties in Latin America, even though the party had been severely repressed during the dictatorship of General Carlos Ibáñez between 1927 and 1931. Here too, the cause of Spain was a bonus for the Chilean Communist Party (PCCh). Intellectuals were attracted to the party because of its defence of the Spanish Republic. The Communist party used the war to attack the Chilean Socialist Party on the grounds that by analogy with Spain, the only true revolutionary party was the Communist party. The 1938 election in Chile fought, and won, by the Popular Front was presented as a struggle between democracy and fascism. Spanish communists in exile soon became members of the Chilean party, and formed its most radical and dedicated militants.[19]

Popular Front tactics were unusually appropriate for the political configuration of Chile. A solid labour movement provided a good base for the party. The existence of an erratic Socialist party gave the Communist party a good adversary against which to define itself, and a potential ally on the left. A powerful Radical party which shared the anti-clericalism of the Communist party, and thought of the Socialist party as a more dangerous competitor, made a good ally for the Communist party. The Communist

[17] Pablo Neruda, *Confieso que He Vivido* (Barcelona, 1983), pp. 186–7.
[18] Robert J. Alexander, *Communism in Latin America* (New Brunswick, N.J., 1957), p. 300.
[19] Paul Drake, 'Chile', in Falcoff and Pike, *The Spanish Civil War*, p. 278.

party took credit for the formation and victory of the Popular Front, but by not taking ministerial responsibility was able to avoid criticism. With a Popular Front government in power it had unusual freedom to operate, and took full advantage of the growth in trade union numbers. Its electoral strength rose from 4.16 per cent of the national vote in the congressional elections of 1937, to 11.8 per cent in 1941 when it elected three senators and 16 deputies. The party claimed that its membership had risen from 1,000 in 1935 to 50,000 by 1940.[20]

The Chilean party loyally followed the Comintern line when the Popular Front strategy was replaced during the Second World War by one of national unity. This new strategy meant subordinating national considerations to the overall task of supporting the war effort, and to this end the party would attempt to forge alliances even with the traditional Right, on the grounds that left-right distinctions had been superseded by fascist-anti-facist ones. This coincided with what became known as Browderism, named after the secretary-general of the North American party who advocated disbanding the party and regrouping in a looser association to function as a pressure group within the dominant U.S. political parties. The Chilean party was uncomfortable with this new initiative, and was pleased when in 1945 Browderism was formally denounced and the party could begin to recapture the ground it had lost especially in the union movement.

The Mexican political system was very different from that of Chile, and while the Chilean Communist Party had little difficulty in adapting to national politics, the Mexican party had enough problem in trying to understand the system let alone operate in it. The Communist party argued that the Mexican revolution was 'incomplete' and could not be finished successfully unless it was led by the Communist party. For a party with weak links with the working class and peasantry, and with a membership rarely above the 10,000 level (except under the Cárdenas government when it rose to perhaps 40,000), such a claim looked very improbable.[21] The party had difficulty in defining itself in relation to the revolution, at times even going so far as to propose merger of the Communist party in the official revolutionary party.

[20] Andrew Barnard, 'The Chilean Communist Party, 1922–1947', unpublished Ph.D. thesis (London, 1977), p. 263.

[21] This, and other sections on Mexico draws heavily on the writings of Barry Carr. See especially, 'Mexican Communism, 1968–1981: euro communism in the Americas?', *Journal of Latin American Studies*, 17, 1 (1985), pp. 201–8.

The Mexican Communist Party reached its greatest influence when the international strategy of the Popular Front coincided with the reformist presidency of Lázaro Cárdenas. The communists played a crucial role in the creation of a number of leading unions – teachers, railways, petroleum workers, miners – and was a dominant force in the most important union federation, the Confederación de Trabajadores de México (CTM). President Cárdenas made use of the unions in the expropriation of the oil companies and the railways, when companies that were largely or partially foreign owned were taken into state ownership. The railways were even placed under worker control in 1938, but the experiment was not a success. President Cárdenas found the communists useful allies in his struggle to reform the Mexican economic and political system, and in his attempt to reform the educational system along socialist lines in an effort to combat clericalism and to instil rationalist values. The Soviet educational model was much admired, and Marxist texts even circulated in the Colegio Militar. Nevertheless, the Mexican version of the Soviet experience stressed development and productivity rather than class consciousness. As Alan Knight has written, 'The Soviets were seen less as carriers of class war than successful exponents of large scale modern industrialization: more Fordist than Ford.'[22] The attempt to imitate Soviet methods was enthusiastically endorsed by those teachers who were members or supporters of the Mexican Communist Party, perhaps a sixth of the total teaching profession. Nevertheless, more teachers were Catholics than communists, and as the popular response to socialist education was tepid or hostile, the experiment began to be abandoned even before Cárdenas left power.

Mexico produced many leftists who, while never joining the party, expressed belief in socialist ideas and who were regarded as 'fellow travellers'. The outstanding example was the intellectual turned union leader, Vicente Lombardo Toledano. In the later 1930s Lombardo increasingly identified with the communist line in the CTM, and became the leading figure in the communist inspired Latin American union confederation, the Confederación de Trabajadores de América Latina (CTAL). But relations between Lombardo and the communist movement were complex. He never joined the party, regarding the local Mexican party as of little real significance, and for fear that joining the party might jeopardize his relations with Cárdenas. Lombardo's industrial base was in the small

---

[22] Alan Knight, 'Mexico, *c.* 1930–1946', in *Cambridge History of Latin America,* Vol. VII (1990), p. 27.

unions and federations, especially in Mexico City, and the weakness of these unions made collaboration with the government attractive. The communists were stronger in the big industrial unions competing with an apolitical syndicalism. Lombardo and the communists struggled for control over individual unions such as the teachers, and for overall control of the CTM. Lombardo had more respect for international communism, and in return the international movement found him more useful as an independent Marxist than as a party member.

Many members of the official party and the official union movement regarded the communists with undisguised suspicion. And with the replacement of Cárdenas by strongly anti-communist presidents – Avila Camacho in 1940 and Alemán in 1946 – the Communist party went into decline. This was also a consequence of internal struggles within the party, in part due to recriminations over its role in the assassination of Trotsky in Mexico in 1940. Fierce anti-communism was also the hallmark of Fidel Velásquez, who dominated the Mexican labour movement for decades, but who never forgot, nor forgave the communists for the bitter battles he fought with them in the 1930s and 1940s. Such anti-communism was notable in a society where although the Communist party was much weaker than its counterpart in Chile, the overall ideological appeal of Marxism in intellectual and political circles was even greater.

Argentina, by contrast, was a society where the Communist party had little influence, and the ideological influence of Marxism, at least until the 1960s was also weak. Except for a base among the construction workers, the party had shallow roots in the labour movement, and was a small organization of a few thousand members. What growth it experienced in the early 1940s was due more to its participation as a liberal democratic organization in the largely middle-class anti-fascist resistance than as any potentially revolutionary agent of the working class.

Whatever the real strength of the left in the labour movement, there was undeniably a real fear among the elite of the potential for a growth of communism. Part of this fear was due to the presence in Argentina of a large immigrant population well aware of developments in, for example, Mussolini's Italy (for the elite a positive example of the way to control labour unrest and the communists) and in Republican Spain (for the elite a negative example of consequences of letting the communists grow unhindered). Although many immigrants were not naturalized, and therefore unable to vote in the 1930s, elite sectors feared that future integration could lead to the growth of radical political ideologies. Communist influence grew after the adoption of Popular Front tactics in 1935. After that date almost all union growth was concentrated in the communist unions, and almost all strikes were led by militants of the party. But what is more striking about Argentina in this period is the strength of the reaction to these movements, and the development of nationalist movements. In the end the power of these anti-communist sentiments would lead sectors of the elite to prefer Perón (however reluctantly) to more radical alternatives. And the ideological contortions of the communists, who went into alliance with parties of the Right to oppose Perón in the 1945 elections, led to labour desertion from the cause of communism to that of Peronism.

Tactical questions of taxing severity faced Communist parties in Colombia and Venezuela. Given the social structure of Colombia, with its dominant economic activity of coffee production more suited to the development of a petty bourgeois individualism than a proletarian collectivism, what should a Marxist party do to develop its base? The Colombian party formed strong links with the Liberal party from 1936 to late 1940. This tactic was criticized by later communist writers for preventing the development of an autonomous labour movement. But it is not clear that there was a viable alternative. The labour movement was weak, and had little influence in the coffee sector, and popular attachment to the Liberal and Conservative parties was strong. The Colombian electoral system also adversely affected the fortunes of the Left. In the Colombian system of proportional representation the chances of winning seats were much greater if a party presented itself as Liberal or Conservative and offered a list of candidates within the overall major party. This tactic might help the Left as a pressure group, but clearly worked against the long-term development of an independent Left party.

In Venezuela, the Communists and Rómulo Betancourt's AD party had worked together against the oil companies. But the erstwhile allies later went separate ways. With the failure of the 1936 strike Betancourt revised his party's strategy away form overtly socialist objectives and concluded that alliance with the Communist party was more of a hindrance than a benefit. The Communist party, brought under more effective Comintern control, allied with the military president General Isaías Medina Angarita (1941–5), and preached industrial peace in the oil fields to maintain supplies for the allied war effort. In the struggle to control the petroleum workers unions, the communists lost to the AD Party which with its moderate nationalism and willingness to back strikes to support workers demands was more in accord with workers demands than the Communist party.

The issue of the Venezuelan party's support for the government of Medina draws attention to the policy for which the Communist parties were most criticized during the early 1940s – their willingness to form alliances with right-wing governments and even with dictators, notably with Somoza in Nicaragua and Batista in Cuba. Such alliances made short-term tactical sense for both sides. In return for their support, the communists were given some freedom to organize the union movement, to develop their party organization, and to create front organizations to capitalize upon the admiration that communism had aroused for its defence of the Spanish Republic, and later for the war effort of the Soviet Union. Dictators gained the benefit of being associated with the leading anti-fascist force, now willing allies in their efforts to eliminate common domestic enemies. Indeed, in the case of Nicaragua, with the choice between a Somoza prepared to accept some socio-economic reforms, and a Conservative party prepared to accept none, even in purely domestic terms the choice of Somoza was far from irrational. Somoza invited Lombardo Toledano to address a rally in Nicaragua in November 1942, and given his need for labour support, he tolerated a labour code and growing communist strength in the labour movement. Not until mid-1945 did Somoza feel strong enough to repress the communist PSN (Partido Socialista Nicaragüense). However, while it is true that the PSN enjoyed a period of open activity under Somoza, the long-term damage to the party was great, not least because the party lost members who later were to form the Sandinista movement.[23]

The Cuban Communist Party struck a similar deal with Batista, though the Cuban party was stronger than that of Nicaragua. It had captured the sympathy of many outstanding Cuban intellectuals, and had dominated the powerful labour unions since the 1930s. In return for the legalisation of the party, a free hand to organize a new union structure, and the promise of a Constituent Assembly, the party agreed to support Batista's presidency. The party benefited. Membership of 5000 in 1937 rose to 122,000 in 1944. The party had its own radio station and daily paper, and dominated the labour movement. By the onset of the Second World War between one-

---

[23] Jeffrey Gould provides an excellent account of the politics of this period in, 'Somoza and the Nicaraguan Labor Movement 1944–48', *Journal of Latin American Studies*, 19, 2 (1987): 353–87, and "Nicaragua', in Leslie Bethell and Ian Roxborough (eds), *Latin American between the Second World War and the Cold War, 1944–1948* (Cambridge, 1992).

third and one-half of the work force was organized, and three-quarters of it belonged to the communist dominated Confederación de Trabajadores de Cuba (CTC). The Cuban union movement was unusual in that almost half was employed in agriculture, and union leaders were often middle-class professionals rather than members of the working class. Two party members, Juan Marinello and Carlos Rafael Rodríquez, became cabinet ministers in 1942 – the first to do so in the western hemisphere. The party had ten members in the Chamber of Deputies, and had elected mayors of provincial cities. With the election of the *Auténtico* candidate, Grau San Martín, in 1944, the party began to suffer repression both because of its association with Batista, and with the onset of the Cold War. Perhaps the rural composition of the union movement meant less ideological sympathy for communism than in urban based union movements, for the *Auténticos* were able to divide the union movement in 1947 and win major control.

The problem for Marxists who could not accept the ideological changes that took place in the communist movement in the 1930s and early 1940s was – where else to go? In Chile there was an attractive Marxist alternative in the Socialist party, but elsewhere the alternatives were scarce. Most countries saw the creation of a small Trotskyist party, but they remained small everywhere, even in Bolivia where Trotskyism did at least exert some influence in the labour movement. There was, unlike the Comintern, no Trotskyist international of any significance that could provide aid, funds and ideological guidance. Trotskyists underestimated the strength of nationalist movements, and had no viable international organization or movement to counter-balance such sentiment. Trotskyists had no better answer than the orthodox parties to the question of the peasantry. They had to suffer not only the persecution of the authorities, but also that of the Communist parties.

Trotskyist parties took sectarianism and dogmatism to new heights, reflecting a desperate search for the formula that would unlock revolutionary support. This desperation led to a search for short cuts, such as entryism into other left-wing parties in order, supposedly, to transform them from within. But often the Trotskyist infiltrators were swallowed up in the party they sought to transform, as occurred in Chile when the Trotskyists entered the Chilean Socialist Party. Trotskyists suffered from the splits in their Fourth International, and fought over whether the party should only participate in national liberation struggle if the proletariat was in command, or whether it should participate in any such struggle, even if led by petty bourgeois sectors.

Trotskyism achieved some political influence in Bolivia. Unusually the Trotskyist party there, the Partido Obrero Revolucionario (POR) was not formed as a result of a split in an existing Communist party. Rather it was formed by a group of intellectuals attracted by Trotsky's writings, and in the late 1930s the group moved towards the political positions of the Fourth International. The POR achieved considerable influence in the miners union, in part because the Communist party was supporting the government in its efforts to maximize tin production even against the interests of the workers – consistent with the international strategy during the Second World War. The Trotskyists at least at this period, put the social question before Bolivia's international role and this had greater appeal to the radical Bolivian miners. But the nationalists of the Movimiento Nacional Revolucionario (MNR), who saw the war as a dispute between distant powers and irrelevant to Bolivia, had even greater appeal, not least to the peasantry excluded by the Marxists from the potential forces for revolutionary change.[24]

FROM SECOND WORLD WAR TO COLD WAR

During the Second World War, communist movements in Latin America enjoyed unusually high prestige and tolerance as a result of their involvement in anti-fascist movements and because of admiration for the war efforts of the Soviet Union. They also benefited from the dissolution of the Comintern which allowed them greater freedom of action. Membership of the Communist parties of Latin America estimated at 100,000 in 1939 had grown to around 500,000 by 1947.

Yet the underlying and fundamental problems of communist strategy remained, even though they were hidden by an unusual international conjuncture. Although the post-war period coincided with an upsurge in industrial militancy from which the Communist parties gained, nevertheless the extent of their gains were limited by the communists advocating industrial peace, and this allowed their rivals such as the Chilean Socialist Party or the Venezuelan Acción Democrática to make substantial gains in the labour movement. There still remained unresolved the problem of how to organize a revolutionary party in a social structure where the working class was weak, the petty bourgeoisie numerous, and the peasantry over-

---

[24] Following the divisions in international Trotskyism at its Berlin conference in 1955 over the question of entryism, the POR split into two and never recovered its previous influence.

whelming. There still remained unresolved the problem of how to define the role of violence in those societies where governments, and armies, and economic elites, however divided over other issues, joined forces when facing radical political movements of the Left. The communist movement adhered to the notion of the party as a revolutionary vanguard even though the central political need was to construct a broadly based multi-class alliance. Perhaps most critically of all, the communists failed to distinguish themselves from reformist governments such as those of Perón in Argentina, Acción Democrática in Venezuela, López Pumarejo in Colombia and others without at the same time appearing to be opposed to reform itself, and without appearing to prefer alliances with the forces of the Right.

Communism went into sharp retreat in Argentina immediately following the war, when the rise of Perón threw the local Communist party into a series of confusions and errors. The party mistakenly saw Peronism as an extension of European fascism into Argentina, and argued that he had merely temporarily fooled the workers. It was not only the Argentine working class that was confused by the line adopted by the local Communist party. The Brazilian Communist Party reproached the Argentine party, and argued that Perón was a populist (with similarities to Vargas), not a fascist. When it became clear that Peronism was no temporary fashion, the party split over whether to ally with him or not. Influential figures like Rodolfo Puiggrós left the party to try to influence Peronism from the inside, but had little impact on the fortunes of that movement. Communism lost its hold over the union movement, and displayed the same kind of uncertainty to the phenomenon of Peronism, as did the Mexican Communist Party to the PRI. The Argentine working class remained resolutely attached at the same time to progressive views on income distribution with quite conservative views on questions of political or social structure – a feature which Perón both recognized and intensified.

Elsewhere in Latin America the years following the war saw a brief period of democracy. The ending of dictatorships coincided with an international climate of support for the establishment of democratic governments. The Communist parties benefited from this new liberal climate. One of the most spectacular advances was made by the Brazilian Communist Party.[25] During the first half of 1945 the Partido Comunista do Brasil

---

[25] This section on Brazil draws heavily on Leslie Bethell, 'Brazil', in Leslie Bethell and Ian Roxborough (eds), *Latin America between the Second World War and the Cold War, 1944–1948* (Cambridge, 1992).

(PCB) organized widely in Brazil. Above all it penetrated the official corporate union structure, though it is not clear if they aimed to control it, or to replace it, with an independent parallel structure. The PCB created a central labour organization, the Movimento Unificador dos Trabalhadores (MUT) which was allowed to function, even though there were legal prohibitions against national union confederations.

In contrast to Argentina, however, the Brazilian urban working class was relatively small and homogeneous; some two million in size in 1945, or about 15 per cent of the work force. More than two-thirds of the work force was still employed in agriculture, cattle-raising, and rural industries. Half the urban work concentrated in two cities – São Paulo and Rio de Janeiro. Of these two million workers, about a quarter was unionized. Unions were closely controlled by the state. During those periods when the state was not uniformly hostile to the PCB, this worked to the advantage of the communists for they could attempt to manipulate state institutions for their own ends. But once the state became totally hostile, as it did in 1947, then it proved relatively easy to dislodge the communists from the control they enjoyed.

In contrast with the tactics of the Argentine CP, the Brazilian party did not oppose the leading populist politician in the country. On the contrary, the PCB tried to benefit from the overwhelming support that Getúlio Vargas enjoyed in the working class. The PCB realized that it was still weakly organized, while the forces opposed to it were powerful. It made sense for the PCB to work with, rather than against, the forces of Getulismo. These tactics brought the PCB impressive electoral success. In the December 1945 elections in Brazil, for example, the Communist party gained 9 percent of the vote and elected fourteen deputies and one senator (Luis Carlos Prestes). Even in the harsher political climate of January 1947 the PCB held on to its share of the vote, becoming the largest single party in the Federal District (the city of Rio de Janeiro) with eighteen out of fifty seats. Perhaps most significant of all, PCB support was decisive in the election of the populist Adhemar de Barros as governor of São Paulo. During immediate the post-war period the PCB had grown substantially: it claimed to have 180,000 members making it by far the largest Communist party in Latin America in 1947.

But under the anti-communist Dutra administration, increasingly severe measures were taken against the party. In May 1947 the PCB was declared illegal. Even in São Paulo, Adhemar de Barros broke with the PCB and began a process of local repression. The Brazilian government realized that the PCB was a real and growing threat, with a powerful base in an increasingly militant labour movement, a rapidly growing membership, and considerable electoral support. The decision to ban the PCB was no mere cosmetic measure designed to placate Washington's increasingly strong anti-communist paranoia. It responded to a real fear that the growth of the PCB, if unhindered, could represent a real threat to the ruling groups of the republic.

In Chile, the U.S. price for granting economic assistance to the government of González Videla after the Second World War was the dismissal from office of the communist ministers. Relations between the government and the Communist party grew steadily cooler, until the government used the occasion of a coal miners strike to outlaw the party, which by now was the most powerful Communist party in the continent, by the 'Law for the Defence of Democracy' passed in 1948. Though the repression of the party was mild compared with what was to happen after 1973, party leaders were arrested and put into concentration camps or sent into exile, and party members lost the right to vote. The party went underground for ten years, and though the experience may have increased the loyalty and commitment of those who stayed the course, the political space on the left was filled by the Socialist party.

The Brazilian and Chilean Communist parties were not the only victims of the Cold War. The Communist party in Cost Rica participated in two governments between 1940 and 1948 in alliance with Social Christian parties. When that alliance was defeated in the Civil War of 1948, the new reformist but anti-communist government of José Figueres banned the Communist party and dissolved the unions where the Communist party had built up an impressive strength. Indeed, communist leaders were purged from unions throughout Latin America. An offensive was launched against the pro-communist Confederación de Trabajadores de América Latina (CTAL) established by Lombardo Toledano in 1938. By 1948 anti-communist leaders had taken power in many unions, and succeeded in disaffiliating unions from the CTAL, though only after bitter disputes.

Latin American governments seized upon the opportunity opened up by the deterioration of relations between the United States and the USSR, to repress popular movements, to break diplomatic relations with the USSR, and to move their countries to the right. President Alemán, elected in Mexico in 1946, sought successfully to out-manoeuvre both Lombardo and the Mexican Communist Party. Alemán turned the wartime crusade against fascism into a peacetime crusade against communism. The positive legacy of the Cárdenas years for the Left was that it was strong enough and legitimate enough for Alemán's government to have to be more subtle and less brutal in its attempts to contain it than in several Latin American countries which fell to military dictatorships.

The role of the United States in this move to the right was not a decisive factor for the major countries of Latin America, though there was encouragement from Washington for Latin America to adopt Cold War policies. However, the power of the United States to influence events in Central America was much greater. The overthrow of the government in Guatemala in 1954 indicated the intensity of U.S. commitment to anti-communist policies.

Was there really the possibility of a communist takeover in Guatemala? The Communist party had only four out of fifty-six congressional seats in 1953. It had, at most, several hundred members and a couple of thousand active sympathizers. It had no cabinet ministers, only eight senior posts in the public administration, and had only been legally recognized in 1952. The first post-war president, Juan José Arévalo, held that the international connections of the Communist party rendered it illegal under the Guatemalan constitution.[26] It did have a following in the labour movement and among intellectuals, largely because of the collapse of other parties. But it had no influence on the military, and little on the overall policies of the Arbenz government. It was still clinging to the idea of the necessary stages for the revolution, which in the case of Guatemala meant the national bourgeois stage first.

The Guatemalan reformist government became a victim of the Cold War paranoia of the U.S. government of the time, and of the right-wing forces in Guatemala, which were only too happy to play along with the United States for their own ends. The tragedy of the coup was that it brought to an end a promising experiment in modest reform, that it posed the future development of the country in terms either of revolution or reaction, that it rendered impossible the establishment of stable govern-

---

[26] Yet Arévalo regarded himself as a socialist, though of a spiritual kind. 'We are socialists because we live in the twentieth century. But we are not materialist socialists . . . We believe that man is above all the will for dignity . . . Our socialism does not aim at an ingenious distribution of material goods or at the stupid equalisation of men who are economically different. Our socialism aims at liberating man psychologically and spiritually. The materialist concept has become a tool in the hands of totalitarian forces. Communism, fascism, and Nazism have also been socialist. But theirs is a socialism which gives food with the left hand while the right mutilates the moral and civic virtues of man.' From Juan José Arévalo, *Escritos Políticos* [Guatemala 1945], cited in James Dunkerley, 'Guatemala since 1930', in *Cambridge History of Latin America*, Vol. VII (1990), p. 220.

ment, and that it created a context in which political violence became a commonplace.

In the popular rebellion in Bolivia that brought to power the MNR in 1952, the communists were on the sidelines. The Communist party was weak and divided, had been founded only in 1940, and was challenged on the left by the Trotskyist POR. The Communist party, the PIR (Partido de la Izquierda Revolucionaria), had supported anti-MNR governments after 1946, and though the Communist party did vote tactically for the MNR in 1951, the military disallowed the electoral results precisely on the ground that the MNR was in alliance with the communists. The MNR had been hostile to the communists from the beginning, refusing to allow that party into the cabinet of Villaroel in 1944 (and the communists had later participated in the coup against Villaroel in 1946). The Communist party had little worker or peasant support: it had only 12000 votes in the 1956 presidential elections to the 750,000 for the MNR. As the communists had been associated with the anti-labour governments before 1952, it could hardly compete with the MNR for the support of labour. The party had even entered into armed conflict with the miners of Potosí in 1947, hitherto the party's stronghold, and the ensuing massacre destroyed the labour base of support for the PIR. The Bolivian Revolution, like that of Cuba later in the decade, was one in which of all the forces on the left, the Communist party was last to realize the significance of what was happening. Communist parties like that of Bolivia showed considerable capacity to survive repression and to keep the party organization alive, but little ability to take political initiatives. The party in Bolivia, and elsewhere in Latin America, showed great caution on those not infrequent opportunities when decisive action could have produced political gains. The dilemma for the communists was that such gains could only have been produced by alliances with other parties, and the Communist parties were generally hostile to alliances in which they were the subordinate elements.

The major ideological challenge on the left to the PIR came from the Trotskyist POR. The POR undoubtedly had influence in the Bolivian union movement, above all in the miners' union. The Bolivian miners were relatively few in number – at their peak in the 1950s only 53,000 – yet their union exercised great power because of the strategic importance of tin to the economy of Bolivia. Partly because of the miners' isolation, their union was not much influenced by anarchism or anarcho-syndicalism. The miners were undoubtedly militant and radical, as was the central union confederation, the Central Obrera Boliviana (COB), created in 1952. But the miners' union tended towards a powerful if narrow syndicalism. The miners union was frequently the battleground between the parties of the Left, but was never captured by any of them. This suspicious attitude to the parties and its pronounced syndicalism helps to explain the appeal of the independent union leader Juan Lechín to the miners, for he was mistrustful of parties and shared the miners' syndicalism. If miners relied on union leaders from the radical Left, at the same time they voted in national elections above all for the nationalist MNR. Even in the militant Siglo XX mine, in the 1956 elections the MNR, which presented a more radical face in the mining camps than it did in the cities, received 4719 votes to the 130 for the Communist party and the 68 of the POR.[27]

At times of crisis and industrial struggle, the miners sought leaders from the Left; at times of elections they voted according to their political preferences, a response not limited to Bolivia. The left-wing parties were never strong enough, nor were the unions wealthy enough, to create a bureaucratized union elite which could control the union. The POR lacked a solid party organization that could move into and colonize the union movement; and after 1953 it lost many members to the MNR, which for all its hybrid ideology did appear to be in the vanguard of the revolutionary movement. The MNR in government after 1952, however, moved sharply to the right, and many of the gains of the revolution were lost. The power base of the Left was gradually reduced as the tin-mining industry declined, and the Left was to suffer from the failure of its misplaced hopes that alliance with progressive military officers would bring it real political power.

THE CUBAN REVOLUTION AND ITS AFTERMATH

The 1950s were lean years for the Left in Latin America. In many countries the communist party was banned. The Bolivian Revolution of 1952 showed the far greater capacity for political mobilization by multi-class nationalist movements than by parties of the orthodox Left, whether inspired by Stalin or by Trotsky. The coup in Guatemala in 1954 was a profound setback. The Cold War saw intense U.S. pressure in Latin America generally, and above all in Central America and the Caribbean, to curb reform movements of any kind that might be identified with the Left.

---

[27] Laurence Whitehead, 'Miners as Voters: the electoral process in the Bolivian mining camps', *Journal of Latin American Studies*, 13, 2 (1981).

At the end of the decade, however, the revolution led by Fidel Castro in Cuba provided a real, and unanticipated, boost to the fortunes of the Left. The story of the Cuban Revolution, and of the hostility of the Communist party there towards Castro until the eve of his success in January 1959 is well known. But if the Communist party played little role in Castro's coming to power, it was closely involved in the consolidation of his rule as Castro needed cadres experienced in political organization once the military phase of the revolution was complete. Any explanation of why the Cuban regime moved towards orthodox communism would also have to stress the international context, the dominance of socialism in intellectual circles, and a fierce anti-Americanism which all combined to make alliance between Castro and the communists if not inevitable at least highly probable. Once the alliance was made, the failure of the regime to develop any degree of international economic autonomy made heavy reliance upon the Soviet Union a matter of time, and the price of that reliance was, eventually, conformity with Soviet practice.

The immediate effect of the success of the Cuban Revolution on the Left in Latin America was electrifying (as indeed it was on the Right, as we shall see). All aspects of dogma, of received wisdom, and of traditional practice were subject to scrutiny in the light of a successful revolution coming from a rural guerrilla without the participation of the Communist party. Central to the new debate on the Left was the need for a reanalysis of the social structure of Latin American countries, especially the vexed question of the nature and role of the so called national bourgeoisie, and of the political potential of the peasantry. Did the revolutionary process have to go through stages; did there have to be a democratic bourgeois revolution first, or could this stage be omitted? What was the relation between the military and political wings of the revolution, and how could the revolutionary force neutralize the military forces of the government? Was Cuba an exceptional case, or could it be repeated elsewhere? The success of the Cuban Revolution undermined the claim of the orthodox Communist parties to be the sole source of Marxist, and therefore revolutionary, legitimacy. It seemed to many young radicals that the revolution could be made by enthusiasm and commitment alone. Most would-be imitators of Castro advocated guerrilla warfare, but even those who did not argued for a political radicalism that would overthrow the existing structures.

Orthodox Communist parties were slow to respond to the challenge of the Cuban Revolution and stuck to their traditional ideas. The communists pointed to Che Guevara's statement on the singularities of the Cuban case, namely that Castro was an exceptional leader, that the United States was unprepared for the revolution, that the national bourgeoisie was prepared to join the anti-Batista front, and that most of the Cuban peasantry was semi-proletarianized through the mechanization of the sugar industry. Of course Guevara himself argued that the absence of these factors in other countries did not preclude the possiblity of revolution, though it did make the work of the political vanguard both harder and more necessary. But the orthodox communists, though they continued to proclaim their belief in the inevitability of the revolution, stressed the need to create a mass urban movement. They argued that socialism in one country was possible, and was not contingent upon a continental revolution. Although the leading role in the revolutionary process would be played by the Communist party and the proletariat, it would be achieved in broad alliance with peasants, intellectuals and the national bourgeoisie. There had to be stages: the revolution must first attack U.S. imperialism and agrarian feudalism. Only then could the revolution proceed to the next stage.

These ideas were rejected by those who wished to apply the Cuban model to other countries. Their argument was that there could be no stages in the revolutionary process because there was no bourgeoisie independent from U.S. domination. The pro-Cuban theorists of the revolution were heavily influenced by the early and crude version of dependency theories in which neo-colonialist exploitation became the universal explanation for the under-development of Latin America. Urban politics was seen as a ghetto. Trade unions were compromised by their participation in politics, towns could easily be controlled by the forces of repression, and elections were a sham. The only way forward was through armed struggle, which would create the leadership, then the rural base and finally the urban support for the revolution. There was no impediment to winning the support of the peasantry, as the countryside was capitalist, and not feudal. And since the military was the armed expression of the oligarchy it had to be – and could be – confronted and defeated by means of guerrilla warfare. Yet as these proponents of guerrilla warfare were to find out to their cost, reality was to disprove most of these assumptions.

The radical Left attacked the miserable record of the communists as agents of insurrection. They criticized the democratic centralist style of party organization of the communists, arguing that it led to the domination of the party by a small bureaucratic elite more interested in controlling the party than in promoting the revolution. They criticized the communists for being more concerned to attack deviants on the Left than the capitalist order. Many of these criticisms were well founded, and they put on the defensive orthodox communists, who continued nevertheless to maintain that attempts at armed insurrection would only lead to further oppression. For the Brazilian leader Carlos Prestes the only conclusion to be drawn from the coup of 1964 was that 'the correct revolutionary attitude was to admit the defeat, draw back, and once more begin the patient work of propaganda on the level of the masses'.[28] For leaders like Prestes, the bulk of the guerrilla left were petty-bourgeois romantics with no links with the popular classes.

The Cuban Revolution coincided with a period of tension in international communism, as relations between the Soviet Union and China deteriorated. The Left in Latin America was to a limited extent affected by the dispute. China had begun efforts to draw Latin American communists away from the Soviet Union as early as 1956, following Kruschev's speech to the 20th Party Congress of the CPSU denouncing Stalinism. Efforts were redoubled as the Cuban missile crisis reflected adversely upon the influence of the Soviet Union. Yet Chinese support for guerrilla movements in Latin America was largely verbal. Indeed, their marked lack of enthusiasm for the Cuban model of peasant rebellion was remarkable considering the origins of the Chinese government. The real aim of the Chinese government was to reduce Soviet influence in Latin America, and in order not to appear sectarian it even advocated a tactic of the broadest possible 'national democratic united front'.

The impact of Chinese efforts – which were in any case very limited – was minor. The Chilean Communist Party issued a warning to its members about the dangers of Chinese communism, but if anything those dangers were more present in the Socialist party than in the Communist. In Brazil the hard line Stalinists in the party objected to Prestes' reforms intended to moderate the party line, and in 1962 they left the Partido Comunista Brasileiro (PCB) to form the pro-Chinese Partido Comunista do Brasil (PC do B), which was consistently intransigent and equally consistently politically marginal. In Bolivia, a group critical of the official policy of approaching the MNR for tactical alliances, broke away and formed the pro-Chinese Partido Comunista Marxista Leninista (PCML). But in many ways the PCML was closer to Cuba than to China, and it

[28] Quoted in Ronald Chilcote, *The Brazilian Communist Party: Conflict and Integration 1922–1972* (New York, 1974), p. 80.

offered aid to Guevara's guerrilla movement – though the offer was not accepted as he would work only with the pro-Moscow party. The first dissident party recognized by the Chinese authorities was in Peru in 1964, and Peru was the only country where Maoism was to assume ideological importance, though not until the 1970s. In general those who formed the pro-Chinese parties were the most dogmatic and sectarian hard liners, who showed no ability to build up a mass party. The prestige of the Chinese communists was damaged when Castro denounced them bitterly in 1966 for having effectively joined the U.S. economic blockade and of trying to subvert the Cuban military and civil service. Mao's cultural revolution did attract the interest of some radical groups, but only in Peru was Chinese communism to be a major political influence.

The debates on the Left in Latin America following the Cuban Revolution were not merely academic. In nearly every country of Latin America during the early 1960s, guerrilla groups were organized, some significant, some not. But the 'lessons' of Cuba were not confined to the Left. The United States and the political Right in Latin America were determined to prevent another Cuba. Between March 1962 and June 1966 there were nine military coups in Latin America. In at least eight of them, the army took preventative action to overthrow a government that was felt to be too weak to take action against popular or 'communist' movements, or against governments that were accused, as in the Dominican Republic or Brazil, of themselves desiring to carry out subversive reforms. President Kennedy, who took office in January 1961, felt that the correct response to Kruschev's support for national liberation movements was the strengthening of democratic systems through a mutual Alliance for Progress, and a strengthening of the military through a massive programme of aid and training. Support for democratic governments was not very successful, but Latin American armies certainly benefited from the help they received from the United States in the interests of containing communism. The armies of mainland Latin America experienced little difficulty in containing the guerrilla movements that broke out in imitation of the Cuban Revolution.

In Colombia, during the *violencia* from 1948 to 1957 both the major parties, the Conservatives and Liberals, had their armed partisans. The Colombian Communist Party also had a small guerrilla group, the Fuerzas Armadas de la Revolución Colombiana (FARC), though rather more as a result of conformity to political practice in the republic than an indication of a desire to seize state power. The FARC controlled some isolated rural municipalities, thus allowing the Communist party to claim that it was pursuing a revolutionary strategy, while in practice finding that electoral politics was a more congenial occupation. The Communist party changed its line in 1967 after President Lleras Restrepo made a permanent trading relationship with the Soviet Union conditional upon Moscow persuading the party to sever its links with the guerrillas, and the Communist party duly announced that in its view there no longer existed a revolutionary situation in Colombia.[29]

The success of Castro set off many would-be imitators in Colombia. The Ejército Popular de Liberación (EPL) was a small Maoist group. The Ejército de Liberación Nacional (ELN) was a Castroite group founded in Cuba in 1963/4 and advocated the *foco* approach of Che Guevara, but had more success, and gained a considerable fortune by its attacks on internationally owned oil installations. The most important of the guerrilla groups to emerge in Colombia was the M-19, formed in 1970 in protest at alleged electoral fraud that prevented the former dictator General Rojas Pinilla from taking power. Such antecedents hardly qualify the M-19 to be counted as a leftist movement, and its programme amounted to little more than a combination of vague nationalism and spectacular armed actions.

Although a relatively weak Colombian state was unable to repress the guerrillas, they did not amount to a serious threat to the status quo – much less than the traditional parties did when they too entered the armed struggle to compete for power. The guerrillas undoubtedly gained some local support in certain areas, such as the banana zone of Uraba with its harsh labour regime, and Arauca where the newly found oil wealth brought few benefits to the poor. But support for the guerrillas remained local, their aims confused, their rivalry endemic, and their power infinitely inferior to the real threat to Colombian democracy that developed with the illegal drugs trade in the 1980s.

The country where the post-Castro guerrillas seemed to have some chance of success was Venezuela, partly because the Communist party itself lent support to the guerrillas, and partly because the democratic system, recently created in 1958, was still fragile. The Venezuelan Communist Party had long exercised a degree of independence from the international line. It maintained an independent stance in the Sino-Soviet conflict, and indeed even sent emissaries to Moscow, Peking and Cuba to try

[29] Christopher Abel and Marco Palacios, 'Colombia since 1958', in *Cambridge History of Latin America*, Vol. VIII (1991), p. 655.

to bridge the gap. It emphasized its support for national liberation struggles, and had close contacts with the Italian Communist Party. Venezuela had recently seen the end of the Pérez Jiménez dictatorship. The Communist party enjoyed high prestige for its role in opposing the dictatorship, and given the level of political instability, the party hoped to collaborate with the other parties in future governments. But the major party, Acción Democrática was opposed to such collaboration, not least because it would have alienated other and more important allies to the right. Yet there were groups inside AD that felt that the party had betrayed its socialist commitment, and there were three splits from AD in the 1960s in which the issue of collaboration with the Communist party was central.

When hostility between AD and the communists ruled out further collaboration, the communists joined the guerrillas in 1963. Expectations on the revolutionary left were high. The new government was still far from firmly established, facing challenges from the right as well as the left. The Venezuelan guerrilla enjoyed the support of Cuba. It was thought that the armed forces were discredited by their participation in the previous dictatorship. Venezuela was a relatively modern and open society, whose class structure, above all the absence of a large traditional peasant class, was assumed to favour the possibilities of successful revolution.

Yet the guerrillas failed disastrously. Although the Communist party, against Moscow's wishes, supported them, it was ill-prepared for such action. Most of the members of the Central Committee were rounded up before the action had started (only six of the eighty strong Central Committee actually fought with the guerrillas). The decision to leave the guerrilla was as abrupt as the decision to join, and it led to dissent in the party, and expulsions from it, including that of Douglas Bravo one of the leading *guerrilleros*.

The party underestimated the extent to which most social groups in Venezuela were committed to democracy and supported the major political parties. The Communist party lost virtually all its former influence in the labour movement, where the nationalist pro-industrialization stance of AD was much more popular. It lost its representation in Congress and in the press. It gained little support among the students, and remained isolated from other parties. It lost whatever ideological initiative it had possessed. Armed struggle made no sense to a working and middle class enjoying the material benefits of oil wealth, and the political benefits of a liberal state.

The Peruvian guerrilla faction was ideologically divided between the

MIR (Movimiento de Izquierda Revolucionaria), which was formed by dissident Apristas, and the ELN (Ejército de Liberación Nacional) formed by dissident communists. Neither had an urban base, and consequently lacked the supplies necessary to maintain themselves. They had little training. They were separated from the peasantry by a huge cultural and linguistic gap, and had little knowledge of conditions in the rural areas, let alone of a programme that might have won over peasant support. The election of President Fernando Belaúnde in 1963, and his promise of agrarian reform, reduced what support they hoped to win in the peasantry. Considerable technical help from the United States allowed the Peruvian army to deal with the guerrillas without too much difficulty.[30] The failings that beset the Peruvian guerrillas affected the Bolivian guerrillas also. The only factor that lent that episode much more international attention was the presence and death of Ernesto 'Che' Guevara in Bolivia in 1967. Even Guevara was unable to win over a suspicious and hostile peasantry.

Between 1959 and 1963, Hugo Blanco, a prominent Trotskyist, had mobilized an estimated 300,000 peasants in the Lares and La Convención valleys in the Cuzco area of Peru. But agrarian conditions there were unusual: labour was scarce, peasant incomes were relatively high from coffee, and the large estates were mostly unoccupied. There was no real guerrilla warfare, and the landowners and the government accepted the peasant occupations with unusual alacrity. Conditions elsewhere in Peru were very different and the movement never spread. Hugo Blanco criticized the revolutionary extremism of some members of his party, and his own syndicalist deviations – both factors leading, in his view, to neglect of the real task of creating a revolutionary party. Trotskyism remained a minority group on the political left in Peru, to be far surpassed in importance by the Maoists.[31]

---

[30] The defeat of the Peruvian guerrilla led to a heated debate inside the Maoist movement in Peru. Most Maoists saw the defeat as demonstrating that the revolution had to be urban rather than rural based. A group led by Abimael Guzmán disagreed and continued to press for armed struggle in the rural areas. They eventually left the party and formed Sendero Luminoso in 1969/1970.

[31] Trotskyism elsewhere in Latin America never disappeared from view: at the very least it was a refuge for those who were disillusioned with orthodox communism, but were not persuaded by the rural guerrilla strategy of the Castroists. A Trotskyist guerrilla movement, the ERP (Ejército Revolucionario del Pueblo), established a base in the Tucumán region of Argentina in the late 1960s and early 1970s. It was eliminated by the military after 1976 when it attempted to confront the army. The Argentine Trotskyist party, the Partido Revolucionario de los Trabajadores (PRT), formally dissolved its military wing in 1977 (although there is some evidence that Trotskyist guerrillas were behind an ill fated assault on a military barracks (in Argentina) in 1989). There are at least four Trotskyist parties active in Argentina, spending much time on mutual recriminations. The existence of these parties partly reflects hostility towards the posture of the pro-Soviet Commu-

The unusual feature of the Guatemalan guerrilla was that the group was founded by young military officers, alienated from their institution by the 1960 coup and the experience of the repressive Ydígoras government. They needed political allies. At first they turned to the Guatemalan Communist Party, the PGT (Partido Guatemalteco de Trabajo), which had in imitation of Cuba even tried its own, ill-fated guerrilla group in 1962. But the young officers found themselves excluded from any decision-taking power by a party that was still essentially orthodox, viewing the armed struggle only as a minor part of an overall strategy. The guerrilla forces led by the former officer Yon Sosa sought alliance with the Trotskyists, but this led to further divisions in the guerrilla movement, and the Trotskyists had no resources to offer comparable to those that could come from Cuba via the PGT. By 1969, the PGT condemned the guerrilla as divorced from the population and influenced by Mexican Trotskyists in the pay of the CIA. The PGT suffered further splits as radicalized sectors of the new left and the Christian Democrats continued to struggle against a series of oppressive military governments. At one stage the guerrillas controlled almost all the departments of Quiche and Huehuetenango, but they forced communities to chose between them and the army in circumstances in which the guerrillas were not strong enough to defend those communities against the army. The result was, predictably, savage reprisals by the military.

By the late 1960s the future of the rural guerrilla looked bleak, and the decade had seen a further decline in the standing of the Communist parties. Either they were criticized for failing to support the guerrilla, as in Bolivia, or they were criticized for participating without real enthusiasm as in Venezuela and Guatemala. The focus of attention now moved from the rural guerrilla in Central America and the Andean republics to the countries of the Southern Cone where a large and powerful urban guerrilla had developed.

Rural rebellion was hardly likely to be a successful strategy for seizing state power in the urban societies of the Southern Cone. In reaction against the dogmatism of the Communist parties, and learning from the failures of the rural guerrilla, two powerful urban guerrilla movements developed in Argentina and Uruguay. In Argentina, the Montoneros

nist party, considered to be too close to the military regime that took power in the coup of 1976. Similarly, in Mexico a Trotskyist party – the PRT (Partido Revolucionario de los Trabajadores) – kept alive the memory of Trotsky exiled there and reflected condemnation of the Moscow orientated Communist party's perpetual uncertainty about its long-term relations with the PRI.

worked explicitly inside the Peronist party; in Uruguay, the Tupamaros, whose origins lay with a rural guerrilla in the north of the country, soon switched to urban operations and eventually participated in a broad movement of the Left, the Frente Amplio, which sought power through electoral means.

These movements rejected the Leninist style of political organization and class-based analysis for an eclectic mixture of ideas drawing upon Third World nationalism, liberation theology, and in the case of the Montoneros some right-wing nationalist ideas that had inspired the neofascist movements of previous decades. As one Tupamaro leader put it, 'We have seen more clearly what not to do than what to do . . . We must try to affirm our political personality by attacking other groups on the left . . . There was no need to make great statements that our policy was the only correct policy: events would show whether that was so or not.'[32]

They did not reject political alliances, but on the contrary, in the tired rhetoric that characterized their pronouncements 'sought allies in the struggle against the dominant sectors and their imperialist allies'. They were successful in attracting support because they tapped resentment against a political system which offered little hope for political change, or economic advancement, either in Argentina or Uruguay, and also because they were audacious. But the Montoneros also repelled other groups on the left through their use of violence and terrorism.

The Montoneros failed to grasp the ambiguity of Perón, and attributed to him revolutionary ideas that were remote from his practice, however occasionally he might give them his verbal blessing. How the Montoneros ever thought that they could capture the sympathy of the Peronist labour movement by killing its leaders is difficult to understand. Once the Tupamaros moved from clandestine military operations to more or less open political activity, they were wide open to infiltration and annihilation at the hands of the military and police. Once the military took power in Argentina in 1976 and decided to take any action that was necessary against them, the Montoneros could not hope to survive.

No government could have permitted groups like the Montoneros or the Tupamaros to operate without attempting to curb them, and the activities of the guerrilla groups set in motion a spiral of violence which culminated in brutally repressive military governments. For all the sophistication of their clandestine military operations, the political analysis of

---

[32] Cited in Regis Debray, *The Revolution on Trial* (London, 1978), p. 205.

the urban guerrilla groups was no more realistic than that of the middle-class intellectuals who had created rural guerrilla movements in the Andean countries.

The failure of the guerrilla movements, both urban and rural, and the seemingly increasing irrelevance of the orthodox Communist parties revealed the inability of both to interpret the world in which they were living. Latin America in the 1960s and 1970s was undergoing a process of multiple change which would alter the economic, social and political context in which the Left operated. In the first place, post-war Latin America saw a prolonged period of economic growth, rapid urbanization and profound changes in the region's class structure. Second, the Catholic Church, for long the bitter opponent of communism, redefined its social message in a way that brought it close, in some countries, to the Left, both ideologically and even organizationally. Third, the coup of 1964 in Brazil was but the first of a series of coups in Latin America that brought to power military governments intent on a thorough restructuring of the economic and political order, accompanied by an ideology of national security that defined the main enemy of the nation as the forces of the Left.

The labour force in Latin America became predominantly urban as it shifted away from agricultural employment. In Mexico, Brazil and Colombia in 1950 the labour force in agriculture was about 60 percent of the total labour force; by the mid-1980s it was down to 30 percent. Yet this urban growth, and import substitution industrialization, was associated with a worsening pattern of income distribution, and a pattern of employment in which the organized labour force was only a small minority of the total employed population. An increasingly large proportion were to be found in the so-called informal sector of the economy. The issues which mobilized this sector had less to do with workplace and control over the means of production, and much more to do with basic conditions of life. Mobilization, when it did take place, was residential or communal, and was directed against the government or municipal authorities rather than against employers, and it involved a variety of social classes and occupations. The extent of mobilization increased under the military governments, for those governments found it easier to control the unions than the shanty towns.

The Latin American Left was slow to recognize the political potential of those who worked in the informal sector. The attitude of the orthodox communists was at best ambiguous and at worse dismissive (the infamous lumpen proletariat in Marxist jargon). A variety of non-Marxist movements, from populist dictators such as Odría in Peru, to progressive parties, such as the Christian Democrats in Chile were quicker to realize that political gains could be made by paying attention to the needs of the urban poor. When, during the military dictatorships of the 1960s and 1970s, unions were repressed, Communist parties began to pay attention to organization in the shanty-towns. But the political base offered by the *pobladores* was much less stable than that offered by organized labour, and much more conditional and volatile, and it was by no means certain that the left-wing parties that built an organizational base in the shanty-towns could hold onto those gains against political alternatives that often had more to offer.

The Church was increasingly aware of the needs of the shanty-towns, and in some countries at least set up a network of local organizations which began to make political demands, and to link their needs to an overall insistence on national political reform. The change in the doctrine of the Catholic Church following the Second Vatican Council (1962–5) and the Declaration of Latin American Bishops at Medellín in 1968 reflected the concern of a church that felt it was becoming increasingly irrelevant in the face of growing secularization and Protestant and Marxist influence. Indeed, Marxist ideas no longer remained the preserve of left-wing parties; they now influenced the analysis and practice of the Church itself, above all through the influential, if numerically very small, theologians of liberation.

The extent of radical rethinking in the Church must not be exaggerated. The Church in Argentina and Uruguay resisted the spirit of Medellín and there was very little innovation. In Colombia the Church remained relatively unchanged by the new ideas and as conservative as before, and some Colombian priests were influential in the watering down of the progressive ideas of Medellín at the next conference of Latin American bishops at Puebla in 1979. But even in countries like Argentina, Uruguay or Colombia, there were some priests and laity who gave their enthusiastic support to the new ideas. Indeed a handful of priests in Argentina formed the Third World movement, and contributed to the ideas that later found expression in the urban guerrilla movement, the Montoneros.

In Brazil the effect of radical Catholicism was much more pronounced, and in Chile, though the Church remained, as it had long been, essentially centrist, it became politically active in opposition to the Pinochet regime. The Church withdrew the support it had extended initially to the coups of 1964 and 1973 in those countries, and denied to those regimes the legitimation that the Church in the past had not infrequently granted to authoritarian regimes. Church activity kept alive a degree of political pluralism, including support for parties of the Left, if not directly, at least indirectly through the support for trade unions, or popular organizations, or research centres where members of radical parties could organize opposition to the military regimes. The challenge by the Church to the economic policies of these regimes was couched in terms that differed little from Marxist critiques. The rethinking of Catholic ideas helped to remove Marxism from a ghetto of Communist parties and restricted intellectual circles. It took place at the same time as a renewal of interest in Marxist ideas, above all in France, and not least in response to the student rebellions of 1968, which replaced dogmatic and mechanical Marxism with a more open and appealing variety, which radical Catholics were to find attractive.[33]

In Nicaragua the influence of progressive Catholicism led the (FSLN – Frente Sandinista de Liberación Nacional), the Sandinistas, to move from narrowly Marxist to much more broadly based perspectives, which in such a profoundly Catholic country as Nicaragua was necessary in order to construct a broad front to overthrow Somoza. The FSLN, at least in public overtures to the Catholic population, recognized the ideological affinity of Christianity and Marxism. According to the Jesuit priest Miguel D'Escoto who later became a minister in the Sandinista government, 'In the beginning, the FSLN was Marxist and anticlerical perhaps because a process of Christianisation had not yet begun in the Nicaraguan Catholic church, and it was identified with the interests of the privileged class. But with our evangelical radicalisation, placing ourselves on the side of the poor and oppressed, and not betraying Christ so much, the Front opened itself to Christians because they believed the Church an important factor in the struggle for liberation, and because they realised they were wrong in believing that only a Marxist could be a revolutionary. Thus the Front acquired maturity and became authentically Sandinista.'[34]

However, it was also frequently the case that revolutionary Christians abandoned the Church to become openly Marxist militants. And there may well have been an element of tactical opportunism rather than real

---

[33] This was period when left wing publishing houses such as Siglo XXI flourished. Two books in particular circulated widely in Latin America and helped to form the political views of a generation of students: Marta Harnecker, *Los Conceptos Elementales del Materialismo Historico* (Mexico, D.F., 1969), and Eduardo Galeano, *Las Venas Abiertas de America Latina* (Mexico, D.F., 1971).

[34] Quoted in Donald Hodges, *Intellectual Foundations,* p. 270.

conviction in the Sandinistas' embrace with Catholicism. It made good political sense for the Sandinista movement to seek allies with the Church in such a strongly Catholic country.

Not all the military regimes of the 1960s and 1970s were at first anti-communist, or anti-Marxist. The Peruvian military that took power in 1968 was clearly influenced by a variety of ideas drawn from Marxism, from dependency theory, from national liberation movements, and from liberation theology. But these ideas were not universal in the Peruvian military and were quickly discarded once the reform programmes ran into major difficulties. There were echoes of Peruvian military reformism in the military government of Rodríguez Lara in Ecuador. Both of these military governments were supported by the respective Communist parties in the expectation that nationalist and reformist military governments would offer the Communist party more opportunities for exercising political influence, especially in the labour movement, than elected governments. Indeed in Peru the most loyal supporter of the military government was the Communist party, which only went into opposition with the general strike in 1977. General Torrijos in Panama also represented a kind of nationalist populist government that the Communist party supported. But the most dramatic episode of military radicalism came with the short-lived government of General Torres in Bolivia. Torres, without much support in the military, earned approval on the left when he expelled the Peace Corps, nationalized the Mathilde zinc mines, and raised the salaries of the miners. But when Torres went along with the Marxist parties and unions in creating a Popular Assembly, he went too far: the military would not accept his system of 'dual power' and he was overthrown in August 1971. In Uruguay the Communist party thought that a military government would be nationalist and reformist, and they did not oppose military intervention in February 1973. They even abandoned a general strike that took place at the start of the military dictatorship in June 1973 in the mistaken hope that they could negotiate with the military. In Argentina, where the brunt of the repression was borne by the Peronist and Trotskyist guerrilla movements, and where there were close trade relations between the USSR and Argentina, the Communist party was very muted in its criticism of the regime.

Nevertheless, the military authoritarian regimes, above all in Argentina, Brazil, Chile and Uruguay, were determined to eliminate any political movement which might challenge their authority. The Left was powerless to resist such military brutality, and militants of the Left suffered repression ranging from exile to assassination. Trade unions were reduced to ineffectiveness, political parties were banned or controlled, the press and media placed under government control, and only the Church enjoyed a very restricted opportunity to defend basic human rights against the repression of the state. (Though it has to be said that in Argentina and Uruguay the Church hardly played any role in defence of those rights).

The ultimate effect on the Left of these authoritarian regimes was profound. In the Southern Cone especially, the Left began a process of re-evaluation whose result was to emphasize the value of democracy. The ideas of Gramsci rather than Lenin became the guide. Democracy was no longer seen as a bourgeois pretence, and elections were no longer considered as a fraud. The Nicaraguan Revolution was seen as a focal point for solidarity, but, unlike that of Cuba, not for emulation. Ideological pluralism was now seen as something desirable. Guerrilla movements were discredited in those countries where guerrilla violence had led to military governments. In some countries, however, the armed struggle continued. In Colombia, which had escaped the wave of military dictatorships, the communist FARC continued to harass civilian governments. In Peru, the Sendero Luminoso (Shining Path) guerrilla gathered strength. In Central America, where elections were rigged, the military was repressive, and civilian parties were weak, and where, especially in Guatemala, racial conflict lent strength to the guerrilla's claims to be the representatives of the poor, guerrilla groups saw no alternative other than to attempt to conquer power through armed struggle.

THE 1970S: DEFEAT IN CHILE, ADVANCE IN NICARAGUA

If the key event of the 1960s for the Left in Latin America was the Cuban revolution, the 1970s began with a very different triumph for the Left when Chile elected a Marxist, Salvador Allende to the presidency. The triumph was short-lived, and the coup against Allende threw the Left into a state of deeper ideological and tactical uncertainty. The 1970s ended with the victory of the Sandinistas in Nicaragua, but although that success had a great impact on the neighbouring countries of Central America, its effects elsewhere were insignificant compared with the triumphalism that had greeted the victory of Castro in Cuba twenty years earlier.

In Chile in 1970 the Left won power in elections, and began a short-lived experiment in trying to create a socialist society through peaceful,

Politics

constitutional means. The Chilean experiment attracted widespread international attention because it posed a question of universal relevance for the
left – could there be a peaceful transition to socialism in a pluralistic and
democratic society? The reasons why the government was ended by a coup
in 1973 have been endlessly debated, and the 'lessons' of Chile have been
used by different groups on the left to justify distinct strategies. There was
no agreement in Chile itself about how to proceed along the 'Chilean road
to socialism', and indeed there was endless debate about means and ends.
But the mere fact of continual internal debate made Chile a focus of
interest for the international Left, for this was no imposition from above of
a rigid revolutionary dogma, but a pluralist and democratic government
attempting to win popular support for the most part by argument and
persuasion. Moreover, there were so many parallels between the Chilean
political system and that of European countries that the experiment was
followed for possible lessons to be applied elsewhere.

With the coup of 1973 however, other lessons were sought: what could
the international Left learn from the mistakes of the Chilean Left? How
could the Left anywhere hope to attain power in the face of opposition
from the national and international Right? The effect of the failure of the
Unidad Popular government was to polarize the Left in Latin America.
The more radical groups, such as the Sandinistas in Nicaragua and pro-
Cuban groups elsewhere, resolved to intensify armed conflict. Their argument was that the coup showed that a peaceful road to socialism was
simply an illusion. Internationally, the more radical groups, such as the
pro-Chinese parties, also drew the conclusion that Chile demonstrated
that the peaceful road was impossible. The far Left argued that facing the
opposition of the Right, the military and the United States that armed
revolution was the only hope of achieving power. This argument was
accepted initially in Chile by the MIR (Movimiento de Izquierda Revolucionaria), but it was soon eliminated by the military government. The
Chilean Communist Party also advocated armed struggle, but did not
adopt the policy until 1980 and only then on a modest scale.

If one response of the Left to the coup was to advocate the need for
violence, another response was diametrically opposite – arguing that the
Left should now moderate its policies and actions so that the conditions
that gave rise to coups would not occur. The revisionists argued that the
Left should stop visualizing power exclusively in terms of force, as something to be physically possessed. The Left should stop concentrating on
property relations to the exclusion of other factors: a simple transference of

ownership to the state would not solve anything, and could indeed create more problems than it resolved. The military could not be defeated by force. A radical government had to achieve such widespread legitimacy that the conditions that gave rise to military intervention – social disorder, political conflict outside the parliamentary and electoral arenas – did not occur. That meant concessions to the Right and a determined effort to win the support of the middle classes and to achieve a working relationship with the business sectors. Political alliances were seen as necessary, and democracy was seen as a value in its own right.

This revisionism had international dimensions. The Italian Communist Party drew the conclusion that there was a need for a historic compromise with the ruling Christian Democratic party to prevent any coup like that in Chile; and the French party used similar arguments in its alliance with the Socialist party. The Chilean case became central to the debate over Eurocommunism, as the proponents of revisonist ideas stressed the need not to create implacable enemies on the right.

The Soviet Union tried to counter the drift towards Eurocommunism by drawing opposite conclusions from the failure of the Allende government. In a series of articles in the *World Marxist Review* analysing Chile, the Soviet line was that 'one of the absolute conditions for defending revolutionary gains' is that 'democracy must serve the people and not allow freedom of action for the counter revolutionary forces'. The paramount role of the working class cannot be replaced by a 'pluralistic approach that forfeits or weakens the leading role of the working class'.[35]

In the same way as the Cuban Revolution set the agenda for the Left in the 1960s in Latin America, the failure of Allende's government did the same for the 1970s. However, whereas Cuba had great influence on the national liberation struggles in the Third World, the lessons of Chile were seen as more applicable to Europe. One of the reasons why Henry Kissinger worried about the Popular Unity government was the effect that its success might have in countries like Italy and Greece. Unlike Cuba, however, the Chilean experiment ended in abrupt failure and so prompted critical analysis on the Left, rather than imitation as in the case of Cuba.

In Central America, whose political history has been marked by frequent and bitter social conflict, tension increased in the 1970s as economic development worsened even further the unequal income distribu-

---

[35] Quoted in Isabel Turrent, *La Unión Soviética en América Latina: el caso de la Unidad Popular Chilena* (Mexico, D.F., 1984), p. 226.

tion. The rural and urban proletariat expanded rapidly while real wages declined and agricultural land was further concentrated. The response of the ruling groups to worker and middle-class demands was violent repression. The response of repressed groups was to form widely based revolutionary coalitions.

The lessons of Chile were not lost on the leaders of the FSLN in Nicaragua, but much more important were the nationalist and revolutionary traditions of the country, and the lessons learnt from the long years of bitter conflict with the government of Somoza. The Sandinista movement, like the FMLN in El Salvador and the guerrilla movement in Guatemala, was far removed from the sectarian *foco* groups of the 1960s. These movements were multi-class, and their ideas drew upon a variety of sources liberation theology, radical Jacobinism, various types of Marxism – and they were flexible enough to adapt their ideas to changing reality. Only in Nicaragua, though, were they able to take power.

The FSLN came to realize, after an initially rather sectarian stance, that a successful movement had to encompass contradictory forces both in the towns and the countryside. It needed not only the support of the landless peasantry, but also that of the middle peasants, for the size of that group and its hostility to large-scale capitalist agriculture made its support critical to the success of the revolution. Similarly, in the towns it needed to draw upon the support of the middle classes, which had grown in the 1960s to encompass about a fifth of the total labour force. This broad social coalition meant that the FSLN's political platform had to be popular, democratic and anti-imperialist. The FSLN stressed that revolution was not seen as deriving from some inescapable economic logic which would determine who were the supporters and who were the opponents of the revolution. Rather the revolutionary process was seen as a conscious political movement, the product of oppression by Somoza rather than the systematic exploitation of a capitalist class.

Traditionally in Central America, leftist insurgent movements have taken the form not of political parties, but of fronts held together at the top by a military command, and involving a wide spread of popular organizations that do not necessarily have a clear ideological unity. The FSLN had support from a wide range of social sectors, though the numbers involved in the fighting were very small. Until the final offensive in 1979 there some three hundred militants divided into three factions. But like the similarly numerically small movement in Cuba, it was able to mobilize wide opposition against an unpopular dictatorship. It drew upon the support of the Catholic Church. It used the language of nationalism and drew upon the memories of Sandino. It relied heavily on the anti-Americanism appropriate to a country that had suffered at the hands of the United States. According to one of its major leaders Carlos Fonseca, the FSLN drew on Marxism for its analysis of social problems, and its capacity to inspire revolutionary organizations, but also upon liberalism for its defence of human rights, and social Christianity for its ability to spread progressive ideas.

Conditions worsened in the 1970s as a revitalized union movement organized strikes against declining wages. Reductions in living standards also led to the growth of militant unions among the white-collar workers such as teachers and health workers. Catholic radicals began to organize peasant unions and base communities, which proliferated after the Managua earthquake. Increasing opposition to Somoza, not least from the business sectors and the United States, and increasing support for the Sandinistas, including even conservatives within the Catholic Church, led to the success of the insurrection in 1979.

The Nicaraguan Communist Party, the PSN, was a spectator to these events, still arguing for a peaceful struggle against Somoza. This caution was subsequently heavily criticized by the Soviet Union, which virtually discarded the PSN to favour relations with the Sandinista government. Unlike the Cuban revolution, the events in Nicaragua produced a revision of the Moscow's political line in favour of armed struggle for Latin America rather than the peaceful road to socialism. While Moscow had waited sixteen months to extend diplomatic recognition to Cuba, it did so to the victorious Sandinistas the day after they took power. But the USSR was cautious in the amount of military and economic aid it gave to Nicaragua – far lower proportionate to Nicaragua's size than that given to Cuba. The USSR was understandably cautious about undertaking another major economic and military commitment in the region on the scale of Cuba.

However, the Left in Latin America did not respond to the success of the Nicaraguan Revolution in the same way as it had to that in Cuba. The Nicaraguan Revolution was seen as a particular form of struggle relevant to that country: it was not for export, at least beyond Central America. The Latin American Left was more conscious than before that each country had its own traditions, local structure of power, and specific problems. The idea that there was a universally applicable formula whether that of the Comintern or the Cuban Revolution was now treated with scepticism.

At the same time as the Sandinistas were victorious in Nicaragua, the guerrilla movement in El Salvador was bogged down in a long war of attrition. It had its origins in splits inside the Communist party and the Christian Democratic Party in the late 1960s. The El Salvador Communist Party clung tenaciously to its beliefs in the necessary stages of the revolution, and it refused to support the armed struggle. It did eventually form its armed wing in 1980, but by then it had lost a great deal of support, and was only a minor force in the overall guerrilla movement. Even with the support of the Communist party the guerrilla could not repeat the experience of Nicaragua. The economic elite in El Salvador was much more united than in Nicaragua, where it had been badly split by the activities of the Somoza dynasty. The army in El Salvador was a more autonomous institution than in Nicaragua. The guerrilla in El Salvador was more sectarian than in Nicaragua. And the United States was massively involved in El Salvador against the guerrilla.

Whatever the reasons for the differences between the movements in Nicaragua and El Salvador, it underlined the point that a strategy that would work in one country would not necessarily work in another. The 1980s began with the Left still absorbing the lessons of the defeat of Allende, the conflicts in Central America, the questioning of ideological orthodoxy by the revisionist Communist parties of Europe, and the increasingly unattractive version of socialism offered by Cuba. If these lessons were difficult enough to absorb, how much more difficult it was to be for the Left at the end of the decade with the collapse of the communist movement in Eastern Europe, and the Soviet Union.

THE 1980S: THE LEFT IN DISARRAY

The Left in Latin America until the 1980s had faced an economy which, in spite of income inequalities, had reasonable levels of overall growth. With the debt crisis of the 1980s growth came to an abrupt halt, and income inequalities worsened. It was no easy task to devise alternative policies to the orthodox adjustment packages being applied. The political context in which the Left had to operate also changed as military governments returned power to civilians in many countries; Peru in 1980, Argentina in 1983, Brazil in 1985, Uruguay in 1985 and Chile in 1990. The international context was changing even more dramatically as the Soviet system was totally rejected in the countries of Eastern Europe, and the Soviet Union embarked upon a series of sweeping reforms.

Although in domestic policy Castro remained an old fashioned Marxist-Leninist, in international policy Cuba emphasized state to state relations and broad questions such as the debt crisis; support for insurrectionary groups was sharply reduced.

If it was always difficult to define the Left in terms of shared policies or behaviour, it became increasingly so in the 1980s. In Chile the Left was still structured around traditional parties and movements, but in other countries it was relatively diffuse, similar to the Mexican Left, which encompassed a large number of parties, political groups, labour unions, organized popular movements and mass publications which continually fluctuated both in form and composition. Grass-roots organizations proliferated in a number of countries and were often suspicious of manipulation by political parties. They expressed powerful demands for citizenship rights; they drew some inspiration from radical Catholicism; and they incorporated groups that had not been politically active in the past, above all women, and the unemployed. Their demands were rarely political in the first instance, but when the political environment was unresponsive or even hostile, then a general demand for democracy was inevitably linked to their specific aims.

Many countries saw the development of an explicitly class-based (*clasista*) unionism, which combined militant action with hostility to the traditional parties of the Left, which still held Leninist assumptions on the subordination of the union movement to the vanguard party. In Colombia a number of *paros cívicos,* organized by a mixture of community associations, trade unions, and leftist politicians, protested against inflation and unemployment, but also against organized crime and the assassination of popular leaders. The Movimiento Cívico founded in Cali in 1977 fought a successful electoral campaign in 1978 when it won 34.9 per cent of the municipal vote. In the nine months between September 1977 and May 1978 there were fifty civic strikes. Several successful strikes brought the whole country to a halt, and the process led to unification in the labour movement, with the formation of the Central Unitaria de Trabajadores in 1985 which brought together some 65 per cent of the organized work force. In Peru, a series of general strikes in 1977 and 1978 organized by a combination of militant unions and community groups led to the decision of the military government to abandon office in 1980.

These so-called new social movements could, and often did, express an explicit rejection of, or disillusionment with, political parties. In Peru, for example, areas where the Left and APRA had been traditionally strong voted in 1990 for the politically unknown Alberto Fujimori as president, and for his untried party, Cambio 90. Fujimori received 40 per cent of his total Lima vote from the twelve poorest districts, far exceeding the vote for the left-wing coalition, Izquierda Unida. The growth of evangelical movements can be seen as part of this same process of rejection of the traditional forms of social organization, whether it be the political parties or the Catholic Church, and in Peru an important base of support for Fujimori came from the evangelical churches.

Nevertheless, popular movements tended to be of protest and of opposition. They flourished when military dictatorships limited political participation. They created a powerful opposition consciousness, with a strongly corporatist element; they believed in the state and not in the market. It is not so clear that they could adapt to the challenges of a different form of participation in a democratic system when political parties were allowed to re-emerge.

The end of dictatorship in a number of countries saw a renewal and redefinition of several Socialist parties. The strategy of these parties of the Left was now less concerned to seize state power than to build up its base in civil society. These parties – the Chilean Socialists, the Brazilian Partido dos Trabalhadores (PT), among others – stressed their national rather than their international roots. They attempted to incorporate democratic practices into their internal organization, far from the democratic centralism of the Soviet model. In some countries, however, new parties developed which might be identified more properly as social democratic rather than socialist. In Bolivia a Socialist party was founded in 1971 explicitly based upon Allende's Socialist party, but never prospered for it attracted little new support and conformed to the Bolivian pattern of severe party infighting. The Bolivian MIR (Movimiento de Izquierda Revolucionario) founded in 1971, also had parallels with the similarly named party in Chile. Abandoning its early extremism, it did appeal to a new generation of Bolivian voters, moved sharply to the right, and even assumed governmental office, though not to pursue policies that could be defined in any sense as socialist. In Ecuador the Izquierda Democrática founded in 1970 appealed at first to urban middle class voters but also won support among unionized labour, and in a broad coalition it won a majority of seats in the 1986 Congressional elections, and elected its leader Rodrigo Borja to the presidency in 1988.

The growth of these new parties and the development of non-party social movements reflected the crisis of the orthodox Marxist parties, above all the Communist party. The electoral record of the Communist parties was unimpressive in the 1980s. The peak vote for the Communist party and its allies in Mexico was 6.5 per cent (in 1985). In Colombia the vote for the Communist party and its allies has ranged from 3.1 per cent in 1974 to 6.8 per cent in 1986. In Costa Rica, when the Communist party (PVP – Partido Vanguardia Popular) allied with three smaller Marxist parties it won 7 per cent of the vote in 1978 and 1982. But when the alliance broke up, even that small vote was sharply reduced.

The reaction of the Marxist parties to the crisis of the 1980s varied enormously. The Mexican Communist Party, for example, moved to embrace a Eurocommunist style revisionism. But the PCM had never been a mass party. At its peak during the Cárdenas presidency it had between 35,000 to 40,000 members, but in normal times rarely more than 10,000. It lost the union base that it had built up in the Cárdenas years, and only in the 1970s with the formation of powerful university unions did it reassert itself in the world of labour. It abandoned the idea that it could transform the PRI (Partido Institucional Revolucionario). It now argued that the PRI had exhausted its progressive potential, and the PCM called for the creation on the left of a democratic and socialist front, though not without strong internal opposition in the party to this change of line.

The PCM had emphasized from the 1970s onwards the struggle for democratic rights – for its own rights as a political party, and for autonomy for the trade unions. It aimed to become a mass rather than an elite party, and advanced a moderate programme of reforms to try to win as much support as possible. Following the example of the Italian Communist Party, it devoted considerable resources to winning power at the local level, though the results were modest (control over the city of Juchitan in Oxacaca with other left groups was the best, though temporary, result). It dropped its anti-clericalism and called for the abolition of the constitutional prohibition on political and electoral rights for the clergy. It recognized that it had a responsibility to encourage the development of autonomous women's organizations.

In November 1981 the Mexican Communist Party dissolved itself, and together with four other parties created the Partido Socialista Unificado de México (PSUM). This was the culmination of ten years of internal debate, and of policy changes that had even led to electoral alliance with the Trotskyist party, the PRT (Partido Revolucionario de los Trabajadores). The Mexican Communist Party denounced the 1968 Soviet invasion of Czechoslovakia, and later that of Afghanistan. It recognized the increase in interest in Marxist ideas following the student rebellion of 1968, and tried to modernize itself to attract the support of those interested in Marxism as an ideology.

The Mexican party had only emerged from semi-legality in 1977, and participated in elections for the first time in 1979 after thirty-two years, receiving about 5.1 per cent of the vote. The attempt at modernization was not without problems. It provoked fierce internal disputes that were resolved in ways that satisfied neither conservatives nor reformers. Only a few days after the formation of the PSUM, the second largest party, the PMT (Partido Mexicano de los Trabajadores) withdrew, and there was continual internal struggle between the parties over their attitude to the government, the ideology of the new party, their attitude to the Soviet bloc, their role in the union movement, and the power that the new party has over its constituent elements.

A complicating feature of the Left in Mexico is the presence of leftist parties such as the Partido Popular Socialista (PPS), which are effectively satellite parties of the PRI. These parties while politically subordinate to the PRI, at the same time espouse a dogmatic Marxism-Leninism, combining Stalinism with belief in the Mexican Revolution. They continue to attract support: in the 1988 elections it was the satellite left which saw its vote sharply increase while that of the independent left fell. Although normally these parties gained only a small vote – 4.7 per cent in 1979, and 2.96 per cent in 1982 – their vote rose to 21.04 per cent in 1988 when they were supporting the Frente Democrático Nacional. The attraction of the FDN coalition was partly its leader and presidential candidate, Cuauhtémoc Cárdenas, the son of the reformist president, and partly its revolutionary nationalism. The coalition emphasized political democracy and the autonomy of mass organizations, but its message was vague enough to create uncertainty as to whether it was simply the left of the PRI, or a genuinely new socialist departure. The coalition was a fragile combination of very disparate elements from the anti-communist Partido Auténtico de la Revolución Mexicana (PARM) to the Stalinist but opportunist PPS. It faced bitter opposition from the PRI because it competed directly for those groups and voters that have been the backbone of the PRI. It is also similar to the PRI in its rather undemocratic internal practices, and it suffers from continuous internal dissent and disagreement. In March 1990 the renamed PRD (Partido Revolucionario Democrático) agreed to incorporate popular movements into the party, but the relationship between the party and the movements is by no means clear and is unlikely to parallel the close organic relationship between the social movements and the PT in Brazil.

If the Mexican party took the route of reform, the Chilean Communist Party went in the opposite direction and after 1980 advocated armed struggle against the dictatorship of General Pinochet. The party was instrumental in creating a small urban guerrilla movement, whose most spectacular action was the almost successful assassination attempt against Pinochet in September 1986. The Chilean party was always a loyal supporter of the Soviet Union; much more so, for example, than the parties in Venezuela or Mexico. It suited Moscow after 1980 to emphasize the armed struggle, and it is not far-fetched to suppose that the change of line in the Chilean party responded to the change of line in Moscow. After all, the party was illegal in Chile and most of its leaders were in exile in the Soviet Union. Undoubtedly the Soviet leadership was embarrassed by the failure of local Communist parties to support successful insurrections as had happened in Cuba and in Nicaragua. The Chilean Communist Party was the best organized party in Latin America, and, according to the Soviet strategists, if any party had the chance of leading rather than following the revolution, then it was in Chile, especially in a country whose ruler was condemned internationally.

The Communist party was also responding to the political isolation that was imposed upon it, not only by the government but also by other parties of the opposition. It had tried initially after the coup to create broad alliances with the Christian Democrats, and also had tried, with more success, to create a common front with the more radical wing of the Socialist party led by Clodomiro Almeyda. Even the more radical Socialists grew uneasy with their alliance with the communists once that party had launched the urban guerrilla group, the Frente Patriótico, and it seemed very unlikely that in the future the party would be able to resurrect the old communist-socialist alliance that had been the basis of left-wing politics in Chile since the 1950s. The Communist party sought to retain its identity by differentiating itself from the renovating process taking place inside the Socialist parties, and stressing its loyalty to orthodox positions. The party was well aware that it was extremely difficult to organize a guerrilla movement in a country with little tradition of political violence and with such an efficiently repressive government as that of Pinochet, and the Frente Patriótico was conceived as a small-scale operation rather than as a massive urban insurrection.

The Soviet leadership, facing the challenge of Eurocommunism, was anxious to show that at least one major party was loyal to the thesis that revolutionary violence had a role to play in political struggle. But the party in Chile was also responding to social change. The traditional base of the party in organized labour was much weaker following the assault on the trade union movement by the Pinochet government. On the other hand, the unemployed youth in the shanty-towns were ready and willing to engage the police and the army in violent conflict once the movement of social protest against the regime broke out in 1983. The Communist party was more likely to capture the allegiance of this group by organizing the violence than by condemning it. The party opposed participating in the plebiscite that in October 1988 led to the defeat of Pinochet's hopes for further eight years of presidential rule. The party did at the last moment accept the plebiscite and urged its members to vote against Pinochet, but it was excluded from the coalition formed to organize that campaign, as it was in the subsequent electoral contest that resulted in a victory for the opposition in the elections of December 1989.

The Chilean experience showed that a policy of isolation and intransigence brought scant benefits in a process of redemocratization, but it was far from clear that there was some alternative strategy that would have brought obviously greater benefits. The Chilean Communist Party like similar parties the world over was deeply shaken by the events in eastern Europe and the former Soviet Union. Like similar parties it went through a crisis of defections of expulsions and spilts, and it faces a future in which its role looks uncertain at best, and marginal at worst.

Peru was the one country in Latin America where communism inspired by China generated popular support, both urban as well as rural. The rural guerrilla movement, Sendero Luminoso (Shining Path) which started operations in 1980, though it was formed a decade before, is the best known of the Chinese inspired movements. Sendero was a faction (Bandera Roja) of the Maoist party till it separated in 1969/70. Sendero grew out of an influential sub-culture of Maoism in Peru. Maoism was ideologically powerful in student circles, and the major schoolteachers union was controlled by the Maoist Patria Roja party.

The pro-Moscow Communist party in Peru, though influential in the union movement, had not created the solid disciplined cadres of the Chilean Communist party. A much weaker industrial base, the counter attractions of APRA and years of repression had led to a party of only modest proportions. It was also a very cautious party. Like most parties of the Left, it welcomed, as we have seen, the military coup of 1968 that brought to power a reformist government led by General Velasco. Unlike other parties of the Left, it continued to support that government long after the reform impulse had finished. Only with the general strike of 1977 did the Peruvian Communist Party join the opposition to the military government. Social sectors that wished to protest against the policies of the government, and the sharp decline in living standards after 1972, turned to other more radical parties. The failure of the Castroite guerrillas in the early 1960s made that particular option seem less attractive, and though the Trotskyists had some support, the imprisonment of their popular leader, Hugo Blanco, and their continual internal squabbling limited their appeal as well.

Following the Sino-Soviet split, a small group had left the orthodox party to form a Maoist party. Though it was soon divided over whether the revolutionary struggle should be primarily urban or rural, it gained support amongst crucial middle sector groups, above all schoolteachers and university students. The general ideological climate created by the Velasco government in its first years was tolerant of radical movements, and allowed the Maoists to create a powerful teachers union, the SUTEP, which before long was confronting the government, sometimes violently, over the pay and working conditions of the teachers.

In the meantime, Sendero Luminoso began patiently to build up cadres and local support in the impoverished Ayacucho region, where economic and social conditions were favourable to its growth. Though poor, even by Peruvian standards, there was no class of large landowners to suppress peasant organizations. Ayacucho had heard many promises of agrarian reform from the Velasco government, but there were few real benefits. In this remote area, the government and police exercised little authority. The population of the area was largely Indian, with strong feelings of resentment again the urban and white rule of Lima. The university in Ayacucho was controlled by Maoists; the most famous professor, and Director of Personnel was none other than Abimael Guzmán, the leader and ideologist of Sendero.

Sendero professed admiration for the ideas of Mao at the height of the cultural revolution – a time when some of the Sendero leadership had been present in China. It also drew on the *indigenista* ideas of Mariátegui. Its largely *mestizo* leadership was hostile to any grass-roots organization other than the party. It recreated the authoritarian structures of Andean society replacing the rule of the landlords by that of the party. It was organized on a highly secretive cell structure, which was difficult to penetrate. It was extremely ruthless and violent, and used terror to impose its rule. The reply of the government initially was to allow the military to impose equally savage counter measures, and the toll of deaths, largely of innocent peasants, amounted to an estimated fifteen thousand between 1980 and 1988. Sendero made a substantial shift in strategy in 1988, declaring that the cities were 'necessary' rather than 'secondary'. Sendero gained some support in the urban shanty towns of Lima, and in some industrial unions. It also published a daily newspaper, *El Diario*. The capacity of Sendero to play havoc with the fragile political system in Peru was not in doubt; but what was in doubt was whether the movement could do more than that. Its extremely simple political propositions and violent methods recalled the Cambodia of Pol Pot.

The growth of Sendero created problems for the mosaic of other parties – orthodox Communist, Trotskyist, pro-Chinese, Castroist – that made up the Left in Peru. The story of the Left in Peru is a never ending process of unification and division. The Left did well in the 1978 elections for the Constituent Assembly, with 29.4 per cent of the vote. But the withdrawal of the Trotskyists weakened the coalition, and there were five separate Left lists competing in the 1980 elections with a combined vote of only 14.4 per cent. Most groups on the left combined to form the Izquierda Unida in 1980, and the Left vote rose to 29 per cent in the council elections of 1983, with the leader of the IU, Alfonso Barrantes taking control of Lima with 36.5 per cent of the vote. Obviously the growth of the Left reflected the grave economic crisis combined with widespread dissatisfaction with the government of President Belaúnde, but it also reflected a great deal of grass-roots organization by the Left, and a serious attempt to devise policies that were more than rhetorical denunciations of the evils of capitalism.

Yet the Left was far from united. As mayor of Lima, Barrantes faced a spate of land invasions organized by the far Left within his coalition. This lack of unity led to a fall in the Left vote to 21 per cent in 1985, though it was still the second electoral force. But the divisions intensified, reflecting on the part of important elements of the IU coalition an ambiguous attitude to democracy (shared, it should be said, by some groups on the right and even by the APRA government). The issue of political violence remained a dividing line between those who wished to collaborate in the democratic process, for all its faults, and those who wished to bring it down and replace it with a different order. Barrantes was criticized by those who argued that the major focus of activity should be the streets and factories and not the Congress. The first national congress of the IU in

January 1989 led to a decisive spilt as Barrantes took with him moderate delegates to form a rival coalition, the Izquierda Socialista. The left vote in the council elections in 1989 collapsed to 11.5 per cent, and the two candidates of the Left contesting the presidential election in 1990 gained only 11 per cent of the vote between them.[36]

One response to the decline of orthodox communism, and the increasing unattractiveness of the Cuban model – and in contrast to the violence associated with the guerrilla movements of countries like Peru, Colombia and El Salvador – was a renewal of interest in socialism of an essentially parliamentary and electoral form. The reaction to years of military dictatorship and the suppression of basic freedoms among some sectors on the Left was a much more positive evaluation of the benefits of formal democracy. The growth of social democratic movements in Europe, notably the Spanish Socialist Party of Felipe González, provided a source of inspiration. The work of the Socialist International in Latin America provided international links, further encouragement, and some financial assistance. Closer analysis of the social structure of Latin America led the more moderate Left to realize the importance of appealing to the middle classes, and to the growing popular organizations that were not trade unions, nor expressions of class struggle, and which owed more to Church inspired institutions than to the Marxist Left.

The Chilean Socialist Party, though always a party that contained a variety of ideological factions, had moved as a whole to the left during the 1960s, partly under the influence of the Cuban Revolution. During the Popular Unity government it was to the left of the Communist party, and supported worker and peasant takeovers of factories and farms. It was savagely repressed after the 1973 coup, and most of the leadership of the party was forced into exile, where the party divided into a moderate wing, and a Marxist-Leninist wing. This difference partly reflected the experience of exile. Those exiled in France or Italy or the Scandinavian countries were influenced by the changes taking place in European social democracy. The more intransigent section, led by Clodomiro Almeyda, were exiled in the eastern bloc, and tended to reflect the ideology of their hosts, including an emphasis on the need for a Socialist-Communist alliance.

The party was forced to a profound reconsideration of the meaning of democracy. The Chilean Left, especially the Socialist party, had taken

---

[36] This section draws heavily on Lewis Taylor, 'One step forward, two steps back: the Peruvian *Izquierda Unida* 1980–1990', *Journal of Communist Studies*, 6, 1 (1990).

democracy for granted. Haya de la Torre had written about Chilean Socialists in 1946, that 'they have contempt for democracy because it has not
cost them anything to acquire it. If only they knew the real face of
tyranny'.[37] After 1973 the Chilean Socialists did know the real face of
tyranny, and one of the consequences of their reconsideration of the value
of democracy was to reject a return to the kinds of policies and political
alliances that had characterized the Popular Unity period.

The moderate Socialist party moved sharply away from an emphasis on
state control over the economy through nationalization of foreign and
local monopolies and large firms, to advocate instead democratic planning, the mixed economy and social pacts between government, workers
and entrepreneurs (*concertación social*). They accepted the need for political
alliances with parties of the centre such as the Christian Democrats and
the Radicals in order to defeat the Pinochet government and to re-
establish democracy in Chile. They criticized the Communist party for
its advocacy of violence.

The radical Socialist party, led by Clodomiro Almeyda, still spoke the
language of Leninism, and formed an alliance with the Communist party,
once the social protests in Chile in 1983 allowed limited party activity in
the country. But the Almeyda Socialists were uneasy with the Communist's justification of violence, and joined with the other Socialists in the
campaign against Pinochet in the plebiscite in 1988, and in the electoral
campaign of 1989. In late 1989, the two Socialist parties came together in
a newly unified party, broadly accepting the policies of the renovating
section of socialism.

The real novelty on the left was an 'instrumental' party the Partido por
la Democracia (PPD) created to contest the 1988 plebiscite and largely of
socialist inspiration. This party presented a more modern image than the
Socialist party, recruited from groups that had little previous involvement
in party activity, and in general aspired to be a Chilean version of the
Spanish PSOE. Relations between the Socialist party and the PPD were
not always easy as the PPD was consciously less ideological than the
Socialist party, and was clearly seen as a vehicle for the political ambitions
of the Socialist leader Ricardo Lagos. It was not at all clear whether the
PPD would absorb the Socialist party, or whether the PPD would be
transformed into a broad political front in which the Socialist party would
be the leading element. This uncertainty and the fact that many leading

[37] Quoted in Jorge Arrate, *La Fuerza Democrática de la Idea Socialista* (Santiago, 1985), p. 82.

Socialists were also members of the PPD reflected the unresolved ambiguities involved in the transformation of Chilean socialism.

The Venezuela Movimiento al Socialismo (MAS) was formed in 1971 by dissident members of the Communist party, and many of them had participated in the 1960s guerrilla movement. Though the party has rarely gained more than 5 per cent of the vote, its importance in the political system has been greater than that figure would suggest, for the ideas it has disseminated have been influential, and it made an important contribution to the consolidation of Venezuelan democracy by advocating reform and not overthrow of the system. The MAS was influenced by the experience of the Italian Communist Party and by the Eurocommunist movement. It emphasized that there must be individual and national roads to socialism, and rejected the idea that there was one correct model. It was critical of the Leninist style of party organization and argued for a participatory party structure. It criticized the Communist party for underestimating the role and importance of the middle classes in the Venezuelan political system. Although many of the members of the MAS came from the Communist party and the far Left, they recognized that the Venezuelan public was committed to democracy. The party presented itself as being committed to democracy, both for the country, and in its own internal structure. MAS emphasized the need for honesty and accountability in public life, and sought to present itself as the true representative of the values that the major parties – AD and COPEI – had once embodied, but which they had compromised in the struggle for political power.

MAS has spent much of its time since 1971 in endless debate about strategy, tactics and organization. It was quite conscious that the major problem of the Left was to find some role at a time when a reformist president (Carlos Andrés Pérez) and increasing oil revenues led to increased support for AD. The answer to this question was not easy: hence the incessant internal debate inside MAS. But the party played a useful role in filtering new ideas into the main two-party system, and in acting as a check on the abuses of power. And it played a more than useful role in helping to create a left in Venezuela that was firmly and publicly committed to parliamentary democracy.[38] MAS gained some additional support as the economic crisis led to disaffection with the major parties, AD and COPEI. In the 1988 elections, running in alliance with another left-wing

[38] Steve Ellner, *Venezuela's Movimiento al Socialismo: From Guerrilla Defeat to Innovative Politics* (Chapel Hill, N.C., 1988) is one of the few scholarly studies of a left wing party in Latin America.

party, it won 10.2 per cent of the vote, and the first direct elections for state governors held in 1989 saw the MAS take the industrial state of Aragua, and come second to AD in several others. But the Venezuelan Left gained relatively little new support from the huge wave of dissatisfaction that led to violent riots in 1989, and to attempted military coups in 1992. Popular discontent took the form of mass street protest, and the real threat to the two-party dominance of Venezuela came from military plotters inspired by grandiose populist visions rather than from the Left. However, a new left-wing party, Causa Radical, based on the union movement, did establish itself in the industrial state of Bolívar. Benefitting from the general rejection of the established parties in the 1993 presidential election, Causa Radical won 22 per cent of the popular vote.

The Left in Uruguay was unusual in the way that it seemed less affected in its ideas and strategy by the long years of military dictatorship than the Left in Brazil or Chile. However, more than the other countries of the Southern Cone, the restoration of democracy in Uruguay was precisely that – a restoration of the previous system. In fact the Left changed rather more than the two dominant parties, Colorado and Nacional. The Left made a strong showing in the 1971 elections when, organized as the Frente Amplio, it won 18 per cent of the vote. In the first elections following military rule in 1984 it won 21.3 per cent of the vote; and in 1989 21.2 per cent. But there were changes in the composition and the politics of the Frente Amplio. In 1973 the main parties in the Frente were the Communist, Socialist and the MLN-Tupamaros. By 1984 the vote going to the radical Left, the MLN, fell as a proportion of the total Left vote from 23 per cent to 6.7 per cent to the communists from 32.9 to 28.2 per cent; while the major gainers were a new moderate Christian Democratic inspired party, the Movimiento por el Gobierno del Pueblo, which won 39.3 per cent of the Frente's vote compared with the 10.3 per cent that had gone to moderate parties in 1971. The Frente Amplio was clearly less extreme than in 1971, and its commitment to electoral politics was firm. It lost the support of the most moderate group in 1989, which formed the Nuevo Espacio party and which took 9 per cent of the popular vote, but its share of the poll remained constant. Moreover, the Frente won a plurality in Montevideo, with 37 per cent of the vote, and elected the mayor.

The Frente Amplio was a wide coalition, held together partly by the peculiarities of the Uruguayan electoral system which encourages broad coalitions of many parties. It gained support partly because it was the only credible alternative to the traditional two party dominance at a time when those parties were increasingly unpopular for their handling of the economy. The Frente Amplio consolidated its hold on the Left by its opposition to the law which grants amnesty to military officers for human rights abuses. The Frente Amplio benefited from the Uruguayan union system which, in contrast to most countries of Latin America, has a history of autonomous development unincorporated into the state machine and not colonized by one of the two major parties. But the Frente Amplio was weak outside Montevideo, where it gained only 9 per cent of the vote, and unionized workers who vote heavily for the Frente constitute only 19 per cent of the adult population of Montevideo and are insignificant elsewhere. The exit from the Frente of the moderate parties reduced its overall chance of electoral gains. To some extent the survival of the Frente was testimony to the overall immobility of the Uruguayan political system, rather than the development of a new and innovative left movement.

The Brazilian Partido dos Trabalhadores (PT) was formed partly because of the perceived inadequacy of the Communist party to express trade union grievances. The PT grew out of the new unionism that developed in the massive metallurgical industries of the São Paulo region. By 1978 after a year of labour militancy the new union leaders, above all Luis Inácio da Silva (Lula), came to believe that workplace militancy was inadequate to achieve their broader aims. In Lula's words 'In my view the Brazilian Left has made mistakes throughout its history precisely because it was unable to comprehend what was going on inside the workers heads and upon that basis elaborate an original doctrine . . . I do not deny that the PCB has been an influential force for many years. What I do deny is the justness of telling the workers that they have to be Communists. The only just course of action is to give the workers the opportunity to be whatever suits them best. We do not wish to impose doctrines. We want to develop a just doctrine which emanates from the organisation of our workers and which at the same time is a result of our own organisation.'[39]

The PT has become the largest explicitly socialist party in Latin America. Its electoral support increased from 3 per cent of the total vote in 1982 to 7 per cent in 1986. In the 1988 elections for mayor, PT candidates took control of thirty-six cities, notably São Paulo, where the candidate was a woman migrant from the impoverished North East, Luiza Erundina. The PT's vote overall in Brazil's 100 largest cities was 28.8 per cent of the total. Though the party had its roots in the urban union movement, it has

---

[39] Quoted in an interview with Lula in *Adelante* (London), January, 1981, p. 6.

also grown in the rural areas where it has the support of the radical Church and the local base communities. In the first round of the 1989 presidential elections Lula, the PT candidate, won 16.08 per cent of the vote, narrowly winning second place over Leonel Brizola (PDT) with 15.74 per cent. In the second round Lula (37.86 per cent) was defeated by Fernando Collor de Mello (42.75 per cent), despite moderating his radical political platform in order to appeal to the centre – a tactic which almost worked.

The PT also sought to adopt a new model of internal organization, that would, unlike that of the PCB, respect the autonomy of the union movement. The party was not to lead the workers, but to express their demands in the political sphere. The organization of the party emphasized participatory democracy. The core organization of the party would be the *nucleo de base* composed of affiliated members either from a neighbourhood, a professional group or work-place or social movement, and engaged in permanent political, rather than occasional electoral, activity. The party was meant to dissolve the differences that normally exist between social movement and party. If, in practice, many nuclei did function largely as electoral bodies, the level of participation of the estimated 600,000 members of the PT was still extraordinarily high by Brazilian party standards.

Such a participatory structure was very appropriate for the oppositional politics made necessary by the imposition of military rule. It was less clear that such a structure was functional for a competitive democracy. Many of the members and leaders of the party came from Catholic radicalism rather than Marxism, and they were more concerned to maintain the autonomy of union and popular organizations than they were to create a disciplined political party. There were many conflicts inside the PT not least between the PT members of congress and the party leaders outside congress. The three Brazilian Trotskyist parties all worked within the PT, even though the largest of them the Convergencia Socialista conceived of the PT as a front to be radicalized under the direction of a revolutionary vanguard, combatting in the PT the influence of the Church and the parliamentary group. Such a variety of political positions did not lead to party discipline, but the defeat of the Trotskyists at the party congress held at the end of 1991 led to a more unified party.

The PT was undoubtedly novel, not just among the parties of Brazil but even among the Socialist parties of Latin America. It was firmly rooted in the working class, and controled some 60 per cent of unions in the public sector, and only slightly fewer in the private sector. In Congress the PT was the party with the largest proportion of deputies linked to organized labour and social movements. It tried to develop new policies and practices; for example, 30 per cent of seats in the Central Committee of the party were to be held by women. But there were problems that it faced for further development. The PT was an ideological party in a party system that was very unideological. It faced the challenge of other parties on the left, notably the old radical populist party of Brizola, and the social democratic PSDB. It reached out to the organized poor in town and countryside, but most poor Brazilians were neither members of unions nor of social organizations and in 1989 these sectors voted more heavily for the right-wing Collor de Mello than for Lula. Like all parties of the Left, the PT had difficulties in proposing policy alternatives for dealing with the economic crisis which did not look either like the unsuccessful formulae of the past, or simple imitations of the orthodox neo-liberal policies. While the PT's attachment to a radical ideology helped to develop committed party members, that very commitment limited its ability to compete in the fluid and populist world of Brazilian party politics.

For all the differences between political systems, there were parallels in Chile, Venezuela, Uruguay and Brazil, and elsewhere in Latin America, in the emergence of a socialism which stressed participation and democracy, which rejected the past orthodoxy of one correct model, and which was firmly based upon national structures rather than international doctrines.

CONCLUSION

'Historically the Left . . . has always presumed the existence of an objective, a program, and organized force capable of carrying out that program, and a theory that explained the logic of the system. The program may have been improvised, the objective unreal, and the organized force nothing of the kind, but this was how the Left though about change, at least how it legitimized its activities. All this is now open to question.'[40]

The 1980s saw momentous changes taking place in international communism, from the monolithic insistence of the time of Brezhnev that there was only one model of socialism even though there might be different routes to it, to the pluralism of socialism accepted by the advocates of *perestroika* in the Soviet Union under Gorbachev, to the final disintegration

---

[40] From an interview with José Aricó in NACLA, *Report on the Americas: the Latin American Left*, Vol. XXV, No. 5, May 1992, p. 21.

of the Soviet Union and with it communism as a viable political ideology. One obvious consequence of these events was the decline of interest and support from the Soviet Union for local communist movements. By the 1980s, however, the amount of Soviet support going to the Communist parties of Latin America was relatively unimportant, with the exception of Cuba. The centre of Soviet operations in Latin America in the 1970s and 1980s was Peru. But the priority for the Soviet Union was an air route to Latin America, and access to the Pacific fishing areas, not the spread of communism in Peru and Latin America. If the Soviet Union continued to maintain interest in the Chilean Communist Party in the 1980s, it was not only because it was the sole Communist party in Latin America which had historically a reasonable electoral record, but also because the Soviet Union was interested in the Pacific area for economic reasons and a friendly party there could be of some benefit to the Soviet Union.

Much more important than the loss of material support was the damage to the ideological standing of Marxism in Latin America. With the collapse of international communism, the Left lost the mobilizing vision of a socialist society to be achieved by revolution. The idea of revolution became not simply unimaginable but even undesirable. The last stand of the Communist movement in Latin America remained the Castro regime in Cuba. This still served as some kind of rallying point for the those who even while disillusioned with Castro's economic failures and lack of respect for human rights, felt that Cuba needed support as the last bastion against U.S. imperialism. That feeling was particularly strong in Central America. There the left had only ever really gained power through force of arms, and still, with good reason, mistrusted the democratic credentials of the political right and centre in the isthmus. It remained unclear, for all the peace negotiations between governments and guerrillas, that the Left in Central America would evolve into some kind of social democracy.

If Cuba still stood as a rallying point for the Left in Central America, that was no longer the case for Nicaraguan revolution which was defeated in the elections of 1990. The Sandinista movement had difficulty in making the change from a vanguard party leading a revolution to a democratic left party fighting a competitive election.[41] Yet it remained testi-

---

41 The confusion of the Sandinista movement is well captured in this statement by José Pasos, deputy chief of the FSLN's international department. 'We have to become a modern party. There are some principles that don't change: political pluralism, non-alignment, mixed economy. Our anti-imperialism stays the same, but it is not the anti-imperialism of Marx or Lenin. For us, it means non-interference in our internal affairs and it's the United States that interferes. We continue to believe in socialism as the goal. But it's definitely not the socialism that has come up in the East,

mony to the loyalty that the Sandinistas aroused that, inspite of an unprecedented economic collapse, and the dreadful consequences of the war against the *contras,* and the hostility of much of the Catholic Church, it could gain over 40 per cent of the vote in the 1990 elections, and still retained substantial power in the new government of Violeta Chamorro. But the fact that the Sandinistas were defeated was a blow to the confidence of the Left in central America and indeed in Latin America. The record of the Left in power was not attractive. Cuba's economic record was dismal, and its political future uncertain. Nicaragua's economic record was, though for different reasons, even worse, and, moreover, the people had voted out the revolution.

Yet it is possible to see some benefits to the Left in Latin America from the collapse of international communism. The Left would no longer have to justify or excuse the undemocratic practices of the Communist bloc. It no longer had to defend regimes that offended liberal democratic beliefs. The Left no longer had to face the same degree of hostility from the United States. It could begin to free itself from the charge that the Left in power will automatically degenerate into authoritarianism.

At the beginning of the 1990s, the Left the world over faced problems as great as or even greater than the Left in Latin America. Indeed it could be argued that, comparatively, for all its reversals, the Latin American Left was in a relatively more favourable situation than elsewhere. At least the Latin American Left was not torn apart by the ethnic conflicts of some other countries. Nor did it have to counter the popular mobilizing force of religious fundamentalism. The Left in many other parts of the world had suffered from being in government at a time of international economic recession. In Latin America the right was in power. It was possible that if neo-liberal economic policies proved less successful than their advocates promised, the advantages of being in the opposition would manifest themselves in the future.

The factors that brought the Left into being in the first place had hardly disappeared. The economic recession of the 1980s accentuated inequality and worsened poverty in Latin America. Political power was still disproportionately controlled by forces of the right. The poor and dispossessed had little recourse to justice within existing legal and institutional systems. It was true that the Left in the 1990s had no distinctive policies to

nor the socialism of Cuba, nor *perestroika.* Perhaps the most acceptable for us would be Swedish socialism, but it's very expensive. What kind of socialism a poor country can have is a discussion that we're now going to begin.' From an interview in *The Guardian* (London), 30 April 1990.

offer that were politically popular. Its strength drew more upon the unacceptable nature of life for the majority of the people than upon the viability of policy options.

The Latin American Left was not alone in finding the new context demanded a new response. European socialist parties responded by moving strongly towards embracing the idea of the market economy and jettisoning most of the policies that they had advocated in the past. But issues that became prominent in Europe, such as ecological or environmental concerns, had not by the end of the decade become important to the Latin American Left in societies where pressing issues of poverty and deprivation were more urgent. Issues like the destruction of the Amazonian rain forest, or the impact of gold mining and other activities on the fate of local native peoples in Brazil aroused more international concern. Nor was the Left in Latin America particularly receptive to the debate on gender inequality. Some parties made a commitment to gender equality in theory, but in practice there was little change in traditional practices. Socialism in the 1980s in Latin America ran the danger of becoming a conservative doctrine, looking to the past, while the ideological initiative was taken up by the political right.

Nevertheless, the Left in Latin America had in the twentieth century established a presence and a prestige that was more solidly based than in many other parts of the world. If the ideas of the Left had been taken over by other parties, that was testimony to the force and relevance of those ideas. The Left created political parties, trade unions and intellectual groups that played central roles in the politics of Latin American countries. The ideas of socialism and Marxism inspired some of the greatest writers and intellectuals of this century in Latin America. Some groups on the Left justified and used violence to achieve their ends, but most did not, and they all bore the brunt of the much greater violence of the state. The Left played an important role in the struggle for democracy against authoritarian regimes in the 1970s and 1980s. Many ordinary men and women joined the Left because they wanted equality and justice and freedom. Those values had only very imperfectly been realized in contemporary Latin America. The Left in the 1990s faced the challenge of devising new forms to achieve old objectives.

3

THE MILITARY IN LATIN AMERICAN POLITICS SINCE 1930

The upheaval in the world economic and political order associated with the 1929 Depression inaugurated an intensely turbulent period in the politics of Latin America in which modern armies – that is to say, armies organized and equipped in imitation of the most prestigious European models and staffed by professional career officers – made their irreversible appearance on the political scene. Between February and December 1930, the military were involved in the overthrow of governments in no fewer than six, widely differing Latin American nations – Argentina, Brazil, the Dominican Republic, Bolivia, Peru and Guatemala. The same year also saw four unsuccessful attempts to seize power by force in other Latin American countries. Over the following two years, Ecuador and El Salvador in 1931, and Chile in 1932, joined the list of countries in which military-provoked political shifts and unscheduled changes of the executive had taken place.

The diversity of situations – indeed, the heterogeneity of Latin American societies and political systems – does not, however, permit easy generalizations. A continent-wide approach must, in the logic of the comparative method itself, be corrected by appropriate attention to nuances, reservations and exceptions. Tendencies seemingly at work in most countries pass others by, and even where they are present may lead to different, even contradictory results. Thus Venezuela, under the iron hand of the 'patriarch' Juan Vicente Gómez, remained untouched by the political crisis which shook the continent, and seems to have entered the twentieth century only on the dictator's death in 1935. In neighbouring Colombia, institutional stability also survived and was consolidated under Liberal hegemony, due in part to the so-called *revolución en marcha* (1934–8), a broad reformist programme within a framework of liberal democracy in which the military played no role. Likewise, in Mexico the revolutionary order grew stronger by demilitarizing itself through the organization of broad popular participation under the aegis of the state. Furthermore, if 1930 represents a far clearer watershed for Argentina and Brazil than for the other nations of the continent, with a 'before' and an 'after' defined in large part by the extent of military involvement in politics, the results of the 6 September and 3 October 'revolutions' would, at least at first glance, seem to be diametrically opposed. In Brazil, the military played a decisive part in the movement that put an end to the oligarchical system of the 'Old Republic', whereas in Argentina it had a role in restoring power to the traditionally dominant classes after a period during which politics had been opened to wider popular participation.

A military wind was, it is true, blowing across the continent. On the eve of the Second World War, the majority of the Latin American republics had military governments, while several nations under ostensibly civilian control either had generals as presidents (Uruguay and Mexico) or were ruled by regimes resulting from 'revolutions' in which the military had played a key role (Brazil and Argentina). This vision must nevertheless be tempered, and not merely because certain countries – like Popular Front Chile, governed by the educator Pedro Aguirre Cerda, or Liberal Colombia presided over by the writer Eduardo Santos – were clear exceptions to the rule. The question should also be raised whether the category 'military', when employed in this fashion, is sufficiently homogeneous or even relevant. The same concept, or equal military rank, may indeed mask profoundly different realities and wholly incommensurable political systems. Cárdenas in Mexico, Baldomir in Uruguay, Ubico in Guatemala, Trujillo in the Dominican Republic, Carías in Honduras, Benavides in Peru, López Contreras in Venezuela, Peñaranda in Bolivia and Estigarribia in Paraguay all bore the title of general. Yet the ways in which they came to power were extremely diverse, as were the regimes over which they presided. A 'military' government cannot be defined merely by the chief executive's profession. (On that criterion, the French Fifth Republic under General de Gaulle could not be considered a constitutional government, while the post-1973 regime in Uruguay, nominally presided over by a civilian, would not appear as the dictatorship of the armed forces that it was.)

In societies with highly disparate levels of state modernization and social complexity, and consequently of functional differentiation, a Latin American general around 1930 might be a primary school teacher turned political chieftain and leader of men in the turmoil of the Mexican Revolution (Calles); or a modest municipal civil servant arbitrarily named captain when he joined the armies of the same revolution (Cárdenas); or a Cuban army typist, a simple sergeant, self-promoted following a coup d'état (Batista); or a courtier owning his gold braid, in Venezuela, to his bureaucratic merits and the 'prince's' favour (López Contreras), or, in Nicaragua, to the grace of a foreign occupying power (Somoza). But a Latin American general of the same period might also be a career officer, sometimes a graduate of a national or foreign military academy, who had climbed the hierarchy through merit or seniority, and whose only occupation had been that of commanding troops. By the same token, very diverse sorts of government are defined by differing degrees of institutional involvement of the standing armed forces in the transmission of power and in the decision-making processes on important political questions.

Do these methodological observations, essential for a student of military political behaviour, imply that the recognition of national and organizational particularities makes it impossible to discover principles of understanding common to all the phenomena to which we have referred? Does the irreducible character of historical realities leave us with no other alternative than to resign ourselves to a purely descriptive approach? So long as the temptation to reduce every case to a single model or line of interpretation is avoided, it is not unprofitable to pose the same set of questions regarding the role of the armed forces and their *modus operandi* in the various Latin American societies since 1930. All the more so since these societies, despite their internal heterogeneity, confronted homogeneous external conditions which gave rise to generally parallel lines of development. The impact of the international context on domestic political phenomena during the 1930s, and above all in the aftermath of the Second World War should not be underestimated, especially when analyzing the behaviour of institutions whose task, by definition, is national defence. A study of the wide range of responses across Latin America to these external constraints is bound to shed light both on the general mechanisms of military power and on national particularities.

THE ARMED FORCES: HISTORICAL EVOLUTION AND NATIONAL EXPERIENCES

Although there is no militarism in the strict sense of the term prior to the birth of standing armies and career officers, military institutions take shape in the image of the nations in which they appear. They not only reflect the particularities of national culture, but are representative of the nature and degree of elaboration of the national state. As the armed branches of the state apparatus, they cannot help but conform to its modes of development. The armed forces of most South American countries cannot, for this reason, be likened to those of certain Caribbean or Central American nations, not only because of their difference in size, but above all because of the belated appearance of the state in the latter countries, and of the colonial context in which it emerged. Thus, Nicaragua, the Dominican Republic, Cuba and Haiti (though not Guatemala or El Salvador), latecomers as far as state construction was concerned, at the beginning of the twentieth century had barely emerged from wars between clans and *caudillos*. They all underwent a long period of United States occupation,[1] intended, according to the 1904 (Theodore) 'Roosevelt corollary' to the Monroe Doctrine, to put an end to what was, in Washington's view, a general breakdown of civilized society. The United States, before withdrawing its 'protection', made efforts to establish local constabularies in these countries, officered by U.S. Marines. These national guards were, in their creator's view, to be independent of the existing local factions and to curb private 'armies', thereby guaranteeing order, peace and the defence of U.S. interests. If the auxiliary forces in question carried out their last mission quite effectively, they did not provide the impulse for a coherent, independent process of state construction. In at least two of the countries which underwent this treatment, the 'national guards' bequeathed by U.S. occupation became, in the patrimonial context of Nicaraguan and Dominican society, their leaders' private armies and, in later years, the 'guardians of the dynasty' of the Trujillos and the Somozas.

In the South American countries and in certain Central American states (at least in Guatemala and El Salvador), three main stages may be distinguished in the military's evolution and their role in politics. Within each of these stages, however, there appear fluctuations, paralleling the vicissitudes of continental diplomacy, and important disparities, rooted in the irreducible particularities of each nation's history. The first period, running roughly from 1860 to the 1920s, saw the creation of modern armies.

---

[1] The United States occupied Cuba in 1898, in the aftermath of its victory over Spain which had led to the island's independence, and again between 1906 and 1909. The Dominican Republic was occupied between 1916 and 1924, as was Nicaragua, on two separate occasions, between 1912 and 1925 and between 1926 and 1933. Haiti was 'protected' by the Marines without interruption from 1915 to 1934.

In the second period, beginning around the 1920s or 1930s, we enter the military era, in which professional armed forces became actors in political life. During the third period, starting in the 1960s, the military's role took on an international colouring, in the framework of U.S. hegemony and under the impact of the Cold War. This last stage may be further broken down into brief, contrasting sequences, determined by the world situation and by Washington's policies.

A country's armed forces are symbols of its national sovereignty. At the turn of the century, they were also emblems of technological progress and of modernity. The creation of standing armed forces endowed with a professional officer corps was part of an outward-looking modernization inseparably linked with the growth *hacia afuera* of the national economies. It was not inconsequential that modernization of the state apparatus should have begun with its military branch. The armed forces of these dependent, unindustrialized nations could, evidently, transform themselves, and in particular raise their technological level, only by imitating foreign prototypes. They realized their dependent modernization not only by purchasing arms from European countries, but also by adopting the advanced countries' models of organization and training and even their military doctrines. At the turn of the century, there existed only two great armies (enemies, what is more), two universally valid military models: that of Germany with its Prussian tradition, and that of France. Between the Franco-Prussian War and the First World War, these two rival powers threw themselves into a ruthless struggle for influence in Latin America as an extension of their European competition. The stakes were not negligible, for a Latin American nation's choice of a military model founded a special relationship in the diplomatic sphere, but above all in the arms trade.

The South American countries' choices in this regard were dictated by their own rivalries as much as by European imperatives. Argentina and Chile requested German military missions to reform their armies, and at the beginning of the century they both sent a substantial number of officers to receive advanced training in German army units. The Argentine and Chilean armies took on, in many respects, a German character. The transformation affected their armaments, uniforms and parade ground steps, but also their internal regulations, the organization of their units and their view of international problems. It was not altogether a coincidence that Chile and Argentina were the two Latin American countries which held out longest against U.S. pressure to embrace the Allied cause during the Second World War. (Neither Argentina nor Chile declared war until 1945). Chile, which became a sort of Latin American Prussia, transmitted the German military model to other countries on the continent, dispatching army missions to or welcoming officers for training from Colombia, Venezuela, Ecuador and even El Salvador. France, for its part, contributed to the modernization of the Peruvian and Brazilian military. The French, drawing on their colonial experience, reorganized and trained the Peruvian army from 1896 until 1940, only interrupting their activity during the First World War. The Brazilians hesitated, awaiting the outcome of that conflict, before deciding in 1919 to invite a French military mission, initially led by General Gamelin, which remained in the country until 1939 and completely transformed the Brazilian army. French training left a deep and lasting mark on the military in Brazil: from 1931 to 1960, virtually every Brazilian minister of war had received French training. Brazilian officers' admiration for their French models was equalled only by the Argentines' respect for their German instructors.

The acceptance of this military assistance, with its enduring consequences, seems not to have been politically uncomfortable for its recipients. Germany and France were not the economically dominant powers in Latin America, although both (and Germany in particular) attempted to establish their presence in various sectors before the First World War and in the inter-war period. Great Britain, the undisputed economic metropolis, limited itself in the military sphere to training naval personnel and building warships. The Latin American nations' dependence during this period was therefore diversified – a state of affairs which was destined to change in the aftermath of the Second World War.

The modernization of Latin American armies involved two key reforms: the recruitment of officers through, and their education in, specialized military academies; and the introduction of compulsory military service. In the 'old army', the men were generally career soldiers, originally impressed, or sometimes ordered into the army by the courts to satisfy a criminal sentence, while the officers were usually the sons of respectable families, furnished with an influential sponsor's recommendation, who learned their profession on the job. The advent of conscription changed the situation. The men henceforth consisted of 'civilians', while it was the officers who were permanent professionals with technical training. Universal military service, moreover, created special responsibilities for the 'new army'. It had to inculcate a civic and moral sense in the future citizens placed in its charge and develop their national spirit. Compulsory military

service, introduced between 1900 (in Chile) and 1916 (in Brazil), preceded universal suffrage in most Latin American countries. The citizen
was thus a soldier before he became a voter, a chronological detail not
without significance. Futhermore, the new officers, recruited on meritocratic criteria and all cast in the common mould of their military academies, assumed a special position in the state. Co-opted by their peers,
liberated in theory from dependence on political or social notables' favour,
academy-trained officers constituted a corps of stable, permanent public
servants with regulated careers, in sharp contrast with the interchangeable
amateurs who predominated in the rest of the state machinery.

The new armies' civic and national responsibilities, and the independence
enjoyed by their officers, hardly predisposed them to remain politically
silent. Those who had believed that professionalization would guarantee
an apolitical military were to be proven sorely mistaken. Soldiers do not
easily remain politically neutral when they find themselves heavily engaged in nation- and state-building tasks and charged with important
internal defence functions. The resources that officers received from the
reforms did the rest. Highly trained technicians, constantly perfecting
their skills, they were now responsible for the annual contingent of conscripts, and thus, in their eyes, for the country's youth and for its future.
Were they not also best qualified to assess the international situation, since
it was their specific task to scrutinize the horizon for foreign threats?
Professional patriots and pioneers of state modernization, these new officers could not but develop a 'consciousness of competence', which would
lead them to intervene with all their great weight in public life.

In the 1920s and 1930s, the political activism of the military as an
institution, altogether different from the traditional *pronunciamientos* of
ambitious or discontented generals, increased remarkably in a large number of countries. Officers generally rose up against the status quo, and it
may thus be said that the armed forces entered politics from stage left.
These interventions, in which only minority sectors of the military participated, as a rule proved extremely effective. In Chile in 1924, a group of
young officers forced a conservative Congress to enact forthwith a series of
socially progressive laws whose passage had been delayed for months or
years. They then called for the dissolution of the legislature, initiating an
era of unrest, instability and reforms. The spirit of the officers involved in
the revolts of 1924–5 was incarnated successively in the dictatorship of
General Carlos Ibáñez del Campo (1927–31), and then fleetingly, though

not without verve, in the short-lived Socialist Republic of June 1932, established by Colonel Marmaduke Grove, a German-trained army officer, commander of the recently formed Chilean Air Force, and a short time thereafter one of the founders of the Chilean Socialist Party.

In Brazil, in 1922, a number of young officers, known as the *tenentes* (lieutenants), took part in a series of sporadic, improvised and uncoordinated rebellions arising out of widespread politico-military dissatisfaction with the corruption and restrictive practices of the 'Old Republic'. The revolt and death of a handful of lieutenants at Copacabana fortress in July 1922, the centenary year of independence, came to symbolize to the Brazilian middle classes their own aspirations for political and social change. In 1924, fresh *tenentista* movements arose in the south of the country. The survivors of one of these failed uprisings struck out across the immense nation on a 'long march' which was to be celebrated as a heroic gesture for the 'regeneration' of Brazil. This was the famous Prestes-Costa column, which failed to recruit the *caboclos* in the interior of the country, and which ended its wanderings in a wretched condition three years later in Bolivia. Luis Carlos Prestes, 'the knight of hope' celebrated by Jorge Amado, abandoned the army for the Brazilian Communist Party which he led from the 1930s to the 1980s. Other *tenentes* supported Getúlio Vargas in the revolution of 1930, which put an end to the oligarchic republic. Certain of them were to be found among the instigators of the coup d'état of 1964 and participated in the military regime of 1964–85. The ambiguity of *tenentismo* itself is revealed in this diversity of personal histories.

Ecuador was also affected by reformist militarism. In July 1925, a league of young officers overthrew the Liberal president, who had relied for support principally on the exporting and financial bourgeoisie of Guayaquil. The *juliana* (July) revolution, the first coup d'état in Ecuadorian history which was not a simple settling of scores between ruling groups, fixed as its goal the establishment of 'equality for all and the protection of the proletariat'. Over the following five years, Ecuador's first social welfare legislation was passed and institutions to implement it were established. In 1931, another military coup d'état, conservative this time and favoured by the most reactionary elements of the sierra, finally put an end to the reformist experiment.

In Bolivia, young officers seized power from traditional politicians, judged incompetent and corrupt, somewhat later, after the country's defeat at the hands of Paraguay in the Chaco War (1932–5). They proposed to implement reforms and to combat the ascendancy of foreign interests, particularly in the petroleum industry, to which they attributed decisive responsibility for the conflict just past. The comradeship of the trenches played no small part in the formation of a Bolivian national consciousness. From 1936 to 1939, Colonels David Toro and Germán Busch thus presided over an anti-oligarchic, progressive authoritarian regime, tinged with xenophobia. However, certain social legislation, as well as measures to extend state control over the financial system and sub-soil resources (Standard Oil was nationalized in 1937) encountered the powerful opposition of the large mining companies. From 1939 generals linked to the mining *rosca* allowed the colonels' innovations to be undone. In 1943, however, Colonel Gualberto Villarroel, supported by the Movimiento Nacionalista Revolucionario (MNR), which expressed the Chaco generation's aspirations for a national resurgence, seized control of the government. Accused of Nazi sympathies, Villarroel strove in an authoritarian manner to mobilize the dispossessed masses around a programme of profound social reforms which directly threatened mining and large landholding interests. In 1946, however, a 'popular' insurrection in La Paz, unleashed by the 'democratic' opposition encouraged by the United States, lynched the president and, to the great satisfaction of the 'tin lords', put an end to the national-military regime.

Argentina strikes a somewhat false note in this military concert which, if not always progressive, was at least always hostile to the status quo. The first coup d'état in this century to overturn a legal, democratically elected government at Buenos Aires was distinctly conservative. In September 1930, General José Uriburu and the cadets of the Colegio Militar, applauded by the oligarchy, drove from power Hipólito Yrigoyen, the Radical president elected by the middle and lower classes. The restoration of the conservative elites was the order of the day. The expanded democratic system adopted in 1912 was replaced by a representative regime based on limited participation and tempered by fraud. General Uriburu was personally favourable to a corporatist revision of the constitution which, however, was never realized. He was flanked by fiery captains with fascist sympathies who reappeared as 'nationalist' colonels or lieutenant-colonels at the time of the coup d'état of June 1943, from which Colonel Juan Domingo Perón and 'Peronism' were to emerge.

Nationalism was perhaps, in this period, the identifiable common denominator of the military's political orientations in the several Latin American countries. The officers' seemingly ambiguous behaviour, often more authoritarian than reformist even in the 'revolutionary' experiments, always had its roots in their underlying concern, even in the pursuit of social justice, to reinforce the human, economic and therefore military potential of their nations. This orientation accorded with the policies of independent, inward-looking development through import substitution industrialization, which were beginning to be adopted at the time. This national-militarist current, which was not systematically opposed to change if carried out in an orderly fashion, nor to improvements in the labouring classes' conditions if accomplished under the state's tutelage, seems to have been dominant in the armed forces. Without multiplying the examples, suffice it to recall that in Brazil, not only did numerous officers show an affinity for *integralismo,* but the Estado Novo itself was founded in 1937 by a general staff imbued with similar attitudes. General Pedro Góes Monteiro, minister of war (1934–7) and army chief of staff (1937–44), who hoped 'progressively to increase state power' and who was said to be a fascist sympathizer and pro-German, listed among the great men of the day, who embodied the political experiments he admired: 'Mussolini, Hitler, Stalin, Mustafa Kemal Pacha, Roosevelt and Salazar'. They had, in his view, each in his own way, succeeded in 'creating new organs and new state institutions, thereby furnishing the state with the means to overcome the domestic crisis'. The political ideal of the Estado Novo's most important military potentate was, in brief, that 'the state must have the power to intervene to regulate the whole of collective life and to discipline the nation'.[2]

This state worship, easily explicable in a federal republic where only in 1937 had the national army secured military ascendancy over local forces, was not however limited to the Brazilian military. South American armed forces, by training and organization, belonged to the state more than to society. Their state-orientated nationalism was in accord with their expanding corporate interests. In Bolivia, officers of the Chaco generation sought the establishment of a strong state to found a new 'nationally orientated socialist' order. Adapted to inter-war conditions in Bolivia, it nevertheless proceeded from the same institutional matrix as the 'national-socialist state' for which, with total historical naïvety, an Argentine industrialist general was still calling more than thirty years later.[3]

[2] General Pedro Góes Monteiro, *A Revolução de 30 e a Finalidade Política do Exército (Esboço Histórico)* (Rio de Janeiro, 1937), pp. 158 and 183.
[3] General E. J. Uriburu, 'El equipamiento de las fuerzas y su relación con el desarrollo nacional', *Estrategia* (Buenos Aires, November 1971), pp. 98–9.

The military's recurrent determination, in this period and later, in various Latin American countries, to 'liberate the state' from civil society, was however also linked to the international situation and the related crisis of the local governing classes. Although the anti-imperialist nationalism of the Bolivian military, outraged at the *demoentreguismo* and the *cleptocracia* of the anti-national mining oligarchy,[4] was not shared at the time by other armed forces on the continent, the contemporary perturbations of the liberal economic system had discredited, in all the continental armed forces, both political liberalism and the capitalist metropolises which practised it. The governing classes' divisions over how to deal with the crisis and with ongoing economic and social transformations also favoured the assertion of military power. The dominant classes became increasingly isolated and progressively lost their capacity to organize the assent of subordinate social groups. The socio-economic elites were divided over the mode of industrialization to adopt and on the attitude to take towards an expanded, newly combative working class. Disorientated, shaken, in some cases completely fragmented, they lacked the means to impose their leadership and a project of their own on society as a whole. The time was ripe for national-militarism. In the absence of a clear general interest defined by the bourgeoisie, the interest of the generals would substitute for it. For a time, it was the military who would define, in accordance with their own state-orientated and authoritarian values, what was best for the nation, in the name of its security and thus of the defence of the essential elements of the status quo.[5]

The overthrow of Vargas in Brazil in 1945 and Villaroel's assassination in Bolivia in 1946, although encouraged by the defeat of the Axis, were both the result of 'democratic' military interventions of a distinctly conservative stripe. The end of the Second World War was, however, marked elsewhere in Latin America by manifestations of a 'popular', indeed leftist, militarism, which differed fundamentally from the national-militarism discussed immediately above. The latter evinced sympathies for the Axis and authoritarian regimes, while the former related to the global popular front constituted by the U.S.-Soviet alliance. This new military reformism

---

[4] As Augusto Céspedes, one of the most outspoken of the MNR's founding members, scathingly put it in his book *El Presidente Colgado* (Buenos Aires, 1966), p. 14.

[5] For a discussion of the limits of military reformism, see Alain Rouquié, 'Le camarade et le commandant: reformisme militaire et légitimité institutionnelle', *Revue Française de Science Politique*, June 1979.

received the blessing of a State Department anxious to be rid of the inconvenient, discredited dictatorships which the United States had continued to support due to the exigencies of the war. It was favoured as well by the restraining influence of Browderism on the Latin American communist movement.

In this short-lived climate of democratic euphoria, soldiers and students in El Salvador, in May 1944, overthrew the dictator Maximiliano Hernández Martínez, who had lost the support of his own army. In July of the same year, Ubico fell in Guatemala, and the general who fleetingly succeeded him was driven from power by a military revolt. In the free presidential vote held in December, the Guatemalan governing junta supported the former opposition's progressive, civilian candidate, Juan José Arévalo, who was overwhelmingly elected. In Ecuador, after the May 1944 revolution, the armed forces, with the agreement of all the left-wing parties, called the popular José María Velasco Ibarra to the presidency and convoked a Constituent Assembly. In Venezuela, the overthrow of Gómez's successor in 1945 in a military coup, and the assumption of power by the Acción Democrática, formed part of the same democratic wave. The times were favourable to political liberalization particularly in the zones under direct U.S. influence. Even Somoza in Nicaragua liberalized his regime, at least superficially, mindful no doubt of the fate of neighbouring dictators.

The Second World War had consecrated the United States' absolute hegemony over the continent. Following the conflict, Washington established, first the diplomatic instruments, then the military dispositions, required for a loose coordination of the Latin American armed forces under the aegis of the Pentagon. In 1947, the Inter-American Treaty of Reciprocal Assistance, signed at Rio de Janeiro and known as the Rio Treaty, established principles of collective solidarity in order to confront any aggression arising from outside the continent. After the outbreak of the Korean War, the United States, between 1952 and 1955, signed bilateral military assistance pacts with a dozen Latin American countries in the framework of the Mutual Security Act passed by the Congress in 1951. Washington was uninterested in creating an integrated defence system for Latin America similar to NATO for the North Atlantic countries, since the region was not considered a high-priority military zone. In Washington's view, despite the Guatemalan 'alert' in 1954, communism did not represent a clear and present danger there.[6]

---

[6] At the Tenth Inter-American Conference, held in Caracas in March 1954, the United States obtained the passage of a resolution condemning communism and declaring that the establishment of

In the early 1960s, however, the shadow of the East-West conflict fell belatedly across Latin America. The Cuban Revolution, the Castro regime's break with the United States in 1960, and the establishment of a communist regime 90 miles from Florida, in the American Mediterranean, created an entirely new political situation in the region. A 'great fear' of Castroism swept across the continent as the Left was revitalized and guerrilla movements sprang up in numerous countries. The United States modified its strategic concepts. The Latin American armies in turn, prompted by the Pentagon, adopted new strategic and tactical hypotheses to adjust to the type of threat they were henceforth supposed to face. The 'Kennedy mutation' in the military's role involved a redefinition of the enemy, and the adoption of doctrines fraught with immediate political consequences. The struggle against the 'internal enemy' henceforth received highest priority. Faced with the danger of 'communist subversion', the armed forces of the continent prepared themselves for counter-revolutionary war. National security replaced national defence. The alarmist vigilance of the military, encouraged by Washington, resulted in their seeing communism everywhere. Any attempt at social change, especially if supported by local leftist parties, was indiscriminately branded as revolutionary. So it was that, between 1962 and 1966, the new Cold War 'crusaders' unleashed a series of nine coups d'état in the region. The armed forces overthrew, as a preventative measure, governments judged 'soft' on communism or lukewarm in their solidarity with the United States.[7] In this period, in accordance with the theory of ideological frontiers, the somewhat ill-defined idea of the 'Christian West' seemed to have replaced the nation-state in the hierarchy of military loyalties.

a communist regime on the continent would endanger peace. This resolution anticipated by a few months the overthrow by mercenaries, trained by the United States in Honduras, of the reformist, democratic government of President Arbenz in Guatemala, which had the support of the Guatemalan Communist Party.

[7] Chronological list of the coups d'état of the 1960s:

Date	Country	President overthrown
March 1962	Argentina	Arturo Frondizi
July 1962	Peru	Manuel Prado y Ugarteche
March 1963	Guatemala	Miguel Ydígoras Fuentes
July 1963	Ecuador	C. Julio Arosemena Monroy
September 1963	Dominican Republic	Juan Bosch
October 1963	Honduras	Ramón Villeda Morales
April 1964	Brazil	João Goulart
November 1964	Bolivia	Víctor Paz Estenssoro
June 1966	Argentina	Arturo Illia

The Cuban regime, for its part, attempted to become a world-wide focal point of revolutionary influence and action. Havana thus played host, in January 1966, to the Tricontinental Conference, a new revolutionary Bandung. In July and August 1967, the conference of the Latin American Organisation of Solidarity (OLAS) met in the Cuban capital to give its official blessing to the numerous attempts to establish guerrilla *focos* in Latin America in accordance with Castroist strategy. However, the failure in Bolivia of a bold attempt to convert the Andes into the Sierra Maestra of South America, which concluded in October 1967 with the death of Castro's legendary lieutenant Ernesto 'Che' Guevara, symbolized the end of a period and marked the beginning of Cuban disengagement.

In 1968, a new conjuncture began to take shape, the effects of which were to make themselves felt in the political orientations of the Latin American military until 1973. This period of detente resulted from a number of different, concurrent causes. Cuba had turned inward on itself, inaugurating a period in which domestic problems were to take precedence over internationalist solidarities. The Soviet Union's pressure on Havana played an important role in Cuba's shelving its hopes of creating 'several Vietnams' or of establishing 'a second Cuba' in Latin America. Moscow's economic, financial and military aid was crucial to the survival of the Cuban experiment, and the USSR had made clear its disapproval of the Cubans' 'adventurist' policy of armed struggle. And, though the United States had by no means forgotten that a communist state existed in the Caribbean, Vietnam and the Middle East overshadowed the 'Castroist threat'. The recently elected Republican administration of Richard Nixon opted for a 'low profile' in Latin America.

It was in these circumstances that the Latin American military, which seized power in a number of states between 1968 and 1972, for a time picked up the threads of the nationalist, reformist militarism of an earlier period. For the Peruvian officers who, led by General Juan Velasco Alvarado, overthrew the country's civilian authorities in October 1968, and for General Omar Torrijos Herrera, who took power almost simultaneously in Panama, the hour of 'revolution by the general staff' had struck. In Bolivia, the opportunistic shift to the left of a conservative militarized regime under General Alfredo Ovando Candia opened the way in 1970 to the fleeting popular government of General Juan José Torres González. A paler version of Peruvian and Panamanian 'radical praetorianism' appeared in Ecuador in 1972. In December of the same year, Honduran officers likewise struck out toward the left, establishing a military government charged with 'bringing the economy and national society up to date', notably through agrarian reform. Parallel developments were to be witnessed elsewhere on the continent. In Argentina, for example, the first months after Peronism's return to power in 1973 witnessed a short-lived breakthrough of military nationalism. That year, at the meeting of the commanders-in-chief of the American armies in Caracas, the Argentine General Carcagno and his Peruvian counterpart General Mercado Jarrín, together supported heretical theories on economic security, autonomous development and social justice, in opposition to the doctrine of national security. These 'brighter days' (or this adventure) proved, however, to be short-lived.

The year 1973, when the Chilean Popular Unity succumbed to soldiers until then respectful of democracy, was also that in which Uruguay, the 'Switzerland of South America', fell under the power of its own legions. In March 1976, a new military intervention in Argentina buried any hopes for the lasting establishment of democracy there: the Argentine military had relinquished power three years earlier only to return in force. The historical conjuncture was again given over to conservative or even counter-revolutionary militarism.

MILITARY REGIMES: MODELS AND MECHANISMS OF CONTEMPORARY MILITARISM

Although all military regimes have a family resemblance if only because of the nature of the institution which usurps power, Latin American military regimes in the period from the 1930s to the 1980s were in fact highly diverse. Nevertheless, a typology of military regimes can usefully be constructed, in terms of a small number of key criteria, which may be helpful in keeping our bearings in the midst of the numerous, empirically unique cases. In doing so, we leave aside the patrimonial or sultanistic Central American and Caribbean dictatorships of the inter-war period, the military nature of which is at the least debatable. Even if the first Somoza, Trujillo and Batista depended upon the praetorian guards they commanded to establish their personal dictatorships, the military origin of their power did not suffice to give it a strictly military nature. The Dominican and Nicaraguan regimes in particular, with their their practice of 'state gangsterism' and familial enrichment, are closer to traditional *caudillismo* than to modern militarism.

We may distinguish, for the purposes of analysis, between reiterated, quasi-institutionalized militarism and so-called 'cataclysmic' or 'break-down' authoritarianism, as well as between military regimes with conservative or counter-revolutionary socio-economic projects and certain forms of reformist or progressive militarism. These distinctions allow us to discern three dominant modes of military power in contemporary Latin America. The first, and doubtless the most characteristic, form is constituted by a virtually permanent, if not stable, military tutelage, in which the exception in constitutional terms has in fact become the rule. Praetorian republics of this sort existed, in one form or another, in Argentina and Brazil, as well as in El Salvador and Guatemala, until the mid-1980s. Second, Uruguay and Chile after 1973 exemplified 'catastrophic militarism', in which soldiers previously respectful of an established democratic tradition attempted to found a counter-revolutionary state. Finally, in the 1970s, military revolutions embracing a wide range of reformist and nationalist attitudes, without mass participation but not without populist connotations, were attempted in Peru, Bolivia and Panama in particular, but also to a certain extent in Ecuador and Honduras.

Praetorian republics: Argentina and Brazil

Contemporary Latin American militarism has been characterized more often by a stable military dominion over the state than by isolated and devastating coups d'état. Lasting military hegemony, where it has existed, dated for the most part from the 1930s. Military tutelage, enduring for half-a-century, became for all intents and purposes institutionalized, and the 'military factor' achieved the status of a quasi-legitimate political partner. This recurrent military role transformed both the state and the armed forces, with the latter, whose participation had become a common-place, constituting truly political forces. Institutionalization of this sort did not need to follow, as occurred in El Salvador after 1948, the canonical model of a 'colonels' party' which dominated politics and legitimized the military's corporatist ambitions. Officers might not even exercise power directly, as in Brazil before 1964, or might periodically hand the government back to civilians, as in Argentina between 1930 and 1983.

In Argentina, military hegemony assumed a wide range of different forms. The military power so brutally established in March 1976 was no more an unforseeable accident or an exceptional infraction of the rules than the more benign dictatorships which preceded it in 1943, 1955, 1962 and 1966. From 1930 to 1983, of the twenty-three presidents, elected or unelected, who governed Argentina, fifteen were military officers. Only two elected presidents completed their legal term of office, and both were generals who would never have reached the presidency had it not been for an opportune coup d'état: General Augustín Pedro Justo, elected in November 1931, after the coup d'état of 6 September 1930 had ousted the Radical president Hipólito Yrigoyen; and General Juan Domingo Perón, constitutionally elected in February 1946 with the backing of organized labour, but who was already the strong man of the military regime established by the 'revolution' of 4 June 1943. In this entire period, no president elected in the framework of a normal succession ever managed to complete his full legal term of office.

The stability of the legally constituted authorities in Argentina was conditioned, among other factors, by their military support. But constant recourse to the armed forces produced a chronic fragility of civilian power. For its part the military, notably by proscribing those who won (or would have won) free elections, made Argentina ungovernable. From 1930 to 1943, the Radical Party was the victim of electoral prohibitions or fraud. Thereafter Peronism, victorious in the 1946 and 1951 presidential elections, was proscribed from 1955, the year of the 'liberating' coup d'état which overthrew Perón, until 1973. The consequence of these military anathemas was a series of coups d'état and a succession of unelected or spuriously elected chief executives. The minority presidents who took office were, moreover, subject to the strict vigilance of armed forces themselves split into groups with determined civilian affinities. For not only did civilians knock on the barracks door in order to resolve their conflicts, but officers also sought civilian allies in order to hold their ground in the internecine struggles within the 'military party'.

Civil-military relations in Argentina, at least until 1983, were conceived of totally differently, and aroused a profoundly different set of expectations, from those prevailing in stable, pluralist, representative systems. Military intervention in politics was, if not legitimate, at least legitimated by broad sectors of public opinion. Every military uprising, far from provoking a holy alliance of the entire political class or of organized civic forces in defence of representative institutions, received the public or private support of the opposition to those in power. Appeals to the military were not merely a means of political revenge available to minority sectors. Militarism spared no party. The armed forces, despite their manifestly conservative tendencies and their historical anti-communism, were not presented in the political class's statements (even after 1976) as adhering, by definition or by nature, to a specific, exclusive ideological or social sector. Not only did both right-wing and left-wing Peronists court the military, but the Communist Party itself and almost every fraction of the non-violent far Left aspired to an alliance with 'patriotic and progressive officers' and continued to hope for an improbable 'Nasserist revolution'. The Argentine armed forces, when they intervened, were thus never unanimously condemned as a danger to the free development of political life or a simple 'tool of the dominant classes'. The military were perceived, rather, as difficult partners, unpredictable great electors in a complex, crafty game in which nothing could be done against them or without them.

In Brazil, the armed forces held power for twenty-one years following the coup d'état of 1964. But, unlike in Argentina, this situation was exceptional, having indeed never occurred since the overthrow of the Empire in 1889. The radical novelty of the Brazilian military's action in institutional terms was nevertheless accompanied by more traditional economic and political ideas and policies, belying the notion of a complete break with the past. Indeed, if we consider the six military interventions in Brazil since 1930 (the five prior to 1964 not having led to a direct seizure of power), the armed forces are seen to have intervened four times against pluralist democracy (in 1937, 1954, 1961 and 1964), and only twice to guarantee constitutional legality (in 1945 and 1955). Two interventions prior to 1964 (those of 1954 and 1961) may equally be regarded as having favoured economically liberal, anti-nationalist development projects. Certain observers have even qualified these interventions as 'trial coups d'état' against the established political system.

This sequence of regulative pressures and interventions, in alternating directions, has buttressed the thesis that the Brazilian armed forces, until 1964, exercised a 'moderating power' inherited from the Emperor. But to reduce the military to this model credits their behaviour with a political coherence and unity of views which it totally lacked. The armed forces did not intervene in public life because they were more united, more effective or better able to maintain continuity in national politics. Rather, the opposite would seem to be true. If, after 1930, the Brazilian military in general, and particularly the army, constituted an authority above the legal authorities, and against whom it was impossible to govern, the armed forces, profoundly politicized or at least 'ideologized', were divided from 1930 to 1964 between two principal tendencies whose public clashes punctuated political life. Changing majorities or, rather, shifting dominant groups within the armed forces, at times favourable to a populist, nationalist line close to that of Vargas and his heirs, at others close to the positions of the conservative liberals, fixed the limits and guarantees of governmental autonomy. Not only did the hegemonic sector within the armed forces sanction and ratify electoral results, but every government had to neutralize its adversaries in the armed forces in order to acquire freedom to act. Without such a *dipositivo militar,* a semi-official term referring to what was virtually an institution, political stability was unattainable.

The activities of political parties and groups extended, moreover, in a more or less institutionalized form, into the armed forces. The conservative party, the União Democrático Nacional (UDN), had its counterpart in the *cruzada democrática,* sometimes referred to as 'the military UDN', whose leaders seized power in 1964. Conversely, the leaders of the armed forces organized civilian clienteles and alliances, and officers constantly passed from military activity to politics. In the 1945 presidential election, for example, the standard-bearers for the two opposing camps were both generals: Major General Eduardo Gomes for the UDN, and General Eurico Dutra, for the *getulistas* of the Partido Social Democrático (PSD). In accordance with praetorian logic, every political group strove to acquire military support in order to increase its own power. Nor was the losers' militarist ardour dampened when their adversaries obtained military favour. Under the Estado Novo, the liberals continued to trust in the military to restore democracy,[8] and even after the 1964 coup d'état, some on the left still proclaimed their faith in the popular and democratic spirit of the national armed forces.

The question has been raised why, in 1964, the Brazilian armed forces did not limit themselves, as they had previously, to a simple corrective intervention. Leaving aside the official or semi-official justifications advanced by both civilians and military, it appears that the determinants of the events of 1964, in the context of the Cold War climate prevailing in Latin America, were extremely complex. The 'crisis of the populist state' – attributable to the exhaustion of its national development project and to the inversion of its relationship with the workers (with the latter, previously under paternalistic control, beginning to exert strong pressure on it) – was indeed a general state crisis. The 'revolution' of 1964 was in a sense a 'coup for the state', that is, an institutional fracture intended to

---

[8] This was the case, for example, of Armando de Salles Oliveira, the leading opposition candidate in the abortive presidential election campaign of 1937, who was forced into exile shortly thereafter. See Thomas E. Skidmore, *Politics in Brazil, 1930–1964: an Experiment in Democracy* (London, 1967), pp. 57–9.

reconstitute, on new foundations, a reinforced state organization. In the military sphere, the nationalist current had likewise lost ground before the ideological offensive of the so-called 'democratic' tendency, which was closely linked to the U.S. armed forces. The Cold War, and the initiation of a new phase of industrial development involving a modification of the income distribution model, strengthened the hand of the liberal 'Atlanticists', among whom predominated former members of the Brazilian Expeditionary Force (FEB) which had participated in the Second World War. These Brazilian officers, who had fought alongside the U.S. Fourth Army Corps in the Italian campaign, were anti-*getulistas* and partisans of free enterprise. They had played an important role in formulating, in the Escola Superior de Guerra, the doctrine of *segurança nacional,* which linked development and security and, by assigning the military the function of defining 'permanent national objectives', justified their political usurpations in the name of Cold War values.

However, in 1964, General Castello Branco, the leader of the 'revolution', did not intend to establish a genuine military dictatorship. The victors of April were authoritarian liberals who sought to reinforce and protect the state by purifying, not by abolishing, the existing democratic system. It was, for them, a question of defending the institutions bequeathed by the constitution of 1946 by proscribing its presumed adversaries, the leaders of the Left and populist politicians. This 'moderate' project for a supervised democracy quickly revealed itself unfeasible, given the strength of the traditional parties and the pressures emanating from the hard-line sectors of the military, and in consequence as well of the economic policies chosen and the popular dissatisfaction they provoked. In the wake of a number of electoral setbacks and of dangerous mass mobilization against the limitations imposed on democracy, Institutional Act No. 5 of December 1968, which granted the president dictatorial powers, sanctioned the march toward an authoritarian regime which nevertheless retained a parliamentary façade. The military-dominated system thus proceeded from a 'manipulated democracy' to a form of modernizing, authoritarian state in which the toleration of marginal political competition lent popular consecration to an emergency regime.

In praetorian republics, the armed forces, once in power, tend to invade the state, whatever respect their leaders continue to accord to representative institutions. In Brazil, the regime, always prompt to modify the rules of the game whenever they proved unfavourable to it, showed no hesitation in concentrating in the executive the attributes of the others

branches. In a parallel development, bureaucratic-military or predominantly military institutions burgeoned as sites of executive authority and
decision-making. Among them, we may note the army high command,
the National Intelligence Service (SNI), and the National Security Council. The SNI came to constitute a sort of 'invisible government', and its
director concentrated such great political resources in his hands that the
post became the high road to the presidency. As for the National Security
Council, created by decree-law only in 1968, the constitutional reform of
1969 entrusted it with nothing less than the task of 'fixing the permanent
objectives and the bases of national policy'.

In Argentina, where military interventions totally suspended representative procedures, militarization was even more patent, but it assumed
varying forms under different military regimes. The bureaucratic-political
institutions established after the 1966 coup d'état were not the same, for
example, as those established after the coup d'état of 1976. In the earlier
regime, the general-president, Juan Carlos Onganía, took all power into
his own hands. The armed forces as such did not govern. This did not
imply that military concerns did not underlie the orientations of the
regime and of its institutions. The monarchical executive established by
General Onganía was legitimated in terms of national defence, and the
new legislation enacted was inspired by the general staff's strategic hypotheses and by national requirements as they defined them. Military
power outside the barracks' walls was also visible in the extensive prerogatives attributed to the CONASE (National Security Council) and to the
SIDE (State Intelligence Service). Nevertheless, until Onganía fell in June
1971, the armed forces were not themselves in power, and officers exercised a relatively limited share of executive functions.

The situation was entirely different in the aftermath of the 1976 coup
d'état. The military's experience under Onganía and, above all, the requirements and consequences of the 'dirty war' against subversion, led to
an inversion in the relationship between the president and the junta of
commanders-in-chief. The military monarchy was replaced by a collegial
body. This new structuring of power reflected the military's decision to
govern for an extended period, their desire to hold on to the initiative in
their relations with civilians, and their concern to assure continuity without discord within the armed forces themselves. The crucial objective was
to avoid intra-military conflicts, or at least to institutionalize them.

Authoritarianism invariably entails an expansion of the political bureaucracy responsible for the surveillance and repression of dissidents and

opponents. But the natural inclination of technocrats in uniform, whatever their proclaimed objectives and ideology, leads them furthermore, in most cases, to favour increased governmental planning and the expansion of the state's economic role. The colonization of the state apparatus by the military is one of the most salient features of praetorian republics in Latin America.

In Argentina, the state was, in this regard, militarized early. The Argentine military, concerned about the 'critical strategic dependency' of a non-industrialized, agricultural country, manifested their interest in industry from the beginning of the century, and played the role of a pressure group for industrialization in opposition to a bourgeoisie convinced of the perfections of laissez-faire and of the permanence of their country's comparative advantages. Military nationalism manifested itself in the persons of Generals Enrique Mosconi and Alonso Baldrich, who insisted that the country should exploit its own petroleum resources, and of General Manuel S. Savio, who argued for an Argentine steel industry, which was however not to be created for many years. Nevertheless, in 1927 General Justo, at the time minister of war in the Alvear administration, inaugurated an aircraft factory in Córdoba which, the following year, began the production in short runs of models under European licence. The key date, however, was 1941, during the Second World War, when a law created the Dirección General de Fabricaciones Militares (DGFM), an autonomous entity within the Ministry of War. Its objectives, as the law defined them, went well beyond the simple production of arms and munitions. The DGFM was to be responsible as well for making good the shortcomings of private industry in the 'area of industrial production for civilian consumption'. The uncontrolled liberalism which characterized the regime presided over by General Videla after 1976, and the anti-statist philosophy of José A. Martínez de Hoz, his minister of economics, although they provoked a grave de-industrialization of the productive apparatus, had virtually no impact on the state's economic responsibilities and, in particular, upon those of Fabricaciones Militares. Monetarist shock treatment and ultra-liberal ideology seem to have collided with the military's statist behaviour, but also with their vested interests, which had increased as a result of a recent colonization of the state.

In Brazil, the regime established following the coup d'état of 1964 propounded ultra-liberal ideas in economic matters. Nevertheless, one of its distinguishing features was the expansion of the public sector and of state capitalism. The growth of the state's industrial responsibilities, in particular, was one of the more paradoxical features of Brazil under the military. If the state's control of savings and distribution gave it enormous power, its role in production, which dated from well before 1964, conferred upon it an apparently overwhelming preponderance. Of the hundred most powerful enterprises in the country, in 1970 forty were under public ownership, forty-six in 1972, and of the almost six hundred enterprises that the state controlled in 1980, approximately two hundred had come into existence after April 1964. This situation prompted certain economic sectors to wage, in 1975–6, a grand *anti-estatização* campaign directed against the 'tentacular state', and some impenitent liberals went so far as to tax General Ernesto Geisel's administration (1974–9) with being 'socialist'! The statist, centralizing activities of the Brazilian armed forces are a historical reality, going back without interruption to the military presidents of the early days of the 'Old Republic'. But the numerous manifestations of similar statist behaviour in other militarized states cannot be ignored.

The counter-revolutionary state: Chile and Uruguay after 1973

In 1973, Chile and Uruguay, despite their long traditions of democratic stability and of military submission to civilian authority, suffered, at virtually the same moment, ferocious and lasting military interventions. In Chile, military subordination had not been seriously challenged since 1932. In Uruguay, the military had never held a share of power in the twentieth century. (In the early 1960s, it has been said, Uruguayans had forgotten that their army existed.) Nevertheless, the military dictatorships established in 1973 in these two former islands of democracy proved among the most repressive on the contintent. In Chile, the coup d'état was among the bloodiest the continent had ever seen.

The radical change in the Chilean military's attitude is to be explained as much by mutations in the political system and the armed forces as by the unexpected election in 1970 of a minority Socialist president. In 1964, to confront the rise of the Left grouped around the figure of Salvador Allende, the Christian Democrats, aided by the United States, had presented an ambitious and innovative programme for a 'revolution in liberty', designed to place Chile on a risk-free 'non-capitalist' path of development, consonant with the 'social doctrine of the Church'. Eduardo Frei, the Christian Democratic candidate, elected president by a huge majority (thanks to the supporters of the Right, who voted for the lesser evil), planned to rely for support on social sectors traditionally excluded from the political process while at the same time modernizing the country's productive apparatus. By promising social justice and steadily increasing wages, Frei raised the expectations of the working population. However, by tampering with the situation of the peasantry, henceforth authorized to form unions, the Christian Democrats unleashed forces which they could neither quickly satisfy nor politically control. The leadership of the business community was uneasy, and the landholding bourgeoisie felt it had been despoiled by an agrarian reform which, though gradual, did liberate its *inquilinos*. The conservatives who had voted for Frei felt betrayed, and the Right came close to thinking that the Christian Democratic president had paved the way for communism. The political spectrum became increasingly radicalized, as social conflicts turned more violent and the Christian Democratic party itself split. By encouraging participation by Chile's traditional outcasts, Frei had opened Pandora's box, violating the 'implicit social pact' on which stability of the Chilean political model rested. The mass mobilization promoted by the Christian Democrats upset the fragile equilibrium which permitted 'the disjunction between the political system and the system of social inequality'.[9] As the social stakes rose, the compromises of the past were no longer feasible.

In these circumstances, there developed and spread among the Chilean Right a 'new' anti-democratic ideology, which assigned the armed forces a role better attuned to the perils of the hour. Its authors challenged the traditional concept of a military blindly submissive to the civilian authorities. Their supposedly Portalian 'neo-corporatism' ascribed to the armed forces an essential place in the structure of a new state. This subterranean ideological development coincided with the promotion to unit commander positions of a generation of officers trained during the Cold War after the shift, inspired by the United States, toward an anti-subversive strategy. These new orientations were particularly pronounced in a country in which, although there were no guerrillas, the Pentagon viewed the 'communist threat' as grave, not only because the Chilean Communist Party was the most powerful on the continent, but also because of the Chilean Socialist Party's evolution toward pro-Cuban positions.

It was in this context that Salvador Allende, the Popular Unity candidate, was elected president of Chile in 1970, with only 36 per cent of the

---

[9] Liliana de Riz, *Sociedad y Política en Chile (de Portales a Pinochet)* (Mexico, D.F., 1979), pp. 60–3.

vote. His programme for a peaceful, parliamentary transition to socialism was subject to paralyzing conditions from birth, since for the Popular Unity government to survive at all, it had to remain within the framework of bourgeois institutions and to respect the constitutional system which had permitted it to accede to power. 'Legality is my strength', Allende is said to have declared, but it was also his weakness, confronted as he was with a Congress, judiciary and civil service, as well as with a majority of the electorate, all hostile to his programme. The armed forces, jealous of their monopoly of violence and of arms, had constituted the touchstone and guarantee of the country's institutions. They now also became terrain for, and the real stake in, the major political confrontations which began to unfold.

The assassination in October 1970 of General René Schneider Chereau, the commander-in-chief of the army, by a group of clumsy rightist conspirators, convinced Congress to ratify Allende's minority election to the presidency. The general's death sanctified in the army the constitutional loyalism which he had defended and which had cost him his life. The 'Schneider doctrine' was undoubtedly, thereafter, a powerful force in neutralizing, or at least in moderating, the putschist impulses of the initally small but growing fraction of the high command won over to seditious, counter-revolutionary positions. The armed forces thus loyally supported Allende for three years, and in the name of the defence of the constitution assured the survival of the socialist experiment. They were then to be the grave-diggers both of Popular Unity and of the democratic regime.

The Chilean armed forces maintained very close ties with the United States. Chile was indeed one of the principal beneficiaries of U.S. military assistance to Latin America, second in importance only to Brazil, and ahead of countries such as Peru, Colombia and Bolivia which had to combat Castroist guerrillas. Chile, where some sixty thousand men were under arms in 1970, received US$169 million in aid from U.S. military programmes between 1946 and 1972 (US$122 million between 1962 and 1972 alone). Between 1950 and 1970, a total of 4,374 Chilean military personnel were sent for instruction to U.S. military installations in Panama or in the United States. About two thousand of these trainees attended programmes between 1965 and 1970, testifying to the extent and intensification of U.S. influence during the Frei administration. Indeed, from 1965 on, practically all Chilean officers spent some time in U.S. military schools. The consequences of such training periods were not, of course, either uniform or automatic.[10] Indeed Carlos Prats González, the 'democratic general', army commander-in-chief under Allende, had himself spent a year at Fort Leavenworth. During the Allende administration, while the United States was reducing or cutting off other sorts of economic support to Chile, they maintained and even increased their military aid. Military assistance to Chile, which had fallen to US$800 thousand in 1970, rose to US$5.7 million in 1971, and to US$10.9 million in 1972, when it was the only U.S. aid granted to Chile.

Allende had few means at his disposal to counteract U.S. influence over the dependent Chilean armed forces. He could count on the constitutionalism of a part of the hierarchy, and upon the strict vertical discipline held in honour in the Chilean army, but he could not prevent junior officers from being imbued with the counter-insurgency mentality taught by the United States. Meanwhile, the Chilean bourgeoisie, its parties as well as its trade and professional organizations, did not remain inactive in face of the structural transformations threatening them. Economic sabotage and parliamentary obstructionism exasperated an already tense social situation, accentuating the nation's polarization. In a climate of civil war, an unrelenting guerrilla campaign was waged in Congress in order to push the government into overstepping legal bounds. The coup d'état was already on the march, but it remained to fabricate its detonating events and to sweep away the final barriers to the movement. The attitude of the far Left, which tried to carry the class struggle into the armed forces themselves, contributed to unifying the officer corps. Finally, on 22 August 1973, the opposition majority in the Chamber of Deputies passed a resolution, addressed explicitly, among others, to the military members of Allende's cabinet, accusing the government of having occasioned, by a systematic course of conduct, the 'grave breakdown of the constitutional and legal order'. The following day, the last obstacle to military action was removed when General Prats, discredited by provocations and left almost without support among his peers, resigned both as minister of national defence and as commander-in-chief of the army. His successor, General Augusto Pinochet Ugarte, who was believed to be a 'democrat', refused to cashier the most notorious putschists. In the following days, the future dictator betrayed his trust, but what he did above all was follow his troops. On the morning of 11 September 1973, instead of the long-awaited civil war, the world was witness to an exercise in brutal White Terror.

---

[10] See Alain Rouquié, *The Military and the State in Latin America* (Berkeley, Cal., 1987), chap. 5.

The violence of the Chilean coup d'état was unexpected. The counter-revolutionary movement in no way resembled the peaceful putsches, akin to ministerial crises in parliamentary regimes, which had punctuated the history of other Latin American countries and in particular that of the praetorian republics of long standing. The political inexperience of the Chilean military, who knew only how to wage war, was not the sole explanatory factor. The sanguinary character of the military operations was dictated by the imperatives of the situation as perceived by the leaders of rebellion. Terror, the imtimidation first of loyal military personnel, then of civilians who had supported the fallen regime, was designed to render later compromises impossible. The blood which had been shed excluded the option of a restoration of the civilized Right. The putschists had not acted to further the interests of the Christian Democrats, despite the important aid the latter had afforded them. Those of Allende's opponents who hoped that the Marxist government's elimination would lead to a return to the pre-1970 'Belle Epoque' were to be sorely disappointed. The coup d'état of 11 September was meant to be a genuine historical rupture. To save the country from the 'Marxist cancer' and to 'protect democracy', the armed forces irreversibly destroyed the 'compromise state' and proclaimed a 'state of siege'. It was clear from the generalized repression and prolonged state terror that the coup d'état did not represent mere rejection of the 'Chilean road to socialism' or a 'technical' response to the impasse in relations between the executive and Congress.

A counter-revolutionary regime took shape which, in the name of the crusade against communism, rejected the guilty weaknesses of representative democracy, and imposed its own socio-economic project. A 'protected', 'risk-free' democracy was to be founded, predicated on a capitalist restructuring and a consequent reorganization of society. The military's anti-Marxist obsession converged, in this regard, with the self-interested ideological concerns of their civilian allies. In Chile, the armed forces' economic role had, historically, always been slight. The adoption and implementation of ultra-liberal Friedmanite principles thus met less military resistance in Santiago than elsewhere in Latin America. The deification of the market was moreover broadly compatible with the logic of the Chilean military in power. The generalized application of market principles, and the resulting destabilization of numerous institutions and activities, were designed to privatize social demands, thereby putting an end to collective action and perhaps even to politics. It was this destructuring of the social fabric by a 'capitalist revolution' which would, in General

Pinochet's eyes, guarantee a worry-free future. The surgery performed by
the armed forces would assure the system's reproduction without any
further recourse to force. To this end, the businesses taken over by the
state under Allende, as well as the land affected by the agrarian reform,
were returned to the private sector. But privatization was also extended to
enterprises long under government control, as well as, within the limits of
the possible, to the public health, education and pension systems. Trade
liberalization damaged local industry but also had the effect of reducing
the size of the proletariat.

If in Chile the existence of a project of socialist transformation prompted
a 180-degree turn under the aegis of the military, Uruguay in 1973, governed by the rightist civilian president Juan María Bordaberry, seemed safe
from a similar institutional breakdown. The issue was, indeed, not the
government's political orientation, but the bankruptcy of a particular mode
of national development. Due to its natural advantages and its relatively
small, homogeneous population of predominantly European origin, Uruguay at the beginning of the century had become an important exporter of
meat and wool. The success of stockrearing allowed the country to introduce
advanced social legislation very early. In this way, the state redistributed a
significant part of the income generated by foreign trade. However, this
city-state's excessive urbanization, and the expansion of the public bureaucracy, contributed to perpetuating traditional agrarian structures with low
productivity. Agriculture had not only financed Uruguayan urban development, but had also contributed significantly to social harmony. The
latifundia were in a sense the base of the welfare state. Large agrarian estates
co-existed with a sort of urban socialism, so that the consumption patterns
of a developed country depended upon an under-developed economy. Social
and political stability had been achieved, but in exchange for low levels of
productive efficiency and a mediocre adaptive capacity in the face of changes
in the economic environment

Immediately after boom created by the Korean War, around 1955, the
drop in demand for wool, and in general the fall in the prices of the
country's principal exports, exposed the system's lack of dynamism and
called into question the validity of the model itself. The various social
groups struggled to increase their share of a frustratingly stagnant national
product, with inflation as one visible result. The 'pauperization' of a
country that was 'European' in its culture and consumption patterns gave
rise to tensions endangering the social consensus. In this context, those
who controlled the principal means of production – the great landholders,

but also the financial and export sector – sought to modify the social and political rules of the game. They voiced opposition to the redistributive policies of the welfare state, as well as to the transfers benefiting wage-earners and favouring industries producing for the domestic market. The dominant groups in Uruguay, seeming to forget the role played by *dirigisme* and state paternalism in maintaining social peace and the status quo, preached austerity and reductions in state expenditures.

Direct control of the government was indispensable if these objectives were to be achieved. After Jorge Pacheco Areco, the leader of the right-wing of the Colorado Party, succeeded to the presidency in late 1967, new men, businessmen and bankers, tried to impose an economic stabilization and recovery plan, including arbitrarily imposed wage restraints. The wave of strikes which shook the country was met by the temporary conscription of the employees of the nationalized banks and the proclamation of a very attenuated state of siege. In this tense atmosphere of decline and fall, there appeared a youthful, clandestine, extra-parliamentary opposition, the Movimiento de Liberación Nacional (MNL) – the Tupamaros, which, through acts of 'symbolic violence', first undermined governmental authority, then finally provoked the disintegration of the regime. The police proved powerless in dealing with the Tupamaros' challenge, which benefited from undeniable popularity, and the political climate degenerated rapidly. Civil liberties were violated under the reigning state of emergency. Uruguay seemed increasingly 'Latin-Americanized' at the approach of the 1971 elections, in which the two traditional parties, the Blancos and the Colorados, faced the competition of a Frente Amplio of the united Left, supported by the Tupamaros. Although Juan María Bordaberry (1972–6), the candidate representing political continuity, won the presidential election, the leftist coalition received 30 per cent of the vote in Montevideo. The Left in all its various guises caused alarm, and the hardening of conservative sentiment, rooted in the fear both of change and of violence, did not bode well for the chances of finding political solutions to the nation's problems.

The Uruguayan armed forces had, until then, been not so much silent as absent. The Colorado Party, which governed without interruption for ninety-three years from 1865 to 1958, as a dominant, modernizing party, created the armed forces in its own image: *civilista* (opposed to military participation in politics) and *colorado*. This has been cited as one reason for the Uruguayan military's non-interventionist history. The armed forces were in fact not autonomous and, linked as they were to a specific political

family, did not regard themselves as situated above parties, with the right
to set themselves up as the supreme authority and guarantor of the national interest. The new responsibilities that Pacheco Areco assigned them
just before the November 1971 elections allowed them finally to assume
such a role. The armed forces henceforth saw themselves entrusted with
responsibility for the suppression of subversive activities.

When, after the electoral defeat of the Left, the Tupamaros plunged
more deeply into armed struggle, attacking the military and the police
directly, the legislature enlarged the military's authority even further. The
armed forces' offensive against the urban guerrillas was indiscriminate and
extremely murderous. Montevideo was placed on a war footing, and the
military terrorized the 'terrorists', who were forced onto the defensive. By
September 1972, the National Liberation Movement had effectively been
dismantled. But, although the MLN was in its death-throes, the armed
forces, far from leaving the political stage, increased their pretensions.
The military's growing indiscipline and arrogance reduced daily the president's already precarious authority. By giving the combined security forces
(armed forces and police) carte blanche to liquidate sedition by any and all
means, the new president, Bordaberry, had taken a political risk which
ultimately would prove fatal to him. The Uruguayan military, convinced
that they were defending the national interest, were not prepared to
accommodate themselves to even the most basic democratic rights and
practices. Official general staff communiqués denounced legislative mo-
tions condemning military exactions as complicity with subversion.

The trial of strength began in July 1972. The army protested against
the appointment of a new minister of defence, fixed its conditions and
announced its programme. The latter was extraordinarily ambiguous,
revealing the diversity of opinion within the military. Certain figures on
the left detected therein the existence of a progressive, 'Peruvian' line. A
number of military communiqués did indeed propose profound structural
reforms. This was not, however, the crux of the matter. The military's
fundamental desire was to achieve representation in every sphere of national life. The creation in February 1973 of the National Security Council
(COSENA), whose secretary-general was the head of the combined forces
general staff, and which was assigned the task of aiding the president in
'the realization of national objectives', institutionalized military power.
On 27 June 1973, the interminable coup d'état culminated in the dissolution of both houses of the legislature and the creation of an appointed
council of state which inherited their powers. But, with a complaisant

Bordaberry still president, the military order preserved a civilian façade. The unions and the leftist parties continued to seek alliances with the elusive 'Peruvian' wing of the armed forces. The political parties which opposed the coup d'état were proscribed at the end 1973, but the Communist Party, although certain of its leaders had been arrested previously, only came systematically under attack beginning in 1975.

As November 1976, the prescribed date for general elections, drew near, the military 'in order to defend democratic traditions', finally dismissed Bordaberry, alleging that he was a partisan of an authoritarian state. The fiction of civilian government was maintained, however, through the appointment of a president of the Council of State who was supposed to incarnate the executive. A series of 'institutional acts' entirely restructured the political system, militarizing it in the name of the 'struggle against sedition'. All opposition was mercilessly crushed. Generalized insecurity reigned in the name of national security. A garrison state had replaced the welfare state. In the economic sphere, the pseudo-civilian regime in Uruguay adopted an ultra-liberal logic similar in many regards to that of General Pinochet's 'Chicago boys'. The neo-liberal policies of the new regime were designed to promote – through the drastic reduction of state expenditures, the opening of the country's borders and the concentration of income – Uruguay's specialization in those industries which could effectively compete in international markets. Some dreamed of transforming Uruguay into a sort of South American Hong Kong, but the hoped-for Uruguayan miracle never materialized.

Military revolutions: Peru, Bolivia, Panama, Ecuador

Self-proclaimed progressive military coups d'état, whose leaders assert that they side with the people, generally inspire profound scepticism when they appear in Latin America. Observers have tended to attribute the armed forces' new stance to a ruse of 'imperialism' or to military opportunism. The Peruvian coup d'état of 3 October 1968 cannot, however, simply be equated with those in Brazil in 1964, in Argentina in 1966 and 1976, or in Chile and Uruguay in 1973. Nor was Peruvian military 'revolutionary nationalism' an isolated case, fruit of an untransferable national singularity. The rise to power in Bolivia of General Ovando in September 1969, then of General Torres a few months later, seemed to confirm the Peruvian experience by divesting it of its uniqueness. The style of action adopted, in the same period, in a very different geopolitical and institutional context, by the Panamanian National Guard at the instance of General Torrijos, showed sufficient resemblance to the two Andean regimes to rule out any narrowly geographical explanation of the phenomenon. The armed forces that seized power in Ecuador in February 1972 also appealed to revolutionary nationalism in promulgating their reforms. And their policies echoed the contemporary programme 'for bringing up to date the economy and national society' which the Honduran military were trying to implement in their country.

This military reformism would seem to be a sort of return to the sources of contemporary Latin American militarism. Yet these experiments were never free from a certain ambiguity. On the honours list of aborted revolutions, those directed by the military would doubtless be found at the top. Progressive experiments conducted by the armed forces have often come to an abrupt halt, or even been transformed into avowed counter-revolution. Military rule would seem to be particularly characterized by brusque regressions, unexpected swings of the pendulum and 180-degree turns. Events in Bolivia, Ecuador and Peru all attest to this tendency, as do those in Honduras, although the shift there was in the politically opposite direction. It is, nevertheless, not without interest to examine the roots and the objectives of these revolutions conducted by the general staff.

In Peru, the military seems to have seized power in order to carry out from a position of strength the reforms which the weak civilian government they overthrew had proved incapable of putting into effect. To this end, the junta which replaced President Fernando Belaúnde Terry was to give battle on two fronts: to modernize Peruvian society, which remained extremely archaic; and to reduce the country's foreign dependency, without losing sight of geopolitical constraints. The new regime's most significant initiative was the preparation and implementation of an agrarian reform law. The guiding lines of the reform, which constituted the keystone of social change, were established in response to the rural dissatisfaction which had fed the 1965 guerrilla uprising, to the massive exodus from the sierra to Lima, and to the insufficiency of national food production which had resulted in growing agricultural imports. The reform was intended to reduce the dualism of Peruvian society, to render it more fluid by destroying the landed foundations of the great oligarchical families, while at the same time constituting an 'economic rationalization' designed to transfer income toward the economy's modern sectors.

The military government implemented a whole series of other measures, founded on the preponderance of the public sector, which were orientated in the same direction. The nationalization of the export trade in certain leading products like minerals and fish meal, the bank reform which limited the participation of foreign capital, and the 'general law on industry' which created a sort of association between capital and labour, were designed to help canalize national investment toward the productive sector by discouraging capital flight and 'denationalization'.

The Peruvian experiment, which some observers have considered unique, did not survive the fall of General Velasco Alvarado at the end of 1975. What were the underlying causes of this unforseen military 'revolution'? Leaving aside fanciful accounts based on the military's supposed instrumental use by outside forces, and restricting ourselves to interpretations centered on the emergence of a 'new military mentality' in Peru, a surprising number of explanatory factors may legitimately be advanced, none of which alone seems to have been decisive but all of which contain an element of truth. Briefly, commentators have cited: the relatively humble origins of Peruvian officers and their social isolation from the upper classes; their thorough acquaintanceship with national realities; the impact on them of the 1965 guerrilla uprising, based in the countryside, which they had had to repress, but which awakened in them a new social awareness; and the circumstantial shift to the right of their traditional adversary, the populist party APRA (Alianza Popular Revolucionaria Americana) (since returned to the fold of Latin American social democracy), which, it is argued, freed them from their past alliance with the oligarchy. Finally, the legendary influence of the Centre for Higher Military Studies (CAEM), where, from 1951 on, Peruvian officers studied national realities, and where economics and sociology were taught, has sometimes been presented as decisive.

A good number of these factors need, however, to be placed in perspective. The social origin of Peruvian officers was no different in the fifty years prior to 1968, during which the military appeared to serve faithfully as 'watch-dogs of the oligarchy'. Chilean officers were, for their part, no less isolated from civilian elites than their northern neighbours. South American armies were, without exception, characterized by the distribution of their garrisons throughout the national territory, and by the human contact and social mixing of officers and men resulting from conscription. And the traumatic experience of guerrilla war in other republics, far from having progressive consequences, had pushed the military in a counter-revolutionary, anti-reformist direction. *Aprista* influence on military ideol-

ogy, and the excellent relations of certain military leaders with those of
APRA, whose alliance with the Right was only tactical, belie as well
explanations founded on a supposed compensating evolution of the two
old, intimately related enemies. As for the CAEM with its progressive
professors, it raises more questions than it answers. It is the eternal
enigma of the chicken and the egg: how did it happen that radicalized
leftist intellectuals came to be teaching in a School for Higher Military
Studies in the first place? We may suggest, summarily, that the doctrine
of 'integral security' (the antithesis of the doctrine of national security in
vogue in the neighbouring armed forces), which assigned pride of place
among military objectives to the struggle against underdevelopment and
poverty, was the product of a specific domestic and international conjuncture. The reformist officers who seized power in 1968, taking advantage of
a political impasse, were in fact only a minority, and the bulk of the armed
forces, rather conservative and passive as elsewhere on the continent,
followed their lead somewhat reluctantly and only for a few years.

In Bolivia, the reformist experience was even briefer, and its denoue-
ment more tragic. The nationalist opportunism of a part of the military
establishment gave rise to the illusion of a revolution by surprise, without
a real base, which was to be quickly replaced by a classic rightist military
dictatorship that lasted for ten years. After the accidental death in 1969 of
General René Barrientos Ortuño, in power since 1964, his principal aide,
General Alfredo Ovando, staged a successful coup d'état. The new president's programme diverged decisively, however, from his predecessor's
strong-arm anti-communist policies. Nationalism and economic liberation became the order of the day. This leftward turn seems to have been
accepted by the Bolivian officer corps in order to protect the military
institutions themselves, whose unpopularity was at its height. Haunted
by the spectre of another '9 April' – that is, of a civilian explosion like
that of 1952 which would again destroy the armed forces – the military
decided to replace a strategy of coercion by one of seduction. The armed
forces were, nevertheless, sharply divided between a 'nationalist' wing
grouped around General Juan José Torres, and what was, in all probabil-
ity, the majority sector, concerned more about public order and the anti-
subversive struggle.

The achievements of Ovando's 'revolutionary-nationalist' government,
in practical terms, were slight. Entangled in paralyzing contradictions, it
only survived until the rightist coup d'état of 4 October 1970, and could
not fulfil the promises of the 'armed forces' mandate' it published, which

had anticipated the recovery of the nation's natural resources, the installation of refineries to process local mineral production, the establishment of heavy industry, an independent foreign policy, and workers' profit-sharing. His government should nevertheless be credited with the repeal of the petroleum code, which had advantaged foreign companies, with the nationalization of Bolivian Gulf Oil, and, above all, with putting an end to the military occupation of the *altiplano* mining towns and with restoring union rights.

Four days after Ovando's fall, General Torres, with the support of a 'union of popular forces' (organized labour, leftist political parties and students) in turn seized power in a counter-coup. Reliance on civilian aid betrayed the intrinsic weakness of the progressive wing of the armed forces. But Torres, isolated and almost bereft of a military base of support, was to take a series of measures strongly desired in popular urban milieux and among the miners. He expelled the Peace Corps, nationalized a zinc mine previously privatized in dubious circumstances, and, above all, increased miners' wages which had been slashed by 40 per cent in 1965 under Barrientos. If Torres was a 'stroke of luck' for the Bolivian Left, he effectively signed a suicide pact with his allies when he accepted the establishment of a Popular Assembly, composed of representatives of trade unions and Marxist parties, which set itself up as an organ of dual power and sacrificed the progressive military, without whom nothing would have been possible, on the altar of revolutionary orthodoxy. On 21 August 1971, the right-wing colonel Hugo Banzer Suárez, supported by business interests (especially from the Santa Cruz region) and initially also by Paz Estenssoro's MNR, overthrew Torres, putting an end to what Augusto Céspedes labelled the 'pyrotechnics of the infantile Left'.[11] Banzer's government, which lasted until 1978, came to resemble other right-wing South American military dictatorships of the period.

In Panama, the nationalist orientation of the government of the National Guard, product of the coup d'état of 8 October 1968, was another 'divine surprise'. The principal objectives of General Omar Torrijos, head of the government junta, which, beginning in February 1969, adopted an intransigent attitude towards Washington, were to reconquer sovereignty over the Panama Canal Zone, occupied by the United States, and to recover the interoceanic waterway. The Panama Canal was the key to the

[11] Augusto Céspedes, 'Bolivia, un Vietnam simbólico y barato', *Marcha*, Montevideo, 1 October 1971.

regime's foreign policy, and may account as well for the policy of mobilization and national harmony which the new government sought to promote domestically. Thus, new labour legislation protected the unions and provided for a minimum wage, collective bargaining agreements, and severance pay. In rural areas, Torrijos promulgated a moderate, gradual agrarian reform which progressively affected unproductive *latifundia* and a great part of foreign-owned landed property.

Like other military revolutions, Torrijos' regime was not concerned with coherence or ideological purity. It flirted with Cuba, and in 1974 resumed diplomatic relations with Castro and with the socialist countries. Panama supported both Salvador Allende and the 'revolution' of the Peruvian military, with whom the National Guard in power maintained close relations. General Torrijos committed himself heavily to the Sandinista cause, affording important direct aid to the guerrillas in their struggle to overthrow Somoza. The government of the National Guard thus seemed to side at every opportunity with 'anti-imperialist' forces and regimes. At the same time, however, taking advantage of the free circulation of the U.S. dollar in Panama, the military regime turned the country into a banking haven by removing all restrictions on currency transfers, by guaranteeing the confidentiality of financial transactions, and by exempting movements of funds from taxation. As a result, Panama became the most important financial centre in Latin America.

In 1977, after prolonged, laborious negotiations, agreement was reached with Washington on a new treaty providing for Panama's complete recovery of the Canal in the year 2000 and the evacuation of the Canal Zone by the United States. But speculation that the treaty would mark the end of the Torrijos era and its nationalist alliance in Panama proved mistaken. Until his accidental death in August 1981, Torrijos was the regime, and the question was even raised whether his government could properly be considered a system of military domination, or whether it was not, rather, the rule of an enlightened *caudillo,* in whom survived many of the characteristics of the traditional model. However, the weight of the National Guard's commanders in the semi-constitutional regime established after Torrijos' death left no room for doubt as to the military nature of the regime itself. Civilian presidents proved ephemeral, interchangeable figureheads, and opposition demonstrations in the late 1980s which demanded the departure of General Manuel Noriega made no mistake as to who really held power in Panama.

We cannot survey here all the more or less abortive attempts to establish a 'radical praetorianism' in Latin America. It is nevertheless worth pausing to consider the apparently very institutional February 1972 coup d'état in Ecuador, which coincided with the country's transitory oil boom. The new regime, under the presidency of General Guillermo Rodríguez Lara, proclaimed itself 'revolutionary, nationalist, social-humanist and for an independent government'. It numbered among its goals an improved distribution of income, the struggle against unemployment, and agrarian and tax reform. It promulgated an 'integral plan of transformation and development' for 1973–7 which provided for the strengthening of the public sector. But it was in the sphere of oil resources that the military proved most active and resolute. In 1972, General Rodríguez Lara created a national administration of hydrocarbons, the Corporación Estatal Petrolera Ecuatoriana (CEPE), to oversee the exploitation of the nation's recently discovered petroleum. At a time when Ecuador had become the fourth-ranking oil exporter on the continent, the state, which revised all contracts and concessions, controlled over 80 per cent of petroleum exploitation. But this manna converted Ecuador into a *rentier* country, and the rhetoric of reform tended to remain a dead letter. The bureaucracy grew. Speculation enriched a 'new class' of which the military formed part. The merchants of Guayaquil accused the government of communism when it sought to check the haemorrhage of foreign exchange by reducing imports. On 11 January 1976, Rodríguez Lara was dismissed by the chiefs of staff of the three services, as a consequence of unrest in the business community and serious social tensions.

These various experiments in military reformism had numerous points in common. The regimes in question were all distinguished by their paternalism. The people were invited to remain onlookers of the changes from which they benefited. In Peru, it was a question of 'humanizing society by decree'. The military-inspired combination of self-management and authoritarianism flowed from an essentially 'anti-political' conception of participation. Thus, General Velasco Alvarado always refused to envisage the creation of a party of the Peruvian revolution, contenting himself with setting up, in 1971, a bureaucratic agency of mobilization dubbed the 'National System for the Support of Social Mobilization' (SINAMOS). The latter's role never exceeded that of an instrument for social manipulation intended to weaken the Marxist and *aprista* unions, and in the course of its existence its failures largely outnumbered its successes. The story was little different in Bolivia and Ecuador, or even in Panama where the official party, a disparate collection of businessmen and intellectuals in-

spired by Marx or Fanon, was united only by its taste for power and by
military tutelage.

Radical or at least progressive minorities existed, of course, in most of
the armed forces on the continent, even in those in which conservative
tendencies always remained predominant. What requires explanation is
why and how, at certain times and places, these minorities managed to
take command, neutralizing the counter-revolutionary or at least conform-
ist inertia of their comrades-in-arms. The characteristics of the period
1968–72 seem, in this regard, to have played a not insignificant role. The
parallel evolutions that we have traced took place at a historically auspicious moment. They would doubtless have been impossible in the absence
of a continent-wide climate of détente. It was the new configuration of
forces in play in the western hemisphere which permitted the undeniable
nationalist upsurge that traversed the continent and which opened the way
to the progressive sectors of certain national armed forces. This hemispheric thaw reflected modifications in the local strategy of the two great
powers, and, more precisely, a change in the attitude of the two regional
poles represented by Cuba and the United States. Havana, following its
setbacks on the continent, had come to accept the doctrine of 'socialism in
one country' and a policy of 'tacit' co-existence with the United States.
Washington, for its part, bogged down in Vietnam and confronted with
the Middle East problem, could henceforth pay less attention to Castroism. A policy of 'benign neglect' required prudence and discretion. The
United States was thus prepared, provisionally, to accomodate itself to the
nationalist wave in Latin America. Only in 1973 did positions in general
begin to harden once again. The military reform movements we have
discussed were, nevertheless, not, as some have suggested, 'imperialism's
second wind', or a 'Pentagon manoeuvre' designed to fabricate a congenial
image for the Latin American armed forces. Radical neo-militarism was
neither a historical curiosity nor a reactionary ruse, but a reflection both of
policies originating in the local armed forces and of fluctuations in the
inter-American situation.

THE LIMITS OF MILITARISM: 'CIVILIAN STATES'

It has sometimes been suggested that the social structures of the Latin
American nations were scarcely favourable to the development of representative democracy. There do exist, however, scattered across the region, a
small number of countries where civilian government has prevailed over

relatively long periods of time. A non-interventionist military is not a completely unknown species in Latin America.

At the end of the 1980s, four Latin American nations stood out as having enjoyed thirty years of uninterrupted civilian government and military subordination. We do not assert that these four favoured countries have been paragons of democratic virtue, nor that they have been immune to attempted coups d'état. It is simply that Costa Rica, Venezuela, Mexico and Colombia are the only Latin American states in which, for over a quarter of a century, civil-military relations have been non-praetorian, and in which putschists, when they have existed, have not met with success.

By what means, and due to what causes, has this civilian supremacy been established? These four 'civilian' states can doubtless teach us some useful lessons on the relations between the military and politics in Latin American societies. Their experience may also furnish clues permitting us better to understand the process of demilitarization which was under way in other states in the region in the 1980s.

Costa Rica obviously wins the palm for democracy in Latin America. This small country, peaceful though situated in a region given over to dictatorship and popular upheavals, has not suffered a military coup d'état since 1917 and, indeed, since 1948 has had no armed forces. Costa Ricans take great pride in the fact that they have twice as many primary school teachers as police (the only security forces). To understand Costa Rica's recent political development, it is necessary to return to the civil war of 1948 which marked a point of rupture and no return in the institutional history of the country. The administration of Rafael Angel Calderón Guardia (1940–4), and that of his successor Teodoro Picado (1944–8), had dissatisfied the grand coffee bourgeoisie, which reacted against their reformist tendencies, but also the new middle classes, which rejected their corruption and disregard for constitutional guarantees. At the close of Picado's administration, the government refused to recognize the results of the recently held presidential election which were unfavourable to Calderón Guardía who, allied to the Communist Party and with the support of the Church, was seeking a second term. As a consequence, in February 1948, the opposition, as disparate in its composition as the governing coalition, having concluded that the electoral route was closed, launched a military uprising which, in the reigning Cold War climate, received the blessing of the United States. The nucleus of the anti-government alliance consisted of a group of modern entrepreneurs and of

urban sectors that advocated reform and defended social-democratic principles. They also had the support, however, of the coffee oligarchy, the
financial sector, large merchants and most of the traditional parties.

The opposition Army of National Liberation, led by José Figueres
Ferrer, carried the day. Only after the collapse of the government's forces,
of mediocre quality and undermined by amateurism, did the real difficulties begin for the opportunistic alliance which had overthrown the former
regime. The grand bourgeoisie had indeed had no other objective than
putting an end to the 'Red Peril'. Figueres and his *liberacionistas,* however,
refused to reverse the reforms carried out by the defeated government. The
victors, moreover, although they banned the Communist Party, also nationalized the banks, enacted a tax on capital, and broadened the state's
economic responsibilities. They hoped as well to institutionalize the army
of 'liberation' which had given them their victory. The grand bourgeoisie
and the conservative groups, so weakened politically that they had been
obliged, in order to recover power, to form an alliance with these 'newcom-
ers', had no military organization at their disposal and wished to reconstitute the standing army. The conservatives dominated the Constituent
Assembly elected in 1949, but Figueres and the *liberacionistas* had force on
their side. The compromise solution finally arrived at involved the legal
abolition of all military institutions. This measure was principally intended to disarm what, in 1951, was to become the Partido de Liberación
Nacional (PLN), but it also offered the victors of the civil war a guarantee
that the oligarchy would not reconstitute a state military force in opposition to them.

The symmetry of this too perfect solution was deceptive. The 'security
forces', a sort of national police force created after the disappearance of the
two armies, were in fact mainly recruited from among the men of the
charismatic 'Don Pepe' Figueres, elected president in 1953. But if the
PLN has since been Costa Rica's leading political formation, it has not
won every presidential election. Historically the largest party, it has never
been a dominant, much less a single, party. Whenever an incumbent's
formation has been defeated in the succeeding presidential election, the
new administration has made use of the spoils system in the officer corps
in order to prevent the surreptitious creation of a one-sidedly partisan
armed force. The officers of the national police thus lack the meritocratic
career guarantees enjoyed by their counterparts in most other Latin American armed forces. The organizational weakness which results does not
favour the transformation into a standing army of a police force with such

slight independence from changing political authorities. The Costa Rican case tends, conversely, to support the hypothesis that the autonomy of armed institutions is indeed one factor explaining their political activism. In Costa Rica, civilian bureaucrats are more highly professionalized than the security forces, making the latter's militarization virtually impossible and, consequently, rendering civilian supremacy absolute.[12]

Venezuela – in the first third of the century the classical land of tropical tyranny – for more than thirty years after 1958 represented a model democracy, where the alternation in power of Social Democrats and Christian Democrats was accompanied by record levels of electoral participation. The change began in 1945. In October of that year, young officers and the social democratic party Acción Democrática (AD) overthrew the government of General Isaías Medina Angarita (1941–5), the second military successor to the dictator General Juan Vicente Gómez, whose long reign, from 1908 to 1935, had ended only with his death. A junta presided over by Rómulo Betancourt, and thereafter president-elect Rómulo Gallegos, attempted for three years to implement an advanced democracy with socialist tendencies, but their efforts were cut short in 1948 by a conservative coup d'état. Colonel Marcos Pérez Jiménez, after eliminating his rivals, established a new dictatorship which was to last a decade, during which Venezuela seemed to have transited from *caudillismo* to praetorianism only to fall back into a barely modernized system of personal power. In January 1958, elements of the armed forces finally drove Pérez Jiménez from power. Since then, civilian government has prevailed.

The vicissitudes of the thirteen troubled years from 1945 to 1958 were not without bearing upon the success of the new regime. The beneficiaries of the coup d'état of 1945, which lacked unanimous opposition support, had monopolized power, while relying on mass mobilization that frightened moderate opinion. Anxious to implement their programme without delay, they had simultaneously launched a series of reforms that increased the number of their adversaries, who came to include the Church as well as the propertied elites, conservative politicians and foreign companies. The overwhelming majorities that the new authorities consistently won at the polls, far from establishing their legitimacy, only increased the fragility of their position. The excessive predominance of AD and its supposed sectarianism were thus its principal weaknesses, and the experience would not be

[12] Costa Rica's lasting demilitarization and therefore singularity in Central America must also, of course, be seen in light of its distinctive colonial past and social formation.

forgotten. The restoration of democracy ten years later and its consolidation owed much to the lessons of this painful learning process. The main priority henceforth was to be the building of a stable, lasting democracy. The various parties reached agreement on a code of conduct and co-existence. Oil wealth is often said to have played a positive role by helping to lower the political stakes. The search for technical solutions to problems, indeed their depoliticization, would not have been possible without this godsend. However, such natural resources do not, in themselves, necessarily possess the virtue of guaranteeing political stability. Mention should rather be made of the crucial role played by prudent and firm political leaders, among them Rómulo Betancourt, elected president in 1958 and, until his death in 1981, the grand old man of Venezuelan democracy. His term of office (1959–64) was, nevertheless, not wanting in putsch attempts from both the right and the left. The constitutional president's tasks were not facilitated either by Castroist guerrilla warfare or the attacks of the Dominican dictator Rafael Leonidas Trujillo. The military Right, favourable to the fallen Pérez Jiménez, and Castroist military elements, each revolted twice during these years. Betancourt always put down military rebels with a firm hand, while at the same time displaying great concern for the armed forces which he treated as his special preserve. He demonstrated consummate skill in using the danger represented by leftist guerrilla bands to rally his party's former enemies – the Church, the armed forces, and business circles – around the country's institutions. The very failure of the guerrillas and, following an amnesty, the reintegration in the democratic concert of the leftist parties which had opted for a strategy of armed struggle, contributed in no small measure to the consolidation of Venezuelan democracy.

From Betancourt's administration until the early 1990s, the Venezuelan armed forces remained politically silent. They did not, however, lack power, and the means employed to assure civilian control were not strictly limited to those spelled out in the nation's constitution. Well-equipped, disposing of an impressive budget, the Venezuelan armed forces were characterized, from the Betancourt period on, by the strong influence of Acción Democrática in the officer corps. The military were also integrated into the world of the decision-makers, which increased their authority. Officers performed numerous extra-military functions in the nationalized sector of the economy and in the management of development programmes. Was the attribution of such tasks to the armed forces simply a sensible use of the military's skills or, primarily, an ambiguous – and perhaps, in the long-term, ineffective or even counter-productive – means of civilian control?

In post-revolutionary Mexico, the strength of the state and the legitimacy of the official party identified with it have been the principal bases of a well-tried stability and civilian preponderance. The Partido Revolucionario Institucional (PRI) is all-powerful, and nothing is considered as falling outside its competence. It is hardly surprising that such a system, which controls the whole of national life, also controls the military. To understand this one-party, civilian preponderance we need to consider briefly the history of the Revolution which began in 1910–11. By 1914–15, the federal army of the dictator Porfirio Díaz had been defeated and dismantled, and the reign of the warlords had begun. Each *caudillo* was master of his own army, and therefore of the territory he occupied. Most of the revolutionary chieftains were originally civilians. It is not surprising that these makeshift generals, who had risen precisely against Díaz's federal police (*rurales*) and his army, manifested a violent anti-militarism, which has never completely disappeared from official ideology. Pancho Villa always opposed the creation of a standing army, while Venustiano Carranza refused the title of generalissimo, and had himself modestly styled 'first chief'. The Mexican warlords were in fact at the head of political parties in arms, not of military institutions.

These predatory armies, which lived off the land and were difficult to demobilize, were expensive. The existence of multiple centres of power and violent political rivalries tore the state apart and weakened a nation economically in ruins. Reconstruction required that the turbulent 'generals' be brought to heel and the numerous centrifugal forces unified. Alvaro Obregón and then, above all, the *caudillo máximo,* Plutarco Elías Calles, whose influence from 1924 to 1935 was considerable, laid the foundations of the modern Mexican system. After the violent elimination of recalcitrant war chiefs (notably Emiliano Zapata and Pancho Villa), they put an end to the regional *caciques'* power by simultaneously creating a genuine army and centralized political institutions. In order to demilitarize politics, it was indeed necessary to militarize the military. However, the essential problem was to compel the 'revolutionaries' to unite and to accept certain rules of the game, the first of which was to settle their differences through political institutions rather than through violence. The unification of the revolutionary family was to be the task of the party of the Revolution.

This party, born of the state and not formed to win elections, had as its first mission to unify and master the armed factions. It was the sole legitimate political forum where the revolutionary forces might discuss their common interests. The party thus put an end to the confusion of military and civilian roles whenever such mingling proved dysfunctional to the strengthening of the state. The newly recast army was even for a time integrated in the Partido Nacional Revolucionario (PNR), the ancestor of the PRI, in accordance with the corporatist model of European totalitarian regimes. The military were thus, paradoxically, politicized in order to demilitarize politics and to neutralize them by incorporating them into the power structure in a subordinate position.

Few armed forces on the continent have since maintained a lower profile. For some time military leaders in Mexico were barely distinguishable from the political class, and did not need to intervene militarily to manifest their power. Once academy-trained officers attained the highest military posts, the armed forces' modest manpower and limited budget indicated that they remained weak. Given the country's importance, the size of its territory, its wealth and its role in the region, these limitations on the military may seem surprising. Mexico, with the second largest population in Latin America, had 175,000 men under arms in 1992 (up from a mere 80,000 in the mid-1970s). It thus possessed the second or third largest armed forces in the region, much smaller than Brazil's and approximately equal in size to Cuba's. However, Mexican defence expenditures ranked only sixth in the region (behind those of Brazil, Venezuela, Argentina, Cuba and Colombia) and Mexico maintained the lowest percentage of its population under arms and dedicated the lowest percentage of its national product to defence of any major Latin American nation. The Mexican military are, of course, not totally absent from the political stage. They are doubtless consulted on all problems concerning public order. But their room for manoeuvre is limited by the party-state's strength and cohesiveness. Officers, far from dominating the political system, are selectively integrated into it through clientelist arrangements.

If economic and social criteria are used as a yardstick, Colombia would have seemed, in the twentieth century, one of the Latin American countries fulfilling the fewest of the requisite conditions for the development of democracy. The country has historically been distinguished by widespread poverty, high levels of illiteracy, poor national integration from both a geographical and a human point of view, a powerful Catholic Church tempted by secular power, large-scale landed estates for a long time immune to change, and a tradition of political violence carried on by ineradicable Marxist guerrilla groups and by drug traffickers. Yet, since the beginning of the century, Colombia has enjoyed a two-party political system which has ensured it a degree of constitutional continuity rare on the continent. Colombian democracy has been, it is often asserted, of a limited, 'Athenian' variety, marked by massive rates of electoral abstention and an oligarchic two-party system. But it has been a democracy nevertheless, suspended only once for a four-year period (1953–7), during which a military dictatorship presided over by General Gustavo Rojas Pinilla was imposed, with the support of a majority of both the traditional parties, Conservatives and Liberals, in order to put an end to the undeclared civil war known as the *violencia.*

The Colombian armed forces have traditionally been weak, poor and lacking in prestige. The creation of a professional military organization was undertaken in Colombia later than in most other major South American countries. Colombian forces have also differed from others on the continent in that, for almost half a century, they have been constantly engaged in active military operations. The development of the military's role was closely linked to the rural, political phenomenon of the *violencia.* As this undeclared confrontation between Liberals and Conservatives, which claimed an estimated 200,000 lives between 1948 and 1956, gradually disappeared, it only gave way to Castroist or Maoist guerrilla warfare. The army has thus always been divided into small units and scattered about the country, engaged in patrolling insecure zones and in combing rebellious or refractory areas. Inured to counter-insurgency warfare, composed of small detachments, it has not been the sort that stages coups d'état. And yet the army is not bereft of power, at least at the local level, where its cadres often replace a civilian administration unable to perform its tasks. It thus has a place in the heart of the power system, but conventional, usurpatory militarism has appeared only once in the history of contemporary Colombia.

The modern Colombian armed forces, though born under the aegis of the Conservative Party, accommodated themselves well to the Liberal-Conservative system. In the post-war period, the military has played the essential role of defender of the two-party framework. Its task has been to liquidate any political alternative which the system has been unable to absorb through co-optation and *transformismo.* The method employed has consisted in closing off all legal outlets to outsiders, with recourse to the armed forces to finish off diehards who have been driven into using violence. This was the fate of the reformist Liberals in 1948, of the ANAPO of former dictator Rojas Pinilla in 1970, and of the Frente Unido of the priest and sociologist Camilo Torres, killed in 1966 while fighting in the ranks of the Ejército de Liberación Nacional (ELN).

The armed forces have thus constituted an important element of the established regime which, it has been said, they respect just so long as the government in turn maintains unchanged its treatment of the military. Within this framework, the Colombian armed forces seem to have possessed sufficient power to satisfy their wishes. Given a free hand, or very nearly, in the struggles against the leftist guerrillas, and endowed with a considerable degree of autonomy in matters of finance and internal organization, the military have readily accepted that the other spheres of the state escape their control. The state in Colombia is weak, hemmed in by business organizations to which it has delegated broad powers, the private sector having charge of many economic responsibilities which elsewhere are governmental. The military seem to manage questions of public order, understood in the broad sense of the term, with almost complete liberty. The political parties share out the spoils of the state and distribute sinecures in the purest clientelist tradition. This parcelling out of power, with each sector receiving its share, has, at least until recently, managed to assure a sort of equilibrium and political stability.

What then may we say, in the light of these four cases, are the principal factors tending to limit militarism? They would seem to be simultaneously military and socio-political, and indeed the presence of elements of both seems generally to be indispensable. On the military side, weak or late professionalization has served, contrary to accepted belief, to reinforce civilian ascendancy. The fusion and confusion of political and military roles, a source of instability in the nineteenth century, have appeared in the twentieth as a means of controlling the armed forces. The strength and coherence of the party system also seem to have played a decisive role, sometimes, as in Colombia, because the deeply rooted system in place has identified itself with civil society, other times, as in Mexico, because the party system has confounded itself with the state, in a situation of historically legitimized monopoly.

Democracy understood as compromise and as agreement, tacit or otherwise, for social co-operation necessarily implies low social stakes and a pact prohibiting recourse to the armed forces against the government in power. To put it differently, a political regime in which the opposition is situated within the institutional system, in which progressive political and trade union forces are weak, and in which mass participation is controlled and channelled, or marginalized, has a somewhat better chance of withstanding militarization. Nonetheless, there are no foolproof methods for assuring civilian ascendancy, just as there is no model for lasting, guaranteed demilitarization. In this regard, the only constant in Latin America has been the ephemeral, unstable character of the region's military regimes.

DEMILITARIZATION? THE 1980S AND BEYOND

At other moments in this century, Latin American military dictatorships have given way to civilian, representative institutions. It is, however, rare to witness a general military retreat from power like that which occurred during the 1980s. Indeed, in mid-1990, not a single military government, in the strict sense of the term, remained in power in Latin America. Only in Paraguay was the president still a general, but one who in 1989 had put an end to General Stroessner's long reign and initiated a process of liberalization. Civilian government was restored in eleven Latin American nations (twelve if Paraguay is included) between 1979 and 1990.[13] Moreover, in 1989 the Duvalier regime in Haiti fell and, after an interlude dominated by the army, the Catholic priest Father Aristide, the victor in free elections, was inaugurated president in February 1991. In these countries, the transmission of power by civilian presidents to elected civilian successors may be taken as one index of the solidity of demilitarization. In 1990, power had already changed hands between elected civilians thirteen times in the first nine 'demilitarized' countries.[14]

The ebbing of the military tide in Latin America was the result of global, regional and local factors. That the return to civilian rule was drawn out over a twelve-year period (1979–90) alerts us that continent-wide causes did not produce simultaneous or uniform effects in each country, and that national characteristics played a key role in determining the timing, as well as the conditions and consequences, of military withdrawal. Two contextual elements, however, can be identified which tended to favour the process of demilitarization in a substantial number of cases.

---

[13] The timetable of democratization was as follows:

Date	Country	First civilian president
1979	Ecuador	Jaime Roldós Aguilera
1980	Peru	Fernando Belaúnde Terry
1982	Honduras	Roberto Suazo Córdova
	Bolivia	Hernán Siles Zuazo
1983	Argentina	Raúl Ricardo Alfonsín
1984	El Salvador	José Napoleón Duarte
1985	Uruguay	Julio María Sanguinetti
	Brazil	José Sarney
1986	Guatemala	Vinicio Cerezo Arévalo
1989	[Paraguay]	[General Andrés Rodríguez Pedotti]
	Panama	Guillermo Endara Galimany
1990	Chile	Patricio Aylwin Azócar

[14] Twice in Ecuador, Peru, Honduras and Bolivia, and once in Argentina, El Salvador, Uruguay, Brazil and Guatemala.

The first of these was the worldwide economic crisis, with its repercussions in Latin America including, notably, the foreign debt problem. Hard times generally favour changes in government. Where the military had come to power promising improved rates of development through a reorganization and modernization, progressive or conservative, of the socio-economic order, the crisis had particularly strong de-legitimizing effects. The erosion of support was reflected, among other ways, in a rise in 'democratic demand' from sectors which previously had given little sign of desiring higher levels of participation.

The second such element was U.S. regional policy in favour of the (at least superficial) predominance of civilian, representative, democratic forms. The Democrat Jimmy Carter (1977–81) gave new importance during his presidency to human rights questions and, despite occasional blunders, his efforts helped launch the demilitarization movement. The Republican presidents Ronald Reagan (1981–9) and George Bush (1989–93) did not share Carter's moralistic, human-rights orientated attitude, but nevertheless did not abandon the Democratic administration's opposition to usurpatory militarism. Indeed, from 1976 to mid-1990, a period embracing Reagan's entire eight years in office and the first year and a half of Bush's presidency, no democracy on the continent succumbed to a military coup d'état, and nine of the eleven Latin American countries (ten of twelve with Paraguay) which returned to civilian control between 1979 and 1990 did so during the Reagan and Bush administrations.

Reagan, Bush and their advisers may have finally concluded, given the counter-productive results of U.S. policy in pre-revolutionary Cuba and Nicaragua, that supporting unpopular dictatorships had a disconcerting tendency to open the way to communist control. Moreover, in the 1980s, elections in Latin America seemed unlikely to result in left-wing victories. But the U.S. position on democratization seem to have been dictated above all, under the two Republican presidents, by Washington's policy requirements in Central America. The Reagan and Bush administrations' activities in the isthmus revolved around two poles: unmitigated hostility toward the Sandinista regime in Nicaragua, and assiduous support for the Salvadoran government against its guerrilla opposition. Washington's Central American crusade, carried on ostensibly in the name of democracy in its struggle with totalitarianism, dictated the creation of regimes respecting at least the forms of democracy among its local allies. (In this regard, congressional pressure on the executive decision-makers in Washington also played a significant role.) The credibility of U.S. policy in Central

America could be further augmented by a South American policy rejecting military dictatorship. The Republican administrations' stance was doubtless the product of a mix of democratic conviction and tactical calculation tinged with hypocrisy. Washington applauded noisily, for example, the May 1984 presidential election in El Salvador, won by Napoleón Duarte, but refused any legitimizing effect to the arguably more democratic presidential election held just six months later, in November, in Nicaragua, in which the Sandinista leader Daniel Ortega triumphed. The Bush administration, furthermore, brandished the restoration of democracy as one justification for its December 1989 invasion of Panama. Nevertheless, policies pursued by Reagan and Bush objectively favoured the trend toward demilitarization throughout Latin America.

If these general factors were at work in many of the transitions from military rule, the unfolding of the process took distinct paths in each of the various countries which returned to civilian government.

In the mid-1970s, Peru and Ecuador were both ruled by progressive military regimes, founded respectively in 1968 and 1972. In both, the reformist programmes were strongly identified with the regimes' initial leaders, both of whom fell – General Velasco Alvarado in 1975, General Rodríguez Lara in 1976 – after losing support within the armed forces. In Quito, the new military Supreme Government Council quickly announced a return to civilian rule. Although Ecuador's petroleum-led economy was fairly strong, the military government had found itself under attack, for conflicting reasons, by both business interests and organized labour, and was particularly concerned by sharpening divisions within the army itself. In Peru, Velasco's successor, General Francisco Morales Bermúdez, also faced opposition from both ends of the political spectrum, the Left demanding an acceleration of the reforms, the traditional parties a return to constitutional government. He had, in addition, to confront a worsening economic situation, attributable in large measure to defects in the regime's initial programme. The Peruvian military, however, at first showed no disposition to surrender power, in part, it seems, because elements in the army remained committed to the revolutionary programme, in part because the armed forces wished to prepare for what they viewed as a likely armed confrontation with Chile.

The military held power for three more years in Quito, but organized a referendum in 1978 on a new constitution, and oversaw elections in 1979. In Peru, the 'second phase' of reforms proved incoherent and ineffectual. Morales Bermúdez, faced with intensifying domestic opposition and a rapidly declining economy, in early 1977 finally announced the calling of a Constituent Assembly which began meeting after a vote the following year. The regime nevertheless managed to put off presidential and legislative elections under the new constitution until mid-1980. In both Ecuador and Peru, the outgoing regimes attempted to guide the choice of the first civilian president. In Quito, manipulation of the electoral laws blocked the candidacy of Assad Bucaram, the military's populist bugbear, but could not prevent the election of Jaime Roldós, the husband of Bucaram's niece. (Roldós, however, soon broke with the Bucaram clan.) In Lima, irony of ironies, the army's preference went to the candidate of its historical enemy, the APRA, which, it felt, would maintain the military regime's reforms without dangerous radicalization. Peruvian voters thereupon elected Fernando Belaúnde, the very man the military had deposed in 1968 and an uncompromising opponent of the former regime. Nonetheless, in both Ecuador and Peru the armed forces retired to their barracks in good order. Continuing to dispose of substantial autonomy, they remained a political actor to be reckoned with.

In Argentina, Brazil, Uruguay and Chile, conservative military regimes had seized power to 'protect' democracy from dangerous 'subversive' movements. They proposed to carry out programmes of national reorganization which were to restore state authority, put an end to social 'disorder' and overcome economic stagnation, thereby permanently eliminating any future leftist threat. The timing and manner of these regimes' retreat from power were determined by a combination of factors. The latter included national political traditions; the nature of the crisis which had provoked the founding coup d'état; the military's success in eliminating the radical Left and the methods employed in doing so; the degree of political institutionalization achieved by the military regime; the divisions in the armed forces resulting from their politicization; the success of the regime's programme to restructure national society and the economy; and, in the case of Argentina, the disastrous Malvinas/Falklands episode.

In Argentina, even before the 1982 war, the regime had been weakened by internecine strife and the bankruptcy of its socio-economic programmes. It was, paradoxically, undermined as well by the very success of the 'dirty war' it had waged against domestic enemies. Those who had promoted the armed forces' seizure of power no longer felt the need for military protection, and the enormous abuses committed provoked repulsion even among certain former supporters of the regime. The attack on the Malvinas/Falklands was itself decided, in large measure, to shore up weakening domestic political support. Without their military defeat, the armed forces would doubtless have been able to prolong their regime for years and negotiate favourable terms for their departure from the government. The surrender in the Malvinas/Falklands precipitated a second, domestic surrender leaving them, at least temporarily, at the mercy of their political opponents.

In Brazil, the semi-authoritarian, semi-competitive regime established in 1964 had never wholly abolished representative procedures or banned political parties. In 1974, the government itself initiated a 'thaw' intended to culminate in the regime's 'legalization' or constitutional legitimation through the use of electoral and juridical subterfuges allowing the official party, though a minority, to retain its grip on power. This institutionalization strategy – which effectively employed pre-existing political arrangements, appropriately modified, on the regime's behalf – and the regime's continuing economic successes allowed the military to prolong their control for more than a decade. In the early 1980s, however, due to sharpening differences of opinion within the armed forces and, above all, to a serious economic crisis, the military gradually lost control of the process. In the indirect presidential election of 1985 (the regime had refused to reintroduce direct voting despite strong popular pressure), the momentum of the democratic movement led, contrary to official intentions and expectations, to the victory of Tancredo Neves, the opposition candidate. As a result of the latter's untimely death, the first president of the 'New Republic' was, however, to be José Sarney, the opposition's vice-presidential candidate but formerly one of the civilian leaders of the military party, who had only recently rallied to the idea of political change. Sarney took office, moreover, under the former regime's constitution, and with the armed forces still ensconced in the positions in the state they had acquired during twenty-one years of military rule.

In Uruguay and Chile, as in Argentina, the military regimes had been extremely repressive. Nevertheless, the two countries' solid democratic traditions in large part survived, and influenced their transition to civilian rule. In Uruguay in 1980, the armed Left had been eliminated, and the regime's liberal economic reforms seemed to be producing results. The collegial military leadership, concerned that excessive politicization was threatening the unity of the armed forces, decided to call a plebiscite on a new constitution, with regular elections promised for 1981. To the astonishment of the regime but also of its opponents, the proposed constitution was massively rejected by the voters. The military never thereafter recovered the initiative, as the pre-existing civilian parties reorganized and the economic situation took a sharp turn for the worse. Within the armed forces, those favouring a negotiated retreat from power managed gradually to get the upper hand. Meetings between military leaders and political party representatives culminated in the famous Naval Club Pact, later officialized in a number of interim constitutional clauses offering the military guarantees for the autonomy of the armed forces and awarding them a temporary right to oversee restored democracy. In the presidential and legislative elections of 1984, the relative strength of the traditional political parties and of the moderate Left approximated their percentage of the vote in the last free ballot in 1971.

In Chile, the personalization of power in General Pinochet's hands diminished the risk of political divisions arising among or within the military organizations and afforded a certain coherence and continuity to the regime's policies. For the armed forces, but also for the civilian sectors which feared a return to the situation prior to 1973, the traditional strength of the Left in Chile argued for prolonging the military regime until the political and socio-economic reforms it had initiated could take root. In 1980, taking advantage of a short-lived economic boom, the regime resolved, as in Uruguay, to call a plebiscite on a new constitution. This text, which was to found a new 'authoritarian' democracy, would not however enter fully into effect until 1989 at the earliest. Interim provisions named General Pinochet president for the period from 1981 to 1989, prolonged his dictatorial powers essentially unchanged, and determined that in 1988 the regime would itself name the single candidate to be proposed to the voters in a presidential plebiscite. Only if the regime's nominee were rejected would an open presidential election finally be held in 1989, with the winner to take office in 1990.

By fair means and foul the Chilean regime won its constitutional plebiscite. For the next decade, the Constitution of 1980 and the timetable it fixed became the centrepiece of the military government's political strategy. The opposition initially rejected the legitimacy of the plebiscite, of the constitution and of its interim provisions. In 1983 and 1984, with the country plunged in a grave economic crisis, it organized huge demonstrations which threatened the regime's survival. But as the economic situation improved, most opposition leaders came grudgingly to recognize that they could only unseat the military by playing by the regime's rules. In the presidential plebiscite of October 1988, General Pinochet, the official candidate, was defeated after the centre and left parties led a vigorous campaign against him. (The general nevertheless received 43 per cent of the vote.) Those in the army who might have refused to accept Pinochet's defeat were neutralized by almost unanimous civilian support for a return to 'normalcy', as well as by the opposition of certain of their peers, in particular the leaders of the other services. Over the following months, government and opposition negotiated several constitutional amendments modifying some of the charter's most aggressively anti-democratic provisions. The Constitution of 1980 nevertheless remained fundamentally intact when Christian Democrat Patricio Aylwin, the opposition coalition's candidate in the December 1989 presidential election, took office in March 1990.

In Bolivia, the process of return to civilian government was particularly chaotic.[15] Military governments reigned in La Paz from 1964 to 1982, interrupted only by three brief civilian interludes. However, during that period Bolivia had no fewer than seventeen presidents, eight of whom (six military officers and two civilians) held office during the final four years of military dominance. The numerous intra-military transfers of power were regularly accomplished by coup d'état. In Bolivia, the dissensions within the armed forces, and notably within the army, thus reached heights not generally attained elsewhere, in part as a consequence of the similar fragmentation of civilian groups.

Hugo Banzer Suárez, the most significant of the military presidents, managed to rule for seven years, from August 1971 when he overthrew General Torres. He assumed office to eliminate an alleged left-wing threat, with the support of elements in the armed forces, but also of business interests and, initially, of Paz Estenssoro's MNR. Banzer's government, increasingly militarized after 1974, often had harsh words for democracy, crushed domestic dissent and proclaimed neo-liberal economic convictions. In November 1977, elections were nevertheless announced for July 1978. On this issue, Banzer appears to have acceded unwillingly to pressure from certain sectors of the military. The latter's discontent had diverse roots, including concern about deepening divisions in the armed forces, dissatisfaction with personal career prospects, and commitment to constitutionalism. Banzer's prestige had also suffered a blow in military circles as a result of the collapse of negotiations with Chile for a corridor to the Pacific. The demand for elections was bolstered by a weak but growing

---

[15] For an analysis of the Bolivian case, see Jean-Pierre Lavaud, *L'Instabilité Politique de l'Amérique Latine: Le Cas Bolivien* (Paris, 1991), *passim*, but particularly pp. 73–142 and 273–82.

civilian opposition and by the Carter administration's influence, though not by economic difficulties which only became serious in 1978. Banzer intended to utilize the electoral process to legitimate his own continuance in office. It was the armed forces, again, which rejected his candidacy and imposed that of Air Force General Juan Pereda Asbún. The elections, however, generated their own dynamic and, despite substantial fraud, Pereda lost the 18 July 1978 vote. The plurality victor was apparently Hernán Siles Zuazo, candidate of the leftist coalition, the Frente de Unidad Democrática y Popular (FUDP or UDP). The election was immediately annulled. Although Banzer was tempted to hold onto power, Pareda disposed of stronger support in the armed forces and, despite the electoral results, was sworn in as president.

Banzer's fall marked the end of coherent military rule. The period from 1978 to 1982 was one of political anarchy.[16] During these troubled years, certain elements in the armed forces, for both ideological and corporate reasons (career interests, fear of further fragmentation and deprofessionalization), tended to support a return to civilian government and democratic forms. These positions were associated, for example, with the name of General David Padilla, who overthrew Pareda in November 1978 and under whom free but inconclusive elections were held in July 1979. Other elements tended to favour continued military control, for an extremely mixed bag of reasons. Among the latter were reticence to turn over the government to left-leaning civilians, the desire to shield the armed forces from civilian reprisals, and personal interest, professional but also pecuniary. General Luis García Meza's year-long reign (July 1980–August 1981) will remain in the annals of military power as an example of right-wing military profiteering and drug-traffic centred gangsterism. Civilian behaviour, however, also played a key role in retaining the military in politics. The fragmentation of civilian political and social forces and the rivalries among them (often deriving from personal ambition) impeded the emergence of a coherent alternative to military rule. Civilians continued, moreover, to knock on the barracks door to resolve their own political disputes.

[16] The two civilian presidents during this period were Walter Guevara Arce (8 August–1 November 1979) and Lidia Gueiler Tejada (16 November 1979–17 July 1980). The five military presidents following Pareda were General David Padilla Arancibia (who overthrew Pareda in November 1978); Colonel Alberto Natusch Busch (who overthrew the civilian Walter Guevara Arce on 1 November 1979), General Luis García Meza Tejada (who overthrew the civilian Lidia Gueiler Tejada in July 1980); General Celso Torrelio Villa (named president by a military junta in September 1981, a month after the fall of García Meza); and General Guido Vildoso Calderón (named president in July 1982 after Torrelio's forced resignation, and who opened the way to Hernán Siles Zuazo's accession to the presidency in October 1982).

García Meza's coup d'état intervened on 17 July 1980, just after the third election in less than than two years (on 29 June 1980) had again given a plurality, on this occasion a substantial one, to Siles Zuazo. When in 1982 the military again turned power over to civilians, the Congress elected in 1980 was convened. Siles was thereupon chosen president, with the support of his own coalition and of all other parties except retired General Banzer's Acción Democrática Nacionalista (ADN). The preceding anarchic period had strengthened both the military and the civilian elements favouring the armed forces' return to their barracks. On the military side, the constant turnover of presidents corroborated the warnings of those who had predicted an exacerbation of institutional fragmentation, and thrust into prominence officers of slight professional prestige, like García Meza, whose conduct had discredited the military institutions. Perhaps more important, the events of the period convinced the civilian electoral losers, and conservative groups more generally, that a UDP government would be less noxious to their interests than continued, disorderly military rule. The electoral weight of Banzer's ADN also served to guarantee the Right an important voice in a Congress in which Siles' UDP did not dispose of a majority.

In Paraguay, General Alfredo Stroessner fell on 3 February 1989, after thirty-four years in power. Stroessner's personalist government had rested on three pillars: the state apparatus, the mass-based Colorado Party and the armed forces (whose officers were also required to join the party). In the 1980s, as the ageing dictator's decline opened a succession crisis, a sharp split in the governing party led to the expulsion of its more moderate faction (the *tradicionalistas*) by that closer to Stroessner (the *militantes*). In early 1989 Stroessner and the *militantes* attempted to extend their purge to the armed forces. When General Andrés Rodríguez Pedotti, the regime's most important military figure after the dictator himself, found himself obliged to choose between involuntary retirement and revolt, he successfully rebelled.[17] Stroessner's overthrow was, of course, not the mere consequence of factional infighting. During the dictator's last years, Paraguay confronted increasing economic and social difficulties, which elements in the business community, the Colorado Party, and the armed forces themselves, recognized could not be overcome without more effective state action, unimaginable under the corrupt old system. General Rodríguez convoked elections for May 1989. The opposition parties, deci-

---

[17] Despite his family ties to Stroessner, whose daughter is married to his son.

mated by decades of repression, were left little time to organize, and Rodríguez himself won the presidency with 73 per cent of the vote. A Constituent Assembly, elected in December 1991, in which the government party held an absolute majority, nevertheless voted to deny the general-president the right to stand for re-election in May 1993. The next president was expected to be a civilian, but would clearly be obliged to seek compromises with a still powerful military attached to its prerogatives and privileges.

Washington's influence weighed most heavily in the return to civilian government in Central America. It was assuredly the dominant factor in ending direct military rule in El Salvador, where in 1984 the army accepted the electoral victory of the same Napoleón Duarte to whom they had refused the presidency in 1972, and in Honduras, where after the 1981 elections a military dictatorship with a civilian bias was replaced by a highly militarized constitutional regime. As for Panama, although General Manuel Noriega faced significant internal opposition, he was only finally toppled on 20 December 1989 by a U.S. invasion force. Guatemala represents a case apart. The Guatemalan military, unlike that in El Salvador, managed brutally to blunt the local guerrilla threat without recourse to U.S. aid (cut off due to human rights violations), and Guatemala, which unlike Honduras has no common border with Nicaragua, could remain relatively aloof from Washington's conflict with the Sandinistas. The Guatemalan military's decision to call elections for a Constituent Assembly in 1984, leading to presidential and legislative elections in 1985, resulted essentially from local causes: economic difficulties, a search for political legitimacy, concern about increasing military politicization and fragmentation. Vinicio Cerezo, the Christian Democrat who won the presidential contest, was not the armed forces' first choice but, sensitive to Guatemalan realities, he acknowledged frankly that he would have to share power with the military.

In the countries where, between 1979 and 1990, civilian rule was restored, the newly installed regimes could indeed not always be said to dominate fully, or even simply to control, their armed forces.[18] The initial period following the military's withdrawal from power was, in particular,

---

[18] We have benefited in the following pages from the insights of Alfred Stepan in his study *Rethinking Military Politics: Brazil and the Southern Cone* (Princeton, N.J., 1988), pp. 68–127, although we have not strictly adhered to his distinction between 'military contestation' and 'military prerogatives'.

often marked by open friction between military and civilian authorities. Where political repression had been especially brutal, the most delicate question confronting the newly elected civilians was that of the sanctions to be imposed for human rights violations committed under the military regime. The civilian government's decision whether to prosecute the perpetrators depended, in each case, on the solidity of its political position, on the gravity of the crimes committed and the public pressure for action, but also on the new leadership's judgement whether criminal prosecution would advance or set back the process of demilitarization. The failure to sanction offenders could validate the military's vision of recent national history, setting a dangerous precedent, but protracted investigations and trials, followed perhaps by prison sentences for the guilty, might retard the military's evolution toward a focus on professional concerns.

In Argentina, where the crimes committed were particularly extensive, and where a military weakened by defeat in war had been forced to abandon power precipitously, Radical president Alfonsín initially took a severe position on human rights abuses, convinced that exemplary treatment of officer-offenders could contribute to breaking the military's half-century stranglehold on power. The civilian government repudiated the amnesty the armed forces had granted themselves in the military regime's final days, commissioned a controversial report on the exactions committed, and prosecuted and jailed the principal leaders of the former regime. The grumbling in the armed forces became louder, however, as the investigations and indictments threatened to implicate hundreds of lower-ranking officers. Alfonsín, who foresaw the impending explosion, took steps to limit the scope of the prosecutions, but an army revolt in April 1987, led by middle-ranking officers, initiated a spiral of military pressures (including two additional uprisings in January and December 1988) and civilian concessions. The Peronist Carlos Menem, who succeeded Alfonsín in 1989, defused the problem on the military's terms by pardoning all the convicted officers, including the leaders of the former regime, and abandoning any further prosecutions. He has, however, shown himself unyielding with the participants in a fourth revolt which broke out in December 1990, when all prior problems were on the point of being resolved.

In Brazil, Uruguay and Chile, the military left power in a stronger position than in Argentina. In Brazil, where the level of repression had been relatively low, the military dominated Congress voted an amnesty in

1979 for crimes committed since 1964. The new civilian government
which took office in 1985 did not question this measure, and offences
committed after 1979 were not vigourously investigated. In Uruguay, the
negotiated withdrawal of the military from power embraced an implicit
amnesty, sanctioned in 1986 in a law voted by the new, democratically
elected Congress. Opponents of this measure, however, collected sufficient signatures to submit the amnesty law to plebiscite. In April 1989,
56.7 per cent of the voters confirmed the amnesty, in part doubtless
because of contemporary troubles in neighbouring Argentina.

In Chile, the Aylwin administration sought to profit from Alfonsín's
experience. A commission was established, as in Argentina, to investigate
crimes committed under the military regime, and, in addition, legislation
was adopted awarding compensation to the victims of human rights violations and their families. The new Chilean government, however, despite
campaign declarations to the contrary, finally opted to accept the amnesty
decreed by the military regime in 1978 for offences committed since the
1973 coup d'état. The broad jurisdiction granted military courts in Chile
also provided cover to the accused in many cases. The Aylwin administration, nevertheless, favoured the prosecution of human rights violations
which occurred between 1978 and 1990, and, furthermore, on the urging
of the executive, Chilean civilian courts increasingly tended to hold that
defendants might benefit from the 1978 amnesty only following a full
judicial investigation of the charges against them. The on-going or potential human rights investigations threatening numerous officers were a
principal cause of a menacing army show of force in December 1990 which
created serious apprehension in civilian circles. The army clearly preferred
to see amnestied offences dismissed without enquiry, and the amnesty
itself extended through March 1990.

In Central America, the treatment of the human rights question in El
Salvador and Guatemala presents a revealing contrast. Given the vital U.S.
role in the Salvadorean civil war, President Duarte and his successor,
Alfredo Cristiani, elected in 1989, could avail themselves of Washington's
influence in their struggles with their own military. Moreover, if the peace
negotiations with the guerrillas, seriously engaged in 1990 with the
support of a substantial fraction of the Salvadorean Right, were to succeed,
the government had to give some satisfaction to the undefeated rebels'
demands for a purge of major human rights violators from the army. The
civilian administrations were thus, in a few cases, able to impose (or to
promise to impose) limited criminal and professional sanctions, with at

least symbolic significance, on the most flagrant military offenders.[19] In Guatemala, where the army crushed the local guerrillas without recourse to Washington's aid, the civilian government of Vinicio Cerezo could not put an end to massive human rights violations, much less prosecute the perpetrators of earlier crimes.

The human rights issue apart, the question may be raised how much general political influence the military retained in those countries where civilian presidents and legislatures were elected. After all, in December 1977 General Morales Bermúdez in Peru spoke unabashedly of the military's intention to transfer 'the government' but not 'power' to civilians.[20] It seems useful, as a loose framework, to distinguish the military's role in matters which, in Western democracies, are normally considered outside their purview from the influence they exercise on questions generally admitted to concern the armed forces. In the latter cases, it is necessary to weigh whether the military are confined to an advisory role or can impose their own points of view. The military's political influence and their inclination to exercise it are furthermore not static phenomena, and may increase or diminish after the military abandons the government.

In Argentina, the military's political power was at a historic low when President Alfonsín was inaugurated in 1983. The new government took advantage of its strong position to retire dozens of high-ranking officers, to create and attribute to a civilian the post of defence minister (reducing the three service heads to sub-ministerial rank), to redefine the armed forces' mission (limiting it to foreign defence), to reorganize the military command structure, and to slash the defence budget and conscription.[21]

---

[19] In conformity with the Esquipulas II accords, adopted by the Central American presidents in August 1987, the Salvadorean government promulgated an amnesty (over the objections of the Left which argued that the measure principally benefited the military). The peace accords signed in January 1992 provided for an *ad hoc* commission to carry out a purge of the army, and also committed the Salvadorean government to effectuating a general reduction and reorganization of the army. On the peace process in El Salvador, see Alain Rouquié, *Guerres et Paix en Amérique Centrale* (Paris, 1992), pp. 362–77.

[20] Cited by Julio Cotler, 'Military Interventions and "Transfer of Power to Civilians" in Peru', in Guillermo O'Donnell, Philippe C. Schmitter and Laurence Whitehead (eds), *Transitions from Authoritarian Rule: Latin America* (Baltimore, Md., 1986), p. 168.

[21] In Argentina, military expenditures were 21 per cent lower in 1983 than in 1982. After a slight rise in 1984, they tended to decline until 1987, when they were 24 per cent lower than in 1983. After two slightly higher years, they declined sharply again in 1990, when they were 33 per cent lower than in 1987. In 1990, military expenditures thus represented only 41 per cent of those in 1982, and 51 per cent of those in 1983. *SIPRI Yearbook 1992: World Armaments and Disarmament*, Stockholm International Peace Research Institute (Oxford, 1992), p. 263. Here and below, we have chosen to compare the changes in real military expenditures from year to year, not their changes as a percentage of total government spending or of the gross national product.

The military revolts of 1987–9, which succeeded in putting an end to human rights prosecutions, also expressed resistance to these civilian-imposed organizational changes and budgetary limitations. However, although the rebellions reinforced the government's wariness in dealing with the military, they did not force the Alfonsín administration into concessions on these structural matters. President Menem, for his part, in certain regards went beyond his predecessor, ordering significant cutbacks in the number of professional military personnel (not just conscripts), and calling a halt to prestigious weapons development projects, notably the missile Condor II. The Argentine military's influence outside the sphere of national defence also declined after 1983. And Menem's neo-liberal economic programme, stressing the transfer of public companies to the private sector, did not overlook traditionally military-controlled enterprises.

In Brazil under President Sarney (1985–90), the armed forces retained great influence. Sarney's cabinet included six general officers on active duty – the three service ministers, but also the chief of the Military Cabinet, the chief of the Armed Forces General Staff and the director of the Serviço Nacional de Informações (SNI). These and other military representatives did not hesitate to intervene in a widerange of matters going well beyond national defence. The military thus played, for example, a key role in thwarting programmes for agrarian reform. Nor did the military have grounds to complain about the government's treatment of the armed forces. The defence budget (which the military regime had kept relatively low) was increased in real terms, and Sarney did not seriously attempt to limit military institutional autonomy. Suggestions for the creation of a unified Defence Ministry, for example, were not pursued, and the military got their way in refusing to reincorporate officers discharged for having opposed the prior regime.[22]

With the passage of time the Brazilian armed forces' high political profile has nevertheless begun to diminish. President Fernando Collor de Mello, who succeeded Sarney in March 1990, limited military representation in his cabinet to the three service ministers. Under Collor the military generally desisted from intervening openly in public debate on controversial issues not directly related to national defence. The armed forces in 1991–2, did, however, overtly express dissatisfaction with reduced de-

---

[22] Brazilian military expenditures were 4 per cent higher in 1985 than in 1984, and 15 per cent higher in 1986 than in 1985. From 1987 to 1989, they fell approximately to the 1985 level, then in 1990 experienced a substantial 26 per cent increase. The military regime, in its final years, had reduced military expenditures. Expenditures for 1984 were 18 per cent lower than in 1982. Only in 1990 did military expenditures finally exceed (by 8 per cent) the figure for 1982. *SIPRI Yearbook 1992: World Armaments and Disarmament*, p. 263.

fence budgets (justified by the government as part of its austerity programme) and low military pay. Their displeasure was made known
through regular channels, but also through other time-tried methods,
including declarations by retired officers' organizations and even public
demonstrations. The decision in April 1990 to abolish the SNI, replaced
by a civilian-directed Secretária de Asuntos Estratégicos (SAE), was also
not well-received. During the 1992 impeachment proceedings against
President Collor, however, the armed forces' leadership maintained a stony
silence, broken only rarely to emphasize their support for constitutional
procedures. Their behaviour contrasted markedly with the military's open
intervention in favour of President Sarney in the late 1980s, when the
shortening of the latter's term was being debated in the Congress.

The new 1988 Brazilian constitution assigns the armed forces a more
restricted political role than its predecessors, but drafters rejected propositions to limit the armed forces' activities solely to foreign defence. They
incorporated among the military's duties 'the defence of the constitutionally established branches of government (*poderes constitucionais*) and, on the
initiative of any one of them, of law and order'.[23] Furthermore, two
successive civilian administrations have not succeeded in reducing significantly the armed forces' autonomy or in evicting the military from certain
of the powerful high- and middle-level non-defence positions they hold.

The Chilean transition to civilian government was unique in South
America. Only in Chile did the military leave power with their confidence
high, unmitigatedly proud of their sixteen-year rule. The country indeed
found itself in the midst of an impressive economic boom which the armed
forces attributed, with some justice, to the economic and social policies
they had dictatorially imposed. And, in Chile, the military had succeeded
in laying to its taste, in the Constitution of 1980, the institutional bases
of the new civilian order and of the latter's relations with the armed forces.
The armed forces, and particularly the army, made no secret of their intention to assure that the new civilian government would continue to respect
'their' constitution. To this end, they could rely on a monopoly of force,
but also on their considerable political leverage, founded somewhat amor-
phously on the prestige they had acquired from the military regime's economic successes, but also more concretely on a de facto alliance with the
Right with which there existed a coincidence of views on a range of issues.

The Constitution of 1980 explicitly attributed to the armed forces and

[23] Article 142 of the Brazilian Constitution of 1988. (The translation is ours.)

Carabineros (police) the mission of guaranteeing *el orden institucional de la República*, and in the months before Aylwin's inauguration in March 1990 the army high command underlined its determination to fulfil this role, if necessary 'by the use of legitimate force'. The Constitution created a National Security Council (four of whose eight members are the three service commanders and the director of the Carabineros) which numbers among its functions 'to call to the attention (*hacer presente*) of any authority established by the Constitution' any threat to the nation's *bases de la institucionalidad* or to national security. The Constitution furthermore restricted the president's choice, in the nomination of the commanders-in-chief of the armed forces and Carabineros, to the five most senior general officers, and provided that, once named, they could not be removed by him during their four-year term of office. A special interim provision allowed the commanders serving when the new constitution came into effect in 1990 to continue at their posts until 1998. (General Pinochet thus remained firmly ensconced as army commander-in-chief.) The constitutional text was supplemented by special 'constitutional organic laws' for the armed forces and the Carabineros, providing, among other things, that the president's power to name, promote or retire officers might only be exercised in accordance with the service commanders' recommendations, and that future defence budgets might not be inferior to that for 1989, adjusted for inflation.[24]

After March 1990, overt civil-military friction, involving particularly the army, focussed in great measure, although not exclusively, on the treatment of human rights violators, questions of past military corruption and General Pinochet's continued tenure as army commander-in-chief. Given the new government's circumspection in dealing with the armed forces, and the latter's awareness of the lack of public support for a new military adventure, these issues did not, however, appear to present a grave menace to restored democracy. At the same time, civilian authorities have proven unable to shake off the yoke of numerous constitutional and quasi-constitutional provisions, not only those directly concerning the military but also others – fixing, for example, the special congressional majorities required to amend the Constitution or the organic laws, providing for the nomination of a significant number of unelected senators and establishing

---

[24] We refer to the text of the Constitution of 1980 as amended in the plebiscite of July 1989. On military questions, see Article 90 (on the role of the armed forces), Articles 95 and 96 (on the National Security Council) and the Eighth Interim Clause (authorizing General Pinochet and the other commanders-in-chief to remain at their posts until 1998).

the rules governing the election of both houses of Congress – which have undercut the new government's capacity to carry out its programmes in many different fields.

In Peru, the course of civil-military relations after 1980 was determined in large part by the unforeseen development of the Shining Path (Sendero Luminoso) revolutionary movement. The first civilian president, Belaúnde, distrusted the armed forces, which had unseated him in 1968, but, perhaps for that very reason, chose from the start to treat them gingerly, abstaining from attempts to impinge on their institutional autonomy and showing himself generous in their budgetary allocations.[25] The military, for their part, disenchanted with their governmental experience and subject to public animosity, seemed disposed to let the civilians govern, as long as their institutional autonomy was respected. The rise of Sendero was, however, to draw the armed forces back to the centre of the political stage. By late December 1982, with the guerrilla movement growing rapidly despite police repression, both Belaúnde and the armed forces' command were constrained to admit that the military, though largely unprepared for the task, would have to take a controlling hand in the counter-insurgency operations.[26] Local military commanders were vested, by decree, with political and military authority over the zones affected by the insurrection. Over the years, these zones have come to encompass a large portion of the national territory.

From 1983, Belaúnde and his two civilian successors, Alan García (1985–90), the first APRA president in the history of Peru, and Alberto Fujimori (1990–), within broad limits gave the armed forces a free hand in determining military counter-insurgency strategy and tactics. The soldiers, however, themselves experienced difficulty in defining a coherent, effective response to Sendero, with certain military leaders preaching, and applying, a classic, lethal 'internal war' approach, while others insisted on the importance of attacking the socio-economic roots of the insurrection. During the García administration's final years, with the country in the

---

[25] In 1981 and 1982 Peruvian annual military expenditures rose in comparison with expenditures for 1979 and 1980. Military expenditures peaked in 1982, when they were 168 per cent higher than in 1979 and 94 per cent higher than in 1980. Though expenditures from 1983 to 1985 were substantially lower than in 1982, they remained significantly higher than those of 1979–80. *SIPRI Yearbook 1989: World Armaments and Disarmament* (Oxford, 1989), p. 187.

[26] The former regime had confidence in its reform programme and had discounted the likelihood of a serious guerrilla uprising. Its expensive armaments programmes had stressed the purchase of heavy weapons adapted to conventional border warfare against Chile or Ecuador, but of limited or no value in the Peruvian sierra.

grip of a grave economic crisis, the counter-insurgency effort suffered as well from a scarcity of resources.[27]

Sendero's intransigent refusal to contemplate a negotiated solution in some measure constrained successive governments to rely on a largely military response to the guerrilla movement. Not that the civilian presidents always simply passively accepted military viewpoints or misconduct. Human rights issues were the most frequent and visible source of civil-military friction, but conflicts over human rights also implicitly involved wider questions about the best manner to get on with defeating the insurgency. Belaúnde showed himself relatively indulgent with the armed forces on these issues. On taking office, Alan García initially emphasized his commitment to reducing human rights abuses. The number of large-scale peasant massacres by government forces seems to have tapered off after 1986, whether because of García's efforts or because the military itself came to find them counter-productive. But, despite the occasional spectacular removal of high-ranking officers, the military continued to dominate the formulation of counter-insurgency policy and to benefit from almost complete impunity in its application. President Fujimori, even before the events of 1992, had amply demonstrated his complaisance toward the military's autonomy in counter-insurgency matters.[28]

On 5 April 1992, Fujimori closed the Peruvian Congress and took power into his own hands in an *auto-golpe,* a coup d'état by those in office. He clearly could not have acted without the foreknowledge and consent of the military high command. A perspicacious analyst of Peruvian affairs has suggested that, after 1980, the Peruvian armed forces were not so much won over to liberal democratic values as convinced that, for them, representative democracy had become an unavoidable 'strategic' choice, since the re-imposition of direct military rule would meet with widespread civilian resistance and might plunge the nation into civil war.[29] The 'civilian' coup d'état of 1992 confirmed in a sense the intuition that the military would

[27] Peruvian annual military expenditures increased substantially in 1985 (+17 per cent) and in 1986 (+13 per cent), fell considerably in 1987 (−17 per cent), rebounded in 1988 to a new high (+51 per cent), then plummeted in 1989 (−38 per cent) and continued to fall in 1990 (−16 per cent). Expenditures in 1990 were the lowest in a decade, representing only 54 per cent of those in 1982, and 52 per cent of those in 1988, the two peak years. *SIPRI Yearbook 1992: World Armaments and Disarmament,* p. 263.

[28] The armed forces may also be less than perfectly neutral in electoral politics. In the late 1980s, when for a time Alfonso Barrantes, the expected candidate of the coalition Izquierda Unida (United Left), appeared the likely victor in the 1990 presidential election, the question was openly discussed in Peru whether the military would accept a victory of even the moderate Left at the polls.

[29] See Cynthia McClintock, 'The Prospects for Democratic Consolidation in a "Least Likely" Case: Peru', *Comparative Politics,* 21, 2 (1989): 127–48.

not risk taking power in their own name. In a population disillusioned by twelve years of democratic rule, the civilian president's seizure of power benefited from public support which might not have been forthcoming had the military taken power directly. Fujimori's rapid decision to hold elections for a new 'Democratic Constituent Congress', to begin meeting in December 1992, reflected his recognition of the need to present at least a democratic façade. His position was reinforced by the capture in Lima in September 1992 of 'Chairman Gonzalo', Abimael Guzmán, the legendary founder and leader of Sendero, whose imprisonment seriously undermined the guerrillas' organization and morale. But Fujimori's relations with the armed forces remained problematic, especially in view of his persistent attempts to increase his personal control over them.[30]

These four cases illustrate, each in its own way, that the demise of military government does not automatically ensure the extinction of the armed forces' political influence or autonomy. Additional examples could without difficulty be cited in other South American nations, and the exercise would prove still easier in Central America.[31] Military government was, furthermore, re-established in Haiti in September 1991, though the army attempted to mask its rule by naming a civilian prime minister. And, most disquieting, in Venezuela, usually cited as the paragon of Latin American democratic institutionalization, two attempted military coups d'état, in February and November 1992, came perilously close to overthrowing the constitutional but highly unpopular government of President Carlos Andrés Pérez. It cannot thus be asserted that the Latin American military have universally resigned themselves to playing a secondary political role, or even simply to exercising from the wings an influence which in some cases remains preponderant.

U.S. influence is, nevertheless, in the 1990s, likely to prove a factor favourable to the maintenance of civilian regimes in Latin America. Support for formal democratic institutions continues to constitute an important instrument of U.S. foreign policy throughout the world. With the passing of the Cold War, the United States may also prove less sensitive to

---

[30] In November 1992 Fujimori had in fact to confront the rebellion of a small number of army troops under the leadership of a prominent retired general, ostensibly favourable to a rapid return to constitutional rule.

[31] Hernán Siles Suazo in Bolivia had to confront no fewer than four attempted military coups d'état during his term of office. In Central America talk of military intervention was particularly abundant in Guatemala and Honduras. In Nicaragua, the Sandinistas' continuing control of the army after their 1990 electoral defeat created the rather unusual situation of a civilian government subject to the surveillance of left-orientated military forces. (The preceding Sandinista government was, of course, not a 'military' regime.)

the security threat supposedly posed by progressive regimes to the south. Washington's concern for the suppression of drug production and trafficking could, however, tend, once again, to create a special relationship between the U.S. military and certain of their Latin American counterparts, while implicating the local armed forces in what are, from their perspective, controversial domestic political issues.

The future political role of the Latin American military will however, in all likelihood, depend primarily on the will and ability of civilians in the various nations to shape orderly, effective political systems, capable of convincingly defining attainable goals, of resolving unavoidable political and social conflicts, and thus of minimizing interested civilian support, or appeals, for military intervention. If, once voters have run the gamut of available political options, elected governments have not proven able to limit popular aspirations appropriately while, at the same time, satisfying their citizens' reasonable demands, the way may be open to more authoritarian governmental forms relying on military backing and participation, even if the armed forces, as in Peru, do not exercise power directly.

In the South American countries where the armed forces held power in the 1970s and 1980s, renewed civilian appeals for direct military political intervention seem relatively unlikely. In all these nations (except Peru) support for radical left-wing solutions to the nation's socio-economic problems has at least temporarily waned. Moreover, earlier military-directed experiments in socio-economic reform having generally failed, civilians seem to have lost whatever confidence they had in the armed forces' capacity to resolve the nation's dilemmas. They possess as well a fresh and searing recollection of military authoritarianism and human rights violations. If, in Venezuela, in the wake of the military uprising of February 1992, a goodly number of citizens seemed to feel that a military regime might be a lesser evil than the ruling civilian government, it was doubtless in part because the armed forces' claims to political neutrality and technocratic competence had not in recent memory been put to the test.

Finally, we should raise the question of the military's attitude toward their own future political role. The 'new professionalism' of the 1960s, which incited the armed forces to take an increased role in domestic questions, was characterized by a certain hubris. The military's confidence in their own problem-solving capacities was thereafter shaken, particularly in the South American countries, by confrontation with intractable realities. Where the armed forces have recently ruled, they do not, in consequence, generally seem eager to reassume the burden of resolving complex, troublesome political and socio-economic questions. Throughout Latin America, the armed forces also discovered from hard experience that the exercise of political power tended to undermine their unity, professionalism, and in consequence their military capacity. In this regard, the Argentine armed forces' humiliating defeat in the Malvinas/Falklands War was exemplary. Despite the purchase of large quantities of modern armaments, the highly politicized Argentine military, consumed by their governmental responsibilities and torn by fierce internecine struggles, proved incapable of planning and executing a co-ordinated war effort or, in most cases, even of mustering the necessary fighting spirit to confront the well-trained British troops. The Argentine catastrophe served a warning on the military throughout the continent.

The military in Latin American seem, nevertheless, not to have ceased thinking of themselves as the bulwark and incarnation of the nation, the guardians of its borders but also of its institutions, of its way of life and, transcendentally, of its very soul. It is revealing that, in the Southern Cone, the armed forces have never institutionally expressed any remorse for the domestic 'dirty wars' they waged in the 1970s and 1980s. To the contrary, they persist in vaunting as their finest hour their role in stamping out 'subversion'. With the end of the Cold War, the military's political ideas could evolve, especially among younger South American officers, toward a more 'anti-Yankee', national-populist stance in response, in part, to the local application of U.S.-inspired neo-liberal economic policies. Such a development would not, however, necessarily alter, and might rather even confirm, the military's underlying conception of the political role which is rightfully theirs in the nation and the state. Indeed, the leaders of the Argentine military revolts of 1987–90 and of the Venezuelan military uprisings of 1992 employed, among other justifications for their actions, precisely this sort of vague national-populist reference.

In 1985 in Argentina, President Alfonsín's defence minister observed that 'the normalization of the armed forces will probably require fifteen to eighteen years'.[32] To effectuate this 'normalization', the civilian and military authorities in each country would have to undertake jointly to redefine military doctrine, establishing a convincing function for the armed forces which would distance them from domestic political concerns. There is little sign that such efforts are widely under way or, where they

---

[32] Cited by Ricardo Sindicaro, 'Trois ans de démocratie en Argentine (1983–1986)', *Problèmes d'Amérique Latine*, 82 (1986), La Documentation Française, Notes et Etudes Documentaires, 4822, p. 15.

have been attempted (as in Argentina), that they have met with much success. But what, precisely, is an appropriate 'military' role for the armed forces in a region in which the extra-continental threat (always somewhat illusory) has vanished, in which border conflicts are rare and limited, and in which physical threats to the state, if they do arise, seem indeed most likely to express themselves through domestic actors?

CONCLUSION

The armed forces and militarism, their socio-political manifestation, seem to be subjects difficult to approach in a scholarly fashion. Observers tend to pass value judgements on the extra-military action of the armed forces, whether to approve it or to condemn it. Certain among them seem to be engaged above all in a search for those responsible for or, rather, guilty of militarist usurpation. Since military rule is perceived as a pathology of political life, an anomaly with respect to the sovereign good of pluralist democracy, in their indignant impatience with it these observers are some-times led to conclude that they have discovered general explanations for, or even the single key to, a phenomenon which they may not have given themselves sufficient time to explore and describe. The loose, instrumen-tal interpretations which have proliferated in this field cannot, however, simply be ignored. All the more so, since our interest in the military as such can only be justified if these metaphorical visions of militarism, ascribing military hegemony to a historical, geographical or social 'else-where', and considering the armed forces themselves as indecipherable 'black boxes', prove to be questionable or, indeed, mistaken.

The historical continuity of militarism, which is not just a contemporary occurrence, seems to have resulted, not in deepening our comparative under-standing of the phenomenon through the confrontation of numerous experi-ences from different periods, but, principally, in obscuring its mechanisms through the simple projection of the present onto the past or, even more commonly, of the past onto the present. The weight of history can be sensed in the importance assumed by determinist interpretations of all sorts, while civic-minded indignation at praetorian treachery has inspired various con-spiratorial accounts of military intervention in political life.

Since much of our lexicon of military power is derived from Spanish (*juntas, pronunciamientos*), and since the majority of Latin American coun-tries were formerly colonized by Spain, the conclusion has often been somewhat hastily drawn that there exists a type of civil-military relations peculiar to the 'Hispanic' world, and that an 'Ibero-Latin' juridical tradition accounts for the chronic incapcity of Latin American states to sustain stable democratic regimes. However, the existence, become commonplace, of military regimes throughout the underdeveloped world, and notably in sub-Saharan Africa, would suffice to indicate the limits of such a thesis. In Latin America itself, examples of military governments in non-'Iberian' countries are not lacking. Surinam, where the army seized power in 1980 and again in 1990, was a colony of the Netherlands until 1975, and the majority of its inhabitants are of Asian descent, while Haiti, basically under military rule since the fall of 'Baby Doc', is a former French colony populated principally by the Creole-speaking descendants of African slaves.

A more elaborate version of this explanation has sometimes been advanced. Contemporary Latin American militarism should be understood, according to this historicist formulation, as the heir to and continuator of yesterday's *caudillismo,* which arose out of the anarchy of the wars of independence. Twenty-one years of military rule in Brazil (1964–85) would alone belie this hypothesis, given the 'negotiated' and peaceful character of that country's emancipation from Portugal in 1822. Furthermore, in a number of those countries where nineteenth-century warlords did play an important role, there is no observable continuity between the predatory power of the old *caudillos* and contemporary forms of national government. In Mexico, where *caudillismo* predominated from the unpredictable President Antonio López de Santa Anna in the middle of the last century to the chiefs of the revolutionary period, no putsch has been attempted for fifty years. Similarly, Venezuela, ruled practically from independence until 1940 by strong men who had seized the central government by force, for more than thirty years after 1958 provided a model of stable, representative democracy. Conversely, other Latin American countries, notorious in recent decades for instability and militarism, in the past, following the disturbances and uncertainties of the independence era, knew protracted periods of civilian ascendancy and unbroken series of legally chosen governments. Argentina from 1862 to 1930, but also Peru, Chile, Bolivia or El Slavador at the end of the nineteenth century, among others, provide examples of this pattern.

To confine militarism to its proper historical limits, it is, moreover, important to insist that the chiefs of armed bands engaged in civil strife, military amateurs though often decked out with bombastic titles, cannot be likened to professional career officers. The *caudillo,* an improvised warrior, was indeed the product of the collapse of the Spanish colonial state and of social disorganization. The officer, to the contrary, is an organization man, and exists only by and for the state. Modern military organizations are public, bureaucratized institutions which hold the technical monopoly of the use of legal violence, while the *caudillos* represented private violence rising up against the state monopoly or upon its ruins. It is not by confusing the actors and their nature that we can utilize the past to facilitate our understanding of the present.

Closer to our own times, conspiracy theories of history, generally accompanied by an uncritical economism, have brought into favour instrumentalist interpretations of military power. After the 1964 coup d'état in Brazil and, above all, after that of 1973 in Chile, the idea has gained currency that the Latin American armed forces are manipulated from abroad. Responsibility for militarist usurpation tends thus to be shifted to the tutelary power. The Latin American military are presented as mere extensions of Washington's military apparatus and as the recognized defenders of U.S. interests. For some, the armed forces of Latin America are scarcely more than the 'political parties of international capital'. The establishment of authoritarian regimes from the 1960s to the 1980s would thus have responded to the needs of the contemporary phase of capitalist development, either because multinational capital and the new international division of labour required strong, repressive governments to curb social movements and guarantee investment, or because the transition from light industry to the production of intermediate and capital goods could not be accomplished within a democratic, civilian framework. According to this hypothesis, the Latin American military had in some sense been 'programmed' to ensure the 'deepening' of the industrialization process.

Such interpretations do, admittedly, have a certain basis in fact. Their proponents properly stress the Latin American military's dependence on the Pentagon in recent decades, and recall the crucial influence exercised by Washington on the Latin American armed forces through the training programmes offered at its military schools, especially in the Panama Canal Zone. They insist on the ascendancy of the national security doctrine, which taught the Latin American general staffs to see the internal enemy as the chief threat, and which, starting in 1960, defined the regional armed forces' principal objective as the defence of 'ideological frontiers'. Finally, the behaviour of certain multinationals towards reformist, democratic governments (for example, ITT's conduct in Chile under Popular Unity), and the active affinity displayed by major foreign economic interests for dictatorships, demonstrate sufficiently the direct role the multinationals played in the advent of the military regimes of the period. Nevertheless, instrumentalist interpretations of this sort have only a very limited analytical reach, insofar as they disregard the specific mechanisms involved in political processes. The assumption that the beneficiaries of a government's actions necessarily instigated and sponsored its rise to power manifests a touching simplicity, and requires a complete disregard for the mediations, for the uncontrolled slippages, and for the unanticipated (and perhaps undesired) consequences characteristic of all collective action.

Authoritarian regimes in Latin America were, moreover, born long before 'the internationalization of domestic markets' characteristic of the recent phase of economic development. If the theory in question reduces itself to the proposition that foreign investment prefers law-and-order regimes to popular governments, it is simply proclaiming a very old truth, in the final analysis, a truism. At the same time, how can it be affirmed that, in recent years, there has been a mechanical correlation between the movements of international capital and the advent of authoritarian regimes, when historical reality bluntly gives the lie to such a largely mythological assertion?

What can be said of the industrial mutinationals' reluctance to invest in Chile despite the Chicago boys, in post-1973 'liberalized' Uruguay, or in the wide-open Argentina of Martínez de Hoz, minister-extraordinary of the economy under the 1976 dictatorship? International capital would seem to be capable of setting up regimes to its liking but not of profiting from them: witness the disinvestment policies pursued in Argentina by the local branches of foreign companies between 1978 and 1982. Finally, how is it possible, in the framework of this rigid conception, to explain the waning of military dictatorship in the period since 1979, which has seen the armed forces return to their barracks in virtually every country on the continent? 'U.S. imperialism' and those cold monsters, the great industrial conglomerates, would appear to be astonishingly fickle. Why would the necessary complementarity, stigmatized in 1976, of capital and repressive militarism, have simply evaporated in the 1980s and 1990s?

U.S. military influence on the Latin American armed forces is undeniable, as is the fact that, since the 1960s, one of Washington's political objectives has been to win over the continent's military elites to U.S. strategic perspectives and to employ them as local relays for U.S. influence. But there is a certain naïvety in the assertion that this project met with complete success, and that the Latin American military, victims of a 'narrow socialization' for the benefit of the U.S. empire, have one and all repudiated their national values. Velasco Alvarado's regime in Peru with its socialist-leaning colonels, Torres' progressive government in Bolivia, and Torrijos' nationalist regime in Panama all emerged, in the late 1960s and early 1970s, despite the Pentagon's role in defining the regional armed forces' missions and despite the training programmes that local military men had attended in Panama. We should also not forget the young Guatemalan officers, fresh from the Pentagon's counter-insurgency courses, who figured among their country's principal guerrilla leaders in the 1960s. That indoctrination, of whatever nature, often produces ambivalent results has long been recognized.

Contemporary militarism was not pre-ordained either historically or geographically. Nor do cultural determinism or foreign manipulation suffice to explain a complex phenomenon in which national and transnational factors intermingle. In endeavouring to evaluate the Latin American military's political role over the longterm, it becomes clear that the region's armed forces have very rarely been simply the passive instruments of domestic or foreign forces, even if such forces have often attempted to co-opt the military's power for their own ends. The political role of the continent's armed forces has varied over space and over time. It has not been determined by single or simple causes. It has reflected social configurations and models of development unpropicious to representative democracy, but has depended as well on the nature of the Latin American armed forces, on their insertion in society and in the state. The deepest roots of military hegemony do not, of course, lie in military society, any more than the armed forces can be held primarily responsible for the chronic instability of certain nations. But the nature of military power in Latin America in the period since 1930 remains unintelligible if proper attention is not accorded to particular historical conjunctures, and if an effort is not made to understand the Latin American armed forces themselves, their original formation, their subsequent evolution, and their specifically political mode of operation.

Part Two

SOCIETY AND POLITICS

4

URBAN LABOUR MOVEMENTS IN
LATIN AMERICA SINCE 1930

INTRODUCTION

The use of the term 'working class' or 'proletariat' in the history of Latin America since 1930 is fraught with difficulty. For some groups of workers, at certain times and places, these terms seem more or less adequate, while for other groups of the working population the phrase 'working class' suggests a greater homogeneity of social origin, location in the world of work, and of attitudes and organization than is warranted. The problem is a real, rather than a merely semantic one. In the changing world of work, certain categories or groups of workers came to define themselves, or to be defined by others, as in some sense a 'working class', and this cultural definition had consequences for the way they thought about the world and acted it it. Classic examples of this are the working classes of Argentina and Chile, where a strong sense of class identity was linked with clear political orientations. However, this was by no means the modal experience, and many Latin American workers saw themselves in much more diffuse terms either as distinctive elites, separate from the rest of the working population, or as subsumed within a larger social category variously labelled 'the poor' or 'the people'. These diverse forms of social identity (and the struggles over the political and cultural definition of the urban work force) have been a central element in the dynamics of working class and popular organization, and comprise one of the links between the labour movement, narrowly defined, and broader social movements. Although this chapter is primarily concerned with the labour movement narrowly defined, there will be a number of references to the links between labour and broader social movements throughout, particularly with regard to the tensions between labour and the pro-democracy movements of the 1940s and with regard to the increasingly close, and still problematic, links between organized labour and urban social movements in the 1960s and 1970s.

The study of Latin America's urban working population must also take into account the terms used, both by elites and by the workers themselves, to refer to this mass of humanity. The 'poor', the 'people', the 'masses', the 'workers' are all rival definitions with vastly different connotations and implications for political action. Added to this semantic ambiguity and contention, is the distinction in Spanish between *trabajador* and *obrero* (and in Portuguese between *trabalhador* and *operário*), distinctions between workers in the most general sense, and manual labourers, factory hands, in a much narrower sense. In Chile, indeed, labour legislation tended to enshrine a similar distinction between monthly paid employees, *empleados* and weekly paid *obreros*. While this distinction often corresponded to that between white and blue collar, it was possible for workers with identical jobs to be categorized differently depending on exactly which industries they were employed in. To add further to this complexity, in Brazil the terms 'class' and 'category' were often used interchangeably as in *a classe metalúrgica* to refer to the category of metal-workers and as in *a classe trabalhadora* (or *operária*) to refer to the working class as a whole. Added to these distinctions were a set of cultural definitions relating to concepts of ethnicity: Black, Indian, *mestizo, caboclo* and so on. This ethnic overlay on the cultural definition of what it meant to be a worker further complicated the situation and hindered the development of class identification. Moreover, while the importance of ethnicity in working-class identity varied from one country to another, the gender composition of the labour force was an important factor everywhere. While women workers in the textile industry, for example, were likely to see themselves as part of a working class, it is by no means clear that this was true for women working as laundresses, domestic servants or in a variety of service occupations. In any case, both class identity and class organization were, until at least the 1970s, largely determined by male workers.

Rapid urbanization after 1940 and the expansion of what is now called the informal sector in the 1960s and 1970s created new categories of the working population that could only with great difficulty be termed 'proletarian'. While most of these people had only their labour power with which to earn a living, this did not necessarily translate into wage employment on a regular basis, much less into any clear sense of class identification. Often employed in small enterprises, or self-employed, outside the realm of labour legislation, such informal sector workers made their living in conditions which were hardly conducive to the development of working-class self-identification.

At the other end of the labour market, the massive and sustained expansion of state employment produced a segment of the labour force which might be described as a white-collar salariat. The conditions of work, the status ascribed to office work, and the pervasiveness of patronage and clientelistic relations in the government sector meant that, even though real wages for this group were seldom very high, there was more likelihood that these workers would describe themselves as 'middle-class' rather than as belonging to a proletariat. With the passage of time, and the massification of state employment, wages and working conditions deteriorated relative to that of other workers, and an increased sense of proletarianization among government workers, leading to industrial and political organization and militancy, was visible by the 1960s and 1970s.

Class formation is a process that takes place in the urban space, and the physical distribution of the labour force, both between cities and within them, has a considerable influence on the formation of social networks, communities and a shared culture. The importance of residential location as a factor in the formation of working-class identity has been explored for mines, company towns and for cities dominated by a single major occupation (such as railways or docks). Here, uniformity of occupational status stimulated strong, but narrowly defined, notions of working-class membership. And as social scientists began their empirical studies of low-income housing settlements in the 1960s they generally found that, while there was considerable diversity among such low-income housing settlements, there also tended to be a mix of occupational categories. Factory workers might live alongside petty traders and informal sector workers.[1] This mixing of different categories of the working poor gave meaning to notions like 'the people' or 'the poor' to describe the working population and, by the 1970s, to changes in the use of the term 'working class' as the concept was broadened to include all those who worked for a living.

Another factor influencing how workers thought of themselves in terms of the larger society is the experience of their parents and their own occupational experiences over their lifetime. The few studies that have been carried out on occupational mobility in Latin America suggest that the boundaries of 'the working class' were often loosely defined and permeable. The present state of research into this difficult and complex topic

---

[1] See, for example, Manuel Castells, *La lucha de clases en Chile* (Buenos Aires, 1971), pp. 250–319.

leaves the historian with more questions than answers. However, both in terms of occupational life-chances and in terms of residential location, the limited evidence currently available suggests a series of links between some core clusters of the urban working class and the more diffuse sectors of the urban working population.

In the countryside, despite the importance of a plantation sector in some countries, and the emergence by the 1930s of active unionism, there still remain doubts as to the extent to which it would be appropriate to describe these groups, let alone landless workers in traditional agriculture, as belonging to a proletariat. It was not until the 1980s, particularly in Brazil, that it became appropriate to treat landless rural labourers as part of the working class. Moreover, as this chapter focusses explicitly on *urban* labour, the specifically rural components of the proletariat will be ignored.

In terms of the organization of the work process itself, we can discern, in most Latin American countries in 1930 three fairly distinct elements of what might be called a working class. First, there were in Chile, Bolivia, Peru and Mexico groups of mine workers, and in Colombia, Venezuela and Mexico groups of workers in the oil industry. Such workers might have close links with rural communities, as was undoubtedly the case in the Andean region, and there might also be a considerable degree of labour turnover and back-and-forth migration between the mining regions and the established urban centres, as happened in Chile. Miners were unlikely to be a purely self-recruiting segment of the labour force. Nevertheless, the spatial isolation of the mining communities and the aggregation of large numbers of (frequently young) men in a compact and relatively homogeneous mass was likely to produce a high level of 'class' identity. This could be further reinforced by management intransigence or by large fluctuations in the demand for labour in the mining sector. Where, as was often the case, the mine-owners were foreign, industrial conflict and class consciousness were also often infused with nationalist demands for state ownership.

A second sector that closely approximated to what might be described as a working class were workers in large enterprises located in small towns or in the countryside. This was often the case with textile factories, for example. Here a homogeneity similar to that of the mining communities was produced, but often with quite significant differences in terms of social organization and industrial militancy. Employers in such one-industry towns were often inclined to attempt various forms of paternalist control over the labour force. Particularly in the textile industry, there was usually employment for women as well as for men, and sometimes also for teen-agers and children. While the more balanced composition of the workforce was no guarantee of tranquility on the industrial relations front, it did mean that chance of a paternalist strategy operating effectively was higher.

Finally, many of the workers in the large towns and cities of the continent could appropriately be described as proletarian. This was particularly so in some of the ports, and among workers on the railways and in municipal transportation and utilities. In Colombia the workers on the Magdalena river should also be included. In addition, many other municipal employees, and many workers in industrial establishments were primarily wage-earners and saw themselves as such. Little is known about artisans and independent workers. The degree to which they were effectively proletarianized, their relationship to the process of industrialization, the extent to which they saw themselves as belonging to a working class, and their attitudes to unions and politics, remain to be explored. Nor is much known about the masses of workers who laboured in small manufacturing establishments and in the expanding service sector.

On the whole, in the early 1930s, it would not be unreasonable, particularly in cities like Buenos Aires, Havana, Mexico City, Santiago or São Paulo to talk about a proletariat with a fairly clearly defined social physiognomy. In Buenos Aires and São Paulo this proletariat was to a substantial degree an immigrant class, with at times tenuous ties of identification with their newly adopted homeland. Large segments of the urban working class in both countries spoke Italian or other non-official languages, though as the waves of massive immigration were interrupted in the 1930s and 1940s, the 'nationalization' of the working classes of Latin America accelerated. Despite the diversity of conditions and degree of self-consciousness, throughout the continent, in the early 1930s, the lineaments of a district working class could be discerned. This working class became more consolidated in the 1940s.

The demographic growth, urbanization and industrialization that occurred in the post-war period in most countries of the region, led to an enormous expansion of the working class, most impressively in Brazil, where industrial employment jumped from 1,600,000 in 1940 to 8,460,000 in 1980, and Mexico, where the industrial labour force rose from 640,000 to 2,580,000 over the same period.[2] As a result, the

---

[2] IBGE, *Estatísticas históricas do Brasil* (Rio de Janeiro, 1987), p. 75; INEGI, *Estadísticas Históricas de México* (Mexico, D.F., 1986), p. 252.

boundaries dividing this working class from the rest of the labouring population became more and more blurred. The rapid growth of cities and of urban employment, and the massive transfer of people from the countryside to urban areas, produced a profound transformation in what it meant to be a worker in Latin America. (The Southern Cone countries remained partial exceptions to the more general pattern, largely because of the slower rate of population growth and growth of urban employment and the earlier and more definitive cultural definition of the working class in those countries.)

In the 1930s some segments of the working class approximated to the notion of an aristocracy of labour: skilled and well-organized, they used their market position to further their own particular interests, and were generally unconcerned to engage in political action on behalf of the working class as a whole. Railway workers and dockers, for example, were among the first groups in Brazil to obtain social security systems, putting them in a clear position of privilege. By the 1980s, however, the union movement in most countries had expanded to a point where there was seldom a clearly definable aristocracy of labour.

High wages by no means always translated into economic satisfaction, industrial peace or political conservatism. Workers in these industries had considerable bargaining power, and were usually well organized, providing them with the potential for militant action. It is frequently much closer to the truth to say that the skilled and well-paid workers have been more likely to act as a militant vanguard than as a conservative aristocracy of labour, though the notion of a 'vanguard' also has its difficulties, as it suggests that there is a coherent and cohesive working class which will follow the political leadership of one of its sections. This has seldom been the case.

Workers in metal-working (including automobile assembly) and electrical supply have tended to earn higher than average wages and to use their industrial muscle to bargain effectively. As these industrial sectors expanded from the mid-1950s onwards, unions in the metal-working sector began to displace railways, docks and utilities as the leading sector of the organized working class, though where there was a significant mining or oil industry, unions in this sector maintained their central position in the labour movement. Some of these unions were attracted to a sort of 'business unionism', avoiding political affiliation and downplaying ties with other groups of workers in order to maximize their own benefits. This was the case for example with electricity supply and metal-working in the city of São Paulo. But workers in these sectors have been equally likely to adopt economically militant and politically radical positions, and to lead opposition movements within unionism as a whole.

Not only were the Latin American working classes diverse, both between and within countries, in terms of their social and industrial composition, there were also significant differences between one city and another. The port city of Santos in Brazil was known as 'Red Santos', and São Paulo became known in the 1940s as a distinctively proletarian city, in clear contrast with the then capital, Rio de Janeiro. In Mexico, the northern industrial city of Monterrey, dominated by tightly knit conservative elite families, remained a bastion of employer-sponsored unionism, and the Federal District the nucleus of the Confederación de Trabajadores de México (CTM) with its host of tiny unions. Regional centres like Puebla or Veracruz, or the towns dominated by mining and oil extraction, were more likely to be centres of industrial conflict. In Argentina in the 1960s the contrast between the mass mobilization of Córdoba and Rosario, with their large metal-working establishments, and the relative tranquility of Buenos Aires was marked. A similar contrast can be seen in Chile between the heavy industry city of Concepción, Santiago with a more diversified occupational structure, and the mining centres of the North. In Peru, the southern working class maintained a distinctive identity and tradition, as did the mining communities in both Peru and Bolivia.

Cities dominated by a few industries or a few employers, and with a preponderance of large establishments, tend to have a clearer class physiognomy than is typically the case in the more occupationally and socially diverse administrative capitals. The working classes of Latin America have been regionally, as well as occupationally, diverse. It is quite problematical whether it is useful to talk of a 'national' working class in any Latin American country, though the Southern Cone countries came the closest to this model.

To all these divisions and distinctions within the urban working classes must be added a fundamental strategic option facing the labour movement that revealed itself in perennial organizational, ideological and political tensions and divisions. This strategic decision was whether or not organized labour should attempt a direct and fundamental assault on the capitalist system with the aim of radical social transformation, or whether the broad outlines of capitalism should be accepted, at least in the immediate present, and labour action be directed towards amelioration of the

condition of the working classes.[3] Usually cast as a dichotomy between
revolution and reform, this strategic decision was inherent in the subordinate situation of the working classes, in their accumulated grievances, and
in their potential organizational and electoral strength. The range of
groups and organizations committed, at least rhetorically, to the revolutionary reconstruction of Latin American society has been diverse.[4] In
practice, however, many of these nominally revolutionary currents, particularly within the labour movement, have adopted postures that have
been indistinguishable from many of those accepted by their reformist
rivals. Thus, although the strategic debates within organized labour have
typically been cast in these ideological terms, the real strategic choices
have been between a largely co-operative strategy on the one hand and a
confrontationist one on the other. There could be no correct *a priori* answer
to the question of whether the long-run interests of the working class
would be better served by a strategy of confrontation in the hope of forcing
concessions from employers and the state, or whether a measure of co-
operation with employers and/or the state would result in a pattern of
growth that would better serve the interests of the working class. There
could be no *a priori* answer to this strategic choice because the eventual
outcome would depend in part on the actions of the other players in the
game, and these could not be foreseen by labour. Given the inherent
necessity for strategic choice, division and conflict within the ranks of
organized labour, expressed in largely ideological terms, was inevitable.
Although this strategic dilemma has been common to all labour movements, the ways in which this choice came to be defined in concrete terms
were quite specific to the Latin American context.

In the first place, the salience of government policy for organized labour
in Latin America has always been high, making the state, rather than
employers, the immediate interlocutor. This has meant that union actions
have been directed as much, or more, at the state as at employers. Second,
given the rapidity of social and economic change in Latin America since
1930, and the rapid recomposition of the industrial labour force in most
countries of the region, these strategic choices between co-operation and
contestation have been taken within quite varying time horizons. In some
cases, indeed, it has been possible for astute labour readers to combine a

---

[3] A recent sophisticated use of this strategic dilemma to analyze labour movements is Ruth Berins
Collier and David Collier, *Shaping the Political Arena: Critical Junctures, The Labor Movement and
Regime Dynamics in Latin America* (Princeton, N.J., 1991).

[4] See chapter by Alan Angell, 'The Left in Latin America since *c.* 1920' in this volume.

strategy of long-term co-operation with a tactic of immediate confrontation, thereby obtaining maximum results from industrial bargaining. The tactical choice of confrontation or co-operation has also, of course depended to some degree on the political complexion of the government of the day. Third, the choice of co-operative strategy has meant, not simply reformist, 'social-democratic' labour policies, but has often led to nearly complete subservience on the part of union leaderships to particular governments, usually in exchange for opportunities for personal enrichment.

These strategic choices within the labour movement, overlaid with the ideological divisions stemming from the wider debates in Latin America (as well as from the international arena), together with the social-structural divisions within the working classes, meant that organizational unity was difficult to attain, frequently covered over profound disagreements, and was constantly in danger of collapse.

Self-identity in the world of work was also bound up with the question of citizenship. By the 1930s adult males in most Latin American countries had the franchise, though in many countries women did not get the vote until the 1940s, and illiterates were excluded from the electorate in Brazil, for example until 1985. With these important exceptions, citizenship for urban workers in contemporary Latin America has not revolved around the question of the franchise. It was, however, focussed on three issues: support for democracy against military dictatorship; favourable labour legislation, including the right to independent union activity; and a diffuse but nevertheless important sense of not being 'second-class citizens'. Organized labour in Latin America has had a varying attitude towards these citizenship issues. While labour movements in the post-war period have generally held a positive position on a broad range of citizenship and human rights issues, there have been occasions when at least some sections of the working class have supported authoritarian and dictatorial governments which have offered not merely material improvements but also a greater sense of dignity to workers.

In the 1930s and 1940s there were close links between demands for an expansion of citizenship and struggles for the institutionalization of labour unions. During this period unions often saw themselves not simply as organizations of special interest groups but also as representing the aspirations of a much broader entity usually referred to as 'the people'. Herein lies one of the roots of populism in Latin American politics. In some aspects, what are usually described as populist movements embodied a somewhat inchoate demand for fuller citizenship. This is clear in the discourse of Peronism, for example, with its celebration of the *descamisados* and its stress on the dignity of labour. Populist ideology, of which Peronism is merely one example, stressed, inter alia, the acceptance of the lower social orders as legitimate actors in the body politic, and hence by extension, the legitimacy of their demands for full citizenship.

Citizenship meant not merely the vote, which in any case was already widely extended to literate males, but also a demand that democratic institutions be respected and that the essential prerequisites of democracy – free press, rule of law, free and fair elections, freedom of association – be guaranteed. Here there were obvious links with the efforts of workers to create viable and durable organizations. But citizenship also meant, for many people in Latin America, the right to personal dignity and an adequate standard of living.

Looking at the history of the urban working class and labour movement in Latin America as a whole, and leaving aside for the moment important variations between countries, the years since 1930 may be divided into five principal periods. The first began with the turmoil and intense mobilization that accompanied the economic crisis of the early 1930s. It continued with Popular Frontism in the mid to late thirties, and ended with the general labour tranquility of the Second World War. A second phase began with the widespread industrial mobilization and renewed assertiveness of organized labour in politics at the end of the Second World War. This was immediately followed by a concerted attack on Communist-led unions in particular in the early days of the Cold War (generally speaking, 1947 and 1948, though in some countries the assault on the left began as early as 1945 or 1946). The conservative victory that concluded this phase introduced a third period marked by political quiescence or tutelage, which extended through the 1950s and the greater part of the 1960s. The fourth phase began towards the end of the sixties in some countries and the second half of the seventies in others, and was characterized by a broad increase in the level of industrial and political conflict. It was during this phase that observers began to refer to the 'new unionism'. This phase also witnessed a growing interconnectedness between labour movements, narrowly defined, and the wider social movements of many kinds, which multiplied during these years. Finally, a fifth phase began with the debt crisis of 1982. It was characterized by a serious decline in wages, by declining employment in the formal sector of the economy, and at least initially in some countries by increasing levels of industrial conflict. The end of the 1980s appeared to witness profound changes in labour legislation and in the operation of labour markets, as well as in economic policy more generally, which pointed in the direction of significant shifts in the relationships between organized labour, employers and the state in many countries in Latin America.

These phases in the development of the labour movements of Latin America were intimately linked with shifts in the occupational and class structures of the region, with changes in political and economic systems, and with the development of social movements more broadly defined.

FROM THE 1929 DEPRESSION TO THE SECOND WORLD WAR

The impact of the 1929 Depression on the working population of Latin America was profound, though its effects varied considerably from country to country, largely depending on the political repercussions of the economic crisis and on the extent to which import substituting industrialization emerged as a stimulus to employment growth. Everywhere the initial impact of the Depression was a sharp reduction in economic activity and political turmoil. While the roots of political mobilization in many Latin American countries in the twentieth century may be traced back to the twenties or beyond, the Depression of 1929 focussed political and economic conflicts in new ways. At the political level a widespread challenge to continued oligarchic domination developed or was strengthened, and organized labour frequently had to reorient itself to these new political movements. In some countries the seeds were set for new, enduring identifications with popular political movements and political parties. The shift in the Comintern line in 1935 in favour of Popular Front policies created conditions more favourable for continental labour unity than ever before. With the exception of the period of the Hitler–Stalin pact (1939–41), the bulk of Latin America's popular and leftist forces found Popular Frontism (and its wartime continuation, National Frontism) a convenient vehicle for papering over internal differences and, in some cases, for achieving a remarkable unity of purpose.

In 1938 Mexican labour leader Vicente Lombardo Toledano formed the Confederación de Trabajadores de América Latina (CTAL) to bring together the bulk of organized labour in the region. Born in 1894 into an upper-middle class family in Puebla, Mexico, Lombardo had become the leading intellectual of the Mexican labour movement and was one of the leaders of the CTM. Although he always denied being a Party member, Lombardo after his visit to Moscow in 1935 adopted a position similar, if not identical, to that of the Comintern, that is to say, he conceived the CTAL as the organizational vehicle for a mass, left-leaning support for Popular Front policies. Within a few years the CTAL became – at least on paper – the dominant labour organization in Latin America. It claimed to represent some three million workers out of a total unionized labour force of less than four million. There were, moreover, friendly relations between the CTAL and the equally recently founded Congress of Industrial Organizations (CIO) in the United States.

In Argentina, the period from 1930 to the military government of 1943 was a largely defensive one for the unions. The conservative governments of this period were hostile to the idea of working-class participation in politics, and a series of basically fraudulent elections effectively blocked the development of broad-based social movements. Union membership, not high to begin with, may have dropped somewhat in the first years of the 1930s and then grew by 40 per cent between 1936 and 1941;[5] strike activity fell off from an average of 104 strikes per year in the period 1920–9 to an average of 70 per year between 1930 and 1944.[6] However, towards the end of the 1930s steady improvements in labour organization began to appear, stimulated in part by the growth of import-substituting industries and in part by the increasing institutionalization of industrial relations through the Department of Labour.

During this period the railway unions, led by moderate socialists, continued to hold a dominant position within organized labour. But the Communist Party made a number of significant advances in the Argentine union movement during the 1930s, gaining important centres of strength in meat-packing, construction, textiles and metalworking.

The thirties also witnessed the beginning of a major social and cultural transformation of the working class in Argentina. Prior to 1930 the weight of immigrants from southern Europe, and in particular from Italy, in the composition of the Argentine proletariat had been marked. Immigrants had played a significant role in labour organization in the first decades of the century and had contributed to the strength and diffusion of anarchist and socialist ideologies. The social composition of the urban working class began to change with the cessation of mass immigration

---

[5] According to Ronaldo Munck, in 1930 the CGT organized 200,000 of Argentina's four and a half million workers. By 1936 CGT membership was 262,000 and had risen to 330,000 by 1941. Membership for the union movement as a whole rose from 369,000 in 1936 to 506,000 in 1941. R. Munck, *Argentina: from Anarchism to Perónism* (London, 1987), pp. 108–115.

[6] R. Munck, *Argentina*, pp. 100, 124.

from Europe and the increase of migration into Buenos Aires from the interior of the country. There is still controversy about the impact of these changes in the social origins of the working class on its culture and on the political attitudes of workers, particularly with reference to the emergence of Peronism in the period 1943–6. Although some scholars have suggested that the Argentine working class was dividing into an older, proletarian segment and a new mass of migrants from the countryside, the evidence for this is far from conclusive, and it is more likely that, at least in terms of political and industrial attitudes, there were few important differences between these segments of the Argentine working class. Perhaps of greater import in these years was the increase in the number of Argentine workers who were native or naturalized citizens and thus had the right to vote.

In Brazil the period from 1930 to 1945 was dominated by the presence of Getúlio Vargas in government and his changing strategy towards organized labour. Brazilian unions in 1930 were weak and divided between anarchist, communist and more moderate currents. Official data indicate 328 unions in existence in 1935, with some 137,000 members.[7] There were a mere ninety strikes in the state of São Paulo during the entire decade.[8] Early efforts to bring labour under the wing of the state were initiated with the creation in 1931 of a National Department of Labour headed by *tenente* Lindolfo Collor. Collor actively sought to incorporate organized labour within the body politic largely through the creation of an increasingly complex body of labour legislation. Despite some vacillation in the regime's attitude to organized labour prior to the establishment of the Estado Novo, throughout this period legal recognition of unions was a central part of the government's control strategy.

What happened in the labour movement, as always, depended very much on national politics. In 1935 the Brazilian Communist Party, together with remnants of the *tenente* movement, launched a series of attempted insurrections, mainly in northeastern cities. The uprising was rapidly put down, and the Communist Party persecuted. The repression, however, seems to have spread to the working class as a whole and made active organizational work more difficult from this date until the over-

---

[7] Antonio Carlos Bernardo, *Tutela e autonomia sindical: Brasil, 1930–1945* (São Paulo, 1982), p. 113. By 1936 the number of unions had risen to 823, and the number of unionized workers to 308,000. However, changing legal requirement for union registration in the 1930s makes it difficult to get an accurate estimate of trends.
[8] Aziz Simão, *Sindicato e Estado* (São Paulo, 1966), p. 142.

throw of the Vargas government in 1945. The imposition of the Estado Novo in 1937 then consolidated the corporatist orientation of Brazilian industrial relations. Increasingly, unions and employers were organized in industry-wide *sindicatos,* with a monopoly of representation, and within a tripartite system of conciliation and arbitration for which the model was Italian labour legislation of the Mussolini period.

During the Estado Novo (1937–45) Brazilian labour lost whatever organizational autonomy it possessed and became largely subordinate to the corporatist state. Union funds were tightly controlled, and the sizeable sums accruing from the *imposto sindical* (a compulsory union tax of one day's wages per year per employee deducted directly from the payroll of all workers, whether or not they belonged to a union) were primarily destined to provide a range of health and welfare benefits for union members. Union leaders were vetted by the political police (the Departamento de Ordem Político e Social, DOPS) and increasingly resembled a timid bureaucratic clique. Labour legislation codified in 1943 in the Consolidação das Leis do Trabalho (CLT) benefited urban workers, particularly those in unions, and the industrial growth of this period did something to push up wages for skilled workers. The CLT was conceived as an attempt by the state to protect as well as to control labour. As such it was fiercely attacked by employers and seems to have elicited widespread, if passive, support from within the ranks of organized labour. However, with strikes an infrequent occurrence, with a ban on any kind of national confederation of labour, and with independent leftist leadership effectively removed, unions were in no position to seek improvements for the majority of the working class.

In contrast to the generally unfavourable political environment of Argentina and Brazil, the Mexican labour movement did well in the second half of the thirties. The end of the twenties had seen Mexican unionism in disarray: the once-powerful Confederación Regional Obrera Mexicana (CROM) had collapsed and Mexican union organizations were fragmented and economically and politically weak. However, the early thirties was a period of sustained efforts on the part of Mexican union organizers to move towards greater unity. This was particularly apparent with the formation of national industrial unions in railways (1933), in mining and metal-working (1934), and in oil extraction and refining (1934). Together with teachers and workers in electricity generating and distribution (which remained divided into a number of competing unions), these big industrial unions were destined to play a major role in the Mexican labour movement in subsequent years. With Lázaro Cárdenas' accession to the presidency in 1934, labour conflict accelerated: while the average annual number of strikes between 1925 and 1933 had been only 23, for the years 1934–40, the average annual strike rate was 439.[9]

Cárdenas, while sharing many of the corporatist tendencies of his Argentine and Brazilian peers, sought to implement them in a radically different political context. The Mexican Revolution had dramatically shifted political power to those with access to the new state. In addition to regional *caudillos,* and to the political bureaucracy, these new power contenders included both organized labour and the organized sectors of the peasantry. Whereas previous presidents had sought to distance themselves from labour, Cárdenas, in part as a strategy to prevent outgoing president Plutarco Elias Calles from exercising continuing power from behind the throne, made organized labour and the peasantry into major bulwarks of his regime. This shift was facilitated by a switch in the line of the Mexican Communist Party in 1935 from opposition to Cárdenas as a 'neo-fascist' to adoption of a Popular Front strategy and support for the new president. This, together with the formation of the national industrial unions and the control by Vicente Lombardo Toledano of a major split from the CROM, provided the conditions for the formation in 1936 of the CTM. With an initial membership of about 600,000, by 1941 the CTM had doubled its ranks to 1,300,00.[10] The CTM has continued to dominate Mexican unionism to this day.

There are considerable difficulties in the interpretation of the data, but it is likely that real wages for most industrial workers rose during the Cárdenas presidency, although the inflation at the end of the thirties may have eroded some of these gains. The beginnings of import substitution industrialization expanded urban employment. At the same time, however, these years also saw a considerable migratory flow to the big cities which undoubtedly did much to worsen labour market conditions.

Unionization proceeded apace, with both communists and independent leftists making substantial gains in influence. Political currents within Mexican unionism at this time may roughly be described as falling into three categories. At the conservative end of the spectrum there was a group of union leaders who came to be known as the *cinco lobitos.* The leader of this group was Fidel Velázquez, born in 1900, who had begun his political

[9] J. Wilkie, *The Mexican Revolution, Federal Expenditure and Social Change Since 1910* (Berkeley, Cal., 1967), p. 184.
[10] D. La Botz, *The Crisis of Mexican Labor* (New York, 1988), p. 61.

career as a Zapatista organizer. He had then moved on to organize the workers involved in milk distribution in Mexico City, and from there had risen to a position of influence among the unions organizing workers in the capital. The other *lobitos* were Adolfo Sánchez Madariaga, Luís Quintero, Jesús Yurén and Fernando Amilpa. This group was inclined towards a pragmatic accommodation with the government of the day, was basically reluctant to foster union mobilization and strike activity, and was suspicious of the rank-and-file. At the radical end of the spectrum were the Communists and a number of independent leftists. These groups controlled perhaps half of the votes in the CTM, and were particularly influential in the national industrial unions.[11] They supported Cárdenas and sought to use their relatively favoured position to further worker mobilization. Straddling the divide, and attempting to raise himself above these factional disputes, was Vicente Lombardo Toledano.

There were a number of major strikes in Mexico during this period. Among the more dramatic were the oil workers' strike of 1937, which Cárdenas then used to push through the expropriation of the industry, and the strikes in the industrial city of Monterrey in 1936, which brought already tense relations between Cárdenas and the conservative *regiomontano* bourgeoisie to fever pitch. Following the nationalization of the oil industry, there was a prolonged tussle between Cárdenas and the union concerning the oil workers' attempts to establish a form of worker control in the industry which, together with increasingly strident demands for higher wages, led eventually to government use of troops to break a strike in 1940 (and nearly to break up the union). Similarly, worker administration on the railways (nationalized in 1937) had been a failure and relations between railway workers and Cárdenas had grown increasingly embittered. Thus, unlike the successful imposition of state control over a relatively weak labour movement in Brazil, Mexico saw the independent mobilization of organized labour which entered into an uneasy, tense relationship with a left-leaning president without being willing to give up its autonomy as the process of consolidation of the revolutionary state continued.

[11] During a temporary split in the CTM in 1937 both sides published claims about their membership. The Communist-led left claimed to control 366,000 workers against 292,000 controlled by the *cinco lobitos*. Lombardo Toledano, at this time allied with the *cinco lobitos*, claimed that the Communist controlled 139,000 workers, and the conservatives 597,000. Despite the considerable discrepancies, which are typical of statistics on unionization (and particularly so for Mexico), these figures suggest an overall membership of about 700,000. J. F. Leal, *Agrupaciones y burocracias sindicales en México, 1906/1938* (Mexico, D.F., 1985), pp. 124–5.

In Chile the impact of the Depression of 1929 was particularly severe, with a dramatic rise in unemployment, particularly in the mining sector. The political turbulence of the 1920s spilled over into the following decade, its most dramatic expression being the short-lived Socialist Republic of 1932. While this had little immediate impact on labour, the subsequent formation of the Socialist Party in April 1933 was important in furthering the development of a ideologically militant labour movement. The conservative administration of Arturo Alessandri (1932–8) was replaced in 1938 by the Popular Front government of Pedro Aguirre Cerda (1938–41). This, and the successor Radical governments of the 1940s, relied heavily on labour support in electoral terms, though this did not prevent the passage of anti-labour legislation towards the end of the decade.

On the whole the 1930s were a period of union growth, with the member of unions increasing from 421 in 1930 to 1,880 in 1940. During the same years, membership increased from 55,000 to 162,000.[12] Prior to the founding of the Confederación de Trabajadores de Chile (CTCh) in 1936, the Chilean labour movement had been divided into three main sections. The anarcho-syndicalist Confederación General de Trabajo (CGT) was, by 1936, a spent force, and the Communist-dominated Federación de Obreros de Chile (FOCh) had been decimated, and was now confined largely to miners in coal and nitrates. The Socialists, however, continued to grow, and came to dominate the union movement in the thirties.

In Peru the Depression of 1929 led to massive lay-offs and an employer offensive against organized labour. During this decade both the Alianza Popular Revolucionaria Americana (APRA) and the Communist Party emerged as rivals for the political representation of Peruvian labour. However, the situation was initially complicated with the seizure of power in August 1930 by the populist Luís Sánchez Cerro in a military coup and his subsequent victory in the presidential elections of 1931 with the support of unemployed artisans and unskilled labour. In so far as it is possible to distinguish Sánchez Cerro's social base from that of APRA, it was formed by the unorganized sections of the working poor, rather than on the somewhat better-off and more organized proletariat and white collar salariat which formed an important part of APRA's constituency.[13] In early 1932 Sánchez Cerro declared an emergency law and embarked on a

[12] Paul Drake, *Socialism and Populism in Chile, 1932–52* (Urbana, Ill. 1978), p. 178.
[13] S. Stein, *Populism in Peru* (Madison, Wis., 1980), p. 114.

wholesale repression of both labour and APRA. The failure of the July 1932 APRA insurrection in Trujillo opened the way for further repressive measures. The recently formed Confederación General de Trabajadores del Perú (CGTP) was dissolved, and the labour movement driven underground. With the assassination of Sánchez Cerro in April 1933 and his replacement by General Benevides, there was some easing up on labour repression and minimum wage and social security legislation was enacted in 1933 and 1936. The government of Manuel Prado (1939–45) tolerated a greater degree of political liberty, but continued the basically anti-labour orientation of the previous administrations. During these years APRA made itself into the principal political current within the labour movement, though this was increasingly challenged by the Communists (who were particularly influential in the strategic mining sector).

In Bolivia the decade opened with the Chaco War (1932–5), and a search for alternatives to oligarchic domination. After the Chaco War the labour movement gradually re-emerged under the military socialist governments of David Toro and Germán Busch. A Ministry of Labour was established in 1936 with a labour leader, Waldo Alvarez, as its head. In the same year the Confederación Sindical de Trabajadores Bolivianos (CSTB) was established, and was to be the most powerful labour organization in Bolivia until the formation of the Confederación Obrera Boliviana (COB) in the course of the 1952 revolution. Politically, union activists were divided between supporters of the nationalist and corporatist Movimiento Nacional Revolucionario (MNR) and adherents of Guillermo Lora's Trotskyist Partido Obrero Revolucionario (POR). Throughout this period there was resistance from the nine owners to unionization, and the army was regularly employed to break strikes. In 1942 a sizeable clash occurred at the Catavi mine, leaving between 40 and 400 miners and family members dead.

The early thirties in Cuba witnessed high levels of unemployment and the beginning of organization against the dictatorship of Gerardo Machado. In March 1930 a general strike of some 200,000 paralyzed the island and was put down with extreme force and the proclamation in November of a state of siege. Discontent was widespread and in August 1933 the Machado government was brought down by a broadly-based movement of opposition, in which a notable role was played by sugar workers, who organized massive strikes, seized sugar mills, and in a number of places formed 'soviets'. The ensuing political turmoil ushered in a brief period of rapid organizational growth, culminating in a massive general strike in February and March 1935. President Carlos Mendieta order the army to suppress the strike, imposed martial law and a subsequent period of repression placed unions on the defensive. It was only towards the end of the decade that organized labour began to recover from the repression of the mid-thirties. The Confederación de Trabajadores de Cuba (CTC) was founded in January 1939 with the support of the CTAL; it claimed some 645,000 members.[14] Cuba, like the countries of the Southern Cone, had a highly urbanized work force, resulting in a relatively high level of unionization. In addition, the seasonal nature of employment in the highly proletarianized sugar sector, together with the dramatic oscillations in the international demand for sugar, produced a working class where rural-urban divisions were less salient than elsewhere in the region, and where a store of accumulated grievances about unemployment, economic dependency and foreign domination, and authoritarian labour relations combined with Cuba's revolutionary experiences to produce a labour movement that readily accepted the leadership of radical parties, first the Communists and later the July 26 Movement.

The immediate impact of the Depression of 1929 in Colombia was to further weaken a labour movement that was as yet still in an early stage of development. Once the immediate effects of the crisis were past, labour organization began to grow and strikes to break out. Between 1933 and 1935 there was a marked increase in strike activity, beginning with workers in the publicly owned transport sector and spreading to the private sector. By 1935 the first truly national organizations began to be formed, and something like 42,000 workers were affiliated with unions.[15] These years were marked by the support given by the unions to the Liberal governments of Alfonso López (1934–8 and 1942–5) and Eduardo Santos (1938–42), though the Communists were also influential in the union movement. In 1936 the change in the political line of the Comintern adopted the previous year paved the way for the creation first of the Confederación Sindical de Colombia and then of the Confederación de Trabajadores de Colombia, affiliated with the CTAL.

Elsewhere in the continent, weak labour movements struggled for survival in the face of difficult economic conditions and general government hostility and repression. Despite widespread popular mobilization and

[14] Aleida Plasencia Moro, 'Historia del movimiento obrero en Cuba', in Pablo González Casanova (ed.), *Historia del movimiento obrero en América Latina,* Vol. 1, (Mexico, D.F., 1984), p. 137.
[15] M. Urrutia, *The Development of the Colombian Labor Movement* (New Haven, Conn., 1969), p. 183. By 1942 union membership had climbed to 95,000.

considerable political turmoil, the record for organized labour in the thirties was generally dismal.

The Second World War might have been expected to produce widespread labour unrest, as unions sought to use the generally tighter labour markets to counter the effects of inflation on real wages. In fact the general trend was in the opposite direction. Labour generally supported the majority of Latin American governments when, in the wake of the Japanese attack on Pearl Harbor, they declared war on the Axis powers. The war was seen largely as a war for democracy against dictatorship, and under the influence of the Communist parties of the region and the CTAL, most labour movements followed up the policies of the Popular Front with no-strike pledges for its duration. While this policy was by no means universally popular among unionists, the CTAL had sufficient authority in most countries for this to result in a fall in strike activity. Argentina and Bolivia had governments which refused until the very end of the war to declare war on the Axis, but in these countries government hostility to the labour movement meant (with the exception of Argentina after 1943) little strike activity in any case. In Brazil, where labour legislation prohibited unions from affiliation with international bodies such as the CTAL, the Vargas government maintained control over the unions for the duration of the war. Strike activity throughout the continent was thus quite limited at a time of employment expansion and significant inflationary pressures on real wages.[16]

FROM THE SECOND WORLD WAR TO THE COLD WAR[17]

Falling real wages combined with no-strike pledges during the Second World War resulted in a build-up of pressure for major change as the end

[16] In the absence of any definitive study, there remains some controversy concerning the trend of real wages during the Second World War. The tight labour market almost certainly led to some wage drift, as workers worked more overtime and as employers competed against one another for categories of labour which were in short supply. The increase in the number of threshold members holding paid employment as a result of the expansion of industrial employment and the entry of women into the labour market also probably had the effect of raising real family incomes. Operating against these factors was an increase in rural to urban migration (counter-acting the tightening of the labour market), and the no-strike pledges of the unions in the face of rising inflation. The net result was probably a substantial decline in working-class incomes. Certainly, available statistics for the wages of industrial workers in this period indicate a widespread and substantial decline in real wages during the war.

[17] This section draws heavily on Leslie Bethell and Ian Roxborough (eds), *Latin America between the Second World War and the Cold War, 1944–8* (Cambridge, 1992).

of the war came in sight. In several countries, beginning in 1943 or 1944, there was a noticeable increase in strike activity. In Brazil there were massive strike waves in 1945 and 1946. It appeared as if the tight state control of the Estado Novo had come to an end and ushered in a period of industrial conflict (as well as a rise in the influence of the Brazilian Communist Party). In Argentina, the rise of Perón to power between 1943 and 1946 was accompanied by mass working-class mobilization. In Mexico there were more strikes (and more workers involved in strikes) in 1944 than at any previous time, even during the period of working-class mobilization under Cárdenas.[18] The strike waves spilled over into the early post-war period. In some countries the increase in labour mobilization at the end of the Second World War was enmeshed in complex and varying ways with the parallel upsurge in demands (in those countries that were dictatorships during the war) for democratization and expanded citizenship rights. In Venezuela, for example, the overthrow of the government of Medina Angarita in October 1945 and the accession to power of Acción Democrática meant not only democratization but also freedom for labour to organize and strike. But while movements for democracy and for improvements in the condition of the organized working class coincided in Venezuela and Peru, in Brazil and Nicaragua organized labour rallied behind dictators Vargas and Somoza against an opposition which was seen by unions as reactionary and oligarchic. Similarly, Argentine labour threw in its lot with Perón, who it regarded as pro-labour, against the democratic opposition to the military dictatorship.

The CTAL had been vociferous in its support of the Allied war effort. At the end of the war the CTAL which, like the communist movement in general, had a significant presence in many countries, was momentarily at a loss as to which direction to pursue. The line adopted by Lombardo was a continuation of Popular Front policies into the post-war period, a strategy that would, at the political level, be described as 'Browderism'. This implied a long-term alliance between labour and the 'progressive national bourgeoisie' around state-led industrialization, and suggested the need to build and strengthen institutions which would enable labour to have a permanent influence on the formation of macroeconomic policy. However, while the CTAL wished to create a working relationship with the state, its

---

[18] Strike frequency under Cárdenas had peaked at 642 strikes in 1935 and 674 in 1936 (with 145,000 workers involved in strikes in the first year and 114,000 in the next). In 1943 and 1944 there were 766 and 887 strikes, respectively, and the corresponding figures for workers involved were 82,000 and 166,000. Wilkie, *The Mexican Revolution,* p. 184.

position remained quite distinct from that of the more conservative currents within Latin American unionism, in that the CTAL was more likely to use militant tactics to promote its aims and in its suspicion of the United States more generally.

Browderism on the part of the left coincided with the increasingly felt need on the part of political elites to foster industrial development through active state intervention. With the end of the war several Latin American governments sought to consciously foster and develop the industrialization that had taken place largely without deliberate planning during the 1930s and the war years. This would mean bringing increasingly restive labour movements under tighter control and, in so far as these governments hoped to attract foreign capital, the promotion of an appropriate 'investment climate'. The need to regulate and institutionalize labour relations had been generally recognized in the previous decade, partly as an attempt to deal with the perceived threat posed by the 'social question', and partly as a way in which new political forces could organize a mass base. Now, in the immediate post-war period, to these concerns was added a series of concerns about macroeconomic stability. More than ever it was now imperative to defeat the militant tendencies in the labour movement and to reach some sort of working agreement with the more conservative factions.

The U.S. State Department viewed the strength of the CTAL and its political project with concern, and supported the efforts of Serafino Romualdi as the 'roving labour ambassador' of the American Federation of Labor (AFL) in Latin America. Romualdi sought to stimulate those forces within the Latin American trade union movement which favoured a more pro-U.S. and 'business-orientated' unionism to split from the CTAL. These efforts were in part a continuation of North American concern (particularly on the part of the AFL) with what was seen as excessively 'political' unionism in Latin America. Throughout the first half of the twentieth century the AFL had attempted to promote a form of bread and butter unionism in Latin America with which it could sympathize. While Romualdi's efforts in Latin America at the end of the war built on this historical tradition, they must also be placed in the context of a global struggle for control of the international trade union organizations between the communist and the non-communist currents in the world labour movement. Global ideological concerns were now superimposed on the fundamental strategic and ideological divisions fermenting within the national labour movements. These struggles culminated in the split of the

World Federation of Trade Unions and the formation of the International Confederation of Free Trade Unions in 1949.

Whatever the purely domestic reasons for the attack on the communist leadership in Latin American labour unions, the Latin American labour movement became caught up in these international struggles at the end of the war. A number of meetings were held between Romualdi and trade union leaders in several countries and at a meeting in Lima, in January 1948, a major split in the CTAL was consummated. The leading figures were Bernardo Ibáñez of Chile, Arturo Sabroso of Peru and Eusebio Mujal of Cuba. A number of national confederations withdrew from the CTAL and in the process provoked splits that had long been latent within them. In one country after another the bitter factional disputes within the principal union organizations (which had been papered over in the interests of working-class unity) now broke out into the open. In some countries (for example, Cuba and Mexico) conservative unionists used armed thugs to challenge leftist control of the union movement. In many countries the government openly sided with the more conservative elements by cracking down on communists within union ranks.

From this date on, the CTAL entered into rapid decline and finally passed into oblivion in 1959. While its strength may well have been exaggerated by friends and foes alike, and while it may have been heavily dependent on the continued good will of the Mexican CTM and the Mexican government for financial support, it would nevertheless be an exaggeration to suggest that the CTAL was a purely paper organization with no effective impact on events in the region. The U.S. government, at least, was sufficiently convinced of the potential threat posed by the CTAL and the union left in Latin America to encourage their systematic repression.

Of course there was more to developments in Latin American labour organizations in the latter half of the 1940s than simply a Cold War struggle over international union affiliation. There were endogenous sources of the growing trend towards conservatism in labour relations, such as the need to promote a good investment climate to attract foreign capital. Moreover, with the end of the wartime alliance with the communists, the stage was set for a return to the routine politics of anticommunism. Increasing hostility towards communist parties coincided with a more general crackdown on organized labour as a whole. Further encouragement, if any was needed, for this conservative turn in government labour policy was derived from the purge of the Communists in the labour movement in the United States (beginning in the CIO and the

United Automobile Workers in 1945 and 1946), president Truman's tough stand against striking mineworkers in 1946, and the passage of the Taft–Hartley legislation in 1947 prohibiting Communists from holding union office. These events were closely followed in Latin America and were widely seen as signals of which way the wind was blowing.

In Brazil where during the first half of the forties labour had remained closely controlled by the corporatist Estado Novo the imminent end of the Second World War, and the general expectation that the Vargas dictatorship was coming to an end, led to a revival of union activity. Both Rio de Janeiro and São Paulo now had substantial industrial labour forces, and the labour vote was clearly important in the new democratic politics. Vargas now hoped to consolidate the support he had gained with the CLT and enlist organized labour on his side in the Partido Trabalhista Brasileiro (PTB) alongside the Partido Social Democratico (PSD), against the conservative opposition União Democrática Nacional (UDN). (All three parties were formed in 1945.)

Strike activity increased substantially during the first half of 1945. In an extremely fluid and confused situation, both the Communists and the *trabalhistas* vied for the support of the organized working class. There was an attempt in August and September 1945 through the *queremista* movement to urge Vargas to retain power, and large rallies organized by Vargas' followers were held in Brazil's major cities. Fears that Vargas might not allow free elections were finally banished when he was overthrown in a military *coup* led by General Góes Monteiro. In the elections of December 1945 General Eurico Gaspar Dutra, the candidate of the PSD, backed halfheartedly by Vargas, won with 55 per cent of the vote.

There followed a renewed upsurge of labour militancy in the first months of 1946 and a brief but intense three-way struggle between the Trabalhista labour activists of the PTB, the Communists, and the Ministry of Labour. Broadly speaking, the PTB drew much of its support in São Paulo from workers who had recently migrated to the city from small towns and rural areas, whereas the Communists predominated among the more established industrial workers. In April 1945 the Communists had set up a union organization outside the control of the Ministry of Labour, the Movimento Unificador dos Trabalhadores (MUT). In September 1946 it played a leading part in the formation of Brazil's first Confederação dos Trabalhadores do Brasil (CTB). The Dutra government moved rapidly to ban both the MUT and the CTB, intervened in more than four hundred unions, removed Communists from union and political positions and eventually proscribed the PCB. The Trabalhistas in the PTB moved into the vacuum left by the Communists. By 1947 the wave of labour mobilization sparked by the end of the Second World War had been contained and reversed. Brazil's new democracy henceforth operated with the corpus of labour legislation inherited from the Estado Novo. Unions continued to be tightly controlled by the state and their autonomy limited. This was clearly demonstrated by the drop in strike activity from an average of fifty strikes per year in 1945 and 1946 to an average of twelve strikes per year for the next decade.[19]

In Mexico there was also an upsurge in union militancy in the closing years of the war, followed by repression. Relations between the CTM and Lázaro Cárdenas had already begun to cool towards the end of his presidency, with large sections of the union movement continuing to demonstrate an independence that brought them into repeated conflict with the government. These tensions were increased during the government of Manuel Avila Camacho (1940–6), with its attempt to rectify the 'excesses' of Cardenismo, but were put in abeyance by the advent of the Second World War and the CTM decision not to strike while the war was in progress. Towards the end of the war inflation brought about general restiveness in the ranks of labour, and in some industries particular problems induced or exacerbated by the war raised industrial conflict to new levels. This was the case with the three biggest national industrial unions.

The railways were suffering from under-capitalization and a run-down in track and rolling stock, as well as from major organizational problems, stemming from the legacy of workers' control, from bad management and from the continued fragmentation of the national rail system. In the oil industry union power and management collusion had led to widespread over-manning and inefficiencies. In mining the end of the war brought with it a decline in U.S. demand and widespread lay-offs. The election of Miguel Alemán to the presidency in 1946 brought into office someone who was concerned to establish the bases for stable economic growth in Mexico. A first step would be a major house-cleaning of the unions.

At the same time that Alemán was preparing for a showdown with the militants in the labour movement, a struggle was coming to a head within the CTM between the *cinco lobitos* and the radicals in the national industrial

---

[19] Salvador Sandoval, 'Strikes in Brazil: 1945–1980', unpublished Ph.D. dissertation (University of Michigan, 1984), p. 29.

unions. The big three industrial unions left the CTM and formed the Central Única de Trabajadores (CUT) in March 1947. At the same time, Lombardo Toledano began systematically to campaign for the formation of a Partido Popular, originally envisaged as a mass pressure group within the official party. Lombardo avoided identification with the militants in the national industrial unions and attempted to maintain an independent role as the grand leader of the Mexican working class. But it was now too late. Since the foundation of the CTAL in 1938 he had left the running of the CTM to the *cinco lobitos* and could no longer count on any substantial organizational strength in that organization. The *cinco lobitos* moved to declare joint membership in the Partido Popular incompatible with CTM affiliation and in March 1948 expelled Lombardo and his few remaining loyal followers. While internal factors are sufficient to explain this course of events, there can be little doubt that Cold War pressures also played some role. With Lombardo out of the way, the CTM could now turn its fire on its rival, the CUT. There was a more or less even balance of force in numerical terms between the CTM and the CUT;[20] a situation that clearly favoured the CUT, with its powerful industrial unions, over the CTM, which had its base in the thousands of small unions in small-scale establishments in Mexico City and elsewhere. The position of the CUT seemed also likely to be reinforced by the establishment of the Partido Popular and the apparently imminent unification of the Mexican left, following the Mesa Redonda de los Marxistas Mexicanos held in January 1947. Some observers began to talk about the imminent demise of the CTM. Before this could transpire, the government of Miguel Alemán moved in to break up the CUT.

The pretext was an accusation of fraud made by Jesús Díaz de León, the new General Secretary of the railwayworkers' union against the previous leader, Luís Gómez Z. When the railwayworkers' union, together with the other two major industrial unions, established the CUT, Gómez Z. had channelled union funds to the CUT and had subsequently resigned his position in the railway union to work full time in the CUT. He had been replaced by an apparently trustworthy lieutenant, Jesús Díaz de León, 'el charro', who could be expected to do as Gómez wished. This turned out to

---

[20] The CTM retained about 100,000 members, whereas the national industrial unions controlled about 200,000 workers. In addition, a Lombardista group, the Alianza de Obreros y Campesinos de México, claimed to represent some 130,000 workers, and the remaining union organizations (CROM, CGT, and so on) claimed the highly inflated figure of 400,000 members. Luis Medina, *Civilismo y modernización del autoritarismo* (Mexico, D.F., 1979), p. 146.

be misplaced confidence. In September 1948 Díaz de León brought charges of misuse of trade union funds against Gómez Z, and after some weeks of confusion the government backed up Díaz de León with the use of police to occupy union buildings. Thousands of workers were fired, and the union became an unconditional supporter of the government's economic policies. Known as the 'Charrazo' because of Díaz de León's penchant for dressing as a 'charro' cowboy (hence his nickname), this event spelled the end of the CUT challenge to the Alemán government. Shortly thereafter the radical leaderships of the oil workers' union (1949) and the miners' union (1950) were overthrown and conservative leaderships installed. 'Charrismo', the recognition by Mexican union bosses that untoward militancy would provoke the ire and subsequent subversion of their unions by the government, was to become the defining feature of Mexican unionism for the next two decades. In June 1949 a last-ditch effort was made by the Lombardistas to create a counterweight to the CTM, the Unión General de Obreros y Campesinos de México. However, both this and the Partido Popular were stillborn.

In Chile during the Popular Front and Radical party governments of the 1940s, as we have seen, the labour movement dominated by the Socialists and Communists actively supported the government, and when Gabriel González Videla, a left-wing Radical, was elected in September 1946 he brought three Communist Party members into his cabinet, though only after privately assuring the U.S. embassy that he would take an early opportunity to ease them out. His task was made easier by the bitter rivalries between the Communists in the labour movement and their Socialist (and to a lesser extent, Radical) rivals. A protracted civil war within the labour movement went on for most of 1946, and ended with the socialists in disarray and decline. When the Communists proved not to be pliable junior partners in the Radical government, and continued to support strikes and the unionization of the countryside, tensions between González Videla and the Communists mounted, leading the president to stage a confrontation over a coal miners' strike in August 1947, push the Communists out of the cabinet, and imprison the party leadership. Under continuing State Department pressure, González Videla launched an anti-Communist campaign which eventually culminated in April 1948 in the passage of the law for the Permanent Defence of Democracy, the so-called 'Ley Maldita', leading to widespread purges of Communist union officials and public employees, and a rapid decline in strikes. Actively participating in these events, and eventually benefitting from them, were a number of moderate trade union leaders led by Bernardo Ibáñez who had been in touch with the AFL since 1943 and sought to precipitate a split within the ranks of the CTAL.

In Cuba the advent of the Cold War produced a major split in the CTC. Leaders of the maritime workers' union were invited to the United States as early as July 1943 by the AFL and convinced to begin the work of establishing a new labour organization to rival the CTC. This initiative failed to prosper, largely because Auténtico candidate Ramón Grau San Martín still needed CTC (and Communist) support in the 1944 presidential elections. The AFL nevertheless retained its close ties with non-Communist Cuban labour readers and after the end of the Second World War the State Department pressured Grau San Martín to begin a purge of the Communists. Finally, in April and May 1947 the Auténticos forced a split in the CTC, with the government predictably refusing to recognize the legal status of the rump CTC led by veteran Communist labour leader Lázaro Peña Rival. Arrests of union activists, assassinations by gangsters and violent clashes on the streets of Havana followed. In short order the communist-led CTC was destroyed, and Communist influence in the labour movement greatly reduced. The subsequent domination of an explicitly pro-regime labour movement by Eusebio Mujal did not, however, bring total labour peace to Cuba. The Communists continued to exercise some influence, and in any case the continuing restiveness of the Cuban working class forced the leaders of the new CTC to support some strikes and push for wage increases, in the process demanding bribes from companies for a speedy settlement of labour disputes. Labour unrest and gangsterism remained dominant characteristics of the Cuban labour scene throughout the fifties, even under the dictatorship of Fulgencio Batista, who continued to rely on the mujalistas to provide him with much-needed support.

In Venezuela the 1945–8 AD government used its power to support unionization efforts (the number of unions in existence rose from 113 in 1936 to 252 in 1945 and to 1014 by 1948)[21] and at the same time effectively displaced the Communists from leadership positions in the labour movement. Although there were several reasons for the overthrow of the AD government in 1948, labour militancy certainly played a part. Despite its anti-communism, AD still proved too radical for conservative forces in Venezuelan society.

[21] Julio Godio, *El movimiento obrero venezolano, 1945–1980* (Caracas, 1982), p. 39.

In Peru, the 1945–8 government of José Luís Bustamante provided the setting for a similar pattern of union growth. The Confederación de Trabajadores de Perú (CTP) had been re-established in 1944, and strikes in 1944, 1945 and 1946 brought real wages back to their pre-war levels. Whereas the Prado government (1939–45) had recognized an average of 24 unions per year, the Bustamante government recognized a further 264 unions in these years, an average of 88 per year.[22] During the Bustamante government APRA increased its hold over the Peruvian union movement at the expense of the Communists. General strikes in 1947 and 1948 added to the increasing levels of tension in Peru and, with the Bustamante regime losing control, as in Venezuela, the military *coup* of 1948, together with the divisions in the CTP, heralded a return to a general weakness of the union movement and its marginalization from national politics.

The Colombian labour movement also experienced some growth during and after the Second World War, though by no means of a spectacular nature. The total number of registered unions rose from 554 in 1940 to 986 in 1947, and from 84,000 union members to 166,000 over the same period.[23] As in most of Latin America, the war brought a fall in real wages in Colombia and the end of the war a re-emergence of labour militancy. However, unions came under government attack; a number of important strikes were defeated. At the end of the war the fate of the union movement became tied up with developments in the party system. Within the Liberal Party Jorge Eliecer Gaitán challenged the established party leadership with a populist programme of moral regeneration. While his following in the unions was relatively modest, Gaitán did attract considerable support in the low income sectors of the urban population. His assassination in April 1948 led to several days of rioting in Bogotá, the *bogotazo*. This is generally seen as one of the key precipitating factors of the *violencia* which was to scar Colombian politics for the next two decades. This context of generalized political violence, with limited options available at the national level, was an unpropitious time for labour organizing. The period of generally tranquil industrial relations which was initiated in the late forties was also heavily influenced by a split in the Confederación de Trabajadores de Colombia (CTC) and by the fact that the Catholic Unión de Trabajadores de Colombia (UTC), formed in 1946, displaced it as the predominant labour organization in the country.

[22] Denis Sulmont, *El movimiento obrero peruano* (*1890–1980*) (Lima, 1980), p. 212.
[23] Urrutia, *The Development of the Colombian Labor Movement*, p. 183.

In Bolivia the 1940s were dominated by the efforts of the MNR to achieve power, and by the vacillating labour policies of a variety of unstable governments. The seizure of power by the nationalist Colonel Gualberto Villarroel in December 1943 had some superficial resemblance to the rise of Perón in Argentina. Labelled a fascist by the United States and facing intense opposition from a variety of social forces including the Communist-dominated Confederación Sindical de Trabajadores de Bolivia (CSTB), Villarroel attempted with MNR support to develop a base among the mineworkers, permitting the formation of the Federación Sindical de Trabajadores Mineros de Bolivia (FSTMB) in June 1944. However, relations between the MNR and the labour movement were always tense. Mounting opposition from pro-democracy middle-class groups finally resulted in an urban insurrection and the ouster and hanging of Villarroel in July 1946. The labour movement failed to come to his rescue. The following *sexenio* of largely conservative governments saw attempted uprisings by the MNR, constant labour unrest, and a series of major strikes, which were usually met with repression. Under the leadership of Juan Lechín, the Bolivian tin miners had, in November 1946, with the thesis of Pulacayo, formally adopted a Trotskyist insurrectional line. The repressive attitude of a series of Bolivian governments (massacres in the mines in Potosí in January 1947 and in Catavi in May and September 1949, leaving perhaps 800 dead), repression following a general strike in La Paz in 1950, together with widespread lay-offs in the mines in 1947 (the 'white massacres'), and the special characteristics of mining communities, had led to a heightened sense of political radicalism among the miners. A combination of miserable living and working conditions and a wealth of cultural traditions enabled the mining communities to develop a series of integrating rituals which blended militant Trotskyism with elements of pre-colonial religion in a highly effective, if somewhat eclectic, brew.[24] This fed into the larger insurrectionary movement headed by the MNR. Bolivia thus differed from most of the rest of Latin America in that the late 1940s did not see the control of labour militancy. Indeed, by April 1952, Bolivia was in the throes of a profound social revolution which would lead labour to a share in governmental power.

Argentina under Perón seemed to stand out from the general pattern of labour repression brought about by the Cold War. But, as we shall see, the

---

[24] June Nash, *We Eat the Mines and the Mines Eat Us* (New York, 1979), pp. 87–120.

mobilization of the early Perón years was rapidly reversed, bringing Argentina more into line with developments elsewhere in the region.

The Argentine military *coup* of 1943 initiated a period of dramatic transformation of the labour movement which emerged from the *década infame* (1930–43) relatively divided and weak.[25] Colonel Juan Domingo Perón, appointed head of the National Department of Labour (which was rapidly elevated to the Ministry of Labour and Social Welfare) in the military government, and his associates, such as Colonel Domingo Mercante, encouraged union organization and put pressure on employers to offer favourable wage settlements, enabling workers to bargain more effectively with employers and to begin to push up real wages (which had been in decline for some years). Perhaps the single most important factor was government tolerance and encouragement of unionization.

At the same time as Perón encouraged union growth, he moved to isolate and weaken his rivals in the labour movement, particularly the Communists who attacked Perón as a neo-fascist because of his identification with a military government which would not break relations with the Axis powers, but also any unionists who showed signs of independence. There were also, of course, strong elements of corporatist thinking in Perón's approach to labour, and he was able successfully to play upon a widely held fear among Argentine elites of Communist-inspired class conflict.

Perón's apparent growing radicalization, and certainly his increasing accumulation of power, brought to a head conflict between him and the rest of the military *junta* and in October 1945 he was arrested and imprisoned. Masses of Argentine workers reacted with spontaneous demonstrations, following what was by now becoming a well-established practice. The CGT responded to this pressure from its rank-and-file by calling for a general strike to demand the release of a Minister who had acted so favourably towards the unions. There were disputes among the union leaders at the CGT meeting between those who wished to remain independent of and aloof from the military government, including its Minister of Labour, and those who wished to give conditional support to what they

---

[25] In 1945 total union membership stood at little over half a million. In 1947 the CGT claimed about a million members, and by 1950 it was claiming five million members, though this is clearly an exaggeration and probably no more than two or two-and-a-half million workers were ever enrolled in the CGT. Ruben Rotondaro, *Realidad y cambio en el sindicalismo* (Buenos Aires, 1971), p. 145; Louise M. Doyon, 'El crecimiento sindical bajo el perónismo', in Juan Carlos Torre (ed.), *La formacíon del sindicalismo peronista* (Buenos Aires, 1988), pp. 174–8.

saw as a clearly pro-labour element within the *junta*. The pro-Perón position prevailed by a vote of 21 to 19, and a strike was called for 18 October 1945.[26] The CGT strike call was, however, anticipated by the workers of Buenos Aires who, on the 17 October streamed across the bridges dividing the working-class districts from the downtown area and marched on the Presidential Palace in the Plaza de Mayo. Contemporary observers were shocked by the spectacle of the 'masses' taking over the streets of bourgeois Buenos Aires; for their part, the evidence suggests a tremendous feeling of empowerment on the part of Argentine workers. Faced with the massive demonstration in the Plaza de Mayo the *junta* backtracked and released Perón from his confinement. His speech later that evening from the balcony of the Casa Rosada marked a significant watershed in the history of the Argentine working class, and the formalization of that class's identification with its leader.

On the basis of this massive wave of working-class support, Perón became a leading contender in the Presidential elections scheduled for 1946. The elections pitted Perón against the conservative opposition, organized in the Unión Democrática and supported by the Communist Party which, following international ideological politics, labelled Perón a fascist. Perón's assumption of a nationalist mantle was further helped by the publication by the U.S. State Department of a 'Blue Book' denouncing the Argentine and Bolivian regimes for Axis sympathies, and by Ambassador Spruille Braden's highly visible efforts on behalf of the Democratic Union and against Perón. Perón turned U.S. hostility to his advantage with the slogan, 'Braden or Perón' and was thereby able to put together a coalition that included organized labour, the Church, nationalist sectors of the military, and sections of the elite who feared communism more than they feared Perón.

Union leaders formed the Partido Laborista to support Perón's candidacy, envisioning this as something rather similar to the British Labour Party. However, immediately after his election, Perón moved to weaken and eventually destroy the Partido Laborista and bring under control or eliminate its leaders. During the next two or three years Perón moved successfully to bring the unions to heel. This was done by attacking the remaining leaders in the CGT and the Partido Laborista, and by bringing the constituent unions of the CGT under increasingly centralized control.

[26] The proceedings of this meeting are reproduced in Torre (ed.), *La formación del sindicalismo peronista*, pp. 153–68.

Using the pretext of a visiting delegation of U.S. labour leaders to impugn the loyalty of independent socialist, Luís Gay, Perón forced him to resign from his position as head of the CGT in January 1947. He was replaced with an unconditional Peronist. The parallel process of driving the Communists out of the union movement had begun early, and had led to intense conflicts with the meatpackers' union, led by Communist José Peter, and later by *laborista* Cipriano Reyes. Peronist tactics were to harass the independent unions, set up parallel unions, and to use the influence of the Ministry of Labour to ensure that the Peronist unions were rewarded with wage increases. Independently-minded working-class militants were forced out of key union positions and the unions were effectively brought into an ideological orbit which linked their fate so closely with the Peronist regime that independent action, let alone opposition, was possible only at great cost. Cipriano Reyes was finally imprisoned in 1948 for allegedly plotting to assassinate Perón, and remained there until the overthrow of the regime in 1955.

Although Perón's rise to power had been accompanied by massive mobilization and an increase in strike activity, as Perón began to consolidate his power in the late 1940s the frequency of strikes dropped dramatically. A combination of political control over the unions, a favourable labour market, and rising real wages were the major factors in the impressive turnaround in strike activity. During the mobilization period the number of strikes was 47 in 1945, 142 in 1946, 64 in 1947 and 103 in 1948. Strike activity then fell off drastically, to 36 in 1949 and remained low for the remainder of the Peronist government.[27] Perhaps the most impressive feature of the Peronist mobilization of the working class was the dramatic rise in unionization. As we have seen, Argentine union membership rose from about half a million in 1946 to over two million in 1950. Unions now had substantial funds, there was an impressive social security system, and unions provided a wide range of fringe benefits, such as medical care and subsidized vacation resorts, to their members. The price was an increasing subservience to the state. At a symbolic level this was most clearly marked by the 1947 promulgation of the 'rights of the worker' which singularly failed to mention the right to strike. By the end of the decade Argentina was back in line with the overall trend in the region. Despite a rhetorically pro-labour government, Argentine unions had been largely domesticated.

[27] Munck, *Argentina*, p. 144.

POST-WAR INSTITUTIONALIZATION: CORPORATISM IN
THE 1950S AND 1960S

The Second World War and its immediate aftermath constituted a major watershed in the development of the labour movement in Latin America. In the larger countries of the region the world recession of the 1930s and then the war itself had stimulated the growth of import-substituting industries. These years had seen the growth of the urban proletariat, and in Argentina and Brazil, its transformation from a largely immigrant to an increasingly national class. These changes in the nature of the working class occurred simultaneously with major shifts in the political system in a number of countries, changes which had implications for the ways in which labour could organize, both at the union level and in terms of national politics.

From 1950 to 1970 the urban labour force of Latin America increased from 46 to 61 per cent of the total labour force (and in 1985 was estimated at 70 per cent of the total). During this period industrial employment expanded from 19 per cent of the total labour force in 1950 to 23 per cent in 1970 (and 26 per cent in 1980); employment in services expanded even more rapidly from 27 per cent in 1950 to 36 per cent in 1970 (and 42 per cent in 1980). The labour force as a whole grew at an annual rate of 2.1 per cent in the period 1950–60, and 2.45 per cent between 1960 and 1970 (and 3.12 per cent between 1970 and 1980). The increase in absolute numbers is even more impressive: the industrial labour force for Latin America as a whole rose from 10,561,000 in 1950 to just under 20 million in 1970 (and to 30,413,000 in 1980). This remarkable expansion was most noticeable in Brazil, Venezuela and Mexico which saw a fourfold increase in the industrial labour force between 1950 and 1980, and least apparent in Argentina, Uruguay and Chile, whose industrial labour forces increased by between 30 and 50 per cent over this period.[28] This period also saw the rise and maturation of new industries, particularly the metalworking complex, which gave rise to the organization of new contingents of the working class.[29]

[28] Inter-American Development Bank, *Economic and Social Progress in Latin America: 1987 Report* (Washington, D.C., 1987), pp. 98–9. The figures are: Brazil, 2,965,000 to 11,767,000; Mexico, 1,482,000 to 6,451,000; Venezuela, 357,000 to 1,406,000. The number of industrial workers more than doubled in Colombia (711,000 to 1,877,000) and Peru (471,000 to 980,000).

[29] See chapter by Orlandina de Oliveira and Bryan Roberts, 'Urban Growth and Urban Social Structure in Latin America, 1930–1990', *Cambridge History of Latin America* Vol VI, Part I for a discussion of occupational change and its relationship to social stratification.

Despite major differences between countries in the ways in which the growing labour movements were linked with the national political systems, many of them had in common during the post-war period more or less serious and enduring experiments with corporatism. Industrial relations in general, and union organization in particular, came increasingly to be regulated by the State. Frequently, this meant a considerable loss of autonomy by unions, though in some cases it also meant an expansion in the role of unions in national life, a solidification and bureaucratization of what had hitherto often been ideologically militant but organizationally feeble unions, and in a number of countries the beginning of a sustained rise in real living standards for at least the better organized sections of the working class. This relative degree of institutionalization on the one hand and repression on the other produced a certain amount of peace on the labour front, though the post-war years were by no means uneventful. Labour conflict was at best contained, and not eliminated, and such control as governments were able to achieve proved increasingly fragile. As the newer industrial sectors of Latin America came to maturity, a new generation of workers and union leaders arose to break the post-war truce and begin a new phase of labour militancy.

No doubt much of this occurred largely in response to changes in the industrial and occupational structure, as well as because of the political alliances entered into by the unions. And such gains as were made were both limited in coverage – the bulk of the working population remained beyond the scope of effective labour and social security legislation – and subject to erosion in periods of economic downturn and political repression. Nevertheless, the post-war period saw an impressive institutionalization of labour movements throughout the continent, often building on previous efforts and continuing a clear historical trajectory, but in many marking a significant break with past traditions. By 1948, in the majority of countries of the region, the institutional forms which would channel labour conflict for the next two or three decades were in place. For this relatively lengthy period, industrial relations systems in Latin America served effectively to channel and contain industrial conflict and prevent it from becoming either a major economic or a major political concern to governments. In so far as there is any single thread running through these years it is the combination of relatively rapid economic growth and a variety of corporatist arrangements for mediating labour conflict.

These corporatist systems varied from country to country. Brazil stands at one end of the continuum, with a highly codified set of labour laws which greatly restricted union activity, and with constant governmental intervention in the regulation of industrial relations. Unions were organized on a territorial and industry-wide basis, so that, for instance, all workers in the textile industry in the state of São Paulo would belong to one union. The system was designed to reduce competition between unions to a minimum. Federations and confederations of unions were strictly controlled and had limited powers. The organization of employers' associations paralleled the structure of the workers' unions. Industrial disputes were mediated through a set of tripartite institutions, with representatives of the employers, the union leadership and the state sitting on key commissions and labour courts. Union funds still came from the *imposto sindical* described above, and were distributed between the local union and the regional and national organizations, with strict legal control over how these funds could be invested and spent. Most of the money was to go towards the provision of a range of welfare services for union members. The *imposto sindical* was, in effect, a social security programme, and Brazilian unions were increasingly seen by their members to function as providers of social security benefits rather than as instruments for collective bargaining. Since most wage increases and individual worker grievances were settled in the complex labour court system, collective bargaining and dispute settlement were largely removed from the sphere of the workplace. Nothing equivalent to shop stewards ever developed and unions had no workplace function.

The corporatist system served to produce a conservative union leadership and a bias against rank-and-file mobilization. Since union finances were independent of the number of union members, but expenditure on union services was directly correlated with the size of union membership, there was no incentive for union leaders to increase membership. There were also direct political controls: candidates for union office were required to provide certificates of good conduct from the DOPS. Finally, the government had the right to intervene in unions to remove union leaders and to replace them with government appointees.

This impressive panoply of labour legislation removed conflict from the shop-floor, where unions had no institutionalized presence, and from direct negotiations between workers and employers, into the vast bureaucracy of the labour courts and the Ministry of Labour where conciliation and arbitration procedures were insulated from the immediate demands of the rank and file. At the same time, the salience of the welfare function of the union for the individual members had the effect of depoliticizing union activity still further. It was during these years that union leaders became a bureaucratic caste and the epithet *pelego* (the sheepskin placed between the saddle and the horse to enable the horse to support the rider's weight without ill effects) came into general use.

Brazil's corporatist labour legislation was more sytematic and allowed for less union autonomy than elsewhere in the continent. In Mexico a similar corporatist body of labour legislation had come into being with the Federal Labour Law of 1931, building on the guarantees of labour rights in the revolutionary constitution of 1917. But the corporatist organization of unions themselves came only in 1936 with the formation of the CTM and its affiliation with the official party. Indeed, Mexican corporatism must be seen as originating largely in the reorganization of the official party in 1938 along corporatist lines. Cárdenas had encouraged the growth of a unified labour confederation, and had brought it into the political system as one of the key components of the revolutionary coalition. At the same time, he had been insistent that a clear line of demarcation be drawn between it and the peasant sector.

To these two sectors were added the military (later abolished as a specific sector of the official party in 1940) and the so-called 'popular sector' (created in 1943) which was a catch-all for government workers, organizations of women and youth, and a host of independent workers such as taxi drivers and small merchants who were ultimately dependent on government patronage for their livelihood. Public employees were organized in the Federación de Sindicatos de Trabajadores al Servicio del Estado (FSTSE) which was affiliated with the popular sector of the official party, rather than with the labour sector. This meant, for example, that the massive teachers' union belonged to FSTSE and had no close links with other unions in the labour sector.

Providing that they did not directly challenge the government, Mexican union leaders had a measure of autonomy to which Brazilian union leaders could not realistically aspire. Instead of being largely a low-status transmission belt for government policy, Mexican labour leaders were an integral, if subordinate, part of the ruling apparatus. As such, individual leaders did not merely exercise political power, but were also able to consolidate personal empires and develop a host of clientelistic relationships with their rank and file and with other political actors. An indicator of the political importance of Mexican union leaders has been their substantial representation in Congress. Between 1937 and 1970 the number of 'worker' deputies in the chamber of deputies oscillated between a high of 52 and a low of 18 (out of a total that varied between 147 and 214).[30]

The complex and varied nature of Mexican union organization also acted in the same direction. Instead of the uniform structure of Brazilian unionism, Mexican unions have been of every shape and size. A key component of union ranks has been the small number of national industrial unions. These have organized all the workers in a given industry throughout the country. The national industrial unions have been large, and have had considerable potential industrial muscle.[31] There are also state-wide industrial unions, unions formed at the enterprise and plant level, and unions of *oficios varios* which bring together workers in a variety of activities in small towns to form a purely territorial basis for unionism. This organizational structure had produced over a thousand unions by the 1960s, dominated by a few very large unions, but with a considerable combined influence of the many extremely small unions. The average size of unions in 1960 was a mere 134 members.

Adding to the complexity of the Mexican union structure has been the freedom to form higher level organizations. While the CTM retained a predominant position in Mexican unionism during most of the post-war period, organizing perhaps two-thirds of the unionized labour force, it had to co-exist with a number of rival federations and confederations. The CROM and CGT, which had seen their heyday in the 1920s, continued to exist, and in 1952 a number of unions formed the Confederación Revolucionaria de Obreros y Campesinos (CROC). Revolutionary in name only, the formation of this rival to the CTM owed much to the continual struggle within the ranks of the union bureaucracy for access to government patronage. A number of smaller confederations also cluttered the organizational landscape. All of these organizations maintained affiliation with the official party, and they were linked together from time to time by umbrella organizations, such as the Bloque de Unidad Obrera (1955) and the Congreso del Trabajo (1966). In addition, a number of unions re-

---

[30] Mario Ramírez Rancaño, *Crecimiento económico e inestabilidad política en México* (Mexico, D.F., 1977), p. 41.

[31] While statistics are notoriously unreliable, estimates of the membership of the railway workers' union in the 1970s put it at between 60,000 and 100,000; the miners' union probably had about 70,000 members, the two unions in the electrical industry together had about 80,000 members, the oil workers' union about 70,000, and the telephone workers' union about 18,000. Francisco Zapata, 'Afiliación y organización sindical en México', in José Luis Reyna, Francisco Zapata, Marcelo Miquet Fleury and Silvia Gómez-Tagle et al., *Tres estudios sobre el movimiento obrero en México* (Mexico, D.F., 1976), p. 123; and Manuel Camacho, *El futuro inmediato* (Mexico, D.F., 1980), pp. 126–7.

mained outside the ranks of the official party. These included the so-called 'white' (employer-sponsored) unions of Monterrey, and the militant 'independent' unions linked to the Frente Auténtico del Trabajo and the Unidad Obrera Independiente, controlling about 10 per cent of total union membership in the 1970s.

Nor were Mexican trade union finances as closely regulated as those in Brazil. Indeed, corruption was rampant and there can be little doubt that some key figures in the union bureaucracy at least, profited from their position to amass considerable personal wealth. Strike legislation and legislation concerning union funds also allowed a great degree of union autonomy than has been the case in Brazil.

While Mexican unions also played an important welfare role, the provision of social security has been more centralized and more directly administered by the state than in Brazil. The flexibility of the Mexican industrial relations system, together with a number of significant rights for organized labour, meant that union leaders had a much more complex relationship with their membership than has typically been the case in Brazil. The Mexican system has been permeated throughout with complex webs of clientelistic relationships in a way that has been much less common in Brazil.

Brazil and Mexico, in their different ways, are the clearest cases of corporatist control of labour relations in Latin America. At times, other countries operated one or other variant of corporatism in their industrial relations systems; in Argentina during Peronist and military administrations, for example, and in Peru during the Velasco Alvarado presidency. But corporatism has by no means been the universal rule in Latin America. In Chile, Colombia, Bolivia and Peru, the norm has been for a more 'liberal' system of industrial relations to prevail. In Venezuela the post-war period saw the emergence of something resembling a social-democratic type of industrial relations system, with the unions generally identified with Acción Democrática, supporting it in an uncomfortable alliance when that party was in power, and when in opposition engaging in a greater degree of direct confrontation with non-AD governments. Even in Brazil and Mexico there have been limits to the corporatist system and it has at times been seriously challenged. In Cuba after 1959 unions were largely subordinated to the Communist regime, but even here they still played important roles in mediating local disputes and in mobilizing worker effort for increased productivity.

Throughout the region the salient feature of the union structures that were established in the postwar period was the high degree of regulation of industrial relations and union activity by the state. And linked with this state-centered organization of industrial relations was the high degree of politicization of union activity. Although the relationship between unions and parties has varied from country to country, in most countries unions tended to be closely related to political parties, sometimes clearly aligned with a particular party, sometimes serving as battlegrounds between competing parties and ideologies. However, given the paucity of historical research on this topic, the degree to which this politicization of the higher reaches of the labour movement directly affected industrial relations on the shop-floor remains a moot point.

The degree to which industrial relations were organized in a corporatist fashion in Latin America varied not only from country to country but also displayed considerable change over time. The military governments that came to power in many countries in the 1960s and 1970s oscillated between direct repression of union activity and efforts to channel it in a revitalized corporatist framework. Similarly, civilian governments were also torn between the use of corporatist mechanisms of negotiation with organized labour, usually in the form of an incomes policy, and attempts to rely exclusively on free collective bargaining to determine wage levels. There was also a tendency, particularly in times of intense political mobilization and/or economic crisis for sections of the labour movement to break away from corporatist control systems and to develop more independent and oppositional organizations. Particularly in those countries with a more politicized labour movement, the implementation of austerity measures as part of a stabilization programme might well trigger widespread labour protest, leading to the development of a political crisis and sometimes to military intervention.

In general, the prevailing import substitution industrialization (ISI) growth model meant that most Latin American governments, most of the time, felt constrained to play an active role in industrial relations as part of a larger process of active economic management. At a macroeconomic level this meant attempts to determine wage and employment levels, and to prevent industrial conflict from frightening away potential foreign investors. At a micro level the institutions of corporatist labour regulation operated largely through the labour courts and the social security systems. In some ways the labour courts functioned as a sort of 'cooling out' system for the grievances of individual workers, displacing the locus of conflict from the workplace to the legal system. The legal processes involved often were protracted and usually resulted in negotiated compromises between workers and employers. This system, both at the macro and at the micro level, heightened the importance within the labour movement of professional labour lawyers, some of whom often came to play an important advisory and leadership role in the labour movement.

These corporatist systems were underpinned by the expansion of wage employment in urban areas and, at least in the more rapidly industrializing countries, by substantial wage growth. This expansion of the urban work-force, however, produced quite diverse results. As a first approximation, it is useful to distinguish those workers who were in the organized, formal, 'protected' sector of the economy from the rest. The size of the formal proletariat was quite variable, both between countries and, indeed, between cities in the same country. For the workers in the formal sector, the post-war years were good years. Not only was there an expansion in the number of jobs in industry, but this was also accompanied in several countries by legislation that favoured job stability. Although job stability was a key feature of employment in the state apparatus and in state-owned industries, it also operated to a substantial degree in the large firms in the private sector. This did not prevent shake-outs and job rotation during recessions, but the overall level of job protection in the formal sector of many Latin American countries throughout much of the post-war period seems to have been relatively high.[32] The increasing role of the state meant a steady expansion of the state and para-state sectors, areas particularly propitious to the development of large-scale unionization.

To expanding employment and a certain measure of job stability must be added a long period of wage growth for many workers. Although there is considerable variation in national experiences, there was a widely experienced decline in real wages during the Second World War in Latin America, followed by a long period of growth of wages. In Peru, Colombia, Mexico and Brazil real industrial wages probably doubled during the 1950s and 1960s; in both Argentina and Chile, on the other hand, wage growth was quite erratic: Argentine wages remained stagnant, and Chilean wages continued to fall during the 1950s, and only recovered the level

---

[32] There has been considerable variation between countries in terms of job protection, with many workers in Mexico enjoying considerable tenure rights, whereas Brazilian employers seem to have resorted much more frequently to layoffs to control labour costs. For examples drawn from the automobile industry, see John Humphrey, *Capitalist Control and Workers' Struggle in the Brazilian Auto Industry* (Princeton, N.J., 1982), pp. 105–14; and Ian Roxborough, *Unions and Politics in Mexico: the Case of the Automobile Industry* (Cambridge, 1984), pp. 61–4.

they had been at the beginning of the period by 1969.[33] This long period
of growth faltered, and in many cases came to an end in the mid-seventies
and generally with the onset of the debt crisis in 1982. Wages rose fastest
and almost continuously for skilled workers, and slowly and at times not
at all for workers at the lower end of the labour market (so that even
during the boom years of the 'Brazilian miracle' unskilled workers failed to
gain the real wage improvements that went to those whose skills were in
short supply). Real wages on the whole rose less rapidly than productivity,
and labour's income share generally deteriorated. But for individual workers, this was by and large a time of real improvement in welfare.

Unionization in the formal sector also tended to be high, particularly in
the state sector and in large manufacturing and transportation establishments. Estimates of the total unionized labour force are notoriously unreliable, and the data must be treated with considerable caution. The total
number of workers unionized in Latin America in 1946 was perhaps 3.8
million. By 1960 it had risen to something like 6.6 million, and 14
million in 1964, with Argentina, Brazil and Mexico accounting for the
lion's share.[34] As a percentage of the total labour force (18.3 per cent), and
more particularly of the urban labour force (where the rate of unionization
was probably double that for the labour force as a whole), this was not
unimpressive. Argentina, Peru, Brazil, Mexico and Venezuela had unionization rates of between 25 and 40 per cent of the total economically active
population (which are not dissimilar to rates for OECD countries). Colombia, Chile and the smaller countries had unionization rates of between 10
and 20 per cent.[35] Unionization rates have been highest in mining, plantations, in the public sector, and in industries dominated by large-scale
manufacturing establishments. During the 1950s and 1960s unions in the
metal-working industries (especially automobile manufacturing) were
highly unionized and played an important leadership role for the union
movement as a whole. The rapid expansion of the service sector (and
particularly of state employment) also led to union expansion and militancy among white-collar workers, particularly in health, banking and
education. Given the importance of the state sector in the economy, it is
not surprising that this has been one of the strongholds of unionism in

---

[33] John Martin, 'Labor's Real Wages in Latin America Since 1940', *Statistical Abstract of Latin America*,
18 (1977), pp. 211–32.

[34] Victor Alba, *Politics and the Labor Movement in Latin America* (Stanford, Cal., 1968), p. 211.

[35] It must be stressed that these are merely orders of magnitude. See Francisco Zapata, *El Conflicto
Sindical en América Latina* (Mexico, D.F., 1986), p. 159.

Latin America. Of particular importance have been state enterprises (railways, communications, public utilities, health, education, energy, mineral exploitation, steel) and municipal workers' unions.

While most places of work remained small and employed fewer than ten workers, a small number of very large enterprises (both in the public and in the private sector) employing a substantial proportion of the labour force, formed the basis for union strength. Unions in these sectors of the economy were able to achieve real gains for their members throughout much of the post-war period, even in those cases where the union leaderships had evolved into a self-serving or pro-government clique. For workers elsewhere in the economy these were also years of generally rising incomes, through job security, working conditions and social security coverage fell far behind those of workers in the 'protected' sector. Wages in entry level jobs, such as construction, generally showed little tendency to rise, though it is likely that for many workers employment in this and similar sectors was simply the first step on a career ladder that would eventually lead to a better job. Teachers, post office and health workers in particular displayed high levels of organization and conflict, and increasingly adopted left-wing political ideologies. Office workers in the central government bureaucracies have been unionized in some countries, though frequently prohibitions on strike activity meant that this section of the workforce remained largely quiescent.

When unions have gone out on strike in Latin America in the post-war period, they have done so overwhelmingly because of wage issues, most frequently at times of contract renewal. General strikes to protest about government economic policy have also been an important part of the repertoire of labour action in nearly all countries. Designating a strike 'general' typically indicates more about the nature of worker demands than about the scope of labour action, which has been quite variable. While general strikes have been called in most countries throughout the twentieth century, they were most common in Bolivia, Chile, Peru and Argentina and, in the 1970s and 1980s, in Colombia and Brazil as well. Conflicts between individual workers and employers have been about a wide range of issues. Data from Mexico suggest that many of these individual conflicts have arisen from worker complaints of arbitrary dismissal.

Strike funds have tended to be small, and the pool of potential replacements high, so strikes typically have been of short duration. Analyses of trends in strike activity indicate that inflation and the general state of the economy have been the principal factors affecting changes in strike activity.[36] Although many scholars have argued that the volume of strikes depends on the political complexion of the government in power, this appears to be a less important factor than was once thought.

Miners have usually had a high strike propensity, and much of the variation in strike rates between countries can be attributed to the presence or absence of a substantial mining sector. In the 1970s workers in metalworking tended to be the most militant, with white-collar workers in the public sector (and in banking) a close second. In the 1980s it appeared as if public sector workers had taken the lead in industrial militancy. This was partly due to the steady process of proletarianization of white-collar work, and to government attempts to reduce the size of the public sector and to hold the line on wage rises by controlling wages in this sector.

The post-war institutionalization of industrial relations, together with long-term growth in both wages and employment, was instrumental in securing two decades of relative labour peace for many countries in Latin America. The success of the conservative consolidations of the late 1940s notwithstanding, this lengthy period of labour peace was broken with some frequency by outbursts of conflict arising from a variety of sources. The most common detonators of widespread labour unrest were bouts of high inflation and the subsequent implementation of stabilization policies. With economic and political instability leading unions to focus on government policy, and with a combination of weakness in terms of workplace bargaining (a result of a generally loose labour market) and the widespread linkages between unions and political parties, the high level of politicization of Latin American labour movements in the post-war period is readily understandable.

The Brazilian labour movement was essential dormant from 1947 to 1952. The number of union members actually declined during this period, from 798,000 to 747,000. In 1951, Getúlio Vargas, elected president the previous year, allowed union elections, cancelling the requirement that candidates for union office swear a loyalty oath. Both the PTB and the Communists did well in these elections and from 1952 onwards labour activity began to pick up. Vargas himself sought, not entirely successfully, to channel labour militancy into nationalist forms and to offer symbolic rather than economic rewards. There were major strike movements in São Paulo in 1953 (the so-called 'strike of the 300,000') and

[36] Francisco Zapata, *El Conflicto Sindical*, pp. 155–75.

again in 1957. The Kubitschek administration (1956–61) adopted a confused and vacillating approach to labour, attempting to promote peace on the industrial relations front and allowing the Communists to function even though they were still denied legality.

The coming to power of João Goulart in 1961 ushered in a brief period of political and economic mobilization in Brazil. Strike activity had been infrequent during most of the post-war period. In 1958 there were only 31 strikes, and in 1959 and 1960, 73 strikes each year. Beginning in 1961 strike activity expanded, with 115 strikes that year, 148 in 1962 and 172 in 1963. Union militants began increasingly to assert their autonomy from the control systems that had operated for most of the post-war period. The Comando Geral dos Trabalhadores (CGT) was formed in 1962 and led the 'strike of the 700,000' in 1963. However, the base of the CGT was largely in Rio de Janeiro, in the unions linked with state employment, and in transport. The industrial unions of São Paulo were largely absent from the national mobilizations called by the CGT. Overall, growing union militancy, and the political salience of strikes called by the CGT, was an important contributory factor in the heightening crisis that led up to the coup of April 1964.

The first action of the military *junta* that put an end to the Goulart presidency in 1964 was to intervene in 70 per cent of the unions with more than 5,000 members (a total of 563 interventions), replacing the existing leaderships with state-appointed (often military) appointees.[37] There now ensued another period of union quiescence. Only at the end of the 1970s did union activity re-emerge as a major factor in national life.

In Mexico efforts to control organized labour – the sequence of *charrazos* – occupied most of the presidency of Miguel Alemán (1946–52). By the end of the decade Fidel Velázquez and his *camarilla* (coterie) were in control of the union movement, and apart from isolated protest movements like the strike and 'caravan of hunger' of the miners of Nueva Rosita, Coahuila in 1953, there was little in the way of labour conflict until 1958. In that year, a grass-roots movement in the railway union led to a series of strikes and finally to an open confrontation with the government, with the use of troops to break the strike, mass dismissals and the arrest of the strike leaders. With this exception, there were no insignificant industrial disputes in Mexico until the early 1970s.

---

[37] Leôncio Martins Rodrigues, 'Sindicalismo e Classe Operária (1930–1964)', in Boris Fausto (ed.), *História Geral da Civilização Brasiliera*, Vol. 10 (São Paulo, 1981), p. 551.

As has been suggested above, labour peace was not due exclusively to the operation of mechanisms of control over rank and file militancy, either by union leaders or by the state. From the early 1950s until the mid-1970s, real wages for industrial workers in Mexico rose at a steady, if not spectacular rate. At the same time, the expansion of industrial employment, while rising sufficiently slowly to give rise to concern, enabled large numbers of new entrants to the urban labour force to find employment in industry, as well as in a great variety of enterprises in the service sector. Workers could feel some satisfaction in that the system was, in fact, 'delivering the goods' in terms of rising wages and growing employment, however low absolute levels of income might be.

There is, of course, very little information on worker attitudes during most of this period; much must remain in the realm of speculation. However, the tremendous growth in the industrial labour force – a three-fold increase over a generation – had a considerable effect in transforming the composition of the Mexican working class. While we do not have sufficiently precise statistics to say with any confidence exactly what changes occurred in the working class, the overall data, together with a number of case studies and small samples, suggest that the vast majority of Mexican industrial workers in the late sixties and early seventies were migrants or children of migrants. While a core of proletarian families helped maintain a sense of working-class tradition, the massive recomposition of the industrial labour force, coming on top of the defeat of labour militancy in the 1940s, almost certainly meant a dilution of class cohesion and militancy. The experience of individual mobility may well have been the primary element of class consciousness for many Mexican workers. Steady progress in individual living standards, the massification of the urban workforce, and the continuous operation of a sophisticated and at times brutal system of political and industrial control together explain the long period of relative industrial peace.

The institutionalization of labour relations in Venezuela, despite the overthrow of the AD government in 1948 and a brief (and unsuccessful) attempt by Pérez Jiménez to create a Peronist labour movement in the mid-fifties, turned out to be a relatively stable form of social-democratic linkage between AD and the Confederación de Trabajadores de Venezuela (CTV). During periods of AD government, Venezuelan unions were willing to consider a variety of incomes policies, and strike activity tended to fall off. When AD was in opposition, however, the CTV was more likely to engage in strikes against government policy.

The story of the post-war period in Colombia was one of division and weakness in the union movement. With the militant unions defeated and repressed between 1945 and 1948, and with a rather timid Catholic organization, the UTC, representing the bulk of organized workers, it is hardly surprising that wages stagnated in Colombia until the end of the 1950s. Thereafter, the continuing good performance of the Colombian economy resulted in steady growth in real wages for most categories of urban workers, including those at the lower end of the labour market.

The 1960s saw a reinvigoration of unionism in Colombia, with the UTC losing its previously dominant position, the CTC recovering some of its strength, the emergence in 1964 of a new Communist confederation, the CSTC (Confederación Sindical de Trabajadores de Colombia), and a marked increase in strike activity. Total union membership grew slowly at first, from 166,000 in 1947 to about a quarter of a million in 1959, and then surged upwards to about 700,000 by 1965. In that year the UTC controlled 42 per cent of unionized workers, the CTC 34 per cent, and the CSTC 13 per cent.[38] A combination of recession and inflation produced a series of strikes in 1963, which, while decisively crushed, marked the beginning of a sea-change in Colombian unionism which would burst forth in a wave of union militancy in the 1970s. Within the UTC, the brand of moderate social Catholicism which had orientated its actions was challenged from within by more pragmatic currents less closely linked to the Catholic Church. A split ensued and in May 1971 the Confederación General del Trabajo (CGT) was formed. Despite rising militancy and increasingly successful attempts at coordinated actions, the Colombian union movement remained divided, with a wide range of union organizations competing for the support of the Colombian working class. Unions remained relatively weak, and were frequently on the defensive as most post-war Colombian governments pursued liberal economic policies.

Unlike the working class in Mexico and Brazil, but in many ways similar to that of Argentina, the Chilean working class of the 1950s and 1960s displayed considerable class unity. Despite intense ideological rivalry between the Socialist and Communist Parties, in 1953 the Central Unica de Trabajadores (CUT) was formed. An analysis of the party political affiliations of delegates to CUT Congresses between 1957 and 1972 shows the Communists as the largest grouping (31 to 46 per cent), fol-

---

[38] Rocío Londoño, 'La estructura sindical colombiana en la década del 70', in Hernando Gómez Buendía, Rocío Londoño Bolero and Guillermo Perry Rubio, *Sindicalismo y política económica* (Bogotá, 1986), p. 109.

lowed by the Socialists (23 to 33 per cent) and the Christian Democrats (10 to 25 per cent).[39] This meant Communist-Socialist leadership, though in 1972 and 1973 Christian Democratic unionists were frequently involved in head-on clashes with the rest of the CUT.

Union membership in the urban sector was 283,000 in 1952, dropped somewhat to 270,000 in 1964, and then grew rapidly under the Christian Democratic administration to 429,000 in 1969. Chilean unions have been small (in 1967 there were 2,796 unions covering urban workers, with a total membership of 361,350 giving an average union size of 129 workers per union), and have relied on political parties to press their demands.[40] The centre of Chilean unionism has been in mining, particularly in the huge copper mines of Chuquicamata and El Teniente, but also in the coal mining district of Lota-Coronel near Concepción. Most factory industry was located either in Concepción or in Santiago, where a number of industrial belts, *cordones industriales,* grew up.

Chilean industrial conflicts during most of the post-war period were marked by two phenomena: (a) a striking duality in the labour force between the small and declining copper mining sector (the labour force employed in mining dropped from 6 to 3 per cent of the total labour force between 1940 and 1980) and the mass of urban workers organized into relatively small and industrially weak unions; and (b) the intense ideological competition between Communists, Socialists and Christian Democrats for the allegiance of the working class. The highly politicized class consciousness of Chilean workers led to intense internal divisions at the national political level, and the legal distinction between *obreros* and *empleados* served to further fragment the Chilean working class at the level of individual workplaces.

Workers in the copper mines enjoyed relatively high wages, though the high cost of living in the mining camps and the harsh conditions of the northern desert had also to be taken into account. Perhaps partly as a result, there was considerable rotation in the Chilean mining proletariat, as well as high levels of both industrial militancy and political radicalism.

Given the troubled state of the Chilean economy during the fifties and early sixties, it is not surprising that strike levels were relatively high and increasing. During the period 1932–42 there had been 21 strikes per year on average. This figure rose to 114 for the period 1943–9, 199 for 1950–

[39] Alan Angell, *Politics and the Labour Movement in Chile* (Oxford, 1971), p. 218.
[40] Angell, *Politics,* p. 54,

7, 243 for 1960–3 and to 937 strikes per year for the period 1964–9.[41] Concern over wages and inflation increasingly brought the CUT into direct conflict with the government, leading to a clash with troops in 1962 which left six dead and many wounded. The Frei government (1964–70) attempted unsuccessfully to build on its base in the union movement to expand its influence, and then attempted to bring the unions under its control, a move which was successfully resisted, not only by the Socialists and Communists but also by the left wing of the Christian Democratic party itself. Strike activity continued to rise and relations with the increasingly radicalized labour movement deteriorated.

In Argentina, in the final years of the first Peronist regime there was an economic recession; real wages fell between 1950 and 1952, recovered in 1953, but fell again in 1954 and 1955. Peronist control over the unions began to weaken somewhat and both 1950 and 1954 saw important strike waves. However, despite growing tensions within the Confederación General de Trabajo (CGT), the corporatist project seemed solid; the identification of the Argentine working class with the *patria peronista* suffered some erosion but was largely intact. It provided both a deep sense of class consciousness and, at least superficially, an impressive unity of working-class action.

Following the overthrow of Perón in 1955, a series of attempted stabilization policies, together with vacillating attitudes towards the unions and the attempt to expunge Peronism from the body politic, brought the working class into constant conflict with the post-Peronist regimes. This period of peronist 'resistance' cemented the identification of the working class with its leader and its organizational embodiment in the trade union movement. The myth of the 'golden age' of the Argentine working class under Perón (1943/6–55) was articulated and diffused in working-class culture.[42]

Some sections of Argentine unionism saw their best strategy as a political struggle for the return of a Peronist government, and reliance on state patronage to raise wages. Other sections sought to deal pragmatically with whichever government was in office, adopting the strategy of using their industrial muscle to obtain improvements for their membership. This

---

[41] Angell, *Politics,* p. 76; and Brian Loveman, *Chile: the Legacy of Hispanic Capitalism* (New York, 1979), p. 266. It should be noted that the high number of strikes in the late sixties may perhaps reflect an increasing number of strikes by agricultural workers.

[42] See Daniel James, *Resistance and Integration: Peronism and the Argentine Working Class, 1946–1976* (Cambridge, 1988), pp. 97–100.

pragmatism was perfectly compatible with militant tactics. Augusto Vandor, for example, leader of the powerful Unión Obrera Metalúrgica (UOM), who set the tone for Argentine unionism in the early 1960s, was not above using armed force and the kidnapping of executives as bargaining tactics during wage negotiations. The pragmatism of these union leaders, however, led to tensions between their desire to reach some sort of working agreement with the existing regimes, and Perón's subordination of the Peronist movement, including the unions, to his continuing efforts to return to power.

During more than ten years between 1955 and 1966, no Argentine government was strong enough to subdue organized labour. The strength of the unions, in an economy with permanent balance of payments problems and inflationary pressures, not to mention the underlying structural problems of inefficiency stemming from the model of import substitution industrialization being followed, was sufficient to frustrate most government attempts to implement stabilization policies. Dissatisfaction with the apparent failure of the civilian political parties to find a way out from Argentina's continuing economic difficulties led in 1966 to the military seizure of power. The Onganía dictatorship suspended collective bargaining and moved to strengthen the corporatist features of Argentine industrial relations. Within a year the unions were in disarray and strike activity declined.

During the 1950s the organized labour movement in Cuba, under the control of Eusebio Mujal, remained largely quiescent, and offered no organized resistance to the Batista dictatorship. This did not mean, however, that individual workers were passive. The broad civic opposition to Batista, led by Frank País in Cuba's cities, included large numbers of workers. Their organizations, however, remained aloof from the struggle and a (rather botched) call by the Fidelista resistance for a general strike in 1958 was a failure. Survey research in Cuba shortly after the triumph of the revolution indicated widespread support among workers for the new regime,[43] though as Castro consolidated his hold on power and moved into the Communist bloc Cuba's unions once more lost their organizational autonomy.

Standing out as an exception to the notion that the fifties and sixties were relatively quiet years for organized labour is the important role played by the labour movement in the Bolivian Revolution of 1952. As we

[43] See Maurice Zeitlin, *Revolutionary Politics and the Cuban Working Class* (Princeton, N.J., 1967).

have seen, continued efforts by the MNR to take power against a background of intense industrial conflict finally led to the insurrection of April 1952 in which the intervention of miners, railwaymen and urban workers was decisive. For some years thereafter the Central Obrera Boliviana (COB) participated in the revolutionary government of the MNR. The mines were nationalized and a system of workers' control was instituted.

However, despite the influence of labour in the revolutionary government, the pressing need to address Bolivia's economic problems, and particularly the secular decline in profitability of the tin mines, led to increasingly tense relations between the partners of this uneasy coalition. There was under-investment and over-manning in the tin mines, and some change in this situation was necessarily a central part of any serious stabilization programme. A first effort at a major stabilization programme was made in 1956. It was followed by the 'Triangular Plan' of 1961. The COB resisted these stabilization efforts and in 1963 overt conflict erupted with a lengthy strike at the Siglo XX mine. This strike led to a breakdown of relations between the FSTMB and the COB on the one hand, and the MNR government on the other. Finally, in November 1964 the army seized power, and in May of the following year moved decisively to break the power of the miners. Juan Lechín was arrested and deported, union leaders were fired, the mining camps occupied by the military, and wage levels driven down. Institutionalization of industrial relations and class conflict, however, remained elusive and such labour tranquility as was attained depended largely on repression.

THE 'NEW UNIONISM' BETWEEN THE LATE 1960S AND THE EARLY 1980S

In the late sixties the period of relatively peaceful and institutionalized labour relations in the two decades following the Second World War gave way to a period of renewed conflict between capital and labour. It has been asserted by some scholars that economic change in at least the larger Latin American countries produced a 'new unionism' marked by increased industrial militancy, though possibly also in some countries by a decline in political radicalism. The argument was that economic growth had brought with it an expansion of employment in newer technologically more modern industries, frequently owned by transnational companies or the state, such as the automobile industry, petrochemicals and steel, and the metal-working sector more generally. The establishments were typically large and tended to employ young men at relatively good rates of pay. Turnover in these industries was often high, but laid-off workers were likely to find other jobs elsewhere fairly rapidly. It was argued that this combination of circumstances made for industrial militancy, just as the concentration of male workforces in mining camps earlier in the period was a principal factor underlying militancy in the mining industry.

The *Cordobazo* in Argentina may be seen as the start of a decade of industrial conflict in a number of Latin American countries. At the CGT congress of March 1968 a new group of militant union leaders, mainly from the interior, elected Raimundo Ongaro as general secretary and advocated a policy of outright resistance to the increasingly authoritarian military regime. A series of plant-level disputes broke out in the newly created automobile and petrochemical industries, most of which were located in Córdoba and the Paraná industrial belt. Mass strikes in the industrial cities of Córdoba and Rosario in 1969 signalled the outbreak of the Cordobazo, which turned into a quasi-insurrectional situation as students and workers took over the centre of the city of the 29th and 30th of May. The Cordobazo had to be put down by the military. Whatever the specific reasons for the revolts in Córdoba and Rosario (and a repetition in 1971 of this confluence of urban and industrial grievances), the pressure exerted by them forced the military regime to begin a withdrawal from power, leading to the re-election of Perón in 1973. The Cordobazo was followed, as we shall see, by the rise of the 'independent unions' and the 'Democratic Current' in the Electricity Workers' union in Mexico in the mid-1970s and the mass strikes in the ABC region of São Paulo in the late 1970s, leading to the formation of the Central Unica dos Trabalhadores (CUT) and the Partido dos Trabalhadores (PT) in Brazil. It remains to be seen, however, to what extent these were related phenomena.

In all these cases young workers in the metal-working industries were prominent in the movements, though workers in other industries were also mobilized. Most of these movements also had in common opposition to an authoritarian regime and to a system of industrial relations and union control that was felt to be unrepresentative. In this way they can be seen as part of a larger development of what some observers have called 'new social movements'. The 1970s was a period of coincidence between specifically labour struggles on the one hand, and wider urban social movements on the other hand. At the most general level, these urban social movements embodied popular struggles for an improvement in their economic and social well-being on the one hand, and for re-democratization and a greater and fuller form of citizenship on the other hand. Concretely, they included such diverse phenomena as neighbourhood-based struggles for access to land, housing and urban services, movements to promote and defend the position of women, gays and ethnic minorities, and a host of sectoral and special interest associations such as students, pensioners and housewives. While many of these social movements were of largely local scope, some developed both protest and pressure at the national level. To some considerable degree, many of these urban social movements involved workers and their families in a new setting parallel to that of industrial action.

Foremost among the struggles for a decent standard of living were those that revolved around the 'urban question'. The rapid urbanization of this period increased the urgency of mundane struggles over urban services (transport, health, water, electricity, refuse collection, sewage, roads, schools, police, and so on), access to land on which to construct housing, and a variety of related issues. Quite often left-wing political parties played a role in providing the organizational support for land seizures, though this varied greatly from country to country. In many places social networks of ethnicity or place of origin provided an alternative framework for organization. In some countries, notably Brazil and some of the Central American countries, radical elements of the Catholic Church provided an important contingent of cadres for the new social movements, as well as scarce organizational resources.

The nature of the linkage between distributive struggle in the sphere of consumption (the urban question) and conflicts at the workplace is a topic that has not been as yet thoroughly explored. In cities and towns with concentrated, large-scale enterprises or a single industry there have often been visible links between the two sets of economic conflicts. These have ranged from community support for strikers to situations bordering on full-scale urban insurrection, as in the Cordobazos of 1969 and 1971. Linking the world of work and the urban question are two key features of the class structure: the degree of residential segregation and homogeneity of various economic groups; and the extent to which family survival strategies interconnect the spheres of work and domestic life. That these sorts of connections have existed is indisputable, as is the fact that they have varied widely from city to city, and from country to country, as well as over time. Beyond this not a great deal is known.

In the post-war period, and most obviously with the wave of authoritarian military governments which came to power in the 1960s and 1970s, organized labour has frequently, though by no means universally, found itself at odds with dictatorships. Although a frequent response of the labour leadership has been to seek some form of accommodation with the military government, the general constraints on union activity and wage compression, to say nothing of episodes of intense repression directed against rank-and-file activists, have stimulated both rank-and-file insurgency and inclined organized labour to participate actively in pro-democracy movements. Social movements aimed at restoring democracy have been important throughout Latin America in this period and have provided labour movements with a bridge between their narrowly defined sectoral interests and a notion of themselves as articulating and representing the citizenship issues of civil society as a whole. These pro-democracy movements of the seventies and eighties deserve the label 'social movements' since their range extended far beyond that of the civilian political parties to include trade unions, employers' associations, students and a host of other groups coalesced in loosely organized efforts to bring pressure on dictatorships to allow free elections. In addition to putting public pressure on dictatorships to release political prisoners, human rights organizations also provided support groups for families of the victims of arbitrary state violence. Throughout the continent labour's struggles to organize and pursue collective bargaining brought it into the mainstream of wider struggles for democratization and a respect for citizenship and civil rights.

The upsurge of rank-and-file militancy threatened to create new union organizations paralleling and challenging existing unions in a number of countries. This was perhaps the most salient aspect of the 'new unionism'. It led either to radicalization of conservative union leadership – unless it could fend off or confront and defeat the insurgents, or to the emergence of new breakaway unions and union confederations. In Mexico, the Unión Obrera Independiente (UOI) and the Frente Auténtico de Trabajo (FAT) expanded to control perhaps 10 per cent of total union membership by the end of the 1970s, including workers in a number of key sectors. In some important unions, like the teachers' union, unions in some auto plants, in some of the steel mills controlled by the mining and metal-working union, and in some sections of the oil industry, militant rank-and-file movements developed and at times appeared to be on the verge of taking over. Among these movements for union independence from the pro-government *charros* the most important was the Tendencia Democrática which was influential among the electrical workers during the first half of the 1970s. The unification of the electricity generating industry brought pressures on the three existing unions to merge. The largest of these unions was a classical *charro* union, but the other two smaller unions had retained both a degree of internal democracy and a commitment to radical nationalism. As the merger movement got under way, the Tendencia Democrática emerged in an effort to prevent the smaller democratic unions from simply being engulfed by the *charros*. The Tendencia Democrática was important not simply because it was the most visible expression of a broad-ranging movement which threatened to break up the conservative institutionalization of the 1948 *charrazo,* bringing into question the whole relationship between the union movement and Mexico's governing party, the PRI, but also because, with its popular nationalist call for a resumption of the *cardenista* heritage of the Mexican revolution, it served as a rallying point for a much larger, if as yet inchoate, movement for political opening in Mexico.

The incumbent union leaderships responded to these challenges by direct attacks on the insurgent rank-and-file movements, by concessions and by verbal radicalization. The Tendencia Democrática was defeated, almost certainly through manipulation of union elections and intimidation. Although this movement had appeared strong in the early 1970s, and had served as a pole around which like-minded unionists could organize, 1975 was its peak and by 1977 the Tendencia Democrática had declined to a shadow of its former self. In the automobile industry insurgent challenges were met with direct opposition by union leaders in Chrysler (successfully) and in Volkswagen (unsuccessfully). Militant movements in steel works controlled by the Mining and Metal-working Union were denied representation at the union's national congress and gradually shunted aside. Another response on the part of conservative trade union leaderships was to co-opt the radical challengers, as was done in the case of insurgent leader Francisco Hérnandez Juárez, who led a number of important strikes in the Telephone Workers' union in the 1970s, defeating the incumbent leadership, but who subsequently accepted the constraints on militancy imposed by the Mexican state.

In Brazil in the second half of the 1970s the ABC region of greater São Paulo emerged as the focus of rising industrial militancy. Despite the rapid growth of the economy during the 'miracle' years, under the military dictatorship the mass of unskilled workers in Brazil had seen their wages stagnate. The rapid growth of the automobile complex in the ABC region, with its huge factories, attracted a workforce of predominantly young males from all over the country. The process of massification of this workforce was accelerated by the high level of labour turnover caused by the widespread employer policy of using layoffs and dismissals to keep wage costs down. After a period of quiescence, a number of massive strikes broke out in 1978 and 1979. The *'pelego'* union leadership was bypassed and new leaders emerged from the rank-and-file, including Luis Ignacio da Silva, 'Lula', who became the leader of the PT (and the PT's presidential candidate in 1989). Mass strikes broke out again in 1980 and, despite harsh measures by the government, union militancy thereafter continued at a high level for the rest of the decade.

The new currents within Brazilians unionism now began preparations to establish a national-level organization. In August 1981 the first of a series of meetings were held with this aim in mind. However, divisions within union ranks led, in 1983, to the emergence of two organizations: the radical Central Unica dos Trabalhadores (CUT) and the Coordenação Nacional da Classe Trabalhadora (CONCLAT), which later became the Central Geral dos Trabalhadores (CGT). Union membership, both in unions affiliated with the CUT and in those linked to the CGT, grew rapidly; 1,602,000 urban workers were members of unions in 1965, 2,132,000 in 1970, 3,224,000 in 1975, 4,271,000 in 1978, and 5,648,000 by 1987.[44]

The 'new unionism' in Brazil was heavily marked by the coincidence of a resurgence of industrial conflict and the beginning of a lengthy process of redemocratization involving broad sections of the population around the demand for an end to the dictatorship and *diretas já*. At the same time, the emergence of the 'new unionism' was also a result of the recomposition of the industrial labour force, primarily in greater São Paulo, following the rapid industrialization of the post-war period and particularly the years of the economic 'miracle' in the late 1960s and early 1970s.

In the marked contrast to the more moderate position espoused by the Metal-workers Union of São Paulo city, the metal-working unions of the ABC region were both industrially more militant, and politically more radical. This difference between the city of São Paulo and the ABC region lends support to the arguments underlying the 'new unionism' hypothesis. The São Paulo workers tended to be older and more established than their counterparts in the ABC region. Moreover, the factories in the ABC

---

[44] Maria Hermínia Tavares de Almeida, 'O Sindicalismo Brasileiro entre a Conservação e a Mudança', in Bernardo Sorj and Maria Hermínia Tavares de Almeida (eds), *Sociedade e Política no Brasil pós-64* (São Paulo, 1983), p. 194.

region were on the whole larger and more recently established than their counterparts in São Paulo. Added to the difference in the composition of the labour force and the structure of the industry, was a difference in the nature of the city itself. The municipalities of Santo André, São Bernardo and São Caetano that formed the ABC region had a much more homogeneous working class composition than did the highly complex and variegated hub of São Paulo itself. It is hardly surprising, therefore, that class identity should have been so strong in the ABC region, or that it should have produced a high level of industrial militancy and political radicalism.

In Argentina, where peronism retained its hold over the mass of the workers, the Cordobazo of 1969, as we have seen, dramatically underscored the changes that had occurred in the industrial working class and heralded an upsurge in rank-and-file insurgency. The restrictions on union activity under the military had the effect of shifting power downwards in the unions, to the factory delegates, which had always been strong in Argentina, enabling the more militant currents of Peronist unionism to prosper. Augustín Tosca of the Luz y Fuerza union probably best represented the 'new unionist' current within Argentina unionism. The growth of rank-and-file union militancy was coincident with the growth of the urban guerrilla detachments of the Montoneros, the Peronist Youth, and the Trotskyist Ejército Revolucionario del Pueblo (ERP) during the military dictatorship of 1966–73. While the two phenomena may have had similar causes, links between the guerrilla movements and rank-and-file union militants appear to have been relatively slender.

The installation of the second Peronist government in 1973 was the signal for the outbreak of bitter internal strife both within the unions and between the unions and the guerrilla groups. The combination of economic chaos and political violence which characterized the Peronist government of 1973–6, and which brought about its collapse, did little for Argentine unionism. In the increasingly polarized political climate the old-style Peronist union bosses were often seen by the radicalized youth movement as betrayers of their class and therefore as enemies of the radical movement. In September 1973, the Montoneros assassinated José Rucci, general secretary of the CGT. For their part, the union bosses went along with the increased repression and the unleashing of the 'dirty war' which was the response to political polarization and increasing violence. When the military finally took over again in 1976 they implemented a ruthless repression of rank-and-file militants in the labour movement as well as in the ranks of the guerrillas.

In Peru the reforming military dictatorship of General Juan Velasco Alvarado (1968–75) had the opposite effect, providing a significant impetus to the development of militant unionism, though the roots of Peruvian labour militancy can be traced earlier. At the end of the 1960s the influence of the Communist party in organized labour had grown and the Confederación General de Trabajadores del Peru (CGTP) had begun to displace the Aprista CTP. Attempts by the military to form their own corporatist union organization were relatively unsuccessful, but the generally sympathetic climate for labour organizing enabled both APRA and the Left to expand. The replacement of Velasco Alvarado by the more conservative General Francisco Morales Bermudez (1975–80) then led to severe conflicts with the unions. In April 1976 the government declared strikes illegal in any sector of the economy that generated foreign exchange, and when the unions responded by calling a general strike, imposed a state of emergency. The radicalization of the Peruvian working class now accelerated, with a variety of left-wing parties (including some Maoists who were particularly important in the teachers' union) displacing APRA as the dominant force in organized labour. In addition to the traditionally militant miners, schoolteachers and other white-collar workers such as bankworkers now began to mobilize, broadening the basis of working-class action. General strikes were held in May 1978, January 1979 and June 1979, forcing the regime to back down and adding to the pressure for re-democratization. This high level of union militancy carried over into the civilian Belaúnde administration (1980–5).

As in Peru, Colombia in the 1970s saw both heightened labour conflict, with the strike rate increasing from an annual average for the 1962–71 period of 58 to an average of 73 for 1972–81. Within the union movement, 1,156,000 strong by 1974, the UTC and the CTC were increasingly challenged by the new labour confederations, the Communist CSTC and the CGT. In 1974 the CTC claimed 25 per cent and the UTC 40 per cent of all union members; by 1980 their respective shares had fallen to 20 and 31 per cent. Three-quarters of all strikes were called by the CSTC and the independent unions.[45] This rising wave of labour unrest was part of a larger movement of 'civic strikes' to protest government

---

[45] Daniel Pécaut, 'Colombia', in Jean Carrière, Nigel Haworth and Jacqueline Roddrick (eds), *The State, Industrial Relations and the Labour Movement in Latin America* (London, 1989), p. 292; Londoño, 'La estructura', p. 109.

inaction and incompetence in the provision of urban services. Between January 1971 and May 1978 there were 132 such civic strikes.[46]

In Venezuela, total work stoppages rose from an annual average of 30 per year between 1961 and 1970, to an annual average of 175 for the period 1971–80. Although the CTV continued its close ties with Acción Democrática (AD), even the brief pro-labour measures of the government of Carlos Andrés Pérez (1974–9) failed to stop a general deterioration of relations between the government and organized labour. This had its effects on AD, as its share of the delegates to the CTV congress dropped from 70 per cent in the 1960s to an average of 46 per cent in the 1970s.[47]

Labour militancy in Chile, while never low, accelerated during the late sixties and early seventies. During the Frei government the union movement became the most effective vehicle of opposition to the government's economic policies, as general strikes were called to protest against austerity measures. When the Popular Unity government came to power in 1970 working-class expectations were raised and, as inflation accelerated, industrial conflict mounted. While wages rose dramatically, so also did the number of strikes. In 1971 and 1972 there were 2,377 and 2,474 strikes, respectively, compared with 977 in 1969. It is probable that many of these were brief affairs aimed at achieving wage increases or establishing a union presence, since neither the total of workers involved nor man-days lost increased markedly.[48] It is also likely that a considerable part of the rise in strike activity was due to increased mobilization in the countryside. With the backing of the more radical parties in the Popular Unity coalition, union activists now began to seize factories and demand their expropriation by the State. This resulted in an uncontrolled and unplanned series of factory seizures which increased political polarization and undermined the legitimacy of the Allende government in the eyes of the Christian Democrats. Unionists also moved to establish *cordones industriales,* organizations that linked together factories in the same industrial district, and these *cordones* became the nuclei for industrial militancy. In Santiago in 1972 perhaps 100,000 people were involved.[49]

[46] Christopher Abel and Marco Palacios, 'Colombia, 1930–1958', *The Cambridge History of Latin America,* Vol. VIII (Cambridge, 1991), p. 664.

[47] Charles Davis and Kenneth Coleman, 'Political Control of Organized Labor in a Semi-Consociational Democracy: the case of Venezuela', in Edward Epstein (ed.), *Labor Autonomy and the State in Latin America* (Boston, Mass., 1989), p. 259.

[48] Alan Angell, 'Chile Since 1958', *Cambridge History of Latin America,* Vol. VIII, (Cambridge, 1991), p. 347.

[49] Ibid., p. 355.

Although the Communists and Socialists predominated in the CUT (with 62 per cent of the vote in the 1972 CUT national election), the Christian Democrats retained an important presence (with 25 per cent of the vote), particularly among white-collar workers (where they gained 41 per cent of the white-collar vote).[50] As political polarization widened, a strike of copper miners in 1973 revealed the deep divisions in the labour movement between Christian Democrats on the one hand and Communists and Socialists on the other. Although the strike had begun largely as a pay demand, the opposition began to mobilize around it and the government appealed for a return to work, with the result that the strike rapidly expressed a largely political division within the mine-workers, reflecting the larger division and politicization of Chilean society. Finally, in September 1973, the Allende government was overthrown by the military and the labour movement severely repressed. After a period during which union activity was practically illegal and in which union militants were jailed and murdered, in 1979 the Pinochet regime promulgated new labour legislation (the 'Plan Laboral') designed to decentralize and depoliticize industrial relations.

In Bolivia, during the military dictatorships of the 1964–83 period, popular discontent led to outbreaks of protest which were repeatedly suppressed. Perhaps the most notable instance was the short-lived Asamblea Popular (June 1971), an attempt at 'dual power' by the unions and the left during the last days of the government of General Juan José Torres (1970–1). Apart from this ephemeral triumph, these years witnessed widespread repression by one military dictatorship after another with considerable loss of life.

Overall, the 1970s saw a rise in labour conflict and a turn to the left on the part of the working class, taking different forms and beginning at different times in different countries. A central differentiating factor, of course, was whether the military had seized power and moved to repress organized labour. These military dictatorships often served inadvertently to foster the emergence of new and more militant leaderships. Military government attempts to weaken what they saw as 'political unionism' focussed on shifting power from the peak national confederations downwards to organizations at the level of the individual enterprise or plant, removing union leaders associated with political activities, improving labour productivity, facilitating the dismissal and lay-off of workers, and

[50] Ibid., p. 352.

restricting strikes. While these policies often had some temporary success, they tended to make it easier for new, younger and more militant leaderships to emerge from the rank-and-file. Where this was so, there was a clear radicalization of the labour movement, and often a confluence of union militancy with more general societal mobilization for a return to civilian rule.

Whether this general rise in militancy can be described as the emergence of a 'new unionism' is, however, contentious. While in some countries, notably Brazil and Mexico, and to some extent in Argentina and Peru, the changing composition of the industrial labour force and the development of rank-and-file challenges to union oligarchs offer support for the 'new unionism' thesis, in other countries (for example Bolivia and Chile) the factors producing labour militancy appear to have been more directly political in character.

The control systems institutionalized at the end of the 1940s had been challenged from time to time in a number of countries; by the late 1960s and early 1970s, often linked with wider resistance to military dictatorship, these challenges had become more frequent and more widespread. The growth of the industrial labour force, together with the continuing political and economic crises of import substitution industrialization, steadily increased the potential for industrial conflict. The result was a general rise in the level of industrial conflict throughout the region. However, the timing, the specific causes, and the specific forms this militancy assumed varied considerably from country to country. In that sense, the hypothesis of the rise of a 'new unionism' only held true for a limited number of countries. More generally, by the 1970s the working class in many countries had 'come of age' and had extended multiple links with the burgeoning broader social movements. The notion of a working class that was in some sense separate from the rest of the working poor, a notion that had prevailed in many countries for most of the earlier period, was now being eroded and wider notions of class identity were coming into play.

THE DEBT CRISIS AND INDUSTRIAL RESTRUCTURING IN THE 1980s

In the 1980s three decades of post-war economic growth in Latin America came to an end. In most countries the impact on the working class and its organizations was profound. The turning point varied from country to country, with the beginnings of economic slowdown in the mid- and late-seventies for some countries, while in others it was delayed until the mid- to late-eighties. The impact of the debt crisis beginning in August 1982 was uneven across the region, and the timing and seriousness of structural reform programmes which governments implemented as a response to the debt crisis also varied from country to country.

The economic crisis of the 1980s produced, in most countries, higher inflation, a sharp decline in real wages, a rise in unemployment, and an expansion of the informal sector. In some countries the debt crisis and government responses either initiated or further stimulated programmes of industrial restructuring, sometimes leading to de-industrialization. In a number of countries, most notably Argentina, Brazil and Peru, 'heterodox shocks' (usually involving wage and price freezes) were implemented in an effort to reduce inflation, and often ended in political and economic failure. In the first years of the decade there was much talk of 'social pacts' (to address the impact of the economic crisis on the poorer sections of society) and political pacts (to help the process of democratic consolidation). By the end of the decade, as governments appeared to have weathered the worst of the economic crisis and fought off challenges to their authority, dealing with the crisis through *concertación* had largely given place to efforts to restructure economies along neo-liberal lines. By 1990 (and in some instances considerably earlier) most governments in the region had, formally at least, committed themselves to a dramatic reversal of the ISI model of development. Structural reform programmes of a neo-liberal kind had been initiated in the majority of countries of the region. A key component of these programmes as far as labour was concerned were efforts to increase flexibility in the labour market, sometimes as a result of considerable modifications in labour law. The aim of the neo-liberal re-formers was to do away with corporatist institutions, de-politicize industrial relations, restore managerial prerogatives in the use of labour, and devolve collective bargaining from the national to the work-place level.

Taking 1980 as a base year, average real wages in Mexico dropped to 71 per cent in 1987, and by 1990 had recovered only to 78 per cent. In Peru, wages dropped to 78 per cent in 1985, recovered their 1980 level by 1987, but then plunged to 43 per cent of that level by the end of the decade. Argentine wages held up reasonably well during the first years of the decade, largely owing to massive increases at the end of the military dictatorship, but then fell to 76 per cent of their 1980 value by 1990. In Chile and Colombia, on the other hand, real wages remained more or less stable during most of the 1980s. Despite significant variation in the experience of Rio de Janeiro and São Paulo, wages in Brazil followed a pattern not unlike that of Argentina, holding up well in the early years, but dropping by 15–25 per cent at the end of the decade. Urban minimum wages (which perhaps are a useful indicator of earnings in the lower end of the labour market) were, again with the exceptions of Chile and Colombia, much lower at the end of the decade than they had been before the debt crisis. In 1990 minimum wages for urban workers, as a percentage of their value in 1980, were 53 per cent for Brazil, 46 per cent for Mexico, 23 per cent for Peru, and 51 per cent for Venezuela.[51] Measured unemployment rose in many countries, and the number of hours worked on average by urban workers declined. All this spelled a serious decline in real living standards, though this may have been compensated in part by a shift of some family members into the informal sector.

In Argentina the military government of 1976–83 had presided over a substantial de-industrialization. The overall size of the manufacturing sector actually declined in these years (from 1,114,000 industrial workers in 1974 to 780,000 in 1981),[52] and with this, there was a drop in real wages. As the military hold on power grew increasingly precarious and the 1983 elections approached, wages were permitted to rise substantially, so that some of the decline had been made up by the time power was handed over to the civilian government of Raúl Alfonsín in December 1983. During the Alfonsín government the level of real wages remained steady, though somewhat erratic, and rose during the Austral plan of 1985–6. The relative stability of wages did not, however, contribute much to lowering tensions between the Peronist unions and the Radical government. At the beginning of 1984, Alfonsín sent legislative proposals to Congress with the aim of breaking the hold of the Peronists on the unions and reducing their control over union welfare funds. The proposal was narrowly defeated, and marked the beginning of a long period of troubled relations between the unions and the government. Despite the appointment in 1987 of a moderate Peronist union leader to the post of Minister of Labour, the CGT continued with a policy of confrontation with the government, carrying out thirteen general strikes during the Alfonsín administration. With the emergence in 1989 of

[51] CEPAL, *Preliminary Overview of the Latin American and Caribbean Economy: 1991* (Santiago, 1992), pp. 41–2.
[52] Héctor Palomino, *Cambios ocupacionales y sociales en Argentina, 1947–1985* (Buenos Aires, 1987), p. 83.

hyperinflation, real wages in Argentina dropped sharply during the last months of Alfonsín's term.

Argentine workers looked to the Peronist president, Carlos Saúl Menem, to implement a promised *salariazo* to compensate for the losses sustained during hyperinflation. However, in his first years in office at least, Menem was to prove no populist. Instead of generalized wage increases, the government adopted a programme of structural reform. Real wages continued their downward course, and a combination of hyperinflation, opening of the Argentine economy to international trade, and recession resulted in widespread unemployment. The metal-working sector of Argentine industry was badly hit, with many jobs being shed, and unions in this sector, including the once-mighty UOM, lost up to half their membership. The radical programme of economic stabilization and restructuring put into effect by the Menem government led (once again) to a split in the ranks of the CGT, with some sectors of the movement supporting and collaborating with the government, while a dissident, and dwindling, group led by Saúl Ubaldini maintained a posture of intransigent opposition.

In Brazil the government of José Sarney (1985–90) did not adopt a clear or consistent policy towards the unions. At times it unsuccessfully appealed for a social pact between labour and management while at other times (indeed, often simultaneously) the government actively repressed strikes. Faced with ambivalence on the part of the government, the labour movement, divided between the radical CUT and the moderate CGT (which itself underwent a number of internal splits), displayed equal ambivalence in its response. While the CUT on the whole took an intransigent position and pressed for general strikes to protest government economic policy, it did on occasion enter into preliminary negotiations (which never came to fruition) over a possible 'social pact'. And the CGT, while consistently favouring a social pact, did join with the CUT in general strikes against the government in 1986 and 1987. Alongside these two major currents in the union movement, the so-called 'unionism of results', led by Luiz Antonio Medeiros of the São Paulo metalworkers' union and Rogerio Magri of the São Paulo electricity generating union, emerged as a third force, forming a new confederation, Força Sindical. Continued rivalry between the different groupings within Brazilian unionism did much to weaken the movement, both during the Sarney administration and during the first years of the government of Fernando Collor de Mello.

During the six to nine months in 1986 when the heterodox Cruzado plan (which, by freezing wages and prices had an expansionary effect on economic activity) seemed to many to be working, the purchasing power of wages rose rapidly, only to fall dramatically in the aftermath. The strike rate shot up, from 79 in 1981 and 126 in 1982, to 843 in 1985, 1,494 in 1986 and 2,369 in 1987. Strike activity dropped slightly the following year, to 1,954, and then rose again to 4,189 strikes in 1989.[53] The closing years of the Sarney administration saw a series of massive strikes, mainly by public sector employees. The collapse of the Cruzado plan led to very high inflation and the transition to the new Collor administration in March 1990 was accompanied by a drop in working-class living standards and a continued defensive attitude on the part of a severely shaken labour movement.

In Mexico the initial impact of the debt crisis stunned the labour movement. As wages and employment plummeted, the CTM proposed an incomes policy, only to be spurned by President Miguel de la Madrid (1982–8). The crisis notwithstanding, union leaderships experienced considerable difficulty in restraining rank-and-file insurgent movements, most notably in the massive teachers' union where a mass movement led to the deposition of the *charro* leader, Carlos Jonquitud Barrios in 1989. Under the impact of mounting inflation, the Mexican government adopted an incomes policy in December 1987 in which representatives of organized labour, the employers' associations and the peasant organizations oversaw a system of controlled wage and price movements. The decline in real wages was slowed down, and by the end of the 1980s it appeared to many observers that Mexico was on the road to recovery.

With the inauguration of president Carlos Salinas de Gortari in 1988 relations between the Congreso del Trabajo (particularly the CTM) and the government were improved, as the wage and price control policy brought them back into the centre of the scene and provided them with arguments to use against an increasingly restive rank-and-file. In January 1989 the police attacked the headquarters of the oil workers' union, and jailed its leader, Joaquín Hernández Galicia, 'La Quina', on what appear to have been trumped up charges. In all likelihood this was a piece of politically inspired vengeance by Salinas for the overt support given by La Quina to opposition candidate Cuauhtémoc Cárdenas in the 1988 elections. This,

[53] International Labour Organization (ILO), *Yearbook of Labour Statistics 1991* (Geneva, 1991), p. 1040.

and the subsequent purge of the corrupt Sindicato de Trabajadores Petroleros de la República Mexicana (STPRM), were widely seen as both a warning to the union movement as a whole not to step outside the traditional bounds of loyalty to the PRI and as an isolated attack on a particularly troublesome union. With new-found confidence the CTM, still under the control of nonagenarian Fidel Velázquez, dealt harshly with insurgent movements within its ranks, breaking strikes in the Modelo brewery and the Ford factory in Cuautitlán in 1991. With union militancy largely confined to rank-and-file movements in health, education and a limited number of other sectors, the Mexican labour movement had little organic connection with the increasingly widespread civic movements pressing for political liberalization. While both the conservative Partido de Acción Nacional (PAN) and the reformist Partido de la Revolución Democrática (PRD), led by Cuauhtémoc Cárdenas, organized a wide variety of civic actions aimed at forcing the Mexican government to allow free and fair elections, the bulk of the labour movement stood aside. The lesson of La Quina's destruction had been learned by the union bureaucrats, and the rank-and-file were in no position to argue.

In Peru the Aprista government of Alán García (1985–90) experimented with a heterodox stabilization policy similar to the Austral and Cruzado plans, and the failure of this policy was also accompanied by a marked worsening of the situation of the working class. As the economy collapsed, widespread labour and popular protest added to the general atmosphere of chaos. Finally, in 1990 presidential elections brought a total outsider, Alberto Fujimori, to office. Rapidly abandoning his promises to avoid the shock treatment proposed by the rival candidate, Mario Vargas Llosa, Fujimori took the road travelled by the majority of Latin American presidents in these years and began a programme of structural reform.

Elsewhere (for example, in Bolivia and Venezuela) governments adopted severely orthodox adjustment programmes, often weakening the labour movement and/or provoking massive, if shortlived, protest. While Colombia had suffered less from the debt crisis than most other countries (largely owing to lower indebtedness, good economic management and early moves towards export promotion), an increasingly militant labour movement in that country also found itself on the defensive as the recrudescence of violence in the 1980s numbered many union leaders among its victims.

The fiscal crisis and general deterioration of government services in the 1980s placed an increasingly heavy burden on the urban population and social movements struggled to cope with the worsening economic situation. A number of neighbourhood associations and women's groups increasingly took on new tasks such as the communal provision of food. Linked with the deteriorating economic situation were a number of incidents toward the end of the 1980s and the beginning of the 1990s in which supermarkets were looted. The most publicized incidents were the looting of supermarkets in Caracas in 1989 and 1992 and Buenos Aires in 1990, though similar events also occurred with some frequency in Brazil. Whether or not these sackings of supermarkets merit inclusion in the category of 'social movement' is debateable: however, they added a new element to the repertoire of popular responses to economic policy.

In Chile the impact of the debt crisis was somewhat different from the experience of many countries. In the first instance, the crisis hit a country that had, under the military government of General Pinochet (1973–90), already implemented orthodox stabilization and restructuring policies. Much of the cost of adjustment had already been born by the working class and, moreover, international investors continued to have considerable confidence in the Chilean economy as a result of the highly orthodox economic policies applied. While the debt crisis did, indeed, have a serious impact on Chile, its repercussions were overshadowed by the presence of a military dictatorship committed to neo-liberal restructuring.

The restructuring of labour relations in Pinochet's Chile had also begun earlier, shifting the focus of union activity to the enterprise, making lengthy strikes very difficult, and facilitating the dismissal of workers. With wages depressed and unemployment up, with a structural shift away from manufacturing employment and towards an increase in the informal sector, and with large numbers of workers employed on government relief schemes, the Pinochet dictatorship had brought about major changes in the Chilean working class. A rapid reversal of this situation by the new Christian Democratic government of Patricio Aylwin was unlikely, given the considerable pressure his government was under not to deviate markedly from the parameters of the neo-liberal model established by the military.

For the region as a whole, by the end of the 1980s there had as yet been no sustained recovery from the situation of generalized recession, though there were widespread expectations that the structural economic reforms being adopted by several governments would stimulate recovery on a sound basis. Given the magnitude of the decline in real wages and the considerable changes in employment, as the decade of the 1990s opened workers and their unions throughout Latin America were in a much worse position than they had been a decade previously.

Throughout the second half of the 1980s (and in some countries the process had begun earlier) attempts to implement stabilization programmes led to increased industrial unrest. Three general strikes were essayed against the Sarney government in Brazil, and no less than thirteen against Alfonsín in Argentina. Many of these strikes were led by workers in the public sector, responding to attempts by governments to reduce the size of the state sector by privatizing government-owned enterprises, to increase efficiency in state enterprises by reducing the workforce, or to impose a wage freeze on the public sector. Workers in the metal-working sector appeared to have lost their central role in the labour movement, as new economic policies promoted massive changes in the occupational structure.

Despite these (largely defensive) reactions, for organized labour as a whole the decade of the 1980s was one of defeat or at least setback. In some countries the economic basis of unionism in manufacturing and state enterprises was undermined by de-industrialization and the rapid privatization of the state sector. In most countries the debt crisis meant rising unemployment and declining wages. Strikes tended to be defensive, and frequently failed to produce material gains. It seemed apparent that labour movements in Latin America were undergoing profound transformations as part of a more general adjustment of these societies to the changed economic and political circumstances of the eighties and nineties. Although a chapter in the history of Latin American labour had clearly come to an end, the lineaments of the emerging system of industrial relations were as yet difficult to discern.

CONCLUSION

It is difficult to find a single, modal pattern of labour movement formation and action throughout Latin America. The diversity of occupational and economic structures on the one hand, and of political systems on the other, make diversity of experience the norm. Moreover, the very notion of a distinct history of labour is problematic. Labour movements are a central and integral part of society, and are linked to developments in the economy, the political system, the organization of industry and work processes, and to broader developments in the social structure (changes in the occupational structure, social mobility, residential patterns, forms of class and occupational identity, and so forth). It is, indeed, this polyvalent aspect of labour history that makes it so difficult to disentangle from the larger processes of historical change.

There is a natural bias in studies of Latin American labour movements to emphasize those countries that are larger, more urban and more industrially developed. This chapter reflects such biases, suggesting a greater degree of commonality of experience than would be the case had more attention been devoted to the smaller countries of the region. Moreover, in the search for an organizing principle, this chapter has used a periodization for the region which can serve only as a first approximation for each of the specifically national experiences.

There are, of course, important underlying trends which provide some unity and coherence to the experience of labour in Latin America between 1930 and 1990. The beginning of the period saw an urban labour force that was a distinct minority in what were still largely rural societies. The twin processes of urbanization and industrialization, coupled with rapid population growth, transformed the nature of the urban labour force over the next fifty years. It became massified, and while the formal sector grew rapidly, so also did the informal sector of the economy, adding new lines of division within the urban working poor to those already in existence.

Moreover, industrialization produced important shifts in the salient occupational characteristics of this urban labour force. In the 1930s the nuclei of working-class formation were (as might be expected in export economies) in transport (railways and docks) and in public utilities (power generation, public transport, municipal services, and so on). Those sections of the workforce employed in large factories were likely to be employed in textile mills, often in single-industry or company towns located outside the main metropoli. In some countries there was also a large mining labour force, comprising the most organized and militant section of the labour movement. To these highly proletarianized categories must be added large numbers of skilled workers and artisans in a variety of urban trades: construction, baking and food processing, breweries, leather and clothing, and so on. Many of these people worked in small establishments.

By the 1970s (and in some countries earlier) in many countries of the region the industrial and occupational landscape had changed. Few of the industries present in the 1930s had disappeared or even experienced a significant decline (though this cannot be said for textiles, which under the pressures of foreign competition, modernized and changed many of its fundamental characteristics as far as labour processes were concerned).

However, alongside these older industries, over-shadowing them and introducing new forms of labour relations, newer industries and forms of
economic activity appeared. The most obvious of these newer industries
was the metal-working complex, centred on the automobile industry but
extending far beyond it. With the expansion of the automobile came road-
building and trucking to rival railway and coastal transportation, and a
host of ancillary industries: gas stations, auto repair workshops, and so on.
Where mining and textiles had once been the principal creators of single-
industry towns, in the 1970s steel mills, petrochemical refineries and oil
wells were more likely to have taken over this role. The growth of government activity had also greatly expanded the number of white-collar jobs,
not merely in the burgeoning bureaucracies, but also in teaching and
health services. Together with the creation of a large number of state-
owned industrial enterprises, this meant that workers in the state sector,
both blue and white collar, were now an important part of the labour
force. With the parallel expansion of professional employment of various
kinds, and a variety of new service sectors, the ranks of the white-collar
labour force expanded considerably over the fifty-year period. Finally,
massive urbanization swelled the ranks of those diverse activities now
generally referred to as 'the informal sector'. In 1980, as in 1930, the
occupational experiences of Latin America's urban work force were extremely diverse. While the numbers of workers employed in large enterprises grew both absolutely and relatively, at no point did this constitute
the average work experience. Nor (despite the attention given to it by
historians and social scientists) was work in a factory ever the most common form of working-class employment in Latin America (just as it never
was in the industrialized countries of Europe and in the United States).

These very general trends worked themselves out in diverse ways in
different countries, taking quite different institutional forms. Given the
multiplicity of channels through which workers could attempt to bring
pressure to bear to improve their situation, this is hardly surprising. To
begin with, the level of unionization of the labour force, and the ways in
which unions were organized and operated, varied considerably, partly as a
result of differences in legal codes, partly as a result of different industrial
structures, and partly as a result of differences in political systems. Given
the economic and political turbulence of many Latin American countries,
lasting and institutionalized forms of labour incorporation were infrequent
(Mexico being a notable exception). Faced with rapidly changing economic and political conditions, union leaders and rank-and-file activists

responded in a variety of ways, sometimes at cross-purposes with each other. At the most general level, labour movements were frequently divided over whether to co-operate with employers and the state in order to maximize the pie that would later be divided, or whether to enter into zero-sum conflict over effort bargains and distributional issues and allow long-term growth to take care of itself. The lack of clear ground rules for the political economy as a whole simply exacerbated this inherent ambivalence of labour action.

To these broad forces hindering stable patterns of incorporation must be added the unsettling effects of industrial change itself. As the *punto neurálgico* of the labour movement shifted from railways, mining, textiles and utilities to the metal-working sector (and then to public employment), the character of labour disputes changed. New industries meant different kinds of labour processes, and hence different kinds of industrial conflicts; new work forces with different sociological characteristics; and new forms of business organization, with different relations both to the state and to their employees. Partly as a result of industrial change, partly as a result of broader demographic processes, the spatial location of the labour force changed, adding yet one more element of complexity to an already highly complex picture.

As the character of industrial conflict evolved, the corporatist mechanisms set up in the very different context of the 1930s and 1940s, and consolidated in the immediate post-war years, came under increasing strain. And pressures developed to recast the links between union organizations and political parties that had emerged in the middle decades of the twentieth century.

Despite the importance of the issue, we know very little about the ways in which workers in Latin America perceived themselves in relation to the larger society. It may be speculated that working people in the 1930s were most likely to see themselves as exercising quite specific trades and occupations, and were likely to accept a highly restricted definition of themselves as bakers, printers, tramdrivers, and so on. Only in the larger enterprises and in some towns were workers likely to think of themselves self-consciously as belonging to a working class. At the same time that they accepted a largely occupational self-definition, workers were also likely to see themselves as part of a larger entity – the 'people' (*el pueblo, o povo*) – in contra-distinction to 'the rich', 'the oligarchy', or 'decent society'. As industrialization proceeded, the use of the notion of working class (*clase obrera, classe operária*) may have become more prevalent by the middle of the century. These terms carried the connotation of manual labour, as in the contrast with *empleado* (employee). By the 1980s, the phrase *clase trabajadora* (*classe trabalhadora*) had come into wider use, indicating a membership broader than that connoted by manual labour in a factory setting. While the term '*el pueblo*' never dropped out of political discourse as a way of defining worker identity, notions of the '*clase trabajadora*', the 'poor', and the working poor increasingly competed with this. And of course, with the significant exception of the immigrant labour forces of São Paulo and Buenos Aires in the 1930s, nationality was universally a transcending form of self-identification for most of Latin America's workers.

If there is any general pattern to labour movement development since 1930, it is one of massification and diversification of the labour force on the one hand, and the increasing homogenization of experiences as citizens on the other hand. The movement was a complicated one, from groups of workers who were a small minority in largely rural societies, and whose sense of working class identity was fairly embryonic, to the creation of a new working class in the forties, fifties and sixties, and then its massification and redefinition as a major social force in the sixties and seventies. At a semantic level the result of these changes may have been a shift towards a broad concept of 'the working poor' (instead of 'the people'), and the '*clase trabajadora*' (instead of '*clase obrera*'). Such semantic shifts were facilitated by the pattern of lower-income residence (which brought people with quite different occupational experiences together in the urban setting), and by common problems with urban services, bureaucracies, authoritarian dictatorships, and a wide range of citizenship issues.

These intertwined processes of massification of the urban labour force, diversification in the occupational sphere, and homogenization in the realm of self-identity took quite different forms in individual countries. This chapter has not sought to locate these in a typology, nor to present a systematic theory which accounts for the range of variation in Latin American labour movements, opting instead to indicate the key factors that have operated in what is, in fact, an enormously complex process of class formation, industrial conflict, and political and economic bargaining. At the beginning of the 1990s new challenges meant that the process of making and remaking the Latin American working classes was likely to continue its complex history.

5

RURAL MOBILIZATIONS IN LATIN
AMERICA SINCE *c.* 1920

INTRODUCTION

Political mobilization and social violence have been recurrent phenomena in rural Latin America in the twentieth century. The enormous diversity in these phenomena represents a major challenge for anyone attempting to analyse them from a single perspective or with the purpose of drawing generalizations. However, it is possible to find a common framework for analysis if we accept that for all its heterogeneity rural unrest has taken place in the context of several great, inter-related processes of societal transformation, an essential ingredient of which has been conflict among contending social actors.

First, the *hacienda* (or *latifundio*) system and the peasant community ceased to be the dominant organizing forms of agricultural production. The *hacienda* owners – in so far as they survived as a class – largely lost their political hegemony. At the local level, this meant that they lost much of their capacity to exert social and political pressure ('extra-economic coercion') over peasants and workers. The persisting peasantries were no longer 'tied to the land'. They gained in influence because of their alliances with the new political elites; but their importance steadily decreased vis-à-vis that of the emerging middle classes and the urban and rural proletariat.

Second, the capitalization of agriculture, which was a result of the increasing integration of the countryside with large urban markets and international channels of distribution, took a wide variety of forms, resulting in the emergence of new types of large and medium-sized farms and ranches but also in the transformation of the traditional family (peasant) unit. Land ownership ceased to be the cornerstone of agricultural production: control of financial and technological resources, as well as commer-

cial channels, became the crucial factor. Such control was also the basis of
the power of multi-national corporations operating in the Latin American
countryside. In addition, its importance reflected the increasing subordination of agriculture to other sectors in the national economies. Because of
these changes, the old plantations lost economic weight: they no longer
represented the main concentration of capital in the countryside. On the
other hand, although proletarianization of the rural labour force was a
salient phenomenon, not all the peasants were becoming proletarians. On
the contrary, it is contended here that peasantries did not simply resist 'the
penetration of capital' – nor did they merely play a passive role as a labour
reserve – but rather they often sought to participate in the construction of
certain forms of capitalism.

A third important change relates to the activities of the state. After the
Second World War there was a general belief – which lasted until the
1980s – in the need for a strong, active state, which would prevent the
fragmentation of a precarious civil society. From a weak and frequently
passive role, the state developed a project or a series of nation-building
projects – sometimes successful, sometimes aborted – the aim of which
was to make state apparatuses co-terminous with the whole of society.
There was a rapid expansion of the 'public domain' in the sense that a host
of social relations and realms of action became subject to government
regulations; additionally, the representatives of the state became effective
power wielders at the local level. Furthermore, government agencies replaced private enterprises in initiating many ground-breaking economic
activities. Equally, state-controlled organizations substituted the institutions of civil society in multifarious fields: labour relations, communications and information, financial services, and even recreation and art.

These processes were neither linear, nor irreversible. They occurred
with irregular rythms and adopted idiosyncratic forms in different countries. And they led by the late twentieth century to the multi-dimensional
configuration in which it was not possible to define rural conflict exclusively in terms of 'the rape of the peasantry' by landowners in collusion
with repressive bailiffs and heartless technocrats. Peasants remained political actors in their own right, who may devise strategies vis-à-vis exploitation, exclusion and harassment. The struggle for land remained very
important; but rural demands became diversified. The category 'peasant'
acquired – more than ever – multiple meanings: it came to refer to highly
mobile tenants and sharecroppers, itinerant part-time proletarians who
maintain a family plot, 'modernized' market-orientated villagers as well as

'traditional' Indians. For all of them, there were many types of connections with the wider society, and many possible coincidences or dissensions with respect to other social actors. It is in this context of societal heterogeneity and multiple convergences – the context of emerging modern nation-states – that rural unrest in the twentieth century has to be understood. The development of a network of relationships cutting across heterogeneous groups, classes and social categories is the central feature of a long and complicated process of nation-building – a process of contention and negotiation. From this perspective, rural mobilizations can be regarded as moments of adjustment in the setting up of formal and informal channels of mediation in emerging national systems.

For the purposes of this discussion, the concept 'mobilization' rather than 'social movement' has been used since in the recent sociological debate the latter has a restricted meaning: it purports the creation of a collective consciousness and a strategy to change the structure of society, at least to a certain degree. 'Mobilization' is a broader concept, referring to 'excessive participation' on the part of a group or social sector; that is, to actions which are not approved of, or predicted, by the existing power structure and social norms. On the one hand, these actions may imply the development of vertical loyalties between popular groups and patron figures operating in the upper echelons of society. This 'mobilization from above' permits the manipulation and inhibition of demands derived from popular grievances and projects of social change, although negotiation with the base is always needed. On the other hand, grass-roots mobilizations (which may become 'social movements') imply the development or reinforcement of collective identities, and the tuning of leadership to popular demands. Grass-roots political awakening is a process where class and ethnic consciousness, as well as 'primordial ties' such as kinship and neighbourhood, are paramount; but it usually occurs at junctures where collective grievances are explicitly imputed to the existing power structure (and to specific dominant groups), and where this structure is not conceived as impossible to change. It goes without saying that the success of any social movement depends on its capacity to articulate its demands with those of other equally mobilized popular sectors – without being devoured by them – in such a way as to influence the institutions of the state in their favour.

The following periodization has been adopted as a tool for analysing the historical events included in this chapter: (a) 1920s and 1930s; (b) 1930s to 1960s and (c) 1960s to 1980s. This periodization is not a succession of stages with clear-cut beginnings and ends. Rather, it is a heuristic device, which attempts to relate rural mobilizations, both regional and national, to certain wider economic and – more significantly – political variables. In this sense, my central hypothesis is that differences in rural unrest are not only related to heterogeneity of actors and demands, but are also derived from differences in the changing societal context. This does not mean that the specific social, economic and political characteristics and situations of rural actors should not be examined, since in the last instance they determine why a given mobilization occurs at a particular moment in a particular place. It is only by examining both the local and the supra-local, the specific and the general, that the crucial features of mobilization – its duration, organizational consistency, goals, scale, and spatial scope – can by fully analysed.

It is impossible to treat all the important rural mobilizations from the 1920s to the 1980s. I shall instead pay particular attention to those countries where the sheer number and scale of uprisings have made the whole world aware of their relevance. But I will also try to show how different social movements represent the variability of social groups in the countryside and the diversity of their grievances, attempted solutions, alliances and outcomes. All rural mobilizations show that these groups become part of national politics; but they do it at different paces and by way of different paths. It is the aim of this chapter to make sense of both similarity and diversity.

1920S AND 1930S

The 1920s and 1930s witnessed the final stage of a long historical phase in which an expanding landed elite had exerted oligarchic control over the apparatuses of incipient, usually weak, national states. The crisis in the international market, of which the 1929 crash was the most dramatic moment, eroded in many countries the economic base of important sectors of the oligarchy: their capacity to export raw materials and selected agro-industrial products. In this context, new political formulas were tried out, for which the emerging elites – the industrial and commercial bourgeoisie and an increasingly independent middle class (professionals, the military, small entrepreneurs, rural and urban) demanding a share of power, mainly through participation in government – required the support of 'disposable' social sectors. But the old patrimonial political economy proved resilient. In the absence of consolidated political structures and systems of

universal representation, new national governments, whatever their programmes and manifest ideologies, were still dependent on the traditional
mechanisms of regional and local domination, in Spanish America
caudillismo and *caciquismo* (two concepts which are often used interchangeably but which should be clearly distinguished),[1] in Brazil *coronelismo*.
Consequently, political actors were not differentiated from networks of
patronage and pressure groups defending private interests. Thus, agrarian
mobilizations were often related to factional disputes over regional and
national power, and to a lack of effective state centralization. However,
particularly in Spanish America, the substratum for unrest was to be found
in the grievances of a vast rural mass – particularly the 'non-white' population, which had been formally incorporated as 'citizens equal before the
law' into national society, while effectively discriminated against and
harassed by the abolition of communal property (in the case of the Indians), new taxation, and anti-vagrancy legislation (in the case of both
Indians and other types of rural workers). The peasants were emerging as
crucial political actors not only because they expressed their grievances
against continuing land expropriation or their claims for a more advantageous participation in the market of labour and agricultural products, but
also in terms of their multiplying possibilities for internal organization
and alliances with old and new protagonists in the arena of national
politics.

The cases presented in this section illustrate different forms of relationships among peasants and rural workers on the old hand, and *caudillos,*

---

[1] In the nineteenth century, *caudillos* were powerful landlords who assumed regional government
functions after the destruction of colonial political institutions. They commanded private armies
and competed for national power. On the other hand, twentieth-century *caudillos* were not only
members of the landowning class but also military officers and even (particularly in the case of
Mexico) aspiring politicians who built independent power domains at the regional level with the
help of massive followings. In contrast, *caciques* emerged from the depths of the rural masses, or
from the lower middle classes. In their villages or towns of origin they fulfilled functions of local
authority but also of political and cultural brokerage. *Caciques* rarely commanded durable armed
retinues but they could induce violent ourbursts (*jacqueries*). In the first half of the twentieth
century, their role was related to the recruitment of rural populace for factional disputes among
caudillos, but also to peasant resistance against taxes, land expropriation or disruption of traditional
village life. Because of the decisive influence and brokerage capacity of *caciques,* grass-roots movements could play an important role in the wider field of factional rivalries. A third leading character
in the rural upheavals of this period, especially in the northeast of Brazil but also, for example, in
the northern Peruvian sierra, was the bandit. Occasionally, he also played the role of political
broker. Often, he was an instrument of the dominant regional interests in their challenges to central
power and their bids in factional politics. But his actions – as those of *caciques* and *caudillos* – were
equally conditioned by the nature and demands of rural popular groups, particularly peasant
groups. For a discussion of the literature on social banditry, which for lack of space has been omitted
from this chapter, see bibliographical essay.

caciques and heterogeneous political actors on the other, in the context of changing national political structures in Spanish America. In Mexico post-revolutionary *caudillos* had to reckon with a peasantry which in many instances had a long tradition of communal organization. Furthermore, the emerging regime used a rather ambiguous agrarianism both as a legitimizing ideology and a centralizing device. Therefore *caudillos* and *caciques* became agrarian brokers lest they be devoured by the formal state apparatus, although they were curtailed in their actions by persisting anti-agrarian forces, both at the regional level and in the midst of the central government itself. In Central America – especially in El Salvador and Guatemala – ethnic communal identity and a fledgeling class consciousness contributed to the articulation of demands for effective social change; but they failed to find effective brokers at the national level and were simply repressed by force. Finally, the struggle for land in the Bolivian highlands and the Peruvian central and southern sierras reveals a combination of ethnic, anti-*caudillo* consciousness and village factionalism confronting a deeply divided political elite and – again – a lack of successful national brokers.

Mexico

By the time Alvaro Obregón assumed the presidency of Mexico in 1920, the large-scale peasant armies which had emerged in the states of Morelos, Tlaxcala and Chihuahua had been virtually dismantled and their leaders co-opted, forsaken or murdered. These peasant armies had well-defined goals: the improvement of living conditions in the countryside, the end of the political power and repressive capacities of the *hacienda* owners, and – most clearly in the case of Morelos – the restitution of communal land to the villagers. In the name of these goals they had fought against the Díaz and Huerta dictatorships; but also against Madero and the *constitucionalistas* – the modernizing northern faction, which was the final winner of the Revolution. The success of Obregón's rebellion against Carranza was partly due to his alliance with the scattered remains of the defeated but still discontented peasant armies. In addition, his discourse in favour of social reform, which varied from moderate to radical, according to the audience, also attracted the support of heterogeneous actors and sympathizers of the revolutionary movement: lesser rural leaders, reformist military officers, radical intellectuals, labour organizers, and even open-minded landowners and entrepreneurs. Obregón shared the nineteenth-century liberals' dream of building a nation of prosperous, mostly middle-size private farmers; but he was willing to implement the 1915 Law of Agrarian Reform, which allowed for the (partial) division of *latifundia* into *ejidos* (land grants given in collective property by the federal government to groups of petitioners, provided these were not full-time *hacienda* workers) and the restoration of communal terrains, in order to appease the peasantry and gain its support. This legislation substituted bureaucratic procedure for direct popular action. In addition, the final decision with respect to the formation of an *ejido* ('dotación definitiva') was placed in the hands of the President of the Republic, whereas state governors' grants were defined as only 'provisional'. Conscious of the need to centralize power in the federal executive, Obregón also wanted to curtail the power of the new labour organizers by taking the rural population out of their control. Thus, he created the Comisión Nacional Agraria with corresponding Comisiones Locales in each state and 'executive committees' at the village level to promote land distribution. He also favoured the foundation of the Partido Nacional Agrarista (PNA), in charge of agrarian agitation. In turn, both the Comisiones and the PNA promoted Ligas Agraristas (or Ligas de Comunidades Agrarias) in each state, some of which became extremely strong and independent.[2]

During the 1920s and early 1930s, the Ligas were responsible for the continuity of rural mobilization related to demands for land distribution. However, the Ligas operated in a context of *caudillismo, caciquismo* and factionalism. At the regional level, the formation of factions in Mexico was related to the persisting economic power, organizing ability and *caudillista* practices of the old oligarchy, the militant presence of the Catholic Church, the political bids of the new military elite and their civil cronies, as well as to the criss-crossing divisions among the labour unions, the PNA, the Ligas and other rural and urban political groups. But these divisions were also dependent on, and nourished by, the importance of factionalism at the national level, where political offices were rancorously disputed by the strongest revolutionary generals. In the process of articulation between regional and national factions a new type of *caudillo* emerged: the radical leader, for whom the attainment and maintenance of unrestricted personal political power and the development of large political

---

[2] See Jesús Silva Herzog, *El agrarismo mexicano y la reforma agraria,* 2nd edn (Mexico, D.F., 1964), pp. 280–7; Armando Bartra, *Los herederos de Zapata. Movimientos campesinos posrevolucionarios en México* (Mexico, D.F., 1985); Jaime Tamayo, *La clase obrera en la historia de México, Vol. 7: En el interinato de Adolfo de la Huerta y el gobierno de Alvaro Obregón (1920–1924)* (Mexico, D.F., 1987).

clienteles was an adequate instrument for social change.[3] We shall briefly examine rural mobilizations under the aegis of such regional *caudillos* as Felipe Carrillo Puerto in Yucatán, Francisco J. Múgica and Lázaro Cárdenas in Michoacán, José Guadalupe Zuno in Jalisco, Adalberto Tejeda in Veracruz, and Saturnino Cedillo in San Luis Potosí.[4] Characteristically, these regions did not present large-scale rural mobilizations during the revolutionary decade (1910–20). But they had hundreds of peasant villages which had suffered expropriation from *haciendas* during the Liberal period, and their effervescence during the 1920s and early 1930s was a necessary condition for the subsequent rise of the centralized mass organizations founded in 1936 by Lázaro Cárdenas – the regional *caudillo* who became a national statesman.

In Yucatán, where more than half of the rural population were *hacienda*-resident, semi-enslaved Maya Indians uprooted from their communities after the bloody Caste War of 1847, a 'revolution from without' had occurred when in 1915 General Salvador Alvarado was sent by Carranza to overthrow the state government, which was clearly a puppet of the powerful landed oligarchy. This oligarchy had become immensely wealthy because of the boom in the international *henequén* (sisal) market at the turn of the century. Yet Alvarado's government meant no harm for the sisal plantations, which he considered an important source of revenue for the Revolution. Thus, he refrained from radical agrarianist discourses and concentrated on improving labour conditions in rural and urban contexts through the organization of unions. However, he allowed one of his lieutenants, Carrillo Puerto, to organize Ligas de Resistencia ('leagues of resistance') in the rural communities located outside the main henequén-producing area. These communities had lost their land to *haciendas,* which benefited from maize, sugar-cane and cattle production through renting and sharecropping arrangements. Thanks to Carrillo Puerto's leagues, peasants were given free access to idle *hacienda* and government land. In the new network of power and patronage, village *caciques* became key

[3] Francisco A. Gómez Jara, *El movimiento campesino en México* (Mexico, D.F., 1970), pp. 30–9, 49–55.

[4] Lack of space prevents discussion of Tomás Garrido Canabal in Tabasco, Emilio Portes Gil in Tamaulipas, Saturnino Osornio in Querétaro, among others. See, on Garrido, Carlos Martínez Assad, 'Los caudillos regionales y el poder central', in Carlos Martínez Assad et al., *Revolucionarios fueron todos* (Mexico, D.F., 1982), pp. 154–60; and Carlos Martínez Assad, *El laboratorio de la revolución: el Tabasco garridista* (Mexico, D.F., 1979); on Portes Gil, Arturo Alvarado, 'Perfil político de Emilio Portes Gil', in Carlos Martínez Assad (ed.), *Estadistas, caciques y caudillos* (Mexico, D.F., 1988), pp. 730–96; on Osornio, Martha García Ugarte, 'Saturnino Osornio: remembranzas de una época en Querétaro', in ibid., pp. 335–62.

elements, hitching local organizations to the state government through the leagues – which soon provided the basis for a new political party, the Partido Socialista del Sureste (PSS).

After Obregón took office, Carrillo Puerto was elected governor of Yucatán. As such, he carried out a programme of land distribution which gave every community a grant of *ejido* land – albeit with only a provisional charter. But he did not allow an independent peasant organization to develop; on the contrary, he strengthened the clientelistic linkages be-tween the government, the PSS, the local leagues, and the beneficiaries of the agrarian programme. However, Obregón was not enthusiastic about dealing with personalistic power structures at the regional level, and he refrained from answering Carrillo Puerto's demands for weapons for his peasants. In 1923, the army garrisons in Yucatán and the neighbouring state of Campeche joined the anti-Obregón, nation-wide rebellion headed by General Adolfo de la Huerta, which was given enthusiastic support by the landowners and their *guardias blancas* (private armed retinues). Many *caciques* switched their loyalty to the rebels, or else remained cautiously passive. Carrillo Puerto was murdered. Even though the rebellion was suffocated, the government of Yucatán fell into the hands of moderate parties, the leagues lost their impetus, and the process of agrarian reform was halted for almost two decades.

The fate of the Yucatán leagues and their caudillo was symptomatic of the awkward relationship between a central government struggling to consolidate its power, and regional elites competing for political suprem-acy and the support of the masses. Both Obregón and his successor Plutarco Elías Calles – who was President from 1924 to 1928 but effec-tively wielded national power until 1935 – carefully undermined the strength of state governors by manipulating local congresses as well as creating centralized agrarian organizations and labour federations, and by naming generals who were independent of, and even hostile to, local authorities, as military commanders in each state. These commanders often became weary of rural agitation and even drawn into alliance with certain landowners (particularly when they had joined their ranks) and the Church. In this context, peasant organizations and village leaders were sometimes obliged to change allegiances and even befriend anti-agrarian forces if they wanted to ensure their own survival.[5]

[5] See Gilbert Joseph, *Revolution from without: Yucatán, Mexico, and the United States, 1880–1924* (Cambridge, 1982); Francisco J. Paoli, *Yucatán y los orígenes del nuevo estado mexicano* (Mexico, D.F., 1984); Gilbert M. Joseph, 'Caciquismo and the revolution: Carrillo Puerto in the Yucatán', in D. A.

The case of Jalisco provides a good example of this dilemma. A radical, state-wide, peasant league (the Liga de Comunidades Agraristas) was fostered by Governor Zuno (1923–6), who also strove to create an aggressive labour movement independent from both the Confederación Regional Obrera Mexicana (CROM) – the labour arm of Calles – and Catholic organizations, which had great importance locally.

When General Estrada, the army commander, became the head of the De la Huertista uprising in western Mexico (Jalisco, Colima and Michoacán) – again, with the sympathy of the landowners and their *guardias blancas* – , Zuno managed to escape alive, and rallied the leagues as well as many aspiring rural leaders against the rebels. The agrarian cause seemed particularly alive in southern Jalisco, where massive village land expropriation had taken place during the second half of the nineteenth century. After the defeat of De la Huerta and Estrada, Zuno returned to office, and allowed the loyal rural *caciques* to seize *hacienda* land. These *caciques* often used this opportunity to enrich themselves, settle personal disputes and get rid of their political rivals. In addition, the governor was unable to engineer an alliance between the two most radical tendencies in the agrarian movement, the Anarchists and the Communists – the latter dominating in the Liga de Comunidades Agraristas de Jalisco. When the anti-revolutionary *cristero* movement broke out in 1926, Zuno was allowed to distribute rifles and pistols to his *caciques* and their followers; but his open quarrels with the CROM and Calles led to his impeachment by the local Congress. At this juncture, Zuno was not supported by his previous friends the rural bosses, nor by the Liga authorities, who chose to switch their loyalty to Calles' men. Moreover, since the latter did not favour the acceleration of agrarian reform, *caciques* used their armed force to prevent rural agitation – until Lázaro Cárdenas became President of the Republic in 1934.[6]

In Michoacán, the agrarian flame was stronger and lasted longer than in Yucatán and Jalisco, because of the presence of more radical, and less

Brading (ed.), *Caudillo and Peasant in the Mexican Revolution* (Cambridge, 1980); see also Rina Ortíz, Enrique Arriola and Pedro Siller, 'Los gobiernos de Alvarado y Carrillo Puerto', *Historia Obrera* (Mexico, D.F., n.d.), and Beatriz González Padilla, 'La dirigencia política en Yucatán, 1909–1925', in L. Millet Cámara et al., *Hacienda y cambio social en Yucatán* (Mérida, 1984), pp. 103–66.
[6] See Jaime Tamayo, 'Los movimientos sociales. 1917–1929', in M. A. Aldana Rendón (ed.), *Jalisco desde la Revolución,* Vol. IV (Guadalajara, 1988) pp. 161–6; Guillermo de la Peña, 'Populism, Regional Power, and Political Mediation: Southern Jalisco, 1900–80', in Eric Van Young (ed.), *Mexican Regions: Comparative History and Development* (San Diego, Cal., 1993), pp. 201–7.

opportunistic, local peasant leaders backed by a militant tradition of communal defence, and because agrarianism continued to be supported by the state government beyond Obregón's presidency.

As in Jalisco, moderate Church-sponsored rural and urban unions were successful in gaining support among the working population; but in addition a number of leftist peasant organizations came to life in the early 1920s. These organizations began to form a militant coalition thanks to the leadership of Primo Tapia, an Indian peasant from the village of Naranja in the heart of the Zacapu valley who had been educated at a Catholic seminary and then migrated to the United States, where between 1907 and 1921 he acquired anarcho-syndicalist ideas through his association with the Flores Magón brothers and with the Industrial Workers of the World (IWW). Tapia had plenty of the traits of a cosmopolitan revolutionary; but he never lost his familiarity with local and regional custom, his taste for and dexterity with the spoken Tarascan language, nor his identity as a member of a respected family and of a wide network of kinsmen and neighbours. Ethnicity therefore remained an important aspect of Primo Tapia's identity, expressed in overt hostility towards non-Indian (*mestizo* and Spanish) families and groups in the vicinity.

In addition to agriculture and traditional crafts, the Indians of the Zacapu valley had a crucial source of livelihood in the marshes and lagoons, from which they obtained fish, mussels, fowl and several types of reed for basket and mat weaving. But after 1880 a vast process of drainage was carried out by two Spanish entrepreneurs, who then seized the rich dessicated soil with the blessing of the federal government. Since a great deal of village land had already been appropriated by *mestizo* families, Indians were forced to make a living by working as day labourers not only in the neighbouring *haciendas* but also in the plantations of the relatively distant *tierra caliente* (hot country) of Michoacán.[7] After the fall of the Díaz dictatorship, Joaquín de la Cruz, an educated Indian and sympathizer of Zapata's agrarianism, who was a maternal uncle to Primo Tapia, led an unsuccessful legal fight to recover the ancestral land of the village – until he was murdered in 1919. A number of local young people joined the

---

[7] This and the following paragraphs are largely based on Paul Friedrich's classic *Agrarian revolt in a Mexican village,* 2nd edn (Chicago, Ill., 1977), and Jorge Zepeda Patterson, 'Los caudillos en Michoacán: Francisco J. Múgica y Lázaro Cárdenas', in Carlos Martínez Assad (ed.), *Estadistas, caciques y caudillos,* p. 248. See also Fernando Salmerón Castro, *Los límites del agrarismo. Proceso político y estructuras de poder en Taretan, Michoacán* (Zamora, 1989), pp. 104–22.

Villista forces when they passed by, and when Primo Tapia came back they formed the backbone of his agrarian movement.

In 1921, Francisco Múgica was Governor of Michoacán. Initially, he had been backed by the urban-based Partido Socialista Michoacano, but he soon attracted the support of incipient peasant leagues as he distributed over 23,000 hectares in provisional grants. In reply, *guradias blancas* from *haciendas* began terrorizing peasants and even killed prominent members of Múgica's party. Taking advantage of Obregón's personal dislike of Múgica – again, because he was too radical and independent – General Estrada and other prominent military officers joined the anti-agrarian factions of Michoacán and managed to overthrow the governor in 1922. Meanwhile, Primo Tapia and his first cousin Pedro López headed a fighting group of relatives, friends and neighbours who organized themselves against *guardias blancas,* drew up a list of land petitioners and started the legal process for the creation of an *ejido*. At the end of 1921, a meeting of agrarian delegations of neighbouring villages in Naranja elected Primo Tapia as their representative for the whole Zacapu district. In 1922, when the Liga de Comunidades y Sindicatos Agraristas de Michoacán was created in Morelia, Tapia became its first Secretary General. In 1923, he attended the First National Agrarian Convention in Mexico City, where he submitted an initiative to reform the 1915 Agrarian Law, so that *hacienda* workers would become eligible as *ejidatarios* and all the large landholdings could be totally expropriated. Such initiative was not well received in the higher circles of the federal government. During the De la Huerta–Estrada attempted coup d'état, Tapia and his men had to fight against both *obregonistas* and rebels; but they took advantage of the turmoil to eliminate more rivals.[8]

When Calles became President of the Republic, he supported a new Michoacán governor who took sides with the *hacendados* and persecuted the agrarian fighters. The villages of the Zacapu valley finally had got their provisional *ejidos* in 1924. Tapia continued his agitation against *haciendas* throughout 1924 and 1925; but he was captured and summarily executed by soldiers in 1926 – apparently under the orders of Calles himself. By this time, Calles had introduced a crucial change in the agrarian legislation: the division of *ejidos* into family plots, so that the land distribution programme might become 'de-socialized'. In spite of this new legislation

---

[8] Gerrit Huizer, *La lucha campesina en México* (Mexico, D.F., 1970), p. 49; Paul Friedrich, *Agrarian revolt in a Mexican village,* pp. 105–12.

and Calles' discourse in favour of economic efficiency in the rural areas (meaning that he would not expropriate productive *haciendas*), the conservative forces in Michoacán did not sympathize with the federal government because of its extreme anti-Catholicism. Moreover, the vast majority of the population in western Michoacán supported the *cristero* armies.[9] To the President's regret, agrarianism had again to be encouraged as a means of attracting peasant loyalty to the government.

In 1928, General Lázaro Cárdenas, a close friend of Múgica's, became governor of Michoacán. He soon founded the Confederación Revolucionaria Michoacana del Trabajo (CRMDT) in order to re-arrange the dispersed socialist unions and peasant leagues into a single organization. In 1930, the Agrarian Conference held in Morelia triggered off intense agitation in the rural areas. In 1932, there were 4,000 agrarian committees (which together boasted 100,000 members) affiliated to the CRMDT. Nearly 150,000 hectares were distributed between 1928 and 1932 to 16,000 *ejidatarios,* even though the largest modernizing *haciendas* still enjoyed the protection of the federal government.[10] But the old radical *caciques* were alive and healthy, particularly since the state government had given them *mausers,* although increasingly their activities had more to do with local factional fighting than with agrarian change. As Paul Friedrich has put it, 'after 1926 the land you fought to obtain was in the hands of your fellow *ejidatarios,* and to that coveted land was tied the rich booty from cash crops, forced loans, and the graft and embezzlement that were assumed to be part of your office'.[11] Nevertheless, Cárdenas used these *caciques* as allies in the process of consolidating both the CRMDT and his personalized power.

At the time of the Revolution, the state of Veracruz had a relatively high proportion of wage labourers, both rural and urban, because of the development of the textile industry in the Orizaba region, oil fields in Minatitlán, Coatzacoalcos and Poza Rica, services of all kinds in the port of Veracruz – the main Mexican port since colonial times – sugar-cane plantations in the lowlands, and coffee plantations in the highlands. It was no coincidence that the 1906 Acayucan uprising – the most important peasant rebellion in the state during the Díaz period – had a peasant, who

---

[9] Luis González, *Pueblo en vilo* (México, 1968); see also his monographs *Zamora* (Morelia, 1978), and *Sahuayo* (Morelia, 1979).

[10] Jorge Zepeda Patterson, 'Los caudillos de Michoacán', pp. 256–61.

[11] Paul Friedrich, *The Princes of Naranja. An Essay in Anthrohistorical Method* (Austin, Tex., 1986), p. 134.

had also been a textile worker, as its main leader. This uprising attracted support not only from Indian villagers who demanded the return of their expropriated communal lands, and from discontented rural workers and tenants, but also from a variety of urban groups who protested against the excessive political power and prerogatives of the landowning class.[12] Throughout the revolutionary period, the main military leader was Manuel Peláez, member of a landowning family and a close ally of the British and American oil companies, whose area of operation, which included the Huasteca sierra and the North of the state, was kept 'free' of the dangers of agrarianism. On the other hand, the *carrancista* governor, Cándido Aguilar, had a moderate agrarian project, similar to Alvarado's in Yucatán, which failed to attract the support of peasants and rural workers.

As governor of Veracruz from 1921 to 1924, Adalberto Tejeda confronted a military commander, Guadalupe Sánchez, who had become a big landowner, openly supported haciendas and encouraged repression by *guardias blancas*. But Tejeda counted on the support of militant urban groups such as the dashing Sindicato de Inquilinos (Union of Tenants), the incipient Communist party, and – because he was a friend of Calles – the CROM. At the same time, he won the sympathy of two young agrarian agitators, Ursulo Galván and Manuel Almanza, who had come as migrant workers to the port and there become influenced by first anarchist and later communist ideas, transmitted by newly arrived European (mainly Spanish) ideologues. With Tejeda's blessing, Galván and Almanza founded groups of *ejido* petitioners in many villages, which later would become unified as the Peasant League of Veracruz.

In order to protect local agrarian committees and emerging unions – and also his own supremacy – Tejeda reinforced the Guardia Civil: a military police, created in the previous decade, which was directly under the command of the governor. After 1922, certain rural areas of the state, particularly on the central coast and in the South, were the theatre of numerous seizures of land by groups of peasants, encouraged by the state government and the Guardia Civil. In 1923, there were several open confrontations between the Guardia Civil and the army. Pressured by General Sánchez, Obregón gave the order that the Guardia should be disarmed. This was obeyed by Tejeda, but then he formally created the Liga de Comunidades Agrarias del Estado de Veracruz (LCAEV) – the most radical in the

---

[12] Leonardo Pasquel, *La revolución en el estado de Veracruz*, Vol. 1 (Mexico, D.F., 1971), pp. 85–7; see also Heather Fowler Salamini, *Agrarian Radicalism in Veracruz, 1920–38* (Lincoln, Neb., 1978).

country – once more with the help of Galván and Almanza. When the De la Huerta rebellion broke out, Tejeda converted the Liga into a set of armed rural guerrillas.

Together with other conservative military officers, Sánchez joined De la Huerta in his aborted coup d'etat, and had to run for his life when the uprising was defeated. The new army commander in the state did not object to Tejeda's agrarian policies, so that Ursulo Galván, now openly affiliated to the Communist Party – he even visited the Soviet Union on several occasions – but maintaining close contact with the governor, was able to continue organizing *ejido* petitioners, who swiftly received *dotaciones provisionales* from the state government. Where local strongmen and caciques had become allies and clients of Tejeda's, they received both arms and his full blessing to establish a stern system of political control.

In 1924, when Calles became President, Tejeda was appointed Minister of Communication; as such, he helped Ursulo Galván and other regional leaders to organize the National Congress of Agrarian Leagues, which purported to create a nation-wide organization. However, just two years later, as Minister of the Interior (Secretario de Gobernación), Tejeda engineered the overthrow of Zuno from the governorship of Jalisco and did not prevent Primo Tapia's assassination.[13] Loyalty to Calles came before his sympathy for the national cause of agrarianism.

From 1924 to 1928, the LCAEV made less spectacular advances, since the new governor, Heriberto Jara, preferred to engineer his own (rather slow) agrarian policy and to support a renewed version of the Guardia Civil; but the league members maintained a military presence in the rural areas and an important political presence in the municipal councils and the local Congress, thanks to a complex and delicate web of alliances with the CROM and the Communist Party. As a federal deputy, Ursulo Galván increasingly spent his time in Mexico City and visiting and encouraging leagues in other parts of Mexico, leaving Manuel Almanza in charge in Veracruz. Although the *cristeros* were much less strong in Veracruz than in western Mexico, their threat was none the less a further reason for the government to respect the old pact with the armed peasants.

When in 1928 Tejeda came back for a second period as governor, he constructed a hegemonic domain for himself and the LCAEV. In 1929, the Liga again provided armed help against a military revolt, headed by

<hr>

[13] Romana Falcón and Soledad García, *La semilla en el surco. Adalberto Tejeda y el radicalismo en Veracruz, 1883–1960* (Mexico, D.F., 1986), pp. 169–70.

Escobar, although the cost was a definite break with the Communist Party – which was angry at Calles's ambiguous policies and unwisely supported the revolt.[14] Thus, during this 'gilded period of agrarianism' (1928–32), Tejeda relied again on a clientelistic network of allies and *caciques* to implement a re-invigorated programme of land distribution and social reforms – he promoted co-operatives, founded schools, instigated anti-monopoly laws, defended unions harassed by employers, and managed to mediate successfully in the turmoil caused in the sugar refineries by the collapse of prices after 1929.[15] However, his relationship with Calles inevitably deteriorated when the Jefe Máximo favoured the emergence of alternative agrarian organizations under his direct control, through the newly created Partido Nacional Revolucionario (PNR). Besides, Ursulo Galván's unexpected death in 1930 left a void in grass-roots leadership which was never filled again. Certain local leaders – as was the case in the *municipio* La Antigua – had left the agrarian struggle for more comfortable political posts or for businesses in the cities, so that in such places the agrarian programme was never really carried out. After he left the governorship in 1932, many local sections and leaders abandoned Tejeda and the Liga. Other leaders were assassinated, and gradually the old allies of the LCAEV were driven out of political offices. The new governor, Vázquez Vela, with Calles's blessing, reverted several *dotaciones provisionales* in favour of landowners.[16]

In contrast with most of his fellow agrarian *caudillos,* Saturnino Cedillo in San Luis Potosí did not come from a lower middle-class family, nor did he merely join the Revolution in a fit of youthful idealism. The son of a freeholding peasant, he and his three brothers started fighting – together with the brothers Carrera Torres, who had acquired radical ideas as students in a teacher-training college – because they were involved in a series of personal conflicts with the *hacienda* elite of their region, known as Valle del Maíz, which also led them to take sides with sharecroppers and wage labourers.[17] Staunchly advocating land distribution from the beginning, their movement paralleled in certain ways Zapata's; but Cedillismo managed to survive not only because it gained massive local support by invad-

---

[14] Carlos Martínez Assad, 'Los caudillos regionales y el poder central', in C. Martínez Assad et al., *Revolucionarios fueron todos* (Mexico, D.F., 1982), pp. 154–60.

[15] Salamini, *Agrarian Radicalism,* pp. 121–36.

[16] Romana Falcón, *El agrarismo en Veracruz. La etapa radical, 1928–1935* (Mexico, D.F., 1977), pp. 214–17.

[17] See Beatriz Rojas, *La pequeña guerra. Los Carrera Torres y los Cedillo* (Zamora, 1983).

ing estates and letting former sharecroppers seize the land, but also thanks to its successive alliances with Villa, Carranza and Obregón.

Under Obregón's presidency, Cedillo organized his followers in *colonias militares,* by which soldiers received plots of cultivable land, and plots for housing, without losing their military status. This allowed Cedillo to maintain a self-supporting peasant army. The *colonias* were not *ejidos,* although their land was also inalienable; their impetus did not come from the demands of organized groups of villagers, but from the initiatives of a regional military leader.[18] This explains both the strong bonds of loyalty established between General Cedillo and his men, and the high degree of autonomy of the organization. In his native ranch of Palomas, the general created the nucleus of a power which a few years later novelist Graham Greene, who visited the ranch in 1938, would define as 'feudal'.[19] In 1923, the *colonos militares* were the decisive force to stop Delahuertismo in San Luis Potosí. Between 1926 and 1929, the *cedillistas* fought and won the most important battles against the *cristeros* all over western Mexico. The creation of *ejidos* became a tool in the hands of Cedillo, who after 1927, when he personally took over the governorship, ensured that the landowners who were ready to support him were in no way disturbed. In turn, his landowner friends donated tracts of land for the creation of new *colonias militares,* or simply to be given to *cedillistas.* The power of Cedillo reached such proportions that, in addition to capturing virtually all public offices in San Luis Potosí for his kindred and protegés, he was even able to exert effective pressure concerning the appointment of mayors and governors in the neighbouring states of Zacatecas and Querétaro.[20]

Yet Calles's designs for centralized hegemony could not tolerate the fact that Cedillo commanded an independent army of between 15,000 and 20,000 loyal men. But the cunning *caudillo* was not easily deposed: he was always willing to support the Jefe Máximo against political rivals. In 1931 he was appointed Minister of Agriculture for a brief period. Meanwhile, the PNR, the party founded by Calles, started building its own base of power in the state. In 1934, Cedillo declared his full support to Lázaro Cárdenas, who afterwards made him Minister of Agriculture for a second time, perhaps mainly to get him out of this territory. From then on,

---

[18] Martínez Assad, 'Los caudillos regionales y el poder central', pp. 187–96.
[19] Graham Greene, *The Lawless Roads* (London, 1987), pp. 52–61. (First published in 1939.)
[20] Lorenzo Meyer, 'El conflicto social y los gobiernos del Maximato', in *Historia de la revolución mexicana,* Vol. 13 (Mexico, D.F., 1978), pp. 307–16; Romana Falcón, *Revolución y caciquismo. San Luis Potosí, 1910–1938* (México, D.F., 1984), ch. IV.

Cárdenas proceeded to dismantle Cedillo's domain, through the PNR political machine and through the new centralized peasant organization, the Confederación Campesina Mexicana (CCM), which became the crucial mediating mechanism for a massive programme of *ejido* creation. It was often the case that the new *ejidos* overlapped the territory of *colonias militares,* creating endless violent disputes.[21] In addition, the *colonos* were put under the direct jurisdiction of the state army commander, no longer a friend of Cedillo's, who in turn started to disarm them. In August 1937, Cedillo resigned from his cabinet post, and a year later attempted to launch a military rebellion, hoping to count on the support of the foreign oil companies, which faced expropriation by the Cárdenas government. This support never materialized, so Cedillo dissuaded his loyal *colonos* from following him into inevitable disaster. The caudillo met his fate in an ambush early in 1939, and the *colonias* were brutally ravaged by the army. Some of them survived under military supervision; others preferred to convert to *ejidos.*

The death of Saturnino Cedillo signalled the end of post-revolutionary regional *caudillismo.* But, before disappearing, *caudillismo* had provided an enormous service both to the centralizing project of Calles and to the controlled incorporation of the masses devised by Cárdenas. It also provided an invaluable channel of mediation for the demands of the peasants and other sectors of the rural populace – demands for land and participation, which also included the displacement of the old political elite – but without letting these demands grow into a serious threat to the supremacy of the new political elite headed by Obregón, Calles and Cárdenas. In fact, a crucial priority for the regional *caudillos* was to be a part of this nascent elite, and therefore they became active players – and bitter rivals – in the factional political contest which extended from the national to the regional and local levels. Similarly, within each region, *caciques* and other local leaders tended to compete among themselves for the favours of the regional caudillos, reproducing the national factional context. Hence the difficulties faced by attempted alliances among peasants, industrial workers and urban sectors, even when (as in Michoacán and Veracruz) such alliances were favoured by the incumbent *caudillo.*

And yet, to repeat, it was precisely this combination of grass-roots demands and community organization, personalized leadership-cum-brokerage, selective repression, and ubiquitous factionalism which laid

[21] Martínez Assad, 'Los caudillos regionales', pp. 196–207.

the foundations of the successful policies of stability – the populist pact – characteristic of modern Mexico. The contrast with the handling of rural unrest and organized communal resistance in certain Central American and Andean countries – where repression of popular rural demands and replacement of the old political elites was not carried out through skilful brokers and did not lead to a real stabilization of the new political regimes – may help to sustain this contention.

Central America

Throughout the early decades of the twentieth century the countries of Central American shared three important characteristics: they all had 'Liberal' modernizing no nonsense governments, inspired by the doctrines of Social Darwinism and the Mexican regime of Porfirio Díaz; they were enthusiastically producing staples for the international market; and they increasingly suffered economic and political interference from foreign powers. The opening up of foreign trade led to the consolidation of coffee and bananas as dominant crops. Situated in the highlands, coffee plantations were in the hands of national entrepreneurs, who – particularly in Guatemala and El Salvador – seized land from the Indian villages and established a mixed labour regime whereby the resident *colonos* would work all year round in the plantations, receiving a meagre salary and a plot of land to grow their own food, whereas seasonal help would be provided by village Indians, whose own subsistence cultivation took place in the steepest, less fertile terrains. Conversely, the coastal banana plantations were in foreign hands, the United Fruit Company being the most important, and attracted a proletarianized migrant labour force – mostly Blacks and *mestizos,* but also Indians. Since the members of the old oligarchies had in many instances supported the ousted Conservative parties, they had largely lost their political influence to a new bourgeois class and an increasingly strong professionalized military establishment, even though many Conservative families re-emerged as coffee planters and international merchants. Political opposition flourished among the emergent urban middle classes, whose banners to attract popular support were the defence of national pride and the struggle against the overexploitation of workers.[22]

Because of the continuous re-investment of its considerable earnings

[22] Ralph Lee Woodward, Jr., *Central America. a Nation Divided,* 2nd edn (New York, 1985), ch. 8, and *passim.* See also James Dunkerley, *Power in the Isthmus. a Political History of Modern Central America* (London, 1988), ch. 2.

from coffee exports, El Salvador had expanded its commercial agriculture – which now included cotton and *henequen* as export crops – and also developed a small but thriving proto-industrial and service economy in cities such as San Salvador and Santa Ana, which in turn attracted further investment from the United States. Nevertheless, the vast majority of the population lived in abject poverty, and suffered chronic food shortages since the land had been seized from the peasants to the benefit of internationally oriented planters. In 1918, President Alfonso Quiñónez founded an organization called Liga Roja ('Red League') as an institutional channel of mediation between the government and the workers, including the peasants, in the absence of trade unions or political parties. But Quiñónez, a member of the coffee bourgeoisie and of a narrow family circle which ruled the country from 1913 to 1931, failed to develop the league into a minimally satisfying form of popular representation.

The peasants and *colonos* in the densely populated central and western highlands had lived a history of violence, ever since their attempts to protest against land expropriation in the period 1880–1900 had been bloodily repressed. Discontent was further nourished by laws which enabled planters to expel tenants and recruit forced labour – with the help of the army – when the needs of production thus demanded.[23] To make things worse, the 1929 crash and the following crisis marked a fall in the price of coffee: the average price per *quintal* fell from a maximum of forty-three *colones* in 1925 to thirty-three in 1929, to just fifteen in 1932. Unemployment increased to as much as 40 per cent in the rural areas after 1929.[24] This created fertile ground for the Marxist preachings of José Agustín Farabundo Martí, the son of a small farmer, sometime law student and founder of the Salvadorean Communist Party; but also for broader ideologies which denounced injustice and demanded straightforward policies to guarantee minimum rights and improve the workers' welfare.

In 1930, President Pío Romero Bosque decided for a democratic opening in order to appease increasing waves of protest throughout the country. A national election was won by the founder of the Labour Party, Arturo Araujo, a progressive entrepreneur educated in England, whose banners included *vitalismo mínimo* (an arithmetically elaborated doctrine which

[23] David Browning, *El Salvador, Landscape and Society* (Oxford, 1971), p. 217; Liisa North, *Bitter Grounds: Roots of Revolt in El Salvador* (London, 1982), pp. 22–4.

[24] Alejandro D. Marroquín, 'Estudio sobre la crisis de los años treinta en El Salvador', in Pablo González Casanova (ed.), *América Latina en los años treinta* (Mexico, D.F., 1978), pp. 142–3.

held that every person had the right to possess and receive at least what he or she needed to lead a minimally satisfactory life), labour reforms and land distribution, and who was therefore massively supported by unions and peasants.[25] Araujo took office in March 1931, but his government proved totally inefficient – both in fulfilling his promises and in coming to grips with the desperate economic crisis. Nine months after his inauguration, in the midst of endless agitation and strikes, he was deposed by a military coup. The new President was General Maximiliano Hernández Martínez. Against his stern disciplinary measures, and after municipal elections were cancelled, a great peasant revolt broke out in the western highlands in January 1932.

This revolt had been incited by the Communist Party, but Farabundo Martí and many other Communist leaders were killed or jailed by Hernández Martínez at the very outset. The real organizational pivot was in the Indian *cofradías* – the old religious sodalities which had been the legal corporate holders of community land and retained their political functions in spite of expropriatory laws – led by village *caciques*. The uprising had a distinct ethnic character. The main goals were extremely clear for all the participants: to recover the land which had been brutally taken away from them, and to restore the formal authority to the *cofradías*. It was in the Departments of Santa Ana, Ahuachapán, and Sonsonate – and particularly in communities such as Juayúa, Izalco, Ahuachapán and Tacuba – which had also been the theatres of conflicts in the late nineteenth century, where the 1932 revolt became most ardent. The rebels occupied estates and town halls, evicting and sometimes killing administrators, bureaucrats and *ladino* (non-Indian) merchants. Their headquarters were located in Juayúa, but in fact each *cacique* was fairly independent to plan his own actions. This lack of co-ordination was one of the reasons why the rebellion was easily suppressed. Other reasons, perhaps more important, were that the Indians were armed with machetes and only a few guns, while they were attacked by a fully equipped army and vigilantes supplied by the planters, and that there was no parallel revolt in the urban areas. Since all Indians were defined as enemies, the soldiers opened fire on multitudes of women and children. According to numerous eye witnesses, when the military took a village they coldly killed everyone who they thought had an Indian look. The number of people killed by the Indians – including soldiers – amounted to little more

---

[25] Rafael Guidos Véjar, *El ascenso del militarismo en El Salvador* (San Salvador, 1980), p. 102; Rafael Menjívar Larín, *El Salvador: el eslabón más pequeño* (San José, 1980), p. 55.

than 100. On the side of the Indians, the most conservative estimate is 10,000 victims; the highest 50,000 – although the number which is usually accepted is 30,000.[26] Consolidated as a dictator, Hernández Martínez ruled by force until 1943.

In other Central American countries (except Costa Rica, where the non-white population is a small minority), there was also a 'conquest tradition' – to use Richard Adams's words[27] – which created segregation, mistrust and even hatred among different ethnic groups, and which from time to time resulted in conflict. The consequences of ethnic conflict were particularly devastating in El Salvador.

The Andes

In the 1920s and 1930s Bolivian society was still sharply divided by a colonial inheritance of ethnic mistrust and hatred. For the old and new ruling classes and urban groups, the Indians represented the menacing face of 'barbarity', which had to be swept away by the advancing forces of 'civilization': this was the ideological justification for the relentless attacks on traditional Quechua and Aymara institutions such as the *ayllú* – the land holding, self-governing Indian community. During the second half of the nineteenth century, the proportion of people having ownership of, or direct access to land had dropped from two-thirds to one-third of the total population.[28] The 1899 civil war led to the consolidation of a Liberal government interested in promoting the exportation of new raw materials such as rubber and tin, in addition to silver, as well as the full commercialization of the economy.

The Liberal years marked the beginning of a cycle of rebellions, initiated by Pablo Zárate Willka, an aymara *mallku* (*cacique*) who in the civil war had commanded an Indian army in support of the Liberals and then demanded restoration of communal lands and recognition of autonomous status for the Indian village authorities within the Republic. Willka's forces were decimated, but from 1900 to 1920 no less than sixty *jacqueries* – attacks on

---

[26] Thomas P. Anderson, *Matanza: El Salvador Communist Revolt of 1932* (Lincoln, Nebr., 1971), pp. 131–6; Rafael Guidos Véjar, *El ascenso del militarismo en El Salvador*, pp. 135–7.

[27] Richard N. Adams, 'The Conquest Tradition of Mesoamerica', *Texas Papers on Latin America*, Institute of Latin American Studies, University of Texas at Austin, 1987.

[28] Silvia Rivera Cusicanqui, 'La expansión del latifundio en el Altiplano boliviano: elementos para una caracterización de una oligarquía regional', in Enrique Florescano (ed.), *Orígenes y desarrollo de la burguesía en América Latina, 1700–1955* (Mexico, D.F., 1985), pp. 357–86; see also Erick D. Langer, *Rural Society and the Mining Economy in Southern Bolivia* (Stanford, Cal., 1989).

haciendas and *mestizo* towns – took place in the Departamentos of La Paz, Potosí, Oruro, Cochabamba, and even in the distant El Chaco.[29]

The common experience of defending the land favoured the re-emergence of an ethnic consciousness beyond community boudaries which had probably all but disappeared in the nineteenth century. This consciousness was also reinforced by a refunctionalization of the *mallkus* or *kurakas* (traditional local authorities) as leaders in the lengthy process of legal defence of community land: for instance, in the southern Departmento of Chuquisaca, several *kurakas* were able to produce colonial documents which actually halted the expropriatory dispositions of the *revisitas,* or land surveying brigades. Also in the South (northern Potosí, Oruro and western Chuquisaca), the *kurakas,* together with *tinterillos* (poor educated *mestizos* who provided services to the Indians in their dealings with the bureaucracy), and instigated by an emerging Socialist 'Pro-Indian Defensive League' (based on La Paz) led a veritable epidemic of conspiracies and mutinies from 1924 to 1927, culminating in a large-scale insurrection, with the participation of about 12,000 *comuneros,* both Aymara and Quechua. Their frustration and rage were again shown in certain acts of unbelievable violence: at one point, a landowner was ritually sacrificed and eaten. Even though the 1927 insurrection was crushed by the army, it showed the possibility of a wide multi-ethnic Indian alliance.[30]

The Chaco War (1932–5) provoked another series of anti-urban, anti-White *jacqueries* in protest against the draft: for instance, on New Year's Day 1933, after conscription agents had forcefully and sometimes brutally taken able men away from their communities, the town of Pucarani, near La Paz, was looted by Indians who lynched the local officials and anyone else who put up resistance.[31] But, at the same time, the war gave the drafted Indians the possibility of a national identity – the realization that they were citizens and their participation was important, as René Zavaleta has emphatically pointed out.[32] The collapse of the Liberals, and the

[29] Gonzalo Flores, 'Levantamientos campesinos durante el periodo liberal', in Fernando Calderón and Jorge Dandler (eds), *Bolivia: la fuerza histórica del campesinado* (Cochabamba, 1984), pp. 121–32; Silvia Rivera Cusicanqui, '*Oprimidos pero no vencidos', Luchas del campesinado aymara y qhechua de Bolivia, 1900–1980* (Geneva, 1986), ch. II.

[30] Erick D. Langer, 'The great southern Bolivian Indian rebellion of 1927: a microanalysis', paper delivered at 46th International Congress of Americanists, Amsterdam, July, 1988.

[31] David Preston, *Farmers and Towns. Rural – Urban Relations in Highland Bolivia* (Norwich, Eng., 1978), pp. 1–2.

[32] René Zavaleta Mercado, *Bolivia: el desarrollo de la conciencia nacional* (Montevideo, 1967); also 'Notas sobre la cuestión nacional en Bolivia', in Marco Palacios (ed.) *La unidad nacional en América latina. Del regionalismo a la nacionalidad* (Mexico, D.F., 1983), pp. 87–98.

arrival of a military government with reformist ideas but few viable projects – and even fewer possibilities of establishing organic contacts with peasants and workers – opened the way for further unrest, but also for the activities of multiple leftist groups, pro-Indian educationists, and union organizers. These emerging actors would become crucial in the rise of a populist organization in the 1940s and 1950s: the Movimiento Nacional Revolucionario (MNR), which for the first time would provide institutional viability to grass-roots demands in rural Bolivia.

What was the social and economic content of the 'defence of community'? In spite of certain nativist discourses, it is doubtful that the Bolivian Indians aspired to the return of the pre-Hispanic, precapitalist world: rather they aimed to preserve the community as a means of securing strategic resources, which would allow them to participate in national society with fewer disadvantages. As for the *kuraka* leaders, they were interested in preserving the communal jurisdiction which provided the basis of their authority *and* their power as privileged brokers. But these facts were often obscured in discussions among intellectuals and politicians – even among the most perceptive and progressive. In Peru, for instance, an intense debate on 'the Indian as a problem' had arisen during the period of Leguía (1919–30), particularly after 1928 when José Carlos Mariátegui, the young pioneer of Latin American Marxist thought and founding member of the Communist Party of Peru, published his influential book, *Siete ensayos de interpretación de la realidad peruana*. For Mariátegui, who died two years later, at the age of 35, Indian reality was the central problem in the 'national biology', for a simple reason: four-fifths of the population were Indians. And, since they were tradionally agriculturalists, the uses and misuses of land were a crucial aspect of the same problem. Mariátegui held that there was a basic contradiction in the organization of land tenure: between the persisting, communalistic *ayllú,* and the feudal *latifundia.* The latter had created a complex political structure for parasitic exploitation, the pivotal point of which was the institution of *gamonalismo.* The *gamonal* (landowner and political boss) had become the articulation point between local bureaucracy and the wider political system, which permitted and protected the functioning of institutions such as the *yanaconazgo* (equivalent to medieval serfdom) and the *enganche* (indentured labour). Thus, liberalism and capitalism were a mere fiction: the landowning class had proved totally incapable of becoming a national bourgeoisie. It would only be through the abolition of the *hacienda* and the evolution of the *ayllú* towards socialist co-operatives – a natural evolution – that this radical, inhuman contradiction would be solved.[33]

The government of Leguía did not sympathize with socialism – much less with communism. But it was interested in the dismantling of 'feudalism', in order to give a final blow to the landowner-sponsored Civilista Party and attract support from the Indians. Leguía formally abolished *yanaconazgo* and *enganche*, and created a Bureau of Indigenous Affairs and a Patronate of the Indigenous Race, in charge of studying ways to solve Indian problems, and to act as mediators in their solution. More importantly, in the 1920 Constitution he decreed the existence of the Indian community as a legal entity: thus, those villages willing to go through the legal procedure of revalidation, would be able to recover or purchase back land expropriated after 1893.[34] However, neither Leguía nor his successors recognized the existence of traditional authorities (the old *varayok* or *alcaldes de vara*), so the leaders in the process were often modernizing local farmers, interested in using communal holdings to expand their own economic ventures.[35] This was particularly the case in the Central Peruvian Sierra, where the local village economies were strongly stimulated by the expansion of comunications in the 1920s; and then (paradoxically) by the world crisis of the 1930s, due to the increasing demand for foodstuffs in the domestic market. Because of their contacts and influences, these emerging leaders often succeeded in gaining access to recovered communal plots.

The effects of Leguía's policies tended to be different in the Southern Peruvian Sierra, where the commercialization and diversification of peasant agriculture (and agriculture in general) was much slower. In the Indian communities of La Mar (Departamento de Ayacucho), the local population found out that the bureaucratic procedures for revalidation of land titles were incredibly complicated, and both the Bureau and the Patronate virtually useless. In addition, they faced increasing taxation, additional labour tasks because of the new conscription for the building of

---

[33] José Carlos Mariátegui, *Siete ensayos de interpretación de la realidad peruana* (Mexico, D.F., 1979), pp. 35–92. (First published in Lima in 1928; English edition published by the University of Texas Press in 1981.)

[34] Richard W. Patch, 'How Communal are the Communities?', *American Universities Field Staff,* Latin America (Peru), 12 June 1959, pp. 11–12; Thomas M. Davies Jr., *Indian integration in Peru: a half century of experience* (Lincoln, Nebr., 1970).

[35] Henri Favre, 'Capitalismo y etnicidad: la política indigenista del Perú', in Claude Bataillon et al., *Indianidad, etnocidio, indigenismo en América Latina* (Mexico D.F., 1988), pp. 118–19.

roads, and renewed harassment by the *gamonales* – virtually all local authorities were members of landed families, and resented Indian attempts to vindicate communal property.

Between 1921 and 1925, a number rebellious outbreaks provoked repression, which in turn bred more discontent and violence. In 1923, a major Indian uprising took place, instigated by lawyers from the city of Huamanga. The rebels burnt *mestizo* towns and *haciendas,* very much in the fashion of the Bolivian *jacqueries;* but in the end they were massacred by the Guardia Civil, although general unrest continued for several years.[36] After these violent episodes, certain Southern Sierra communities got their old property or part of it back from *haciendas;* but this land was often insufficient for subsistence. The *comuneros* had to resort to renting pasture land (often paid in labour) from the big landowners; their condition was again one of dependence and subordination.[37] On the other hand, many communities never recovered any land; on the contrary, they continued losing it to *haciendas,* as it was depicted in Ciro Alegría's great testimonial novel, *El mundo es ancho y ajeno* (1941).

1930S TO 1960S

The period from 1930 to 1960 was one of profound economic and political change in Latin America. Formal political actors, including competing parties and bureaucratic agents, sought to create a relatively autonomous space by establishing links with popular sectors and by controlling popular organizations. Factionalism and patronage networks were still important; but negotiations with the base now had to include institutional responses to the demand for universal enfranchisement. These negotiations usually presented a renewed threat to the structure of landed property, in so far as the *latifundio* system began to be perceived as a formidable obstacle to individual social mobility as well as to the development of a free market of labour, products and means of production at the national level. (In the context of 'import substitution industrialization' (ISI), in the 1950s especially, internal market formation seemed a necessary condition for national development.) Thus, in many a political discourse, agrarian reform not only became a crucial strategy for the legitimization of the state – and a symbol of the breaking-down of the old power blocks – but it also became a blueprint for

[36] Eric Mayer, 'State Policy and Rebellion in Ayacucho: the campesino movement in La Mar, 1922–1923', paper delivered at 46th International Congress of Americanists, Amsterdam, 1988.
[37] Patch. 'How Communal are the Communities?', pp. 12–17.

agricultural modernization, an important premise for a State-led programme which would include public investment in irrigation and transport, as well as credit and marketing re-organization. Moreover, during the 1950s, the Economic Commission for Latin America (ECLA) 'model' of development included the setting up of income-levelling mechanisms. And agrarian reform was paramount among them. Finally, in the early 1960s, the Kennedy-sponsored Alliance for Progress also gave its blessing to programmes of 'non-revolutionary' distribution of land to peasants as a deterrent to Communism.

Alliances among political actors and rural popular groups became (at least temporarily) viable when new governments and political parties, usually progressive but not radical – of the kind known as 'populist' – gained the support of sizeable sectors of the emerging bourgeoisie and the middle classes by playing them off against the landed oligarchy. On the other hand, such alliances were frustrated when both urban-industrial groups and new political actors (including the military) found it convenient to avoid confrontations with the old agrarian elite. This was the case where the economic context allowed for agricultural modernization without reform, or without incorporating the peasantry, as in the Brazilian frontier expansion. The role of foreign, particularly U.S., investors could also be determinant. In Central America, for example, U.S. capitalists whose interests were in agriculture rather than industry or finance, exerted pressure through their government to avoid drastic agrarian changes. Moreover, the United States in several cases openly intervened against 'the threat of communism', when processes of social change seemed out of control.

The groups advocating agrarian change, including the peasantries, did not always agree about what type of innovation should be implemented, or by what means. Since the range of options varied from mildly reformist to radically revolutionary, rural mobilizations occurred in a context of wider alignments and conflicts, which in certain cases led to extreme polarization and violence. In this connection, the role of emerging political parties with different agrarian strategies was important: mobilizations were not now typically led by *caudillos* or strongmen (except in certain instances of the Colombian *violencia*) but by political groups which aspired for national recognition and competed to become the bearers of alternative projects of nation-building. These groups had to contend with both the traditional oligarchic parties – Liberal, Conservative and their functional equivalents – and the new nationalist military leaders. They often included members of the military but had a pred civilian orientation, since their appeal was to actors in the emergent civil society: urban middle classes, industrial workers, 'disposable' peasants. Some sought institutional identity in the 'European' parties (Socialist, Radical Communist, Christian Democrat) but those with a mass appeal – the 'populist' organizations mentioned above – were ideologically flexible and innovative (although they might use a Marxist vocabulary) and, because of their multi-class composition, achieved or aspired to achieve a position of overwhelming dominance vis-à-vis other parties.

It was often through alliances with such parties that grass-rooots mobilizations could transcend local, highly specific demands and articulate viable long- or medium-term strategies. Yet there was a drastic difference between, on the one hand, the mobilized rural groups of the pre-Second World War period, which (with the exception of the Mexican peasant leagues) had a rather loose organic identity and, on the other, the unions (*sindicatos*) and leagues which mushroomed all over Latin America in the 1940s and 1950s, since the latter (particularly in Mexico, Bolivia and Brazil) often managed to establish their own structure and leadership and to weave intra- and inter-class alliances. This is not to propose a type of Leninist perspective in which party leadership becomes a *sine qua non* for focussed mass action. In fact, the mobilizing parties were an instrument for institutionalizing the combined grass-roots efforts and *also* for controlling or even thwarting them. Thus, an analysis of contradictions within broad alliances is needed to understand the historical outcome of specific mobilizations.

The two processes of agrarian populism that were obviously successful took place in Mexico under President Cárdenas in the late 1930s, and Bolivia under the Movimiento Nacional Revolucionario (MNR) in the early 1950s. It was not only that a pact was achieved between the new political elite, the peasantry and the rural workers (through comprehensive parties which also incorporated middle-class groups and industrial workers, as well as certain groups of the new industrial bourgeoisie), but in addition the institutions of the state were reformed in favour of the rural populace. Although the old landowning class in Mexico had been much stronger and more capitalized than in Bolivia, its strength had been undermined both by the triumph of the revolutionary armies and by the depression in the 1930s, whereas the Bolivian oligarchy was unable to rally the support of a divided army in order to confront simultaneous waves of discontent from peasants and mining workers. In both cases, a clientelistic structure re-emerged which ensured nevertheless that the rural population remained in a subordinate position. Mexico's early corporatist structures were increasingly unable to respond to popular demands. Significantly, at least two of the large-scale rural opposition groups that emerged in the 1940s and 1950s grew out of splits within the corporatist sector of the ruling party.

Four other attempted populist alliances failed: in Colombia, Guatemala, Brazil and Peru. In Colombia and Brazil, where the peasantries had become heavily involved in commercial agriculture without gaining political status, populist alliances were frustrated by persisting structures of oligarchic patronage, divisions within the Left, and military intervention. In Guatemala, a populist coalition was actually in power for more then a decade, and an agrarian project germane to the Mexican and Bolivian models was put into practice; but the alliance between the middle classes and the peasantry was hindered by distrust based on caste-type divisions, by fear of 'communism' and in the end by a U.S.-backed military coup. In Peru, as in Guatemala and Brazil, the importance of foreign capital was of considerable help in maintaining the bond among old and new elites and the army. At the same time the Peruvian Alianza Popular Revolucionaria Americana (APRA), one of the great populist parties in Latin America, nevertheless proved incapable of offering a viable alternative to the rural masses, whose leadership instead was eventually provided by the extreme Left – and the army itself.

Mexico

In 1929, Plutarco Elías Calles, the *de facto* head of the Mexican post-revolutionary government, created the Partido Nacional Revolucionario (PNR). The PNR functioned as a relatively efficient mechanism for neutralizing *caudillos* and individual power seekers; but its conception did not contemplate any systematic way of incorporating and controlling large popular groups except through their leaders, who could be repudiated by their bases if demands were not met. In relation to rural organizations, the PNR was initially unable to attract the massive support of the peasant leagues. (Throughout 1929 President Emilio Portes Gil confirmed many provisional land grants which the agrarianist governors had conceded in their states in the 1920s, but the puppet presidents of the Jefe Máximo, Ortiz Rubio and Rodríguez, soon put a brake on the land distribution policy.) The leagues had united in the 1926 Congress and then split into three main factions: one of them joined the Confederación Sindical

Unitaria, affiliated to the Communist Party; another became the independent Liga de Comunidades Agrarias Ursulo Galván, and the third remained within the PNR. In 1931, a re-unification of the old leagues crystallized in the creation of the Confederación Campesina de México (CCM), which became linked to progressive figures within the PNR, and then acquired a massive dimension as supporter of the presidential candidacy of Lázaro Cárdenas. In 1938 Cárdenas transformed the PNR into the Partido de la Revolución Mexicana (PRM), which purported to be a party of organized masses. Soon afterwards, the CCM gave way to the Confederación Nacional Campesina (CNC), its main function being the articulation of the *ejidos* with the PRM: by statute, every *ejidatario* became a member of the CNC, and therefore a member of the party.

To attract what was left of the peasant leagues, Cárdenas adopted a policy of mass distribution of land to the village committees. Moreover, during his lengthy presidential campaign, which had taken him even to the most isolated regions, he saw first hand the desperate plight of rural wage labourers – made doubly critical by unemployment and over-exploitation after the 1929 crash – and promoted their organization, both through the CCM and through his loyal labour arm: the Confederación de Trabajadores de México (CTM), created in 1936. From 1933 to 1937, he favoured agitation, union formation, and strikes among the workers of the most modernized *latifundia*: in the rice and cotton fields of the Michoacán *tierra caliente* and the region of La Laguna in Coahuila; in the sugar-cane plantations of Morelos (Zacatepec), Puebla, Tamaulipas (El Mante) and Sinaloa (Los Mochis); in the *henequén* kingdom of Yucatán; and in the rich cereal and pulse producing areas of Mexicali in Baja California and the Yaqui Valley in Sonora. Probably the most spectacular strike was that of the cotton cultivators of the La Laguna plantations, against whom the planters sent their armed vigilantes and even counted on the support of the army. When President Cárdenas personally intervened, the conflict was resolved in favour of the workers, which gave a new impetus to mobilizations in other modernized *haciendas*.[38] Furthermore, the workers in these areas began to seize the land, since the new Agrarian Law for the first time included them among the people who had the right to petition for land. In the end they became *ejidatarios* in co-operative organizations.[39] Another legal change brought by Cárdenas permitted the creation of *ejido colectivos* – thus subvert-

[38] Gerrit Huizer, *La lucha campesina en México*, pp. 63–7.
[39] Francisco Gómez Jara, *El movimiento campesino en México*, pp. 72–94; Gerrit Huizer, *La lucha campesina en México*, pp. 59–72.

ing Calles's project of favouring discrete family units. This was the form adopted by most of the expropriated plantations – in, for example, La Laguna, the Michoacán *tierra caliente* and Yucatán.

During the period of office, President Cárdenas distributed over 18,000,000 hectares to over a million families. Not suprisingly, he was able to mobilize massive rural support at critical moments: when he openly quarrelled with Calles and exiled him in 1936, and when he expropriated the foreign oil companies in 1938. Furthermore, Cárdenas maintained that *ejidatarios* should be given arms when they were in danger of attacks from *guardias blancas* and hostile *caciques,* so he ordered the distribution of at least 60,000 rifles to peasants in strategic areas, organized in mounted brigades.[40]

The strategy of massive land distribution also had the purpose of stimulating the growth of the national market. The prices of cotton, *henequén* and sugar had collapsed at the beginning of the 1930s, and probably many *haciendas* and processing industries would have disappeared anyway. (Significantly, land devoted to cattle ranching, a business of uninterrupted prosperity, was not the object of massive expropriations.) But at the outset of the Second World War, the international market showed signs of recovery, and the agrarian distribution programme slowed down. At the same time, the government was aware of the necessity for policies of national reconciliation, in the context of an impending presidential election in 1940, and possible war in alliance with the United States. Thus, in many instances, *ejidatarios* found themselves faced by a recovering private agricultural and agro-industrial sector which, as in the case of the Atencingo sugar refinery in the state of Puebla, would re-occupy its position of superiority *vis-à-vis* the peasantry: a superiority no longer based on the control of vast tracts of land, but on the manipulation of irrigation, technology, and credit – and alliances with politicians and *caciques.*[41] Moreover, the paucity, or absence, of government credit and technological assistance to a sizable proportion of *ejidatarios* (that is, those who were not producing export crops) made them easy prey to private capital, since the only alternative to poverty was migration to the cities or the United States. For example, in the erstwhile prosperous sugar-cane and cereal producing region of Yautepec-Cuautla (Morelos), poverty and corruption had caused countless *ejidatarios* to become cyclical emigrants, so they were

[40] Gerrit Huizer, *La lucha campesina en México,* pp. 69–73.
[41] David Ronfeldt, *Atencingo. The Politics of Agrarian Struggle in a Mexican Ejido* (Stanford, Cal., 1973), ch. 3.

only too pleased to become dependent again on the sugar refineries, re-opened after 1940.[42] Repressed discontent as well as rivalries among local *caciques* and aspiring leaders begot many small-scale mobilizations, of which perhaps the most publicized was the so-called *bola chiquita* ('tiny upheaval') in the states of Puebla and Morelos, where anger at the failure of *ejidos* combined with mistrust caused by the new policy of universal military draft and rumours of young people being sent to fight in favour of the *gringos*.[43]

There was, however, one large-scale organization which staged massive mobilizations against the government. Founded in 1937 by middle-class Catholic lawyers with populist leanings, the Unión Nacional Sinarquista (UNS), thus named because it purported to represent the opposite of anarchy, boasted 900,000 members in the mid-1940s (although 550,000 in perhaps a more realistic figure). This membership mostly came from the rural areas of central-western Mexico, where the Cristero movement had also gained its greatest support. Like the *cristeros*, the Sinarquistas opposed the anti-Church, anti-religious legislation brought about by the Revolution; but their platform also included a fierce critique of govern-ment corruption – manifest in the sudden, scandalous enrichment of most politicians – and the failure of the *ejido* as a solution to rural poverty. One of the most powerful Sinarquista slogans was: *Ejidatario, la Revolución te ha traicionado* (the Revolution has betrayed you!).[44] Significantly, the breed-ing grounds for Sinarquismo such as the Altos de Jalisco, Aguascalientes, the Michoacán southern sierra, and the Bajío, were characterized by a dominance of medium-sized and small private landholdings which already existed before the Revolution. Since the Indian population had always been scarce, the tradition of communal property was weak in these re-gions. Hence, agrarian reform had not been a popular demand but often an imposition from above. Sinarquistas did not favour restoring *haciendas*, but they claimed that *ejidos* should become private property, and that *ejidatarios* should not be subject to the control of the PRM. Its centralized,

[42] Eyler N. Simpson, *The Ejido: Mexico's way out* (Chapel Hill, N.C., 1937), p. 339; Guillermo de la Peña, 'Commodity Production, Class Differentiation and the Role of the State in the Morelos Highlands: an historical approach', in B. S. Orlove, M.W. Foley, and T. F. Love, *State, capital, and rural society. Anthropological perspectives on political economy in Mexico and the Andes* (Boulder, Col., 1989), pp. 87–92.

[43] Ramón Ramírez Melgarejo, 'La bola chiquita: un movimiento campesino', in Arturo Warman et al., *Los campesinos de la tierra de Zapata, I: Adaptación, cambio y rebelión* (Mexico, D.F., 1974), pp. 165–221; G. de la Peña, *A Legacy of Promises. Agriculture, Politics and Rituals in the Morelos Highlands of Mexico* (Austin, Tex., 1981), pp. 101–2.

[44] Nathan L. Whetten, *Rural Mexico* (Chicago, Ill., 1948), ch. XX.

hierarchical, militaristic structure allowed the UNS to convoke tens of thousands of people within days: hence the multitudinous quality of their demonstrations in cities such as León and Morelia, which unnerved the PRM. More importantly, they started winning municipal elections in Michoacán and the Huasteca – even in Indian areas – and capturing local *ejido* committees, notwithstanding the (sometimes murderous) agressions they suffered from *caciques* and armed *ejidatarios* loyal to the PRM.[45]

By subordinating peasant leagues to the bureaucratic structure of the ruling revolutionary party Lázaro Cárdenas had sowed the seeds of authoritarianism. After Cárdenas it became clear that the government was using the separate mass organizations for peasants (CNC) and urban industrial workers (CTM) not to respond to popular demands but rather to manipulate and even suppress them. But since the number of rural problems was legion, demands and protests never ceased to multiply. We shall examine three important anti-government mobilizations in the Mexican countryside in the 1940s and 1950s: the protests organized by the Unión General de Obreros y Campesinos de México (UGOCM), *jaramillismo,* and the militancy of the Central Campesina Independiente (CCI).

President Avila Camacho (1940–6) proclaimed the need to substitute distribution of productive lands with colonization of unused terrains, particularly in the coastal areas, in what was called *la marcha al mar* (the march to the sea). The pace of land distribution diminished significantly. Under President Miguel Alemán (1946–52) several collective *ejido* societies were dismantled, on grounds of real or supposed inefficiency and corruption (admittedly, in many cases the *ejidatarios* enthusiastically welcomed the process of de-collectivization).[46] Both Avila Camacho and Alemán courted capitalist investment for industry and agriculture: they intro-

---

[45] Gonzalo Aguirre Beltrán, *Formas de gobierno indígena* (Mexico, D.F., 1953), pp. 201–7; Jean Meyer, *El sinarquismo ¿un fascismo mexicano?* (Mexico, D.F., 1979), pp. 185–97. After 1940, the moderate policies of the Avila Camacho administration convinced some prominent Sinarquistas to establish a pact of co-operation with the government. The orthodox wing, led by Salvador Abascal, organized a campaign of agricultural colonization on the desert shores of the Gulf of Cortés. A sort of millennaristic society was created, inspired by the Gospel and the doctrine of Thomas Aquinas. The colonies were visited by Lázaro Cárdenas (then Minister of Defence) in 1942, who manifested sympathy towards the idea of colonization. But the experiment was rather unsuccessful: the biggest colony had less than sixty families living in dire economic conditions. Sinarquismo was weakened by slanderous accusations of being at the service of the Axis. On the pretext of their violent anti-government (labelled 'anti-patriotic') demonstrations, the Sinarquistas were banned from public political activity in several states. But they often reappeared with other names, winning some local elections and suffering frequent repression – such as the massacre which took place in León in 1946.

[46] See Susana Glantz, *El ejido colectivo de la Nueva Italia* (Mexico, D.F., 1974), chs. 7 and 8, and *Manuel. Una biografía política* (Mexico, D.F., 1979).

duced new decrees and Constitutional reforms protecting large producers of selected key crops and cattle breeders from expropriation. Under Alemán Congress passed the Ley del Amparo Agrario (Law of Agrarian Injunction), under which the Supreme Court was allowed to challenge all decisive instances of land expropriation (including by the President of the Republic himself). Even the CNC proclaimed the need for the growth of 'democratic capitalism' in Mexican agriculture.[47] This did not mean that the expansion of the *ejido* simply stopped. *Ejido* fields represented nearly 60 per cent of the spectacular growth of the area under cultivation between 1940 and 1960 – from aproximately four million to fourteen million hectares – but the best land often remained in private hands. It also happened that both private and public investment overwhelmingly benefited private producers in terms of irrigation, roads, technical assistance and credit. For instance, the lion's share of irrigation and communication schemes in the 1950s went to private landholdings in the northwestern states of Sonora and Sinaloa, producing for the U.S. market.[48] In any case, the result was a sharp polarization between the 'modern' and the 'peasant' sector, in which the latter provided cheap maize for their families and some surplus to be sold in the cities, and in addition cheap seasonal labour for capitalized farms, both in Mexico and the United States. This situation has been labelled *neolatifundismo:* the peasant is still exploited, not by feudal *hacendados* but by modern entrepreneurs, thanks to an ingenious system of control which makes him grateful to a manipulative State.[49]

In 1948, Vicente Lombardo Toledano, a Marxist lawyer and labour organizer, was expelled from the CTM and then from the PRI (formerly PRM). Lombardo (perhaps with Cárdenas's blessing) created a new opposition party, the Partido Popular (PP) (later Partido Popular Socialista, PPS), which attracted rural workers and *ejidatarios,* mostly in the sugarcane fields and refineries, and in the cotton-growing areas. In 1949, Lombardo founded the Unión General de Obreros y Campesinos de México (UGOCM), which at the outset boasted the support of more than 300,000 affiliates, including the powerful Unión de Sociedades de Crédito Colectivo Ejidal of the La Laguna region, where Cárdenas's popularity had been stronger. The aims of UGOCM were ambitious: to restore the radical orientation of the Revolutionary government by removing popular organi-

[47] Armando Bartra, *Los herederos de Zapata*, p. 72.
[48] See Gerrit Huizer, *La lucha campesina en México,* ch. 3; Cynthia Hewitt de Alcántara, *The Modernization of Mexican Agriculture, 1940–1970* (Geneva, 1973).
[49] See Arturo Warman, *Los campesinos, hijos predilectos del régimen* (Mexico, D.F., 1972).

zations from the PRI's control. However, Alemán's government soon devised legal mechanisms to weaken the new federation: for instance, the Ministry of Labour did not recognize the UGOCM as a lawful mediator in the negotiation of labour contracts. Later, under Ruiz Cortines's presidency (1952–8), the Congress changed the law of rural credit to ban the functioning of the Sociedades de Crédito Ejidal. In addition, persisting UGOCM leaders and organizations were consistently repressed – for example, in Michoacán.

But the UGOCM continued campaigning in Sinaloa and Sonora, where the concentration of capital in agriculture was strongest. In 1957, the UGOCM staged a massive meeting in Los Mochis (the site of a large sugar refinery where the local society of collective *ejidos* had recently been dissolved). From 1958 to 1960, Jacinto López, a prominent ex-CNC leader who joined the UGOCM, led seizures of land by thousands of landless peasants and casual rural workers, in Sonora, Sinaloa, Chihuahua, Nayarit and Colima (which cost him two or three spells in gaol). Even though these squatters were on each occasion swiftly evicted and disbanded by the army, the actions had an important symbolic value, and in fact a handful of landholdings (mainly those in the hands of foreigners) were eventually converted into *ejidos*.

Jaramillismo – named after its leader, Rubén Jaramillo – rallied the unified support of rural proletarians, *ejidatarios* and industrial workers in the sugar producing areas of Morelos and Puebla, in protest of the malfunctioning of the post-revolutionary agrarian system. As a young man, Rubén Jaramillo had joined the armies of Zapata. During the 1920s, he became an *ejido* organizer and then a member of a Freemason lodge, where he acquired radical ideas and met with followers of Cárdenas (who was himself a Mason). Later, his conversion to Methodism gave him a sense of mission and a deep commitment to fight injustice. In 1938, he was elected as delegate of the CNC in the sugar-cane and rice-producing areas of Tlalquiltenango and Jojutla, and organized demands for the creation of a co-operative sugar refinery, which was founded in Zacatepec. But, after 1940, Jaramillo became the voice of protest against corruption in the management of the refinery, which had become a political booty for the friends of President Avila Camacho. In 1943, he led a group of armed men who held fields and offices to ransom until delayed credits were handed over to the peasants. In 1944, his group founded the Partido Agrario Obrero de Morelos, which endorsed Jaramillo's unsuccessful candidacy for governor in 1946. After 1947, Porfirio Jaramillo, Rubén's brother, led a co-operative in the refinery of Atencingo (not far away from Zacatepec), which was supported by Rubén's armed groups in its confrontations with management and authorities.[50] In 1951–2, these groups mobilized again in protest against new state taxes imposed on the rural areas for the benefit of the cities, and against the stratagems by which the management of the refinery forced *ejidatarios* to lease their plots to private entrepreneurs. Throughout 1952, Jaramillo, together with many land-demanding peasant groups, joined the Henriquista Party, a dissident faction of the PRI led by opposition presidential candidate Miguel Henríquez Guzmán. *Henriquismo* – the coalition formed around the Henríquez candidacy, which apparently had Cárdenas's consent – could have become a nation-wide, institutionalized expression of Jaramillos's ideals, but was repressed and disbanded. Throughout the 1950s, particularly after Porfirio Jaramillo was murdered in 1953, Lázaro Cárdenas himself tried to mediate between the government and Rubén. The latter accepted the amnesty offered to him by President López Mateos in 1959; but later he headed a new mobilization with road blocks and land seizures in 1961–2, when a tract of land already colonized by *ejidatarios* was re-privatized as part of a tourist scheme. In May 1962 Rubén Jaramillo, along with his pregnant wife and two stepdaughters, was captured by soldiers (apparently acting without authority) and killed.[51] The regional character and strongly personalized leadership of *jaramillismo* made it particularly vulnerable to repression, which probably would have come sooner if Cárdenas had not protected Jaramillo.

In 1959, the Central Campesina Independiente (CCI) was founded by another charismatic leader, Alfonso Garzón, previously head of the CNC for the state of Baja California. He represented the discontent of *ejidatarios* whose crops had been ruined by the salinity of the Colorado River, and whose demands had received no attention from the government or the CNC. The CCI attracted other peasant groups as well, including those led by Ramón Danzós Palomino, a former rural teacher and Communist Party member, in Sonora and La Laguna. It goals included the completion of agrarian distribution and the democratization of rural organizations. These goals were endorsed by a nation-wide coalition of leftist organizations which, in 1961, under the leadership of Lázaro Cárdenas, took the name of Movimiento de Liberación Nacional. The

[50] Ronfeldt, *Atencingo,* pp. 82–105.
[51] See Froylán C. Manjarrez, 'La matanza de Xochicalco', in *Rubén Jaramillo. Autobiografía y asesinato* (Mexico, D.F., 1957).

coalition never consolidated, however, and was disbanded by Cárdenas himself in less than a year. In 1963–4, the CCI clusters joined the Frente Electoral del Pueblo, which staged several spectacular demonstrations against the PRI and in support of their own candidates for the presidency and several mayorships and seats in the Federal Congress. Soon after, the CCI split in two: one part, led by Garzón, made friends with the PRI and became dominant in Baja California; the other, Communist-orientated faction, headed by Danzós, continued its agitation against the PRI and the CNC in Sonora, La Laguna and Puebla. The growth of the independent faction was deterred by sheer repression, but the government was never able to destroy it.

Colombia

As elsewhere in the Andean region, the history of Colombian *haciendas* throughout the colonial period and the early years of independence was one of encroachment on Indian land and of subordination of the labour force from the highland communities. However, during the second half of the nineteenth century, a growing demand for commercial crops – mainly coffee – provoked a process of intensive colonization of the mountain slopes and the central-western valleys. This implied the occupation of more land, communal but mainly vacant and public; huge population movements; the construction of roads and railways; the mechanization of production; and general social dislocation. In the coffee-producing areas, tenants and smallholders (*colonos*) who had become totally incorporated into the market economy led isolated actions of resistance and protest against expanding *haciendas* and monopolizing merchants. In certain Indian areas, such as Nariño, Northern Cauca and Southern Tolima, emerging communal organizations, notably the one led by Manuel Quintín Lame in Cauca, demanded political autonomy and the devolution of patrimonial (*resguardo*) land.[52]

During the early decades of the twentieth century, the two traditional elite-dominated patronage machines, the Liberal and the Conservative parties, competed bitterly for hegemony. The Partido Socialista Revolucionario was created in 1927 and then transformed into the Partido Comunista, which from its inception had links with the rural areas: previously some of its founders had been members of the Cauca Indian move-

---

[52] See Diego Castrillón Arboleda, *El indio Quintín Lame* (Bogotá, 1973).

ment. After the Conservatives had proved incapable of curbing the rising wave of strikes except by exercising sheer force – as in the case of the repression of Tropical Oil workers in 1927 and the massacre of United Fruit workers in 1928 – the Liberals achieved control of the Presidency and the Congress from 1930 to 1946. They attempted to implement a project of social reform in order to curb Communist influence and gain popular support from burgeoning organizations of both rural and urban labourers. Whereas Colombian industrialists sympathized with the Liberal project, landowners manifested increasing malaise, particularly after new taxation was imposed on large landed estates and the Congress passed an Agrarian Reform Law – the *Ley 100* of 1936 – that allowed *colonos* (tenants and sharecroppers) to claim the land they were cultivating as their own, provided this land had not been formally registered by other owner. Since a great deal of previously vacant *hacienda* land was *de facto* owned but not formally titled, the Law meant trouble.[53] However, a regulation of 1938 gave *de facto* owners the possibility of registering their land to avoid expropriation, which was taken as a provocation by militant peasant groups.

In the end these reforms met opposition from within the Liberal Party itself, which split into two factions: the traditionalists and the populists. The latter found a charismatic leader in Jorge Eliécer Gaitán who, although attacked by the left as 'a fascist' in the beginning, in the mid-1940s managed to create a convergence of popular forces – the Unión Nacional de Izquierda Revolucionaria (UNIR). The rest of the story is well known: the Conservatives won the 1946 presidential election; the mild social reforms of the Liberals were undone (for example, many of the sales of haciendas to smallholders were declared illegal); open conflict began in the cities and villages; Gaitán led a protest movement and was murdered; in 1948 an infuriated mob looted the national capital (the *bogotazo*); between 1946 and 1966, the period known as *la violencia,* more than 200,000 people died violent, often horrific deaths, mainly in the rural areas.[54] In the 1940s and 1950s, notwithstanding Ley 100, 50 per cent of the rural population were landless. In 1954, when the first comprehensive agrarian survey was carried out in Colombia, of those possessing land, 55 per cent were smallholders (*minifundistas*) cultivating plots of two hectares and less which as a whole amounted to just 3.5 per cent of the total area

[53] Salomón Kalmanovitz, *Economía y nación. Una breve historia de Colombia* (Bogotá, 1985), pp. 268–73.
[54] Paul Oquist, *Violence, Conflict, and Politics in Colombia* (New York, 1980), pp. 4–11.

under cultivation; and 35 per cent were medium-sized holders with an average plot of 15 hectares, controlling 20 per cent of the cultivated area. In contrast, haciendas of 100 hectares or more represented 10 per cent of landholders and 76.5 per cent of the cultivated area. Of these, the larger *haciendas,* usually devoted to cattle and using traditional techniques for production and labour control, were mostly situated on the coast, the Llanos (plains) in the east, and in the Andean highlands. Modernized *haciendas* were smaller and used wage labour: those located in the western regions of Valle, Cauca, Tolima and Córdoba grew sugar-cane, cotton, or rice, whereas coffee was the main product in Cundinamarca and parts of Tolima and Cauca. Medium holdings dominated in most of the coffee zones in Caldas, Antioquia, Quindío, but not in Cundinamarca where *haciendas* and *minifundios* were also found, although the latter were more frequently devoted to subsistence crops.[55]

There were several distinct types of situations which generated rural *violencia.* The first has been termed 'the revenge of the *hacendados*' against peasants who had previously invaded *latifundios* or claimed vacant terrains and attempted to challenge the domination of the landowning class.[56] This revenge was often intertwined with partisan divisions – between Liberals and Conservatives. The second, frequent in areas with medium-sized and small holdings, was related to rivalries among families and villages over land tenure and political control. The third type could be found in areas where the main landowners and patrons had fled, leaving their clients entangled in endless, unsolvable disputes over economic and political resources. Finally, a fourth less well documented type occurred when rebellious Liberal *hacendados* (for instance, in the Eastern Llanos) rallied their workers against the Conservative authorities and their allies. A frequent consequence of all these generative situations at the local level was the development of banditry and partisan guerrillas. The overall result was a self-perpetuating, but highly fragmented, intra- and inter-class civil war.[57]

The case of the municipio of Chaparral in southern Tolima, studied by Medófilo Medina, is a good illustration of the type of class violence

[55] Hernán Toro Agudelo, 'Planteamiento y soluciones del problema agrario', in Gonzalo Cataño (ed.), *Colombia: estructura política y agraria* (Bogotá, 1971), pp. 164–9.
[56] Pierre Gilhodes, *La question agraire en Colombie* (Paris, 1974).
[57] Oquist, *Violence,* p. 17. See also Darío Fajardo, 'La Violencia, 1946–1964. Su desarrollo y su impacto', paper presented at a seminar, La Cuestión Regional y la Cuestión Nacional en América Latina, El Colegio de México, November, 1981.

described as 'the landowners' revenge'.[58] Prior to 1880, this area had been dominated by livestock *haciendas*, but the rise of coffee prices provoked both the conversion of the old *fincas* to coffee cultivation and the incorporation of unchartered land in the eastern slopes of the Cordillera Central, mainly through the labour of newly arrived *colonos*. Many of these *colonos* came in the 1920s and 1930s from Indian communities dispossessed of their *resguardo* land, and some of them had had connections with the Indian communal-agrarian movement led by Manuel Quintín Lame in Cauca.[59] In Chaparral, the landowners assumed that the newly opened plots belonged to them, and exerted control over *colonos* through monopolizing the commercialization of the product. Between 1932 and 1942, the production of coffee in the municipio doubled. After 1936, several leagues and unions were created, promoted by schoolteachers and by *colonos* or rural workers linked to the Liberal or the Communist Parties, or to Gaitán's UNIR. These organizations launched protests and threatened strikes against landowners who cheated in the weighing of coffee. But the unions also encouraged *colonos* to take advantage of the 1936 Agrarian Law and apply for the titles of the land they were cultivating. In the following years, 1500 titles of land plots were adjudged to *colonos* by the national agrarian authorities (the Juzgado de Tierras); but these titles were immediately contested by the landowners, who renewed their ardent allegiance to the Conservatives and had the support of local judges – often their kinsmen, friends or clients. Reprisals against militant union members included the refusal of loans for cultivation (from bank officials) and the delaying of payment for their products. Moreover, the *hacendados* set up bands of armed vigilantes who expelled rebellious *colonos* from their plots and forced labourers to return to their place in *hacienda* coffee production. An old Law of Vagrancy and Theft was used by authorities to place reluctant workers in jail.

Throughout the 1940s, Chaparral became the theatre of open class confrontation, particularly after the Liberal defeat in 1946, when on the one hand the landowners felt they had become unpunishable and on the other the leagues and unions decided to resist harassment with force. After the national election of 1949 – in which the Conservatives retained power – local police forces became directly dependent on the national authorities; this new police stormed several *veredas* (hamlets) in December

---

[58] See Medófilo Medina, 'La resistencia campesina en el Sur de Tolima', in *Ensayos sobre la Violencia* (Bogotá, 1983), pp. 233–65.
[59] See Castrillón Arboleda, *El indio Quintín Lame*.

1949, burning twenty-eight houses, imprisoning numerous people and murdering eight men who had openly campaigned for the Liberals. But, in April 1950, a small-scale Liberal uprising in the *municipio* freed all prisoners. Meanwhile, the union leaders had organized groups of self-defence. One of these leaders, Isauro Yossa, maintained links with the Communist Party in Bogotá, which provided guns and military training. Reinforced by Liberal families and harassed peasants, Yossa founded a batallion that frequently clashed with the police and the army, and eventually took refuge in the mountains, where in 1951 a guerrilla camp was established in the district of El Davis. However, El Davis became the object of hatred of neighbouring Liberal landowners. At the national level, the Liberal Party disowned those members who, allied with the Communists, had embarked on open class struggle. Yet even some of the Communists in Bogotá publicly denounced guerrilla action as an obstacle to political negotiation. After 1952, the Colombian army increased its military efficiency thanks to technical advice and more sophisticated arms donated by the United States, and kept El Davis in a state of siege. In 1953, El Davis came to its end. Whereas many guerrillas fled to more distant zones and became bandits or joined emergent rebel groups, others accepted the conditions of amnesty offered by the new military government. Some of the latter became collaborators of the army. But a large number of survivors put themselves at the orders of the Communist Party.

The second and third types of violence were common in some of the main coffee-producing areas – parts of Cundinamarca, Tolima and El Quindío – where the period of colonization had witnessed a paradoxical phenomenon: within the *hacienda* lands there was a strengthening of peasant forms of production and eventually a differentiated peasantry emerged, including tenants who became small-scale entrepreneurs, *agregados* (middlemen) who hired labour to clear new ground for the coffee bushes, and sharecroppers *cum* seasonal labourers.[60] In such areas, it was the emerging rich peasants, and not the peasant unions or leagues, who contested the legitimacy of the occupation of vacant land by *haciendas;* but these new entrepreneurs were divided by multiple economic rivalries and partisan loyalties. In addition, they were not interested in defending the less fortunate peasantry who provided cheap labour.

The pattern of events in the Department of Quindío, studied by Carlos

---

[60] Marco Palacios, *Coffee in Colombia, 1850–1970. An Economic, Social and Political History* (Cambridge, 1973), pp. 68–70.

Enrique Ortiz, illustrates the parochial character and cross-cutting alliances of *la violencia* in this region. At the outbreak of the conflict, local power rested with the landowners, Liberal or Conservative, who maintained extensive networks of clients. People of a particular locality were dependent upon each other for providing services, keeping law and order and maintaining local religious cults. Allegiance to one party or another was mainly a question of where you were born. In everyday life, these rooted allegiances were more relevant than class divisions.

In the absence of *hacendados,* who had fled the instability, the main beneficiaries of violence in the Quindío were the *agregados* or richer tenants. They were left in charge of vast properties and dealt directly with the coffee traders (*fonderos*) located in the small townships. These traders also profited from the high cash circulation resulting from the absence of landowner control, and from the fact that they were buying cheap coffee stolen from abandoned plantations. The old clientelist pattern was reproduced under the new leadership of *agregados* and *fonderos,* who used their armed retinues (*pájaros*) as bands of robbers in plantations and as factors of local political control and murderous vengeance. In this context, the offensive against the Liberals after 1946, and the responses to it, did not have a clear class focus. It was the day labourers, irrespective of their party affiliation, who were the most frequent victims, though the survivors enjoyed higher wages than previously. On the other hand, there were also local clashes among Liberal and Conservative entrepreneurs competing for land, commercial control and political influence. Religion seemed to be a more important factor than class, with the clergy seizing the opportunity to lead a preaching crusade against the Liberals. After 1950, groups of persecuted Liberals fled to the high sierra and became guerrillas, waging a lonely war of banditry; but they had no alternative political project of land redistribution or land reform. They were fighting for the restoration of the *statu quo ante,* for the return of their lands and their old patrons.[61]

The situation of violence was not alleviated by the attitude of President Laureano Gómez (1949–52), who wanted to eradicate all possible Liberal and leftist influences. Confronting national dissolution, the army threw its support behind General Rojas Pinilla (1953–7) who courted unions and began a strategy of reconciliation. This strategy was far from successful: in 1954, the army killed protesting students in the centre of Bogotá,

---

[61] See Carlos Miguel Ortiz Sarmiento, *Estado y subversión en Colombia. La Violencia en el Quindío, años 50* (Bogotá, 1985).

and reassumed the persecution of peasants. In addition, Rojas Pinilla won the animosity of the bourgeoisie, and particularly of the ever powerful coffee sector, when he tried to curb inflation by taxing exports. He also failed in his attempt to create a sort of Colombian version of Peronism, since his manipulated 're-election' in 1957 was universally repudiated. The only possible alliance at this point seemed to be between the moderate wings of the old parties – Liberals and Conservatives – who established a joint government from 1958 to 1962. In this year, a Liberal scion, Alfonso López Michelsen, won the Presidential election – not as a traditional Liberal candidate, but as a self-styled populist. Yet López Michelsen and his Movimiento Liberal Revolucionario failed to unite moderate and popular forces. As we shall see, his government had to face guerrilla warfare which he and his successors could only deal with by outright military repression.

Guatemala

In 1945, twenty-two families owned one half of the cultivable land in Guatemala. Most of the rest belonged to 300,000 peasants, mostly members of Indian communities, but there was also a significant number of independent *ladino* (non-Indian) small farmers. The big landholdings produced mainly coffee on the highlands and bananas on the coastal lowlands for the world market, and used both permanent and seasonal labour, the latter coming from the Indian communities. President Juan José Arévalo, democratically elected in December 1944 after fourteeen years of dictatorship, declared his intentions of starting a process of social reform. His predominantly middle-class government devised a blueprint for agrarian reform, though without showing much eagerness to put it into practice. Arevalo's successor, Jacobo Arbenz, promoted the spread of urban and rural labour unions and took the Agrarian Reform decree to the Congress, where it was approved in 1952. Its main point was to expropriate and redistribute landholdings larger than ninety hectares, particularly those standing idle or undercultivated. Its first experimental field was the Department of Escuintla, the richest in the country, where the United Fruit Company had major interests. In all Departments, local Agrarian Committees, fashioned after their Mexican counterparts, were created at the village level. In the Indian communities, these Committees together with the delegations from the political parties and peasant leagues, became important foci for social change. From 1952 to 1954, nearly 500 *fincas* (commercial *haciendas*) and plantations were legally affected, and nearly 700,000 hectares were expropriated for redistribution (of which 300,000 were taken from the United Fruit Company). But, in 1954, a military revolt, financed by United Fruit and engineered by the U.S. State Department and the CIA, ended the Arbenz administration and handed over power to a group of army officers whose primary task was to dismantle the reforms of the previous years, and to repress and murder its supporters.[62]

Although some kind of rural unions existed in the 1920s and 1930s, playing an important part in several uprisings (like one in Suchitepéquez), the Ubico dictatorship had all but abolished them. Their legal status was recovered thanks to the 1945 Constitution, and then to the 1947 Arévalo Labour Code (strengthened by a 1949 Decree which eliminated all restrictions against rural unions). They staged several major strikes – two famous examples being the 1948–9 strikes at United Fruit plantations in Tiquisate and Bananera. In 1954, there were several hundreds of *sindicatos de finca* (unions of wage labourers) and *sindicatos campesinos* (Peasant Leagues or associations of independent small farmers). These *sindicatos* in turn became dominated by two large national federations: the Confederación General de Trabajadores de Guatemala (CGTC) and the Confederación Nacional Campesina de Guatemala (CNCG) which together monopolized popular representation during the Arbenz government.[63] Like other labour organizations in the country, both of them, and particularly the CGTC, became heavily influenced by the Communist Party, legalized in 1949. However, there were some *sindicatos de finca* with a high degree of initiative and independence, particularly those of United Fruit workers. Local branches of peasant leagues were also very active among *ladino* independent farmers, particularly in the East, where high population growth did not have an established outlet of seasonal labour migration to *fincas* – as happened in the Indian communities.

The main tasks of the federations at the local level were first to provide assistance in finding legal channels for the solution of pressing problems; and second to indoctrinate and agitate for strikes demanding improvements in wages and labour conditions. But, after 1952, they also pro-

---

[62] Neale J. Pearson, 'Guatemala: the peasant union movement, 1944–54', in Henry A. Landsberger (ed.), *Latin American peasant movements* (Ithaca, N.Y., 1969), pp. 323–73.

[63] Brian Murphy, 'The Stunted Growth of Campesino Organizations', in Richard N. Adams, *Crucifixion by Power. Essays on Guatemalan national social structure, 1944–1966* (Austin, Tex., 1970), pp. 441–8, 454–9.

moted the creation of land-demanding agrarian committees at municipal and departmental levels. The spontaneous land invasions, like the one which took place in Patzicía, Department of Chimaltenango, shortly after the downfall of Ubico, were not approved of by the regime.[64] Nevertheless, the *finqueros,* grouped in the Association of Agrarian Entrepreneurs, claimed that anarchic land invasions were a widespread phenomenon, that anarchy was rampant in the rural areas, and that Communist infiltration of the government should be blamed for such a serious threat to national prosperity. Even the middle-class sectors who sympathized with Arbenz had misgivings about the growth of peasant consciousness, particularly when associated with 'the rise of the Indians against civilization'. This type of justification was used when massive repression against rural activists was unleashed in 1954, which perhaps caused as many as 9,000 deaths.[65]

Less than five years after the pustch, 90 per cent of the affected finca land had been given back to their previous owners. By 1961, there were only seven *sindicatos de finca* which survived the purges. According to the new dispositions, to be legal, a syndicate had to 'prove' that it was totally free of communist infiltration and did not engage in any political activities. As to the Peasant Leagues, they disappeared altogether until 1961, when the Christian Democrats began reorganizing them on the basis of a new Labour Code.[66] One could hypothesize that, in addition to suffering violence from the military, the grass-roots organizations dissolved for lack of local leadership and autonomous dynamism. This may also be related to the split created in many communities between the traditional authority of the elders and the new electoral and associational procedures established by the Revolution.[67] In any case, the populist experiment was unable to devise effective means of mass mobilization in its defence, since Arbenz's government had to compete for the favour of the masses with its own divided supporters – particularly the Communist Party, whose increasing influence was a decisive factor in provoking the military coup.[68]

[64] Luis Cardoza y Aragón, *Guatemala: las líneas de su mano* (Mexico, D.F., 1955), pp. 272–3.
[65] Julio Castellanos Cambranes, 'Origins of the crisis of the established order in Guatemala', in Steve C. Ropp and James A. Morris (eds), *Central America. Crisis and Adaptation* (Albuquerque, N.Mex., 1984), pp. 140–3.
[66] Bryan Murphy, 'The stunted growth', pp. 449–52.
[67] See Richard N. Adams (ed.), *Political Changes in Guatemalan Indian Communities* (New Orleans: Middle American Research Institute, 1957).
[68] Ralph Lee Woodward, *Central America,* pp. 236–40.

Bolivia

As early as 1936 – one year after the end of the Chaco war – a *sindicato campesino* was created in the province of Cliza, Valley of Cochabamba, where agricultural commercialization, communications and then army recruitment had resulted in the emergence of class and civic consciousness among the peasantry. The aim of the *sindicato* was to negotiate better conditions for *colonos* (tenants) and *pegujaleros* (sharecroppers), who in practice were still subject to feudal-type labour obligations with landowners. Advised by rural teachers, the *sindicato* was moderately successful and extended to other provinces, but in 1939 a coalition of landowners bought those *haciendas* where activism was strongest, and proceeded to evict tenants and sharecroppers. This unchained a violent if finally defeated grassroots reaction. In the same years and throughout the 1940s, in the neighbouring Ayopaya sierra, there were numerous incipients of violence between peasant freeholders and *colonos* on the one hand, and *haciendas* on the other. Certain *sindicato* leaders established initial contacts with *kurakas* in the Altiplano who had also headed strikes against landowners.

Colonel Gualberto Villarroel who seized power in December 1943 not only counted on the support of discontented young officers but also attracted Movimiento Nacional Revolucionario (MNR), which purported to be a nationalist, multi-class, pluralistic movement. The MNR was led by moderate Socialist intellectuals and eventually became allied with the Federation of Unions of Bolivian Miners, which had 50,000 affiliates, dominated by the workers of the tin mines, who were in turn influenced by the Trotskyist left (that is, by the Partido Obrero Revolucionario, POR). Villarroel, a native of Cochabamba who spoke Qhechwa, encouraged emerging groups in the countryside to organize *congresos regionales indígenas,* and then a National Indigenous Congress in 1945.[69]

In the Congresses, the trans-communal ethic consciousness created in the previous decades – in contrast to Mexico, Guatemala, and Peru, where Indians still manifested a strong 'community ethnocentrism', as Gonzalo Aguirre Beltrán has put it[70] – expressed itself in resolutions against discriminatory anti-Indian laws, regulations and usages (forced labour services were still taken for granted, as was Indian exclusion from

[69] Richard W. Patch, 'Bolivia: U.S. assistance in a revolutionary setting', in Richard N. Adams et al., *Social Change in Latin America Today* (New York, 1960), pp. 108–76; Jorge Dandler, *El sindicalismo campesino en Bolivia: los cambios estructurales en Ucureña (1935–1952)* (Mexico, D.F., 1969).

[70] Gonzalo Aguirre Beltrán, *El proceso de aculturación* (Mexico, D.F., 1957).

public urban places). But it was the symbolic power of Indian multitudes marching in the centres of the cities, particularly in La Paz, which frightened the anti-reformist forces – what was known as *la rosca:* the parasitic landowners and tin barons, and their allies in the high military circles. In the national Congress, personally inaugurated by President Villarroel, a number of projects of agrarian change were put forward, which ranged from the moderate MNR blueprint for colonizing idle lands, to the Partido de Izquierda Revolucionaria (PIR) (a Marxist, pro-Soviet group) project for dismembering and re-distributing all private landholdings. However, in the end the land question was not resolved. And the landowners often refused to obey the dispositions abolishing Indian labour obligations, which provoked a wave of strikes throughout the country, and even an uprising (in Las Canchas, Potosí) suppressed by the government itself. In July, 1946, an urban mob instigated by *la rosca* looted La Paz and lynched the President; soon afterwards, military repression against peasant mobilizations permitted the return of forced labour. The PIR, which had supported the anti-Villarroel rabbles, lost the sympathy of many peasant organizations, whose members mourned the lynched President as a mythic hero. Six months after his death, his name was used as a battle cry by the participants in the great uprising of Ayopaya (Cochabamba), where several thousand Indians, whose leaders had contacts with the mining unions, attacked *haciendas* and were only stopped a week later. The army even bombed them from the air. After Ayopaya, there were also uprisings in the Altiplano and the South, at times supported by La Paz-based Troskyist and Anarchist labour groups.[71]

MNR candidates, Víctor Paz Estenssoro and Hernán Siles Zuazo, won an overwhelming victory in the national elections of May 1951. Although a military coup prevented a peaceful transition of government, divisions within the army finally allowed Paz Estenssoro to assume the presidency in April, 1952. Juan Lechín, the tin miners' leader, was appointed Minister of Mines and Petroleum, and directed a programme to nationalize the big mining consortiums. However, the new government included among its members a group of military officers opposed to agrarian reform, and no steps were taken in this direction until the peasantry forced the process.

The pivot of the new peasant mobilization was Ucureña, in Cochabamba, where the old coalition of teachers and peasant unions had sur-

---

[71] Jorge Dandler and Juan Torruco, 'El Congreso Nacional Indígena de 1945 y la rebelión campesina de Ayopaya (1947)', in Calderón and Dandler (eds), *Bolivia: la fuerza histórica del campesinado,* pp. 133–200; Silvia Rivera Cusicanqui, *'Oprimidos pero no vencidos',* ch. IV.

vived since 1936, and where two local leaders, Sinforoso Rivas and José Rojas, had a long experience in social and political struggle. It is interesting to note that traditional communal institutions and systems of authority were much weaker in Cochabamba than in, for example, the Altiplano or Northern Potosí. Thus, the unions did not replace or compete with any existing popular organizations: rather they filled a void. Rivas created a Federación Campesina and established contacts with Lechín and his newly created Central Obrera Boliviana (COB), through which he channelled petitions and proposed legal changes. Rojas on the other hand developed a more independent and fighting organization, the Central Sindical Campesina del Valle, whose followers became armed militiae, seized *haciendas,* and expelled landowners. In fact, the latter had become convinced of their defeat and fled to the cities or even out of the country. Both Rivas and Rojas, with the patronage of the MNR, fostered the creation of militant unions in other regions of the country – through which they developed clientelistic networks – which also presented demands for land distribution to the government, and seized *hacienda* land. But parallel peasant militiae flourished everywhere, often founded by MNR students from La Paz, as was the case in the province of Nor Yungas, where spontaneous mobilizations had not existed previously.[72] Finally, on 2 August 1953, Paz Estenssoro signed the Decree of Agrarian Reform in Ucureña, before an assembly of 100,000 peasants from all parts of Bolivia.[73]

The *latifundio* structure ceased to exist and *colonos* became the rightful owners of *hacienda* land: 200,000 families received almost 10,000,000 hectares. Although the law recognized the traditional landholding rights of communities, most of those who benefited from the distribution of *haciendas* held their land in private property. Agricultural productivity did not suffer from distribution, since most land continued to be cultivated as before. The name 'Indian' was abolished from the official vocabulary because of its colonial connotations: now there would be only *campesinos,* full citizens as anyone else. Rural education expanded prodigiously. The banning of compulsory services stimulated the labour market, increased social mobility and helped alleviate labour shortages in the lowlands. On the other hand, most peasants still had very little good

---

[72] D. B. Heath, 'Peasant syndicates among the Aymara of the Yungas – a view from the grass roots', in Landsberger (ed.), *Latin American peasant movements,* pp. 170–209.

[73] Jorge Dandler, 'Campesinado y reforma agraria en Cochabamba (1952–3): Dinámica de un movimiento campesino en Bolivia', in Calderón and Dandler, *Bolivia: la fuerza histórica del campesinado,* pp. 201–39.

arable land, and – as happened in many Mexican *ejidos* – very restricted access to credit, technology and marketing channels. The old land-owning class reappeared in the cities as moneylenders and commercial middlemen, and they often re-functionalized relationships of patronage with 'their Indians'. But a new web of political patronage and factional-ism was being formed by the MNR itself, around leaders who at differ-ent levels bitterly competed for political offices and influence. People like Lechín and Rojas – who later was appointed Minister of Peasant Affairs – were now the big bosses who created dangerous cleavages not only within the MNR cadres but also between the working class and the peasantry in general. Such cleavages only increased when peasant unions refused to lend support to miners' protests against the government, which was now the owner of a rather disastrous mining industry. Con-comitantly, the U.S. State Department, having decided that the Bolivian Revolution – unlike in Guatemala – was not 'communist-orientated', al-lowed U.S. aid to pour into the country, on the condition that the moderate line would prevail.[74] When Hernán Siles Zuazo became Presi-dent in 1956 after a highly manipulated election, he applied himself to the task of marginalizing the left wing of the MNR. In 1964, barely a decade after the Revolution, a military coup put General René Barrientos in the presidency. The divided MNR was not able to offer meaningful resistance; but the Agrarian Reform was sustained.

Northeastern Brazil

In the Northeast of Brazil the impunity of the *coroneis* for recruiting private armies decreased considerably during the Estado Novo (1937–45). But both their dominance of the regional economy, and the nature of regional labour relationships, remained virtually untouched. Sugar-cane and cotton plantations were still based on the work of *moradores* and *foreiros* (sharecrop-pers and tenants), subordinated through institutions such as the *cambão* (unpaid labour duties) and the *barracão* (a sort of 'company store').[75] After the Second World War, a radical transformation began in the structure of the sugar economy, brought about by the opening up and expansion of the

---

[74] Richard W. Patch, 'Bolivia: U.S. assistance in a revolutionary setting', pp. 124–37; Jonathan Kelley and Herbert S. Klein, *Revolution and the Rebirth of Inequality. A theory applied to the national revolution in Bolivia* (Berkeley, Cal., 1964); D. B. Heath, 'Bolivia: peasant syndicates among the Aymara of the Yungas'.

[75] See Francisco Julião, *Cambão: la cara oculta del Brasil* (Mexico, D.F., 1968).

international market. The old *senhores de engenho* and even the relatively modernized *usineiros* began to specialize in the production of cane, leaving the industrialization process largely to the more technologically advanced refineries in the central-south. In order to enlarge the area of sugar-cane cultivation and increase productivity, it was urgent to end the old system of tenancy and sharecropping, and bring about the proletarianization of the labour force. But the new situation did not prove advantageous for the workers: salaries were lower than the national average, the cane cutters lacked any kind of secondary benefits, and unions were practically forbidden.[76] In turn, independent farming by peasant freeholders became increasingly and often disadvantageously dependent on urban markets and middlemen.[77] The rise of the Ligas Camponesas in the 1950s and 1960s expressed the discontent of a dislocated population, as well as the resistance of *moradores* and *foreiros* fighting eviction. Significantly, an initial aspect of their emerging collective ideology was an idealization of the past – an idyllic vision of the paternalistic relationships in the old plantations.[78]

The first league was born in 1955, among *foreiros* at the Engenho Galileia, in the state of Pernambuco, as a burial and mutual benefit society: the Sociedade Agrícola de Plantadores e Pecuaristas de Pernambuco (SAPPP). The SAPPP found an adviser in Francisco Julião, a Recife lawyer and socialist deputy, supported both by the Partido Socialista Brasileiro (PSB) and the semi-legal Communist Party. Julião – who happened to be the scion of a well-known landowning family – managed to register the Sociedade as a civil association (a non-profit, assistance-orientated institution, in the Iberian legal tradition), since formal recognition as a union would have been virtually impossible. Julião also brought the situation of Galileia to the attention of a wider, influential public. The Congresso Camponés de Pernambuco, convoked by the SAPPP in September 1955, attracted more than 3,000 people, including *foreiros, moradores,* salaried workers, and some freeholders. Under Julião's leadership, the association assumed state-wide importance: its centralized structure, with head office in Recife and delegations in *engenhos,* villages and towns, permitted effective agitation, marches, and massive meetings, despite continuous harassment from the state government. In 1958, events such

---

[76] See Fernando Antonio Azevedo, *As Ligas Camponesas* (Rio de Janeiro, 1982), ch. 2.

[77] See D. E. Goodman, 'Rural Structure, Surplus Mobilisation, and Modes of Production in a Peripheral Region: the Brazilian North-east', *Journal of Peasant Studies,* 5, 1 (1977): 3–32 for a critical summary of the debates on the nature of agricultural changes in the region.

[78] Azevedo, *As Ligas Camponesas,* pp. 50–1.

as the March of Hunger in Recife, and the multitudinous Congresso de Lavradores, Trabalhadores Agrícolas e Pescadores, both organized by SAPPP, were widely reported by the main national newspapers. There were also a significant number of legal victories for the *foreiros,* not only in matters of eviction and rent increases, but also concerning their rights over improvements made on the land.

Under the reformist presidency of João Goulart (1961–4), there was no legislation for reforming the structure of land tenure, although a new rural labour code was passed in 1963. This code fostered unionization of rural wage labourers, which to a certain extent competed with other forms of association, as the SAPPP had only a minority of proletarianized follower.[79] From the early 1950s, and particularly since the Pernambuco movement came to national attention, the Catholic Church – to create an alternative to 'communist agitation' – had organized its own leagues and unions in the Northeast, among *bóiafrias* (casual workers) in the São Paulo region, and evicted *posseiros* (squatters on idle land) in the Minas Gerais. Padre Melo and Padre Crespo, organizers of the Federation of Rural Workers of Pernambuco and advocates of non-violent strikes, emerged as important new social leaders – possible rivals of Francisco Juliao.[80] In turn, the Communist Party, particularly after its 1960 Congress, had veered away from, and then quarrelled with, the Pernambuco peasant leagues and their sister associations. The party's new position was that rural unions should be formed but the revolution could not begin in the countryside; rather, a broad alliance was needed between the proletariat (urban and rural) and the progressive bourgeoisie in order to destroy the feudal rural order – of which the peasantry was a part. From this perspective, only idle *latifundia* should be expropriated. In contrast, the leagues, while lacking a specific programme for the organization of land use (individual/family plots, or collective entities), defended the need for a wholesale agrarian reform which would put all land under peasant control.

A federal deputy since 1961, Julião himself was not very clear on which model of agrarian reform should be followed. But he was persuaded that the peasantry was a revolutionary class, probably *the* revolutionary class in Brazil. At the time of the 1964 military coup, he was preparing two alternative strategies: on the one hand, he had converted the SAPPP into a national organization: the Ligas Camponesas do Brasil, which easily could

[79] Azevedo, *As Ligas Camponesas,* pp. 82–5.
[80] Shephard Forman, *The Brazilian Peasantry* (New York, 1975), pp. 188–9.

become a Socialist Agrarian political party; on the other hand, he was training some of his followers for guerrilla warfare. In Pernambuco, the Ligas backed Miguel Arraes, the new governor, who came to office representing a successful popular coalition, in his defence and strict application of the Rural Labour Code; but their disagreement concerning land expropriation was obvious when Arraes did not support the occupations of two *engenhos* – although finally one of them was expropriated by decree, to avoid open violence. Both in this region and at national level, the Ligas were losing cohesion and membership, as the government favoured the unions, both Catholic and Communist. When military repression came, and most leaders were jailed or went into exile (Julião himself spent several months in a federal prison before he made his way to Mexico), only the Catholic Federation of Rural Workers was able to survive, but without its previous impetus and mystique.

Peru

In Peru in 1956, following the end of the dictatorship of General Manuel A. Odría (1948–56), President Manuel Prado ended the ban on rural unionization and allowed both APRA and the Communists to operate freely. The main beneficiaries of this political opening were the coastal agro-industrial proletarians, who became formally organized in two large federations: the Federación de Trabajadores Azucareros del Perú (FTAP), and the Federación Nacional de Campesinos Peruanos (FENCAP). Both were dominated by APRA, and both were rather indifferent to the demands of the peasantry of the Sierra, where *latifundistas* still owned perhaps as much as 70 per cent of the land, for land distribution and abolition of labour services. Like the Brazilian Communists, the *Apristas* regarded peasants as a feudal lag for which total proletarianization was not only inevitable but highly desirable. However, Haya de la Torre's party was not advocating a proletarian revolution; in fact, since the Prado government managed to co-opt APRA leadership, the coastal unions restricted their claims to job security, improved wages, and better living and working conditions, without pushing too much for them. In 1959–60 there were two great mobilizations and strikes in Casagrande – the largest sugar plantation in the country – and Paramonga, which attracted bloody police repression. But after 1960 plantation strikes became extremely rare. When a wave of land invasions began in the Sierra in the early 1960s, only a small dissident sector of the *Apristas* (the sympathizers of the Cuban revolution, known as *APRA rebelde*) supported them.[81]

It might be hypothesized that conditions were ripe in Peru for a populist agrarian revolution similar to that in Bolivia, but that it was prevented by APRA's extreme prudence (or opportunism?), lack of significant ties among different sectors of peasants and workers, and a major strength on the part of the Peruvian military – as compared to the Bolivian army, which had been in a state of disarray at the time of the large-scale land seizures. And, in these circumstances, the road was open for the radical left to operate freely among the highland peasantry. In addition, the political awakening of the peasants was influenced by their participation as occasional wage labourers in the big mining enclave of Cerro de Pasco and the steel refineries of La Oroya – both in the Central Sierra, and both with militant unions; by their exposure to city life as temporary migrants in Lima; by their contact with relatives and fellow villagers who had gone to work or study in the coast and stayed there; and because of the increase in literacy and political information.[82]

The first radical peasant organization emerged in the Eastern highland valleys of La Convención and Lares – a frontier region within the Department of Cuzco, which was sparsely settled until the 1930s when malaria was erradicated and a railroad was built. The land was entirely owned by huge *haciendas* (nearly 100 of them) and partially cultivated by *arrendires* (tenant farmers), who received plots in the mountain slopes to grow their food in exchange for a fixed number of labour days, and whose access to the market was mediated by the landowners. In the 1940s, the *hacendados*, responding to the booming demand for coffee in the international market, encouraged its cultivation in the best land for it, which was precisely in the mountain slopes; but after a while the *arrendires* – as it had happened in Colombia – discovered that they could expand their coffee production on vacant terrain and sell it directly to middlemen. Thus, they began to refuse to perform labour duties in the flatland, where less valuable crops (sugar-cane, cocoa, coca) were grown. The population of the valleys doubled between 1940 and 1960 (from 30,000 to more than 60,000 people,

---

[81] Mariano Valderrama, 'Historia política del movimiento campesino peruano en el siglo XX', in Pablo González Casanova (ed.), *Historia política de los campesinos latinoamericanos,* Vol. 3 (Mexico, D.F., 1985), pp. 136–8.

[82] H. Handelman, *Struggle in the Andes. Peasant Political Mobilization in Peru* (Austin, Tex., 1975), ch. 4; Julio Cotler and Felipe Portocarrero, 'Peru: peasant organizations', in Landsberger (ed.), *Latin American Peasant Movements,* pp. 299–300.

of which about 10,000 were tenant farmers), because of immigrants attracted by the possibility of making money out of the expanding agricultural market. Quillabamba, the main town in the valleys, became a thriving market center, where credit was available to farmers from *rescatistas* (middlemen).[83] A new social category became important: the *allegados,* usually recent Indian immigrants working for *arrendires* during the planting and harvesting seasons and receiving small subsistence plots from them.

As early as 1951, the *arrendires* tried to create an union, looking for the help of the Cuzco Labour Federation, influenced by Communists, and Cuzco lawyers to press their demands for better working conditions before the Ministry of Labour. In fact, in spite of the landowners' angry claims, the government did not send troops to enforce labour obligations, and in 1958 the Provincial Peasant Federation of La Convención, comprising eight *hacienda* unions, was recognized as legal by the Prado government. In 1960, there were already 130 unions and over 11,000 members (*arrendires* and *allegados*) in the Federation. An investigation by the Labour Ministry recommended that wage-labour contracts substituted the institution of forced labour services. The fulfillment of this recommendation, which also meant that vacant land would be available for rental arrangements, became the Federation's main goal. However, a turning point occurred when a twenty-five-year-old agronomist and Trotskyist agitator, Hugo Blanco – the son of a Cuzco lawyer – became head of one of the unions and persuaded his followers to demand the total expropriation of *haciendas* and their distribution among actual agricultural producers. This caused a serious cleavage between Blanco's supporters and those *arrendires* whose aim was to become coffee entrepreneurs and did not sympathize with the idea of a regional agrarian revolution led by a Trotskyite. Rallying the most radical unions under the slogan Tierra o Muerte ('Land or Death'), Blanco won the 1962 election for Secretary General of the Peasant Federation; but his victory was challenged, and unchained a series of violent incidents, in which several policemen were killed. Hugo Blanco was held responsible for the violence and gaoled at the end of 1962; nevertheless, the two opposite fractions of the Federation agreed to stage a boycott on the *hacendados,* refusing both to perform labour duties and to pay rent for their parcels. Surprisingly, the military Junta which toppled Prado in July, 1962, decided to put a brake on

[83] Eric J. Hobsbawm, 'La Convención, a Case of Neo-feudalism', *Journal of Latin American Studies,* I, 1 (1969): 31–50.

the rising conflict, and ruled that farmers could obtain the legal title of the land they were working, by simply paying the recorded value to the government, which in turn would pay compensation to the previous landowners. This decision was sustained by President Fernando Belaúnde, elected in July, 1963. However, the impetus of the Federation declined, since new divisions emerged, particularly between the *arrendires* and the less fortunate *allegados*.[84]

Meanwhile, many other areas of the central and southern Sierras were shaken by strikes of *colonos* (sharecroppers), and even more by invasions of *haciendas*. Whereas strikers demanded the end of labour obligations, invading *comuneros,* such as the villagers of Yanacancha, Rancas and Yanahuanca, in the Department of Pasco, claimed the land to be formally recognized as communal property. In the years between 1959 and 1963 there were no less than 100 seizures, and most of them took place in the months between Prado's fall and Belaúnde's election, when the agrarian issue was vehemently debated at the national level. In the Departments of Pasco and Junín, the presence of the left-wing of *Aprismo* conditioned that these mobilizations were encouraged by the FENCAP; elsewhere, it was the Communist-influenced Confederación Campesina de Perú (CCP), founded in 1956, which provided advice and organizational support. However, factional disputes within both organizations as well as repression prevented them from becoming full-fledged, overarching fronts for the defence of peasant demands. In many cases, as in the valley of Yanamarca (Jauja) and the village of Huasicancha (Junín), local organizations were strong enough to negotiate and choose their alliances with the federation or the party which best suited their interests.[85] In the Department of Puno, peasant demands concerning labouring conditions and devolution of communal lands were mainly channelled through two Christian-Democrat orientated federations, the Frente Sindical Campesino and the Movimiento Sindical Cristiano del Peru, both of which gained political offices for their leaders, but without achieving real changes in the agrarian structure.[86] In sum, in 1963, even if local and regional conflicts and

[84] Wesley W. Craig, 'The Peasant Movement of La Convención', in Landsberger (ed.), *Latin American Peasant Movements,* pp. 274–96.

[85] Handelman, *Struggle in the Andes,* pp. 62–5; Cotler and Portocarrero, 'Peru: peasant organizations', pp. 315–17; William F. Whyte, 'Rural Peru – peasants as activists', in D. B. Heath (ed.), *Contemporary Cultures and Societies in Latin America,* 2nd edn. (New York, 1974), pp. 528–30; Gavin A. Smith and Pedro Cano, 'Some Factors Contributing to Land Occupations in Peru: the example of Huasicancha, 1963–1968', in Norman Long and Bryan Roberts (eds), *Peasant Cooperation and Capitalist Expansion in Central Peru* (Austin, Tex., 1978), pp. 168–71.

[86] See Edward Dew, *Politics in the Altiplano. The Dynamics of Change in Rural Peru* (Austin, Tex., 1969).

mobilizations had effective results in certain instances, there was not a nation-wide alliance which might put pressure on the Belaúnde government to embark on a serious agrarian reform programme. In spite of Belaúnde's campaign promises and of the actual approval of an Agrarian Law in 1964 which allowed for the expropriation of large *haciendas* in favour of *colonos* and landless communities, the land-tenure situation changed very little. In fact, after an initial policy of conciliation, the regime became increasingly repressive against rebel peasants, and the new legislation was all but forgotten.

A note on indigenismo

In virtually all the cases of rural mobilization in Latin America from the 1930s to the 1960s there was a significant development in the nature of peasant demands – from abolition of labour obligations of a 'feudal' type to expropriation of *haciendas* and land distribution. This development was duly acknowledged and sometimes directly fostered by populist organizations and also by certain sectors of the left. But, as Mariátegui had forcefully argued, the issue of *latifundia* expropriation was also closely related to 'the Indian question', that is, to the recognition of the grievances unjustly caused to indigenous peoples, which in countries such as Bolivia, Peru, Ecuador and Guatemala, and in certain regions of Colombia and Mexico, still formed the bulk of the population. Thus, the positive evaluation of the Indians and their crucial contribution to national identity became an important aspect of populist discourses. Equally important was to find a correct methodology to assess and alleviate their problems, which supposedly would be devised by professional anthropologists, sociologists and historians. *Indigenismo* was then the name received by this mixture of social analysis and political planning which purported to mobilize the indigenous population in a process of nation building. Invariably, *indigenismo* defended the rights of the Indians over the land they cultivated, not merely because it was historically theirs, but fundamentally because their dependence on landlords was a factor of poverty and exclusion which prevented them from becoming equal citizens. However, *indigenismo* also proclaimed the need for the Indians to become full members of national society – that is to lose their Indian identity. In the words of the leading *indigenista* ideologist in Mexico, Manuel Gamio, the *incorporation* of the Indians was a most urgent obligation of any progressive government.

In 1940, the first Inter-American Indigenista Congress met in Pátz-cuaro, Mexico, under the auspices of the government of Lázaro Cárdenas, and with the presence of delegates – scientists, politicians and social leaders – from the whole continent, but without any Indian group formally represented. In his inaugural address, President Cárdenas insisted on the importance of *mestizaje* – the new mixed race, the new mixed culture – for national identity; as far as the government of Mexico was concerned, he said, the goal was not to 'Indianize' the nation but to 'Mexicanize' the Indians. The Congress resolved that special institutions should be created in each country, in charge of representing the Indian population, lobbying for protective laws, and promoting and implementing aggressive social, economic and educational programmes. Agrarian reform, including the recognition and protection of collective property, was a crucial recommendation. A direct result of the Congress was the foundation of the Instituto Indigenista Interamericano, which has promoted research, publications and discussions on Indian problems and solutions. In many countries, similar institutes or offices were put into operation, but they were not always very effective.[87] For instance, the Office for Social Integration in Guatemala was unable to stop the genocidal anti-Indian actions of the army and the planters after the 1954 coup d'etat. In Mexico, where the Instituto Nacional Indigenista (INI) had ample support from the government, its main function was of social control and brokerage between the indigenous groups and the State apparatus, and therefore any attempt of developing political representation based on communal traditions or new autonomous institutions created inevitable tensions. Notwithstanding the efforts of well-meaning INI anthropologists such as Julio de la Fuente, Maurilio Muñoz and Gonzalo Aguirre Beltrán, Indian areas in Mexico were (and are) still marked by lack of public assistance, extreme poverty and over-exploitation of labourers. In Peru, the Indigenista Institute became a rather weak and ineffective agency for community development. In Bolivia, the MNR, after rallying massive Indian support, explicitly refused to recognize Indian identity and communal authorities. Not surprisingly, all emerging independent Indian (ethnic) organizations in Latin America maintained ambiguous relationships both with populist parties and *indigenista* policies.

[87] Marie-Chantal Barre, *Ideologías indígenas y movimientos indios* (Mexico, D.F., 1983), pp. 34–41.

1960S TO 1980S

After 1960, government, army, new and old elites, and foreign economic and political interests in many Latin American countries realigned against real or potential popular unrest. Among the ruling classes, the victory of Castroism in Cuba – a populist Revolution which became Communist – reinforced fears of leftist subversion and misgivings about popular organizations. In the context of the consolidation of centralizing nation-states, the army had become a privileged actor, not only in countries like Paraguay, El Salvador and Nicaragua, where traditional authoritarianism persisted, but also in countries where popular and middle-class groups had gained political recognition. Durable military regimes came to power in Guatemala in the 1950s, in Brazil, Bolivia, Argentina and Peru during the 1960s; and in Uruguay and Chile (supposedly havens of civilian democracy) in the 1970s. Most of the new military governments abolished political parties and opposition groups, suppressed manifestations of popular dissent and systematically violated human rights. They did not take the trouble to create alternative systems of political representation. Nevertheless, they invariably claimed to rule in the name of the middle classes and the popular sectors.

The relationship between the new authoritarian governments and agrarian organizations varied from country to country. More often than not, repression was a feature of these relationships. Corporatist organizations were now more manipulative than representative. With the notable exception of the Peruvian army, the military mistrusted agrarian reform policies, believing that only 'modern', highly capitalized private enterprises with a disciplined labour force could create an agricultural surplus and compete in the international market – a belief shared after 1970 by technocrats in non-military governments (in Mexico and Venezuela, for instance).

In truth, at the end of the 1960s, it was clear that existing agrarian-reform programmes had failed to solve the problems of rural unemployment, food scarcity and poverty. The U.S.-sponsored Alliance for Progress had also failed. In turn, ECLA doctrines were denounced. The economic context of rural Latin America had changed, partly because of the reforms introduced by populist alliances, but also because of the internationalization of agriculture. Even certain sectors of the Left had misgivings about agrarian reform programmes which they condemned as 'mystifications' and as mechanisms for 're-peasantization', perpetuating reserves of cheap labour and passive politics. The left frequently invoked the example of Cuba – a source of intense fascination during the 1960s and 1970s – in agrarian as well as political matters: Cuba did not develop a reformist agricultural programme but a revolutionary programme of total collectivization.

The weakening or dismantling of populist programmes – and the subversion of the standing rules of participation and political fair play – did not necessarily mean that a new hegemony was consolidated. Peasants and rural workers continued struggling for land and access to credit, technology and commercialization channels, as well as demanding a better deal in the labour market, without being clear on what were the possibilities for negotiation. Their main visible enemy was no longer the landowning class – which in Mexico, Bolivia and even Venezuela had been successfully neutralized or even destroyed – but rather the government apparatuses, since the structure of heavily centralized state intervention in the countryside had been actually fortified by the new authoritarian regimes. Thus, a number of militant rural organizations emerged (or re-emerged), whose relationship with the government was often made difficult by defficient mechanisms of representation or brokerage. In several countries, the displaced forces of opposition resorted to organized guerrilla warfare, which in only a few cases attracted significant support from the inhabitants of villages and hamlets and which had only a partial and ambiguous endorsement from the Left.

In 1979, the fall of Somoza marked the beginning of a new period of democratization in Latin America. As authoritarian governments crumbled and new civilian governments emerged, the countryside became alive again with multiple mobilizations. But their structure was changing: instead of unions and leagues linked to political parties and national organizations, there was a proliferation of autonomous groups whose demands and strategies were defined by means of a high degree of local grassroots participation. Often their goals were no longer expressed in terms of class interests, but rather in terms of human rights, religious values, gender equality, ecological awareness, citizenship, and emerging or recovered ethnic and communal identities. Agrarian reform was still a crucial demand of certain mobilized rural groups; but it was no longer necessarily tied to plans for co-operative production under the management of a centralized state. Instead, the 1980s witnessed the emergence of a sector of capitalized small and medium farmers united through flexible networks of reciprocal aid. Mistrust toward state dependence was related to the generalized corruption and inefficiency of public institutions during the authoritarian years, and to the financial collapse of many governments during the

1980s, which resulted in privatization of public enterprises and the suspension of development and welfare schemes.

This section begins with the impact that the example of Cuba and the *foquismo* doctrine had on the relationships between the organized political left and armed rural mobilizations which failed to develop into mass movements in Venezuela, Colombia and Bolivia in the early 1960s. In these three countries, military repression was crucial in determining the fate of popular protest, but at the same time the opposition forces were unable to articulate an alternative political programme which could win massive support. Following the failure of the guerrilla movement, the emergence of the ANUC in Colombia in 1967 represented the last important effort to create a large-scale rural organization in the hemisphere. The ANUC explicitly (and rather successfully in the beginning) dealt with the heterogenous nature of grass-roots demands. Its eventual demise has to be explained by its ambiguous relationships with a state which wavered between clientelistic and authoritarian practices, and also by internal competition for a centralized leadership. In contrast to Venezuela, Colombia and Bolivia, rural insurgency in three Central American countries – Guatemala, El Salvador, Nicaragua – enjoyed the sympathy and active support of the popular sectors, partly because of the intervention of an unlikely actor: the Catholic Church, which openly denounced the structural causes of social injustice in the hemisphere, after the renovating winds of the Second Vatican Council (1962–5) and particularly the Conference of Bishops in Medellín in 1968. After the failure of the guerrillas in Peru in the early 1960s the military regime (1968–80) itself implemented an agrarian reform programme. The return to civilian rule in 1980, however, coincided with the emergence of a new insurrectionary movement called The Shining Path (Sendero Luminoso) which found support among a dislocated rural population. There were significant rural mobilizations in Chile during the administrations of Eduardo Frei (1964–70) and Salvador Allende (1970–3) before the establishment of the repressive Pinochet regime (1973–90). In Mexico the attempt by President Echeverría (1970–6) to create a new mass organization in the rural areas was a failure, and his successors proved unable to co-opt the multitude mobilizations that came into existence in the late 1970s and 1980s.

Venezuela, Colombia, Bolivia

Between December 1956 and January 1959 a revolutionary uprising headed by Fidel Castro was successful in overthrowing the dictatorial, corrupt government of Fulgencio Batista in Cuba. The Communist Party, which in the 1920s had had an important role of agitation among the abundant rural proletariat, but was later weakened and reduced to a semi-clandestine status, was extremely suspicious of Castro's adventure. The first supporters of Castro's guerrillas in the Sierra Maestra came from a rather unusual sector of the rural population: the squatters expelled from sugar-cane plantations in the plains, who had migrated to highland areas in search of vacant lands. For its part, Castro's group made it clear that with the triumph of the revolution there would be a thorough redistribution of land. In September 1958, in the midst of the guerrilla campaign, an Agrarian Congress was held, and less than a month later, the Agrarian Law of the Sierra was passed, which purported to fulfill the commitment made by Castro himself in his famous 1953 speech, *History will absolve me*.[88] Once in power the former rebels kept their promise of giving land to squatters, tenant farmers and rural labourers. In the following years (after a new Agrarian Law was passed in 1963) they devised a complex apparatus in charge of promoting and administering collective production in the countryside.

From the Cuban experience, a new theory of revolution was proclaimed by Ernesto 'Che' Guevara. This theory had two main points: 'a small group of resolute men' with a revolutionary ideology and operating in clandestine conditions could create a *foco,* a powerful spark from which the fire of radical change would spread to a whole country, leading to the defeat of the professional army; and this revolution in Latin America must start in the rural areas.[89] Guevara – from the beginning an avowed Marxist, unlike Castro – developed these ideas in his treatise on *Guerrilla Warfare.* Later, they were given a philosophical flavour by French professor Regis Debray's *Revolution in the Revolution? Foquismo,* challenging as it did the Leninist principle of the supreme rule of the Party, was initially denounced as irresponsible adventurism by the orthodox Left. But there were some Communist parties, such as those in Venezuela, Colombia and Bolivia, on which the Cuban experience left a deep mark and led to a transformation in their attitudes and methods.

In Venezuela, the ten-year-old repressive dictatorship of Marcos Pérez Jiménez came to an end in 1958. Elected President in December, 1958, Rómulo Betancourt, the leader of Acción Democrática (AD), formed a

---

[88] Eric R. Wolf, *Peasant Wars of the Tentieth Century* (New York, 1969), pp. 260–3, 269–73; Adolfo Martín Barrios, 'Historia política de los campesinos cubanos', in González Casanova, *Historia política de los campesinos latinoamericanos,* pp. 79–82.

[89] Quoted in Richard Gott, *Rural Guerrillas in Latin America* (London, 1973), p. 30.

coalition government with the the Christian Democrats (COPEI) and the centre-left Unión Republicana Democrática (URD). However, the URD left the coalition after a year, partly because the AD had lost its radical impetus. Moreover, the most radical among AD members abandoned their party to create the Movimiento de la Izquierda Revolucionaria (MIR), and Betancourt's main agrarian adviser led another dissenting group, the AD-ARS. When AD had been in power, from 1945 to 1948, a programme of agrarian reform was put into practice, through which idle lands could be expropriated and leased by the government to peasants. The AD government in 1958 was, however, convinced that restraint was necessary: it did not want to alienate the U.S. nor to lose the lucrative revenues received from the U.S. oil companies. The agrarian legislation passed in 1960 expropriated only vacant (uncultivated) *haciendas* – whose owners were generously reimbursed – and public land, which was then distributed in private holdings. Unproductive *latifundia* in steep mountains were left alone; instead, peasants were encouraged to open new lands to cultivation in the flat coastal region. Within five years Betancourt and his successor Leoni managed to halt land seizures by peasants. The agrarian programme established 700 settlements and granted nearly three million hectares to more than 100,000 families, who also got credit, extension services, technical aid, and the blessing of the Alliance for Progress.[90] At the end of the 1960s, an independent observer hailed the Venezuelan Reform as more successful in economic terms than its Mexican and Bolivian forerunners.[91] Politically, it was even more successful: the programme had re-invigorated the web of patron–client ties between the AD and the rural population. Still, the problem of rural poverty continued, and one obvious result was the massive rural-urban exodus, as well as the visible proliferation of shanty-towns on the outskirts of the cities.

The Marxist Left – the Communists and the MIR – did not share Betancourt's theses. In 1960, both declared their approval of armed struggle in Venezuela. In January, 1962, the first signs of guerrilla activity appeared in the mountains of both the East (Turimiquire, in the state of Sucre) and the western state of Lara. During the following months, at least a dozen guerrilla bands were tracked down – and severely beaten – by the army, but a number of members of the Armed Forces joined the rebels. In

[90] John Duncan Powell, 'Venezuela: the peasant union movement', in Landsberger (ed.), *Latin American Peasant Movements*, p. 571.
[91] Charles Erasmus, 'Agrarian Reform Versus Land Reform: three Latin American countries', in D. B. Heath (ed.), *Contemporary Cultures and Societies in Latin America*, pp. 143–57.

February, 1963, five insurgent groups, combining the MIR, Communists, and former members of the military, convened to set up formally the Fuerzas Armadas de Liberación Nacional (FALN). Concomitantly, the Communists founded the Frente de Liberación Nacional (FLN), a civilian political front, in charge of devising broad, long-term strategies. But the peasant support for the revolution was nowhere in sight. The radical enthusiasm of urban groups had declined, whereas the army grew in influence and strength. Many leaders, both insurgent and civilian, were captured and put in jail. When Leoni, the new AD presidential candidate, was elected and took office in 1964, he offered legal political status to all non-violent organizations. This caused a split in the urban FLN, although the rural FALN continued under arms. In 1965, the Venezuelan Communist Party, apparently influenced by the opinions of orthodox European parties, officially withdrew its support for the armed struggle, which resulted in a drastic re-arrangement of the FLN/FALN. In spite of many bold actions undertaken by the surviving guerrillas, their belligerent capacity became insignificant by the end of the decade.[92]

Contrary to their Venezuelan counterparts, rural guerrillas in Colombia, as we have seen, had a long history and a strong leadership which was both Communist and of peasant origin. They drew on the support of relatively large numbers of mobilized, anti-Conservative peasants. After El Davis had been dismantled in 1953 (see above) other guerrilla encampments had been established in Marquetalia (southern Tolima), Río Chiquito (northeastern Cauca), El Pato and Guayabero (eastern Huila), Viotá (eastern Tolima), Tequendama and Sumapaz (Cundinamarca), which became known as 'the independent peasant republics'. They were in fact veritable redoubts of Communist rule, with their own systems of production, police, armed forces and administration of justice. Marquetalia was the largest: it covered about 5,000 square kilometres and harboured as many as 4,000 families. Its famous leaders, Fermín Charry ('Charro Negro'), Manuel Marulanda ('Tirofijo') and Isauro Yossa were all El Davis veterans and members of the Central Committee of the Communist Party of Colombia. Yet until the mid-1960s the official line of the party was not in favour of armed insurgency. Against this passivity and inspired by the Cuban Revolution, a group of Bogotá students founded the Movimiento de Obreros, Estudiantes y Campesinos (MOEC) in 1960. Almost at the

[92] Gott, *Rural Guerrillas in Latin America,* pp. 195–255; Robert J. Alexander, *The Communist Party of Venezuela* (Stanford, Cal., 1969).

same time, a group of intellectuals, led by Gloria Gaitán (the daughter of populist leader Eliécer Gaitán), created the Frente Unido de Acción Revolucionaria (FUAR). Both the MOEC and the FUAR conducted unsuccessful guerrilla actions. Meanwhile, the successive governments of the National Front, pressured by the U.S. and assisted by CIA money and advisers, started a heavy counter-insurgent offensive, which aimed at the total destruction of the guerrilla strongholds. In 1964, 'Operation Marquetalia' involved 16,000 soldiers (a third of the whole Colombian army), as well as dozens of helicopters and warplanes, which forced the disbandment of Marquetalia. The rest of the 'peasant republics' fell throughout 1964–5. But the operations again put thousands of peasants on the move, many of whom became brigands. Others organized mobile guerrilla bands. These bands held several conferences under the chairmanship of Tirofijo; and in 1966 – now with the formal blessing of the Tenth Congress of the Communist Party – they decided to set up a comprehensive organization: the Fuerzas Armadas de la Revolución Colombiana (FARC).[93]

The Communist Party openly favoured rural insurgency due, on the one hand, to the increasing prestige of the Cuban regime among progressive forces in Latin America and its friendship with the Soviet Union, and on the other, to the fear of being displaced by other radical groups (for example, the Maoists), in the context of the widespread dissapointment of the Colombian left with the National Front. A particular source of frustration was the ineffective Instituto Colombiano de Reforma Agraria (INCORA), founded in 1961 to re-organize the land tenure system and change the social dynamics of agriculture. Meanwhile, in the mountains of Santander, another *foco* had been created in 1964–5 by students (former members of MOEC) and peasants: the Ejército de Liberación Nacional (ELN), whose head, Fabio Vásquez, subsequently tried to establish an alliance with Tirofijo and the FARC. Vásquez was told, however, that the ELN should subordinate itself to the Central Committee of the Communist Party, but he refused. Nevertheless, the ELN became world famous when it acquired a new member, the young Catholic priest Camilo Torres, who had emerged as the most charismatic figure in Colombia.

Trained as a sociologist in Louvain (Belgium), Father Torres conducted critical research, university seminars and discussion groups on the social and political conditions of Colombia. As a result, he became convinced

---

[93] Gott, *Rural Guerrillas*, pp. 279–320.

that the government was unwilling and unable to break with the reactionary oligarchy and that the traditional parties had lost their capacity to create social awareness among the masses. In March 1965 he published a *Platform for a Movement of Popular Unity* summarizing his ideas on agrarian reform and economic nationalization, and calling for a non-partisan coalition of progressive forces. This document created a big stir in the cities. As a result, he lost his job at the university and was later stripped of his clerical functions by Church authorities. Throughout 1965, Camilo Torres campaigned all over the country in favour of his incipient, non-sectarian United Front. Trying to win as broad a support as possible, he negotiated with Communists and radicals as well as the left wing of the Liberals and progressive Catholics. This very flexibility, however, alienated the organized Left.[94] In spite of the priest's enormous personal popularity, the United Front made very little progress. Disillusioned, Torres retreated to the mountains and joined the ELN. In his view, the ELN shared his ideals of non-sectarian commitment to the masses, and he expected that his campaign for agrarian reform would win the enthusiasm of the peasantry. But on 15 February 1966, he was killed in an ambush by the army.

In reality, neither the FARC, nor the ELN, nor the Maoist Ejército Popular de Liberación (EPL) which sprung up in 1968 enjoyed the broad participation of the peasant uprisings during the years of *la violencia*. Moreover, by the late 1960s they had become small, marginalized, badly organized bands. The army, whose budget increased to nearly 30 per cent of the GNP during the 1960s, had become specialized in hunting guerrillas. In addition, the military forces and the National Front used an anti-violence, anti-banditry discourse which had a strong appeal for a frightened rural population, after nearly thirty years of continuous horror.[95]

The hardest blow to the *foquista* theory was the defeat in 1967 of its standard-bearer, Che Guevara, in Bolivia. Bolivian rural unions were still connected with the State through negotiating alliances and clientelistic ties, even though a military junta headed by Generals Barrientos and Ovando had replaced the MNR in 1964. The military had serious confrontations with the miners, but they gained the sympathy of the peasants.

---

[94] Excerpts from Camilo Torres's main writings, including his *Platform,* his famous message to students, and the personal *manifesto,* which announces his decision to join the ELN, are reproduced in Germán Guzmán, *Camilo. Presencia y Destino* (Bogotá, 1967). See also Adolfo Gilly, *La senda de la guerrilla* (Mexico, D.F., 1986), pp. 157–76.

[95] Francisco Leal Buitrago, *Estado y política en Colombia* (Bogotá, 1984), pp. 213–20; Jesús Antonio Bejarano, 'Campesinado y luchas agrarias en Colombia', in González Casanova (ed.), *Historia política de los campesinos latinoamericanos,* Vol. 3, pp. 59–61.

The peasant unions even signed what came to be known as the *Pacto Militar-Campesino,* and it was through their support that Barrientos was elected President in 1966. It has to be remembered that the post-revolutionary army, re-organized by the MNR, was of popular extraction. Its soldiers were well-regarded in many rural areas, where they had participated in development and social assistance projects. Barrientos himself – as did General Gualberto Villarroel, the promoter of the Indigenous Congresses in the 1940s – came from a Quechua-speaking Cochabamba family. However, the military government proceeded to disarm the peasant militias, in order to prevent trouble. Whereas the top MNR leaders went to exile, the parties of the left were openly persecuted, particularly those with more influence among the miners, such as the Trotskyist Partido Revolucionario and Juan Lechín's Partido Revolucionario de Izquierda Nacional (PRIN), a split of the MNR; but also the pro-Soviet Communist Party of Bolivia (PCB), which replaced the weakened Partido de Izquierda Revolucionaria (PIR).

Early in 1966, the Secretary General of the PCB, Mario Monje Molina, agreed in principle to collaborate with Che Guevara in the creation of a revolutionary *foco* in the Bolivian jungle. At least two members of the PCB Central Committee, the Peredo brothers, were sent to Cuba to be trained in the tactics of guerrilla warfare. However, after December, 1966, the relationship between Che and Monje became strained over the issue of leadership. As a result, recruitment of Bolivians for the fighting force was done through the personal networks of the Peredos and among unemployed miners. In early 1967, the force had fifty men: twenty-nine Bolivians, seventeen Cubans, three Peruvians, and Che Guevara himself. An isolated, mountainous area, situated to the south of the city of Santa Cruz, was chosen for guerrilla operation. Its sparse population of farmers and seasonal migrant labourers (who found relatively attractive jobs in the oil fields of Camirí) did not show sympathy for the guerrillas. After the first clash between rebels and the army in March 1967, Barrientos – who was advised by U.S. 'experts on counter-insurgency' and by CIA agents – placed the whole southeast of the country under direct military rule. People found serving as contacts between the guerrillas and the outside world (the Bolivian cities and the international scene) were killed or – as in the case of Regis Debray, who had come to Bolivia, ostensibly as a journalist – captured by the army. In spite of this, groups of miners showed open support for the guerrilla cause, and some unions collected money for it. In the big tin mine of Siglo Veinte there was even a training camp for guerrilla warfare, which provoked a bloody raid by soldiers in June 1967, leaving dozens of dead people. Other possible supporters of the guerrillas were unwilling or unable to act. On 8 October 1967, his group reduced to only seventeen men, Che Guevara was injured in battle and captured by a military patrol. A few hours later, he was shot dead, in cold blood.[96]

The failure of guerrilla groups in Venezuela, Colombia and Bolivia to become genuine *focos* – that is, attract broad support from other mobilized sectors – seems to have been related to three main factors. First, the population in general did not perceive the guerrilla goals as being a part of a comprehensive programme of acceptable social, economic and political change. This was related to the ability of governments to present guerrillas as bandits or crazy extremists, and also to the inability or unwillingness of political organizations of the left (which often were badly divided) to publicize those goals in a favourable light. Second, people had not lost faith in legal/peaceful means of attaining desired changes. This was particularly the case in Venezuela where formal democracy had returned after ten years of dictatorship; the AD government combined repression with negotiation and patronage; and a moderate agrarian reform was implemented. Even in Colombia, where 75 per cent of the electorate abstained from voting in 1966, people knew that non-peaceful means had proven to be disastrous, after a seemingly endless civil war. And in Bolivia, in spite of an uneasy political climate, civic mobilizations were preferred to civil war. Third, the ruling groups and their armies – in part, because of U.S. help – presented an image of strength, even though in the Colombian and Bolivian regimes internal rifts were deep and persistent.

In Colombia, the democratic opening after 1966 permitted the emergence of the ANUC (Asociación Nacional de Usuarios Campesinos), which became probably the most important mass organization in rural Latin America during the late 1960s and early 1970s. Its outstanding characteristics were: (a) the consolidation of institutional, representative legitimacy at the national level; (b) the co-ordination of heterogeneous demands (claims for land, access to credit and markets, political participation, ethnic revivalism) into a single united front; (c) the creation of an independent political position from which the ANUC could negotiate with both the state and the political Left. As León Zamosc has made clear in his brilliant

[96] Gott, *Rural Guerrillas in Latin America*, pp. 480–561.

study of the ANUC, these characteristics are the result of a convergence of multiple historical forces, including the exhaustion of guerrillas, the new hegemonic strategies of the National Front, and the continuation of massive rural mobilizations.[97]

For the first time in the history of Colombia – and with the support of the industrialist class – Liberal President Carlos Lleras Restrepo (1966–70) devised a plan in which the rural population would be encouraged to participate in a state-sponsored organization as users of government services in the countryside. This required the invigoration of INCORA, the Agrarian Reform Institute, which was impelled by the government to develop effective measures of agrarian reform: in the years between 1966 and 1970, INCORA redistributed twice as much land as in the previous presidential period. It also meant the institutional channelling of rural popular demands. These demands were clearly diversified, in terms of regions and productive structures. For the landless peasants (the combination of tenants, sharecroppers and labourers) of the traditional *haciendas* on the Atlantic Coast and the eastern plains, the main demand was expropriation and redistribution of *latifundia,* particularly in those areas where peasants were being evicted from the land they had opened for cultivation. For people in the indigenous municipalities of Cauca and southern Tolima, land redistribution would have to go hand in hand with the restoration of the old communal *resguardos.* In the areas of commercially orientated smallholdings – the slopes of the Andean range and the interior valleys – the main issues were access to credit, technology, markets and fair prices. Communications, marketing and basic services were also demands made by small and medium holders in the newly colonized areas on the Pacific Coast and along the Venezuelan border. Finally, the rural proletariat of the modernized *haciendas* in the north and west wanted job security and fair salaries – and land redistribution if those claims were not duly answered. ANUC was created in 1967 to fulfill the important functions of co-ordination and negotiation with the State.

In 1968, the number of ANUC members was 600,000; three years later, it was almost a million – of which 50 per cent were smallholders – grouped in 634 municipal and twenty-eight departmental associations. Its success was related to the fulfillment of demands and the atmosphere of participation at all levels, which in turn gradually led to the multiplica-

[97] See León Zamosc, *La cuestión agraria y el movimiento campesino en Colombia. Luchas de la Asociación Nacional de Usuarios Campesinos, 1967–1981* (Geneva, 1987). See also Silvia Rivera Cusicanqui, *Política e ideología en el movimiento campesino colombiano. El caso de la ANUC* (Geneva, 1987).

tion of public petitions and marches, and the escalation of land seizures. After 1970 Conservative President Misael Pastrana showed much less sympathy for the ANUC. On the one hand, the landowning class – the backbone of Pastrana's party – argued that large-scale agricultural exploitation was necessary in order to take advantage of the new booming conditions in the international market. On the other hand, after the relative calm and prosperity of the Lleras period, the industrial bourgeoisie was no longer convinced of the necessity of a radical agrarian reform. Faced with this situation, the ANUC leadership was divided: the followers of ex-President Lleras as well as the Christian Democrats defended the need to maintain a negotiating relationship with the government, whereas the left (Trotskyites and Communists) pushed for a strategy of non-violent confrontation. At the Second National Assembly of the ANUC (January 1971), the radical position gained strength, which led to a new wave of seizures of land and government offices (particularly on the Atlantic Coast), as well as public demonstrations, campaigns of civil disobedience, and radical statements concerning the necessity of abolishing *latifundia* altogether. In January 1972, the so-called Pact of Chicoral established that INCORA would not expropriate those landholdings which duly payed their taxes, fixed in accordance with the values of a revised land census. When the government called for an ANUC national congress in Armenia, in November 1972, the anti-government majority organized its own congress in Sincelejo, which was attended by delegates from all Departments, and opened with a demonstration of more than 10,000 peasants. The authorities then declared the Sincelejo congress illegal, and responded to land seizures with the use of public force. In spite of this, both ANUC factions rejected the programme of violence proposed by two pro-Chinese groups: the Marxist-Leninist Leagues, and the Marxist-Leninist Communist Party of Colombia, which had gained a certain following among displaced sharecroppers in Sucre, Córdoba, Bolívar and Antioquia, and believed in the existence of a 'situation of insurrection' in Colombia.

The López Michelsen government (1974–8) attempted to strike a compromise with both the landowners and the rural populace. On the one hand, it launched a programme of credit and technical assistance for smallholders, as well as services such as education and electricity for all rural areas, including isolated *veredas* (hamlets). Also, the 1975 *Ley de Aparcería* (Sharecropping Law), established protective regulations for sharecroppers, and forced large landowners (over 200 hectares) to provide their labourers with subsistence plots. On the other hand, immunity against land expropriation was offered to landowners who complied with these provisions.[98] The Sincelejo ANUC denounced the Sharecropping Law as a shameless manoeuvre, and made a renewed call for the struggle for land. This prompted a new repressive response from the government, and even a wave of murders by landowners, police, and army – just as in the days of *la violencia,* although not in exactly the same areas. However, the weapon of land invasions was often very effective, as in several municipalities of Tolima, Huila and Córdoba, where squatters held out for several weeks, until INCORA representatives negotiated a settlement with the landowners.[99]

Yet the radical ANUC lost strength after 1976. The majority of ANUC members were smallholders, and many of them adopted a moderate, pro-government stance because of the services provided to them in the previous years. They were also mellowed by favourable market conditions, particularly for coffee growers. Even though only 66,000 families had become beneficiaries of the agrarian reform programme – a smallish number compared to Mexico, Bolivia and even Venezuela – the Sharecropping Law succeeded in defusing the militancy of many land-petitioning groups, especially in the areas of new colonization along the Venezuelan border, where landless peasants had settled en masse, and where many of them were making a comfortable income cultivating marijuana.[100] Other factors that led to the waning of the association and scattering of its members were a rigid central bureaucracy and internal quarrels among factions competing for leadership.

In the late 1970s new guerrilla groups like the Movimiento 19 de Abril (M-19) formed by former militants of the Alianza Nacional Popular (ANAPO, founded in 1966 by former president Rojas Pinilla) and old guerrilla groups like the FARC – linked to the Communist Party since the 1960s – and the EPL again found support among the dislocated rural population. Together with the drug barons, thus reduced the Colombian state to a situation of weakness almost as critical as the 1940s. President Belisario Betancur (1982–6) offered amnesty to the guerrillas, which was pragmatically accepted by a segment of the FARC; but not by the M-19, which renewed and widely publicized its insurgent

---

[98] Alcides Gómez, 'Política agraria de López y Ley de Aparcería', *Ideología y Sociedad* (Bogotá), 14–15 (1975), pp. 47–63.

[99] Zamosc, *La cuestión agraria,* pp. 143–9.

[100] León Zamosc, 'Peasant Struggles of the 1970s in Colombia', in Susan Eckstein (ed.), *Power and Popular Protest: Latin American Social Movements* (Berkeley, Cal., 1989), pp. 120–3.

actions.[101] The governments of Presidents Barco (1986–90) and Gaviria (1990–) also sought to negotiate with guerrillas and even with the drug barons. The EPL and the M-19 seemed to have laid down their guns – the M-19 actually transformed itself into a legal political party – but the violence continued. The suspension of agrarian reform and rural development policies since the late 1970s had not contributed to the process of peace in the countryside.

Central America

In Central American countries (with the exception of Costa Rica), notwithstanding periods of aggregate economic growth (mainly during the 1960s and early 1970s) due to booming export agriculture and relatively prosperous import-substitution industrialization, the expanding population faced the perennial inequality, racism, social fragmentation, anti-democratic governments, and dependence on the United States. The armed insurgencies in Guatemala, El Salvador and Nicaragua, in spite of internal quarrels, gained the support of sizeable sectors of the population, both urban and rural, as representing the only feasible strategy to achieve social justice and national liberation. However, the history of these struggles is also tragic, and their actual effect on social reforms has yet to be evaluated.

The guerrillas in Guatemala had their origin in an aborted military revolt, on 13 November 1960, in which a group of nationalist officers attempted to prevent the government of General Miguel Ydígoras Fuentes from letting anti-Castro Cubans and the CIA set up secret military training camps in Guatemalan territory. Three survivors, Marco Antonio Yon Sosa, Luis Turcios Lima and Alejandro de León, escaped to Mexico – with the help of sympathetic peasants – and then returned to Guatemala to organize a rebel fighting force.[102] The three had previously received military training by the U.S. army, which did not prevent their strong opposition to U.S. intervention. De León was located and killed by the political police in July 1961. In February 1962 the Movimiento Revolucionario 13 de Noviembre (MR-13), led by Yon Sosa and Turcios Lima, started operating from Sierra de Minas, in the eastern Department of Izabal. A month later, Colonel Paz Tejada founded another rebel group, the Frente 20 de Octubre (the date of Arévalo's 1944 revolution); and during the following months there were

---

[101] Fernando Rojas, 'Crisis económica y crisis política bajo el gobierno de Betancur', in Fernando Calderón (ed.), *Los movimientos sociales frente a la crisis* (Buenos Aires, 1986), pp. 225–62.
[102] Adolfo Gilly, *La senda de la guerrilla,* pp. 62–7.

peasant riots and student marches in support of the guerrillas. But General Ydígoras crushed all opposition in the cities, and the rebels confined themselves to the mountains. In December 1962 the MR-13 promoted the formation of an alliance, the Fuerzas Armadas Revolucionarias (FAR), with the Partido Guatemalteco del Trabajo (PGT) – the Communist Party, reduced to clandestine status – and with a student group called Movimiento 12 de Abril (the date of recent student riots in Guatemala City). In March 1963, Ydígoras was deposed by Colonel Peralta Azurdia, who called off the announced elections, and put the whole country under a virtual state of siege, which lasted until 1966. Meanwhile, the FAR, and particularly the MR-13, managed to organize underground armed peasant committees in the Northeast, mainly in those areas which had suffered from the reversal of Arbenz's agrarian reform after 1954 coup. By 1964, the MR-13 leaders, particularly Yon Sosa and Francisco Amado Granados, had come under the influence of Trotskyism – which caused a split with the pro-Soviet PGT, and also misgivings on the part of the segment led by Turcios Lima, who was sympathetic to Castro but assumed a non-Communist stance.

A national election in May 1966 was won by the Partido Revolucionario (PR), the legal heir of Arévalo's revolution, with the support of the PGT. The new President, Julio César Méndez Montenegro, offered amnesty to the insurgents, but the groups of both Yon Sosa and Turcios Lima refused, arguing that the army and the landowning class would not let Méndez develop his programme of democratic reforms. They were right. Throughout the 1960s, the army established a network of 'military commissioners' in charge of co-ordinating the actions of spies and armed vigilantes provided by local landowners. At the same time, a number of right-wing secret terrorist organizations, such as the Mano Blanca and the Frente de Resistencia Nacional, often under the protection of the 'commissioners', undertook the task of assassinating those people suspected of supporting the guerrillas or having subversive ideas. Possibly, the car crash in which Turcios Lima lost his life on October, 1966, was engineered by the army and its spies. In 1967–8 the army, assisted by U.S. Green Beret 'Special Forces', worked to destroy armed peasant groups, particularly in the northeastern mountains (the Izabal-Zacapa-Alta Verapaz-Chiquimula area), and to locate and kill the *guerrilleros de la noche* ('night guerrillas': those who led a normal life during the day time and joined armed actions at night). In the coastal area of Escuintla, these 'night guerrillas' were co-ordinated by a new radical organization that grew out of the unions of the Arbenz years, the Partido de Unión Revolucionaria. By the end of Méndez Montenegro's period of office

(1970), the country was 'effectively in a state of clandestine civil war'. The rebel forces obtained money and arms through raiding military posts and kidnapping hostages for ransom; but they also received help from rural and urban civilians (students, for instance) as well as from contacts in Mexico and friendly socialist governments.[103] There is no evidence that strong ties existed between the rebels and the surviving legal rural unions and leagues (which were less than 100 in the whole country and had a weak situation vis-à-vis employers and landowners); nevertheless, these legal organizations were harassed by military commissioners and rightist terrorist bands.[104]

In 1970 Yon Sosa was killed by the Mexican army when he was crossing the border; but the FAR, re-uniting the guerrillas, continued operating until 1975, when it was disbanded by counter-insurgent forces. During that same year, a new rebel front, the Ejército Guerrillero de los Pobres (EGP), took over in northern Quiché. In the late 1970s, a resuscitated FAR and the emerging Organización del Pueblo en Armas (OPA) found substantial following among impoverished Indian migratory labourers in the western areas of El Quiché, Huehuetenango, Quetzaltenango and San Marcos, where subsistence cultivation had been seriously disrupted by invading estates devoted to export crops.[105] In the villages, it was through traditional ritual organizations and kinship networks, as well as Christian Base Communities – the associations promoted by the progressive Catholic clergy – that EGP, FAR and OPA were able to establish mechanisms of communication and recruiting.[106]

After 1970 a succession of military governments continued the massive and indiscriminate repression against rural areas where rebels actually or supposedly operated. Lucas García (1978–82) and Ríos Montt (1982–3) launched a genocidal offensive against Indian villages – 150,000 people were killed in seven years – nourished by a racist discourse against 'the barbarians' similar to the ideological justifications of Indian massacres in Bolivia at the turn of the century and El Salvador in 1932. Thousands of terrified people fled to Chiapas in Mexico, where 149 camps with almost 200,000 Guatemalan refugees existed in 1984.[107] However, popular resis-

---

[103] See Adams, *Crucifixion by Power,* pp. 142–3, 214–17, 267–77. The quotation is from p. 142.

[104] Brian Murphy, 'The Stunted Growth of Campesino Organization', in Richard N. Adams, *Crucifixion by power,* pp. 476–7.

[105] Jeffrey M. Paige, 'Social Theory and Peasant Revolution in Vietnam and Guatemala', *Theory and Society,* 12 (1983): 699–737; James Dunkerley, *Power in the Isthmus,* pp. 73–5.

[106] Antonio Bran, 'Guatemala: organización popular y lucha de clases en el campo', in González Casanova (ed.), *Historia política de los campesinos latinoamericanos,* Vol. 2, pp. 14–17.

[107] Woodward, *Central America. A Nation Divided,* pp. 242–5.

tance endured, and not only among Indian communities. On the coastal plantations and modernized highland *fincas,* a new federation of rural labourers, the Comité de Unidad Campesina, founded in 1978, successfully mobilized both Indians and Ladinos in strikes and marchers – such as the national strike of March, 1980, when 80,000 labourers paralysed fourteen sugar refineries and seventy large *fincas* – and negotiated better working conditions, in spite of constant aggressions from the army and vigilante groups.[108]

In Guatemala, peasant support for guerrillas was rooted in the profound resentment caused by the dismantling of Arbenz's agrarian reform and the repression of unions and leagues after 1954. Such support was more intense among the less fortunate rural groups: those precarious cultivators who had to leave their villages periodically as casual labourers and move from estate to estate in search of badly paid work, and who in addition suffered racist discrimination from the non-Indian (*ladino*) population. In contrast, permanent estate labourers and smallholders were less prone to join the rebels. In El Salvador, the radicalized rural groups which emerged in the 1970s were also composed mainly of seasonal migratory labourers. But in the Salvadorean case we find a more accelerated process of rural pauperization and even 'de-peasantization', related to high population density and a renewed voracity on the part of the landowning class for land to grow export crops – sugar-cane as well as coffee and cotton. In 1975, 40 per cent of the rural families were landless, and 50 per cent of landholdings were of less than one hectare.[109] There was a chronic scarcity of grains and basic foodstuffs, since growing of such crops was pushed off to marginal fields. Concomitantly, there was a surplus of labour; strictly speaking, there was not a full proletarianization, since employers were not offering many full-time jobs; and rural wages were kept at a very low level. When more than 100,000 Salvadorean migrants were expelled by the Honduran government – the incident which provoked the so-called 'football war' in 1969 – rural unemployment intensified.

The Federación Cristiana de Campesinos Salvadoreños (FECCAS) was the first independent rural organization to emerge in a country where civil liberties had been virtually non-existent for nearly forty years. Protected by the Catholic Church, FECCAS established local committees to defend

[108] Antonio Bran, 'Guatemala: organización popular y lucha de clases en el campo', pp. 18–20.
[109] David Browning, *El Salvador: Landscape and Society,* pp. 225–35; Carlos Rafael Cabarrús, *Génesis de una revolución. Análisis del surgimiento y desarrollo de la organización campesina en El Salvador* (Mexico, D.F., 1983), pp. 58–9.

the rights of peasants and rural workers. It had close ties with other progressive Catholic movements, such as the Delegates of the Word and the Christian Base Communities, which worked to raise individual and social awareness among their members. After 1974, FECCAS participated in a broad rural-urban front of protest against low salaries and the high cost of living, the Frente de Acción Popular Unificada (FAPU). This front developed links with the Christian Democratic Party (PDC) – which had been founded in 1960, and since 1964 had control over several municipal councils, including San Salvador, and one-third of legislative seats at the National Assembly – as well as with urban unions sponsored by the Catholic Church and the semi-clandestine Confederación General de Trabajadores de El Salvador (CGTS).[110]

In January, 1970, the National Assembly convoked an Agrarian Reform Congress, which was also championed by José Napoleón Duarte, the PDC mayor of San Salvador; by Guillermo Ungo, leader of the Social-Democratic Movimiento Revolucionario Nacional (MRN); and even by Archbishop Luis Chávez y González. All sectors and organizations of Salvadorean society sent delegates. But when the Congress recommended a number of measures, including 'massive expropriation in favour of the common good', business representatives walked out, and the government simply ignored the issue. Meanwhile, a number of landowners and military officers had created a paramilitary group in the countryside, the Organización Democrática Nacionalista (ORDEN), devoted to fighting 'communism'. This organization attracted peasants through clientelistic mechanisms, and was reinforced after the 1970 Agrarian Congress.[111] When national elections were held in 1972, integral agrarian reform was a prominent banner in the campaigns of the Unión Nacional Opositora (UNO), a coalition of the three most important opposition parties: the DC, the MNR, and the Unión Democrática Nacional (UDN). (The underground Communist Party, banned since 1932, also supported the UNO.) No candidate received a majority of votes, and the National Assembly appointed Colonel Arturo Armando Molina, the candidate of the ruling Partido de Conciliación Nacional – the party of the armed forces – among widespread accusations of fraud, since polling in the countryside had been closely controlled by the National Guard, ORDEN and the landowners.

Meanwhile, thanks to the information network provided by Catholic

---

[110] Rafael Menjívar, *Formación y lucha del proletariado industrial salvadoreño* (San Salvador, 1979), pp. 90–2.

[111] North, *Bitter Grounds: Roots of Revolt in El Salvador,* pp. 68–71.

grass-roots organizations, both the electoral fraud and measures blocking agrarian reform were known and widely discussed in the rural areas. For instance, in the sugar-cane producing region of Aguilares in the centre-east – where most peasants had been driven out of the valleys by the large estates and lived on precarious subsistence plots in the hills with seasonal employment as cane cutters – members of the Christian Base Communities decided to send delegates to FECCAS seminars and FAPU demonstrations, with the explicit purpose of joining in the political struggle for social justice and in favour of land redistribution. A similar mobilization took place in the coffee-growing area of San Martín. According to Carlos Cabarrús's careful study of both cases (Aguilares and San Martín), the peasants most easily mobilized (mostly against the regime but also by ORDEN) were those who retained community affiliation and a certain economic autonomy reinforced by kindred solidarity, but had become semi-proletarianized and faced harassment by planters and landowners. From 1972 to 1975, FECCAS carried out a successful recruiting campaign, founding local committees and regional councils in several areas of the country. In July, 1975, FECCAS and the Union of Rural Labourers – which had begun as a mobilization sponsored by students and grew into a well-coordinated organization of wage labourers – joined in a meeting at the San Salvador Cathedral to form the Bloque Popular Revolucionario (BPR). The BPR drew up a comprehensive political programme, including: (a) democratic freedoms, clean elections and the end of military repression; (b) agrarian reform; (c) alliances between urban and rural labourers, and with teachers and students, for better salaries and working conditions, and in favour of a regime of justice and equality.[112]

By 1976 open hostility had grown between the military and the Church, many of whose members were involved in the defence and organization of the dispossesed classes, particularly the peasants. After a new fraudulent election in 1977, through which Molina's Minister of Defence, General Carlos Humberto Romero, became President, a right-wing vigilante organization, the Unión Guerrera Blanca (UGR), began murdering and threatening priests.[113] The newly appointed Archbishop, Mgr Oscar Arnulfo Romero (who had the same last name as the President but was his ideological opponent), voiced his profound rejection of the regime violence. A group of students and workers then founded the Popular Leagues

---

[112] Cabarrús, *Génesis de una revolución*, pp. 174–94, 234–40.
[113] North, *Bitter Grounds: Roots of Revolt in El Salvador*, pp. 74–7.

(LP-28), linked to a guerrilla organization of radicalized Christian Democrats, the Ejército Revolucionario del Pueblo (ERP), which existed since 1971 but had until then lacked substantial following. Other emerging guerrilla groups also developed alliances with popular coalitions during 1977. For instance, the Communist-led Fuerzas Populares de Liberación Farabundo Martí (FPL-FM) established a working link with the BPR. Similarly, the FAPU became the civilian wing of the Fuerzas Armadas de Resistencia Nacional (FARN), product of a split in the ERP. In April, 1977, the organized peasants peacefully seized large landholdings in the region of Aguilares and strikes were declared in other plantation areas, demanding a wage increase. Both types of mobilization prompted brutal reactions, particularly after the Law of Defence and Guarantee of Public Order was passed in December, 1977. As repression of popular organizations increased, support for armed insurgency increased as well. The FPL-FM had frequent clashes with ORDEN; the FARN raised substantial amounts of money through kidnapping foreign businessmen; and the ERP chose members of the security forces as its target. It had become widely accepted by the militant opposition that popular revolution was the only real alternative to military terror.[114] Two other insurgent groups emerged in the late 1970s: the Fuerzas Armadas de Liberación (FAL) and the Partido Revolucionario de los Trabajadores Centroamericanos (PRTC).

Appalled by General Romero's record of brutality and violation of human rights, U.S. President Carter gave his blessing to a coup which installed a civilian-military junta, in October, 1979. Ungo's MNR initially supported this *junta,* until became clear that the new government could not control the right-wing paramilitary forces or death squads which continued devastating and pillaging the rural areas (they killed over 3,000 peasants in 1980 alone) as well as terrorizing the working-class neighbourhoods in the cities. (These forces murdered Archbishop Oscar Arnulfo Romero in March, 1980.) In 1980, the various guerrilla groups and the popular coalitions, as well as the MNR, converged to form the Unified Revolutionary Directorate and then the Frente Democrático Revolucionario and the Frente Farabundo Martí de Liberación Nacional (FDR/FMLN). In 1982, as U.S. President Reagan stepped up military and technical aid to the Salvadorean government, the FDR/FMLN had military control over 20 per cent of the rural areas. In 1983, in spite of

---

[114] Cabarrús, *Génesis de una revolución,* pp. 281–326; North, *Bitter Grounds: Roots of Revolt in El Salvador,* pp. 77–84.

frequent clashes between different guerrilla factions, the insurgents were winning the war. They had made vast purchases of arms with ransom money; and were receiving arms, medicines and funds from Ethiopia and Vietnam (transported by Cuban and Nicaraguan aircrafts), as well as from civil associations in Western Europe, United States and Mexico. It was widely believed that the government could not stand without the help of the United States. At the end of the decade, the FDR/FMLN virtually reigned over one-third of the country, including the northern Departments bordering Honduras and the western portion of the Salvadorean Pacific coast, while vast areas of the Centre West were the theatre of endemic confrontations between rebels and government.

The leaders of the rural guerrillas of the 1960s and 1970s in Latin America had a heterogeneous social background: middle-class intellectuals, dissident members of the military, students and radical clergymen; but also people of peasant origin, as in the Colombian 'peasant republics' and the fighting groups derived from the Christian Base Communities of El Salvador and Guatemala. In Nicaragua, the spread of Christian grass-roots groups was also decisive both for the emergence of peasant leaders and for the growth of popular resistance. In the early 1970s, poet-priest Ernesto Cardenal became a symbolic figure of the new Church. At the same time, Christian Base Communities proliferated in the rural area of Zelaya under the leadership of the Capuchin Fathers, and the Jesuits created the Centre for Agrarian Education and Promotion (CEPA), which operated in the west, particularly in the departments of Carazo, Masaya and Estelí. These organizations provided a space where the Frente Sandinista de Liberación Nacional (FSLN) could meet with socially awakened rural groups. Created in 1962, the clandestine FSLN articulated an ideology combining Marxism, *foquismo,* anti-imperialist nationalism – its emblematic figure was Augusto César Sandino – and Christianity. During the 1960s and 1970s a number of both CEPA-inspired and spontaneous peasant mobilizations and land seizures took place, mainly on the Pacific coast, where the expansion of cotton plantations had led to the forceful eviction of smallholders. In order to put a brake on popular protest, increase control over the peasantry and stimulate food production, the regime implemented an agrarian reform which consisted of colonizing unsettled areas on the Atlantic Coast – a project very similar to the Venezuelan one, which also received full support from the Alliance for Progress. Although the reform permitted a re-accommodation of the rural population, land seizures continued. The trend toward export production caused a scarcity of basic grains, whilst real rural wages declined. Despite repression from the National Guard, thousands of plantation labourers joined the Asociación de Trabajadores del Campo (ATC), which was promoted throughout the late 1970s by the FSLN. In Las Segovias – Sandino's area of operation in the 1920s – the FSLN guerrillas found support among impoverished smallholders and evicted peasants who never benefited from the agrarian reform.[115]

In January 1978, after the assassination of Pedro Joaquín Chamorro, editor of the Conservative newspaper *La Prensa* and founder of the Unión Democrática de Liberación (UDEL), the Frente Amplio de Oposición (FAO) replaced the UDEL and eventually forged a strong alliance with the FSLN, aimed at overthrowing Somoza, who had lost the sympathy of the Carter administration. A wave of rural and urban strikes marked the beginning of a mass insurrection, which led to the seizure of Carazo, Chinandega and the city of León, and to the control of northwestern Nicaragua by the FSLN. To solve the problem of food supply in the liberated areas, the rebels organized the Comunas Agrícolas Sandinistas (CAS), again with the help of existing Christian popular groups. The CAS in fact constituted a structure of local and regional government and implemented a programme of land redistribution. After Somoza fell in July, 1979, following a general strike and a successful military offensive against the remains of the National Guard, the CAS were the model for a nation-wide organization of rural co-operatives.[116]

However, the Sandinista government did not attempt a total expropriation of land nor a collectivization of agriculture. The agrarian decrees of the new government in 1979–80 expropriated the holdings of the Somoza family and their immediate collaborators – which amounted to one million hectares – and created new rules for sharecropping and tenancy. The expropriated holdings formed the Area de Propiedad del Pueblo, which was reorganized into state enterprises. In July, 1982, a rather moderate Agrarian Reform Law established the distribution of abandoned terrains, as well as large landholdings which were idle or deficiently cultivated, or cultivated through sharecroppers and tenants. At the end of 1982, aproximately 6,000 rural families had received nearly 150,000 hectares.

---

[115] Woodward, *Central America,* pp. 259–62; Orlando Núñez Soto, 'Los campesinos y la política en Nicaragua', in González Casanova, *Historia política,* Vol. 2, pp. 122–6.

[116] Orlando Núñez Soto, 'Los campesinos y la política en Nicaragua', pp. 127–31; Rafael Menjívar, Sui Moy Li Kam and Virginia Portuguez, 'El movimiento campesino en Nicaragua', in Daniel Camacho and Rafael Menjívar (eds), *Movimientos populares en Centroamérica* (San José, 1985), pp. 418–20.

Four years later, the goals of the Sandinista reform concerning land alloca-
tion were virtually met: nearly 100,000 families were in possesion of two-
million hectares. The ATC became the mass organization of Sandinismo
for rural wage labourers, and the Unión Nacional de Agricultores y
Ganaderos (UNAG) was created for medium and small-scale landholders,
who could join either the CAS or an alternative co-operative organization
for credit and services. These organizations and institutions did not have
the strong clientelistic/corporatist bent of their counterparts in Mexico,
Bolivia and Venezuela; but they still provided a readily mobilized base of
support for the revolutionary regime, in so far as much of the rural
population had actually participated in, and identified with, the anti-
Somoza insurrection.[117]

Peace for Nicaragua was slow and hard to achieve. Several anti-
Sandinista groups – the *Contras,* ranging from discontented liberals to
former Somocistas – waged war against the regime, with funds openly
provided by the United States. The war ended when opposition leader
Violeta Chamorro (Pedro Joaquín's widow) won a national election in
1990, although political stability was still at stake, since the country faced
enormous economic problems. Meanwhile, a new President in El Salvador, Alfredo Cristiani, who took office in June 1989, began negotiations
with the rebels, pressured by UN Secretary General Javier Pérez de
Cuéllar. On 15 January 1991, the Chapultepec Peace Agreement was
signed by the Salvadoran government, the guerrilla representatives, and
distinguished witnesses: the UN representatives and several Latin American Presidents and ambassadors. The Agreement led to a ceasefire and to a
process of bilateral disarmament, although one of its crucial points, land
distribution to former insurgents, was left unresolved. In turn, violence in
Guatemala also seemed to be decreasing. Jorge Serrano, President since
1990, offered amnesty to political exiles and fugitives; and the army and
elite received a slap in the face when Rigoberta Menchú, a Guatemalan
Indian and human rights activist, was awarded the Nobel Prize for Peace
in 1992.

Peru

Although the Peruvian highlands was the stage for multiple peasant mobilizations in the early 1960s, a number of APRA dissidents – members of

---

[117] Rafael Menjívar, et al., 'El movimiento campesino en Nicaragua', pp. 420–35.

APRA Rebelde, which later became the Movimiento de Izquierda Revolucionaria (MIR) – adopted the doctrine of *foquismo,* carrying out guerrilla actions in the central Sierra in 1964–5. Earlier, in 1962, MIR leader and ideologist Luis de la Puente had met with Hugo Blanco, the Trotskyist leader of La Convención, without reaching an agreement. The Communist Party of Peru declared its sympathy for the guerrilla cause, but was not sure about which would be the best moment to act; and the emerging Maoist groups vehemently disapproved of MIR links with 'revisionists' and Trotskyites.[118] The only firm alliance was between MIR and the Ejército de Liberación Nacional (ELN); yet their joint actions were short-lived and ended with the defeat and killing of several prominent revolutionaries, including Luis de la Puente. De la Puente had actually chosen the rugged mountains of La Convención as his theatre of operation, but found little local sympathy, and in the end was informed on to the army by a peasant woman.[119]

Lack of support for guerrillas was related to the high expectations aroused by promises of agrarian reform from President Fernando Belaúnde, elected in 1963. However, five years later, only 2,625 families had actually received land, usually of bad quality; and the proliferating (though highly divided) rural leagues and unions were again showing signs of unrest. In October 1968 Belaúnde was deposed by a military coup which justified itself by promising social change and appealing to Peruvian pride. On this occasion the nationalist, reformist discourse of the military was really put into practice: they nationalized oil companies and agro-mining enclaves, and in June, 1969 implemented an Agrarian Reform Law. The rationale behind this law was fourfold: the modernization of 'feudal' Sierra agriculture, the recovery of foreign-owned modern plantations for the national interest, the definitive overthrow of the parasitic class of *hacendados,* and the appeasement of the rural population, increasingly discontented because of their limited opportunities to participate in the expanding market economy. In addition, the law would provide credibility to the social programme of the military, and both APRA and the left would be cut out from popular leadership.

Without exception, the Agrarian Law expropriated landholdings having more than 150 hectares of irrigated land (or the equivalent in rain-fed and pasture land). From 1969 to 1974, 175,000 families received nearly

---

[118] Gott, *Rural Guerrillas in Latin America,* pp. 448–57.
[119] Whyte, 'Rural Peru – Peasants as Activists', in D. W. Heath (ed.), *Contemporary Cultures and Societies of Latin America,* pp. 534–6.

four and a half million hectares. These figures had doubled by 1977.[120] Landholdings were not divided up but converted into formally autonomous co-operatives: Cooperativas Agrícolas de Producción (CAPS), for the coast, and Sociedades Agrícolas de Interés Social (SAIS), for the Sierra; the latter including both former *hacienda* and community land. Then years after the Agrarian Law, there were still at least 250,000 landless rural labourers: it was physically impossible to give land to everybody, and the agrarian programme had to create ways of excluding people. For instance, only full-time labourers on *haciendas* and plantations and resident members of communities affiliated to the SAIS were entitled to become members of the co-operatives; casual and seasonal workers as well as temporay sharecroppers and tenants did not change their status. Village rights over communal land were not automatically taken into account. Often, a sizable area of hacienda land was claimed by a neighbouring village; thus, old hostilities persisted, now directed against the co-operatives. Within many SAIS, hostilities were also common between *comuneros* and former *hacienda* workers. Peasants who previously had rented fields from adjoining *haciendas* were now unable to continue using those fields – unless that land had become part of the same SAIS where they were recognized as members, which often was not the case – nor were they able to rent other tracts of land from a co-operative. This had particularly harmful effects on *huacchilleros* – tenants of pasture in the highlands – who in the old times had enjoyed a relatively thriving business raising sheep.[121] In this context, the left organized leagues of landless or unsatisfied peasants, which joined together in the Confederación Campesina del Perú (CCP). These leagues seized land in poor areas such as Piura, and had frequent armed clashes with the new landholders. But for most landless people, the real alternative was to emigrate to the cities, particularly Lima, to which during the 1970s and 1980s hundreds of thousands of highlanders flocked, surviving by means of the informal economy.[122]

The main public device for social control, Sistema Nacional de Apoyo a la Movilización Social (SINAMOS), was a gigantic, institutionalized mobilization from above. Among the goals of SINAMOS, which co-opted old cadres from the APRA and even former guerrilla leaders, and whose agents

---

[120] Cynthia McClintock, *Peasant Cooperatives and Political Change in Peru* (Princeton, N.J., 1981), pp. 60–2.

[121] See Juan Martinez Alier, *Los huacchilleros del Perú* (Madrid, 1973).

[122] See Hernando de Soto, *El Otro Sendero: la revolución informal* (Lima, 1986); Eng. trans. *The Other Path* (London, 1989).

were often students and teachers, was to assist popular groups in their productive and organizational tasks. It also was to act as a corporative mediator in cases of conflict, together with the broad rural organization founded under the auspices of the military government: the Confederación Nacional Agraria (CNA), which represented the interests of those benefited by Agrarian Reform. In practice, SINAMOS sought to compete with the APRA and the left as a rallying mechanism for rural and urban labourers, although in the most isolated areas it established pragmatic alliances with the CCP in order to accelerate local organization for land redistribution. After two or three years, the authoritarian nature of SINAMOS was clear: its leaders were never elected but appointed from above, and they were accountable only to the government. It was often accused of inefficiency and corruption, or at least of extreme bureaucratization. The Peruvian military regime was not bloodily repressive; but it was intolerant: mass media were nationalized or placed under strict control, and outspoken opponents were jailed or deported from the country. Through SINAMOS, this intolerance extended from the national to the local level.[123]

After 1974, as inflation increased, international prices fell and the export economy declined, not only the CCP but even the CNA became critical of SINAMOS and the regime. Autonomous grass-roots actions proliferated, including mobilizations for services and collective forms of local security and mutual help. In many cases, the emergence of an ideology which favoured new types of solidarity, as well as social awareness and equalitarian participation, was in fact the result of practices instituted through the rural co-operatives, where members learned the importance of establishing horizontal links among themselves, and where all had the right to voice their opinions and vote in public meetings. And yet the official running of the co-operatives was after ten years almost universally rejected. Also, their economic performance had deteriorated, partly because of lack of incentives for individual productivity.[124] In 1980 the military decided to relinquish power and convoke a national election. The winner was Belaúnde, who dismantled SINAMOS but respected the structure of Agrarian Reform. Neither he nor his successor – Alan García, the

---

[123] Penny Lernoux, 'Los generales como revolucionarios', *Plural,* 39 (1974), pp. 38–43; Cynthia McClintock, *Peasant Cooperatives,* pp. 42–59; 296–313.

[124] Cynthia McClintock, *Peasant Cooperatives,* pp. 217–8, 252–5; cf. Eduardo Ballón, 'El proceso de constitución del movimiento popular peruano', in Daniel Camacho and Rafael Menjívar (eds), *Los movimientos populares en América Latina* (Mexico, D.F., 1989), pp. 328–38.

first APRA President in the history of Peru – were able to improve agricultural production or recover the trust of the rural population. Instead, they faced a new guerrilla outburst which developed into a mass insurrection and shook the foundations of the State.

Sendero Luminoso (Shining Path) is the name by which the Partido Comunista del Perú Marxista-Leninista Pensamiento Mao Tse-tung is popularly known. It was created at the Universidad Nacional San Cristóbal de Huamanga (Department of Ayacucho, in the southern Peruvian highlands), during the late 1960s to early 1970s, by a group of young lecturers at the Faculty of Education, led by Manuel Abimael Guzmán Reynoso (*nom de guérre:* comrade Gonzalo, or Chairman Gonzalo). The *Sendero* ideology combines Mariátegui's analysis of Peru as a 'feudal society' with the revolutionary strategies devised by Mao for the transformation of feudal China. In other words: since democracy cannot exist under feudalism, the defence of democratic institutions is a farse, a disguise for the ascent of Fascism. The only possibility for change is the violent overthrow of the standing order by the masses – where the peasantry, the oppressed class *par excellence,* will lead the way. Paradoxically, these ideas flourished precisely at the time when the great landed estates were being dismantled. But, according to the Sendero, agrarian reform has to be seen simply as a stratagem of the fascist state.[125]

The first cadres of the revolutionary movement were recruited among university students, and particularly among those who would become teachers of secondary schools in the rural areas. Subsequently, recruitment took place at secondary schools. The most likely converts were students whose families resided in villages with a high degree of economic diversification, where the aspirations of the young could not be met by traditional occupations, and where peasant production was often in a state of disarray. Villages of this type have sent hundreds of thousands of migrants to the cities, and also many aspiring young men and women to intermediary and higher education.[126] However, the mounting crisis in Peru has cruelly thwarted expectations of upward social mobility for these young people. Since the public sector has been the largest employer of people with educational credentials, the financial crisis of the state – expressed, for instance, in a contracting demand for bureaucrats and teachers, and in a drastic decline in real salaries – became a major source of frustration for

[125] See Henri Favre, 'Perú: Sendero Luminoso y horizontes ocultos', *Cuadernos Americanos,* 4, 4 (1987), pp. 41–8.
[126] Ibid., pp. 56–7.

the 'disposable' youth. On the other hand, the preachers of revolution also found fertile ground in at least some isolated peasant communities in the *puna,* the upper regions of the highlands. It should be remembered that under the Agrarian Reforms these peasants had received land of inferior quality – if they received any land at all. Nor had they had not benefited from state development programmes. Thus, Sendero activists were regarded by the *puna* peasants as eager young people who in addition to speaking Quechua and scrupulously fulfilling communal obligations, including religious tasks, gave voice to many of the villagers' just complaints against the government.

In May 1980, the Sendero Luminoso received publicity for the first time after they burned the electoral lists at the small village of Guschi. In the following months, a number of dynamite explosions took place in several towns, mainly in the southern highlands. From November 1980 on, the incidents became more frequent and violent: public buildings and farms were taken over or burned, bridges were demolished, electricity and water pipes were cut, and many people were killed. In the department of Ayacucho, and then in Huancavelica and Apurímac, many rural outposts of the Guardia Civil were systematically destroyed, so that members of this corps, as well as civil servants, had to flee to avoid lynching. Thus, for all practical purposes, the Peruvian state ceased to exist in vast areas of the sierra. Meanwhile, in Lima itself, multiple acts of sabotage and terrorism, including a spectacular black-out on New Year's eve – made it clear that the Sendero also had sympathizers in the capital itself. The central government reacted very slowly to the rapidly expanding movement until the end of 1982, when the Army was finally given the mission of fighting the rebels.

In spite of its quick success, the Sendero Luminoso also roused hostility and deep resentment among the populace. Its methods have remained authoritarian: to participate is to obey; the party is always right because it represents the true interests of the people; to protest is treason; traitors must be punished and even executed. In the rural areas, the 'feudal enemies' – the old *gamonales* and tax collectors – had largely vanished with the Agrarian Reform, so 'the revolution' often took the form of petty revenges and rekindled old quarrels among local families, and also among villages with ethnic or economic rivalries. In addition, the *Sendero* sought to impose a kind of autarchic agrarian economic system in the areas it controlled: it forbade peasants to attend the *ferias* (rural market places) in neighbouring towns and provincial capitals. For many villagers, this constituted a heavy blow to their welfare, since their local economies had historically been based not on subsistence agriculture but on a complex combination of production for subsistence and the market, on specialized trades and traditional manufacturing, *and* on commercial activities within a wide area. Whether such a strategy was inspired by the Khmer Rouge or by the marriage of Mariátegui and Mao, it sometimes led to violent reactions from villagers.

The Belaúnde government was unable to control the situation by force, or to devise any kind of social and economic policy which could overcome the widespread discontent. Furthermore, at the end of his mandate, Belaúnde seemed to have yielded to military pressure and allowed for an increase of repressive army raids throughout the sierra. After 1985, a new government, headed by the APRA, failed to establish a truce or any kind of negotiations with the rebels. From the late 1980s, Sendero Luminoso found a new area of operation in the upper Huallaga Valley, in eastern Peru, thanks to its alliances with peasants involved in the growing and smuggling of coca, who were violently persecuted by the army. Sendero was reportedly receiving lavish financial help from the so-called Drug Barons.

APRA was defeated in the 1990 national elections, amidst accusations of corruption and inefficiency. Alberto Fujimori, the new President, gave a renewed power to the military, who managed to capture several important *senderista* leaders, including 'Chairman Gonzalo' himself, who was jailed in September, 1992. But Sendero Luminoso remained alive and well, and continued to spread terror among civilians.

Chile

In Chile the peasantry represented only 30 per cent of the labour force. Up to the 1950s it was highly scattered over extensive, traditionally run landed estates (*fundos*), which followed a de-centralized pattern of cultivation: the land was given to tenants (*inquilinos*) who in turn delivered a part of their produce plus labour services to the landowner. Rural unions – made legal in 1937, but subject to many complex technicalities – were all but inexistent. To attract peasant votes, the banner of universal unionization and agrarian reform had been used by different national candidates since the 1920s, particularly by the Popular Front's first triumphant president, Pedro Aguirre Cerda (1938–42), and by the old nationalist *caudillo* Carlos Ibáñez del Campo (1952–8). But it was not until the administration of Christian Democrat Eduardo Frei Montalva (1964–70), that this banner was converted into an effective political blueprint. As soon as Frei took office, his agencies organized a massive campaign for unionization (a campaign supported by the Radical Party, the Socialists, and the Communists). The enthusiastic response of rural dwellers was probably related to the fact that, at least since 1955, many *fundos* in the rich Central Valley underwent a process of modernization and capitalist expansion, taking away land from *inquilinos* to expand land under direct cultivation, creating a proletarianized population, and even expelling surplus labourers from their old work places. This meant the breakdown of the old paternalistic link between labourer and boss.[127] Initially, the emerging unions fought to establish their negotiating status, to increase wages and improve working conditions as well as to protect *inquilinos* from eviction. But soon they were organizing strikes to pressure for agrarian reform because it took Frei three years to generate his own legislation and a feasible programme. Faced with such sluggishness, some militant peasant groups started seizing *latifundia*. As is shown in the case of the Central Valley *fundo* of Culiprán, studied by James Petras and Hugo Zemelman, this type of mobilization occurred under certain specific conditions. In Culiprán, the decision of the *inquilinos* and labourers to seize the land (in February, 1965) followed a series of confrontations with the landowner due to the latter's refusal to pay minimal wages and his demand of rent for the use of pasture land and draft animals (which previously were included in the tenancy contract). Through the campaigns of the political parties, and from their own literacy and access to the press, the Culiprán peasants also knew that the President was committed to the idea of land distribution; that there were government agencies (CORA: Corporación de la Reforma Agraria, and INDAP: Instituto de Desarrollo Agropecuario) in charge of planning and eventually executing such distribution; and that public opinion was generally in their favour. Thus, they refused to obey the police forces sent by the landowner to expel them. In fact, the police did not dare to use violence against the squatters. In November, 1965, the landowner himself had to leave, after the government recognized Culiprán as a pioneering *asentamiento agrario,* or settlement instituted under the Agrarian Law, with 250 peasants holding collective rights over 10,500 hectares, of which 2,500 were irrigated.[128]

The example of Culiprán was followed by labourers on more than fifty

[127] Leonardo Castillo and David Lehmann, 'Chile's Three Agrarian Reforms: the inheritors', *Bulletin of Latin American Research,* I, 2 (1982), pp. 23–5.

[128] James Petras and Hugo Zemelman, *Peasants in Revolt. A Chilean Case Study, 1965–71* (Austin, Tex., 1972), esp. pp. 14–34.

fundos between 1966 and 1969. There were also indigenous communities in the South which, supported by the emerging Peasant and Indian Federation (PCI), seized their old communal lands from *latifundia* and gained recognition as rightful owners.[129] Yet by 1970 the number of agrarian reform beneficiaries only amounted to 20,000, not the 100,000 that Frei had promised in his campaign. This despite the fact that the new legislation allowed the government to expropriate all landholdings having more than eighty 'standardized' hectares (a standard hectare being defined as a highly productive one). Not surprisingly, the PDC years were characterized by literally hundreds of local strikes, orchestrated by the growing federations of peasant unions – mainly influenced by the Left – which culminated in a national strike in May, 1970. In September, Salvador Allende, candidate of the Unidad Popular (UP) coalition formed by Socialists, Communists and Radicals, won the presidential election, and inherited a situation of virtual insurgency in the countryside.

In three years, the UP government increased the number of agrarian beneficiaries to 75,000. It also intervened in those *fundos* where quarrels between landowners and strikers had not been resolved. But at least 150,000 peasants still remained landless, and in many new *asentamientos agrarios* there were more members than the land could reasonably support. There were also mounting tensions between, on the one hand, the UP organizers who promoted collective ownership and management, as well as equal pay for all members, and on the other many beneficiaries who wanted individual ownership and management of their plots, and consequently were in favour of differential distribution of profits. Other tensions within Allende's camp were created by groups of ultra-radical students affiliated to the Movimiento de Izquierda Revolucionaria and the Federación de Estudiantes Revolucionarios, who headed dozens of wildcat land seizures in Southern Chile. Meanwhile, the demand for food increased in the cities, because of generalized wage improvement and the social welfare policies implemented by the UP; but agricultural productivity fell. Throughout 1972, to make things worse, scarcity of hard currency made it impossible to import agricultural products which had been available for more than twenty years. Credits were suspended, and an inordinate amount of rainfall, together with persisting strikes of transport

---

[129] Gerrit Huizer, *El potencial revolucionario del campesino en América Latina* (Mexico, D.F., 1973), pp. 74–91.

and commercial entrepreneurs (financed by the CIA) ensured inefficient food supply and high inflation.[130] By 1973, the UP was internally divided by acute partisan quarrels, which had repercussions in the political management of the increasingly militant rural organizations. The military putsch of September, 1973, did not meet significant resistance from the mobilized peasantry. In any case, the overthrow of the legitimate government was followed by the murder of hundreds, and the imprisonment and torture of thousands, of members of unions and *asentamientos agrarios*.

Between 1973 and 1976, the military returned to their previous owners all intervened and illegally occupied farms, as well as some 25 per cent of the land affected by agrarian reform. But they did not dismantle the agrarian reform apparatus altogether: they substituted an office of 'agrarian normalization' for CORA; and they allocated plots to supporters of the new regime – for which the beneficiaries were expected to pay – while ousting people suspected of leftist allegiances from the *asentamientos*. In accordance with General Pinochet's neo-liberal leanings, the new system favoured the emergence of privatized, economically viable family units, although co-operatives were not banned. Government subsidies for productive inputs, however, were drastically reduced, and credit rates were kept well above inflation. In these circumstances, the new farmers had scant possibilities of participating in profitable export production (fruits and vegetables), which requires high investment. Many farmers sold the plots they had received, since they were finding it very difficult to pay their debts. Although the Chilean economic elite did not recover their dominant position as quasi-feudal lords, they re-emerged in a new sector of modernized, middle-sized farms. Some of these farms were highly capitalized; others specialized in labour-intensive cultivation; but they all benefited from the heavy-handed military policies of social and political control, and they developed close ties with multinational corporations. Thus, even if the regime tried to gain a rural cliente by maintaining the principle of land distribution, in the end it lost political support – as was shown both in the 1988 plebiscite and the 1990 national election – since the real heirs of Pinochet's 'reform' had mostly been the same old privileged minority.[131]

---

[130] Jacques Chonchol, 'La reforma agraria en Chile (1964–1973)', in Antonio García (ed.), *Desarrollo agrario y la América Latina* (Mexico, D.F., 1981), esp. pp. 763–5.

[131] Castillo and Lehmann, 'Chile's Three Agrarian Reforms', pp. 37–40.

Mexico

During the period of President Echeverría (1970–6), the over-populated Mexican countryside went through a new crisis caused by the continuation of poor structural conditions (in financing, technology and marketing) and the impact of international market fluctuations on key products such as cotton, fruits and vegetables. By 1974, the country was no longer self-sufficient in basic foodstuffs, due to population increase and the channelling of investment to more profitable crops.[132] The gap between pauperized smallholders and prosperous farmers and ranchers – who were often the PRI authorities in their localities and regions – was wider than ever. The number of landless peasants – the numerous children of *ejidatarios* and smallholders who might not inherit any land – grew every year. In 1970, agrarian reform beneficiaries represented only 27 per cent of the rural labour force (against 40 per cent in 1940).[133] Meanwhile, rural unrest became a common phenomenon in all regions of Mexico; however, as in Colombia and other Latin American nations, it was characterized by extreme heterogeneity and dispersion. In the northern areas of highly capitalized agriculture, wage labourers demanded better salaries and also expropriation of disguised *latifundia*. In the centre and southeast, *ejidatarios* producing sugar-cane and sisal protested against delays in state credits and low prices for their products. In many southern states, peasants orchestrated land seizures and occupied government offices protesting against invasion of their lands, corrupt *caciques*, political manipulation, and police brutality. Marches and road blockages occurred everywhere, as a sign of discontent with lack of credits and bad marketing conditions. The army was often sent to break up mobilizations, sometimes with astonishing brutality (as when a village in Puebla was bombed with napalm). Only the mountains of Guerrero, one of the poorer areas of the country, experienced armed insurrection: the guerrilla movement led by two rural teachers, Genaro Vázquez and Lucio Cabañas, which had been totally wiped out by 1975.[134]

Worried about the state's loss of legitimacy, Echeverría attempted to rekindle the populist alliances of the Mexican state by announcing a revitalization of land distribution, an increase in public investment in the country-

---

[132] See David Barkin and Blanca Suárez, *El fin de la autosuficiencia alimentaria* (Mexico, D.F., 1985).
[133] Susan R. Walsh Sanderson, *Land Reform in Mexico, 1910–1980* (New York, 1984), pp. 90–9.
[134] Bartra, *Los herederos de Zapata*, pp. 103–11, 120–5; Orlando Ortiz, *Genaro Vázquez* (Mexico, D.F., 1974); Luis Suárez, *Lucio Cabañas, el guerrillero sin esperanza* (Mexico, D.F., 1984).

side, and the creation of new state enterprises for regional development and the promotion of specific crops. The idea of collectivist *ejidos* was resurrected by Echeverría, and his government began to put it into practice. He also visited hundreds of peasant communities (following the example of Cárdenas) and used a radical rhetoric, even manifesting his approval for land seizures in cases of extreme monopolization of land or exploitation of labourers. In 1971 new agrarian and water control legislation was passed to strengthen *ejido* property and put further restrictions on the concentration of private property (through explicitly banning the common practice of dividing up a large landholding among members of the same family).[135] In addition, the president favoured the creation of a new intermediary mass organization, the Congreso Permanente Agrario, which brought together the CNC, the non-Communist CCI, the UGOCM, and the CAM (Congreso Agrario Mexicano, a PRI-controlled organization of landless peasants) into the Pact of Ocampo (1974). Yet this organization (in contrast with the ANUC in its initial stages) was unable to co-opt most of the existing mobilized groups, for three main reasons: it did not offer a comprehensive, viable platform for the negotiation of rural demands; it was perceived as dominated by the same old clique of opportunist leaders who competed among themselves for political and economic prizes; and it was often confronted by local and regional associations which valued their autonomy and were not interested in being devoured by a large bureaucracy. It should be noted that emerging organizations on the left, such as the Communist-led Central Independiente de Obreros Agrícolas y Campesinos (CIOAC, which grew out of the Danzós's CCI), supported many mobilizations, but did not absorb local autonomous groups.

Echeverría's institutional reforms as well as his ambiguous handling of popular unrest alarmed the business community, which rallied to the defence of private landed property and the post-revolutionary political and economic dominance of the class of private farmers.[136] Echeverría agreed to create a National Consulting Agrarian Commision with representatives of government, landowners – the emerging Unión Agrícola Nacional (UNAN), and official agrarian organizations – the Pact of Ocampo. But independent peasant groups were not satisfied: in April 1976, one such group in Sonora founded the Frente Campesino Independiente (FCI) and

---

[135] Steven E. Sanderson, *Agrarian Populism and the Mexican State. The Struggle for Land in Sonora* (Berkeley, Cal., 1981), pp. 172–5.
[136] Fernando Rello, *Burguesía, campesinos y estado en México: el conflicto agrario de 1976* (Geneva, 1987), pp. 25–36.

proceeded to seize irrigated tracts of land in the Yaqui and the Mayo Valleys. Echeverría himself travelled to Sonora and condemned the invasions (which were also taking place in Sinaloa, Veracruz, Chiapas and Jalisco), but he also announced the creation of new *ejidos*. Throughout the summer of 1976, Sonora became an arena of confrontation between the UNAN and the federal government. In November, a few days before leaving office, Echeverría decreed the expropriation in Sonora of over 100,000 hectares, and of nearly 500,000 more nation-wide on his last day of office. At the same time, rural organizations – within and outside the Pact of Ocampo – seized large landholdings in Durango and Sinaloa.[137] The government seemed to be losing its grip on rural groups; even in Yucatán, a traditional CNC stronghold, the sisal-producing *ejidatarios* staged successful independent protests in demand of better pay from the official Rural Bank.[138]

Echeverría ended his *sexenio* in the midst of widespread discontent. His successor, José López Portillo, sought a reconciliation with the business sectors, paid compensation to expropriated landowners, and distanced himself from 'populist demagoguery'. With the rural popular groups, he carried out a typical policy of stick and carrot. On the one hand, López Portillo did not hesitate in sending the army to evict squatters or throwing independent leaders in jail. For all practical purposes, the Pact of Ocampo was dismantled. On the other hand, he took advantage of booming international oil prices and foreign loans to invest lavishly in the countryside and particularly to launch a vast programme of subsidies for *ejidatarios* and private smallholders with the purpose of regaining food self-sufficiency (the so-called Sistema Alimentario Mexicano). With his Ley de Fomento Agropecuario he allowed for the association of *ejidos* with private landowners in order to produce selected crops and raise livestock. In practice, this opened the door for the legal incorporation of *ejido* land into private businesses, which often implied the exclusion of *ejidatarios* from all administrative decisions.

Nevertheless, the burgeoning of independent rural groups of all sorts continued. An interesting case is that of the new Coalition of Collective Ejidos of the Yaqui and the Mayo Valleys, which broke with the CNC, refused to contribute any compensation to former landowners, and successfully negotiated with public agencies to obtain credit and technical assis-

---

[137] Sanderson, *Agrarian Populism*, pp. 191–200.
[138] Eric Villanueva, *Crisis henequenera y movimientos campesinos en Yucatán, 1966–1983* (Mexico, D.F. 1965), pp. 154–61.

tance.[139] Similarly, militant associations from all states convened in 1979–80 – without losing their independence and organic identity – to form the Coordinadora Nacional Plan de Ayala (CNPA), which held a monthly audience with the Minister of Agriculture. Other organizations clearly identified with the established Left, such as the CIOAC, also established links with numerous local mobilizations by offering legal counsel and joining their meetings and demonstrations.[140] Finally, the López Portillo years witnessed the emergence of rural unions of wage labourers, whose importance was such that the CNC attempted to develop its own version – without much success, since it did not enjoy the sympathy of the president.

By 1980, it was clear that the CNC had lost its clout as a corporatist mechanism of control. It was not through its mediation but thanks to popular pressure that land distribution had occurred in the previous decade. Because of the proliferation of government development agencies reaching from the national to the local level, rural groups could do without the CNC in their negotiations with authorities concerning credit and technical assistance.[141] Moreover, rural communities ceased to accept the legitimacy of mayors and municipal officers imposed by the CNC. To protest against such impositions, hundreds of villages mobilized in the form of marches and seizures of municipal buildings which sometimes lasted for months until the government agreed to replace the authorities with new officers. After more liberal electoral legislation was passed in 1978, many municipal mobilizations were organized by parties of the left, which brought together peasants and urban groups such as students and industrial workers, and even managed to win municipal elections. This happened in places such as Juchitán (Oaxaca), Ciudad Cuauhtémoc (Chihuahua), Alcozauca (Guerrero), and Tuxcueca (Jalisco).[142] In spite of persisting harassment and blatant electoral fraud, the political awakening of villagers and the fight against the PRI *caciques* continued into the 1990s.

Under the presidency of Miguel de la Madrid (1982–8), the Mexican government confirmed its intention of favouring private farmers, particu-

---

[139] See Gustavo Gordillo, *Campesinos al asalto del cielo: De la expropiación estatal a la apropiación campesina* (Mexico, D.F., 1988).

[140] See Luisa Paré, 'Movimiento campesino y politica agraria en México, 1976–1982', *Revista Mexicana de Sociología*, XLVI, 4 (1985): 85–111.

[141] See Clarisa Hardy, *El Estado y los campesinos: la Confederación Nacional Campesina (CNC)* (Mexico, D.F., 1984).

[142] See Adriana López Monjardín, 'Los procesos electorales como alternativa para la disdencia rural', in Jorge Zepeda Patterson (ed.), *Las sociedades rurales, hoy* (Zamora, 1988), pp. 449–64 and *La lucha por los ayuntamientos: una utopía viable* (Mexico, D.F., 1986).

larly livestock ranchers, and encouraging the association between *ejidos* and private businesses. De la Madrid, in a context of rampant economic crisis, also scrapped the policy of subsidies and let both basic agricultural products and input prices rise freely, with disastrous results for small producers.[143] Rural mobilizations continued, emphasizing de-corporatization and de-centralization, and combining diversified demands, both economic and political, under umbrella organizations such as the CNPA, the CIOAC, and the Unión Nacional de Organizaciones Campesinas Autónomas (UNORCA), created in 1985. Throughout the 1980s, new types of demands and social identities defined rural mobilizations: not only the quest for democracy, but also for gender equality, education, and the recognition of ethnic values. The importance of democratic demands was obvious when in 1988 most independent popular organizations backed the presidential candidacy of Cuauhtémoc Cárdenas – the son of Lázaro Cárdenas – against the PRI. Following his much disputed election victory, President Carlos Salinas resurrected the Permanent Agrarian Congress not as a corporatist organization but as a space for negotiation with independent groups.[144]

A note on ethnic mobilizations

During the 1970s, organizations representing Indians throughout the Americas organized a series of international conferences, despite the disapproval of their governments.[145] All these conferences insisted upon three points. First, the problem of the physical survival of the Indian groups cannot be stated as something separate from their cultural survival. In this sense, ethnocide is no less of a crime than genocide; moreover, to force a human group to part with its culture often means to condemn it to death. Second, a central aspect of Indian culture in general is the sacred value placed on the link between the Indian and the land; this link was violently broken by the Conquest and needs to be repaired, but not by development programmes imposed by non-Indian governments, but by the free action of the Indians themselves. Third, the so-called nations of Latin America are artificial entities; the real nations are the Indian ones, which should be

---

[143] See José Luis Calva, *Crisis agrícola y alimentaria en México, 1982–88* (Mexico, D.F., 1988); John Heath, 'El financiamiento del sector agropecuario en México', in Zepeda Patterson (ed.), *Las sociedades rurales, hoy*, pp. 129–42.

[144] See Neil Harvey, *The New Agrarian Movement in Mexico, 1979–1990* (London, Institute of Latin American Studies, 1990), Research Paper 23.

[145] Marie-Chantal Barre, *Ideologias indigenistas y movimientos indios*, pp. 153–60.

granted political autonomy. Class struggle, though important, is not the single key which would open the door for a new, free society; for the Indians, cultural struggle is even more important.[146]

The new Indianism (as it was called, to distinguish it from the old *indigenismo*) was not related to mass movements but to regional and local mobilizations and organizations. As we have seen, in northern Guatemala ethnic consciousness was an important element in the development of armed resistance in Indian villages to the military government. In Nicaragua, the Sandinista government was also challenged by the Miskitos of the Atlantic coast when it tried to impose a rigid system of economic, political and ideological control upon them.[147] In Colombia, the Regional Council of the Cauca Indians (CRIC), created in 1971 in the Department of Cauca, supported the ANUC in its demands for land distribution; but the CRIC also fought for the necessity of combining the recovery of the ancestral *resguardos* with a strong cultural and political programme, including research on indigenous languages and culture, the training of teachers who would introduce children to the study of their own history, the debate on legislation affecting Indian land and customs, the strengthening of local bodies of government (*cabildos*), and the creation of a body of political representation at the regional level. When the ANUC was repressed and virtually disbanded, the CRIC continued its actions through a network of cooperatives and *cabildos*.[148] During the 1980s, in spite of harassment by the army on the pretext of alliances between the M-19 and the CRIC, the Cauca Indians continued the fight for regional and cultural autonomy.

The movement known as *katarismo* in Bolivia represented an attempt at re-democratizing peasant unions while simultaneously re-creating Aymara ethnic solidarity. It was formed in the early 1970s by students of Aymara descent in La Paz and by young Aymara peasants in the highlands who had been educated in the schools founded by the MNR government. Although the movement had infiltrated the national leadership of the powerful National Federation of Peasant Workers of Bolivia (CNTCB), it did not have a centralized structure. In July 1973, the network of groups which had adopted the name *katarismo* convened in La Paz and published the famous Tiwanaku Manifesto, in which Bolivian Indians defined themselves as 'for-

---

[146] Guillermo Bonfil Batalla (ed.), *Utopía y revolución. El pensamiento político contemporáneo de los indios en América Latina* (Mexico, D.F., 1981).

[147] Marie-Chantal Barre, 'La presencia indígena en los procesos sociopolíticos contemporáneos de Centroamérica', *Cuadernos Americanos* (Nueva Epoca), III, 6 (1989): 120–46.

[148] Christian Gros, 'Una organización indígena en lucha por la tierra', in C. Bataillon et al., *Indianidad, etnocidio e indigenismo en América Latina*, pp. 235–58.

eigners in their own fatherland'. The Manifesto repudiates both the integrationist policies of the MNR governments, in which the ethnic identity of at least 60 per cent of the Bolivian population was flatly denied, and the repressive Military-Peasant Pact of Barrientos and Bánzer.[149] After the January 1974 repression and killing of mobilized peasants who protested against Bánzer's neo-liberal policies in the Cochabamba Valley, the influence of independent *katarista* leaders in peasant unions took a new strength. Meanwhile, a myriad of actions in favour of Aymara language and culture were promoted by *kataristas* in combination with non-governmental organizations. A notorious example was the publication and distribution of a biography of Tupac Katari, the emblematic hero, to a massive public, through leaflets and radio programmes produced by the Centre of Peasant Research and Promotion, an institution sponsored by the Jesuits. After 1978, *katarismo* became linked to an independent peasant movement which adopted the name of Tupac Katari; to a new hegemonic federation of peasant unions (Confederacíon Sindical Unica de Trabajadores Campesinos de Bolivia, CSUTCM); and to numerous civic associations in urban and rural areas, which became crucial factors for the triumph of a renewed MNR when stable electoral democracy returned to Bolivia in the 1980s. An important innovation in the movement was the emergence of 'Bartolina Sisa' (that was the name of Tupac Katari's wife), an organization for peasant women, which in several congresses and mobilizations demanded better treatment for Indian women, not only in the realms of work, unionization and politics, but also in the domestic realm. The *katarista* movement as a whole was not able to develop a substantial non-Aymara (that is, Qhechwa and Camba) following, and it suffered internal divisions associated with partisan and ideological affiliations. However, it was perhaps its lack of bureaucratic centralization that gave *katarismo* a flexible and multiple presence in the building of a new national consensus, after almost twenty years of military dictatorship.[150]

In Mexico, President Echeverría attempted to co-opt emerging ethnic mobilizations through the creation of intermediary bodies, or 'supreme councils', in the different Indian regions of Mexico. These bodies in fact became branches of the PRI or clientelist agencies for the Instituto

[149] Yvon LeBot, 'Extranjeros en nuestro propio país. El movimiento indígena en Bolivia durante los años 70', in Claude Bataillon et al., *Indianidad, etnocidio e indigenismo en América Latina*, pp. 222–32.

[150] See Silvia Rivera Cusicanqui, *Oprimidos pero no vencidos*, pp. 117–53; Rosario León, 'Bartolina Sisa': la organización de mujeres campesinas en Bolivia', in Elizabeth Jelin (ed.), *Ciudadanía e identidad. Las mujeres en los movimientos sociales latino-americanos* (Geneva, 1987), pp. 223–52.

Nacional Indigenista. At the same time, ethnicity reappeared as an essential component in many land-demanding mobilizations, including those in Sonora in 1976. In 1974, the Coalición Obrero Campesino Estudiantil del Istmo (COCEI) was founded in the town of Juchitán, situated on the Isthmus of Tehuantepec, Oaxaca, which had a long tradition of revolt in defence of communal land.[151] The Zapotecs, the dominat ethnic group in this region, were both rural and urban dwellers. Although fully integrated into the commercial economy of Oaxaca, they maintained their language, traditional dress, and syncretic rituals. The COCEI began as an attempt at recovering Indian land from private ranchers, but soon decided to present independent candidates for municipal elections – whose triumph was prevented by fraudulent means both in 1974 and 1977. From 1974 to 1980, however, the COCEI constructed a well-defined identity while articulating a host of demands: the return of land to the communities; electoral democracy; an end to repression against independent candidates and their supporters; defence of Zapotec culture and of the natural resources of the Isthmus; and recovery of the regional economy. Its membership included landless peasants, workers in the local rice plants, students of Zapotec descent from the local technical institute, and students and intellectuals living in the capital city of Oaxaca and in Mexico City. In 1980 the COCEI joined forces with the Communist Party in the creation of a sort of Popular Front for local elections in the state of Oaxaca. Again, the PRI was given the triumph in all municipalities. In Juchitán the fraud was so blatant that, after massive acts of protests – including the occupation of the town hall – and accusations in the national press, a new election was held, and the COCEI candidate became mayor of Juchitán.[152] From 1981 to 1984, the region became a theatre of confrontation between the COCEI and the PRI, and also a laboratory for the revival of Zapotec culture: the mayor gave speeches in Zapotec; official communications were published both in this language and in Spanish; the great *juchiteca* painter Francisco Toledo returned from Mexico City to found and direct the Institute of Art and Culture of Juchitán, where sophisticated artistic techniques were used to recover local forms and traditions; literary and historiographic texts in Zapotec were published and distributed to children. This revival was also directed at strengthening regional identity: the reference group was not the Zapotec in general (for there are Zapotecs in other places of

---

[151] John Tutino, 'Rebelión indígena en Tehuantepec', *Cuadernos Políticos,* 24 (1980); Víctor de la Cruz, 'La rebelión de los juchitecos y uno de sus líderes: Che Gómez', *Historias,* 17 (1987): 57–82.
[152] López Monjardin, *La lucha por los ayuntamientos: una utopía viable,* pp. 120–5.

Oaxaca), but the people of Juchitán. However, the wealthy Zapotec commercial class in the township felt threatened by the escalation of mobilization and COCEI radical discourse, and went back to support the PRI. In
fact, the structure of the COCEI had little room for rich merchants; it
consisted of committees of artisans and informal vendors in the town,
peasants in the villages, and workers in the local and neighbouring agro-
businesses (rice plants and sugar-cane refineries) and in the emerging oil
works near the Isthmus port of Salina Cruz.[153] It was perhaps the eruption
of industrial unrest and the serious challenge posed to the PRI unions in a
region of strategic value for the expansion of the oil economy which in
August 1984 led the government of the state, with the help of the army,
to overthrow the Juchitán municipal authorities, accused of subversion.
But the movement continued.

Both *katarismo* and the COCEI included in their rank and file students
and intellectuals for whom ethnic and regional identity had perhaps a
greater value than class affiliation, but their organizational demands can
only be understood in the context of class confrontation. The persistence
of a discourse articulated in terms of ethnic and regional values highlights
the importance of cultural mediation in the emergence of grass-roots
movements, but also the possible exhaustion of traditional class or populist parties. A similar discourse is found in the Unión de Comuneros
Emiliano Zapata (UCEZ), one of the organizations associated to the
CNPA network. The UCEZ was created in 1979 by representatives of
Indian communities and *ejidos* of western Mexico in a meeting at Tingam-
bato, Michoacán, with the explicit purpose of defending communal cultural traditions and landed property. Its main following developed from
villages of the Purhepecha (or Tarascan) region in the state of Michoacán,
where forestry businesses in the highlands, cattle ranchers in the valleys,
and tourist schemes on the shores of Lake Patzcuaro had encroached on
communal land. From its inception, the UCEZ, whose leader was a
lawyer of peasant origin, defined its role as provider of legal assistance to
communal organizations, and as organizer of mass meetings and demonstrations where people from many communities joined together in discussing and presenting their demands to government agencies. These
meetings (which often ended with the occupation of public buildings)
were supported by progressive Catholic priests and leftist political parties,

---

[153] Hélene Riviere d'Arc and Marie-France Prevot-Schapira, 'Les zapoteques, le PRI et la COCEI.
Affrontements autour des interventions de l'Etat dans l'Isthme de Tehuantepec', *Amérique Latine*,
15 (June 1983), pp. 64–71.

but the UCEZ carefully avoided identification with any religious or partisan group. From 1979 to 1983, the movement succeeded in stopping violent actions against *comuneros* and *ejidatarios,* sending murderers of Indians to jail, expelling invaders from communal land in several villages, and even forcing the resignation of the corrupt delegate of the Ministry of Agrarian Reform in Michoacán. In 1983–4, the UCEZ became known nation-wide as one of the leading members of the CNPA, and it began to provide legal help and train cadres for other organizations.[154] By 1984, however, it had developed a strong ethnic identity based on the use of purhepecha language. This probably weakened its national influence, but strengthened its regional roots. In addition, ethnic affiliation provided a strategic criterion for legitimizing access to communal resources such as arable land, water, forest and lumber mills. Even if the UCEZ has been criticized for its refusal to participate in electoral politics as an organization, its independence, pragmatic goals and cultural appeal contributed to its success and growth. The leader of the movement was accused of playing the role of a *cacique* – his personal success derived from his abilities as a cultural broker – but at the same time he respected the autonomy of grass-roots organizations at the village level and refused to convert the UCEZ into a corporatist entity. In this case, as in those of COCEI and the *katarista* organizations, ethnic pride – the positive valuation of local and regional culture – became an antidote to manipulation by external agents.

A note on mobilizations in the Brazilian Amazon

Mobilizations in the Brazilian Amazon in defence of the forest were given world coverage in 1988, when the murder of Chico Mendes, pacifist leader of the rubber tappers in the Brazilian state of Acre, raised protests from human rights and ecological associations in the United States and Europe. But the history of the struggle began with the decision of the military government twenty years earlier to colonize the Amazon, converting thousands of hectares of rain forest into farmland and cattle ranches. Throughout the 1970s, the forest was burned and cleared. This led to confrontation with existing settlers, such as the rubber tappers, whose source of livelihood was being destroyed, and the eviction and killing of Indians –

---

[154] Jorge Zepeda, 'No es lo mismo agrario que agrio, ni comuneros que comunistas, pero se parecen. La UCEZ en Michoacán', in Jaime Tamayo (ed.), *Perspectivas de los movimientos sociales en la región centro-occidente* (Guadalajara, 1986), pp. 323–78.

which the Indian National Foundation (FUNAI), the official *indigenista* institution, could do little to prevent.[155]

The official *indigenista* policies of the military government in Brazil insisted on the inevitability of Indian integration.[156] But for the Indians the opening of roads and clearing of forest in the Amazon did not mean integration: it really meant their disappearance. It was again the progressive wing of the Church which undertook the task of proposing a new type of policy for the Indians. Created in 1973 by Jesuits supported by a group of bishops, the Indigenous Mission Council (CIMI) organized meetings for Indian chiefs in 1974, 1975 and 1976; suggested reasonable development projects to FUNAI; and denounced massacres of Indians such as the killing of *bororos* by ranchers in General Carneiro, in the state of Mato Grosso in 1976.[157]

In 1975, the Catholic Church created a Pastoral Commission for the Land, which established chapters in several Amazonian towns, and certain priests felt encouraged to undertake the defence of the forest and its inhabitants. The spread of Christian Base Communities meant that people could come together and discuss their problems and possible solutions, including how to obtain judicial injunctions against invading ranchers and organize unions of harassed peasants and labourers. The Union of Rubber Tappers in Acre was a salient example of such unions. Its founder, Wilson Pinheiro, entered into conflict with both ranchers and rubber bosses, since from the latter he demanded better payment and equipment for the tappers. For this he was murdered in 1977.

Pinheiro's successor, Chico Mendes, continued the fight. With the help of several anthropologist friends he organized a national meeting of rubber tappers in 1985, and even forged an alliance between their unions and Indian groups. The unions and the Christian Base Communities, however, remained independent. With the coming of democracy to Brazil, Mendes became an active member of the socialist Workers' Party (PT). In 1987, he further attracted the attention of the media when he travelled to the United States, met with officers of the Inter-American Development Bank and the World Bank, and persuaded them to stop funding a trans-

[155] Patrick Menget, 'Reflexiones sobre el derecho y la existencia de las comunidades indígenas en Brasil', in Bataillon et al., *Indianidad, etnocidio e indigenismo en América Latina*, pp. 183–96; Shelton H. Davis, *Victims of the Miracle: development and the Indians of Brazil* (Cambridge, 1977); Darcy Ribeiro, *Fronteras indígenas de la civilización* (Mexico, D.F., 1971), pp. 108–10, 242–57.
[156] Ismarth Araujo Oliveira, 'Política indigenista brasileña', *América Indígena*, 37, 1 (1977): 41–63.
[157] Greg Urban, 'Missions and Indians in Brazil', *Cultural Survival Quarterly*, 7, 3 (1983), pp. 18–19; Margarita Zárate and Florence Rosemberg (eds), *Los indios de Brasil. Su proceso de lucha. (Documentos)* (Mexico, D.F., 1989), pp. 49–58, 79–80, 95–105, 110–7, 130–1.

Amazonian road – which would have increased the wave of destructive colonizers – and support a productive scheme of agro-forestry. Chico Mendes did not live to see its beginning: he was murdered by a right-wing association of ranchers. But his union, together with many other groups, continued the campaign to protect human rights in the Amazon and save one of the richest natural treasures in the world.

The proliferation and persistence of rural mobilizations all over Latin America, despite of the wave of authoritarianism in the 1960s and 1970s, left an important, multidimensional legacy. First, the old landed oligarchy all but disappeared as an important political and economic force in the hemisphere – except perhaps in Guatemala, Paraguay and El Salvador (and in the latter a land-distribution programme began in the mid-1980s). Even in Brazil, where land reform never took place, the power of the *coronéis* was a matter of the past. Second, it was no longer possible for a national political party or organization to ignore the demands of the rural population or to minimize the strength of peasants and organized labourers in the countryside. Third, rural popular groups gained visibility: they forged links with many areas of civil society, which allowed their voices to be heard in the national and international arenas. Even during the worst periods of repression, rural actors could not be silenced or excluded altogether, thanks to spaces created by institutions such as the Catholic Church. On the other hand, rural mobilizations had not changed the fact that, taken as a whole, the rural popular sectors, and particularly the peasantries, although highly differentiated, were still the most underprivileged sector in Latin American society. The differentiation of rural people and their alliances has meant that their causes for unrest have multiplied – hence the extreme heterogeneity of contemporary mobilizations and organizations. Such heterogeneity has not simply led to dispersion and chaos, but has also resulted in a growing desire for political pluralism and social flexibility. The debate on agrarian development has been re-opened, but there is no clear-cut answer. Although populist dogmas have not regained their appeal, technocratic certainties have been questioned by reality itself.

CONCLUSION

A central task in this chapter has been to explore the relationships between specific rural mobilizations and the wider political and economic context at different periods of time. Special attention has been paid to the alliances and contradictions between local groups of peasants and agricultural labourers of various kinds, and other political actors who operate at the national level and use or change the institutions of the state in accordance to their own particular purposes. The economic context has been taken into account in so far as political pacts or conflicts are often related to the differential capacity of rural producers to respond to opportunities for the appropriation of strategic resources, including land, capital and access to the market. A basic contention throughout this chapter was that rural grass-roots groups have not been passive recipients but active participants in the vast political and economic changes characteristic of Latin American contemporary history.

The surveying of rural mobilizations has also shown that it is misleading to characterize them by a sweeping formula such as 'resistance to modernization'. It is true that a great deal of peasant unrest has entailed rejection of the damaging effects of capital concentration: protests against eviction of sharecroppers and tenants, as in the Bolivian Cochabamba Valley and northeastern Brazil in the 1940s and 1950s or against disadvantageous conditions of trade and credit for smallholders, as in the Mexican upheavals of the 1970s. But such protests did not imply that people were refusing to participate as citizens in their respective national polities, or as individual producers and labourers in a wider economy. Moreover, a frequent grass-roots demand has been direct access to land and marketing in order to increase participation in periods of national economic expansion. The cases of southern Tolima (Colombia) in the 1940s and the Convención Valley (Peru) in the 1960s typify the struggle of the peasantry to gain control of those resources which would allow them to cultivate profitable crops and sell them without costly intermediation. Even the 'peasant republics' of the Colombian guerrillas were connected to the outside market; in fact, internal stratification arising from commercial links generated problems among their dwellers. Since 1930, the only significant experiments in economic isolation have been the Sinarquista colonies in Baja California, and the autarchic villages strictly controlled by Sendero Luminoso in highland Peru. In both cases, this forced isolation led to acute discontent.

Certain compelling symbols and myths adopted by mobilized rural groups as markers of identity – such as the legendary character of Tupac Katari, the use of indigenous languages and dress, the myth of the ancestral land – should not too readily be interpreted as signs of a 'pre-modern' mentality. The leaders of the great Indian revolts in the Andes and El Salvador before Second World War may have articulated a utopian nativist discourse; but the real issues were agrarian legislation, free commerce, local elections, discriminating taxation and military draft: all of them referred to the insertion of the Indian population into emerging modern polities. Similarly, the Indianist discourse of the last twenty years may proclaim the illegitimacy of non-Indian nations; but the relevant new ethnic movements (in Colombia, Bolivia, Mexico) point to a re-emergence of grass-roots solidarity as a tool for the construction of political and economic democracy within a wider societal context. This is not to say that ethnicity can be reduced to a sort of pragmatic stratagem in class struggle. The failure of monolithic theories of progress have forced us to re-evaluate the importance of diversified cultural identities and plural solutions to human problems. But these identities (ethnic, regional, religious, philosophical) are not passports to the fragmented past but keys to a converging future.

On the basis of the evidence presented in this chapter, it is impossible to define types of rural dwellers in terms of their proclivity for mobilization or reluctance to mobilize. We have encountered mobilized *comuneros* in the Andes, Central America and Mexico; tenants and sharecroppers in Brazil, Mexico, Colombia and Peru; squatters in Cuba; migrant labourers in Central America; smallholders in Colombia and Mexico. Differences in economic status help to explain the varying nature of the objective grievances which may lead people to manifesting their discontent. However, the variables of opportunity, explicit motivation, leadership, existing solidarity, and cultural-ideological relevance are needed not only to discern whether people would take action or not, but also to establish the specific goals, strategies and scope of such action.

A tentative periodization was adopted to help us understand certain patterned variations in the articulation of local groups to national politics. The collapse of the oligarchic republics and their highly personalized and fragmented systems of public order in the 1920s and 1930s unchained conflicts between old and new types of patrons and brokers competing for clienteles and relevance. In spite of their differences in ideology and status, *coronéis, gamonales,* agrarian *caudillos,* bandits and revolutionary *caciques* equally defined a type of mobilization 'from above', which negotiated the management of popular demands in a context of unstable state institutions. At the same time, other mobilizations with a high degree of non-manipulated grass-roots participation, such as the Indian revolts of the 1930s, lacked access to institutional or personal mediation to negotiate their demands, and often were repressed by the state or directly by the old hegemonic class. Then, from the 1930s to the 1960s, new national power groups and emerging hegemonic classes founded political parties with a gigantic double task: to strengthen the institutions of a new, centralized state, based on an all-inclusive social pact; and to incorporate the popular sectors through education, land distribution, unionization and political enfranchisement. Land distribution was the main banner mobilizing rural followers in support of populist parties which attained power in Mexico, Columbia, Guatemala, Bolivia, and later Venezuela and Chile; but only in Mexico and Venezuela did such parties manage to establish a relatively stable social pact. The bulk of rural mobilizations in this period were related to some kind of partisan politics. Even class struggle often adopted the form of conflicts between or within parties. Concomitantly, as agrarian reform and/or bureaucratic expansion undermined the power of the landowning class, rural protests became increasingly directed against the agencies of the state. The ascent of the military and the explicit use of public force instead of political negotiation throughout the 1960s and 1970s reflected the failure of populist reformism. Armed mobilizations in the countryside proliferated; in Guatemala, Nicaragua, El Salvador and later Colombia these revolts acquired national dimensions.

In the 1970s and 1980s the continuing effervescence of rural Latin America did not find a new, well-defined structure of mediation. Attempts to recover the old populist alliances between mass parties and rural groups (mainly in Colombia, Nicaragua, Peru and Mexico) failed. The economic crisis of the 1980s imposed drastic limitations which had not existed in the period 1940–60. The heterogeneity of agricultural production demanded complex policies and nuanced mechanisms of consensus. The earlier faith in centralized states, large-scale organizations and clear-cut solutions had been lost. Cuba was no longer the paradigm – but rather a painful lesson. The pertinence and modalities of agrarian reform were again open questions. The network of emerging autonomous groups which were gaining momentum in the context of a nascent democratic pluralism in the late 1980s and early 1990s faced the daunting task of designing viable paths of consensus for the future.

BIBLIOGRAPHICAL ESSAYS

I. DEMOCRACY IN LATIN AMERICA SINCE 1930

In spite of the apparently vast bibliography dealing with democracy in Latin America, there are many surprising gaps in the literature, particularly in terms of the development of truly comparable studies across countries and through time. The study of governmental and political institutions, which attracted attention especially among U.S. political scientists studying Latin America in the 1940s and 1950s, increasingly fell into disfavor through the 1960s and 1970s. This was a consequence initially of the sometimes excessive formalism of the earlier literature and of the onslaught of behavioralist perspectives (which did lead to many electoral studies); subsequently, it reflected the effects of dependency approaches which often viewed political processes as epiphenomenal, and then of the wave of military governments that swept through the region in the late 1960s and 1970s. With the transitions to civilian rule in the late 1970s and in the 1980s, and a concomitant revalorization of political democracy and of the importance of the study of institutions, there was a burgeoning literature on democracy in individual Latin American countries, as well as in a comparative perspective.

This essay focuses almost exclusively on comparative publications, apart from a selected list of constitutional works. Several of the social or corporate actors central to democracy, such as labour, the Left and the military, receive special attention in other bibliographical essays and are barely noted here. The bibliographical essays in *The Cambridge History of Latin America* vols. VII, VIII and IX provide references to the country-specific literature on such issues as the history of democracy, political parties and elections.

Constitutionalism and presidentialism

Most Latin American countries have useful compendia and analyses of their constitutions, as the study of constitutional law has a long history in the region. Although extremely useful, many of these studies do not go beyond a formal analysis of constitutional doctrines and rules. For Argentina, for example, see José Roberto Dromi, *Constitución, gobierno y control* (Buenos Aires, 1983); Arturo Enrique Sampay, *La reforma constitucional* (La Plata, 1949); Arturo Enrique Sampay (ed.), *Las constituciones de la Argentina, 1810–1972* (Buenos Aires, 1975); Germán José Bidart Campos, *Historia política y constitucional argentina* (Buenos Aires, 1976); Segundo V. Linares Quintana, *Derecho constitucional e instituciones políticas: Teoría empírica de las instituciones políticas* (Buenos Aires, 1970); and Jorge R. Vanossi, *Teoría constitucional,* 2 vols. (Buenos Aires, 1975–6). For Brazil, see *Constituições do Brasil* (Rio de Janeiro, 1976) and Odacir Soares, *A nova constituição* (Brasília, 1988). For Chile, see Alejandro Silva Bascuñán, *Tratado de derecho constitucional,* 3 vols. (Santiago, Chile, 1963), Enrique Silva Cimma, *Derecho administrativo chileno y comparado,* 2nd ed. (Santiago, Chile, 1969), and Sergio Carrasco Delgado, *Génesis y vigencia de los textos constitucionales chilenos* (Santiago, Chile, 1980). For Colombia, see Diego Uribe Vargas, *Las constituciones de Colombia: Segunda edición ampliada y actualizada, Volumen 1, 2, y 3* (Madrid, 1985), Jaime Vidal Perdomo, *La reforma constitucional de 1968 y sus alcances jurídicos* (Bogotá, 1970), and Luis Carlos Sáchica and Jaime Vidal Perdomo, *Aproximación crítica a la constitución de 1991* (Bogotá, 1991). Costa Rican constitutional sources include Marco Tulio Zeldón et al., *Digesto constitucional de Costa Rica* (San José, C.R., 1946), Marco Tulio Zeldón, *Historia constitucional de Costa Rica en el bienio, 1948–49* (San José, C.R., 1950), Oscar R. Aguilar Bulgarelli, *Evolución político-constitucional de Costa Rica: Síntesis histórica* (San José, C.R., 1976), and Mario Alberto Jiménez, *Historia constitucional de Costa Rica* (San José, C.R., 1979) and *Constitución política de la República de Costa Rica: Anotada y concordada* (San José, C.R., 1985). For Peru, see Lizardo Alzamara Silva, *Derecho constitucional general y del Perú* (Lima, 1942), Enrique Chirinos Soto, *La nueva constitución al alcance de todos* (Lima, 1979), and Moisés Tambini del Valle, *Las constituciones del Perú* (Lima, 1981). Uruguayan constitutional texts are compiled in Héctor Gros Espiell, *Las constituciones del Uruguay* (1956; 2nd ed., Madrid, 1978). And, for Venezuela, see Ernesto Wolf, *Tratado de derecho constitucional venezolano,* 2 vols. (Caracas, 1945), Esteban Agudo Ereytes et al., *Estudios sobre la constitución,*

4 vols. (Caracas, 1979), and Allan Randolph Brewer-Carías, *Instituciones políticas y constitucionales,* 2 vols. (Caracas, 1985) and *Problemas del estado de partidos* (Caracas, 1988).

Studies of comparative Latin American constitutionalism are rare. Antonio Colomer Viadel, *Introducción al constitucionalismo iberoamericano* (Madrid, 1990) provides a useful introduction to comparative Latin American constitutionalism. Jorge Mario Eastman, *Constituciones políticas comparadas de América del Sur* (Bogotá, 1991) gives a valuable comparative summary of South American constitutions in the light of the reforms of the Colombian Constitution. An impressive treatment of the constitutional and legal treatment of human rights and national security in Latin America is Hernán Montealegre, *La seguridad del estado y los derechos humanos* (Santiago, Chile, 1979).

The classic study on constitutionalism and presidentialism in Latin America is 'The balance between legislative and executive power: A study in comparative constitutional law', *The University of Chicago Law Review,* 5 (1937–8), 566–608. Another early analysis of the presidential and semi-parliamentary nature of different Latin American governments may be found in Russell H. Fitzgibbon (ed.), 'Latin America looks to the future', a special section of the *American Political Science Review,* 39 (June 1945), 481–547, especially the articles by Russell H. Fitzgibbon, 'Constitutional development in Latin America: A synthesis', 511–21, and William S. Stokes, 'Parliamentary government in Latin America', 522–35. See also Carl J. Friedrich, *Constitutional Government and Democracy: Theory and Practice in Europe and Latin America* (Boston, 1941), and W. W. Pierson (ed.), 'Pathology of democracy in Latin America: A symposium', *American Political Science Review,* 44 (March 1950), 100–49, especially the articles by Arthur P. Whitaker, 'Pathology of democracy in Latin America: A historian's point of view', 101–18; and Russell Fitzgibbon, 'A political scientist's point of view', 118–28. See also William W. Pierson and Federico G. Gil, *Governments of Latin America* (New York, 1957), Harold Davis (ed.), *Government and Politics in Latin America* (New York, 1958) and Thomas Dibacco (ed.), *Presidential Power in Latin American Politics* (New York, 1977).

The distinguished Mexican journal of constitutional law, *Boletín Mexicano de Derecho Comparado,* has published valuable articles on presidential regimes on the continent. See Salvador Valencia Carmona, 'Las tendencias contemporáneas del ejecutivo latinoamericano', 11/31–2 (1978), 133–56 and Monique Lions, 'Referéndum, la delegación del poder legislativo y la responsabilidad de los ministros en América Latina', 5/15 (1972), 463–85.

A recent comprehensive attempt to evaluate presidential regimes, with considerable attention to the Latin American cases, is Richard Moulin, *Le presidentialisme et la classification des régimes politiques* (Paris, 1978).

Interest in presidentialism in Latin America increased enormously in the late 1980s and early 1990s. Consejo para la Consolidación de la Democracia (eds.), *Presidencialismo vs. parlamentarismo: Materiales para el estudio de la reforma constitucional* (Buenos Aires, 1988) is a useful compilation of articles; one published in English in slightly revised form is Juan Linz, 'The perils of presidentialism', *Journal of Democracy*, 1 (1990), 51–69. See also Dieter Nohlen and Mario Fernández (eds.), *Presidencialismo versus parlamentarismo, América Latina* (Caracas, 1991). Juan Linz, Arturo Valenzuela and collaborators examine general issues and individual countries in Linz and Valenzuela (eds.), *The Failure of Presidentialism: The Latin American Experience* (Baltimore, 1994); see also Scott Mainwaring, 'Presidentialism in Latin America', *Latin American Research Review*, 25/2 (1990), 159–79.

There has been remarkably little comparative work on Latin American legislatures. Three edited books which include several comparative chapters on Latin American legislatures are Allan Kornberg and Lloyd Musolf (eds.), *Legislatures in Developmental Perspective* (Durham, N.C., 1970); Weston H. Agor (ed.), *Latin American Legislatures: Their Role and Influence* (New York, 1971); and Joel Smith and Lloyd D. Musolf (eds.), *Legislatures in Development: Dynamics of Change in New and Old States* (Durham, N.C., 1979). See also Steven Hughes and Kenneth Mijeski, *Legislative-Executive Policy-Making: The Cases of Chile and Costa Rica* (Beverly Hills, Calif., 1973).

Participation, parties and elections

There is currently no centralized Latin American electoral data base, or depository for Latin American public opinion polls. One useful source of political statistics is the annual *Statistical Abstract of Latin America* (Los Angeles), published since 1955. The Roper Center, University of Connecticut in Storrs, Connecticut, and the Institute for Research in the Social Sciences, University of North Carolina in Chapel Hill, North Carolina, are beginning to collect Latin American public opinion polls in a form accessible to all scholars.

Political participation has usually been studied either in a country-specific fashion or by comparing the political activities of particular groups, such as labour or the peasantry. One valuable compilation of articles is John A. Booth and Mitchell Seligson (eds.), *Political Participation in Latin America,* 2 vols. (New York, 1978–9). See also Howard Handelman, 'The political mobilization of urban squatter settlements', *Latin American Research Review,* 10 (1975), 35–72. The best sources on populism are also largely country specific. However, see Torcuato S. Di Tella, 'Populism and reform in Latin America', in Claudio Véliz (ed.), *Obstacles to Change in Latin America* (New York, 1965); Helio Jaguaribe, *Political Development: A General Theory and a Latin American Case Study* (New York, 1973); A. E. Niekerk, *Populism and Political Development in Latin America* (Rotterdam, 1974); Octavio Ianni, *A formação do estado populista na América Latina* (Rio de Janeiro, 1975; 2nd ed., São Paulo, 1989); Michael L. Conniff (ed.), *Latin American Populism in Comparative Perspective* (Albuquerque, N.Mex., 1982); and Robert H. Dix, 'Populism: Authoritarian and democratic', *Latin American Research Review,* 20/2 (1985), 29–52.

There has been extensive research on individual parties and party leaders. See the bibliographical essays for specific countries. An important volume, which includes some Latin American case studies, is Seymour Martin Lipset and Stein Rokkan (eds.), *Party Systems and Voter Alignments: Cross-National Perspectives* (New York, 1967); see especially the chapter by Lipset and Rokkan, 'Cleavage structures, party systems, and voter alignments: An introduction'. See also Giovanni Sartori, *Parties and Party Systems: A Framework for Analysis* (Cambridge, Eng., 1976). General works focused on Latin America include Robert J. Alexander, *Latin American Political Parties* (New York, 1973); Ronald McDonald, *Party Systems and Elections in Latin America* (Chicago, 1971); Jean-Pierre Bernard et al., *Guide to the Political Parties of South America* (Hammondsworth, Eng., 1973); Robert J. Alexander (ed.), *Political Parties of the Americas* (Westport, Conn., 1982); Ernest A. Duff, *Leader and Party in Latin America* (Boulder, Colo., 1985); Rolando Peredo Torres, *Partidos políticos en América Latina* (Lima, 1986); Ronald McDonald and J. Mark Ruhl, *Party Politics and Elections in Latin America* (Boulder, Colo., 1989); and Scott Mainwaring and Timothy Scully (eds.), *Building Democratic Institutions: Parties and Party Systems in Latin America* (Stanford, Calif., 1994). Extensive material on political parties and their development, particularly with regard to labour incorporation, for eight Latin American countries, may be found in Ruth Berins Collier and David Collier, *Shaping the Political Arena: Critical Junctures, the Labor Movement, and Regime Dynamics in Latin America* (Princeton, N.J., 1991). On Southern Cone parties, see Marcelo Cavarozzi and Manuel Antonio Garretón (eds.), *Muerte y resurrección: Los partidos políticos en el autoritarismo y las transiciones en el Cono Sur* (Santiago, Chile, 1989); see also, on Argentina and Chile, Karen

Remmer, *Party Competition in Argentina and Chile: Political Recruitment and Public Policy, 1890–1930* (Lincoln, Nebr., 1984). Christian Democratic parties are examined in Edward J. Williams, *Latin American Christian Democratic Parties* (Knoxville, Tenn., 1967). Changes in Central American parties are reviewed in Louis W. Goodman, William M. LeoGrande and Johanna Mendelson Forman (eds.), *Political Parties and Democracy in Central America* (Boulder, Colo., 1992).

Early comparative articles include Robert J. Alexander, 'The Latin American *Aprista* parties', *Political Quarterly,* 20 (1949), 236–47; Federico G. Gil, 'Responsible parties in Latin America', *Journal of Politics,* 15 (1953), 333–48; and Russell H. Fitzgibbon, 'The Party Potpourri in Latin America', *Western Political Quarterly,* 10 (March 1957), 3–22. Subsequent efforts to characterize Latin American parties include John D. Martz, 'Studying Latin American political parties: Dimensions past and present', *Journal of Politics,* 26 (1964), 509–31; Alan Angell, 'Party systems in Latin America', *Political Quarterly,* 37 (1966), 309–23; Robert E. Scott, 'Political parties and policy-making in Latin America', in Joseph LaPalombara and Myron Weiner (eds.), *Political Parties and Political Development* (Princeton, N.J., 1966); Peter Ranis, 'A two-dimensional typology of Latin American political parties', *Journal of Politics,* 38 (1968), 798–832; Douglas Chalmers, 'Parties and society in Latin America', *Studies in Comparative International Development,* 7 (Summer 1972), 102–28; Robert Kaufman, 'Corporatism, clientelism, and partisan conflict: A study of seven Latin American countries', in James M. Malloy (ed.), *Authoritarianism and Corporatism in Latin America* (Pittsburgh, Pa., 1977); and Mary J. R. Martz, 'Studying Latin American political parties: Dimensions past and present', *Journal of Latin American Studies,* 12 (1980), 139–67. More recent comparative articles include Liliana De Riz, 'Política y partidos: Ejercicio de análisis comparado: Argentina, Chile, Brasil y Uruguay', *Desarrollo Económico,* 25 (January 1986), 659–82; Scott Mainwaring, 'Political parties and democratization in Brazil and the Southern Cone', *Comparative Politics,* 21 (October 1988), 91–120; and Robert H. Dix, 'Cleavage structure and party systems in Latin America', *Comparative Politics,* 22 (October 1989), 23–37. Finally, see three useful bibliographies: Harry Kantor, *Latin American Political Parties: A Bibliography* (Gainesville, Fla., 1968), Alejandro Witkes Velásquez, *Bibliografía latinoamericana de política y partidos políticos* (San José, C.R., 1988), and Manuel Alcántara, Ismael Crespo and Antonia Martínez, *Procesos electorales y partidos políticos en América Latina (1980–1992): Guía bibliográfica,*

Duke- University of North Carolina Program in Latin American Studies, Working Paper no. 8 (Durham and Chapel Hill, N.C., 1993).

There is an extensive literature analysing elections in Latin American countries, although again most of it is country specific. From 1963 to 1969, the Institute for the Comparative Study of Political Systems published 'election factbooks' of varying quality analysing specific elections in Argentina, Chile, Colombia, Costa Rica and Uruguay as part of its *Election Analysis Series*. Enrique C. Ochoa, 'The rapid expansion of voter participation in Latin America: Presidential elections, 1845–1986', *Statistical Abstract of Latin America,* 25 (1987), 869–911, provides a valuable compendium of statistics on electoral turnout in the region. The most complete analysis and compilation of electoral laws, participation rates and voting results may be found in Dieter Nohlen (ed.), *Enciclopedia electoral latinoamericana y del caribe* (San José, C.R., 1993).

Beginning in the 1980s, the Centro Interamericano de Asesoría y Promoción Electoral (CAPEL), based in San José, Costa Rica, began publishing what has become a lengthy list of publications examining different features of constitutionalism, electoral laws and procedures, parties and party systems in Latin America and in specific Latin American countries. Among the general publications published by CAPEL are: Marcos Kaplan, 'Participación política, estatismo y presidencialismo en la América Latina contemporánea', *Cuadernos de CAPEL,* 1 (San José, C.R., 1985); Francisco Oliart, 'Campesinado indígena y derecho electoral en América Latina', *Cuadernos de CAPEL,* 6 (San José, C.R., 1986); Rolando Franco, 'Los sistemas electorales y su impacto político', *Cuadernos de CAPEL,* 20 (San José, C.R., 1987); Augusto Hernández Becerra et al., *Legislación electoral comparada: Colombia, México, Panamá, Venezuela y Centroamérica* (San José, C.R., 1986); Jorge Mario García Laguardia, *El régimen constitucional de los partidos políticos en América Latina* (San José, C.R., 1986); Dieter Nohlen, *La reforma electoral en América Latina: Seis contribuciones al debate* (San José, C.R., 1987); Manuel Aragón Reyes et al., *Elecciones y democracia en América Latina* (San José, C.R., 1987); and Juan Jaramillo, Marta León Roesch and Dieter Nohlen (eds.), *Poder electoral y consolidación democrática: Estudios sobre la organización electoral en América Latina* (San José, C.R., 1989). See also Jorge R. Vanossi et al., *Legislación electoral comparada: Argentina, Bolivia, Brasil, Chile, Ecuador, Paraguay, Perú y Uruguay* (Montevideo, 1988); and Gabriel Murillo Castaño and Marta María Villaveces de Ordoñez (eds.), *Conferencia interamericana sobre sistemas electorales* (Caracas, 1990).

With the transitions to democracy of the 1980s, a number of comparative studies of elections appeared, including Paul W. Drake and Eduardo Silva, (eds.), *Elections and Democratization in Latin America: 1980–1985* (San Diego, Calif., 1986) and John A. Booth and Mitchell A. Seligson (eds.), *Elections and Democracy in Central America* (Chapel Hill, N.C., 1989). Several Latin American cases are included in Myron Weiner and Ergun Ozbudun (eds.), *Comparative Elections in Developing Countries* (Durham, N.C., 1987).

Articles with a comparative focus on aspects of elections in Latin America include Ronald H. McDonald, 'Electoral fraud and regime controls in Latin America', *Western Political Quarterly,* 25 (1972), 81–93; Martin C. Needler, 'The closeness of elections in Latin America', *Latin American Research Review,* 12 (1977), 115–21; and Scott Mainwaring, 'Politicians, parties and electoral systems: Brazil in comparative perspective', *Comparative Politics,* 24 (1991), 21–43.

Theoretical perspectives

One strand of literature views Latin American presidentialism, centralism and possibilities for democracy primarily through a cultural prism. A particularly valuable exposition is Richard Morse, 'The heritage of Latin America', in Louis Hartz (ed.), *The Founding of New Societies* (New York, 1964). See also Claudio Véliz, *The Centralist Tradition of Latin America* (Princeton, N.J., 1980); Howard Wiarda, *The Continuing Struggle for Democracy in Latin America* (Boulder, Colo., 1980), and *Political and Social Change in Latin America: The Distinct Tradition* (1974; 2nd ed., Amherst, Mass., 1982; 3rd ed., Boulder, Colo., 1992); Glen Dealy, *The Public Man: An Interpretation of Latin America and Other Catholic Countries* (Amherst, Mass., 1977); and Lawrence Harrison, *Underdevelopment Is a State of Mind: The Latin American Case* (Lanham, Md., 1985).

More empirically-based studies on political culture, or in a different philosophical tradition, include Susan Tiano, 'Authoritarianism and political culture in Argentina and Chile in the mid-1960s', *Latin American Research Review,* 21 (1986), 73–98; Norbert Lechner (ed.), *Cultura política y democratización* (Santiago, Chile, 1987); and Susan C. Bourque and Kay B. Warren, 'Democracy without peace: The cultural politics of terror in Peru', *Latin American Research Review,* 24 (1989), 7–34.

Generally more optimistic interpretations regarding Latin American democracy, built around a modernization perspective, emerged in the late

1950s and 1960s. An interpretation inspired by the structural-functionalist school, may be found in George Blanksten, 'The politics of Latin America', in Gabriel Almond and James Coleman (eds.), *The Politics of Developing Areas* (Princeton, N.J., 1960). Perspectives broadly in the modernization school, combining culturalist, institutional and behavioural views, include John J. Johnson, *Political Change in Latin America: The Emergence of the Middle Sectors* (Stanford, Calif., 1958); Charles W. Anderson, *Politics and Economic Change in Latin America* (Princeton, N.J., 1967); Jacques Lambert, *Latin America: Social Structure and Political Institutions* (Berkeley, 1967); Seymour Martin Lipset and Aldo Solari (eds.), *Elites in Latin America* (New York, 1967); Harry Kantor, *Patterns of Politics and Political Systems in Latin America* (Chicago, 1969); and Kalman Silvert, *Essays in Understanding Latin America* (Philadelphia, 1977).

In the 1960s, a strong reaction to modernization, structural-functionalist and behavioural perspectives that appeared to downplay the impact of the role of the United States and of social class conflict emerged from Latin America. Views underscoring dependency, imperialism and class domination tended to dismiss political democracy as a facade, as unviable or as a possible instrument toward revolutionary socialism. Two classic, and quite different, interpretations are André Gunder Frank, *Capitalism and Underdevelopment in Latin America* (New York, 1967) and Fernando Henrique Cardoso and Enzo Faletto, *Dependency and Development in Latin America* (Berkeley, 1979), the latter first published in Portuguese and in Spanish in the 1960s. See also Theotonio Dos Santos, *Socialismo o fascismo: Dilema latinoamericano,* 2nd ed. (Santiago, Chile, 1972) and Rodolfo Stavenhagen, 'The future of Latin America: Between underdevelopment and revolution', *Latin American Perspectives,* 1 (1974), 124–49. Important collections of articles include James Petras (ed.), *Latin America: From Dependence to Revolution* (New York, 1973); James Petras and Maurice Zeitlin (eds.), *Latin America: Reform or Revolution?* (Greenwich, Conn., 1968); and Ronald H. Chilcote and Joel C. Edelstein (eds.), *Latin America: The Struggle with Dependency and Beyond* (New York, 1974).

The wave of military coups in the 1960s and the early 1970s, including among the more industrialized countries in Latin America, led to new interpretations about the difficulties of democracy in the region. The most significant was Guillermo O'Donnell, *Modernization and Bureaucratic-Authoritarianism: Studies in South American Politics* (Berkeley, 1973); its arguments were extensively and critically reviewed in David Collier (ed.), *The New Authoritarianism in Latin America* (Princeton, N.J., 1979). Non-culturalist corporatist interpretations of the problems of democracy in Latin America also appeared at this time; one of the most influential was Philippe C. Schmitter, 'Still the Century of Corporatism?', *Review of Politics*, 36/1 (1974), 85–131. A noteworthy structuralist interpretation of the reasons for variations in democratic experiences in Latin America in a comparative framework also examining European cases is Dietrich Rueschemeyer, Evelyne Huber Stephens and John D. Stephens, *Capitalist Development and Democracy* (Chicago, 1992). Goran Therborn, 'The travail of Latin American democracy', *New Left Review*, No. 113–14 (1979), 77–109, is an interesting contribution. More focused on social movements is Alain Touraine, *Actores sociales y sistemas políticos en América Latina* (Santiago, Chile, 1987). A valuable, if eclectic, interpretive framework and chapters examining the democratic record of ten Latin American countries can be found in Larry Diamond, Juan J. Linz and Seymour Martin Lipset (eds.), *Democracy in Developing Countries*, Vol. 4: *Latin America* (Boulder, Colo., 1989).

Central to many of these debates about democracy in Latin America is how to understand the role of the United States. On first the advance and then the retreat of democracy and the influence, direct and indirect, of the United States on both during the period immediately after the Second World War, see Leslie Bethell and Ian Roxborough (eds.), *Latin America between the Second World War and the Cold War, 1944–1948* (Cambridge, Eng., 1992). A skeptical view of U.S.-sponsored elections as democracy is Edward S. Herman and Frank Brodhead, *Demonstration Elections: U.S.-Staged Elections in the Dominican Republic, Vietnam, and El Salvador* (Boston, 1984). Diverging views may be found in Julio Cotler and Richard R. Fagen (eds.), *Latin America and the United States: The Changing Political Realities* (Stanford, Calif., 1974). Also useful are the articles by Howard J. Wiarda, 'Can democracy be exported? The quest for democracy in U.S.–Latin American Policy', and Guillermo O'Donnell, 'The United States, Latin America, democracy: Variations on a very old theme', both in Kevin Middlebrook and Carlos Rico (eds.), *The United States and Latin America in the 1980s: Contending Perspectives on a Decade in Crisis* (Pittsburgh, Pa., 1986), and several articles in Robert A. Pastor (ed.), *Democracy in the Americas: Stopping the Pendulum* (New York, 1989). A detailed examination of the issues of the United States and democracy in Latin America in the twentieth century may be found in Abraham F. Lowenthal (ed.), *Exporting Democracy: The United States and Latin America* (Baltimore, 1991). See also Thomas Carothers, *In the Name of Democracy: U.S. Policy Toward Latin America in the Reagan Years* (Berkeley, 1991).

Another focus of attention especially in the 1980s and early 1990s has been the relationship between economic problems and democracy. See Jonathan Hartlyn and Samuel A. Morley (eds.), *Latin American Political Economy: Financial Crisis and Political Change* (Boulder, Colo., 1986); John Sheahan, *Patterns of Development in Latin America: Poverty, Repression, and Economic Strategy* (Princeton, N.J., 1987); Barbara Stallings and Robert Kaufman (eds.), *Debt and Democracy in Latin America* (Boulder, Colo., 1989); Jeffry A. Frieden, *Debt, Development and Democracy: Modern Political Economy and Latin America, 1965–1985* (Princeton, N.J., 1991); and Stephen Haggard and Robert Kaufman (eds.), *The Politics of Economic Adjustment: International Constraints, Distributive Conflicts and the State* (Princeton, N.J., 1992).

Alongside culturalist and structuralist views of democracy in Latin America have been others emphasizing political and institutional features and processes during critical turning points. Juan Linz and Alfred Stepan (eds.), *The Breakdown of Democratic Regimes* (Baltimore, 1978) focuses on when, how and why democracies fail. See the general introduction by Juan Linz, a book-length chapter on Chile and the 1973 breakdown by Arturo Valenzuela, and chapters by other authors, some more historical-structural in interpretation, on five additional Latin American countries.

Literature that is more process-oriented and focused on questions of institutional and political choice is especially evident in the analysis of democratic transitions, particularly the wave of transitions of the late 1970s and the 1980s. An early, influential article was Dankwart Rustow, 'Transitions to democracy: Toward a dynamic model', *Comparative Politics*, 2 (1970), 337–63.

An essential source is Guillermo O'Donnell, Philippe C. Schmitter and Laurence Whitehead (eds.), *Transitions from Authoritarian Rule* (Baltimore, 1986), which includes several comparative chapters, discussion on eight Latin American countries and a lengthy concluding discussion. Samuel P. Huntington, *The Third Wave: Democratization in the Late Twentieth Century* (Norman, Okla., 1991) includes many Latin American cases. See also Enzo Faletto (ed.), *Movimientos populares y alternativas de poder en Latino-américa* (Puebla, 1980); Robert Wesson (ed.), *Democracy in Latin America: Promises and Problems* (Stanford, Calif., 1982); Archibald Ritter and David Pollack (eds.), *Latin American Prospects for the 1980s: Equity, Democracy and Development* (New York, 1983); Francisco Orrego Vicuña et al., *Transición a la democracia en América Latina* (Buenos Aires, 1985); Alain Rouquié, Bolivar Lamounier and Jorge Schvarzer (eds.), *Como renascem as democracias*

(São Paulo, 1985); Scott Mainwaring and Eduardo Viola, 'Transitions to democracy: Brazil and Argentina in the 1980s', *Journal of International Affairs,* 38 (1985), 193–219; Karen Remmer, 'Redemocratization and the impact of authoritarian rule in Latin America', *Comparative Politics,* 17 (1985), 253–75; James Malloy and Mitchell Seligson (eds.), *Authoritarians and Democrats: Regime Transition in Latin America* (Pittsburgh, Pa., 1987); Enrique Baloyra (ed.), *Comparing New Democracies: Transitions and Consolidations in Mediterranean Europe and the Southern Cone* (Boulder, Colo., 1987); 'Transición y perspectivas de la democracia en Iberoamérica', *Pensamiento Iberoamericano, Revista de Economía Política,* 14 (1988), 7–317; Dieter Nohlen and Aldo Solari (eds.), *Reforma política y consolidación democrática: Europa y América Latina* (Caracas, 1988); Edelberto Torres Rivas, *Repression and Resistance: The Struggle for Democracy in Central America* (Boulder, Colo., 1989); Carlos Barba Solano, José Luis Barros Horcasitas and Javier Hurtado (eds.), *Transiciones a la democracia en Europa y América Latina* (Mexico, D.F., 1991); Manuel Alcántara Sáez (ed.), 'Número monográfico sobre política en América Latina', *Revista de Estudios Políticos,* 74 (1991); and John Higley and Richard Gunther (eds.), *Elites and Democratic Consolidation in Latin America and Southern Europe* (Cambridge, Eng., 1992).

An effort to measure democracy in Latin America, based on the opinions of a panel of experts, was initiated by Russell H. Fitzgibbon and has been periodically updated. See Russell H. Fitzgibbon, 'Measuring democratic change in Latin America', *Journal of Politics,* 39/1 (1967), 129–66; Kenneth F. Johnson, 'Measuring the scholarly image of Latin American Democracy: 1945 to 1970', in James W. Wilkie and Kenneth Ruddle (eds.), *Methodology in Quantitative Latin American Studies* (Los Angeles, 1976); Kenneth F. Johnson, 'Scholarly images of Latin American political democracy in 1975,' *Latin American Research Review,* 11/2 (1976), 129–40; and Kenneth F. Johnson, 'The 1980 Image-Index Survey of Latin American political democracy', *Latin American Research Review,* 17/3 (1982), 193–201.

One of the most difficult challenges remains the conceptualization of political democracy and the development of typologies of democracy. An essential initial source is the work of Robert A. Dahl, *Polyarchy: Participation and Opposition* (New Haven, Conn., 1971). Many of the above-cited authors (including Linz and Stepan; O'Donnell, Schmitter and Whitehead; Diamond, Linz and Lipset; Rueschemeyer, Stephens and Stephens; Wiarda; and Johnson) have attempted to develop typologies of democracy, based on factors ranging from stability, to the extent of respect for civil liberties and political rights, to the degree of inclusiveness of the population in the democratic polity, to the degree of civilian control over the armed forces, to the extension of democracy into the social or the economic realm.

2. THE LEFT IN LATIN AMERICA SINCE C. 1920

For the early years of the communist movement in Latin America, see Robert Alexander, *Communism in Latin America* (New Brunswick, N.J., 1957) and *Trotskyism in Latin America:* (Stanford, Calif., 1973); and Rollie Poppino, *International Communism in Latin America: A History of the Movement, 1917 to 1963* (New York, 1964). For excellent collections of documents, see Stephen Clissold (ed.), *Soviet Relations with Latin America, 1918 to 1968: A Documentary Survey* (London, 1970) and Luis Aguilar (ed.), *Marxism in Latin America* (Philadelphia, 1978).

Relations between Latin America and the Comintern are treated in provocative fashion by Manuel Caballero, *Latin America and the Comintern, 1919–1943* (Cambridge, Eng., 1986). Quite outstanding is the detailed analysis of the Comintern in Central America in Rodolfo Cerdas, *La Internacional Comunista, América Latina y la revolución en Centroamérica* (San José, C.R., 1986); Eng. trans., *The Communist International in Central America, 1920–1936* (London, 1993). Two books provide comprehensive coverage of relations between Latin America and the Soviet Union; Nicola Miller, *Soviet Relations with Latin America, 1959–1987* (Cambridge, Eng., 1989), and Eusebio Mujal-Leon (ed.), *The USSR and Latin America: A Developing Relationship* (London, 1989). See also the article by Rodolfo Cerdas Cruz, 'New directions in Soviet policy towards Latin America', *Journal of Latin American Studies,* 21/1 (1989), 1–22; and Fernando Bustamante, 'Soviet foreign policy toward Latin America', *Journal of Inter-American Studies and World Affairs,* 32/4 (1990), 35–65. Cole Blasier examines Soviet perceptions of Latin America in *The Giant's Rival: The USSR and Latin America* (Pittsburgh, Pa., 1983). See also J. G. Oswald (ed.), *The Soviet Image of Contemporary Latin America: A Documentary History 1960–1968* (Austin, Tex., 1970); William E. Ratliff, *Castroism and Communism in Latin America, 1959–1976* (Washington, D.C., 1976); Augusto Varas (ed.), *Soviet–Latin America Relations in the 1980s* (Boulder, Colo., 1986); and Robert Leiken, *Soviet Strategy in Latin America* (Washington, D.C., 1982). For the activities of the Socialist International in Latin America, see Felicity Williams, *La Internacional Socialista y América Latina* (Mexico, D.F., 1984).

The polemic between Mariátegui and the Comintern was the first of many debates between orthodoxy and 'heresy' in the world of Latin American communism. On this debate, see Alberto Flores Galindo, *La agonía de Mariátegui: La polémica con la Komintern* (Lima, 1980); Carlos Franco, *Del Marxismo eurocéntrico al Marxismo latinoamericano* (Lima, 1981); Harry Vanden, 'Mariátegui, Marxismo, Comunismo and other bibliographical notes', *Latin American Research Review*, 14/3 (1979), 61–86 and *National Marxism in Latin America: José Carlos Mariátegui's Thought and Politics* (Boulder, Colo., 1986); and Ricardo Martínez de la Torre, *Apuntes para una interpretación Marxista de la historia social del Perú* (Lima, 1947). Mariátegui's best-known book is *Seven Intrepretive Essays on Peruvian Reality* (1928; Eng. trans., Austin, Tex., 1971).

Discussions of the importance of Marxism as an ideology in Latin America are rather few and disappointing. There are exceptions, however, notably in the writing of José Aricó: see *Marx y América Latina* (Lima, 1980); and 'El Marxismo en América Latina', in Fernando Calderón (ed.), *Socialismo, autoritarismo y democracia* (Lima, 1989). Another acute observer is Tomás Moulián, *Democracia y socialismo en Chile* (Santiago, Chile, 1983). An excellent and detailed exposition of Marxist ideas on underdevelopment is Gabriel Palma, 'Dependency: A formal theory of underdevelopment or a methodology for the analysis of concrete situations of underdevelopment', *World Development*, 6/7–8 (1978), 881–924. Sheldon Liss, *Marxist Thought in Latin America* (Berkeley, 1984) is detailed but rather uncritical. A useful anthology is Michael Lowy (ed.), *El Marxismo en América Latina de 1909 a neustras días* (Mexico, D.F., 1982), Eng. trans., *Marxism in Latin America from 1909 to the Present* (London, 1992). An attempt to rescue the Marxist tradition for the contemporary Latin American Left is Richard Harris, *Marxism, Socialism and Democracy in Latin America* (Boulder, Colo., 1992). See also the articles contained in NACLA Report, *The Latin American Left: A Painful Rebirth*, 25/5 (1992).

Although not directly concerned with Marxism, there is interesting discussion of the relationship between the Left and culture in Jean Franco, *The Modern Culture of Latin America: Society and the Artist* (London, 1967), and in her book on the Peruvian poet, *César Vallejo: The Dialectics of Poetry and Silence* (Cambridge, Eng., 1976). Gerald Martin, *Journeys Through the Labyrinth: Latin American Fiction in the Twentieth Century* (London, 1989), amongst its many other qualities, explores the political commitment of Latin American writers. One of the few specific studies to take ideas and ideologies seriously, odd though some of those ideas were, is Donald

Hodges, *Intellectual Foundations of the Nicaraguan Revolution* (Austin, Tex., 1986). The ideological and political significance of the Spanish Civil War for the countries of Latin America is well treated in Mark Falcoff and Fredrick Pike (eds.), *The Spanish Civil War: American Hemispheric Perspectives* (Lincoln, Nebr., 1982). For the important period following the Second World War, see Leslie Bethell and Ian Roxborough (eds.), *Latin America between the Second World War and the Cold War, 1944–1948* (Cambridge, Eng., 1992).

There are relatively few memoirs by Marxists, or former Marxists, and they are not always reliable. But well worth reading for Chile are Elías Lafertte, *Vida de un comunista* (Santiago, Chile, 1961); Pablo Neruda, *Confieso que he vivido: Memorias* (Barcelona, 1983); and the ex-Comintern agent turned militant anti-communist, Eudocio Ravines, *The Yenan Way* (New York, 1951). For Mexico, see Valentín Campa, *Mi testimonio: Experiencias de un comunista mexicano* (Mexico, D.F., 1978). Quite outstanding is Roque Dalton's recounting of the life of the veteran Salvadorean communist, available in English translation, *Miguel Marmol* (Willimantic, Conn., 1986). On another leading Salvadorean figure, see Jorge Arias Gómez, *Farabundo Martí: Esbozo biográfico* (San José, C.R., 1972). For Argentina, see José Peter, *Historia y luchas de los obreros del carne* (Buenos Aires, 1947), and *Crónicas proletarias* (Buenos Aires, 1968). For the memoirs of a leading Comintern agent who was active in Mexico, see M. N. Roy, *Memoirs* (Bombay, 1964). And for the memoirs of a labour activist from the opposite side of the political spectrum, see Serafino Romualdi, *Presidents and Peons: Recollections of a Labor Ambassador in Latin America* (New York, 1967).

On Chinese communism in Latin America after the Sino–Soviet split, see Cecil Johnson, *Communist China and Latin America, 1959–1967* (New York, 1970) and 'China and Latin America: New ties and tactics', *Problems of Communism,* 21/4 (1972); J. L. Lee, 'Communist China's Latin America policy', *Asian Survey* (November 1964); Alain Joxe, *El conflicto chino–soviético en América Latina* (Montevideo, 1967); and Alan Angell, 'Classroom Maoists: The Politics of Peruvian schoolteachers under military government', *Bulletin of Latin American Research,* 1/2 (1982), 1–20. See also Ernst Halperin, 'Peking and the Latin American Communists', *China Quarterly* (January 1967).

The guerrilla movements that sprang up following the Cuban Revolution are discussed in great, if uncritical, detail in Richard Gott, *Rural Guerrillas in Latin America* (London, 1973). The strategy of such movements derived from Regis Debray's influential if partial account of the success of the Cuban Revolution in *Revolution in the Revolution?* (London, 1968). Debray later wrote, in two volumes, *A Critique of Arms* (London, 1977 and 1978), which sets out his revised theories and includes case studies of guerrillas in Venezuela, Guatemala and Uruguay. Very revealing of the problems facing rural guerrilla movements are the diaries of Che Guevara in Bolivia, edited by Daniel James, *The Complete Bolivian Diaries and Other Captured Documents* (London, 1968). See also I. L. Horowitz, *Latin American Radicalism: A Documentary Report on Left and Nationalist Movements* (London, 1969). A more recent account of the revolutionary Left is Ronaldo Munck, *Revolutionary Trends in Latin America,* Monograph Series no. 17, Centre for Developing Area Studies, McGill University (Montreal, 1984). See also the perceptive article by Steve Ellner, 'The Latin American Left since Allende: Perspectives and new directions', *Latin American Research Review,* 24/2 (1989), 143–167.

The literature on the Cuban Revolution is huge. Amongst the works which look at the Cuban Revolution in comparative or theoretical perspective are James O'Connor, *The Origins of Socialism in Cuba* (Ithaca, N.Y., 1970); K. S. Karol, *Guerrillas in Power* (New York, 1970); D. Bruce Jackson, *Castro, the Kremlin and Communism in Latin America* (Baltimore, 1969); Andrés Suárez, *Cuba, Castro and Communism, 1959–1966* (Cambridge, Mass., 1967); Bertram Silverman (ed.), *Man and Socialism in Cuba* (New York, 1972); Jorge Domínguez, *Cuba: Order and Revolution* (Cambridge, Mass., 1978). Marxism in Cuba before Castro is described in Sheldon Liss, *Roots of Revolution: Radical Thought in Cuba* (Lincoln, Nebr., 1987). On the pre-Castro Communist party, see Harold Sims, 'Cuban labor and the Communist Party, 1937–1958', *Cuban Studies,* 15/1 (1985); and Antonio Avila and Jorge García Montes, *Historia del Partido Comunista de Cuba* (Miami, 1970). Maurice Zeitlin, *Revolutionary Politics and the Cuban Working Class* (New York, 1967) explores the political ideas of ordinary Cubans.

The literature on left-wing movements in individual countries varies greatly in quality. In general, too much is written by passionate supporters or by no less passionate opponents.

Argentina

An unusually scholarly treatment of the urban guerrilla in Argentina is Richard Gillespie, *Soldiers of Perón: Argentina's Montoneros* (Oxford, 1982);

but see the review article of the book by Celia Szusterman, in *Journal of Latin American Studies*, 16/1 (1984), 157–70. Relations between Argentina and the USSR are well treated in Mario Rapoport, 'Argentina and the Soviet Union: History of political and commercial relations, 1917–1955', *Hispanic American Historical Review*, 66/2 (1986), 239–85; and in Aldo Vacs, *Discrete Partners: Argentina and the USSR* (Pittsburgh, Pa., 1984).

For the politics of the Left in Argentina in the inter-war period, see Horoschi Matsushita, *El movimiento obrero argentino, 1930–1945* (Buenos Aires, 1983); and David Tamarin, *The Argentine Labor Movement, 1930–1945: A Study in the Origins of Peronism* (Albuquerque, N.Mex., 1985). Also useful on the labour movement is Samuel L. Baily, *Labor, Nationalism and Politics in Argentina* (New Brunswick, N.J., 1967); and Ronaldo Munck, *Argentina from Anarchism to Peronism* (London, 1987). The best assessment of the way that Peronism captured the support of the Argentine working class is Daniel James, *Resistance and Integration: Peronism and the Argentine Working Class, 1946–1976* (Cambridge, Eng., 1988). A savage attack on the Argentine Communist Party is Jorge Abelardo Ramos, *Historia del estalinismo en Argentina* (Buenos Aires, 1969). A more recent study is Ricardo Falcón and Hugo Quiroga, *Contribución al estudio de la evolución ideológica del Partido Comunista Argentino* (Buenos Aires, 1984). For the official account of the Communist party's relations with Peronism, see Oscar Arévalo, *El Partido Comunista* (Buenos Aires, 1983). For a Left Peronist view, see Rodolfo Puiggrós, *Las Izquierdas y el problema nacional* (Buenos Aires, 1973). On the Socialist Party, see Richard J. Walter, *The Socialist Party of Argentina, 1890–1930* (Austin, Tex., 1977). For Trotskyism, see Osvaldo Coggiola, *El Trotskismo en la Argentina, 1960–1985*, 2 vols. (Buenos Aires, 1986).

Brazil

There are several good studies of the Brazilian Left. For the early years, see Astrojildo Pereira, *Formação do PCB* (Rio de Janeiro, 1962); John W. F. Dulles, *Anarchists and Communists in Brazil, 1900–1935* (Austin, Tex., 1973); and Sheldon Maram, 'Labor and the Left in Brazil, 1890–1921', *Hispanic American Historical Review*, 57/2 (1977), 259–72. For a careful and critical examination of a longer period, see Ronald Chilcote, *The Brazilian Communist Party; Conflict and Integration 1922–1972* (New York, 1974). On the Communist party see also Leôncio Martins Rodrigues, 'O PCB: Os Dirigentes e a organização', in Boris Fausto (ed.), *História geral da civilização brasileira,* vol. 10 (São Paulo, 1981). The problems facing the Brazilian Left in trying to cope with the important post–Second World War conjuncture is well illustrated in Leslie Bethell's contribution in Leslie Bethell and Ian Roxborough (eds.), *Latin America between the Second World War and the Cold War, 1944–1948* (Cambridge, Eng., 1992); and John French, 'Workers and the rise of Adhemarista populism in São Paulo, Brazil 1945–1947', *Hispanic American Historical Review,* 68/1 (1988), 1–43. For the way that the Brazilian state controlled labour, see Kenneth P. Erickson, *The Brazilian Corporate State and Working Class Politics* (Berkeley, 1977). See also John W. F. Dulles, *Brazilian Communism 1935–1945: Repression during World Upheaval* (Austin, Tex., 1983). An advocate of armed struggle is João Quartim, *Dictatorship and Armed Struggle in Brazil* (London, 1971); and a participant, later killed in a confrontation with the army, is Carlos Marighela, *For the Liberation of Brazil* (London, 1971). See also Jacob Gorender, *Combate nas trevas: A Esquerda brasileira; das ilusões perdidas à luta armada* (São Paulo, 1987). On the Partido dos Trabalhadores, see Rachel Menegnello, *PT: A Formação de un partido, 1979–1982* (São Paulo, 1989), and Leôncio Martins Rodrigues, *Partidos e sindicatos* (São Paulo, 1990). Two recent studies of the Partido dos Trabalhadores are Emir Sader and Ken Silverstein, *Without Fear of Being Happy: Lula, the Workers Party and Brazil* (London, 1991); and the outstanding book by Margaret Keck, *The Workers Party and Democratization in Brazil* (New Haven, Conn., 1992).

Chile

The Chilean Left has received considerable attention, reflecting its importance in the politics of the country. An excellent overall interpretation is Julio Faúndez, *Marxism and Democracy in Chile: From 1932 to the Fall of Allende* (New Haven, Conn., and London, 1988). The pioneer of labour studies in Chile wrote extensively on the politics of the union movement: See Jorge Barría, *Trayectoria y estructura del movimiento sindical chileno* (Santiago, Chile, 1963), and the *Historia de la CUT* (Santiago, Chile., 1971). Relations between the parties of the Left and the unions is also discussed in Alan Angell, *Politics and the Labour Movement in Chile* (Oxford, 1972). A brilliant account of a worker seizure of a factory under the Allende government is Peter Winn, *Weavers of Revolution: The Yarur Workers and Chile's Road to Socialism* (New York, 1986).

Hernán Ramírez Necochea gives the official PC interpretation in his influential *Orígen y formación del Partido Comunista de Chile* (Santiago, Chile, 1965). An excellent unpublished doctoral thesis is Andrew Barnard, 'The Chilean Communist Party, 1922–1947' (unpublished Ph.D. thesis, University of London 1977). More recent studies include Carmelo Furci, *The Chilean Communist Party and the Road to Socialism* (London, 1984); Eduardo Godard Labarca, *Corvalán, 27 horas* (Santiago, Chile, 1973); and Augusto Varas (ed.), *El Partido Comunista en Chile* (Santiago, Chile, 1988). Ernst Halperin deals with relations between the Socialists and Communists in *Nationalism and Communism in Chile* (Cambridge, Mass., 1965). On the Socialists, see Julio César Jobet, *El Partido Socialista de Chile,* 2 vols. (Santiago, Chile, 1971); Fernando Casanueva and Manuel Fernández, *El Partido Socialista y la lucha de clases en Chile* (Santiago, Chile, 1973); and Benny Pollack and Hernán Rosenkranz, *Revolutionary Social Democracy: The Chilean Socialist Party* (London, 1986). Three books develop Socialist rethinking in Chile: Jorge Arrate, *La fuerza democrática de la idea socialista* (Santiago, Chile, 1987) and edited by the same author, *La renovación socialista* (Santiago, Chile, 1987); and Ricardo Lagos, *Democracia para Chile: Proposiciones de un socialista* (Santiago, Chile, 1986). The most thorough account of the development of the Socialist party is Paul Drake, *Socialism and Populism in Chile, 1932–1952* (Urbana, Ill., 1978). A stimulating more recent account is Ignacio Walker, *Socialismo y democracia: Chile y Europa en perspectiva comparada* (Santiago, Chile, 1990).

There is a huge literature on the Allende government. For accounts relevant to this chapter, see Eduardo Labarca Godard, *Chile al rojo* (Santiago, Chile, 1971), which gives a fascinating account of the origins of the government. For a good review of the literature see Lois Hecht Oppenheim, 'The Chilean road to socialism revisited', *Latin American Research Review,* 24/1 (1989), 155–83. Allende's ideas are explored in Regis Debray, *Conversations with Allende* (London, 1971). An interesting account by an aide of the president is Joan Garcés, *Allende y la experiencia chilena* (Barcelona, 1976). The best account of the political economy of the period is Sergio Bitar, *Transición, socialismo y democracia: La experiencia chilena* (Mexico, D.F., 1979), translated as *Chile: Experiment in Democracy* (Philadelphia, 1986). Relations with the Soviet Union are well treated in Isabel Turrent, *La Unión Soviética en América Latina: El caso de la Unidad Popular Chilena* (Mexico, D.F., 1984).

Uruguay

For the history of communism in Uruguay, see Eugenio Gómez, *Historia del Partido Comunista del Uruguay* (Montevideo, 1961). For the trade union movement, see Francisco Pinto, *Historia del movimiento obrero del Uruguay* (Montevideo, 1960); and Héctor Rodríguez, *Nuestros sindicatos, 1865–1965* (Montevideo, 1965). For the armed struggle in Uruguay, see the overly sympathetic account of Alain Labrousse, *The Tupamaros* (London, 1973).

Bolivia

The basic text on the Bolivian Left is the work by the Trotskyist historian and activist, Guillermo Lora, accessible in an English translation by Christine Whitehead and edited by Laurence Whitehead, *A History of the Bolivian Labour Movement* (Cambridge, Eng., 1977). A rather different book is by a USAID official, John Magill, *Labor Unions and Political Socialization: A Case Study of the Bolivian Workers* (New York, 1974). A detailed examination of the problems of the contemporary Left in Bolivia is James Dunkerley, *Rebellion in the Veins: Political Struggle in Bolivia* (London, 1984). The electoral behaviour of the most radical sector of the work force is examined in Laurence Whitehead, 'Miners as voters: The electoral process in Bolivia's mining camps', *Journal of Latin American Studies,* 13/2 (1981), 313–46.

Colombia

The official version of Colombian modern history as seen by that country's Communist party is *Treinta años de lucha del Partido Comunista de Colombia* (Bogotá, 1960). The party's views of the union movement are expressed in Edgar Caicedo, *Historia de las luchas sindicales en Colombia* (Bogotá, 1977). A Marxist account of popular struggles is Manuel Moncayo and Fernando Rojas, *Luchas obreras y política laboral en Colombia* (Bogotá, 1978). Two important works on labour from a different perspective are Miguel Urrutia, *Development of the Colombian Labor Movement* (New Haven, Conn., 1969) and Daniel Pecaut, *Política y sindicalismo en Colombia* (Bogotá, 1973). A classic account by a communist activist in the 1920s and 30s is Ignacio Torres Giraldo, *Los Inconformes* (Bogotá, 1978). For the early period, see also Gonzalo Sánchez, *Los 'Bolcheviques' de El Líbano* (Bogotá,

1976). On Gaitán, see Herbert Braun, *The Assassination of Gaitán: Public Life and Urban Violence in Colombia* (Madison, Wis., 1985). On violence, see Paul Oquist, *Violence, Conflict and Politics in Colombia* (New York, 1980).

Peru

A good article on the Peruvian Left is Evelyne Huber Stephens, 'The Peruvian military government, labor mobilization, and the political strength of the Left', *Latin American Research Review,* 18/2 (1983), 57–93. See also Jorge Nieto, *Izquierda y democracia en el Perú, 1975–1980* (Lima, 1983), and Guillermo Rochabrún, 'Crisis, democracy and the Left in Peru', *Latin American Perspectives,* 15/3 (1988), 77–96. An excellent article on the guerrilla is Leon Campbell, 'The historiography of the Peruvian guerrilla movement, 1960–1963', *Latin American Research Review,* 8/1 (1973), 45–70; and for an account by a participant see Héctor Béjar, *Perú 1965: Apuntes sobre una experiencia guerrillera* (Lima, 1969). The Trotskyist union organiser gives his version of the peasant struggle in Hugo Blanco, *Land or Death: The Peasant Struggle in Peru* (New York, 1972); and on Hugo Blanco, see Tom Brass, 'Trotskyism, Hugo Blanco and the ideology of a Peruvian peasant movement', *Journal of Peasant Studies,* 16/2 (1989), 173–97. The secretary-general of the Communist party, Jorge del Prado, has written 40 *años de lucha* (Lima, 1968). On Sendero Luminoso, see Gustavo Gorriti, *Sendero: Historia de la Guerra Milenaria en el Perú* (Lima, 1990); and Cynthia McClintock, 'Peru's Sendero Luminoso rebellion: Origins and trajectory', in Susan Eckstein (ed.), *Power and Popular Protest,* (Berkeley, 1989); and Carlos Iván Degregori, *Ayacucho 1969–1979: El surgimiento de Sendero Luminoso* (Lima, 1990).

Venezuela

On Venezuela, Rómulo Betancourt, *Venezuela, política y petróleo* (Mexico, D.F., 1956) is a basic source for many aspects of the politics of that country. See also the biography by Robert Alexander, *Rómulo Betancourt and the Transformation of Venezuela* (New Brunswick, N.J., 1982). A communist activist gives his account in Juan Bautista Fuenmayor, *Veinte años de historia* (Caracas, 1980). For the early period of the communist movement, see Manuel Caballero, *Entre Gómez y Stalin* (Caracas, 1989). For the struggle between Acción Democrática and the Communist party in the unions, see Steve Ellner, *Los partidos políticos y su disputa por el control del movimiento sindical en Venezuela, 1936–1948* (Caracas, 1980); and, by the same author, 'The Venezuelan Left in the era of the Popular Front', *Journal of Latin American Studies,* 11/1 (1979); Héctor Lucena, *El movimiento obrero y las relaciones laborales* (Carabobo, 1981); and Alberto Pla et al., *Clase obrera, partidos y sindicatos en Venezuela, 1936–1950* (Caracas, 1982). An account of the guerrilla experience by a disillusioned participant is Angela Zago, *Aquí no ha pasado nada* (Caracas, 1972). An outstanding study of the Venezuelan Left in more recent years is Steve Ellner, *Venezuela's Movimiento al Socialismo: From Guerrilla Defeat to Innovative Politics* (Durham, N.C., 1988). A leading member of the new Left, Teodoro Petkoff, has written *Socialismo para Venezuela?* (Caracas, 1970), *Razón y pasión del socialismo* (Caracas, 1973) and *Del optimismo de la voluntad: Escritos políticos* (Caracas, 1987).

Mexico

The major work on the Mexican Left is Barry Carr, *Marxism and Communism in Twentieth-Century Mexico* (Lincoln, Nebr., 1992). An excellent set of essays on Mexico, covering the whole period, is Arnoldo Martínez Verdugo (ed.), *Historia del comunismo en México* (Mexico, D.F., 1983). The early years of the Mexican Left are thoroughly examined in Barry Carr, *El movimiento obrero y la política en México, 1910–1929* (Mexico, D.F., 1981); and see also Arnaldo Córdoba, *La clase obrera en la historia de México;* Vol. 9: *En una época de crisis, 1928–1934* (Mexico, D.F., 1980) and Manuel Márquez Fuentes and Octavio Rodríguez Araujo, *El Partido Comunista Mexicano, 1919–1943* (Mexico, D.F., 1973). For the crucial Cárdenas years, see Samuel León and Ignacio Marván, *La clase obrera en la historia de México: En el Cardenismo 1934–1940* (Mexico, D.F., 1985), and Arturo Anguiano, Guadalupe Pacheco and Rogelio Viscaino, *Cárdenas y la izquierda mexicana* (Mexico, D.F., 1975). The influential artist and leading Communist party member David Alfaro Siqueiros has written his memoirs, *Me llamaban el coronelazo* (Mexico, D.F., 1977). A good account of the early Left is Gaston García Cantú, *El socialismo en México* (Mexico, D.F., 1969). There is no satisfactory biography of the influential Lombardo Toledano; see, however, R. Millon, *Mexican Marxist: Vicente Lombardo Toledano* (Chapel Hill, N.C., 1966). Karl Schmitt, *Communism in Mexico* (Austin, Tex., 1965) has some useful information. Barry Carr, 'Mexican Communism, 1968–1981: Euro–Communism in the Americas?' *Journal of Latin American Studies,* 17/1 (1985), 201–28, is an important article. Middle class fears of Marxism are well described in Soledad Loaeza, *Clases medias y política en México* (Mexico, D.F., 1988). For the recent period see Barry Carr and Ricardo Anzaldua Montoya (eds.), *The Mexican Left, the Popular Movements, and the Politics of Austerity* (San Diego, Calif., 1986); and also by Barry Carr, 'The creation of the Mexican Socialist Party', *Journal of Communist Studies*, 4/3 (1988).

Central America

A superb study of Central America with many insights for the successes and the failures of the Left in that region is James Dunkerley, *Power in the Isthmus: A Political History of Modern Central America* (London, 1988); see also Robert Wesson (ed.), *Communism in Central America and the Caribbean* (Stanford, Calif., 1982). A good review essay is John Booth, 'Socioeconomic and political roots of national revolts in Central America', *Latin American Research Review*, 26/1 (1991), 33–74. For European Socialist interest in Latin America, see Eusebio Mujal León, *European Socialism and the Crisis in Central America* (Washington, D.C., 1989).

On the tragic events of 1932 in El Salvador, see Thomas Anderson, *Matanza: El Salvador's Communist Revolt of 1932* (Lincoln, Nebr., 1971) and Vinicio González, 'La insurreción salvadoreña de 1932 y la gran huelga hondureña de 1954', *Revista Mexicana de Sociología*, 40/2 (1978). On El Salvador, see also Tommie Sue Montgomery, *Revolution in El Salvador* (Boulder, Colo., 1982); Enrique Baloyra, *El Salvador in Transition* (Chapel Hill, N.C., 1982); James Dunkerley, *The Long War: Dictatorship and Revolution in El Salvador* (London, 1982); and Jenny Pearce, *Promised Land; Peasant Rebellion in Chalatenango, El Salvador* (London, 1986), an account sympathetic to the guerrillas. On Honduras, see Victor Meza, *Historia del movimiento obrero hondureño* (Tegucigalpa, 1980), and Mario Posas, *Lucha ideológica y organización sindical en Honduras* (Tegucigalpa, 1980).

The standard biography of Sandino in Nicaragua is Neill Macaulay, *The Sandino Affair* (Chicago, 1967); see also Gregorio Selser, *Sandino: General de hombres libres* (Buenos Aires, 1959); and Sergio Ramírez, *El pensamiento vivo de Sandino* (San José, C.R., 1974). An official view of the Sandinista movement is Humberto Ortega, *50 años de lucha sandinista* (Managua, 1979). Of the huge number of accounts of the revolution, the book by George Black is useful for its concentration on ideological aspects, *Triumph of the People: The Sandinista Revolution in Nicaragua* (London, 1981). On Costa Rica, the important civil war of 1948 is examined in John P. Bell, *Crisis in Costa Rica: The 1948 Revolution* (Austin, Tex., 1971). See also Gilberto Calvo and Francisco Zuñigo (eds.), *Manuel Mora: Discursos 1934–1979* (San José, C.R., 1980). Though written from a decidedly Cold War standpoint, there is a great deal of useful information in Ronald Schneider, *Communism in Guatemala 1944–1954* (New York, 1958). A rather distinct view is offered in Eduardo Galeano, *Guatemala: Occupied Country* (New York, 1969).

3. THE MILITARY IN LATIN AMERICAN POLITICS SINCE 1930*

Few political institutions or social groups in Latin America have attracted as much sustained scholarly interest as the military. The corpus of academic literature consists mainly of studies of institutional, behavioural and cultural aspects of the armed forces as political actors. To a lesser extent, the corpus also contains institutional military histories as well as sociological studies of the military organizations as social groups.

The focus of this bibliographical essay is primarily on academic literature dealing with the domestic political role of Latin American military establishments. Conventional military histories that deal with the military institutions exclusively in their military personae – the Chaco War, the Brazilian Expeditionary Force, and, more significantly, the Falklands/ Malvinas War – are not included. Also excluded are the institutional histories and biographies officially sanctioned by the various military establishments themselves. Official military publications and in-house journals comprise a corpus of literature quite distinct from academic studies. For a superb academic analysis of the official corpus of military literature in Latin America and elsewhere, see Frederick M. Nunn, *The Time of the Generals: Latin American Professional Militarism in World Perspective* (Lincoln, Nebr., 1992). This exclusion, however, does not cover books written by military personnel in their individual capacity, such as academic works and autobiographies.

Latin America

The decade of the 1960s was a time of pioneering academic work in the new multi-disciplinary field of Area Studies. These years also represented

---

*This essay was written by Varun Sahni.

the zenith of the 'behavioural revolution' then underway in the discipline of political science in North American academe, with its emphasis on analytical studies that were empirical, quantitative, comparative and inter-disciplinary. It is in this intellectual climate that the classical literature on military politics in Latin America was written. In the region itself, the 'twilight of the tyrants' in the late 1950s had been swiftly followed by another wave of military coups, resulting in the establishment of a new breed of military regimes that appeared to be more durable than their predecessors. In other parts of the world, decolonization from European rule had given rise to a host of new polities in which the military establishments soon came to dominate the political process, thereby laying the ground for comparative regional studies of military politics in Asia, Africa and Latin America.

It is interesting that despite the prevalent academic fashion, the literature on Latin American military politics in the 1960s was never dominated by quantitative analytical works, and in the main remained rooted firmly in the historical analytical tradition. When compared with present-day standards of academic rigour in social and political research, the classical literature frequently seems impressionistic, besides being riddled with factual errors. This, however, should not detract from the pioneering nature of these works. John J. Johnson, *The Military and Society in Latin America* (Stanford, Calif., 1964) represents the classical literature on Latin American military politics at its very best. Edwin Lieuwen's two books, *Arms and Politics in Latin America* (New York, 1961) and *Generals vs. Presidents: Neomilitarism in Latin America* (London, 1964) were both extremely influential in their time. Other works of significance in this academic genre are Gino Germani and K. H. Silvert, *Estructura social e intervención militar en América Latina* (Buenos Aires, 1965); Willard F. Barker and C. Neale Ronning, *Internal Security and Military Power: Counter-Insurgency and Civic Action in Latin America* (Columbus, Ohio, 1966); and José Nun, *Latin America: The Hegemonic Crisis and the Military Coup* (Berkeley, 1969). Also noteworthy in this context are Irving L. Horowitz, 'The military elites', in Seymour M. Lipset and Aldo Solari (eds.), *Elites in Latin America* (New York, 1967); José Nun, 'The middle-class military coup', in Claudio Véliz (ed.), *The Politics of Conformity in Latin America* (New York, 1967); and Lyle McAlister, 'The Military', in John J. Johnson (ed.), *Continuity and Change in Latin America* (Stanford, Calif., 1964).

Apart from academic works specifically on Latin American military politics, a number of other studies on military politics in general were published in the 1960s. Of these, Samuel Finer's *The Man on Horseback: The Role of the Military in Politics* (London, 1962) remains a classic. Morris Janowitz, *The Military in the Political Development of New Nations: An Essay in Comparative Analysis* (Chicago, 1964) is another fine work. Both Finer and Janowitz allude to Latin American examples frequently in their books. William Gutteridge, *Military Institutions and Power in the New States* (London, 1964) is based far more on African examples, but is nevertheless worthy of study. See also John J. Johnson (ed.), *The Role of the Military in Underdeveloped Countries* (Princeton, N.J., 1962). Another significant work in this area is Samuel P. Huntington (ed.), *Changing Patterns of Military Politics* (New York, 1962). In his later works, *The Soldier and the State: The Theory and Politics of Civil–Military Relations* (Cambridge, Mass., 1967) and *Political Order in Changing Societies* (New Haven, Conn., 1968). Huntington came to emphasize institutional weaknesses in civilian polities as a causal factor for military takeovers, an analysis that many of his contemporaries held to be both normative and tautological.

Academic works on military sociology comprise an important part of the classical corpus on military politics. Two studies by Morris Janowitz, *Sociology and the Military Establishment* (New York, 1959) and *The Professional Soldier: A Social and Political Portrait* (Glencoe, Ill., 1960) can be regarded as precursors. Morris Janowitz (ed.), *The New Military: Changing Patterns of Organization* (New York, 1964) and two books edited by Jacques Van Doorn, *Armed Forces and Society: Sociological Essays* (The Hague, 1968) and *The Military Profession and Military Regimes: Commitments and Conflicts* (The Hague, 1969), contain many valuable contributions. The literature was taken forward and consolidated in the two companion volumes co-edited by Janowitz and Van Doorn, *On Military Ideology* and *On Military Intervention* (Rotterdam, 1971).

Finally, the classical literature on Latin American military politics also consists of comparative case studies of specific countries. See, for example. Luigi Einaudi and Alfred C. Stepan, *Latin American Institutional Development: Changing Military Perspectives in Peru and Brazil* (Santa Monica, Calif., 1971); Liisa North, *Civil–Military Relations in Argentina, Chile and Peru* (Berkeley, 1966); Lyle N. McAlister, Anthony Maingot, and Robert Potash (eds.), *The Military in Latin American Sociopolitical Evolution: Four Case Studies* (Washington, D.C., 1970); and Charles D. Corbett, *The Latin American Military as a Socio-Political Force: Case Studies of Bolivia and Argentina* (Miami, 1972).

The study that most clearly marks a break with the classical literature on

Latin American military politics is Guillermo O'Donnell, *Modernization and Bureaucratic-Authoritarianism: Studies in South American Politics* (Berkeley, 1973). O'Donnell's BA model had an enormous influence on subsequent literature. Two scholarly responses are Karen L. Remmer and Gilbert W. Merkx, 'Bureaucratic-Authoritarianism revisited', *Latin American Research Review,* 17/2 (1982), 3–40 and Fernando Henrique Cardoso, 'On the characterization of authoritarian regimes in Latin America', in David Collier (ed.), *The New Authoritarianism in Latin America* (Princeton, N.J., 1979).

Apart from Guillermo O'Donnell, a number of other academic studies of Latin American military politics were published in the heyday of military governments. Among them, the more noteworthy are Virgilio Beltrán, *El papel político y social de las FFAA en América Latina* (Caracas, 1970); Philippe C. Schmitter (ed.), *Military Rule in Latin America: Function, Consequences and Perspectives* (Beverly Hills, Calif., 1973); Jacques Van Doorn, *The Soldier and Social Change* (Beverly Hills, Calif., 1975); Guido Vicario, *Militari e politica in America Latina* (Rome, 1978); Mauricio Solaún and Michael A. Quinn, *Sinners and Heretics: The Politics of Military Intervention in Latin America* (Urbana, Ill., 1973); Issac Sandoval Rodríguez, *Las crisis políticas latinoamericanas y el militarismo* (Mexico, D.F., 1976); Mario Esteban Carranza, *Fuerzas armadas y estado de excepción en América Latina* (Mexico, D.F., 1978); James M. Malloy (ed.), *Authoritarianism and Corporatism in Latin America* (London, 1977); and Irving Louis Horowitz and Ellen Kay Trimberger, 'State power and military nationalism in Latin America', *Comparative Politics,* 8/2 (1976). Roberto Calvo, *La doctrina militar de la seguridad nacional: Autoritarismo político y neoliberalismo económico en el Cono Sur* (Caracas, 1979) is a particularly stimulating book. Denis Martin, Alain Rouquié, Tatiana Yannapolous and Philippe Decraene, *Os Militares e o poder na América Latina e na Africa* (Lisbon, 1975) presents a fascinating comparison between the two regions.

Other significant studies from the 1970s on military politics which include Latin American cases are: Bengt Abrahamson, *Military Professionalism and Political Power* (Beverly Hills, Calif., 1972); Edward Feit, *The Armed Bureaucrats: Military Administrative Regimes and Political Development* (Boston, 1973); Eric A. Nordlinger, *Soldiers in Politics: Military Coups and Governments* (Englewood Cliffs, N.J., 1977); Catherine McArdle Kelleher (ed.), *Political–Military Systems: Comparative Perspectives* (Beverly Hills, Calif., 1974); Claude E. Welch, Jr. (ed.), *Civilian Control of the Military: Theory and Cases from Developing Countries* (Albany, N.Y., 1976); Sheldon W. Simon (ed.), *The Military and Security in the Third World: Domestic and*

International Impacts (Boulder, Colo., 1978); Morris Janowitz, *Military Institutions and Coercion in the Developing Nations* (Chicago, 1977); Amos Perlmutter, *The Military and Politics in Modern Times: On Professionals, Praetorians and Revolutionary Soldiers* (New Haven, Conn., 1977); and Alain Rouquié (ed.), *La Politique de Mars: Les processes politiques au sein des partis militaires* (Paris, 1981).

With the reemergence of democracy in the region in the 1980s some excellent books have been published on military politics in Latin America. Frederick M. Nunn, *Yesterday's Soldiers: European Military Professionalism in South America, 1890–1940* (Lincoln, Nebr., 1983) provides essential historical background. Alfred Stepan, *Rethinking Military Politics: Brazil and the Southern Cone* (Princeton, N.J., 1988), is outstanding. Alain Rouquié, *L'etat militaire en Amérique latine* (Paris, 1982); Sp. trans. *El estado militar en América Latina* (Buenos Aires, 1984); Eng. trans. *The Military and the State in Latin America* (Berkeley, 1987) is one of the finest books ever published on Latin American military politics. Also important is Genaro Arriagada Herrera, *El pensamiento político de los militares: Estudios sobre Chile, Argentina, Brasil y Uruguay,* 2nd ed. (Santiago, Chile, 1986). Other works include George Philip, *The Military in South American Politics* (London, 1985); Karen L. Remmer, *Military Rule in Latin America* (Boston, 1989); Paul Cammack and Philip O'Brien (eds.), *Generals in Retreat: The Crisis of Military Rule in Latin America* (Manchester, Eng., 1985); Augusto Varas, *La política de las armas en América Latina* (Santiago, Chile, 1988); Pablo González Casanova, *Los militares y la política en América Latina* (Mexico, D.F., 1988); Augusto Varas (ed.), *La autonomía militar en América Latina* (Caracas, 1988); and Abraham F. Lowenthal and J. Samuel Fitch (eds.), *Armies and Politics in Latin America* (New York, 1986). Robert Wesson's two edited books, *New Military Politics in Latin America* (New York, 1982) and *The Latin American Military Institution* (New York, 1986) are also worth reading. Finally, John Markoff and Silvio R. Duncan Baretta, 'What we don't know about military coups: Observations on recent South American politics', *Armed Forces and Society,* 12/2 (1986) is a well-written and thought-provoking article.

Brian Loveman and Thomas M. Davies, Jr. (eds.), *The Politics of Antipolitics: The Military in Latin America,* 2nd ed. (Lincoln, Nebr., 1989) is a useful compilation of reading materials on Latin American military politics. Amos Perlmutter and Valerie Plave Bennett (eds.), *The Political Influence of the Military: A Comparative Reader* (New Haven, Conn., 1980) includes material on other regions as well.

Alain Rouquié, 'Demilititarization and the institutionalization of military-dominated polities in Latin America', in Guillermo O'Donnell, Philippe Schmitter and Laurence Whitehead (eds.), *Transitions from Authoritarian Rule: Prospects for Democracy* (Baltimore, 1986), is one of the best pieces on the process of transition from military authoritarian rule to some form of civilian democratic governance from the perspective of the military establishments. James M. Malloy and Mitchell A. Seligson (eds.), *Authoritarians and Democrats: Regime Transition in Latin America* (Pittsburgh, Pa., 1987) is another useful work on this subject. Also worth reading are Martin C. Needler, 'The military withdrawal from power in South America', *Armed Forces and Society*, 6/4 (1980) and Karen L. Remmer, 'Redemocratization and the impact of authoritarian rule in Latin America', *Comparative Politics*, 17/3 (1985), 253–75. Samuel E. Finer, 'The retreat to the barracks: Notes on the practice and theory of military withdrawal from seats of power', *Third World Quarterly*, 7/1 (1985) and Talukder Maniruzzaman, *Military Withdrawal from Politics: A Comparative Study* (Cambridge, Mass., 1987) are the best multi-regional studies of military withdrawals from power.

In post-authoritarian political situations, the relations that the civilian democratic regime establishes with its military institutions is a factor of cardinal importance in the consolidation of democracy. By far the best work on this crucial subject is Louis W. Goodman, Johanna S. R. Mendelson, and Juan Rial (eds.), *The Military and Democracy: The Future of Civil–Military Relations in Latin America* (Lexington, Mass., 1990). Merilee S. Grindle's article, 'Civil–military relations and budgetary politics in Latin America', *Armed Forces and Society*, 13/2 (1987) looks at an important area of civil–military disputation. Another excellent book is Paul W. Zagorski, *Democracy vs. National Security: Civil–Military Relations in Latin America* (Boulder, Colo., 1992), which contains comparative analyses of civil–military relations in the areas of human rights, internal security, military reform and reform of the state. The novelty of this book lies in the systematic manner in which it focuses upon the various areas of civil–military disputation that arise in the post-authoritarian period. Finally, Morris Janowitz (ed.), *Civil–Military Relations: Regional Perspectives* (Beverly Hills, Calif., 1981) presents a comparative view with other regions.

The annual publications of the International Institute of Strategic Studies (IISS), London, and the Stockholm International Peace Research Institute (SIPRI) contain updated information on the related issues of military expenditures and arms purchases. *World Military Expenditures and Arms Transfers,* the official publication of the U.S. Arms Control and Disarmament Agency (ACDA), is also a useful source of information. Significant works over the years on Latin American military expenditures include Joseph E. Loftus, *Latin American Defense Expenditures: 1938–1965* (Santa Monica, Calif., 1968) and Gertrude E. Heare, *Trends in Latin American Military Expenditures, 1940–1970: Argentina, Brazil, Chile, Colombia, Peru, and Venezuela,* U.S. Department of State, Office of External Research, Publication 8618 (Washington, D.C., 1971). Another worthwhile contribution is Geoffrey Kemp, 'The prospects for arms control in Latin America: The strategic dimension', in Philippe C. Schmitter (ed.), *Military Rule in Latin America: Function, Consequences and Perspectives* (Beverly Hills, Calif., 1973). Josef Goldblat and Victor Millan, *The Falklands/Malvinas War: Spur to Arms Buildup* (Stockholm, 1983) is also useful. Augusto Varas, *Militarization and the Internal Arms Race in Latin America* (Boulder, Colo., 1985) is the best book on the subject. Robert E. Looney, *The Political Economy of Latin American Military Expenditures: Case Studies of Venezuela and Argentina* (Lexington, Ky., 1986) is a fine comparative study.

John Child, *Unequal Alliance: The Interamerican Military System, 1938–1978* (Boulder, Colo., 1980) is a superb history of the U.S.-dominated multilateral military arrangement in the Western Hemisphere. Jan Knippers Black, *Sentinels of Empire: The United States and Latin American Militarism* (New York, 1986) is another useful study of U.S.–Latin American military relations. Lars Schoultz, *National Security and United States Policy Toward Latin America* (Princeton, N.J., 1987), also contains important material on this subject. Philippe C. Schmitter, 'Foreign military assistance, national military spending and military rule in Latin America', in Schmitter (ed.), *Military Rule in Latin America: Function, Consequences and Perspectives* (Beverly Hills, Calif., 1973) is an important contribution. A related publication of interest is 'Some relationships between U.S. military training in Latin America and weapons acquisition patterns: 1959–1969', Arms Control Project, Center for International Studies, MIT (February 1970). J. Samuel Fitch, 'The political impact of U.S. military aid to Latin America', *Armed Forces and Society,* 5/3 (1979) makes interesting reading.

In the Latin American military tradition an important place has been assigned to books on geopolitics, and it is one of the favourite topics on which the generals and admirals of the region have written books. The names of the Brazilian generals Golbery do Couto e Silva (*Geopolítica do*

Brasil [Rio de Janeiro, 1967]) and Carlos de Meira Mattos (*A Geopolítica e as projeções do poder* [Rio de Janeiro, 1977]); the Chilean generals Chrismar Escuti (*Geopolítica: Leyes que se deducen del estudio de la expansión de los estados* [Santiago, Chile, 1968]) and Augusto Pinochet Ugarte (*Geopolítica: Diferentes etapas para el estudio geopolítico de los estados* [Santiago, Chile, 1968]) and the Argentine general Juan E. Guglialmelli (numerous articles in *Estrategia* [Buenos Aires]) stand out. John Child, *Geopolitics and Conflict in South America: Quarrels Among Neighbors* (New York, 1985) is an excellent work that summarizes the various national views. Argentine and Chilean admirals have written innumerable books and articles on Antarctica and the disputed insular territories in the South Atlantic. Virginia Gamba-Stonehouse covers these different standpoints superbly in her book, *Strategy in the Southern Oceans: A South American View* (London, 1989).

Military Balance, the annual publication of IISS, London, is the standard source on comparative arsenals. Adrian J. English's two books, *Armed Forces of Latin America: Their Histories, Development, Present Strength and Military Potential* (London, 1984) and *Regional Defence Profile No. 1: Latin America* (London, 1988), are superb.

There is no academic study of the training and socialization process in Latin American military educational establishments, either comparative or country-specific. However, Michael D. Stephens (ed.), *The Educating of Armies* (London, 1989) contains a chapter on military education in post-Revolutionary Cuba.

Nearly all the literature cited above relates to Latin American *armies,* a word which is mistakenly treated by most scholars as being synonymous with *military.* Robert L. Scheina, *Latin America: A Naval History 1810–1987* (Annapolis, Md., 1987) is therefore a valuable addition to the corpus on Latin American military politics.

Argentina

There are two excellent studies of the Argentine army. Robert A. Potash, *The Army and Politics in Argentina,* is the result of many years of sustained and focussed scholarship. The first volume, subtitled *Yrigoyen to Perón* (Stanford, Calif., 1969), covers the years 1928–45. *Perón to Frondizi* (Stanford, Calif., 1980) analyses events up to 1962; a further volume in the future is to be devoutly wished for. Alain Rouquié, *Poder militar y sociedad política en la Argentina* (Buenos Aires, 1981/1982); original Fr. *Pouvoir*

militaire et société politique en république argentine (Paris, 1978) is also published in two volumes, with the first volume covering the period up to the
GOU coup of 1943 and the second volume taking the story forward to the
return of Perón in 1973. Potash and Rouquié have both written superb
political histories, but they differ in perspective: the former approaches
the topic as a historian, the latter as a political scientist. Taken together,
they provide the reader with what is easily the most authoritative academic coverage of any Latin American military institution and its role in
politics. See also F. Lafage, *L'Argentine des dictatures, 1930–1983: Pouvoir
militaire et idéologie contre-révolutionnaire* (Paris, 1991).

Argentine military politics in the period between the fall of Perón in
1955 and the fall of Frondizi in 1962 are examined in Carlos A. Florit, *Las
fuerzas armadas y la guerra psicológica* (Buenos Aires, 1963) and Rogelio
García Lupo, *La rebelión de los generales* (Buenos Aires, 1963). J. Ochoa de
Eguileor and Virgilio R. Beltrán, *Las fuerzas armadas hablan* (Buenos
Aires, 1968) is a useful study of a slightly later period. A left-wing
perspective on Argentine militarism can be found in Jorge Abelardo Ramos, *Historia política del ejército argentino* (Buenos Aires, 1973). Jorge A.
Paita (ed.), *Argentina: 1930–1960: Sur* (Buenos Aires, 1961) contains an
excellent chapter on the armed forces by Horacio Sueldo. Marvin Goldwert, *Democracy, Militarism, and Nationalism in Argentina, 1930–1966: An
Interpretation* (Austin, Tex., 1972) is another worthwhile study of Argentine military politics. Goldwert's analytical classification of the Argentine
armed forces into the two opposing camps of 'liberal nationalists' and
'integral nationalists' is both interesting and illuminating.

Guillermo O'Donnell, *Bureaucratic Authoritarianism: Argentina, 1966–
1973, in Comparative Perspective* (Berkeley, 1988) and William C. Smith,
Authoritarianism and the Crisis of the Argentine Political Economy (Stanford,
Calif., 1989) are both distinguished books on the military regimes of the
'revolución argentina'. Like Potash and Rouquié, they are a couple of
scholarly studies that are best read together. However, far from comple-
menting each other, O'Donnell and Smith view Argentine military politics in general, and the period 1966–73 in particular, from radically
different perspectives. And unlike O'Donnell, whose book focusses on the
period 1966–73, Smith analyses the period 1976–83 as well. Other books
worth reading on the 1966–73 period are Roberto Roth, *Los años de
Onganía: Relato de un testigo* (Buenos Aires, 1980); Rubén M. Perina,
Onganía, Levingston, Lanusse: Los militares en la política argentina (Buenos

Aires, 1983); and Carlos Alberto Quinterno, *Militares y populismo* (*La crisis argentina desde 1966 hasta 1976*) (Buenos Aires, 1978).

Darío Cantón, *La política de los militares argentinos: 1900–1971* (Buenos Aires, 1971) is superb in its analysis of Argentine military politics in the twentieth century as viewed from the vantage point of the ouster of General Onganía and the collapse of the so-called Argentine Revolution of 1966. Robert Potash looks at the same period from the viewpoint of military professionalism in 'The impact of professionalism on the twentieth century Argentine Military', Program in Latin American Studies, Occasional Papers Series No. 3, University of Massachusetts (Amherst, Mass., 1977). Félix Luna, *De Perón a Lanusse* (Buenos Aires, 1972), deals with the period from the fall of Perón to his final return from exile. One of the best general articles on Argentine military politics is James Rowe, 'Argentina's restless Military', in Robert D. Tomasek (ed.), *Latin American Politics: Studies of the Contemporary Scene* (New York, 1970). Philip B. Springler, 'Disunity and disorder: Factional politics in the Argentine military', in Henry Bienen (ed.), *The Military Intervenes: Case Studies in Political Development* (Hartford, Conn., 1968) analyses fissures and divisions within the Argentine military institutions. See also Silvio Waisbord, 'Politics and identity in the Argentine Army: Cleavages and the generational factor', *Latin American Research Review,* 26/2 (1991), 157–70.

Nunca Más (London, 1986), the official report of the Comisión Nacional sobre la Desaparición de las Personas (CONADEP), which was set up by the Alfonsín administration to investigate the 'disappearences' of the 'dirty war', is by far the best account of the extra-legal terror unleashed by the military state during the Proceso de Reorganización Nacional (1976–83). Juan E. Corradi, 'The mode of destruction: Terrorism in Argentina', *Telos,* 54 (Winter 1982–3), is a good article on this grim topic. Other articles that are useful for the Proceso period include Ronaldo Munck, 'The "modern" military dictatorship in Latin America: The case of Argentina (1976–1982)', *Latin American Perspectives,* 12/4 (1985), 41–7, and David Pion-Berlin, 'The fall of military rule in Argentina: 1976–1983', *Journal of Inter-American Studies and World Affairs,* 27/2 (1985), 55–76. See also Andrés Fontana, 'Political decision making by a military corporation, 1976–1983' (unpublished Ph.D. dissertation, University of Texas, Austin, 1987).

A number of articles have appeared on the process of transition from military authoritarian rule to civilian democratic governance in Argentina.

Of these, the most useful and interesting are Alain Rouquié, 'Argentina, the departure of the military: End of a political cycle or just an episode?', *International Affairs* (London), 59/4 (1983), 575–86, and Ronaldo Munck, 'Democratization and demilitarization in Argentina, 1982–1985', *Bulletin of Latin American Research,* 4/2 (1985), 85–93. See also Andrés Fontana, *Fuerzas armadas, partidos políticos y transición a la democracia en Argentina* (Buenos Aires, 1984). An important area of civil–military disputation during the Alfonsín administration was the question of military reform. Carlos J. Moneta, Ernesto López and Aníbal Romero, *La reforma militar* (Buenos Aires, 1985) and Augusto Varas, 'Democratización y reforma militar en la Argentina', Documento de Trabajo, FLACSO (Santiago 1986), are the most thought-provoking academic contributions on this topic. Civil–military relations during the Alfonsín administration itself are analysed superbly in David Pion-Berlin, 'Between confrontation and accommodation: Military and government policy in democratic Argentina', *Journal of Latin American Studies,* 23/3 (1991), 543–71.

Félix Luna, *Golpes militares y salidas electorales* (Buenos Aires, 1983) is a brief summary of Argentine military politics since 1930. Scholarly studies of Argentine military politics are severely handicapped by the lack of memoirs by Argentine military officers. General Alejandro Lanusse's latest memoirs, entitled *Protagonista y testigo (Reflexiones sobre 70 años de nuestra historia)* (Buenos Aires, 1989), are a welcome exception to this general rule. This book supercedes his earlier memoir, *Mi testimonio,* not only on account of the later publishing date but also because the second version is far less self-serving than the first. Rogelio García Lupo, 'Los Alsogaray: Una dinastía militar', *Política,* 7/71–2 (1968) is an excellent article on one of Argentina's patrician military families.

While the in-house journals of Argentina's military institutions frequently carry articles and essays on military sociology, this is an area that has been grossly understudied by academics. The one obvious exception in this regard is the tiny chapter on the military in José Luis de Imaz, *Los que mandan (Those Who Rule)* (Albany, N.Y., 1970). Since the mid-1980s *La Nación* (Buenos Aires) has carried a number of newspaper articles on military sociology written by retired naval captain Carlos Raimondi. However, the study by General Benjamin Rattenbach, *Sociología militar: Una contribución al estudio* (Buenos Aires, 1958), remains the best contribution on this topic by a military officer in book form.

Finally, most of the literature on Argentine military politics focuses on the Army and tends to ignore or marginalize the part played by the other military institutions. For a different perspective on the role of the military in Argentine political history, see Varun Sahni, 'The Argentine navy as an autonomous actor in Argentine politics' (unpublished D.Phil. dissertation, University of Oxford, 1991).

Brazil

The academic literature on Brazilian military politics since the 1930s is vast in quantity and of a consistently high standard. Understandably, most of this literature deals with the 1964–85 military period. Fortunately, the preceding period has not been completely neglected by scholars. José Murilo de Carvalho, 'Armed forces and politics in Brazil: 1930–1945', *Hispanic American Historical Review,* 62/1 (1982), 193–223, is excellent. See also Frank D. McCann, 'The Brazilian army and the problem of mission, 1939–1964', *Journal of Latin American Studies,* 12/1 (1980), 107–26. Thomas Skidmore, *Politics in Brazil, 1930–1964* (New York, 1967) is indispensable. John W. F. Dulles, *Unrest in Brazil: Political Military Crises 1955–1964* (Austin, Tex., 1970) also looks at Brazilian military politics in the period preceding the coup of 1964. Nelson Werneck Sodré, *História militar do Brasil* (Rio de Janeiro, 1965) is a pro-military book written by a leftist historian in the immediate aftermath of the coup. One of the best studies of the overthrow of the Goulart administration in 1964 is Phyllis R. Parker, *Brazil and the Quiet Intervention, 1964* (Austin, Tex., 1979).

The single most important work on the 21 years of military rule that followed the 1964 coup is Thomas E. Skidmore, *The Politics of Military Rule in Brazil, 1964–1985* (Oxford, 1988). During the military period itself a number of useful studies of the regime were published outside Brazil and, after the *abertura* initiated by the Geisel administration, in Brazil as well. Of these, the most notable are Alfred Stepan, *The Military in Politics: Changing Patterns in Brazil* (Princeton, N.J., 1971); Ronald M. Schneider, *The Political System of Brazil: The Emergence of a 'Modernizing' Authoritarian Regime* (New York, 1971); Alfred Stepan (ed.), *Authoritarian Brazil: Origins, Policies, Future* (New Haven, Conn., 1973); Eliezer Rizzo de Oliviera, *As Forças armadas: Política e ideologia no Brasil, 1964–1969* (Petrópolis, 1976); Edmundo Campos Coelho, *Em busca de identidade: O Exército e a política na sociedade brasileira* (Rio de Janeiro, 1976); Alfredo Amaral Gurgel, *Segurança e democracia* (Rio de Janeiro, 1975); and Henry H. Keith (ed.), *Perspectives on Armed Politics in Brazil* (Tempe, Ariz.,

1976). An interesting analysis of the first decade of military rule can be found in Barry Ames, *Rhetoric and Reality in a Military Regime: Brazil since 1964* (Beverly Hills, Calif., 1975). See also Carlos Castelo Branco, *Os Militares no poder,* 2 vols. (Rio de Janeiro, 1977/1978). Alain Rouquié (ed.), *Les Partis militaires au Brésil* (Paris, 1980) and Philippe Faucher, *Le Brésil des militaires* (Montreal, 1981), are both significant books on Brazilian military politics and the best contributions on this subject in the French language. Other important contributions on Brazilian military politics written during the military years include the doctoral dissertation by Alexandre de Souza Costa Barros, 'The Brazilian military: Professional socialization, political performance and state building' (University of Chicago, 1978) and Frank McCann's article, 'Origins of the "new professionalism" of the Brazilian military', *Journal of Inter-American Studies and World Affairs,* 21/4 (1979).

Much has been made of the ideological role of the Escola Superior de Guerra in the 1964 coup and the subsequent military period. Antônio de Arruda, *ESG: Historia de sua doutrina* (Rio de Janeiro, 1980) is a useful work on the subject. In conjunction with this study, the following publications of the ESG are also worth reading: *Doutrina básica* (Rio de Janeiro, 1979), *Complementos da doutrina* (Rio de Janeiro, 1981), and *Fundamentos da doutrina* (Rio de Janeiro, 1981).

During the Costa e Silva and Medici administrations the Army intelligence agency, the Serviço Nacional de Informações (SNI), became a virtual 'army within an army'. An excellent work on this topic is Ana Lagda, *SNI: Como nasceu, como fonciona* (São Paulo, 1983). Alfred Stepan's *Rethinking Military Politics: Brazil and the Southern Cone* (Princeton, N.J., 1988) is a remarkable comparative study that illuminates the 1964–85 military period with much-needed hindsight. A good book on the Brazilian military institutions in the immediate post-authoritarian period is Eliezer Rizzo de Oliviera (ed.), *Militares, pensamento e açao política* (Campinas, 1987). Stanley Hilton, 'The Brazilian Military: Changing strategic perceptions and the question of mission', *Armed Forces and Society,* 13 (1987) is another worthwhile contribution.

For a wide-ranging political history of the Brazilian army, see Frank D. McCann's fine study, *A Nação armada: Ensaios sobre a história de exército brasileiro* (Recife, 1989). Frederick M. Nunn, 'Military professionalism and professional militarism in Brazil, 1870–1970', *Journal of Latin American Studies,* 4/1 (1972), 29–54, is another significant contribution. Robert A. Hayes, *The Armed Nation: The Brazilian Corporate Mystique*

(Tempe, Ariz., 1989) will likewise be read by students of Brazilian military politics with much profit.

Chile

Despite Chile's long history of stable representative government and strong institutionalised political parties, the Chilean military institutions were not neglected by academic scholars in the period before the coup of 1973. Roy Allen Hansen's unpublished doctoral dissertation, 'Military culture and organizational decline: A study of the Chilean Army' (University of California, Los Angeles, 1967), and Alain Joxe, *Las fuerzas armadas en el sistema político chileno* (Santiago, Chile, 1970), were important pre-1973 studies of the Chilean military institutions and military politics. Also worth mentioning in this context is Frederick M. Nunn, *Chilean Politics, 1920–1931: The Honorable Mission of the Armed Forces* (Albuquerque, N.Mex., 1970). Published soon after the 1973 coup, Liisa North's *The Military in Chilean Politics* (Toronto, 1974) was an important addition to the literature on Chilean military politics. Another excellent book covering the period before the coup is Frederick M. Nunn, *The Military in Chilean History: Essays on Civil–Military Relations, 1810–1973* (Albuquerque, N.Mex., 1976).

On the 1973 coup Paul E. Sigmund, *The Overthrow of Allende and the Politics of Chile, 1964–1976* (Pittsburgh, Pa., 1977) and Arturo Valenzuela, *The Breakdown of Democratic Regimes: Chile* (Baltimore, 1978) are the best academic works. Less objective studies of the coup are Pio García (ed.), *Fuerzas armadas y el golpe de estado en Chile* (Mexico, D.F., 1974) and James Petras and Morris Morley, *The United States and Chile: Imperialism and the Overthrow of the Allende Government* (New York, 1975). Nathaniel Davis, *The Last Two Years of Salvador Allende* (Ithaca, N.Y., 1985) is a remarkably honest account by the U.S. ambassador to Chile during the Allende administration.

One of the best studies of the Pinochet period is Samuel Valenzuela and Arturo Valenzuela (eds.), *Military Rule in Chile: Dictatorship and Oppositions* (Baltimore, 1986). Brian Loveman, 'Military dictatorship and political opposition in Chile, 1973–1986', *Journal of Inter-American Studies and World Affairs,* 28/4 (1986–7), 1–38, covers similar ground. The chapter by Augusto Varas, 'The crisis of legitimacy of military rule in the 1980s', in Paul W. Drake and Iván Jaksic (eds.), *The Struggle for Democracy in Chile, 1982–1990* (Lincoln, Nebr., 1991) is superb. The second part of Karen L. Remmer's book, *Military Rule in Latin America* (Boston, 1989), focuses on the Pinochet period and presents a useful analysis of the military regime's policy initiatives and their impact on Chile. Manuel Antonio Garretón, *El proceso político chileno* (Santiago, Chile, 1983); Eng. trans. *The Chilean Political Process* (Boston, 1989) is also deserving of study.

The characteristic that most differentiates the post-1973 military regime in Chile from its counterparts in the region is the personalist nature of the dictatorship. The best study of the monopolizing of power by Pinochet is Arturo Valenzuela, 'The military in power: the consolidation of one-man rule', in Drake and Jaksic (eds.), *The Struggle for Democracy in Chile.* A fascinating book in this context is Ascanio Cavallo, Manuel Salazar and Oscar Sepúlveda, *La historia oculta del régimen militar* (Santiago, Chile, 1988). Genaro Arriagada, *La política militar de Pinochet* (Santiago, Chile, 1985); Eng. trans. *Pinochet: The Politics of Power* (Boston, 1988) is another interesting and stimulating work. The most significant political struggle within the Chilean armed forces after the 1973 coup was between Pinochet and the Air Force commander General Gustavo Leigh. With the latter's dismissal in 1978 Pinochet's position became unassailable. This crucial episode is covered in Florencia Varas, *Gustavo Leigh: El general disidente* (Santiago, Chile, 1979), a series of interviews.

Some of the best studies of Chilean military politics during the Pinochet period were published by the Santiago-based Facultad Latinoamericana de Ciencias Sociales (FLACSO) in the period following the Constitution of 1980: Augusto Varas, Felipe Agüero, and Fernando Bustamante, *Chile, democracia, fuerzas armadas* (Santiago, Chile, 1980); Varas and Agüero, *El proyecto político militar* (Santiago, Chile, 1982); Hugo Frühling, Carlos Portales and Varas, *Estado y fuerzas armadas en el proceso político* (Santiago, Chile, 1983); and Varas, *Los militares en el poder: Régimen y gobierno militar en Chile, 1973–1986* (Santiago, Chile, 1987). Stephen Suffern, 'Les forces armées chiliennes entre deux crises politiques: 1973–1989', *Problèmes d'Amérique Latine,* 85/3 (1987) is a useful contribution.

For a dictator's-eye view of Chilean politics, see Augusto Pinochet Ugarte, *Política, politiquería, y demagogia* (Santiago, Chile, 1983). See also his *El día decisivo: 11 de septiembre de 1973* (Santiago, Chile 1980). The first two volumes of Pinochet's autobiography are of little interest: *Camino recorrido: Memorias de un soldado* (Santiago, Chile, 1990). The first volume covers the period to 1973, and the second 1973–80; there will no doubt be more. Another noteworthy military autobiography is by Pinochet's predecessor, General Carlos Prats González, *Memorias: Testimonio de un soldado* (Santiago, Chile, 1985).

On civil–military relations during and after the transition to democracy, see Brian Loveman, '¿Misión cumplida? Civil–Military relations and the Chilean political transition', *Journal of Inter-American Studies and World Affairs*, 33/3 (1991). *Informe Rettig (Informe de la Comisión Nacional de Verdad y Reconciliación)*, 2 vols. (Santiago, Chile, 1991) is the Chilean equivalent of the Argentine *Nunca Más*. The commission was set up by the Aylwin administration to report officially on human rights violations during the military regime.

Peru

Military politics in Peru has come to be closely identified with the reformist military regime that came to power after the 'left-wing' coup in 1968. On the military before 1968 the best book is Victor Villanueva, *El militarismo en el Perú* (Lima, 1962). See also Allen Gulach, 'Civil–military relations in Peru: 1914–1945' (unpublished Ph.D. dissertation, University of New Mexico, 1973). Jorge Rodríguez Beruff, *Los militares y el poder: Un ensayo sobre la doctrina militar en el Perú, 1948–1968* (Lima, 1983) is an excellent study of Peruvian military politics before General Velasco's 1968 coup. Another important contribution in this context is Frederick Nunn, 'Professional militarism in twentieth century Peru: Historical and theoretical background to the Golpe de Estado of 1968', *Hispanic American Historical Review*, 59/3 (1979), 391–417. Luigi Einaudi's book, *The Peruvian Military: A Summary Political Analysis* (Santa Monica, Calif., 1969), written soon after the 1968 coup, also makes for good reading. Daniel M. Masterson, *Militarism and Politics in Latin America: Peru from Sánchez Cerro to Sendero Luminoso* (New York, 1991) is excellent.

A string of interesting books on Peruvian military politics were written by Victor Villanueva in the first few years of the Revolutionary Government of the Armed Forces, including *¿Nueva mentalidad militar en el Perú?* (Buenos Aires, 1969) and *Ejército peruano: Del caudillaje anárquico al militarismo reformista* (Lima, 1973). Two articles by Julio Cotler are essential: 'Political crises and military populism in Peru', *Studies in Comparative International Development*, 6/5 (1970–1) and 'Concentración del ingreso y autoritarismo político en el Perú', *Sociedad y Política*, 1/4 (1973); the latter piece actually led to Cotler's expulsion from the country. See also José Z. García, 'Military government in Peru, 1968–1971' (unpublished Ph.D. dissertation, University of New Mexico, 1973); Luigi Einaudi, 'Revolution from within: Military rule in Peru since 1968', *Studies in Comparative*

International Development, 8/1 (1973); Jane S. Jaquette, 'Revolution by Fiat: The context of policy-making in Peru', *Western Political Quarterly,* 25/4 (1972); and Carlos A. Astiz and José Z. García, 'The Peruvian Military: Achievement orientation, training, and political tendencies', *Western Political Quarterly,* 25/4 (1972). The ideological role attributed to the Centro de Altos Estudios Militares (CAEM) in post-1968 Peru is identical to that of the Escola Superior de Guerra in the post-1964 Brazil. Victor Villanueva's book on the subject, *El CAEM y la revolución de las fuerzas armadas* (Lima, 1972), is therefore a work of some significance. Villanueva's *Cien años del ejército peruano: Frustraciones y cambios* (Lima, 1971) and Francisco José del Solar, *El militarismo en el Perú* (Caracas, 1976) are both long-term studies of Peruvian military politics written during the reformist military period.

The post-1968 military regime generated an enormous scholarly interest overseas. Three superb studies that emerged during the military period are Abraham F. Lowenthal (ed.), *The Peruvian Experiment: Continuity and Change Under Military Rule* (Princeton, N.J., 1975); K. J. Middlebrook and D. Scott Palmer, *Military Government and Political Development: Lessons from Perú* (Beverly Hills, Calif., 1975); and Alfred Stepan, *The State and Society: Peru in Comparative Perspective* (Princeton, N.J., 1978). George Philip, *The Rise and Fall of the Peruvian Military Radicals* (London, 1978) is another useful contribution on post-1968 military politics. See also David Booth and Bernardo Sorj (eds.), *Military Reformism and Social Classes: The Peruvian Experience, 1968–90* (London, 1983).

A thoughtful and thought-provoking look back at the reformist military period is presented in Cynthia McClintock and Abraham Lowenthal (eds.), *The Peruvian Experiment Reconsidered* (Princeton, N.J., 1983). Evelyne Stephens, 'The Peruvian military government, labor mobilization, and the political strength of the Left', *Latin American Research Review,* 18/2 (1983), 57–93, takes a much-needed look at the crucial issue of the position of leftist groups during the Revolutionary Government of the Armed Forces. Alan Angell, 'El gobierno militar peruano de 1968 a 1980: El fracaso de la revolución desde arriba', *Foro Internacional,* 25 (1984) is a useful summary of the military period.

Central America and Caribbean

Richard Millett's study of the Somocista National Guard, *Guardians of the Dynasty: A History of the Guardia Nacional and the Somoza Family* (Maryknoll, N.Y., 1977) is perhaps the finest work on a military institution in

Central America. Constantino Urcuyo Fournier's doctoral dissertation, 'Les Forces de sécurité publique et la politique au Costa Rica, 1960–1978', (Université de Paris-V, 1980), is a valuable contribution on military politics in a country that officially abolished its armed forces four decades ago. Useful pieces on Guatemalan military politics include Kenneth J. Grieb, 'The Guatemalan Military and the Revolution of 1944', *The Americas,* 32/4 (1976); Richard N. Adams, 'The Guatemalan Military', *Studies in Comparative International Development,* 4/5 (1968); and George Black's contributions in 'Garrison Guatemala', *NACLA's Report of the Americas,* 17/1 (1983). The picture of Salvadorean military politics presented in Charles W. Anderson, 'El Salvador: The Army as reformer', in Martin C. Needler (ed.), *Political Systems of Latin America* (New York, 1970) should be compared with the view presented a decade later in William M. LeoGrande and Carla Anne Robbins, 'Oligarchs and officers: The crisis in El Salvador', *Foreign Affairs,* 58 (Summer 1980). An important recent contribution is Alain Rouquié, *Guerres et paix en Amérique Centrale* (Paris, 1992). Steve C. Ropp, *Panamanian Politics: From Guarded Nation to National Guard* (New York, 1982) is an excellent study of the Omar Torrijos period. Renato Pereira, *Panamá: Fuerzas armadas y política* (Panama City, 1979) is another worthwhile book on Panamanian military politics before Noriega. G. Pope Atkins, *Arms and Politics in the Dominican Republic* (Boulder, Colo., 1981) is an excellent work. See also Howard J. Wiarda, *Dictatorship and Development: The Methods of Control in Trujillo's Dominican Republic* (Gainesville, Fla., 1968). Marvin Goldwert's comparative study, *The Constabulary in the Dominican Republic and Nicaragua* (Gainesville, Fla., 1962) makes for interesting reading. Luis Humberto Guzmán, *Políticos en uniforme: Un balance de poder del EPS* (Managua, 1992), is the only book-length study of the Sandinista army.

The U.S. role in Central America and the Caribbean remains a factor of paramount importance. A fine study on this subject is Don L. Etchison, *The United States and Militarism in Central America* (New York, 1975). John Saxe-Fernández, 'The Central American Defence Council and Pax Americana', in Irving Louis Horowitz (ed.), *Latin American Radicalism: A Documentary Report on Left and Nationalist Movements* (New York, 1969) complements Etchison's study well. In this context the book by the overthrown Dominican leader Juan Bosch, *El pentagonismo: Sustituto de imperialismo* (Mexico, D.F., 1968), is interesting despite being polemical.

Cuban military politics in the period before the Cuban Revolution is covered superbly in Louis A. Pérez, Jr., *Army Politics in Cuba, 1898–1958* (Pittsburgh, Pa., 1976). Another worthwhile study is Rafael Fermoselle,

The Evolution of the Cuban Military, 1492–1986 (Miami, 1987). Jaime Suchlicki (ed.), *The Cuban Military Under Castro* (Coral Gables, Fla., 1989), and Jorge I. Domínguez, 'The civic soldier in Cuba', in Catherine Kelleher (ed.), *Political–Military Systems: Comparative Perspectives* (Beverly Hills, Calif., 1974) analyze civil–military relations in the Castro period.

Bolivia

Gary Prado Salmon's study of Bolivian military politics, *Poder y FFAA, 1949–1982* (La Paz, 1984), could well become a minor classic. James Dunkerly, *Orígenes del poder militar: Historia política e institutional del ejército boliviano hasta 1935* (La Paz, 1987), already is one. Although this book only covers the period up to the end of the Chaco War, it nevertheless merits a mention in this post-1930 bibliography because it goes a long way in explaining the historical background for the military interventions that have plagued Bolivian politics from the late 1940s onwards. Herbert S. Klein's articles, 'David Toro and the establishment of "Military Socialism" in Bolivia', *Hispanic American Historical Review*, 45/1 (1965), and 'Germán Busch and the era of "Military Socialism" in Bolivia', *Hispanic American Historical Review*, 47/2 (1967) take a close look at the brief 'military socialist' period following the Chaco War. Dunkerley's *Rebellion in the Veins: Political Struggle in Bolivia, 1952–1982* (London, 1984) contains an excellent treatment of Bolivian military politics. Guillermo Bedregal, *Los militares en Bolivia: Ensayo de interpretación sociológica* (La Paz, 1971) is well worth study. William H. Brill, *Military Intervention in Bolivia: The Overthrow of Paz Estenssoro and the MNR* (Washington, D.C., 1967) has not lost its academic appeal over the years. Jean-Pierre Lavaud, *L'instabilité politique de l'Amerique Latine: le cas bolivien* (Paris, 1991) is an excellent recent contribution, a large part of which deals specifically with the military.

Colombia and Ecuador

A useful article on military politics in Colombia in the period following *La violencia* is J. León Helguera, 'The changing role of the military in Colombia', *Journal of Inter-American Studies and World Affairs*, 3/3 (1961), 35–8. Richard Maullin's book, *Soldiers, Guerrillas, and Politics in Colombia* (Lexington, Mass., 1973), remains a classic study of Colombian military politics. J. Mark Ruhl, *Colombia: Armed Forces and Society* (Syracuse, N.Y., 1980) was a welcome addition to the literature. Other noteworthy books in recent years on military politics in Colombia include Alvaro Echeverría, *El poder y los militares: Un análisis de los ejércitos del continente y Colombia* (Bogotá, 1978) and Alfredo Peña, *Democracia y golpe militar* (Bogotá, 1979). A useful history of Colombian military politics is provided in Gonzalo Bermúdez Rossi, *El poder militar en Colombia: De la colonia al Frente Nacional* (Bogotá, 1982). Olga Behar, *Las guerras de la paz* (Bogotá, 1985) deserves to be read. The former commander-in-chief of the Colombian Army, General Fernando Landazábal Reyes, wrote a series of interesting books on various aspects of military politics in the 1980s, including *Conflicto social* (Medellín, 1982); *Páginas de controversia* (Bogotá, 1983); *El precio de la paz* (Bogotá, 1985); and *La integración nacional* (Bogotá, 1987).

J. Samuel Fitch, *The Military Coup d'Etat as a Political Process: Ecuador, 1948–1966* (Baltimore, 1977) is a useful study of military politics in Ecuador in the post-war period. It is well complemented by Augusto Varas and Fernando Bustamante, *Fuerzas armadas y política en Ecuador* (Quito, 1978) and Anita Isaacs, *Military Rule and Transition in Ecuador, 1972–1992* (Oxford, 1993). See also Anita Isaacs, 'Problems of demo-cratic consolidation in Ecuador', *Bulletin of Latin American Research,* 10/2 (1991), 221–38.

Mexico

Although Mexico is one of the most important countries in the region and shares a long land border with the United States, the Mexican military establishment has been sorely understudied. The reason for this neglect is obvious: the Mexican military institutions have been peripheral to the political process since the late 1930s. David Ronfeldt (ed.), *The Modern Mexican Military: A Reassessment* (La Jolla, Calif., 1984) and Roderic A. Camp, *Generals in the Palacio: The Military in Modern Mexico* (New York, 1992) thus fill a yawning gap in the political science literature on Mexico. Edwin Lieuwen, *Mexican Militarism: The Political Rise and Fall of the Revolutionary Army, 1910–40* (Albuquerque, N.Mex., 1968) is a fine study of the political power of the Army in the years following the Mexican Revolution and its ultimate marginalization following the 'insti-tutionalization' of the revolution in the 1930s. Other books of signifi-cance on the Mexican military establishment are Jorge Alberto Lozoya, *El ejército mexicano: 1911–1965* (Mexico, D.F., 1971) and Guillermo Boils, *Los militares y la política en México: 1915–1974* (Mexico, D.F., 1975). Franklin D. Margiotta's article, 'Civilian control and the Mexican Military: Changing patterns of political influence', in Claude E. Welch, Jr., (ed.), *Civilian Control of the Military: Theory and Cases from Developing Countries* (Albany, N.Y., 1976), is a useful contribution to the literature on military politics in Mexico.

Paraguay and Uruguay

For Paraguay, Andrew Nickson, 'The overthrow of the Stroessner regime: Re-establishing the status quo', *Bulletin of Latin American Research,* 8/2 (1989), 185–209 not only covers the February 1989 coup against Stroessner but also includes an excellent historical overview of the relations between the military and the Colorado Party.

Written amidst the gathering storm that finally led to direct military intervention in Uruguay in 1973, Gabriel Ramírez, *Las FFAA uruguayas y la crisis continental* (Montevideo, 1972) makes interesting retrospective reading. In recent years the literature on military politics in Uruguay has received an enormous boost with the writings of Carina Perelli and Juan Rial. Perelli and Rial, *De mitos y memorias políticas: La represión, el miedo y después . . .* (Montevideo, 1986) is a superb book on the repression of the military period. See also Paul C. Sondrol, '1984 revisited? A reexamination of Uruguay's military dictatorship', *Bulletin of Latin American Research,* 11/2 (1992), 187–203. Rial, *Las FFAA: Soldados políticos garantes de la democracia?* (Montevideo, 1986) and Perelli, *Someter o convencer: El discurso militar en el Uruguay de la transición y la redemocratización* (Montevideo, 1987) are excellent contributions on the military in the democratic transition. Charles G. Gillespie, *Negotiating Democracy: Politicians and Generals in Uruguay* (Cambridge, Eng., 1991) is superb. See also Cristina Torres, 'Las fuerzas armadas en la transición hacia la democracia', in Charles Gillespie (ed.), *Uruguay y la democracia* (Montevideo, 1985). Carina Perelli, *Los militares y la gestión política* (Montevideo, 1990) and Juan Rial, *Las fuerzas armadas en los años 90: Una agenda de discusión* (Montevideo, 1990) present thought-provoking views on the future of civil–military relations in Uruguay.

Venezuela

In spite of the passage of years since its publication, Winfield J. Burggraaff, *The Venezuelan Armed Forces in Politics, 1935–1959* (Columbia, Mo., 1972) remains the classic study of military politics in Venezuela.

Angel Ziems, *El Gomecismo y la formación del ejército nacional* (Caracas, 1979) is a fine historical work. José Vicente Rangel, Luis Esteban Rey, Pompeyo Márquez, and Germán Lariet, *Militares y política* (*Una polémica inconclusa*) (Caracas, 1976) is a stimulating contribution to the subject. Another noteworthy book is Aníbal Romero, *Seguridad, defensa y democracia* (Caracas, 1980). Gene E. Bigler, 'The armed forces and patterns of civil–military relations', in John D. Martz and D. J. Myers (eds.), *Venezuela: The Democratic Experience* (New York, 1977) is an easily accessible and comprehensive study. Luis Enrique Rangel Bourgoin, *Nosotros los militares* (Caracas, 1983) deserves mention.

There is a tendency for scholars of Latin American military politics to ignore those countries in which the armed forces seem to be firmly under civilian control. The danger inherent in this scholarly neglect is that an unstudied military institution can over a period of time become a 'no-go zone' for scholars, and consequently a *terra incognita*. This danger is well illustrated by the Venezuelan case. The paucity of academic studies on Venezuelan military politics over the years has led to a woeful inadequacy of our collective knowledge on the subject. The inability of scholars to explain the events of 1992 is all too evident.

4. URBAN LABOUR MOVEMENTS IN LATIN AMERICA SINCE 1930

The literature on labour movements and the working class in Latin America in the period since 1930 is most abundant for Brazil and Mexico, followed by Argentina, Chile, Colombia and Peru. There is a limited literature on the remaining countries. Works dealing specifically with occupational structure, and with the political parties of the Left, have been omitted; they are covered in other bibliographic essays in this volume. Works dealing with labour law have also been omitted, unless these have a specific historical or substantive focus.

There are a number of general surveys of the field. Of these, perhaps the most interesting (though also highly debated) are R. B. Collier and D. Collier, *Shaping the Political Arena* (Princeton, N.J., 1991), and C. Bergquist, *Labor in Latin America* (Stanford, Calif., 1986). The former is a massive interpretative effort of the political incorporation of labour and its effects on political development in eight countries: Argentina, Chile, Brazil, Uruguay, Colombia, Venezuela, Peru and Mexico. The latter, employing an interpretative scheme drawn from dependency and labour process theories, compares Chile, Argentina, Venezuela and Colombia. An earlier work which is still a useful and reliable introduction is Hobart Spalding, Jr., *Organized Labor in Latin America* (New York, 1977). See also Moisés Poblete Troncoso and Ben Burnett, *The Rise of the Latin American Labor Movement* (New York, 1960); R. J. Alexander, *Labor Relations in Argentina, Brazil and Chile* (New York, 1962); Victor Alba, *Politics and the Labor Movement in Latin America* (Stanford, Calif., 1968); Carlos Rama, *Historia del movimiento obrero y social latinoamericano contemporáneo* (Barcelona, 1976); and Moisés Poblete Troncoso, *El movimiento obrero latinoamericano* (Mexico, D.F., 1976). A careful Marxist account is J. Godio's *Historia del movimiento obrero latinoamericano,* 3 vols. (San José, C.R., 1979–85). There is also a four-volume collection of country studies (of uneven quality): Pablo González Casanova (ed.), *Historia del movimiento obrero en América Latina* (Mexico, D.F., 1984).

Historiographical and theoretical discussions on Latin American labour history include Kenneth Paul Erickson et al., 'Research on the urban working class and organized labor in Argentina, Brazil and Chile: What is left to be done?', *Latin American Research Review,* 9/2 (1974); Charles Bergquist, 'What is being done? Some recent studies on the urban working class and organized labor in Latin America', *Latin American Research Review,* 16/2 (1981), 203–23; and Emília Viotti da Costa, 'Experience versus structures: New tendencies in the history of labor and the working class in Latin America – What do we gain? What do we lose?, *International Labor and Working-Class History,* 36 (Fall 1989). An historically-oriented survey of the sociological literature is Francisco Zapata, 'Towards a Latin American sociology of labour', *Journal of Latin American Studies,* 22/2 (1990), 375–402. See also, from a sociological perspective, two general books by Francisco Zapata: *Trabajadores y sindicatos en América Latina* (Mexico, D.F., 1988) and *El conflicto sindical en América Latina* (Mexico, D.F., 1986). The first contains a series of essays on general topics and some case studies of Chilean and Mexican unions. The second is the only sustained comparative work on strike activity in Latin America.

Several works dealing specifically with women workers are mentioned below in the review of the literature on individual countries. In addition, June Nash and Helen Icken Safa (eds.), *Sex and Class in Latin America* (New York, 1980) has several papers on women workers, as does Magdalena León (ed.), *Sociedad, subordinación y feminismo,* vol. 3 (Bogotá, 1982).

Two articles deal in a systematic way with the diversity of Latin American experiences and offer typologies: Samuel Valenzuela, 'Movimientos obreros y sistemas políticos: Un análisis conceptual y tipológico', *Desarrollo Económico*, 23/91 (1983), and Ian Roxborough, 'The analysis of labour movements in Latin America: Typologies and theories', *Bulletin of Latin American Research*, 2/2 (1981), 81–95.

On labour in the period at the end of the Second World War and the beginning of the Cold War, see Leslie Bethell and Ian Roxborough (eds.), *Latin America Between the Second World War and the Cold War, 1944–1948* (Cambridge, Eng., 1992). A number of works focus on the international dimensions of Latin American labour in the period from the 1930s to the 1950s. See J. Kofas, *The Struggle for Legitimacy: Latin American Labor and the United States, 1930–1960* (Tempe, Ariz., 1992), which relies heavily on United States archives; L. Quintanilla Obregón, *Lombardismo y sindicatos en América Latina* (Mexico, D.F., 1982) on the CTAL; and two works which deal with Latin America as part of a larger international political project: Ronald Radosh, *American Labor and United States Foreign Policy* (New York, 1969) and Gary Busch, *The Political Role of International Trade Unions* (London, 1983). The autobiographical account of Serafino Romualdi, *Presidents and Peons: Recollections of a Labor Ambassador in Latin America* (New York, 1967) also deserves mention.

Edward Epstein (ed.), *Labor Autonomy and the State in Latin America* (Boston, 1989) provides an overview of labour relations in the 1970s and 1980s. Francisco Zapata et al., *El sindicalismo latinoamericano en los ochenta* (Mexico, D.F., 1986) contains essays on the 1980s by some of the leading specialists in Latin America.

Mexico

On Mexico, single-volume interpretations which serve as a useful point of departure include I. Bizberg, *Estado y sindicalismo en México* (Mexico, D.F., 1990). A more ambitious work is the 17-volume collection under the general editorship of P. González Casanova, *La clase obrera en la historia de México* (Mexico, D.F., 1980–8). Vols. 9–15 cover the period since 1930. See, in particular, A. Córdova, *En una época de crisis (1928–1934)* (Mexico, D.F., 1980); J. Basurto, *Del avilacamachismo al alemanismo (1940–1962)* (Mexico, D.F., 1984); and J. L. Reyna and R. Trejo Delarbe, *De Adolfo Ruiz Cortines a Adolfo López Mateos (1952–1964)* (Mexico, D.F., 1981). Published collections of conference papers on Mexican labour history include: José Woldenberg et al., *Memorias del encuentro sobre historia del movimiento obrero,* 3 vols. (Puebla, 1980–1); Miguel Angel Manzano et al., *Memoria del primer coloquio regional de historia obrera* (Mexico, D.F., 1977); Guillermina Bahena et al., *Memoria del segundo coloquio regional de historia obrera,* 2 vols. (Mexico, D.F., 1979); and Elsa Cecilia Frost et al. (eds.), *El trabajo y los trabajadores en la historia de México* (Mexico, D.F., 1979).

The 1930s, and in particular the Cárdenas presidency (1934–40), is a period which has attracted researchers and has produced a polemical literature. Works with a focus on labour include A. Anguiano, *El estado y la política obrera del cardenismo* (Mexico, D.F., 1975); J. Basurto, *Cárdenas y el poder sindical* (Mexico, D.F., 1983); J. Ashby, *Organized Labor and the Mexican Revolution under Lázaro Cárdenas* (Chapel Hill, N.C., 1963). Two volumes of the series under the general direction of Daniel Cosío Villegas and published by the Colegio de México, *Historia de la Revolución Mexicana,* 23 vols. (Mexico, D.F., 1977–), are of interest for their interpretations of the labour movement: L. Meyer, *El conflicto social y los gobiernos del Maximato,* vol. 13 (Mexico, D.F., 1978); and A. Hernández Chávez, *La mecánica cardenista,* vol. 16 (Mexico, D.F., 1979).

The events of the 1940s and the 1948 Charrazo are detailed in three fine works: V. M. Durand Ponte, *La ruptura de la nación* (Mexico, D.F., 1986); V. M. Durand Ponte et al., *Las derrotas obreras, 1946–1952* (Mexico, D.F., 1984); and R. Loyola (ed.), *Entre la guerra y la estabilidad política: El México de los 40* (Mexico, D.F., 1986). There are also important comments on labour in this period in three of the volumes in the *Historia de la Revolución Mexicana* series: L. Medina, *Del cardenismo al avilacamachismo,* vol. 18 (Mexico, D.F., 1978); B. Torres, *México en la Segunda Guerra Mundial,* vol. 19 (Mexico, D.F., 1979); and L. Medina, *Civilismo y modernización del autoritarismo,* vol. 20 (Mexico, D.F., 1979).

A useful survey of the 1950s is O. Pellicer de Brody and J. L. Reyna, *El afianzamiento de la estabilidad política* (Mexico, D.F., 1978), vol. 22 of the Colegio de México series. The various works cited below on the railway workers are also worth consulting for this period.

The period of union militancy in the 1970s is dealt with by R. Trejo Delarbe, *Este puno si se ve* (Mexico, D.F., 1987). The same author has also produced the very helpful *Crónica del sindicalismo en México (1976–1988)* (Mexico, D.F., 1990), which is an industry-by-industry account of labour conflict in this period. Another chronology is the four volumes of José Luis Cecena Gamez (ed.), *Movimiento obrero, 1970–1980 (Cronología)* (Mexico, D.F., 1981).

For Mexico there are a number of studies of particular industries, unions and labour confederations. The most thorough study of union organizations in the 1970s is a work produced by the research department of the Ministry of Labour: C. Zazueta and R. de la Peña, *La estructura del Congreso del Trabajo* (Mexico, D.F., 1984). A useful collection, based largely on periodical and secondary sources and dealing with the major unions, is the five volumes under the editorship of J. Aguilar, *Los sindicatos nacionales* (Mexico, D.F., 1986–9). There is also J. Aguilar (ed.), *Historia de la CTM, 1936–1990*, 2 vols. (Mexico, D.F., 1990), though this also relies heavily on periodical and secondary sources. Also on the CTM there are A. Aziz Nassif, *El estado mexicano y la CTM* (Mexico, D.F., 1989); S. Yanez Reyes, *Genesis de la burocracia sindical cetemista* (Mexico, D.F., 1984). None of the other confederations has received nearly as much attention, though the excellent book by F. Barbosa Cano, *La CROM de Luis N. Morones a Antonio Hernández* (Puebla, 1980) does devote a few pages to the CROM in the 1930s and 1940s. On oil workers, see A. Alonso y R. López, *El sindicato de trabajadores petroleros y sus relaciones con PEMEX y el estado, 1970–1985* (Mexico, D.F., 1986); and V. Novelo, *La difícil democracia de los petroleros* (Mexico, D.F., 1991). On miners, see J. L. Sariego, *Enclaves y minerales en el norte de México: Historia social de los mineros de Cananea y Nueva Rosita, 1900–1970* (Mexico, D.F., 1988); and L. Reygadas, *Proceso de trabajo y acción obrera: Historia sindical de los mineros de Nueva Rosita, 1929–1979* (Mexico, D.F., 1988). There are a number of works on the railway workers, most of which focus on the strikes of 1958, including: A. Alonso, *El movimiento ferrocarrilero en México, 1958/1959* (Mexico, D.F., 1972); and E. Stevens, *Protest and Response in Mexico* (Cambridge, Mass., 1974). Union militancy in the steel industry in the 1970s is dealt with by I. Bizberg, *La acción obrera en Las Truchas* (Mexico, D.F., 1982). The unions in the electricity-generating industry are analysed by S. Gómez Tagle, *Insurgencia y democracia en los sindicatos electricistas* (Mexico, D.F., 1980) and Mark Thompson, 'Collective bargaining in the Mexican electrical industry', *British Journal of Industrial Relations*, 8/1 (1970). For secondary school teachers and their unions, see A. Loyo Brambila, *El movimiento magisterial de 1958 en México* (Mexico, 1979); Enrique Avila Carrillo and Humberto Martínez Brizuela, *Historia del movimiento magisterial, 1910–1989* (Mexico, D.F., 1990), and two books by G. Peláez: *Las luchas magisteriales de 1956–60* (Mexico, D.F., 1984) and *Historia del Sindicato nacional de Trabajadores de la Educación* (Mexico, D.F., 1984); as well as Stevens, *Protest and Response,* mentioned above. There are several works on the automobile industry. I. Roxborough, *Unions and Politics in Mexico: The Case of the Automobile Industry* (Cambridge, Eng., 1984), and J. Aguilar, *La política sindical en México: Industria del automóvil* (Mexico, D.F., 1982) deal with the industry in the 1970s. An extended comment on these is Kevin Middlebrook, 'Union democratization in the Mexican automobile industry: A reappraisal', *Latin American Research Review*, 24/2 (1988), 69–93. Two more recent studies with a labour process perspective are J. Carrillo (ed.), *La nueva era de la industria automotriz en México* (Tijuana, 1990); and Y. Montiel, *Proceso de trabajo, acción sindical y nuevas tecnologías en Volkswagen de México* (Mexico, D.F., 1991).

There is a useful two-volume collection of papers on women in the labour force: Jenifer Cooper et al. (eds.), *Fuerza de trabajo feminino urbano en México* (Mexico, 1989). Also worthy of note are Vicki Ruiz and Susan Tiano (eds.), *Women on the U.S.–Mexico Border* (Boston, 1987), Lourdes Benería and Martha Roldan, *The Crossroads of Class and Gender: Industrial Homework, Subcontracting, and Household Dynamics in Mexico City* (Chicago, 1987); and María Patricia Fernández-Kelly, *For We Are Sold. I and My People: Women and Industry in Mexico's Frontier* (Albany, N.Y., 1983).

Many important labour leaders have yet to find a biographer, and most of the existing biographies lack balance and objectivity. On Vicente Lombardo Toledano there is the hagiographic R. Millon, *Mexican Marxist – Vicente Lombardo Toledano* (Chapel Hill, N.C., 1966) and the almost diametrically opposed F. Chassen de López, *Lombardo Toledano y el movimiento obrero mexicano (1917/1940)* (Mexico, D.F., 1977). A number of largely journalistic books have more recently appeared on Fidel Velázquez, including Fernando Amilpa Trujillo, *Fidel Velázquez: Mi amigo Amilpa* (Mexico, D.F., 1991); Agustín Sánchez González, *Fidel: Una historia de poder* (Mexico, D.F., 1991); Jorge Mejía Prieto, *Fidel Velázquez: 47 años de historia y poder* (Mexico, D.F., 1980); and Carlos Velasco, *Fidel Velázquez* (Mexico, D.F., 1986). An interesting autobiography is Valentín Campa, *Mi testimonio: Memoria de un comunista mexicano* (Mexico, D.F., 1978). Campa was a leader of the railway workers and has much to say about the forties and fifties.

On the history of wages in Mexico, there are two careful studies: P. Gregory, *The Myth of Market Failure: Employment and the Labor Market in Mexico* (Baltimore, 1986) and J. Bortz, 'El salario obrero en el Distrito Federal, 1939–1975', *Investigación Económica* (October–December 1977). Finally, there is a book of photographs, Victorial Novelo (ed.), *Obreros somos: Expresiones de la cultura obrera* (Mexico, D.F., 1984).

Brazil

There are no satisfactory substantial published English-language surveys of Brazilian labour since 1930, though the doctoral dissertation of Timothy Harding, 'The political history of organized labor in Brazil' (Stanford University, 1973) can be recommended as a place to start. In Portuguese a very good introduction is provided by Leôncio Martins Rodrigues, 'Sindicalismo e classe operária (1930–1964)', in B. Fausto (ed.), *História geral da civilização brasileira,* vol. 10 (São Paulo, 1981). An orthodox Marxist interpretation, with considerable detail and a sensitive periodization, is provided by L. Werneck Vianna, *Liberalismo e sindicato no Brasil* (Rio de Janeiro, 1978). A classic work dealing with the state of São Paulo is A. Simão, *Sindicato e estado* (São Paulo, 1966). Eder Sader et al., *Movimento operário brasileiro,* 1900–1979 (Belo Horizonte, 1980) is a series of short interpretative essays. Kenneth Paul Erickson, *The Brazilian Corporative State and Working-Class Politics* (Berkeley, 1977) focuses on the question of corporatism and state control. Leôncio Martins Rodrigues has produced two interesting general essays: *Trabalhadores, sindicatos e industrialização* (São Paulo, 1974) and *La clase obrera en el Brasil* (Buenos Aires, 1969).

The period between 1930 and 1945 is, in historiographical terms, a veritable minefield. Historians of this period have disputed the relationship between organized labour and the state, with some seeing the Estado Novo as a political project largely independent of organized social forces, and with others taking the view that both labour and industrialists exerted some important influence on policy-making during the Estado Novo. Among the more important published works are: Robert Rowland, 'Classe operária e estado de compromisso', *Estudos CEBRAP,* 8 (1974); R. Barbosa de Araujo, *O Batismo do trabalho: A experiência de Lindolfo Collor* (Rio de Janeiro, 1981); Angela Maria de Castro Gomes, *A Invenção do trabalhismo* (Rio de Janeiro, 1988); R. Antunes, *Classe operária, sindicatos e partido no Brasil: Da revolução de 30 até a Aliança Nacional Libertadora* (São Paulo, 1982); and the brief but interesting Kazumi Munakata, *A Legislação trabalhista no Brasil* (São Paulo, 1981), all of which concentrate on the 1930s. Zélia Lopes da Silva, *A Domesticação dos trabalhadores nos anos 30* (São Paulo, 1990) and René Gertz, 'Estado Novo: Um inventário historiográfico', in José Luiz Werneck da Silva (ed.), *O Feixe e o prisma: uma revisão do Estado Novo* (Rio de Janeiro, 1991), discuss some of the historiographical issues. Angela de Castro Gomes, *Burguesia e trabalho: Política e legislação social no Brasil,* 1917–1937 (Rio de Janeiro, 1979), although mainly dealing with an earlier period, is also very useful. João Almino, *Os Demo-cratas autoritários: Liberdades individuais, de associação política e sindical na constituinte de 1946* (São Paulo, 1980) discusses the debates around the 1946 Constitution, with particular emphasis on labour. A survey of the period of the Estado Novo is contained in A. C. Bernardo, *Tutela e autonomia sindical: Brasil, 1930–1945* (São Paulo, 1982). The crucial period of the mid-forties is dealt with in considerable detail by John French's *The Brazilian Workers' ABC* (Chapel Hill, N.C., 1992), which, as the title indicates, is a study of the ABC region of São Paulo. A careful study of the period between 1945 and the late 1960s is Heloisa Helena Teixeira de Souza Martins, *O Estado e a burocratização do sindicato no Brasil* (São Paulo, 1979). Filling a gap is J. A. Moisés, *Greve de massa e crise política* (São Paulo, 1978), which is a study of the 'strike of the three hundred thousand' in São Paulo in 1953–4, making the point that even in the 'quiet years' there was still considerable union militancy.

The period of labour insurgency during the Goulart presidency in the early 1960s is discussed in a number of general works covering this period, including Erickson, *The Brazilian Corporative State and Working Class Politics,* cited above. Specifically on the PTB and the CGT (and sometimes covering a broader historical span) are Lucília de Almeida Neves Delgado, *CGT no Brasil, 1961–1964* (Belo Horizonte, 1981) and *PTB: Do Getulismo ao reformismo, 1945–1964* (São Paulo, 1989); Luis Alberto Moniz Bandeira, *Brizola e o trabalhismo* (Rio de Janiero, 1979); Maria Victoria Benevides, *O PTB e o trabalhismo* (São Paulo, 1989); and Maria Andrea Loyola, *Os Sindicatos e o PTB: Estudo de um caso em Minas Gerais* (Petrópolis, 1980).

The definitive work on trends in Brazilian wages is John Wells, 'Indus-trial accumulation and living standards in the long-run: The São Paulo industrial working class, 1930–75', parts 1 and 2, *Journal of Development Studies,* 19/2–3 (1983).

A number of early case studies by sociologists provide an insight into industrial relations in the fifties and sixties. J. Brandão Lopes in *Crise de Brasil arcaico* (São Paulo, 1967), deals with the textile industry in 1958 and in *Sociedade industrial no Brasil* (São Paulo, 1964) he reports two cases of factories studied in 1957. L. Martins Rodrigues, *Industrialização e atitudes operárias* (São Paulo, 1970) reports the results of a survey in a São Paulo car factory in 1963. More recent studies by sociologists and anthro-pologists which deserve mention are V. M. Candido Pereira, *O Coração da fábrica* (Rio de Janeiro, 1979) and textile workers in Rio, and J. S. Leite Lopes, *O Vapor do diabo* [Rio de Janeiro, 1978] on the sugar industry in Pernambuco). J. S. Leite Lopes, *A Teçelagem dos conflitos de classe* (São Paulo, 1988) is a study of the textile city of Paulina, Pernambuco, relying heavily on anthropological fieldwork to reconstruct the history of a mill-town in the mid-twentieth century.

Union organization and leadership in Brazil has been well covered. J. A. Rodrigues, *Sindicato e desenvolvimento no Brasil* (São Paulo, 1968) is a general study of Brazilian union organization with data up to 1961. O. Rabello, *A Rede sindical paulista* (São Paulo, 1965) gives a useful snapshot of union organizations in São Paulo in 1964, and can be supplemented with a survey of São Paulo union leaders, carried out in 1963, by J. V. Freitas Marcondes, *Radiografia da lideranca sindical paulista* (São Paulo, 1964). There is a helpful study of the Confederação Nacional dos Trabalhadores na Industria (CNTI) in S. A. Costa, *Estado e contrôle sindical no Brasil* (São Paulo, 1986). On the union organizations of the 1980s, there are four excellent short studies by L. Martins Rodrigues: *Partidos e sindicatos* (São Paulo, 1990), *CUT: Os militantes e a ideologia* (São Paulo, 1990), *Força Sindical* (São Paulo, 1993), and *Retrato da CUT* (São Paulo, 1991). There is also M. Grondin, *Perfil dos dirigentes sindicais na Grande São Paulo* (São Paulo, 1985).

The importance of São Paulo, particularly in the 1970s and 1980s, has led to a massive output of work on the metalworking industries. Many of these works are listed below in the section on the insurgency of the 1970s and 1980s. In addition, there is Braz José de Araujo, *Operários em luta: Metalúrgicos da Baixada Santista (1933–1983)* (Rio de Janeiro, 1985), Dennis Linhares Barsted, *Medição de forças: O movimento grevista de 1953 e a época dos operários navais* (Rio de Janeiro, 1982), and José Ricardo Ramalho's study of a state-owned automobile factory which concentrates on the 1940s and 1950s, *Estado-patrão e luta operária* (São Paulo, 1989). The metalworkers' union of São Bernardo published a fascinating collection of photographs: Aloízio Mercante Oliva (ed.), *Imagens da luta, 1905–1985* (São Bernardo, 1987).

An excellent history of a Brazilian mining union is Y. de Souza Grossi, *Mina de Morro Velho: A Extração do homen* (Rio de Janeiro, 1981). A history of the São Paulo bankworkers between 1923 and 1944 is L. Bicalho Canedo, *O Sindicalismo bancário em São Paulo* (São Paulo, 1978). The history of the chemical and pharmaceutical workers' union of São Paulo has been written by A. Troyano, *Estado e sindicalismo* (São Paulo, 1978). Dock-workers are treated by Barsted, cited above (for Rio de Janeiro) and Ingrid Sarti, *Porto Vermelho* (Rio de Janeiro, 1981) (for the port of Santos).

The union insurgency of the late 1970s onward has received extensive treatment, mainly by social scientists. Many of these works focus on the metalworkers of Greater São Paulo. Among the more useful works are J. Humphrey, *Capitalist Control and Workers' Struggle in the Brazilian Auto Industry* (Princeton, N.J., 1982), V. M. Durand Ponte, *Crisis y movimiento obrero en Brasil: Las huelgas metalúrgicas de 1978–1980* (Mexico, D.F., 1987), Eder Sader, *Quando novos personagens entraram em cena: Experiências e lutas dos trabalhadores da Grande São Paulo, 1970–1980* (Rio de Janeiro, 1988) and Maria Hermínia Tavares de Almeida, 'O Sindicalismo brasileiro entre a conservação e a mudança', in Bernardo Sorj and Maria Hermínia Tavares de Almeida (eds.), *Sociedade e política no Brasil pós-64* (São Paulo, 1983).

On the situation in the 1980s, two useful works are Armando Boito, *O Sindicalismo de estado no Brasil* (São Paulo, 1991), and Armando Boito (ed.), *O Sindicalismo brasileiro nos anos 80* (São Paulo, 1991). In English a helpful survey is Margaret Keck, 'The new unionism in the Brazilian transition' in Alfred Stepan (ed.), *Democratizing Brazil* (New York, 1989). An interesting and broad-ranging essay is Antonio Guimarães and Nádya Araujo Castro, 'Espacios regionales de construcción de la identidad: La clase trabajadora en Brasil después de 1977', *Estudios Sociológicos, 7/21* (1989).

Women workers have been relatively well studied in Brazil. Rosalina de Santa Cruz Leite, *A operária metalúrgica* (São Paulo, 1984) reports extensive interviews with women metalworkers; Jessita Martins Rodrigues, *A mulher operária* (São Paulo, 1979) is a study of women textile workers in San José dos Campos, in the state of São Paulo. A thorough sociological treatment is John Humphrey, *Gender and Work in the Third World: Sexual Divisions in Brazilian Industry* (London, 1987).

Argentina

A useful introduction in English to the history of the labour movement in Argentina from a Marxist perspective is R. Munck, *Argentina: From Anarchism to Peronism* (London, 1987). In Spanish, also from a Marxist perspective, there is Julio Godio's five-volume overview, *El movimiento obrero argentino* (Buenos Aires, 1987–91). A special number of the *Boletín de Estudios Latinoamericanos y del Caribe* 31 (December 1981) is dedicated to historical perspectives on the working class of Argentina and Chile. Carlos Waisman, *Modernization and the Working Class* (Austin, Tex., 1982) is a theoretically oriented discussion by a sociologist of the process of labour incorporation in Argentina, Germany and Britain.

Most of the work on Argentine unionism is, of course, closely bound up with the debates on the origins and nature of Peronism. The 1930s are usually viewed either as a prelude to Peronism or as the last stages of an alternative project of (potentially) Socialist unionism. On the origins of Peronism, an older but still useful work is Samuel Baily, *Labor, Nationalism, and Politics in Argentina* (New Brunswick, N.J., 1967). The view of Peronism stressing the importance of recent migration to the city and the 'massification' of the working class was challenged by a wave of revisionist historiography. The pioneering work was M. Murmis and J. C. Portantiero, *Estudios sobre los orígines del peronismo* (Buenos Aires, 1971), where they argued that popular support for Perón came as much from the established working class as from recent immigrants to the city. This line of argument was strengthened by the publication of Juan Carlos Torre's article, 'Sobre as origens do peronismo – a CGT e o 17 de outubro de 1945', *Estudos CEBRAP*, 16 (1976). Another important article is Daniel James, 'October 17th and 18th, 1945: Mass protest, Peronism and the Argentine working class', *Journal of Social History*, 21 (1988), 441–61. This gave rise to a lively debate, conducted largely in the pages of *Desarrollo Económico*. Several of the articles in this debate have been reproduced in Juan Carlos Torre (ed.), *La formación del sindicalismo peronista* (Buenos Aires, 1986). Accounts of the origins of Peronist unionism taking account of both orthodox and revisionist positions include J. C. Torre, *La vieja guardia sindical y Perón* (Buenos Aires, 1990), H. Matsushita, *Movimiento obrero argentino, 1930–1945* (Buenos Aires, 1983), Elena Susana Pont, *Partido Laborista: Estado y sindicatos* (Buenos Aires, 1984), and H. del Campo, *Sindicalismo y peronismo* (Buenos Aires, 1983). A study which concentrates on the railway workers is D. Tamarin, *The Argentine Labor Movement, 1930–1945* (Albuquerque, N.Mex., 1985). Also on railway workers, see Joel Horowitz, 'Los trabajadores ferroviarios en la Argentina (1920–1943): La formación de una elite obrera', *Desarrollo Económico*, 25/99 (1985).

Paul Buchanan, 'State corporatism in Argentina: Labor administration under Perón and Onganía', *Latin American Research Review*, 20/1 (1985), 61–95, examines the role of the Ministry of Labour. Some of the articles published in Torre (ed.), *La formación del sindicalismo peronista*, cited above, treat the period of the first Peronist governments (1946–55) and Alvaro Abós, *La columna vertebral: Sindicatos y peronismo* (Buenos Aires, 1983) take a broad look at unionism in Argentina from 1946 to 1976.

The international projection of Peronist unionism via the Agrupación de Trabajadores Latinoamericanos Sindicalistas (ATLAS) is covered by most works dealing with international unionism cited above, and has been specifically covered by Manuel Urriza, *CGT y ATLAS: Historia de una experiencia sindical latinoamericana* (Buenos Aires, 1988) and Daniel Parcero, *La CGT y el sindicalismo latinoamericano* (Buenos Aires, 1987).

The relations between the military government that overthrew Perón in 1955 and the unions are discussed in Juan Carlos Torre and Santiago Senén González, *Ejército y sindicatos (los 60 días de Lonardi)* (Buenos Aires, 1969). The most important work on the Peronist 'resistance' period between the overthrow of Perón in 1955 and the return of the Peronists to power in 1973 is Daniel James, *Resistance and Integration: Peronism and the Argentine Working Class, 1946–76* (Cambridge, Eng., 1988), which has a subtle and sophisticated analysis of the factors creating a specifically Peronist working-class identity. Another general survey of the same period is Graciela Ducatenzeiler, *Syndicats et politique en Argentine, 1955–1973* (Montreal, 1980). An important work on the Frondizi government of the late 1950s is Marcelo Cavarozzi, *Sindicatos y política en Argentina* (Buenos Aires, 1984). Ernesto Salas has written a detailed study of the occupation of a meatpacking plant by the workers in 1959: *La resistencia peronista: La toma del frigorífico Lisandro de la Torre,* 2 vols. (Buenos Aires, 1990). A sociological study of the Argentine working class carried out in the mid-1960s has recently been republished: Torcuato Di Tella, *Política y clase obrera* (Buenos Aires, 1983).

The 1960s and 1970s are covered by Osvaldo Calello and Daniel Parcero, *De Vandor a Ubaldini,* 2 vols. (Buenos Aires, 1984). The relationship between unions and the military dictatorship of 1966–73 is treated by Alvaro Abós, *Las organizaciones sindicales y el poder militar (1976–1983)* (Buenos Aires, 1984). Focussing more directly on the Radical and Justicialista parties is Daniel Rodríguez Lamas, *Radicales, peronistas y el movimiento obrero (1963–1973),* 2 vols. (Buenos Aires, 1989). Arturo Fernández has also published a study of the ideology of the Peronist union leadership during this period: *Ideologías de los grupos dirigentes sindicales (1966–1973),* 2 vols. (Buenos Aires, 1986).

The events of the 'Cordobazo' of 1969 are covered by F. Delich, *Crisis y protesta social: Córdoba, mayo de 1969* (Buenos Aires, 1970), and by Beba C.

Balvé and Beatriz S. Balvé, '69: *Huelga política de masas* (Buenos Aires, 1989). The second round of 1971 is the subject of B. Balvé et al., *Lucha de calles, lucha de clases* (Buenos Aires, 1973).

Juan Carlos Torre, *Los sindicatos en el gobierno, 1973–1976* (Buenos Aires, 1983) is the most reliable and useful work on the labour movement during the short-lived Peronist government of 1973–6.

The military dictatorship of 1976–83 is covered in Bernardo Gallitelli and Andrés Thompson (eds.), *Sindicalismo y régimenes militares en Argentina y Chile* (Amsterdam, 1982), and by Pablo Pozzi, *Oposición obrera a la dictadura* (Buenos Aires, 1988).

There are a number of works by social scientists on the period since the return to democracy in 1983. The most useful of these is R. Gaudio and A. Thompson, *Sindicalismo peronista/gobierno radical: Los años de Alfonsín* (Buenos Aires, 1990). The article by James McGuire, 'Union political tactics and democratic consolidation in Alfonsín's Argentina, 1983–1989', *Latin American Research Review*, 27/1 (1992), 37–74 is particularly helpful in explaining the complex factional line-up in the CGT. On labour-management relations, O. Moreno, *La nueva negociación: La negociación colectiva en la Argentina* (Buenos Aires, 1991) is very helpful. The Ministry of Labour published two useful collections of statistical data: *Sindicatos: Elecciones 1984–1986* (Buenos Aires, 1988) and *Estructura sindical en la Argentina* (Buenos Aires, 1987).

Union organization is dealt with in detail in Ruben Zorrilla, *Estructura y dinámica del sindicalismo argentino* (Buenos Aires, 1974). Studies of the leadership and its political tendencies include Alejandro Francisco Lamadrid, *Política y alineamientos sindicales* (Buenos Aires, 1988); Rubén Zorrilla, *Líderes del poder sindical* (Buenos Aires, 1988) and, by the same author, *El liderazgo sindical argentino* (Buenos Aires, 1988). Working-class living standards are considered in Adriana Marshall, 'La composición del consumo de los obreros industriales de Buenos Aires, 1930–1980', *Desarrollo Económico*, 21/83 (1981).

Given the importance of organized labour in Argentina, it is perhaps somewhat surprising that there are not more studies of individual industries or unions. Notable exceptions are I. M. Roldán, *Sindicatos y protesta social en la Argentina: Un estudio de caso: El Sindicato de Luz y Fuerza de Córdoba (1969–1974)* (Amsterdam, 1978); Federico Neiburg, *Fábrica y Villa Obrera: Historia social y antropología de los obreros del cemento*, 2 vols. (Buenos Aires, 1988), and Natalia Duval, *Los sindicatos clasistas: SiTraC (1970–1971)* (Buenos Aires, 1988), a study of auto workers. A study of working conditions for teachers in the 1970s is Mariano Narodowski and Patricio Narodowski, *La crisis laboral docente* (Buenos Aires, 1988).

Uruguay and Paraguay

On Uruguay, see Enrique Rodríguez, *Un movimiento obrero maduro* (Montevideo, 1988), and Francisco Pintos, *Historia del movimiento obrero del Uruguay* (Montevideo, 1960). On Paraguay, see Ramiro Barboza, *Los sindicatos en el Paraguay: Evolución y estructura actual* (Asunción, 1987).

Chile

The monograph by Alan Angell, *Politics and the Labour Movement in Chile* (London, 1972) is still a standard reference for the structure and organization of Chilean labour to the 1960s. See also Jorge Barría, *El movimiento obrero en Chile* (Santiago, Chile, 1971), and James Petras and Maurice Zeitlin, *El radicalismo político de la clase trabajadora chilena* (Buenos Aires, 1969). On copper miners in the 1960s, see Jorge Barría, *Los sindicatos de la gran minería del cobre* (Santiago, Chile, 1970) and Manuel Barrera, *El conflicto obrero en el enclave cuprífero* (Santiago, Chile, 1973). Francisco Zapata has a chapter of his *Trabajadores y sindicatos en América Latina* (Mexico, D.F., 1987) devoted to copper miners during the Pinochet dictatorship. He has also written two other short works: *Los mineros de Chuquicamata: Productores o proletarios?* (Mexico, D.F., 1975) and *Las relaciones entre el movimiento obrero y el gobierno de Allende* (Mexico, D.F., 1974). Information on strikes and on the attitudes of union leaders in the 1960s is available in Manuel Barrera, *El sindicato industrial como instrumento de lucha de la clase obrera chilena* (Santiago, Chile, 1971). A minor classic is Torcuato Di Tella et al., *Sindicato y comunidad* (Buenos Aires, 1967), which compares union militancy in the coal mines of Lota and the steel plant of Huachipato, based on field work in the mid-fifties.

The most interesting work on the Allende period is Peter Winn, *Weavers of Revolution* (New York, 1986). A detailed study of a textile mill which was expropriated during the Popular Unity government, it describes the way in which the micropolitics of the factory articulated with national-level politics. The results of a survey of worker participation in management in 35 enterprises during the Allende government are analysed in Juan Espinosa and Andrew Zimbalist, *Economic Democracy: Workers' Participation in Chilean Industry, 1970–1973* (New York, 1978).

On the Pinochet period, see Jaime Ruiz-Tagle, *El sindicalismo chileno después del Plan Laboral* (Santiago, Chile, 1985); Guillermo Campero and José Valenzuela, *El movimiento sindical chileno en el capitalismo autoritario* (Santiago, Chile, 1981); Manuel Barrera et al., *Sindicatos y estado en el Chile actual* (Geneva, 1985); Manuel Barrera and Gonzalo Falabella (eds.), *Sindicato bajo régimenes militares* (Geneva, 1989) (which deals with Argentina, Brazil and Chile); Francisco Zapata et al., *El sindicalismo latinoamericano en los ochenta* (Santiago, Chile, 1986); J. Samuel Valenzuela and Arturo Valenzuela (eds.), *Military Rule in Chile* (Baltimore, 1986); and Rigoberto García (ed.), *Chile 1973–1974* (Stockholm, 1985).

Bolivia

Bolivian labour history is dominated by the five-volume work of Trotskyist Guillermo Lora. This is available in an abridged version in English: *A History of the Bolivian Labour Movement* (Cambridge, Eng., 1977). See also Jorge Lazarte, *Movimiento obrero y procesos políticos en Bolivia* (La Paz, 1989), and Steven Volk, 'Class, union, party: The development of a revolutionary union movement in Bolivia (1905–1952)', *Science and Society,* 39/1 (1975). John Magill, *Labor Unions and Political Socialization: A Case Study of Bolivian Workers* (New York, 1974) deals specifically with the miners. Also on miners is Laurence Whitehead, 'Sobre el radicalismo de los trabajadores mineros de Bolivia', *Revista Mexicana de Sociología,* 42/4 (1980). June Nash, *We Eat the Mines and the Mines Eat Us* (New York, 1979), is an interesting account by an anthropologist of the role of belief-systems in creating community and occupational cohesiveness among tin miners. Domitla Barrios de Chungara, *Let Me Speak!* (London, 1978), is a powerful testimony by a female activist from the mining camps.

Peru and Ecuador

For Peru the obvious place to start is Denis Sulmont, *El movimiento obrero peruano (1890–1980)* (Lima, 1980). An early and influential analysis of Peruvian labour, based on the notion of 'political bargaining', is James Payne, *Labor and Politics in Peru* (New Haven, Conn., 1965), with a focus on the late 1950s and early 1960s. A study of the textile labour force in the late fifties is David Chaplin, *The Peruvian Industrial Labor Force* (Princeton, N.J., 1967). Piedad Pareja, *Aprismo y sindicalismo en el Perú* (Lima, 1980), is the best source for the Bustamante government of 1945–8. The structure of the working class in the 1970s is discussed in Pedro Galín et al., *Asalariados y clases populares en Lima* (Lima, 1986), and a sophisticated analysis of the self-identity of workers is Jorge Parodi, *'Ser obrero es algo relativo': Obreros, clasismo y política* (Lima, 1986). Other general works are José Barba Caballero, *Historia del movimiento obrero peruano* (Lima, 1981), and Alberto Moya Obeso, *Sindicalismo aprista y clasista en el Perú (1920– 1956)* (Trujillo, Peru, 1977). Specifically on mineworkers there are Jaysuno Abramovich, *Análisis socioeconómico del trabajador minero en el Perú* (Lima, 1983), Julian Laite, *Industrial Development and Migrant Labour* (Manchester, 1981); Heraclio Bonilla, *El minero de los Andes* (Lima, 1974); Dirk Kruijt and Menno Vellinger, *Labor Relations and Multinational Corporations* (Assen, Neth., 1979). Two works deal with the role of worker management in the industrial communities established under the military government of Velasco Alvarado: Giorgio Alberti et al., *Estado y clase: La comunidad industrial en el Perú* (Lima, 1977) and Evelyne Huber Stephens, *The Politics of Workers' Participation* (New York, 1980).

On Ecuador, Osvaldo Albornoz, *Historia del movimiento obrero ecuatoriano* (Quito, 1983); Osvaldo Albornoz et al., *28 de mayo y fundación de la CTE* (Quito, 1984), concentrating on Ecuador in the 1940s; and Juan-Pablo Pérez Sainz, *Clase obrera y democracia en el Ecuador* (Quito, 1985).

Colombia

A good introduction to labour in Colombia is Daniel Pécaut, *Política y sindicalismo en Colombia* (Bogotá, 1973). Also worth consulting are Edgar Caicedo, *Historia de la luchas sindicales en Colombia* (Bogotá, 1982), and Victor Manuel Moncayo and Fernando Rojas, *Luchas obreras y política laboral en Colombia* (Bogotá, 1978). Another survey, using Payne's notion of 'political bargaining', is Miguel Urrutia, *The Development of the Colombian Labor Movement* (New Haven, Conn., 1969). Mauricio Archila Neira has written two works focussing on the cultural identity of the early Colombian working class: *Aquí nadie es forastero: Testimonios sobre la formación de una cultura radical: Barrancabermeja, 1920–1950* (Bogotá, 1986), and *Cultura e identidad obrera: Colombia, 1910–1945* (Bogotá, 1991). Focussing on the Catholic church and the formation of the Unión de Trabajadores de Colombia in 1946 and its subsequent development, is Kenneth Medhurst, *The Church and Labour in Colombia* (Manchester, 1984). The condition of the working class of Bogotá in the 1950s is outlined by Camilo Torres, *La proletarización de Bogotá* (Bogotá, 1987).

An interesting and detailed study of factory workers in Medellín in the 1960s is Charles Savage and George Lombard, *Sons of the Machine: Case Studies of Social Change in the Workplace* (Cambridge, Mass., 1986). Another useful study from the 1960s, this time of an oil town, is A. Eugene Havens and Michel Romieux, *Barrancabermeja: Conflictos sociales en torno a un centro petrolero* (Bogotá, 1966). The union situation in the 1970s and early 1980s is covered by a series of fine case studies in Hernando Gómez Buendía et al., *Sindicalismo y política económica* (Bogotá, 1986).

Venezuela

Julio Godio has written a three-volume work on Venezuelan labour which reproduces and summarizes a large number of documents: Julio Godio, *El movimiento obrero venezolano,* 3 vols. (Caracas, 1980, 1982 and n.d.). The first volume covers 1850–1944, the second, 1945–80, and the third, 1965–80 in more detail. Godio has also written a history of the *Confederación de Trabajadores de Venezuela: 50 años de la CTV (1936–1986)* (Caracas, 1986). On the crucial period of the 1930s and 1940s the best source is Steve Ellner, *Los partidos políticos y su disputa por el control del movimiento sindical en Venezuela 1936–1948* (Caracas, 1980). A study of oil workers, focussing on the years between 1936 and 1957, is Héctor Lucena, *El movimiento obrero petrolero* (Caracas, 1982). A survey of labour organization in the 1970s is Cecilia Valente, *The Political, Economic, and Labor Climate in Venezuela* (Philadelphia, 1979).

Central America

A general discussion of the labour market in Central America in the postwar period was produced under the auspices of the ILO: Guillermo García Huidobro et al., *Cambio y polarización ocupacional en Centroamérica* (San José, C.R., 1986). Manning Nash, *Machine Age Maya: The Industrialization of a Guatemalan Community* (Chicago, 1958) is an anthropological study of the adaptation of workers to industrial discipline in a textile mill in the Guatemalan highlands in the 1950s. On Honduras, see Mario Posas, *Luchas del movimiento obrero hondureño* (San José, C.R., 1981). On El Salvador, see Rafael Menjívar, *Formación y lucha del proletariado industrial salvadoreño* (San Salvador, 1979); For Costa Rica there is Daniel Camacho (ed.), *Desarrollo del movimiento sindical en Costa Rica* (San José, C.R.,

1985), which, after a brief historical survey, deals mainly with the postwar period.

A standard account of the history of Nicaraguan labour is Carlos Pérez Bermudez and Onofre Guevara, *El movimiento obrero en Nicaragua* (Managua, 1985). An interesting revisionist account of the relations between labour and the early Somoza regime is Jeffrey Gould, ' "For an organized Nicaragua": Somoza and the Labour Movement, 1944–1948', *Journal of Latin American Studies,* 19/2 (1987), 353–87. The role of labour in the 1979 revolution is treated by Carlos Vilas, 'The workers' movement in the Sandinista Revolution', in Richard Harris and Carlos Vilas (ed.), *Nicaragua: A Revolution Under Seige* (London, 1985).

Cuba

There is, not surprisingly, little scholarly work on the history of the Cuban labour movement. Jean Stubbs, *Tobacco on the Periphery: A Case Study in Cuban Labour History, 1860–1958* (Cambridge, Eng., 1985) stands out as an exception, and indicates both what can be done and what still remains to be done. A sociological study based on a survey carried out in 1962 by Maurice Zeitlin, *Revolutionary Politics and the Cuban Working Class* (Princeton, N.J., 1967), provides us with a detailed view of Cuban workers' attitudes in the early phase of the revolution. A stridently anti-communist account is Rodolfo Riesgo, *Cuba: El movimiento obrero y su entorno socio-político* (Miami, 1985). A series of essays focussing on the economic condition of the Cuban working class between 1933 and 1958 is Carlos del Toro, *Algunos aspectos económicos, sociales y políticos del movimiento obrero cubano* (Havana, 1974). The post-revolutionary period is covered in Linda Fuller, *Work and Democracy in Socialist Cuba* (Philadelphia, 1992).

5. RURAL MOBILIZATIONS IN LATIN AMERICA SINCE C. 1920

Three well-known attempts to build a typology of peasant movements in Latin America in the twentieth century are Aníbal Quijano, 'Contemporary peasant movements', in Seymour Lipset and Aldo Solari (eds.), *Elites in Latin America* (New York, 1967); Henry A. Landsberger, 'The role of peasant movements and revolts in development', in H. A. Landsberger (ed.), *Latin American Peasant Movements* (Ithaca, N.Y., and London, 1969), and Gerrit Huizer, *El potencial revolucionario del campesinado* (Mexico, D.F., 1973).

Other useful collections of articles on rural unrest are Rodolfo Staven-hagen (ed.), *Agrarian Problems and Peasant Movements in Latin America* (New York, 1970); Ernest Feder (ed.), *La lucha de clases en el campo: Análisis estructural de la economía latinoamericana* (Mexico, D.F., 1975), and Henri Favre (ed.), 'Les mouvements indiens paysans aux XVIIIe, XIXe et XXe siècles', *Actes du XLIIe Congrès International des Américanistes* (Paris, 1976). But the most complete and up-to-date collective work, including chapters on every Latin American country, is Pablo González Casanova (ed.), *Historia política de los campesinos latinoamericanos,* 4 vols. (Mexico, D.F., 1984–85). An illuminating synthesis is Henri Favre, 'L'Etat et la paysannerie en Mésoamérique et dans les Andes', *Etudes Rurales,* 81–2 (1981), 25–55. In a more abstract vein, a model for the changing nature of the rural social order and the increasing diversification of rural actors is provided by Eric R. Wolf, 'Fases de la protesta rural en América Latina', in Feder (ed.), *La lucha de clases en el campo.*

On the significance of *caudillos* and *caciques,* see the pioneering essays by Eric R. Wolf, 'Aspects of group relations in a complex society: Mexico', *American Anthropologist,* 58 (1956), 1065–78, and François Chevalier, ' "Caudillos" et "caciques" en Amérique: Contribution a l'étude des liens personnels', *Mélanges offerts a Marcel Bataillon par les hispanistes français, Bulletin Hispanique,* 51 (1962). See also Eric R. Wolf and Edward C. Hansen, 'Caudillo politics: A structural analysis', *Comparative Studies in Society and History,* 9 (1967), 168–79, and Guillermo de la Peña, 'Poder local, poder regional: Perspectivas socio-antropológicas', in Jorge Padua and Alain Vanneph (eds.), *Poder local, poder regional* (Mexico, D.F., 1986), 27–56.

The classic 'pre-revisionist' account of banditry in the Brazilian North-east is Maria Isaura Pereira de Queiroz, *Os cangaceiros: Les bandits d'honneur brésiliens* (Paris, 1968; Portuguese trans. São Paulo, 1977), on which Eric J. Hobsbawm drew for his portrait of *Bandits* (London, 1969). The revi-sionist literature includes Peter Singelmann, 'Political structure and social banditry in Northeast Brazil', *Journal of Latin American Studies,* 7/1 (1975), 59–83; Billy Jaynes Chandler, *The Bandit King: Lampião of Brazil* (College Station, Tex., 1978); and Linda Lewin, 'The oligarchical limitations of social banditry in Brazil: The Case of the "Good Thief" Antonio Silvino', *Past and Present,* 82 (1979), 116–46. In an otherwise commendable work,

'Los campesinos y la política en Brasil', in P. González Casanova (ed.), *Historia política de los campesinos latinoamericanos,* vol. 4 (1985), 9–83, José de Souza Martins seems to ignore the revisionist literature and supports the vision of Pereira de Queiroz and Hobsbawm. An intelligent, moderately anti-revisionist synthesis is Gilbert Joseph, 'On the trail of Latin American bandits: A re-examination of peasant resistance', *Latin American Research Review,* 25/3 (1990), 7–53. Lewis Taylor's exhaustive study of *Bandits and Politics in Peru: Landlord and Peasant Violence in Hualgayoc, 1900–30* (Cambridge, Eng., 1988) is the most valuable source for a history of conflict in the northern Peruvian Sierra during the Leguía period.

General accounts of the agrarian situation and the activities of peasant leagues in post-revolutionary Mexico are Eyler N. Simpson, *The Ejido: Mexico's Way Out* (Chapel Hill, N.C., 1937); Gerrit Huizer, *La lucha campesina en México* (Mexico, D.F., 1970), and Armando Bartra, *Los herederos de Zapata: Movimientos campesinos posrevolucionarios en México* (Mexico, D.F., 1985). There is a vast bibliography on Mexican *caudillos agraristas.* Felipe Carrillo Puerto has been eulogized by Francisco José Paoli and Enrique Montalvo in *El socialismo olvidado de Yucatán* (Mexico, D.F., 1980). A more critical (though still sympathetic) view on the same character can be found in Gilbert Joseph, 'Mexico's "Popular" Revolution: Mobilization and myth in Yucatán', *Latin American Perspectives,* 6/3 (1979) 46–65; see also his *Revolution from Without: Yucatán, Mexico and the United States* (Cambridge, Eng., 1982). José Guadalupe Zuno's memoirs, *Reminiscencias de una vida* (Guadalajara, 1956), is a useful document on his governorship of Jalisco. A good biography of Francisco J. Múgica (written when the *caudillo* was 55) is Armando de Maria y Campos, *Múgica* (Mexico, D.F., 1939). More analytical accounts are those by Heather Fowler Salamini, 'Revolutionary caudillos: Francisco Múgica and Adalberto Tejada', in D. A. Brading (ed.), *Caudillo and Peasant in the Mexican Revolution* (Cambridge, Eng., 1980), and Jorge Zepeda Patterson, 'Los caudillos en Michoacán: Francisco J. Múgica y Lázaro Cárdenas', in Carlos Martínez Assad (ed.), *Estadistas, caciques y caudillos* (Mexico, D.F., 1988). Paul Friedrich's *Agrarian Revolt in a Mexican Village,* 2nd ed. (Chicago, 1977), is not only the best characterization of Primo Tapia and his following but also a lucid analysis of *caciquismo* in post-revolutionary Michoacán. Equally valuable is the sequel to this book, also by Friedrich: *Princes of Naranja: An Essay in Anthrohistorical Method* (Austin, Tex., 1986). On Adalberto Tejeda and the Veracruz peasant leagues, Heather Fowler Salamini has written an outstanding monograph: *Agrarian Radicalism in Veracruz, 1920–38* (Lincoln, Nebr., 1978); Romana Falcón and Soledad García adopt a biographical approach in *La semilla en el surco: Adalberto Tejeda y el radicalismo en Veracruz* (Mexico, D.F., 1986). Saturnino Cedillo's peasant army is well portrayed in several books: Beatriz Rojas, *La pequeña guerra: Carrera Torres y los Cedillo* (Zamora, 1983); Dudley Ankerson, *Agrarian Warlord: Saturnino Cedillo and the Mexican Revolution in San Luis Potosí* (DeKalb, Ill., 1984), and particularly Romana Falcón, *Revolución y caciquismo: San Luis Potosí, 1910–1938* (Mexico, D.F., 1984). The social conditions for the emergence of the Cedillista movement are analysed by Mari-Jose Amerlinck, 'From hacienda to ejido: The San Diego de Río Verde case' (unpublished Ph.D. dissertation, State University of New York, Stony Brook, 1980), and Victoria Lerner, 'Los fundamentos socioeconómicos del cacicazgo en el México posrevolucionario: El caso de Saturnino Cedillo', *Historia Mexicana*, 23/3 (1980).

Of the many studies on the agrarian strategies of Lázaro Cárdenas, see in particular Eyler N. Simpson, *The Ejido: Mexico's Way Out* (Chapel Hill, N.C., 1937), an honest testimony and a rigourous analysis; Arnaldo Córdova, *La política de masas del cardenismo* (Mexico, D.F., 1974); Luis González, *Los días del presidente Cárdenas* (Mexico, D.F., 1981) (*Historia de la revolución mexicana*, 15), and Nora Hamilton, *The Limits of State Autonomy: Post-revolutionary Mexico* (Princeton, N.J., 1982). A critical point of view on the relations between Cardenismo and the peasants is provided in Marjorie Becker, 'Black and white and color: Cardenismo and the search for a Campesino ideology', *Comparative Studies in Society and History*, 29 (1987), 453–65. On Sinarquismo, Nathan Whetten wrote a lucid chapter in his *Rural Mexico* (Chicago, 1948). Recent analyses are provided by Jean Meyer, *El sinarquismo ¿un fascismo mexicano?* (Mexico, D.F., 1979); Servando Ortoll, 'Las legiones, la base y el sinarquismo: ¿Tres organizaciones distintas y un solo fin verdadero?', in Jorge Alonso (ed.), *El PDM, movimiento regional* (Guadalajera, 1989), 17–64, and Rubén Aguilar and Guillermo Zermeño, *Hacia una reinterpretación del sinarquismo actual* (Mexico, D.F., 1988). César Moheno gives the point of view of the peasant supporters of the movement in *Las historias y los hombres de San Juan* (Zamora, 1985).

James Dunkerley, *Power in the Isthmus: A Political History of Modern Central America* (London, 1988), includes examination of rural mobilizations in the 1920s and 1930s. On Sandino, see Gregorio Selser, *Sandino: General de hombres libres*, 2nd ed. (San José, C.R., 1972). Some information about Sandino's army is given by Jaime Wheelock Román, *Imperialismo y dictadura: Crisis de una formación social* (Mexico, D.F., 1975); but a thorough study of the internal organization of the movement is still lacking. On the 1932 Salvadorean uprising and ensuing massacre, see Thomas P. Anderson, *Matanza: El Salvador Communist Revolt of 1932* (Lincoln, Nebr., 1971) – which has good data but a misleading title: the revolt was more ethnic than 'Communist' – and Rafael Menjívar Larín, *El Salvador: El eslabón más pequeño* (San José, C.R., 1980). Roque Dalton constructed an ironic collage with different versions of the massacre in his *Historias prohibidas del Pulgarcito* (Mexico, D.F., 1977). Dalton also transcribed and edited the memoir of one of the Communist leaders of the revolt: *Miguel Mármol: Los sucesos de 1932 en El Salvador* (San Salvador, 1972).

On Indian resistance in the Bolivian Andean region between the two World Wars, see the opening chapters of two comprehensive books on the subject: Fernando Calderón and Jorge Dandler (eds.), *Bolivia: La fuerza histórica del campesinado* (Cochabamba, 1984), and Silvia Rivera Cusicanqui, *'Oprimidos pero no vencidos': Luchas del campesinado aymara y qhechwa de Bolivia, 1900–1980* (Geneva, 1986). Two excellent accounts of the changes in the Central Peruvian Sierra are Norman Long and Bryan Roberts (eds.), *Peasant Cooperation and Capitalist Expansion in Central Peru* (Austin, Tex., 1978) (the chapter by Carlos Samaniego being particularly relevant for the understanding of the 1930s), and Florencia E. Mallon, *The Defense of Community in Peru's Central Highlands* (Princeton, N.J., 1983). Compulsory and compulsive reading is José Carlos Mariátegui's classic, *Siete ensayos de interpretación de la realidad peruana* (Lima, 1928, English trans. Austin, Tex., 1975). On the rural impacts of Leguía's reforms, see François Chevalier, 'Official indigenismo in Peru in 1920: Origins, significance, and socio-economic scope', in Magnus Mörner (ed.), *Race and Class in Latin America* (New York, 1970); and Wilfredo Kapsoli and Wilson Reátegui, *El campesinado peruano, 1919–1930* (Lima, 1987).

On the historiography of rural upheaval and politics in Colombia, see Jesús Antonio Bejarano, 'Campesinado, luchas agrarias e historia social en Colombia: Notas para un balance historiográfico', in P. González Casanova (ed.), *Historia política de los campesinos latinoamericanos*, vol. 3, 9–72. A classic description of La Violencia is Germán Guzmán, Orlando Fals Borda and Eduardo Umaña Luna, *La Violencia en Colombia*, 2 vols. (Bogotá, 1963–4). In his article 'Violence and the break-up of tradition in Colombia', in Claudio Véliz, ed., *Obstacles to Change in Latin America* (New York, 1965), Orlando Fals Borda emphasized intra-elite conflict as the main detonator of endemic conflict. Paul Oquist's *Violence, Conflict and Politics in Colombia* (New York, 1980) is a study on the historical roots and heterogeneous structural causes of this period. John Walton uses the Colombian case to exemplify the relationships between seemingly parochial peasant movements and national political conflicts in his *Reluctant Rebels: Comparative Studies of Revolution and Underdevelopment* (New York, 1984). A detailed and innovative regional study is Carlos Miguel Ortiz Sarmiento, *Estado y subversión en Colombia: La Violencia en El Quindío, Años 50* (Bogotá, 1985). On the importance of banditry, see Darío Betancourt and Martha L. García, *Matones y cuadrilleros: Origen y evolución de la violencia en el occidente Colombiano*, 2nd ed. (Bogotá, 1991).

The best overall view of the social and political history of Guatemala during the years of populist reforms and their tragic aftermath remains Richard Newbold Adams, *Crucifixion by Power: Essays on Guatemalan National Social Structure, 1944–1966* (Austin, Tex., 1970), which includes a chapter by Brian Murphy on 'The stunted growth of campesino organizations' (438–78). Equally useful as a source of economic and social data is Nathan L. Whetten, *Guatemala: The Land and the People* (New Haven, Conn., 1961). Whetten explicitly compares the Mexican and the Guatemalan agrarian reform programmes. A lyrical defence of the Guatemalan Indian and the need for agrarian reform is to be found in *Guatemala: Las líneas de su mano* by Luis Cardoza y Aragón (Mexico, D.F., 1955). Neale J. Pearson's 'Guatemala: The peasant union movement, 1944–1954', in H. Landsberger (ed.), *Latin American Peasant Movements,* includes a good deal of useful data on the federations. In turn, Stokes Newbold's (pseudonym of Richard N. Adams) post-coup interviews of jailed peasants – supporters of Arbenz and members of *sindicatos* – show that the Guatemalan revolution included a broad spectrum of ideas on social reform, and political ideology and affiliation ('Receptivity to Communist-fomented agitation in rural Guatemala', *Economic Development and Cultural Change,* 5/4 (1957). Thomas and Marjorie Melville, who lived several years as missionaries in rural Guatemala, provide a moving chronicle of both the changes under Arbenz and the ruthless repression against thousands of Indians after the military coup in *Guatemala: The Politics of Land Ownership* (New York, 1971). An indispensable recent study is Piero Gleijeses, *Shattered Hope: The Guatemalan Revolution and the United States, 1944–54* (Princeton, N.J., 1991).

On the agrarian mobilizations which followed the Bolivian revolution, Robert J. Alexander, *The Bolivian National Revolution* (New Brunswick,

N.J., 1958) maintained that they were not spontaneous but organized from above, whereas Richard W. Patch, 'Bolivia: U.S. assistance in a revolutionary setting', in Richard N. Adams et al., *Social Change in Latin America Today* (New York, 1960), 108–76, defended exactly the opposite view. Subsequent research has shown that the nature of mobilizations varied according to region. For instance, the strength of grassroots organizations in Cochabamba and the clarity of their demands has been thoroughly documented by Jorge Dandler in *El sindicalismo campesino en Bolivia: Los cambios estructurales en Ucureña* (Mexico, D.F., 1969); see also his chapters (with Juan Torruco), 'El Congreso Nacional Indígena de 1945 y la rebelión campesina de Ayopaya (1947)' and 'Campesinado y reforma agraria en Cochabamba (1952–3): Dinámica de un movimiento campesino en Bolivia', in F. Calderón and J. Dandler (eds.), *Bolivia: La fuerza histórica del campesinado*. Dwight B. Heath shows a situation of peasant passivity in the eastern lowlands, in 'Bolivia: Peasant syndicates among the Aymara of the Yungas – a view from the grass roots', in H. A. Landsberger, *Latin American Peasant Movements*. See also Silvia Rivera Cusicanqui, *Oprimidos pero no vencidos,* cited above. On the consequences of agrarian reform, see Jonathan Kelley and Herbert S. Klein, *Revolution and the Rebirth of Inequality: A Theory Applied to the National Revolution in Bolivia* (Berkeley, 1966), and Andrew Pearse, 'Campesinado y revolución: El caso de Bolivia', in Calderón and Dandler (eds.), *Bolivia.*

The history of the Ligas Camponesas in Brazil has been written with great sympathy by Clodomiro Santos de Moraes, 'Peasant Leagues in Brazil', in R. Stavenhagen (ed.), *Agrarian Problems and Peasant Movements in Latin America.* Moraes, himself a participant, bitterly regrets the internal quarrels among peasant members and frequent strategic blunders of the leadership. Still sympathetic but more analytical are the works of Cynthia N. Hewitt, 'Brazil: The peasant movement of Pernambuco, 1961–1964', in H. Landsberger (ed.), *Latin American Peasant Movements,* cited above, 374–98; Shepard Forman, *The Brazilian Peasantry* (New York, 1975), and Fernando Antonio Azevedo, *As Ligas Camponesas* (Rio de Janeiro, 1982). Francisco Julião provides his own version in three books: *Que são Ligas Camponesas* (Rio de Janeiro, 1962); *Cambão: La cara oculta de Brasil* (Mexico, D.F., 1968), and *Brasil: Antes y después* (Mexico, D.F., 1968). A critical assessment of the organization and its main leader can be found in Anthony Leeds, 'Brazil and the myth of Francisco Julião', in Joseph Maier and Richard Weatherhead, *Politics of Change in Latin America* (New York, 1964), 190–204. To Leeds's accusations – that Julião was a careerist, that his methods were highly paternalistic, that there were no genuine popular leaders in Brazil, and that the whole Pernambuco mobilization was the consequence of élite internal quarrels – José de Souza Martins, in 'Los campesinos y la política en Brasil', cited above, opposes a view in which rural unrest is explained in terms of the deep contradictions existing in Brazilian agrarian economy – and not only in the Northeast – although he recognizes the divisions and hesitations of the political parties and urban groups competing for the support of the rural population.

An overview of rural violence in the sierra before the 1968 military takeover is provided by Howard Handelman, *Struggle in the Andes: Peasant Mobilization in Peru* (Austin, Tex., 1975). See also Edward Dew, *Politics in the Altiplano: The Dynamics of Change in Rural Peru* (Austin, Tex., 1969), on peasant mobilizations in the Department of Puno. The best analysis of the movement at La Convención and Lares is Eduardo Fioravanti, *Latifundismo y sindicalismo agrario en el Perú* (Lima, 1972). See also Wesley W. Craig, Jr., *From Hacienda to Community: An Analysis of Solidarity and Social Change in Peru* (Ithaca, N.Y., 1967). Eric Hobsbawm analyses the situation of the haciendas and the labour conditions from which the movement sprang in 'A case of neo-feudalism: La Convención, Peru', *Journal of Latin American Studies*, 1/1 (1969), 31–50. William F. Whyte uses the case of La Convención, among others, to argue against the thesis of 'the political passivity' of the peasants in 'Rural Peru – peasants as activists', in D. B. Heath (ed.), *Contemporary Cultures and Societies in Latin America*, 2nd ed. (New York, 1974), and Hugo Blanco (the Trotskyist leader) gives his own account in *Land or Death: The Peasant Struggle in Peru* (New York, 1972). An interesting account of the agrarian struggle in a single village throughout the 1960s is Gavin Smith and Pedro Cano, 'Some factors contributing to peasant land occupations in Peru: The example of Huasicancha, 1963–1968', in Long and Roberts, *Peasant Cooperation and Capitalist Expansion in Central Peru*.

A very useful reader on the history of *indigenismo*, written from a critical point of view, is Claude Bataillon et al., *Indianidad, etnocidio e indigenismo en América Latina* (Mexico, D.F., 1988); see also Marie-Chantal Barre, *Ideologías indigenistas y movimientos indios* (Mexico, D.F., 1983), and Instituto Nacional Indigenista (ed.), *INI: 40 años* (Mexico, D.F., 1940). The writings of Gonzalo Aguirre Beltrán are an intelligent defence of the official Mexican *indigenismo;* see for instance his *Teoría y práctica de la educación indígena* (Mexico, D.F., 1973), and his classic *El proceso de aculturación y el cambio sociocultural en México* (Mexico, D.F., 1970). On the

Peruvian case, see Thomas Davies, *Indian Integration in Peru: A Half Century of Experience* (Lincoln, Nebr., 1974).

On the situation in the Mexican countryside from 1940 to 1970, the writings of Arturo Warman, *Los campesinos, hijos predilectos del régimen* (Mexico, D.F., 1972) and *Ensayos sobre el campesinado mexicano* (Mexico, D.F., 1980), and Roger Bartra, *Estructura agraria y clases sociales en México* (Mexico, D.F., 1974) and *Campesinado y poder político en México* (Mexico, D.F., 1982) are still useful as representatives of two opposite theoretical tendencies: Warman defends a 'peasantization' of Mexican agriculture whereas Bartra sees the future in 'proletarianization'. In addition, Warman wrote an outstanding regional study of Morelos: '. . . *We Come to Object', Mexican Peasants and the State* (Baltimore, 1980). On the taming of the CNC, see Moisés González Navarro, *La Confederación Nacional Campesina: Un grupo de presión en la reforma agraria mexicana* (Mexico, D.F., 1968). There are no detailed studies of the regional functioning of the UGOCM and the CCI, but good case material can be found in monographs such as Fernando Salmerón Castro, *Los límites del agrarismo: Proceso político y estructuras de poder en Taretan, Michoacán* (Zamora, 1989). On Jaramillo, see Rubén M. Jaramillo and Froylán C. Manjarrez, *Rubén Jaramillo: Autobiografía y asesinato* (Mexico, D.F., 1967); Raúl Macín, *Rubén Jaramillo: Profeta olvidado* (Montevideo, 1970), and Carlos Fuentes's reporting in *Política* magazine, included in his *Tiempo mexicano* (Mexico, D.F., 1973). David Ronfeldt, *Atencingo: The Politics of Agrarian Struggle in a Mexican Ejido* (Stanford, Calif., 1973) chronicles repression against peasants and peasant resistance from 1940 to 1970. On the Guerrero guerrillas, there are only a brief article by Francisco Gómezjara, 'El proceso político de Genaro Vázquez hacia la guerrilla campesina', *Revista Mexicana de Ciencias Políticas y Sociales*, 88 (1977), and two journalistic accounts: Orlando Ortiz, *Genaro Vázquez* (Mexico, D.F., 1974), and Luis Suárez, *Lucio Cabañas, el guerrillero sin esperanza* (Mexico, D.F., 1984).

For a brilliant synthesis on the conditions of rural Cuba at the end of the 1950s, see Eric Wolf, *Peasant Wars in the Twentieth Century* (New York, 1969) chap. 6. For an official and rather rhetorical version of peasant participation in the Cuban revolution, see Adolfo Martín Barrios, 'Historia política de los campesinos cubanos', in Pablo González Casanova (ed.), *Historia política de los campesinos latinoamericanos*, vol. 1, 40–92. A descriptive overview and also a passionate and fascinating testimony of the armed struggle in Latin America throughout the 1960s is Richard Gott's *Rural Guerrillas in Latin America* (London, 1970). Adolfo Gilly, journalist and militant Trotskyite, also wrote a personal testimony of the guerrillas in those years: *La senda de la guerrilla* (Mexico, D.F., 1986). For an interesting analysis of the guerrillas' conditions of viability, see Timothy P. Wickham-Crowley, 'Winners, losers, and also-rans: Toward a comparative sociology of Latin American guerrilla movements', in Susan Eckstein (ed.), *Power and Popular Protest: Latin American Social Movements* (Berkeley, 1989), 132–81. See also Regis Debray, 'Latin America: The Long March', *New Left Review*, 3 (1965). (Ten years later, Debray wrote a self-critical analysis, *La crítica de las armas* [Mexico, D.F., 1975], 2 vols.) On the Venezuelan Peasant Federation, see John Duncan Powell, *Political Mobilization of the Venezuelan Peasant* (Cambridge, Mass., 1971). A personal, highly emotional eulogy of Camilo Torres, which includes letters and private documents, is Germán Guzmán Campos, *Camilo: Presencia y destino* (Bogotá, 1967). The disastrous adventure of Che Guevara in Bolivia was recorded by its two main protagonists: see *El diario del Che en Bolivia* (Mexico, D.F., 1967), and Inti Peredo, *Mi campaña con el Che* (Mexico, D.F., 1971). An unsympathetic but thorough account is Robert F. Lamberg, 'El Che en Bolivia: La "Revolución" que fracasó', *Problemas del Comunismo*, 27/4 (1970), 26–38.

The Central American tragedy of repression and violence from the 1960s to the 1980s is recorded in the (already cited) books by Adams, North, Gott, and Dunkerley. A useful reader is Daniel Camacho and Rafael Menjívar (eds.), *Movimientos populares en Centroamérica* (San José, C.R., 1985); the comparative perspective is also explicitly used by John Booth, 'Socioeconomic and political roots of national revolts in Central America', *Latin American Research Review*, 26/1 (1991), 33–74. A thorough study of the Salvadorean peasant revolution in two specific regions is Carlos Rafael Cabarrús, *Génesis de una revolución: Análisis del surgimiento y desarrollo de la organización campesina en El Salvador* (Mexico, D.F., 1983); less analytical but equally instructive is Jenny Pearce's *Promised Land: Peasant Rebellion in Chalatenango, El Salvador* (London, 1986). On the situation of El Salvador after 1980, see Ignacio Medina Núñez, *El Salvador: Entre la guerra y la esperanza* (Guadalajara, 1990). On the crucial revolutionary role played by migrant labourers, see two articles by Jeffrey Paige: 'Social theory and peasant revolution in Vietnam and Guatemala', *Theory and Society*, 12 (1983), 699–737, and 'Cotton and revolution in Nicaragua', in Peter Evans, Dietrich Rueschemeyer, and Theda Skocpol (eds.), *State versus Market in the World System* (Beverly Hills, Calif., 1985). An official but well-informed version of the Nicaraguan agrarian reform is

Jaime Wheelock Román, *Entre la crisis y la agresión: La reforma agraria sandinista* (Managua, 1985).

The best data on the initial steps in the Peruvian agrarian reform are still those provided by José María Caballero and Elena Alvarez, *Aspectos cuantitativos de la reforma agraria* (Lima, 1980); see also José Matos Mar and José Manuel Mejía, *La reforma agraria en el Perú* (Lima, 1980). Cynthia McClintock conducted an in-depth study of nine co-operatives and a control community, which allowed her to write a lucid book: *Peasant Cooperatives and Political Change in Peru* (Princeton, N.J., 1981). A detailed local-level analysis of the functioning of new government agencies can be found in Norman Long and David Winder, 'From peasant community to production co-operative', *Journal of Development Studies*, 12/1 (1975), 75–94. A reappraisal of the process of social reform after ten years is in Abraham Lowenthal and Cynthia McClintock (eds.), *The Peruvian Experiment Reconsidered* (Princeton, N.J., 1983). A longer time span is covered by Tanya Korovkin, *Politics of Agricultural Co-operativism: Peru, 1969–1983* (Vancouver, Can., 1990), though she concentrates on the analysis of three cotton estates.

On the background of peasant agitation in Chile, see Almino Affonso et al., *Movimiento campesino chileno* (Santiago, Chile, 1970), and Arnold Bauer, *Chilean Rural Society to 1930* (Cambridge, Eng., 1975). Robert Kaufman's *The Politics of Land Reform in Chile* (Cambridge, Mass., 1972), dissects the rather complicated alliances and divisions among classes and groups in the Chilean countryside. See also Brian Loveman, *Struggle in the Countryside: Politics and Rural Labor in Chile, 1919–1973* (Bloomington, Ind., 1976). A grassroots view of Frei's agrarian reform is James Petras and Hugo Zemelman, *Peasants in Revolt: A Chilean Case Study, 1965–1971* (Austin, Tex., 1972). On the Chilean Socialist experiment, a good overview is in J. A. Zammit (ed.), *The Chilean Road to Socialism* (Brighton, 1973). See also Fernando Mires, *La rebelión permanente: Las revoluciones sociales en América Latina* (Mexico, D.F., 1988), chap. 6. A critical appraisal covering the agrarian situation under Frei, Allende and Pinochet is Leonardo Castillo and David Lehmann, 'Chile's three agrarian reforms: The Inheritors', *Bulletin of Latin American Research*, 1/2 (1982), 21–44, which complements Lehmann's earlier account of Frei's period, 'Agrarian reform in Chile: An essay in contradictions', in D. Lehmann (ed.), *Agrarian Reform and Agrarian Reformism* (London, 1974). A broad analysis of the Pinochet years was written by Sergio Gómez and Jorge Echenique, *La agricultura chilena: Las dos caras de la modernización* (Santiago, Chile, 1988).

The rise and decline of the ANUC in Colombia is lucidly chronicled and analysed by León Zamosc, *The Agrarian Question and the Peasant Movement in Colombia* (Cambridge, 1986). An updated synthesis of the same work is 'Peasant struggles in the 1970s in Colombia', in Susan Eckstein (ed.), *Power and Popular Protest*. See also Silvia Rivera Cusicanqui, *Política e ideología en el movimiento campesino colombiano: El caso de la ANUC* (Geneva and Bogotá, CINEP, 1987), and Cristina Escobar and Francisco de Roux, 'Movimientos populares en Colombia (1970–1983)', in Daniel Camacho and Rafael Menjívar (eds.), *Los movimientos populares en América Latina* (Mexico, D.F., 1989).

The diversification and capitalization of peasant agriculture is analysed in Guillermo de la Peña, *A Legacy of Promises: Agriculture, Politics and Ritual in the Morelos Highlands of Mexico* (Austin, Tex., 1981). An overview of rural unrest in Mexico from 1970 to the mid-1980s is Blanca Rubio, *Resistencia campesina y explotación rural en México* (Mexico, D.F., 1987); see also a more analytical interpretation in Michael W. Foley, 'Agenda for mobilization: The agrarian question and popular mobilization in contemporary Mexico', *Latin American Research Review*, 26/2 (1991), 39–74. The crisis of CNC control in a particular region is narrated in Eric Villanueva, *Crisis henequenera y movimientos campesinos en Yucatán, 1966–1983* (Mexico, D.F., 1985); see also Clarisa Hardy, *El estado y los campesinos: La Confederación Nacional Campesina (CNC)* (Mexico, D.F., 1984). On the Echeverría years, see Steven E. Sanderson, *Agrarian Populism and the Mexican State: The Struggle for Land in Sonora* (Berkeley, 1981), and Fernando Rello, *Burguesía, campesinos y estado en México: El conflicto agrario de 1976* (Geneva, 1987). On the struggle for local political control, see Adriana López Monjardín, *La lucha por los ayuntamientos: Una utopía viable* (Mexico, D.F., 1986). The expansion of wage rural labour is documented in Luisa Paré, *El proletariado agrícola en México: ¿Campesinos sin tierra o proletarios agrícolas?* (Mexico, D.F., 1977), and Enrique Astorga Lira, *Mercado de trabajo rural en México: La mercancía humana* (Mexico, D.F., 1985). On the last decade, see Luisa Paré, 'Movimiento campesino y política agraria en México, 1976–1982', *Revista Mexicana de Sociología*, 47/4 (1985), 85–111; Gustavo Gordillo, *Campesinos al asalto del cielo: De la expropiación estatal a la apropiación campesina* (Mexico, D.F., 1988). Jonathan Fox and Gustavo Gordillo, 'Between state and market: The campesinos' quest for autonomy', in Wayne Cornelius et al., *Mexico's Alternative Political Futures* (La Jolla, Calif., 1989), 131–72; and most of all Neil Harvey, *Peasant Movements and the Mexican State, 1979–1990* (London, 1991). The (less than fortunate) lot of Mexican agriculture and smallholding groups during the years of De la Madrid is described by José Luis Calva, *Crisis agrícola y alimentaria en México, 1982–1988* (Mexico, D.F., 1988).

The extent of peasant unrest and resistance to SINAMOS *after* the Peruvian agrarian reform is reviewed in Diego García Sayán, *Tomas de tierras en el Perú* (Lima, 1982). Information on the rise of Sendero Luminoso is provided by the reporting of Raúl González in his articles 'Por los caminos de Sendero', *Quehacer* (Lima), 19 (October 1982), and 'Las batallas de Ayacucho', *Quehacer,* 21 (February 1983). Carlos Iván Degregori deals with the regional origins, social context and development of the movement in two lucid and informative essays: 'Sendero Luminoso: Los hondos y mortales desencuentros', Instituto de Estudios Peruanos, Documentos de Trabajo, Serie Antropología, No. 2 (Lima, 1985), and 'Sendero Luminoso: Lucha armada y utopía autoritaria', Instituto de Estudios Peruanos, Documentos de Trabajo, Serie Antropología, No. 3 (Lima, 1985). A broad analytical perspective, linking Sendero with the development of the Peruvian state, is adopted by Henri Favre, 'Perú: Sendero Luminoso y horizontes ocultos', *Cuadernos Americanos,* 4/4 (1987), 29–58; see also the interview with Henri Favre (conducted by Carlos Iván Degregori y Raúl González) in *Quehacer* (Lima), 54 (1988), 48–58. In turn, Cynthia McClintock's emphasis is on the particular situation of impoverishment of the southern highlands peasantry, in her paper 'Why peasants rebel: The case of Perú's Sendero Luminoso', *World Politics,* 37/1 (1984), 48–85. On the renewed crisis of the Colombian state, see Comisión de Estudios sobre la Violencia (ed.), *Colombia: Violencia y democracia: Informe presentado ante el Ministerio de Gobierno* (Bogotá, 1987) (which includes a discussion of rural problems, 190–210), Fabio Castillo, *Los jinetes de la cocaína* (Bogotá, 1987), and Jenny Pearce, *Colombia: Inside the Labyrinth* (London, 1990), especially part 3; see also the review article by Wolfgang Heinz, 'Guerrillas, political violence, and the peace process in Colombia', *Latin American Research Review,* 14/3 (1989), 249–58.

A good deal of the literature on the 'new social movements' is reviewed in the collection of papers edited by David Slater, *New Social Movements and the State in Latin America* (Amsterdam, 1985); see also Fernando Calderón (ed.), *Los movimientos sociales ante la crisis* (Buenos Aires, 1986), and Elizabeth Jelín (ed.), *Ciudadanía e identidad: Las mujeres en los movimientos sociales latino-americanos* (Geneva, 1987). On the invasion of the Brazilian Amazon after 1970, see Joe Foweraker, *The Struggle for Land: A Political Economy of the Pioneer Frontier in Brazil from 1930 to the Present Day* (Cambridge, Eng.,

1981), and two books by José de Souza Martins, *Expropriação e violencia: A questão política no campo* (São Paulo, 1980), esp. chap. 4, and *A militarização da questão agrária no Brasil* (Petrópolis, 1984). Abundant documentary evidence on the new Indian organizations throughout Latin America can be found in Guillermo Bonfil (ed.), *Utopía y revolución: El pensamiento político contemporáneo de los indios en América Latina* (Mexico, D.F., 1981). See also Claude Bataillon et al., *Indianidad, etnocidio e indigenismo en América Latina,* and Marie-Chantal Barre, *Ideologías indigenistas y movimientos indios,* cited above. On the emergence of new political actors (including the *katarista* movement) in Bolivia, see James M. Malloy and Eduardo Gamarra, *Revolution and Reaction in Bolivia, 1964–1985* (New Brunswick, N.J., 1988). On *katarismo,* the best account is still Silvia Rivera Cusicanqui, *Oprimidos pero no vencidos . . .* cited above, part 3. See also Xavier Albó, 'From MNRistas to Kataristas to Katari', in Steve J. Stern (ed.), *Resistance, Rebellion and Consciousness in the Andean World, 18th to 20th Centuries* (Madison, Wis., 1987). On the COCEI in Oaxaca, see Mari-France Prevot-Shapira and Helène Riviere D'Arc, 'Les zapoteques, le PRI et la COCEI: Affrontements autour des interventions de l'état dans l'Isthme de Tehuantepec', *Amerique Latine,* 15 (1983), 64–71. On the UCEZ in Michoacán, see Jorge Zepeda Patterson, 'No es lo mismo agrio que agrario ni comunero que comunista, pero se parecen', in J. Tamayo (ed.), *Movimientos sociales en el occidente de México* (Guadalajara, 1986). A more critical perspective on the UCEZ and the new ethnic political organizations is in Luis Vázquez León, *Ser indio otra vez: La purepechización de los tarascos serranos* (Mexico, D.F., 1992).

INDEX

Mujal, Eusebio, 241, 246, 268
multinational corporations, 214–15, 292
Muñoz, Maurilio, 347
Mussolini, Benito, 154
Mustafa Kemal Pacha, 154
Mutual Security Act of 1951, 156

Napoleonic codes, 12–13
narcotics trade, 47, 53, 188
National Congress of Agrarian Leagues, Mexico, 305
National Consulting Agrarian Commission, Mexico, 381
National Falange, Chile, 28
National Federation of Peasant Workers of Bolivia (CNTCB), 385
National Guard, Panama, 179, 180
National Intelligence Service (SNI), Brazil, 165, 205
National Party, Uruguay, 50–1
National Security Council (CONASE), Argentina, 174
National Security Council, Brazil, 165
National Security Council, Chile, 206
National Security Council (COSENA), Uruguay, 174
National System for the Support of Social Mobilization (SINAMOS), Peru, 181, 372–3
nationalism, 70, 153–5
nationalization, 77, 153, 179, 184, 234
Naval Club Agreements of 1984, Uruguay, 50, 196
Neruda, Pablo, 80, 93–4
Neves, Tancredo, 61, 195
new unionism, 228, 269–79
Nicaragua
    Catholic Church, 119–20, 125, 143
    Communist Party, 125
    democracy, 193
    dictatorial re-election, 19
    elections, 72
    labour movement, 99, 125, 239
    Left, 79, 90–1, 94, 99, 119–22, 124–6, 142–3
    military, 69, 159, 348
    rural mobilization, 350, 361, 368–70, 394
    Sandinista movement, 79, 90–1, 99, 119–22, 124–6, 142–3, 180, 192, 193, 200, 368–70, 385
    Somoza government, 99, 124, 156
    Soviet Union and, 125
    United States and, 56, 148, 192, 193, 200, 370
Niemeyer, Oscar, 80
Nixon, Richard, 158

Noriega, Manuel, 180, 200
North Atlantic Treaty Organization (NATO), 156
Nuevo Espacio Party, Uruguay, 138

Obregón, Alvaro, 187, 296, 297, 299, 301, 302, 307, 308
occupational mobility, 221–2
O'Donnell, Guillermo, 46, 56
Odría, Manuel A., 21, 44, 58, 59, 118, 342
oil
    Bolivia, 153, 179
    Ecuador, 181
    Venezuela, 54, 98
    workers, 222, 224, 232, 234, 243, 328
oligarchical democracy, 8
'one man, one vote', 6, 13
Onganía, Juan Carlos, 56, 165, 268
Ongaro, Raimundo, 270
Operation Marquetalia, Colombia, 354
Organización del Pueblo en Armas (OPA), Guatemala, 363
Organización Democrática Nacionalista (ORDEN), 365–7
Organization of Solidarity (OLAS), 158
organized labour *see* labour movements
Ortega, Daniel, 193
Ortiz, Carlos Enrique, 331–2
Ortiz Rubio, Pascual, 319
Ovando Candia, Alfredo, 158, 175, 178–9, 355

Pacheco Areco, Jorge, 173, 174
Pact of Chicoral of 1972, Colombia, 359
Pact of Ocampo of 1974, Mexico, 381, 382
Pact of Punto Fijo of 1958, Venezuela, 22
Padilla, David, 198
País, Frank, 268
Palma, Gabriel, 77
Panama
    military, 158, 160, 176, 179–81
    Torrijos government, 120, 158, 176, 179–80, 216
    United States and, 179, 180, 193, 200, 214
Panama Canal, 179, 180
Paraguay
    Chaco War (1932–5), 152, 236, 313
    demilitarization, 199–200
    military, 149, 191, 348
    Stroessner government, 199
parliamentarism, 13
Partido Agrario Obrero de Morelos, Mexico, 325
Partido Auténico de la Revolución Mexicana (PARM), 130